Macedonia

the Bradt Travel Guide

Thammy Evans

edition
4

www.bradtguides.com

Bradt Travel Guides Ltd, UK
The Globe Pequot Press Inc, USA

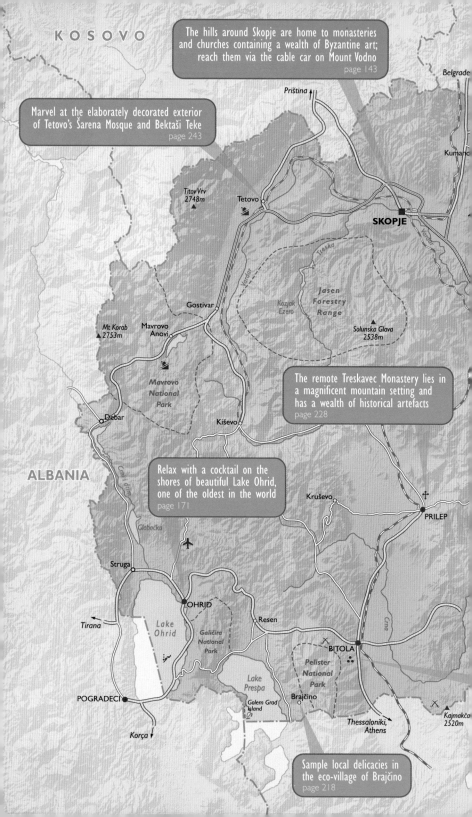

KOSOVO

The hills around Skopje are home to monasteries and churches containing a wealth of Byzantine art; reach them via the cable car on Mount Vodno
page 143

Belgrade

Marvel at the elaborately decorated exterior of Tetovo's Šarena Mosque and Bektaši Teke
page 243

Priština

Kumanc

Titov Vrv
2748m

Tetovo

SKOPJE

Vardar

Treska

Jasen
Forestry
Range

Gostivar

Kozjak
Ezero

Mt Korab
2753m

Mavrovo
Anovi

Solunska Glava
2538m

Mavrovo
National
Park

The remote Treskavec Monastery lies in a magnificent mountain setting and has a wealth of historical artefacts
page 228

Debar

Kiševo

ALBANIA

Crni drim

Relax with a cocktail on the shores of beautiful Lake Ohrid, one of the oldest in the world
page 171

Kruševo

PRILEP

Globočka

Struga

Crna

Tirana

OHRID

Resen

Lake
Ohrid

Galičira
National
Park

BITOLA

Pelister
National
Park

Lake
Prespa

Brajčino

POGRADECI

Golem Grad
Island

Thessaloniki,
Athens

Kajmakčo
2520m

Korça

Sample local delicacies in the eco-village of Brajčino
page 218

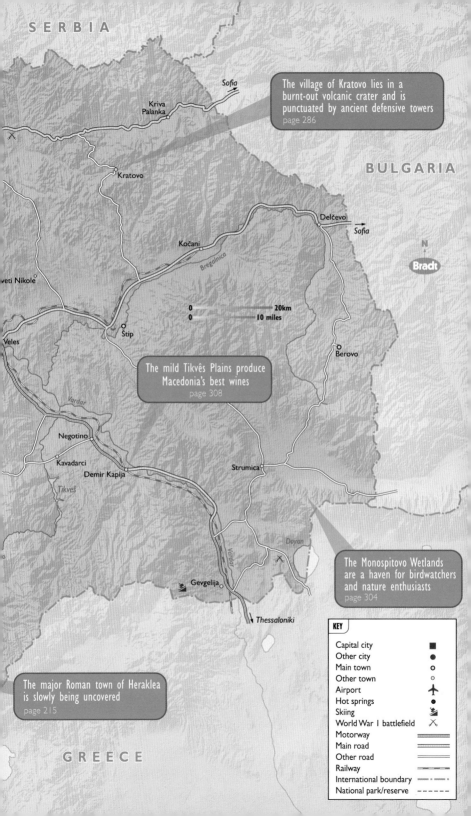

SERBIA

BULGARIA

Sofia

Kriva
Palanka

The village of Kratovo lies in a
burnt-out volcanic crater and is
punctuated by ancient defensive towers
page 286

Kratovo

Delčevo

Sofia

Kočani

N

Bregalnica

Bradt

veti Nikole

0   20km
0   10 miles

Berovo

Štip

Veles

The mild Tikvês Plains produce
Macedonia's best wines
page 308

Vardar

Negotino

Kavadarci

Demir Kapija

Strumica

Tikveš

Dojran

Vardar

The Monospitovo Wetlands
are a haven for birdwatchers
and nature enthusiasts
page 304

Gevgelija

↟ *Thessaloniki*

The major Roman town of Heraklea
is slowly being uncovered
page 215

GREECE

KEY	
Capital city	■
Other city	●
Main town	○
Other town	○
Airport	✈
Hot springs	●
Skiing	🎿
World War I battlefield	✕
Motorway	
Main road	
Other road	
Railway	
International boundary	
National park/reserve	

Macedonia
Don't
miss...

Wineries The rich Tikveš Plain running from Veles along the River Vardar to Demir Kapija is renowned for its wines
(BJ) page 308

People and culture
The future mother-in-law hosts a dance in traditional dress with the closest relatives at the Galičnik wedding festival (SL) page 251

**Ohrid Lake
and town**
Lake Ohrid is the jewel
of the Macedonian
crown — both the
lake and Ohrid town
are UNESCO World
Heritage sites
(JC) page 171

**Art and
architecture**
Over 30,000 eggs
were used to make
the paint and
glaze for Tetovo's
beautifully preserved
Šarena Mosque
(SS) page 243

Hiking
Macedonia is
brimming with
beautiful countryside
that makes splendid
hiking for a range of
fitness and experience
levels (BJ) page 321

left

Kale Fortress, Skopje — continuing excavations of the site have revealed artefacts dating back to the Thracian era of 200BC (BJ) page 146

below

Čifte Amam National Art gallery is a former Turkish bathhouse that now houses various travelling exhibitions (BJ) page 144

bottom

The 214m Kamen Most was first built in the late 15th century and joins the old Turkish town to the new centre of Skopje (BJ) page 147

above Lake Ohrid, like many of Macedonia's lakes and rivers, offers choice fishing opportunities, although fishing for Ohrid trout is prohibited (JC) page 106

below Skiing at Popova Šapka – the resort offers 20km of groomed ski runs and over 35km² of terrain for off-piste skiers (TE) page 245

AUTHOR

Born in London, of Welsh and Malay Chinese parents, **Thammy Evans** has travelled and lived abroad for over 20 years, especially in China and southeast Europe. Professionally, her career lies in the field of political analysis. Her first overseas trip was to Malaysia at the age of eight, and she has been dabbling in numerous foreign languages ever since. Amongst her many other travels, her most memorable are the Trans-Mongolian Railway from Tianjin to Moscow in 1991, mountaineering in Bolivia in the summer of 1999, and doing the field  research for her second Bradt travel guide *Great Wall of China* in 2005. Despite many forays to far-off lands, she feels most at home in the southern climes of wider Europe and has lived and worked in Macedonia for five years. She and her family now have a small stone house by the sea in Istria.

DEDICATION

To my mother

AUTHOR'S STORY

I ended up back in the Balkans (which is another story), with my husband in Macedonia. Not good at twiddling my thumbs, I had already sought advice from a travel writer friend (Cam Burns) about doing some freelance travel writing. 'Why don't you update a travel guidebook on Macedonia?' he suggested. 'What a brilliant idea!' I replied; and off I went to Stanford's, the biggest map and travel bookshop in the UK, to survey the many guidebooks on Macedonia and to choose the one closest to my style of writing to update. After about five minutes of research in the Europe section, I quickly came to the conclusion that there was a grand total of zero guidebooks on Macedonia, and that ipso facto I myself would be writing the very first one! Another five minutes of research led me to the further deduction that the only publishing house crazy enough to tackle such a proposition would be Bradt Travel Guides.

I contacted Bradt, and to cut a very long story short, the then chief editor, Tricia Hayne, wrote back and said 'Yes!' Bradt was looking to expand its Balkan titles and I was very lucky to be in the right place at the right time.

Gathering accurate information on Macedonia, however, was not easy. In 2003 there was little published in English, and what was on the internet was sparse, outdated and contradictory. More was available in Macedonian, but was hyperbolic and did not meet the needs of an independent traveller. So, armed with tip-offs, mostly from the international community there at the time, I set off every weekend to conduct primary research. The result, several editions later and with much fact-checking by some very knowledgeable Macedonians, is the guide you have in your hands today. Enjoy!

PUBLISHER'S FOREWORD   *Hilary Bradt*

Macedonia remains the Cinderella of the former Yugoslavia, attracting fewer visitors than its high-profile neighbours. Readers are fortunate to have Thammy Evans to guide them; she is one of our most highly praised, enthusiastic and conscientious authors. Users of this new edition have a treat in store.

Fourth edition May 2012   First published 2004

Bradt Travel Guides Ltd, IDC House, The Vale, Chalfont St Peter, Bucks SL9 9RZ, England
www.bradtguides.com
Published in the USA by The Globe Pequot Press Inc,
PO Box 480, Guilford, Connecticut 06437-0480

Text copyright © 2012 Thammy Evans
Maps copyright © 2012 Bradt Travel Guides Ltd
Photographs copyright © 2012 Individual photographers (see below)
Project Manager: Maisie Fitzpatrick

ISBN-13: 978 1 84162 395 5
British Library Cataloguing in Publication Data
A catalogue record for this book is available from the British Library

Photographs Alamy: Borderlands (B/A); Julian Cartwright (JC); Dreamstime: Anriphoto (A/DT); Thammy Evans (TE); FLPA: Malcolm Schuyl (MS/FLPA), Jürgen & Christine Sohns (J&CS/FLPA); Blagoja Jankoski (BJ); Samir Ljuma (SL); Kamelia Sojlevska (KS); SuperStock (SS); Wikimedia Commons (WC)

Front cover Lake Ohrid (BJ)
Title page Woman with local headdress (KS); Copper pots, Tetovo (KS); Mosque, Skopje (A/DT)
Back cover Tetovo Arabati Baba Teke (KS); Frescoes in Monastery of Sv Naum, Ohrid (SS)

Maps David McCutcheon

Typeset from the author's disk by Wakewing, High Wycombe
Production managed by Jellyfish Print Solutions; printed in India

Foreword

Macedonia offers huge variety within a relatively compact area. So whether you fancy a stroll up to the heights of Mount Vodno in Skopje to enjoy the panoramic views of the city and countryside, or taking a dip in the waters of Lake Ohrid in the South of Macedonia, the surroundings provide a majestic backdrop to your journey around the country.

The towns are diverse too – from Tetovo and Struga in the west, with a strong Albanian cultural dimension, to the vineyards of central Macedonia and fabulous hiking trails to explore. The south, including Bitola and the striking scenery around Mount Pelister, provide hidden treasures to discover and an altogether different feel to your stay in Macedonia.

Enjoying Macedonia at its best means taking advantage of the varied opportunities to explore the outdoor terrain where you can test your wits at mountain biking, skiing, horseriding and other outdoor pursuits. From capital city to countryside, the variety of towns across Macedonia provide the opportunity to explore at first myriad historical sites including fortresses, ancient monasteries, churches and mosques. The array of galleries and museums provide plenty of illumination into the country's fascinating history and culture.

You will find the people of Macedonia to be among the friendliest, most welcoming hosts in the world. The food matches the diversity of the country, with exciting flavours and thrilling concoctions to interest your palate throughout the year.

I hope you will find Macedonia a genuine pleasure to visit. To help you plan a safe trip please do take time to visit the travel advice on offer at www.fco.gov.uk, which is regularly updated to help you get the most out of your journey here. I wish you a thoroughly enjoyable stay.

Christopher Yvon
British Ambassador

Acknowledgements

So many people have helped with this fourth edition, especially all the friendly people of Macedonia who have willingly or unwittingly helped me.

Specifically for this edition I would like to thank (any mistakes in the text are purely my own) Mimoza Gligorovska for her contribution to the education section and for chasing endless questions; Gerard and Sonja McGurk for the section on travelling with children, and for hosting me in Skopje; Lucy Abel Smith for the box on Renaissance art; Ray Power for the section on Business; Eric Manton for the box on rakija; Aubrey Harris for the box on traditional medicines; Phil Lampron for my beautiful author photograph and for much improving the Bitola section; Samir Ljuma, Goran Miševski, Zoran Bogatinov, Ana Novakova, Silvana Boškovska Georgievska, Beni Arjulai, Sally Broughton, Jennifer Arnold, Luke Hillier, Kim Reczek, Andriana Dragovik, Paško Kuzman; Sašo Dimeski of SAGW for help with the maps; Romeo Drobarov, Bingo, and John Durance for succeeding in getting to Dojran battlefield; my apologies to Simon Roberts for getting his name wrong in the last acknowledgements; Lazar Petrov and Jordan Trajkov at Popova Kula winery; Aleksandar Ristovski at Tikveš; Borče for another suit; Anastas Dudan for a truthful mirror; Pece and Renata at Villa Dihovo; Stevče, Valentina and Jakim from Kratovo Rock Art Centre; Ema of Macedonia Travel; Dimitar Gjorgievski and Nikola of Go Macedonia; Džingis Patel; Dr Dagoli of Dea Tours; Maya and Ace of Simonium Travel for my flight back to Pula; Alison White of Regent Holidays for flights to Skopje; my book distributor in Macedonia, Sašo Kuzmanovski; Bridget for chauffering Dani; and my mother for her tireless care of my affairs and family.

I am particularly thankful to all those readers who have found the time to write in with corrections: Eigil Christiansen, Keith Arnold, Michael Slatnik, Colin Groom, Darrin Erwin, Gunnar Olesen, Joan Joesting, Ines Aparicio, Sally Osment, Myles Munsey, Julian Cartwright, Bill Evans, David Golber, Sandra Brouwer, Alan Prytherch, Lena J. I'm also dearly grateful to all of the Bradt team for their help and understanding throughout the writing and sale of the book.

Finally I must once again thank my husband, Vic, for conducting last-minute primary research; and for the first time I must thank my daughter, Daniella (aged four), for doing the field research on travelling with children.

OOPS!

Apologies – we messed up! A few days after printing thousands of copies of this book, we noticed that – due to a mistake by us (rather than by Thammy) – many of its cross-references were wrong. Cue frantic discussions in the Bradt office: should we pulp all the books and reprint? 'What about the trees?' said the Commissioning Editor. 'What about the cost...?' said the Finance Director. Thammy herself was admirably understanding. It would break her heart to pulp so many books, she said. And so we agreed that adding an errata slip was the better, less-wasteful option. We hope that you understand our decision, and that it doesn't detract from your enjoyment of Thammy's excellent guide. You'll find below and overleaf a list of corrections to the offending cross-references, which fall mainly in the first two chapters.

Page 6
page 194 → page 197
Page 11
page 291 → page 305
Page 12
page 192 → page 196
page 213 → page 215
page 233 → page 235
page 248 → page 250
Page 17
page 144 → page 146
page 186 → page 188
Page 21
page 5 → page 6
box, page 160 → box, page 162
page 254 → page 256
Page 22
box, page 200 → box, page 202
page 211 → page 213
Page 26
page 64 → page 213
box, page 205 → box, page 207
box, page 294 → box, page 296
Page 27
page 256 → page 258
Page 29
box, page 226 → page 228
Page 32
box, page 42 → box, page 34

Page 37
page 125 → page 127
Page 39
page 357 → page 359
Page 41
page 360 → page 361
Page 42
box, page 253 → page 255
Page 43
box, page 253 → page 255
Page 44
see opposite → see below
page 162 → page 164
box, page 164 → box, page 166
Page 46
page 162 → page 164
Travelling positively on page 117 →
Travelling positively on page 118
Page 51
page 183 → page 185
Page 55
page 102 → page 103
box, pages 160–1 → box, pages 162–3
page 185 → page 187
Page 56
page 160 → page 162
page 162 → page 164
page 183 → page 185
page 193 → page 223

page 205 → page 207
page 273 → page 275
Page 58
page 103 → page 104
page 137 → page 139
Page 59
page 171 → page 173
page 195 → page 197
page 249 → page 251
page 311 → page 313
Page 60
page 125 → page 127
Page 61
page 155 → page 157
Page 62
page 100 → page 306
page 145 → page 148
page 187 → page 189
page 196 → page 198
page 220 → page 222
page 221 → page 223
page 226 → page 228
page 228 → page 230
page 249 → page 251
page 253 → page 259
page 254 → page 256
page 267 → page 227
page 281 → page 285
page 287 → page 289
page 301 → page 303

Contents

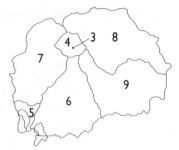

LIST OF MAPS

FEEDBACK REQUEST

At Bradt Travel Guides we're aware that guidebooks start to go out of date on the day they're published – and that you, our readers, are out there in the field doing research of your own. You'll find out before us when a fine new family-run hotel opens or a favourite restaurant changes hands and goes downhill. So why not write to us and tell us about your experiences? We'll include you in the acknowledgements of the next edition of *Macedonia* if we use your feedback. Contact us on ☎ 01753 893444 or e info@bradtguides.com. Alternatively you can add a review of the book to www.bradtguides.com or Amazon.

Periodically our authors post travel updates and reader feedback on the website. Check www.bradtguides.com/guidebook-updates for any news.

NOTE ABOUT MAPS

Several maps in this book use grid lines to allow easy location of sites. Map grid references are listed in square brackets after listings in the text, with page number followed by grid number, eg: [130 B2].

Introduction

There is so much in this small land. It is not a place of extremes, but it is an area filled with intoxicating untold stories. Its outdoors is its jewel — bijou, pristine and almost untouched. Long lost in the battles of neighbouring states, the tangible evidence of previous rulers is only now being unearthed. Most people don't even know where Macedonia is and it was once described to me as the greatest 'non-destination' country. But if you care to scratch the surface, you will find a Macedonia brimming with history, artefacts, rich local culture and beautiful scenery.

From a visitor's perspective, Macedonia has come a long way since the last edition. It has now started to offer western European standards. Aurora Resort and Spa, and the Ramada Plaza are the first true luxury hotels; at the other end of the scale there are a lot more hostels now and places giving Youth Hostel Association discounts. There are biking-tour operators, horseriding tours and western European hiking companies entering the market. Skopje is undergoing a complete facelift with new museums, buildings, statues and an arc de triomphe being built. Budget flights have now made it to Skopje (surely a sign that Macedonia is now mainstream!), and so much more information is available on the web (as well as Facebook).

I am still discovering new places and new experiences in Macedonia. In this fourth edition, there is more on rakija, early Renaissance art, archaeology, Macedonia's Jewish history, travelling with children; a dedicated guide to Macedonia's fantastic wines; and a much needed improved section on the Bitola area.

This guide, however, is just a starter kit, leaving plenty to be discovered, and much to be created. Geographically and historically there is much more to Macedonia if you veer off the tarred and hardened road, and you will only ever be rewarded for taking the bumpy side track. A Macedonian friend is invaluable to help you find your way around and introduce you to your own adventure, especially once you wander off the edges of this book. You will pick up many of these friends along the way who will go out of their way to help as if it is really nothing at all, and many of whom will speak excellent English or German. Talk to the people and you will find them a fount of knowledge on the region, happy to give you their version of events – for what is written here is certainly not the last word on the subject.

Part One

GENERAL INFORMATION

Country name (as recognised internationally) Former Yugoslav Republic of Macedonia (FYROM)

Constitutional name Republika Makedonija (Република Македонија)

Status Independent republic since 1991 through referendum

Languages Macedonian (Cyrillic alphabet), Albanian, Turkish dialects, Roma, Serb dialects

Population 2,077,328 (2011 estimate): ethnic Macedonian 64.2%, Albanian 25.2%, Turkish 3.9%, Roma 2.7%, Serb 1.8%, other 2.2%

Religion Orthodox Christian, Sunni and dervish Muslim, Roman Catholic, Methodist

Government Parliamentary democracy

Main political parties Governing coalition: VMRO-DPMNE (Internal Macedonian Revolutionary Organisation-Democratic Party of Macedonian National Unity), DUI (Democratic Union of Integration); in opposition: SDSM (Social Democratic Party of Macedonia), NDR (National Democratic Revival) and DPA (Democratic Party of Albanians)

President Gjorge Ivanov (next presidential elections 2014)

Prime minister Nikola Gruevski (next parliamentary elections 2015)

Municipalities 84, plus the City of Skopje = 85 (next municipal elections 2013)

Capital Skopje

Other major towns Bitola, Kumanovo, Ohrid, Prilep, Štip, Strumica, Tetovo

Border countries Albania, Kosovo, Serbia, Bulgaria, Greece

Area 25,713km^2

National parks Mavrovo, Galičica, Pelister

UNESCO protected area Ohrid Lake and town

Total length of roads 10,591km (surfaced: 6,000km)

Total railway 922km

Airports 17 (international airports are Skopje and Ohrid)

Highest point Mount Korab 2,753m, bordering Albania

Lowest point River Vardar at Gevgelija border crossing: 45m above sea level

Time GMT+1

Currency Denar (MKD)

Exchange rate £1 = 72.97MKD; US$1 = 46.55MKD; €1 = 60.54MKD (February 2012)

GDP Official: US$9.12bn (World Bank, 2010); Purchasing Power Parity (PPP): US$19.46bn

Average annual income US$4,520 (World Bank, 2010)

International telephone code +389

Electricity 220 volts AC. Sockets are round two-pin.

Flag A yellow oval at the centre emanating eight yellow segments against a red background

National anthem 'Today above Macedonia' (Денес над Македонија)

National flower Poppy

National animal Lion (*Panthera leo*); Balkan lynx; Ohrid trout

National holidays 1–2 January (New Year), 7 January (Orthodox Christmas), April (usually) (Easter), 1–2 May (Labour 'Day'), 2 August (Ilinden), 8 September (Referendum Day), 11 October (National Day)

Endangered indigenous species Ohrid trout

Background Information

And she, Deucalion's daughter,
of Zeus, the thunderer,
bore two sons:
Magnet and Macedon – a cavalryman, a warrior …

Hesiod, *Catalogue of Women*, 7BC

GEOGRAPHY

Geographically speaking, Macedonia is bounded by the Šar and Osogovska mountains to the north, Lake Ohrid and the Pindus Mountains to the west, the Rhodope Mountains to the east, and by Mount Olympus and the Aegean Sea to the south. This area was divided into four parts after the Berlin Treaty of 1878, and although Vardar Macedonia in particular (the land around the upper reaches of the River Vardar) may have changed hands several times since then, the division of the four parts has largely stayed the same. The four parts are now Vardar Macedonia in the northwest, Pirin Macedonia encompassing the Pirin Mountains in the

GEOGRAPHICAL MACEDONIA

3

northeast (now part of Bulgaria), Aegean Macedonia to the south as part of Greece, and a tiny sliver of land north and south of Debar and part of Lake Ohrid, which now belong to Albania.

Vardar Macedonia is divided from Pirin Macedonia in the east by the peak of Mount Ruen and the Vlaina Mountains above the River Struma in Bulgaria. The mountain ranges of Kožuf and Nidže divide the northern Vardar region from the southern plains. This area is completely landlocked and is split almost in half by the River Vardar, which runs south to the Aegean Sea. Only the River Crni Drim, which starts in Lake Ohrid and ends in the Adriatic, and the Strumica, which drains into the Struma in Bulgaria, also lead to a sea port.

As is already evident, there are numerous small mountain ranges in Vardar Macedonia, and in fact 80% of the country is considered mountainous. This is due to the fact that three tectonic plates, African, Asian and European, meet in this region. It is mostly the work of the African plate sliding beneath the Eurasian plates under Greece that caused the geographic formation of Macedonia that we see today, and it is also the reason why there are frequent earthquake tremors in the region and many hot springs.

The friction between the plates has brought about a number of fault lines that run across Macedonia approximately along the course of riverbeds. The one under Kočani along the River Bregalnica contributed to the 1904 earthquake, and the Skopje fault line along the Vardar contributed to the 1963 earthquake that destroyed most of the city. The earliest well-recorded earthquake in the region was in AD518 when Heraklea was destroyed. Scientists claim that these earthquakes are moving eastward in intensity; and with the earthquake of 2011 in Spain, this doesn't bode well for Italy or Macedonia.

There are eight well-developed hot springs in Vardar Macedonia and dozens more that are undeveloped. The former have all been developed for medicinal purposes, although moves are afoot to open them up for recreational use. The medicinal qualities of the water depend on the mineral deposits beneath the spring, which the water has been forced through in order to reach the surface. Yugoslavia put a lot of research into understanding the medicinal properties of these hot springs and Macedonian doctors will frequently prescribe a sojourn at a particular hot spring for its healing qualities in relation to all sorts of maladies, from broken bones to pneumonia. Only Katlanovska Banja near Skopje offers western European spa-type standards, although there are plans also for Negorski Banja near Gevgelija and Kožuf ski resort, and for Kežovica Banja near Štip. Capa Spa's two facilities near Debar have recently been renovated although they are still largely medicinal in nature.

The border of Vardar Macedonia shares three tectonic lakes, Ohrid, Prespa and Dojran, with its neighbours Albania and Greece. As their names imply, these lakes were formed millennia ago from movements in the tectonic plates. Lake Ohrid in particular is so old and its life forms so unique that it is comparable to Lake Baikal in Russia and Lake Titicaca in Peru/Bolivia, and it is under UNESCO protection. There are also ten manmade lakes, which were formed to create a hydro-electric production capability under Yugoslav Macedonia, and a number of glacial lakes high up in the mountains of the Baba, Jablanica and Šar ranges.

The longest river in Macedonia is the Vardar, which starts in the mountains above Gostivar and drains out at Thessaloniki in Greece. The Vardar collects 80% of the water run-out of Macedonia. The next longest rivers are the Bregalnica and Crna, both of which empty into the Vardar.

The highest peak in Macedonia, at 2,753m, Mount Korab is on the border with Albania. The highest peak wholly within Macedonia is Titov Vrv at 2,748m in the Šar Planina range, which is surpassed in the former Yugoslav states only by Mount Triglav in Slovenia. The lowest point in Macedonia is where the River Vardar exits into Greece at 45m above sea level.

Years of communist neglect and a poor economy have done little to improve transportation lines within the country. The only international railway line that presently runs through Macedonia, stopping in Skopje, is from Ljubljana to Thessaloniki. The lines to Priština and Kičevo have been sporadic since hostilities in the 1990s, and the line to Greece via Bitola does not run trains beyond Bitola. The original line to Ohrid was not updated with the wider-gauge rails beyond Kičevo and so stops there. The line from Kumanovo, planned to go to Bulgaria, stops 40km short of the border. A working passenger line runs from Veles to Kočani via Štip, but the side line from Prilep to Sopotnica is no longer working.

In line with preparation for EU entry, the European Agency for Reconstruction is pouring money into the main highways through Macedonia, so Motorway 1 (E75) along the Vardar, Motorway 2 from Kumanovo into Bulgaria and the E65 from Skopje through Tetovo, Gostivar and Kičevo to Ohrid and Bitola are in good condition, with dual carriageways on portions of those roads leading out of Skopje. There are plans to build a new tunnel around Demir Kapija to join up the motorway through to Greece. With decentralisation other roads are being improved, but some are still in a bad state of repair and some are cobbled (which have the advantage at least of being hard wearing). A great many villages in Macedonia are still only accessible by dirt track or goat path, although these tend to be way up in the mountains where village life is dying out (partially because of lack of accessibility).

ANCIENT ROADS IN MACEDONIA

As Rome advanced its empire across the Balkan peninsula and beyond, a number of key trade and military routes were developed. Serving these routes were

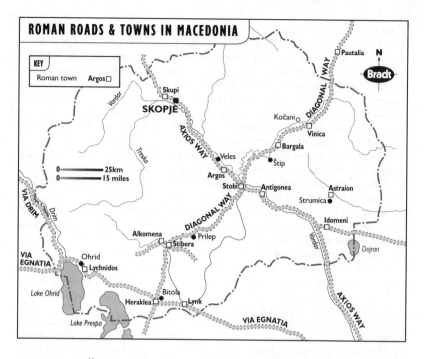

ROMAN ROADS & TOWNS IN MACEDONIA

KEY
Roman town   Argos□

numerous small towns and settlements. Their whereabouts are well documented in Macedonian, but little information is available on them in English and their full significance is even less understood (see box, pages 14–15). Key ancient towns are detailed in individual chapters of this book, but roads are described below.

VIA EGNATIA The Via Egnatia connected Italy via the port of Durres in Albania to Elbasan and Ohrid, mostly along the River Shkumbin on the Albanian side. The Via Egnatia entered Macedonia near the village of Radožda on the western side of Lake Ohrid, then went around the north side of the lake to Ohrid and around the north side of the Galičica and Baba mountains to Heraklea near present-day Bitola. The road exited Vardar Macedonia via the ancient city of Lynk on the River Crna and then went on to Edessa, Pella and Thessaloniki, and eventually to Constantinople (today's Istanbul; Carigrad or Tsar's Town in Macedonian).

Most of the Roman surfaces in Macedonia are either buried or have been resurfaced. The most well-known section of the road in Macedonia is the cobbled section between Magarevo and Turnovo to the west of Bitola. This road was cobbled by French troops during World War I offensives. Some of it can still be seen but the remainder has since been tarmacked. A small section is still visible at the back of Radožda (see page 194). The Via Egnatia Foundation (*www.viaegnatiafoundation.eu*) aims to reinvigorate the Via Egnatia and some of its work has helped to mark the Via Egnatia trail. The Macedonia section of the Via Egnatia is due to be marked in 2012.

There are claims that sections of the Via Egnatia are visible between Oktiši and Gorna Belica at a stopping point called Vajtos, which some believe is the eighth stopping point on the road. But this location would be a complete dog-leg off the Radožda to Ohrid route and it is more likely that this section of ancient Roman road belonged to the road that followed the River Crni Drim from Enchelon (now Struga) via Debar to the mouth of the Crni Drim in present-day Albania.

VIA AXIOS AND THE DIAGONAL WAY The Diagonal Way linked Heraklea with Stibera, which lies halfway between Bitola and Prilep, with Stobi, Bargala near Štip and Pautalija (now Kustendil) in present-day Bulgaria. It was an important road linking the Vardar Valley with the Struma Valley (now in Bulgaria) and crossed other important roads along the way. At Stibera it met the road from the mining town of Demir Hisar which followed the River Crna. At Stobi it crossed the Via Axios (the ancient Greek name for the Vardar River), which ran along the Vardar, and at Bargala it crossed the road from Strumica to the Ovče Polje plains around Sveti Nikole.

CLIMATE

Macedonia has a relatively dry Mediterranean climate with the full array of four seasons, although spring can be quite short, and each season is tempered by the altitude. In the Vardar Valley, Ovče Polje and the lower Pelagonia plains, temperatures are roasting hot in the summer and relatively mild in the winter. Skopjites tend to empty out of the capital during the hottest months of July and August, when temperatures can reach 40°C. These summer highs are infrequently punctuated by summer storms, but they do occur, especially in the mountains. Favourite summer retreats to the cool and welcoming mountains are Mavrovo National Park, Pelister National Park, Popova Šapka, Kriva Palanka, Berovo and Kruševo. Bitola, a mere 380m above Skopje, is usually a good 10–12°C lower in temperature year round than the city itself.

Although the winters are mild in the low areas along the River Vardar, rarely getting below freezing, there are occasionally freak winters, such as in 2001–02, which saw Skopje come to a standstill when snow and ice blocked the roads for weeks. The mountains, however, regularly see 1–2m of snow. This makes for decent skiing, limited only by the standard of facilities or a skier's own abilities to go off-piste. Regions above 2,000m will see pockets of snow as early as August, and the peaks are certainly dusted with a light coat of snow by early November.

September and April may see longer spells of cloud and rain. In general though, the weather is warm and sunny from March through to November and perfect for outdoor sports. October to November is when the mountain trees turn colour before they shed their leaves and this is the time to take a drive or hike through the ravines of Mavrovo, the Radika, Treška, Babuna and Maleševo. Skopje can get caught in fog during this time, but 20 minutes outside of the capital usually reveals bright sunny weather.

FLORA AND FAUNA

Due to Macedonia's location between the Mediterranean and Euro-Siberian regions, the variety of flora and fauna is extensive. During the 1970s and 1980s research and records were made of all the animals and plants in the Yugoslav Federation. Since then, however, Macedonia has had few resources to spend on maintaining these records and so even approximate figures on how many of each type of animal there are in Macedonia are few and far between. Macedonia has worked jointly with other countries, such as Greece, to try to establish approximate numbers of wolves for instance, but more research needs to be done in order to confirm these figures.

A number of hotels and travel agencies, such as Hotel Bistra in Mavrovo, Go Macedonia and Adventure Guide Macedonia in Skopje, can arrange wildlife observation trips by jeep if you are interested. Lake Dojran and Golem Grad Island in Prespa Lake are havens of water wildlife, insects and birds, and there are

Sanne van den Heuvel

If you leave early for a hike in the Macedonian mountains, you will definitely meet a couple of old folks collecting whatever the season offers. Macedonians still use a wide variety of herbs and teas for their medicinal properties and most people will be able to inform you about the characteristics of these plants, where to find them and how to use them.

The pleasure of collecting nettle in early spring, wild strawberries in high summer and chestnuts in autumn creates an intimate relationship with nature, enriching the experience of walking in the mountains. Collecting herbs must be done in agreement with existing regional and national laws for protection and sustainable usage of plant species. Always pick only small parts from each plant to make sure that it is still able to grow.

An excellent book on collecting edible wild plants and mushrooms is Richard Mabey's *Food for Free* (Harper Collins, 2003). The overview below (courtesy of the Berovo Hiking Trail map) provides a list of the most common herbs in Macedonia and their uses. The Berovo map is published by the Tourism Information Point (☏ 033 471 287; www.berovo.gov.mk). They offer programmes on rural and eco tourism and can arrange activities such as hiking, walking, biking and camping.

Latin name	Common name in English and Macedonian	What and how it is collected	Uses
Thymus spp.	Thyme *Majčina dušica*	Young, green parts of the stem with leaves and flowers	Pneumonia, bronchitis and sore throat, nervousness, insomnia
Convalaria majalis	Lily of the valley *Momina solza*	Section above ground when buds begin to show	Heart problems
Rosa canina	Rose hip *Šipka, diva roza*	Mature and hard fruits without stem, clean or sift out the centres which contain sharp hairs	In jams and tea, rich in vitamin C
Primula veris	Primrose *Jaglika aglička*	Flowers in dry, sunny weather; the plant is rare and should only be collected in small batches	Cough, runny nose, cleaning of the blood
Chamomilla vulgare	Chamomile *Kamilica, vrtipop*	Flower and section about ground from spring until end of the summer	Inflammation of the mouth, dry lips, sore throat

dedicated wetlands at Ezerani (near Resen) and Blato (near Strumica). If you take a guided tour in one of the national parks, such as from the village of Brajčino, your guide will be able to show you the tracks and beds of the local animals. Bats can often be seen in the evening around many of Macedonia's caves such as at Leskoec, Matka and Treskavec.

If you just want a quick overview of Macedonia's wildlife then the Natural History Museum in Skopje houses everything (stuffed) in one convenient location. Although the museum is in desperate need of attention and a good English brochure,

Latin name	Common name in English and Macedonian	What and how it is collected	Uses
Origanum vulgare	Wild marjoram Planinski čaj, rigjen	Section of plant above ground and the flower	For the throat, pains in the kidney, and stomach
Urtica dioica	Nettle Kopriva	Leaves and herb are collected in July and August; roots are collected in the autumn and in the spring	Cleaning of the blood, a homeostatic and for kidney disorders
Sambucus nigra	Elder Bozel	Collected when blossoms begin to open in May and June	Given for colds, flu, pneumonia and other respiratory illnesses
Achillea millefolium	Common yarrow Bela rada, ajdučka treva	Above ground section collected when it blossoms from May to September	Pains from diabetes and in the liver
Juniperus communis	Juniper Cmreka	Fruits are collected when they become dark blue from the end of August to September	Improving appetite, pains in gastro-intestinal track and respiratory illnesses
Plantago lanceolata	Narrowleaf plantain Tesnolisten tegavec	Leaves are collected from May to October when the plant blossoms	Cold, diarrhoea and ulcers
Viscum album	Mistletoe Bela imela	Leaves and the stem are collected from November to March; plant grows very slowly and large collections are tough on the plant	Regulation of blood pressure, makes blood vessels more elastic, increases metabolism and processes in the digestive tract
Rubus idaeus	Raspberry Malina	Leaves are collected in summer from June-July to September	Nervousness, pre-menstrual tension, diarrhoea and dysentery
Mentha piperita	Peppermint Nane	Leaves are collected before blossoming in May	Used against gastro-intestinal pains and gases
Erythraea	Centaury/ red gentian Crven kantarion	The upper section is collected before blossoming	Increasing appetite and gastro-intestinal pains
Hypericum	St John's wort Kantarion	Leaves and flowers	In tea and as an oil; an all round immune booster, antiseptic and anti-depressant

it is quite interesting and also houses the skeletons of prehistoric animals that used to roam through Macedonia. For the most current information on Macedonia's wildlife contact Dr Ljupčo Mejolovski or Slavčo Hristovski at the Macedonian Ecology Society (*Bul Kuzman Josifovski-Pitu 28/III-7, 1000 Skopje;* ✆ *02 2402 773/4;* e *contact@mes.org.mk; www.mes.org.mk*).

MAMMALS There are several protected mammal species in Macedonia, including brown bears, jackals and Balkan lynx. Macedonia is still in the process of producing its National Red List, and latest efforts can be found on the website of the Ministry of Environment and Physical Planning (*www.moepp.gov.mk*).

The last study in 1997 on **brown bears** (*Ursus arctos*) assessed their figures at somewhere between 160–200, of which there were around 70 in Mavrovo National Park, 30 in Pelister and only three or four in Galičica. Since brown-bear hunting became illegal in 1996, it is believed that the bear population has slowly increased.

For the **jackal** (*Canis aureus*) there are no available numbers; the **Balkan lynx** (*Lynx lynx martinoi*) is the national animal, depicted on the back of the five denar coin. The Balkan lynx itself is poached for its gorgeous spotted golden-brown fur, even though poaching lynx can bring a sentence of up to eight years' imprisonment. Its habitat, however, is also under continuous threat from illegal logging. In continuing decline, its numbers are believed to be fewer than 100 across Macedonia and Albania, with even fewer in Serbia and Kosovo. In an effort to reverse this phenomenon, the Balkan Lynx Recovery Programme (*www.catsg.org/balkanlynx;* e *catsglib@kora.ch*) has been established across the Balkans to monitor and assist with protection. Thirty cameras have been set up in Galičica National Park alone, where the programme is monitored by Dime Melovski of the Macedonian Ecological Society (see contact details, page 9).

Wolves, on the other hand, are not protected as they are considered a pest, preying on sheep and other farm livestock. Some 350 are killed every year, but their population remains stable at around 700. Since the government decreased the

ENCOUNTERING BROWN BEARS

Taken from Bradt's Central and Eastern European Wildlife, *by Gerard Gorman*

Much has been written and said about what a person should and should not do when meeting a bear face to face. In most cases nothing at all needs to be done as bears usually do their utmost to avoid confrontation with humans. However, in the event of a physical confrontation humans stand almost no chance at all, as brown bears are incredibly powerful and fearless. Most confrontations between humans and bears involve animals who have been startled when feeding or mothers who sense their cubs are at risk.

- Give bears plenty of respect and space
- Never run from a bear; instead speak and move your arms to indicate you are human
- Alternatively, back away slowly and carefully
- If a bear stands up on its hind legs do not panic, it is merely assessing the situation
- Never walk directly towards a bear
- Never approach seemingly 'lost' cubs
- If a bear moves towards you stand your ground and stand as tall as you can
- Never look an approaching bear directly in the eye
- If a bear moves to attack hit the ground face-down and put your hands over the back of the neck
- When on the ground stay still, silent and 'play possum'
- Do not climb a tree to escape from a bear unless you are sure you can get above 4m high

amount paid for a wolf skin (now about 700MKD), it has been assumed that the wolf population will increase.

The national parks and Jasen Forestry Reserve are home to many of the hunted species in Macedonia such as wolf, marten, wild boar, chamois, roebuck and other deer, and their numbers are meant to be regulated through the use of a hunting licence system. Despite this, however, many of these animals are in decline. According to the Open Society Institute (*www.soros.org.mk*) most of the hunted animals' stocks have been reduced to less than 25% of their former numbers, and sightings are definitely not as common as they used to be. The deer populations in some gaming areas are less than 7% of their former numbers.

REPTILES AND INSECTS Macedonia does have some poisonous insects and reptiles, including some snakes and a few species of **spider**. Like most wild creatures, these will go in the opposite direction of a human being if given enough chance to do so. Many types of **lizard** will be seen scurrying from footpaths as you walk through the mountains, and **frogs** are abundant at Lake Prespa. A rare fish-eating spider lives in the wetlands near Strumica (see page 291). **Mosquitoes** are common in marshy areas in the lowlands, but these areas are few and far between. Watch out also for **tortoises** or **turtles** crossing the roads – these are as much of a hazard and victim here as hedgehogs are in Great Britain.

Among Macedonia's 17 different types of **snake** are the common (and poisonous) adder, field viper and sand viper (known as *poskog* or 'jumping snake' in Macedonian), as well as non-venomous water snakes and other more unusual species. The javelin sand boa, found in sandy areas around Lake Dojran, can reach up to 70cm in length and is one of the smallest of the boa and python family usually found in warmer parts of the world. The largest European snake, which can be found in the lowlands of Macedonia, is the large whip snake, *Coluber caspius*, which reaches up to 3m in length. Although non-venomous, it will bite in captivity or when frightened.

Two 'semi-venomous' snakes also live in Macedonia. The Montpelier snake, *Malpolon monspessulanus*, is found up to 2m in length in rocky limestone areas with dense vegetation. The cat snake *Telescopus falax* reaches up to 1m in length and prefers dry rocky lowlands, old walls and ruins. Both snakes are semi-poisonous because their venom produces only localised swelling and numbness and is difficult to eject from the small mouths of these snakes into a human arm or leg. Fingers might be tempting, though.

FISH Macedonia's freshwater fish include carp, bream, catfish, barbell and perch. Dojran bleak, Strumica bleak and Macedonian dace are some that are peculiar to Macedonia, as is the Dojran roach, *Ratilus ratilus dojrovensis*, and Ohrid trout, *Salma trutto letnica*. The latter are now endangered and fishing for them is illegal. The 10 August 2005 article from the Balkan Investigative Research Network (BIRN) highlights the problems of poaching and tourist demands (*www.iwpr. net/?p=bcr&s=f&o=257050&apc_state=henibcr200508*). Ohrid trout is one of four protected fish species in Macedonia. Another type of Ohrid trout, *belvica*, is also served in restaurants and is a tasty alternative for a law-abiding tourist.

Eel, *jagula* in Macedonian, is common in Macedonia and a favourite dish of the locals. The eel from Lake Ohrid used to spawn in the Sargasso Sea until dams were built along the Crni Drim River. It is not yet clear how this is affecting their population, but they still seem abundant. Of the many small fish in Lake Ohrid, the *plašica* is the most famous, for its scales are used to make Ohrid pearls, using a painstakingly intricate technique the secret of which is fiercely guarded by the artisans of Ohrid.

BIRDS There are over 330 kinds of bird in Macedonia, and almost 100 migratory bird species that spend some of the year in Macedonia. Of Macedonia's native birds, 56 are protected. Amongst those protected are vultures and eagles. Despite this status and efforts to increase numbers, vulture populations have halved over the last decade. In 2010 there were estimated to be 19 or 20 pairs of Griffin vultures, 26–8 pairs of Egyptian vultures, and only one solitary male bearded vulture and one male black vulture. Both these last birds lost their mates well over a decade ago, and as they are monogamous creatures it is extremely unlikely that they will find new mates. There are plans afoot through the Black Vulture Conservation Foundation (*www.bvcf.org*) to introduce new pairs of bearded and black vultures into the country, but once again resources to fund such initiatives are limited.

Although eagles used to be abundant in Macedonia, only a dozen or so pairs can be found now around Mount Korab and the Šar mountain range. Storks, both white and black, are also on the decline, but you will still see them nesting in a number of villages and towns. Macedonian folklore claims they bring luck especially with regard to childbearing.

Pelicans and cormorants are quite common and fishermen use cormorants to catch fish on Lake Prespa. A wetland reserve at Ezerani is home to many of Macedonia's birds. Imported birds include peacocks, to be found at the monastery of Sveti Naum; swans, introduced to Lake Ohrid in the early 1970s; black turkeys at the Monastery of Zrze; and ostriches farmed near Tetovo and Gostivar.

PLANTS AND BUTTERFLIES There are over 3,500 different plants in Macedonia. These include alpine flowers such as gentian and furry alpine bluebell as well as imported stocks of kiwi, pomegranates and rice, usually the preserve of more tropical climates. The great variety of flowers here also attracts an incredible number of different butterflies and moths. Look out particularly for the humming-bird hawk-moth, *Macroglossum stellatarum*, which is not commonly found in northern Europe.

NATIONAL PARKS There are three national parks in Macedonia and one forestry reserve; these are covered in more detail in their respective chapters: Galičica (page 192), Pelister (page 213) and Mavrovo (page 248) national parks and Jasen Forestry Reserve (page 233).

Over 35% of the country is forest, most of which is deciduous. Less than 10% of Macedonia's forests are evergreen, but amongst that 10% is the Molika pine, which is unique to the greater Macedonia region, Bulgaria and Albania. In Macedonia the Molika pine is mostly found in Pelister National Park.

ENVIRONMENTAL EFFORTS

Despite views to the contrary, the communist period of Macedonia's history had gone a long way, both deliberately and inadvertently, towards helping preserve Macedonia's rich wildlife and unspoilt natural environment. All three national parks, Pelister (1948), Galičica (1949) and Mavrovo (1958), were set up during this time, as well as Jasen Forestry Reserve (1958), and 48 natural monuments were designated for protection. Inadvertently also, Macedonia's poor economy, low levels of tourism and lack of urbanisation have helped to preserve many areas of natural beauty.

Industrial pollution has been and still is a problem, as is the Macedonian disregard for litter, especially the non-biodegradable kind. The Macedonians may try to blame the government for a lack of litter bins and anyone to take the litter away (which is true) but Macedonians don't help themselves. As every responsible hiker knows, if you pack it in with you, then pack it out with you, and get rid of your rubbish through the waste disposal service rather than leave it as an eyesore and health hazard. There are efforts under way by NGOs to move the government towards better waste management, but it may be a few more years before the effects are seen.

Macedonia does have some environmental groups, which go back to the communist era of social awareness, and even more are springing up now in the wake of international money earmarked for building civil society and civil participation. Although these groups do good work, and go some way towards educating local communities about environmental concerns in their area, to be effective a nationwide effort really needs to be led by the government.

RECYCLING Recycling does exist in Macedonia, although the service doesn't come to the door, and won't even be in a nearby street. Newspaper and magazine recycling is the most ubiquitous, with large bell-like green drums in main streets in which you can slot papers and magazines. These are picked up by Skopje's paper recycling company, Komuna (*Ul Romanija bb, 1040 Skopje, behind the Skopje Fair;* \ *02 2551 081;* e *info@komuna.com.mk; www.komuna.com.mk;* ⏱ *08.00–14.00 daily*). They also collect office paper and will supply special cardboard cartons for offices for that purpose. Cardboard is also recycled there, and when you see it being collected by people on the streets, you'll be glad to know that it is not for the homeless to build a cardboard house under a bridge, but to be sold to Komuna for recycling.

Large blue cages are sometimes visible on main streets for plastic bottle recycling, and a service is available for companies through a USAID-assisted project (*www. plasticrecycling.org.mk*).

Whether you are living in or just visiting Macedonia, don't add to the rubbish which is already here, but follow these simple points:

- Reduce the amount you have to throw away, such as packaging
- Reuse disposable items, such as bags, paper and containers
- If possible, recycle what you need to throw away
- If you pack it in, then pack it out
- Take your own bags (preferably cloth) with you to the shops
- Buy recycled and biodegradable products

LOCAL ENVIRONMENTAL ORGANISATIONS Macedonia's environment is at a critical point in its development and so now is the time to ensure that it is saved for the likes of you and me to enjoy when we come to visit another day. If you would like to find out more about how you could get involved with environmental protection in Macedonia, contact one of the following groups:

Eco-sense 11 Oktomvri 125/12, 1000 Skopje; \ 02 3217 245/247; e info@ekosvest.com. mk; www.ekosvest.com.mk. Regularly seeks volunteers to help with clean-up days & other larger projects.
Eko.net Kozle 100, PO Box 360, 1000 Skopje; \f 02 3090 400; e contact@eko.net.mk; www. eko.net.mk. Dedicated to informing people about the environmental efforts ongoing in Macedonia.
Proaktiva Contact Slavjanka Miladinova at Venjamin Macukovski 2/1-1, PO Box 695, 1000

Skopje; \f 02 2465 963; e info@proaktiva.org. mk; www.proaktiva.org.mk. A young enthusiastic group that has worked hard to increase public awareness of the importance of resource efficiency to Macedonia's environment.
Vila Zora 22 Trajko Panov, 1400 Veles; \ 043 233 023; e vilazora@mt.net.mk; www.vilazora. org.mk. Does major advocacy in remediating soil around the Veles area that has been contaminated by local industry. Also does a lot on preserving & presenting natural habitat & trails.

HISTORY

The Republic of Macedonia achieved independence from Yugoslavia on 8 September 1991. The word 'Macedonia', however, has been associated with a much larger area than that represented by today's republic. 'Macedonia' has meant many things and had a multitude of changing boundaries across the millennia, but at its core is a geographical area upon which most historians and geographers are united. Geographical Macedonia, covering a large swathe of land from the source of the River Vardar (Axios in Greek) to its estuary at Solun (Thessaloniki in Greek), has a very rich and varied history, which is reflected in the present-day political climate and division of the geographical region.

Macedonia had its heyday during the build-up of its ancient empire, ending with the sudden death of Aleksandar III of Macedon (also known as Alexander the Great). Macedonia's claim today to this period of history is hotly disputed by the Greeks (see pages 35–7). As a recognised state, Macedonia rose for a short

(see pages 35–7)

AN UNTOLD STORY – ARCHAEOLOGY IN MACEDONIA

Andriana Dragovic and Nikica Korubin

Macedonia has a rich and varied archaeological resource. Of all the periods to be found in the country (from the Mesolithic to the more recent archaeology of the cold war) it is the Roman sites that are the most monumental and most visible in the landscape. Remarkably little archaeological research has been undertaken however, and the management, curation and presentation of archaeological sites are universally poor. Nevertheless the situation is changing (though maybe not for the better) and a great deal of state funding is pouring into excavation campaigns. Conversely, work in the realms of heritage management and resource quantification is being undertaken largely by the NGO sector with geo-physical surveys at sites such as Skupi, Bargala near Štip and Konjuh near Kumanovo.

Macedonia sits astride the land routes from western Europe into Asia and indeed the conquest of Macedonia was the key to the spread of Roman influence and later military occupation in the east. The ancient territories of Macedonia and Alexander the Great were of particular significance to the Romans because the emulation and surpassing of the feats of Alexander were a visible testament, both in the wider world and more importantly at home in Rome, to the greatness of Rome, the Senate (and later the emperor) and Roman civilisation.

The Romans were extremely familiar with the Hellenic way of life, thought, architecture and urban living, and claimed much of it as their own. Hellenic colonies were interspersed in the western Mediterranean and much of southern Italy was influenced by Macedonian colonies, the most famous of which being the city of Pompeii. Much of the design of Roman houses aped Greek or Hellenic forms. As a result, the Hellenistic world created by Macedonian military might have appeared familiar to the Romans, as if Macedonia itself was a part of Rome's backyard. When Augustus conquered the modern-day areas of Serbia and Bulgaria, establishing the province of Moesia, the frontier of the Roman world in the Balkans became the River Danube. Macedonia in the hinterland of this important frontier was thus one of the keys to military and civilian control of both the northern frontier of the Balkans and a gateway to the ancient Mediterranean world.

while again in the 11th century during the reign of Tsar Samoil (hotly disputed by the Bulgarians, see page 22). The region exerted an influence variously through its status as the Archbishopric of Bitola and Ohrid, but as an independent state, Macedonia did not emerge again until the ten-day Kruševo Republic of 1903.

Geographical Macedonia is now made up of four political entities: Vardar Macedonia, which is the Republic of Macedonia; Pirin Macedonia, which is in Bulgaria; Aegean Macedonia, which is in Greece; and a tiny sliver north and south of Debar, which is in Albania.

CHRONOLOGY

Pre-9500BC	Palaeolithic (Old Stone Age) findings yet to be confirmed at Cocev Kamen
9500–6000BC	First traces of human existence in northern Macedonia date back to the Mesolithic (Middle Stone Age) period

The significance of the archaeology in Macedonia is global, not least because the historical region of Macedonia was Alexander's manor and he still occupies a pre-eminent role in the psyche of northwest Europe and the US.

Funding for archaeological research is derived entirely from the Ministry of Culture. In a country with serious economic problems the realisation of the potential of the archaeological resource to entice the tourist dollar is growing, but as yet lacks the sophistication of approach found in many other European countries. Local archaeological organisations and NGOs are trying to build international co-operation with foreign institutions, with some success. There are a number of examples of collaborative archaeological excavations with foreign (usually American) and Macedonian teams working in tandem.

Looting of archaeological sites is a big problem in Macedonia but identifying the scale is difficult for two reasons. Firstly, looted artefacts are whisked away to foreign markets in Europe, America and the Far East and secondly, the precise provenance of any artefacts can seldom be established because so many of the sites of discovery are unknown to the archaeological community in Macedonia and thus cannot be policed. There is a robust legal framework to protect the archaeological sites of Macedonia, but the actual process of enumerating, identifying and characterising where the undiscovered archaeological sites are is yet to commence with any seriousness and the possibility of state provision for such a process has been called, from within the archaeological community of Macedonia itself, a 'science fiction'. There are, however, many iconic archaeological sites to visit, with excavations under way at Plaošnik in Ohrid; Markovi Kuli, Visoka and Stibera in the Prilep region; Stobi near Veles; Heraklea in Bitola; and Skupi outside Skopje.

Opportunities to excavate at a number of sites in Macedonia can be arranged through the **Balkan Heritage Field School** (e *balkanheritage@gmail.com; www.bhfieldschool.org*) or **Crnobuki Summer Archaeological School** (e *cai@macedonianarchaeology.org; www.crnobuki.macedonianarchaeology.org*).

If you come across an archaeological find, by law it must be reported to the **Cultural Heritage Protection Office** (*Gjuro Gjakovič 61, Skopje;* 02 3211 495, 02 3289 703; e *contact@uzkn.gov.mk*). The Law on Protection of Cultural Heritage, Official Gazette 20/04, can be downloaded from the CHPO website (uzkn.gov.mk).

6000–4000BC	Neolithic (New Stone Age) period, Gorlevo seal and Golemata Majka found near Skopje
4000–2200BC	Aneolithic (Bronze Age), including the use of Kokino observatory
2200–600BC	Iron Age and rock paintings in Cocev Kamen
600–217BC	Paeonian kingdom
Mid-4th century BC	Paeonia vassaled to the Macedon royal dynasty
294–168BC	Antigonid dynasty
168BC–AD**395**	Roman period
395–1204	Byzantine period
6th century	Invasion of Goths, Huns and Avars
7th century	Beginning of Slavic immigration
976–1014	Reign of Tsar Samoil
1018–1767	Archbishopric of Ohrid
1096–97	Crusaders cross Macedonia
1371–94	King Marko's Kingdom of Macedonia
1394–1912	Ottoman rule
1877–78	Russo–Turkish war
March 1878	Treaty of San Stefano gives most of Macedonia to 'Big Bulgaria'
July 1878	Treaty of Berlin returns Macedonia to the Ottoman Empire
1893	Formation of the Internal Macedonian Revolutionary Organisation (VMRO) separatist movement
3 September 1901	Kidnapping of American missionary Miss Ellen Stone
3–10 August 1903	The Kruševo Republic
1912	First Balkan War sees Serbia, Greece and Bulgaria defeat Turkey; Macedonia is divided between Serbia and Greece
1913	Second Balkan War – Bulgaria tries to retake Macedonia
1914–18	Macedonia ruled by Bulgaria during World War I in return for supporting Axis
1918–41	Came under the rule of the Kingdom of Serbs, Croats and Slovenes
1920	Ruled for six months by the Yugoslav Communist Party
1941–44	Ruled again by Bulgaria
1944–91	Socialist Republic of Macedonia (within Federal Republic of Yugoslavia)
1991–present	Independent (former Yugoslav) Republic of Macedonia
2001	Six-month internal conflict between the National Liberation Army (ethnic Albanian) and state security forces
13 August 2001	Signature of the Ohrid Framework Agreement ends the conflict
15 December 2005	Macedonia receives EU candidacy status
April 2008	Greece vetoes Macedonia's accession to NATO due to their name dispute
5 December 2011	The International Court of Justice declares that Greece violated its 1995 Interim Accord with Macedonia by vetoing Macedonia's accession to NATO

STONE AGE PREHISTORY Information on this period of Macedonian history is sketchy. However, there is increasing speculation and some evidence that prehistoric Macedonia (6500–3500BC) may have had a matriarchal society worshipping female lineage and deity until their demise through the arrival of male-dominated Vinca-Turdas Neolithic tribes around 4500BC (established through pottery findings). The discovery of the Golemata Majka (Great Mother, not to be confused with the much later Magna Mater worship of the Romans from around the 2nd century BC) statue of 6500BC in Tumba Madžari in southeast Skopje in 1981 is cited as evidence of this.

The Aneolithic stilt water village, the Bay of Bones (see page 186), near Gradište, Ohrid, is another example of human settlement in Macedonia from prehistory.

Paeonia According to Homer's rendition of mythical times in the *Iliad,* before Macedonia and the Macedonians came Paeonia and the Paeons. This land stretched from the source of the River Vardar to its estuary at Thessaloniki and across the River Struma to the Rhodope Mountains in the east. The legend goes that the Paeons themselves were direct descendants of the river god Axios. They were culturally quite close to their Illyrian, Thracian and Greek neighbours, and even took part in the siege of Troy around 1200BC. Later, other Greek historians such as Herodotus, Livius, Strabo and Thucydides described Paeonia and the Paeons in their writings.

It is now known that the Paeonian tribe existed from at least the late 6th century BC when the tribe started to issue its own coins, some of which are on display in the Museum of Coinage (see page 144) in Skopje. The first known capital of the Paeonians was Vilazora (today's Veles), and this was later moved to Stobi. By that time (mid 4th century BC) Philip II (Alexander the Great's father) brought Paeonia under his rule as a vassal state. It was completely subsumed into Macedonia by 217BC. Traces of their walled towns can still be found around Macedonia, where tumbled piles of limestone blocks tell of the Cyclopean masonry techniques used to build their mighty fortresses. Vajtos, Matka, Mariovo and Demir Kapija were four such sites.

There is also mention during this time that in the southwest of the land lay an area called Pelagonia. Named after Pelagon, the son of Axios, this land was located around the River Crni Drim, which runs from Struga at Lake Ohrid through Debar into present-day Albania.

Further descriptions are made of other tribes bordering on, and fighting with, the ancient Macedonians who came to dominate the region. These tribes include the Lyncestis, who used to live in the area around Heraklea (now Bitola); the Brigians, who spread out in pockets all over Macedonia, modern-day central Albania and northwest Greece; the Enhelians centred around southeast Macedonia; the Dassaretians settled around Ohrid (then Lichnidos); the Illyrians who moved into present-day Albania and therefore bordered on western Macedonia; and finally the Dardanians who originated from a similar area to the Illyrians, and who some believe may have been related to the Illyrians. All these tribes are mentioned by Thucydides in his *History of the Peloponnesian War*, a war fought between Athens and Sparta in 431–404BC.

HOUSE OF MACEDON Legend says that the Macedonians came from Macedon, the grandson of Zeus (the Greek god of thunder) by his first daughter. Hesiod's epic, *Catalogue of Women*, says that Zeus's second daughter bore two sons: Graecian and Latin. Thus the Greeks and the Romans, according to legend, were brothers, and cousins to the Macedonians. Some might say this is the origin of the animosity between the Greeks and the Macedonians. Indeed, at the time, the Greeks had gone to some lengths to keep their 'barbarian' cousins out of the Delphian Amphyctionic Council and from participating in the Olympic Games. Only in the early 5th century BC was the Macedonian royal family finally permitted into the Olympics, having been ordained 'sufficiently' Greek because of their common ancestry and worship of the same Greek gods. Common Macedonians were not allowed to compete until another century later.

How much the Macedons mixed with the Paeonians after they were made a vassal state by Philip II is not known. Philip II, who ruled 359–336BC, did found the city of Heraklea, near Bitola, and this probably brought with it a certain amount of associated Hellenic city culture.

Compared with other tribes in the Balkans, the Macedonians, allegedly by virtue of being mountain people, were renowned hunters and fighters, who also took a liking to drink and dance. These traits were equally matched by their desire for political power, which allowed the Macedonian dynasty to expand its empire

ALEKSANDAR III OF MACEDON (THE GREAT)

Born in Pella (in modern-day Greece) in 356BC, Aleksandar III of Macedon was the son of King Philip II and his wife Olympias, a Molossian princess from neighbouring Epirus. Although both of the royal houses of Macedon and Molossia were probably begrudgingly accepted as Greek by ancestry by the time Aleksander was born, it remains much debated in today's Hellenic Republic and the Republic of Macedonia as to whether Aleksandar was half Macedonian and half Epirian/Molossian or truly Greek. In either case, his father Philip II, who learnt to highly appreciate the Greek military and diplomatic education he was given as a hostage in Thebes, passed his love of Greek culture and education on to the young Aleksandar.

Aleksandar became famous for continuing his father's dream of a united and expanded pan-Hellenic empire. Philip was assassinated in 336BC before he could realise his plans. But, at the age of 20, Aleksandar continued to strengthen his father's gains. A fearless fighter and far-sighted tactician, he spoke both Greek and his native Macedonian, and had been taught in his early years by Aristotle. In the name of spreading Hellenic culture and practices, Aleksandar's empire stretched all the way to the River Ganges in India. In his reign of 12 years his victories were numerous and are legendary:

336BC	Wiped out all remaining contenders to the Macedonian throne from within Macedon
335BC	Destroyed the town of Thebes in Greece
334BC	Defeated the Persians in Asia Minor
333BC	Defeated Darius, King of Persia, at Issus
332BC	Conquered Egypt and founded the town of Alexandria
331BC	Defeated Darius again at Babylon, which Aleksandar then made capital of his empire
327BC	Defeated King Pora, thereby acquiring the Punjab
325BC	Died on 10 June on his return to Babylon

His body was eventually interred by Ptolemy in Alexandria in Egypt. However, his tomb has since disappeared without trace. Some believe his body now lies at Idomena near Gevgelia in Macedonia, but it has yet to be discovered.

The 2004 Oliver Stone movie, *Alexander the Great*, and the 1998 Michael Wood BBC documentary, *In the Footsteps of Alexander*, are two succinct, popular sources on the man and his achievements. A website pooling a vast number of sources on Aleksandar is www.isidore-of-seville.com/alexander.

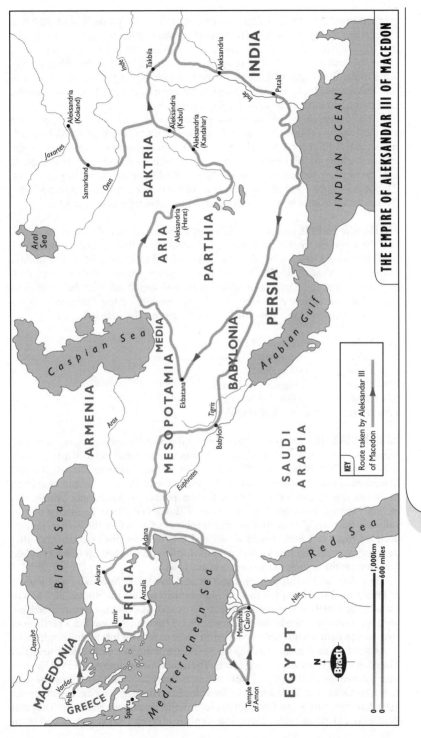

THE EMPIRE OF ALEKSANDAR III OF MACEDON

KEY

Route taken by Aleksandar III
of Macedon

19

gradually over the course of almost seven centuries. At the pinnacle of its existence during the reign of Aleksandar III of Macedon (known to Hellenites as Alexander the Great), the former Macedonian dynasty had gone forth in the name of spreading Hellenism and encompassed geographical Macedonia, most of the Hellenic city-states under the League of Corinth, the Aegean islands, Egypt, Asia Minor, eastern Iran and western India. In 331BC, Babylon (now in modern-day Iraq) was made the capital of Aleksandar's vast pan-Hellenic empire.

In the course of his ambitious campaigning, Aleksandar had squandered the previously good relations with the Greeks won by his father Philip II. Aleksandar's sudden death from fever left behind a weak and unprepared heir, and without the mighty backing of the Greek city-states the empire soon crumbled as a result of fighting between Aleksandar's generals. Eventually divided into four main territories, Aleksander's empire was already in the care of the Regent Antipater. Antipater's son, Cassander, ruled after him, but on his death the empire fell into civil strife.

ANTIGONID EMPIRE With the ancient royal house of Macedon long in tatters and the kingdom in civil war, another of Aleksandar III's generals, Antigonus I Monophthalmus, tried to retake Macedon. He had been ruler of Syria and Asia Minor after Aleksandar III, but was not able to recapture Macedon and died fighting for it at the Battle of Ipsus in 301BC. His son, Demetrius, did succeed in taking Macedon a few years later and thereby established the Antigonid Empire over Macedon and many of the Hellenic city-states for the next 125 years.

294–277BC	Demetrius I Poliorcetes
277–239BC	Antigonus II Gonatas
239–229BC	Demetrius II
229–221BC	Antigonus III Doson
221–179BC	Philip V of Macedon
179–168BC	Perseus of Macedon

ROMAN RULE The Antigonid dynasty was no match for the emerging empire of Rome. Three devastating Macedonian–Roman wars ensued over a 50-year period: 215–205BC, 200–197BC and 171–168BC. On 22 June 168BC, Perseus, the last Macedonian king, was finally defeated at the Battle of Pydna. The land of ancient Macedon was incorporated into the Roman prefecture Macedonia, which also included Epirus, Thessaly, Vetus and some of Thrace and Illyria. Pondering how to rule over the unruly Macedonians, the Amphipolis Council of the Roman Empire declared that Macedonia would be divided into four regions (*meriden*) but that each region would be free to elect its own magistrates and laws. It was forbidden, however, for the regions to co-operate at any level.

Unused to, and unhappy with these limited freedoms, Andriskos, also known as Phillip the False, led a rebellion of Macedonians against the Roman dictators in 149BC. The rebellion was resolutely put down and Macedonia's former freedoms were revoked. The Macedonians themselves were largely left alone, but a garrison of soldiers was permanently stationed there in order to fight off marauding neighbours.

As the Roman Empire grew bigger, so did the importance of various towns in Macedonia that lay on key trading routes. The most famous route was the Via Egnatia, which joined the Illyrian port of Durres (now in Albania) with Pelagonia on the Crni Drim, Heraklea near Bitola and on to Thessaloniki on the Aegean coast. Later the road extended even further to Constantinople. Another important route, the Diagonal Way, linked Heraklea with Stibera near Čepigovo (Prilep), Stobi, Bargala and on to

Pautalija (now Kustendil in Bulgaria). There was also the Axios Road linking Skupi near Skopje with Argos south of Veles, Stobi and Dober near Valandovo. (See ancient roads in Macedonia, page 5.) These important trade and military routes developed significant garrison and trading depots which soon morphed into an intricate system of towns and villages throughout Macedonia, the stories of which remain largely untold. See the box on pages 14–15 for more on Roman archaeological sites and page 6 for a map of Roman roads and towns in Macedonia.

The expansion of the Roman Empire under Illyrian-born Diocletian (who killed St George, see page 254) reduced the size of the prefecture of Macedonia to make way for the new prefectures of Thessalia and Novus Epirus. Later, Macedonia was divided into Macedonia Prima, covering most of present-day Macedonia, and Macedonia Secunda, which covered Heraklea and Dober and the land to the south of these cities.

BYZANTINE MACEDONIA In AD395, the Roman Empire was divided into west and east, with the Greek-language-dominated eastern empire becoming commonly known as the Byzantine Empire. At this time, Macedonia became part of the Byzantine Empire and was ruled from Constantinople.

After Diocletian's death in AD305, Christianity slowly settled in Macedonia. Early in the 4th century, Skupi became the seat of the bishopric for the province of Dardania. In the year AD325, Stobi also acquired its own bishop at the Council of Nicea. Finally, Heraklea was also appointed a bishop later in the century. The ruins of their early Christian basilicas can be found now in Heraklea, Stobi, Skupi and Ohrid.

After over 800 years of Roman and Byzantine rule, the orderly life of the Roman towns in Macedonia fell victim to the Huns, the Goths and the Avars. Attila the Hun and his men ransacked almost a hundred towns in the year AD447. Stobi and Heraklea survived these attacks fairly well, but a few decades later they fell to the Goths of Theodorik the Great. What the Huns and the Goths hadn't destroyed, the Avars (tribal brothers of the Mongolian hordes) finished off. And then, as if to add fate's final signature, the earthquake of AD518 undermined any attempt by the formerly great Roman towns to re-establish themselves.

SLAVIC MACEDONIA After the Huns, Goths and Avars had left the land in ruins, life in Macedonia fell to subsistence farming around small mountain towns and churches. Into this unguarded territory towards the end of the 6th century roamed the Slavic tribes from beyond the Carpathian Mountains (today's Poland, Ukraine and Moldova). The Draguvite and Brysak tribes of the south Slavs settled in the northern Macedonian and western Bulgarian regions. Over the next three centuries they integrated with the local Greek-speaking tribes and eventually adopted Christianity, which had already taken a strong hold on the indigenous population. Some Macedonian historians claim that Macedonia's Slavs came from a unique Slav tribe and had their own language and aspirations for a nation-state. There is little evidence, however, to back this.

Shortly after the fall of Tsar Samoil's empire (see box, page 22), the Normans came riding into Macedonia under Robert Giscard (1016–85) to plunder and loot. The crusaders followed in 1096–97 on their way to pit the strength of Christ against that of Muhammad in the Middle East, levying war taxes as they went. Later on, Giscard's son, Boemund of Tarent (1050–1111), returned in 1107, replaying the plundering and looting of his father.

All the while, the locals tried repeatedly to rise up against their Byzantine rulers. Late Byzantine art flourished in the churches in the area (see box, page 160), and carried by traversing crusaders ushered in the 12th century Renaissance in western

By the end of the 10th century AD, one family's aspirations for their own state were such that the four sons of the Bryzsak Duke Nikola started to rebel against the feudal rule of the Bulgarian authorities that were also ruling over Macedonia. Embroiled in its own fight with Byzantium, Bulgaria had little time for the four brothers, Aron, David, Moses and Samoil. But Bulgaria fell to Byzantium in 971 and with it Macedonia came under Byzantium rule. Five years later in 976, the Byzantium emperor John I Tzimisces died, and the four sons succeeded in taking Bulgaria and Macedonia back.

After David was killed by Vlach travellers and Moses was killed in the Battle of Serres, Aron and Samoil quarrelled. Soon Samoil had Aron and his family killed, leaving Samoil as the sole ruler of an expanding empire. He brought most of Bulgaria under his rule and most of Macedonia minus Thessaloniki, as well as large parts of Greece, Albania, Dalmatia, Bosnia and Serbia as far as the Danube.

Samoil was crowned king by Pope Gregory V at Golem Grad on Lake Prespa. For many Macedonian historians this symbolises the official break with the Bulgarian, quasi-Russian, Orthodox Church, and marks the start of a Macedonian branch of the Church headed by the archdiocese of Ohrid. Others see Samoil and his achievements as the first of many attempts at Bulgarian domination. Weighing slightly more in favour of the argument that Samoil was seen by himself and others as Bulgarian is the evidence of the Bitola inscription (found in 1956, see page 211) and the fact that Samoil's arch-enemy, Emperor Basilius II, was known by the nickname Bulgar Slayer, 'Boulgaroktonos'.

Tsar Samoil later moved his capital to Ohrid, where he built the great fortress being rebuilt today. But by 1014, the new Byzantine emperor Basilius II had had enough of this young upstart and sent troops to take back Samoil's empire. At the Battle of Belasica on 29 July 1014, Samoil's troops were resoundingly crushed by the Byzantines. Basilius (also written as Vasilius, Vasilie and Basil) then ordered that the 15,000 troops remaining should be blinded, leaving only one eye per 100 soldiers so that they could make their way back to Samoil (who had escaped during the battle) and he could see their defeat. The battle was at present-day Vodoča near Strumica. Vodoča means 'plucked eye'.

It is believed that when Samoil saw his blinded troops returning to him at Prilep on 6 October, he collapsed from a heart attack and died shortly afterwards. Macedonia then fell under Byzantine control and the people had to pay severe reparations to Constantinople for several decades to come.

Europe. In 1204, the Norman crusaders succeeded in sacking Constantinople and the Byzantine Empire fizzled into a few renegade dukes in Epirus and Nicea. The new states of Bulgaria and Serbia moved in to try to re-conquer parts of Macedonia.

FIVE HUNDRED YEARS OF OTTOMAN RULE The fall of Byzantium was eventually replaced by another empire, this time the Ottoman (for more on the Ottoman rulers, their rules and the ruled see box, page 43). Despite King Marko of Prilep's brave attempts to keep back the Turks (see box, page 200), his defeat at their hands in 1394 signalled the completion of Ottoman victory over Macedonia. Skopje had already been taken, in 1392. Debar regained some independence under Gjergj Kastriot's Albania from 1444 to 1449, but then fell to Ottoman rule along with all Albania.

With the Ottomans came Islam and the building of mosques, covered markets, balconied houses, an increase in trade and eventually clock towers and railways. As when the Romans arrived all those centuries earlier, Macedonians did not take kindly to these new foreign rulers and many fled the country. Whilst the Ottomans encouraged the rule of the Orthodox elite over its millet (see box, *The millet system of governance and its aftermath*, page 52) and even went to some lengths to help preserve and protect some churches, such as Lešok and Joakim Osogovski, other churches of particular significance, such as Sveti Sofia and Sveti Pantelejmon in Ohrid, were converted into mosques.

In the wake of emigrating Macedonians, the Turks themselves moved into fertile Macedonia in droves to build new villages and towns. This influx built up ethnic tensions and despite the superficial improvement in trade and town life, Macedonians rose up repeatedly against their new masters. Macedonian bandits did all they could to oust the Turks and many were outlawed and hunted down by Ottoman *janissaries* (the military elite, see page 25) and their *arnauts* (special forces largely recruited from Albanian communities).

The Ottoman rulers adhered to the Sunni school of Islam, and therein to the Hanafi legal code. They also, however, tolerated and legitimised the Sufi side of Islam, which hailed from the more folklorish beliefs of Islam and emphasised the mystic communion of its disciples with Allah. Many Macedonians converted to

THE FIVE VILAYETS OF THE OTTOMAN EMPIRE IN 1880

KEY TO BOUNDARIES
1880 Vilayet bdy
1880 Historic bdy
1991 International bdy

Islam during the Ottoman period, either as Sunnis, or to a Sufi order. The Sufi orders, being less strict and more tolerant of individual expression, were more open to converts from other faiths. This was particularly true of the Bektaši order who were appointed the priests of the *janissaries*.

Towards the end of the heyday of Ottoman power, the British landscape artist and travel writer Edward Lear, better known today for his nonsense poetry and limericks, travelled through the Balkans in 1848 and 1849. He spent one week painting and writing in Monastir (Bitola) and Akhrida (Ohrid – at that time a part of Albania) in September 1848. His travelogue reveals a Macedonia demographically very different from today's, in which Lear had to appeal for a guard from the local *bey* to protect him while he drew. (Because the sultan had banned life-drawing – only patterns were allowed – the local peasantry considered his paintings to be the devil's work, and threw stones at him for it.)

The treaties of San Stefano and Berlin By the second half of the 19th century, the Ottomans' iron-like grip over their empire was beginning to loosen. The Habsburg Empire had won back Serbia and Bosnia, and Greece was also independent again. The newly freed states in turn wanted their share of Macedonia. This played itself out first of all in the sphere of the Church. In 1870, Russia ordained the independence of the Bulgarian Orthodox Church, with rights of influence over Macedonia. The Greek Orthodox Church took umbrage with this turn of events, and pushed Turkey into taking the issue up with Russia. Among many other issues this prompted war between the two nations.

The Treaty of San Stefano was the result of Turkey's defeat by Russia in the Russo–Turkish war ending in March 1878. The treaty allowed Romania, Montenegro and Serbia to extend their borders to include much of the land that they now have. Bulgaria, however, was made an autonomous new state, whose new borders extended as far as Niš and Vranje in present-day Serbia, Mount Korab and Ohrid in today's Macedonia, and to the far side of Prespa and Mount Gramos in Greece.

The great European powers of Austro-Hungary, France and Great Britain were dissatisfied with Russia's new extended spheres of influence through Bulgaria, and

KING OF KUMANOVO

In 1689, Austrian emperor Leopold I of the Habsburg Empire sent General Piccolomini towards Macedonia to beat off the Ottoman army which had been encroaching upon Habsburg lands. Karpoš, chief of a band of outlaws based in the mining village of Kratovo, was quick to respond to the general's call for war and decided to rebel against the Ottoman overlords. The outlaws first rose up against the Ottoman stronghold of Kriva Palanka, and this started what came to be known as the Karpoš Uprising. More bandits joined Karpoš and the rebellion next took Kumanovo, then spread east towards Kustendil (now in Bulgaria) and west towards Skopje.

When Leopold heard that Karpoš had taken Kumanovo, the emperor promoted him and named him King of Kumanovo. But Leopold's further assistance to the new king, after Piccolomini had to beat a hasty retreat later that year, came too late. Six weeks after taking Kriva Palanka, Karpoš and 200 of his men were brutally killed and then impaled on the Stone Bridge in Skopje. Leopold's letter of encouragement to the Macedonian people a year later in 1690 fell on deaf ears.

THE DEVŠIRME TAX AND THE JANISSARIES

When the Ottomans expanded into the Balkans they started to run out of the manpower needed to manage their expanding empire, keep order and conquer new lands. As a result the they implemented a tax system in the 1380s that was levied on non-Muslim families within the new territories. This tax, called *devširme*, required between 2.5% and 10% of boys aged seven to14 (not usually the first born) to be taken for education and training to run the Ottoman Empire. The boys were encouraged to convert to the Islam faith and could be enrolled in either a civilian or a military capacity. For many non-Muslim families this tax was understandably extremely unpopular, and certainly did not help to ingratiate the new rulers with their new subjects, no matter what other 'freedoms', donations and perks may have been given in return. But as time went on, non-Muslim families found that the devširme was also a means of advancement within the Ottoman system, and soon selection criteria were attached to the devširme in order to keep down the number of applicants.

On the military side these boys went into the elite troops of the janissary (literally 'new troops' from the Turkish *yeni čeri*). Their training was harsh; once in the janissary it was forever; and they were forbidden to marry. But these elite troops soon realised their own importance and in 1449 they rebelled, demanding higher pay, pensions and other rights. It took another century before, in 1566, they won the right to marry. By the middle of the 17th century the demand to enter the janissary, particularly from Albanian, Bosnian and Bulgarian families, was so high that the devširme could be abolished.

Although these troops were formed, supposedly as a more loyal section of the army, in order to serve as the sultan's personal household troops and bodyguards, they proved in the end to be no more loyal than the rest of the Ottoman army, which was also made up of conscripted soldiers and tribal warriors. By the 18th century the janissary practically held the sultan hostage against his own imperial affairs and even his daily household. The Bekteši order of dervishes, the appointed priests of the janissary, supported them in their efforts.

The empire was already beginning to shrink due to the ineffectiveness of combat troops and many of the janissary weren't even serving soldiers. By 1826 the janissaries were so out of control that Sultan Mahmoud II finally abolished them, after several years of wresting back power from them and creating a totally new army. Their end, in a bloody revolt of the old 'new troops' against the new 'new army', was a sign of things to come over the next century: the demise of the Ottoman Empire.

they convinced Russia to redraw the map. The new treaty, put together in Berlin in June and July 1878, essentially returned Macedonia to the Ottoman Empire, but on the condition, under Article 23, that new statutes of governance be drawn up for all the provinces of European Turkey. Each statute was to be drawn up by a majority of local members and then submitted to the Sublime Porte (as the Ottoman government was known) to be enacted, but only after receiving the opinion (and implied approval) of a European commission on the issue. Such arrangements are not dissimilar to the process that new countries today still need to go through to gain international recognition. Bulgaria was duly annoyed at its loss and saw this as an affront to its long-standing kinship with Macedonia.

The seeds of Macedonian nationalism Some see the Berlin Treaty as the seed for a sovereign Macedonian state. A statute for the *sanjaks* (districts) of European Turkey, however, was never implemented not least because the Great Powers could not agree on how to use the powers they had accorded themselves. The region languished in ever greater misrule and some started to feel that the only way out was full independence. Macedonian nationalism grew and there were repeated protests and armed clashes by Macedonians throughout the three Macedonian *vilayets* (administrative regions) of Skopje (now lacking Kosovo and Metohia, which had gone to Serbia), Bitola and Thessaloniki. At the same time, Bulgarian forces worked to annex Macedonia to Bulgaria. It was during this time that Pasha Kemal Attaturk attended military school in Bitola (see page 64), and the revolutionary mood of time must have had an influence on him.

The various uprisings against the Ottoman rulers led eventually to the formation of a group of intellectuals under the name of the Internal Macedonian Revolutionary Organisation (VMRO). The founding members, Dame Gruev, Petar Pop Arsov, Anton Dimitrov, Ivan Haži Nikolov, Hristo Tatarčev and Hristo Batanžiev, founded the organisation on 23 October 1893 in Thessaloniki, with the goal of creating an independent Macedonia according to its historical and geographical boundaries. Other Macedonian heroes joined up, such as Pitu Guli and Goce Delčev.

It took another ten years of internal and external dispute for VMRO to engineer the uprising that would hopefully secure Macedonia's independence. It was during this effort that Jane Sandanski engineered the first international hostage crisis of our modern era by kidnapping an American missionary in Macedonia, Miss Ellen Stone, in return for US$63,000 (see box, page 294). Finally, at the Congress of Smilevo (20km northwest of Bitola) the Bitola Revolutionary District set the ball rolling for an uprising in their district. This was later expanded to a general uprising throughout all of Macedonia set for the auspicious date of Sv Elijas Day (literally *Ilij den/Ilinden* in Macedonian), 2 August 1903.

In the end it was the Kruševo Revolutionary District, led by Nikola Karev, that gained the upper hand over the ruling Ottomans, and on 3 August they announced the formation of the Republic of Kruševo. Unfortunately, it was only to last ten days before a detachment of the Ottoman army, outnumbering the 1,200 rebels 16 to one, surrounded Kruševo and brought it to heel. Pitu Guli among many others died in the fighting. Goce Delčev had already been killed three months earlier.

The terror wrought on the local population thereafter was without precedent and much of it was recorded in the photography of the Manaki brothers (see box, page 205). But this repression only succeeded in indelibly marking in the minds of the Macedonian consciousness that freedom and independence from foreign rule was the only way out.

20TH-CENTURY MACEDONIA
The first and second Balkan wars By the 20th century, weakened at last by economic fraud, political in-fighting and a costly war with the Italians in 1911, the Ottoman Empire fell prey to the territorial ambitions of its remaining Balkan neighbours. Serbia, Montenegro, Bulgaria and Greece declared war on Turkey on 18 October 1912, and signed up the help of the Macedonian people by declaring that their anti-Ottoman league was for the liberation of the Macedonians. No such thing was to transpire, but instead the four nations divided Macedonia amongst themselves as soon as the defeated Ottoman armies finally retreated to Turkey.

Bulgaria, with rekindled memories of a Greater Bulgaria, took the lion's share of Macedonia, to the annoyance of the remaining nations of the anti-Ottoman league.

Macedonian expatriate communities appealed to the Great Powers in London, and the Macedonian refugees in St Petersburg, Russia, even sent ahead a map made by Dimitrija Čupovski proposing the ethnic and geographical boundaries of an independent Macedonia in order to bolster their case. The neighbouring Balkan states, however, would have none of it. Serbia was vying for an outlet to the Aegean Sea, and Greece wanted control of Thessaloniki. Thus they decided the following year to challenge Bulgaria militarily for the land.

Unlike the first Balkan War of 1912, which had the strategic goal of ousting the Ottomans in order to divide the land up later, the second Balkan War of 1913, ending with the Treaty of Bucharest, was all about gaining land back from Bulgaria's spoils in the 1912 Balkan War. Macedonian villages were razed and their inhabitants massacred in an effort to eliminate insurgents. It was during this time that the founder of Save the Children, Eglantyne Jebb, made her journey to Macedonia for the Macedonian Relief Fund to deliver relief from the UK to war-torn Macedonians (see box, page 28). The land exchanged may have passed to a new government, but Macedonia's new masters (Greece and Serbia) continued to suppress any hint of independence by the Macedonian people.

The Great War In 1914 war broke out following the assassination of the Austrian archduke Ferdinand in Sarajevo. The Central Powers of Germany and Austro-Hungary sided with Bulgaria against Serbia and Greece over the division of Macedonia. Macedonia, for the most part, chose the lesser of two evils by siding with only one of its former oppressors (Bulgaria) against Serbia (backed by France) and Greece. In reality, Macedonians were drafted into all three armies to fight against each other. But Germany also enlisted the help of VMRO by financing the formation of a 'Macedonian' army, which fought alongside the Bulgarians on the condition of independence for Macedonia.

But the Central Powers lost the war, and the Paris Peace Conference set to negotiating the 'Macedonian Question', already an institution and a headache since the Berlin Treaty 40 years earlier. Of the three proposals put forward by Great Britain, France and Italy, it was the French proposal in favour of the Serbs that won out. The British proposal that Macedonia become a protectorate of the newly formed League of Nations, and the Italian proposal for autonomy were rejected as too risky. Thus Macedonia was returned to the 1913 borders of the Treaty of Bucharest. Vardar Macedonia belonged once again initially to the Kingdom of Serbs and then later to the merged Kingdom of Serbs, Croats and Slovenes (later Royal Yugoslavia). A colonisation of Macedonia by the Serbs began.

VMRO, however, would not be silenced and continued to fight for freedom. This led in 1934 to the assassination of the Yugoslav king Aleksandar Karagjorgjevic I by the Macedonian-born Vlada Georgiev. The fighting continued and when in early 1941 Yugoslavia refused to side with the Germans, Germany declared war on Yugoslavia, bringing Vardar Macedonia into the fray.

THE COMMUNIST STRUGGLE FOR VARDAR MACEDONIA Inviting its allies to re-divide Macedonia yet again, the Germans, Italians and Bulgarians surrounded and then moved into Vardar Macedonia in April 1941. A secret British military organisation (see page 256), established to bring down the Axis forces through sabotage and subversion, was parachuted into Macedonia in order to help fight the fascist forces. Working initially with VMRO they later switched to the partisan forces of the Communist Party of Macedonia (CPM), set up in October 1941, when it became clear that the communist forces were the more coherent and successful.

MACEDONIA AND THE RIGHTS OF THE CHILD

Abridged text from The Woman Who Saved the Children: A Biography of Eglantyne Jebb, *by Clare Mulley*

Eglantyne Jebb was born in 1876 to a family of social reformers in Shropshire, England. Her brother-in-law Charlie Buxton, a Liberal Member of Parliament, had founded the Balkan Committee in 1902 to campaign against the repressive policies of the Ottoman government in Macedonia. The committee's independent relief arm, the Macedonian Relief Fund (MRF), was set up a year later.

In February 1913, between the two Balkan wars, Eglantyne travelled to Macedonia and Kosovo to deliver aid to the tens of thousands of mostly Muslim refugees displaced as the Balkan League (of Serbia, Bulgaria, Greece and Montenegro) advanced south to oust the Ottoman administration. This Orthodox Christian League resented Muslims for supporting Turkey, and resented Catholics for supporting Austria, a country with its own designs on Macedonia. Thousands of Muslims and Catholic Albanians were massacred by the victorious Serbian army and, in a systematic programme of what would now be called ethnic cleansing, villages and crops were also destroyed.

Eglantyne delivered funding and provided assistance to the MRF agents in Üsküb (Skopje), Prizren and Monastir (Bitola). Over half of the refugees in Monastir were on the verge of starvation. Some 5,000 were being fed by the MRF, through the distribution of 100,000 loaves of bread between January and April 1913, and the provision of a soup kitchen for 200 children daily for a month between February and March. Monastir was at that time a city of 50,000 inhabitants, and would have to absorb 30,000 refugees before the end of the conflict. But funds were never enough, despite the fact that, as the British Consul told her, just two pence a day could keep a man alive.

'Practically all the babies died,' Eglantyne wrote in her reports. Among the misery of starvation and disease, her most powerful recollection was that of 30 Turkish boys who had been abandoned at a boarding school when their teachers went to fight. When their food ran out the boys had simply gone to bed to die.

Narrowly escaping her own death from influenza on her return to England, Eglantyne did not venture back to the Balkans. She saw her role very much in policy development rather than in service delivery, and immediately urged the MRF to organise repatriation and resettlement of refugees in addition to relief work. From now on international security, sustainable development and citizenship became a fundamental part of her vision, without which relief, however essential, could only be a palliative measure.

Frustrated by the short-term effect of relief work, and spurred by the further agony wrought on German and Austrian orphans of the Great War, Eglantyne co-founded Save the Children in 1919 with her sister Dorothy. In 1923 she authored the five principles of the Declaration of the Rights of the Child, which was adopted by the League of Nations (the precursor to the UN) a year later.

Promising national liberty, the CPM managed to recruit many Macedonians to swell their ranks, despite the fact that it was formerly a sub-group of the Communist Party of Yugoslavia under Tito. Most Macedonians feared returning to a rule under anything relating to Royalist Yugoslavia and fought with the CPM, therefore, for the liberation of their nation rather than for any communist ideology. Under the auspices of the CPM, the Macedonians even set up their own government, the Anti-fascist Assembly of the National Liberation of Macedonia (ASNOM), on 2 August 1944, exactly 41 years after the Ilinden uprising of 1903. The government was headed by the pro-independence politician Metodija Andonov, more commonly known as Čento.

One month later, in September, the Bulgarians withdrew from Vardar Macedonia, suffering heavy losses to partisan forces. The Germans followed in their wake, beating a hasty retreat towards Greece, and ordering the deaths of hundreds of Macedonians after the failed attempt to bring a puppet government into Macedonia through the right-wing faction of VMRO. As it turned out, fewer than 300 Macedonians were actually killed under the German captain Egbert's orders, as many German soldiers let the Macedonians escape.

With the end of World War II the CPM, with a decidedly pro-Yugoslav leadership, reneged on its promises of independence for Macedonia. The new borders around Vardar Macedonia enclosed the new People's Republic of Macedonia (later the Socialist Republic of Macedonia – SRM) firmly within communist Yugoslavia. Čento and his supporters were removed from office and replaced by the pro-Yugoslav Lazar Koliševski, who remained in power until the fall of Yugoslavia 55 years later.

As the capital of the SRM, Skopje, formerly a political backwater, was firmly orientated towards Serbia for leadership, and its pro-Serb partisan leaders were not well versed in government. Meanwhile, Bitola, traditionally the powerhouse of the region, languished in the shadows. Cut off from its usual orientation towards the southern regions of geographical Macedonia, Bitola's previous political and intellectual capacity was lost on the partisan government of the SRM. Any hint of dissension by Macedonia's pro-independence intellectuals was firmly put down.

Under Tito's communist Yugoslavia (1945-1980), although the SRM was nominally given the status of a federal republic, thereby giving it the right to decentralised government of its own people, this was not the case in reality. Limited autonomy was a move by Tito to divide up Serbian ambitions to take over Yugoslavia as a whole. Interdependence was brought to the federation, however, by dividing up its economic capabilities among the republics. The SRM became a popular tourist destination as part of the Yugoslavia package. Mining and tobacco production were encouraged, and Tito even started a tobacco museum in Prilep in 1973 to celebrate 100 years of the tobacco industry there (see box, page 226).

For the first time in the region's history, ethnic Macedonian arts and literature were encouraged, for which a distinct Macedonian language was recognised and strengthened. The man most known for this was Blaže Koneski (1921–93, confusingly also known under the names Blagoje Konjevic when studying in Belgrade, and Blagoy Konev when studying in Bulgaria), who became the head of the Macedonian Academy of Arts and Sciences (MANU). Some have criticised him for deliberately 'Serbifying' the Macedonian language in order to further differentiate it from Bulgarian influences. Others herald him as one of the greatest Macedonian poets and writers in living history.

Despite efforts to revitalise SRM's economy, Macedonia remained the poorhouse of Yugoslavia. This was not helped by the isolation of SRM by three of its neighbours: Albania became deeply introverted, Bulgaria shunned the pro-Serb authorities, and civil war raged in northern Greece until 1949. At the end of the civil war, the border with Greece was closed as Greek authorities tried to stamp out any further spread of communism or secessionist claims by Aegean Macedonians for an independent Aegean Macedonia.

Life in communist Macedonia followed a similar path to that of many other communist countries, although to much lesser extremes. The 1950s saw experimentation with collective production farms and state ownership of land and property. Many officials used these measures to line their own pockets, and although collective production had to be abandoned and a limited private business model was re-introduced in 1965, corruption in state-owned industries remained endemic.

Yugoslavia's break from Soviet tutelage allowed Macedonia to benefit from Yugoslavia's greater freedom of movement and other civil liberties. Nevertheless, one-party rule remained and any talk of an independent Macedonia or a reunification with the other parts of Macedonia was not entertained.

From Tito's death in 1980 and the decline of the Yugoslav economy throughout the 1980s, the Yugoslav republics and their many nationalities started to vie for greater degrees of autonomy and power in the federation or even out of it. As Serbia's president, Slobodan Milošević, became more belligerent at the end of the 1980s, the end of Yugoslavia became increasingly inevitable. Despite Lazar Koliševski's attempts to keep the federation together, the decision to move to a multi-party democracy in 1990 essentially spelt the end of one-party communist ideals in Macedonia.

In January 1991, Kiro Gligorov was appointed president of the SRM by the new multi-party parliament of Macedonia, and on 8 September 1991 the people of Macedonia voted in a referendum for the independence of the Republic of Macedonia and bloodlessly left the Federation of Yugoslavia. The Yugoslav army, taken elsewhere in dying Yugoslavia to fight Croatians and Bosnians, left Macedonia in April the next year.

Turnout for the referendum was 74%, of which 95% voted for independence. The Albanian community claims that most of the remaining 26% of the non-voting citizenry was ethnic Albanians who did not want to live under the alternatives being offered, ie: as a minority within an independent Macedonia, or as a minority within Yugoslavia. It was later to turn out significant that this hefty percentage of Macedonia's citizens felt disenfranchised from the political developments of the country.

THE FORMER YUGOSLAV REPUBLIC OF MACEDONIA

Troubled first years With the additional difficulties of a disenfranchised Albanian community, the infant years of the Republic of Macedonia have been fraught with the usual transitional problems of high corruption and over-centralisation in what was essentially a 'nanny state'. In Macedonia's case this was compounded by its formerly strong dependence on Belgrade. In the first multi-party elections of 1991, voters were faced with a bewildering plethora of parties and candidates, who were divided along political as well as ethnic lines.

The election produced neither a clear winner, nor a clear opposition, so a governing coalition of three parties was formed (the Social Democratic Party of Macedonia (SDSM), and the Liberal Democratic Party (LDP), both from the old communist leaders, along with the leading Albanian party, Party for Democratic Prosperity (PDP). The nationalist centre-right Internal Macedonian Revolutionary Organisation-Democratic Party of Macedonian National Unity (VMRO-DPMNE) took up parliamentary seats in opposition along with several other parties. As head of the leading party in the coalition, Branko Crvenkovski, at the young age of 27, became prime minister.

Two and a half years of political in-fighting ensued until October 1994 when new elections were held. But the bickering continued over the cast of the votes and it was not long before the main party in opposition, VMRO-DPMNE, and others withdrew from the election altogether. As a result, the existing governing parties, presenting themselves for one vote together, won three-quarters of the vote. Forming a government in coalition with the Albanian majority vote, the new government took 112 of the 120 seats in parliament, leaving any form of opposition essentially untenable.

The Albanian community had long been unhappy with their representation in the new Macedonia, which many had not voted for in the first place. In November 1993, Macedonia's police force, strongly linked to the SDSM, arrested 12 people in Tetovo, allegedly for attempting to form an Albanian paramilitary force. The police claimed to find hideouts, weapons caches and other incriminating evidence. Nine of the 12 were jailed for conspiracy and other related charges.

This did not deter the Albanian community, however, who continued to demand greater representation and started to set up their own university in Tetovo in 1995. Considering this a breach of the constitution, in which Macedonian was the only officially recognised language of the new republic, the authorities declared the university illegal and tried to close it down. In the ensuing public demonstrations, three Albanians were killed and ten policemen injured. Shortly thereafter an assassination attempt on President Kiro Gligorov was carried out. He lost one eye in the incident and his driver was killed outright. The unknown assassin has still not been apprehended, even after the government offered US$530,000 in 1999 for information leading to his arrest.

Despite the Liberal Party leaving the governing coalition in early 1996 in order to join the non-parliamentary opposition of VMRO-DPMNE and the attempt by the opposition to call for new parliamentary elections, the governing coalition continued to hold onto power. But international observers were at last allowed to monitor the local elections held that year, which resulted in an even greater division between the ruling coalition in parliament and the opposition, who had won most of the main local elections. Tensions increased and in 1997 the mayors of Tetovo and Gostivar were jailed for raising the double-headed eagle flag of Albania over government buildings in their respective towns.

During the course of 1998, the National Liberation Army (NLA), a newly formed rebel group fighting for the liberation of Albanians, made its first public announcement by claiming responsibility for the bombings of several police stations and judicial courts in the lead-up to the internationally observed parliamentary elections of autumn 1998. Their tactics did not succeed in bringing greater autonomy to the Albanian community, but the ineffectiveness of the ruling coalition to alleviate tensions between ethnic communities and to curb the economic difficulties of the transition to a post-communist system brought the electorate to vote in a new government. The winners, VMRO-DPMNE and the DPA (Democratic Party of Albanians), were both right-wing nationalist parties. Ljubčo Georgievski, aged 32 and leader of VMRO-DPMNE, became prime minister.

The new government was not given an easy start. A crisis was raging in neighbouring Kosovo. In spring 1999, some 360,000 Kosovar Albanians fled into northwestern Macedonia before the NATO bombing of Serbia later that year brought an end to Milošević's offensive in Kosovo. Although most refugees eventually returned to Kosovo or went on to other countries, the Macedonian authorities still feared a rise in the number of Albanians claiming citizenship in Macedonia and forcibly bussed tens of thousands of refugees into neighbouring

Albania in April of that year. This fear was aggravated by several factors: firstly, the Albanian community claim that they made up to 40% of the population in Macedonia (as opposed to 19% in the 1994 census); secondly, the unclear status of ethnic Albanians who had failed to change their Yugoslav passport to a Macedonian one in the allotted timeframe of the early 1990s, but who were still claiming citizenship; thirdly, widespread electoral fraud in northwestern Macedonia in the local elections of 2000.

Throughout 2000, attacks on the police continued until, on 26 February 2001, the Macedonian authorities retaliated against suspected armed rebels in the village of Tanuševci, north of Skopje on the border with Kosovo, for an attack by the NLA on the police station there. Armed conflict between the authorities and the NLA raged for the next six months, both sides taking casualties and alleging war crimes for the deaths of civilians and the desecration of churches and mosques.

A peace deal and amnesty After President Trajkovski (elected after Gligorov stepped down in 1999) requested help from NATO on 20 June 2001, the international community brokered a ceasefire and a peace agreement. The Ohrid Framework Agreement (OFA) was signed on 13 August 2001 by a new unity government, comprising VMRO-DPMNE, the SDSM, DPA and PDP. It gave the Albanian community much greater representation in state institutions as well as recognition of their language and culture (see box, page 42).

At the end of August, Operation Essential Harvest was launched by NATO troops upon invitation by the government to collect arms from rebel forces. Almost 3,500 weapons were collected in the month-long operation, which was half the number that the government had claimed were out there, but twice what the rebels had claimed they had. Another 7,571 were handed in to authorities in another weapons amnesty in 2003.

In addition to the Ohrid Framework Agreement, the government agreed an amnesty for all former rebel fighters except for those who had committed war crimes. The Albanians read this, as was clear in their negotiations with NATO, to mean an amnesty on all crimes except those cases taken up by the International Criminal Tribunal of Yugoslavia (ICTY) in The Hague. The Macedonian authorities interpreted the amnesty clause to mean that they could prosecute those cases not taken up by ICTY. Of the 100+ alleged cases, most were thrown out of court for lack of evidence.

Only five war crimes allegations were considered serious enough to be taken up by ICTY. These included the massacre at Ljuboten, north of Skopje, where at least six men of Albanian ethnicity were found shot in suspicious circumstances; and the mass grave found in Neprošteno containing four Macedonian bodies. After UN Security Council Resolution 1534(5) requested the ICTY consider only the most senior and most responsible leaders in all Yugoslav wars for further indictments, only one indictment was made from the 2001 conflict. This was against the former Minister of Interior, Ljube Boškovski, for his involvement in the massacre at Ljuboten. His command responsibility over the crime could not be established by the ICTY, however, and so he was acquitted in 2008. The remaining four allegations were returned to national jurisdiction in late 2007, despite vocal disagreement by the Albanian community. In the 2011 parliamentary elections, VMRO-DPMNE was returned to government only through coalition with the Democratic Union of Integration, the political party who emerged from the NLA. In return VMRO-DPMNE agreed to give amnesty to the remaining four alleged war crimes.

In comparison, over 40 indictments for war crimes committed in Bosnia during the early 1990s were prosecuted at the ICTY. These include that of the massacre at Srebrenica, where almost 8,000 Bosnian men and boys are alleged to be buried. Many hundreds of bodies have been found, but up to 20,000 remain missing from the war. Twenty-two people went missing in the Macedonian conflict, of which six are ethnic Albanians and one a Bulgarian national. Eight bodies have been found to date.

Accession years Parliamentary elections were held in September 2002. The electorate, disillusioned by the nationalist rhetoric of the VMRO-DPMNE coalition with the DPA and by the ineffectiveness of the unity government to move forward the Ohrid Framework Agreement, brought back the SDSM government of Branko Crvenkovski. Together with a new party, the Democratic Union for Integration (DUI), led by the former rebel leader Ali Ahmeti representing the majority of votes from the Albanian community, the new government made significant inroads in achieving the Ohrid agenda.

The country's situation has improved, although economic growth has not caught up with pre-conflict figures, and many would say that standards of living have still not achieved pre-conflict standards. Post-conflict agencies are moving out, or have scaled down considerably. NATO's forces turned their security mandate over to the first EU military deployment ever under Operation Concordia (350 soldiers), which was deployed on 31 March 2003. This was replaced on 15 December 2003 by an EU police mission, Proxima, comprising only 200 mostly unarmed EU police. Proxima

THE OHRID FRAMEWORK AGREEMENT

In the relative calm and cool of the breezes off Lake Ohrid the international community brought the government and rebel leaders together to thrash out their differences around a table and a piece of paper. The result brought greater rights for the Albanian community and hopes of guaranteed peace for all Macedonians. Although adoption of all the legal provisions envisaged in the agreement was completed with the Law on Flags and Symbols in July 2005, there is still a long way to go on full implementation of these laws in the spirit of the agreement.

CONSTITUTIONAL CHANGES The preamble of the new constitution of November 2002 deleted references to Macedonia as the 'national state of the Macedonian people' whereby Albanians and other minorities were singled out as only having rights as equal citizens, without being acknowledged as actual Macedonian people. The new constitution refers to all Macedonia's population as 'citizens of the Republic of Macedonia', equal before the law.

DEVOLUTION OF AUTHORITY In line with the wishes of the Albanian community for more say over their own affairs and also in line with European Union requirements for increased local self-government, limited powers of authority are being decentralised to the local administrative level throughout the country.

BADINTER MECHANISM Laws directly affecting culture, language, education and issues of local self-government are required to go through the Badinter mechanism in parliament. Named after Robert Badinter, born in 1928 and an experienced leading legal expert on minority rights, the mechanism requires a double majority to pass these laws: an outright majority, as well as a majority of those claiming to belong to the communities not of the majority population of the country.

EQUITABLE REPRESENTATION Equitable representation is now sought throughout all state institutions, and especially in the judiciary and the police. With a lack of sufficiently qualified minority citizens due to previous educational biases, it is proving difficult to increase minority participation in state institutions. It has been even more difficult with the need to downsize bloated institutions, effectively resulting in jobs for Albanians and job losses for ethnic Macedonians. Nevertheless, advances in ethnically mixed policing, for instance, are returning citizens' confidence to institutions of law enforcement.

THE RIGHT TO MINORITY EDUCATION AND LANGUAGE USE Non-majority ethnicities of at least 20% of the population have the right to use their language in state institutions alongside Macedonian (but not in foreign affairs). Although the Albanians are not singled out in the Ohrid Framework Agreement document, this provision has essentially brought the right for the use of Albanian in parliament amongst other institutions, in bilingual identity papers and other official documents, and has eventually legitimised the long-disputed Albanian University of Tetovo.

was reduced to a 30-man police advisory team one year later, which by mid-2006 was replaced by a two-year twinning project with the German police of Brandenburg.

In August 2004, the country succeeded in passing a controversial law to reduce the then 123 municipalities to a more manageable 84. Of the 84 municipalities, 15 are run by ethnic Albanian mayors and one by a Roma mayor. Since local elections in March 2005, the government has been moving slowly towards decentralising power. So far, limited decentralisation seems to be having the desired effect of some rejuvenation of the local economy. Some fear that decentralisation will increase the opportunities for institutional corruption, which is already high at the central level. Some also fear that greater autonomy is in fact polarising the ethnicities rather than uniting them.

Macedonia received EU candidacy status on 15 December 2005, but may not get a start date for negotiations until it has resolved its name dispute with Greece (see page 35), regardless of how well it achieves reforms in the 35 chapters of the EU *acquis* (areas of legal conformity). Macedonia's accession path to NATO was blocked by Greece for the same reason at the April 2008 Bucharest NATO summit, as a result of which Macedonia fell behind the other Adriatic Partnership countries (Albania and Croatia) who joined NATO in 2009. The European Agency for Reconstruction, which has been in the country since June 2001, has poured significant funds into Macedonia to help bring its institutions towards European standards. This has been matched by bilateral financial aid from other EU nations as well as by America.

The parliamentary elections of July 2006 brought in the opposition, VMRO-DPMNE, who were re-elected in a snap election in 2008 after Greece blocked Macedonia's entry to NATO, and again in early elections in 2011. DUI has been VMRO-DPMNE's Albanian partner in government for most of that time.

The transition from one-party rule to multi-party democracy has brought its usual share of troubles to Macedonia, compounded by inter-ethnic problems and a lack of support from neighbouring countries. Some of the hurdles to progress faced by Macedonia are a lack of a fully participating civil society, the lack of independence of state institutions and with that the lack of public faith in those institutions, the problems of transition from state to private ownership and an antiquated education system. Finally, the lack of an independent civil service able to keep the country running effectively whilst parties argue out their differences deprives the country of the continuity needed to keep policy agendas on track.

NOT TO BE CONFUSED WITH GREECE Greece and Macedonia have had strained relations since time immemorial. Most Hellenic city-states viewed Macedonians as drunken barbarians from the north. (The word 'Greek', incidentally, was not used until the Romans used this name of a single Hellenic tribe and the closest geographically to Rome to refer to all of the Greek-speaking tribes on the Balkan peninsula.) Philip II brought Paeonia (the upper Vardar region), Pelagonia (the Prilep area) and Lyncestis (the Bitola area) into his expanding empire and united the constantly warring Greek city-states in the League of Corinth in 338BC to fight the Persians. Upon Philip's assassination, Aleksandar III of Macedon (see box, page 18) completed his father's dream in the name of a new pan-Hellenic era, and the Greeks have since claimed him as Alexander the Great. While most Greek historians would not dispute Aleksandar's lineage from the royal house of Macedon, they see Aleksandar's Macedon firmly as part of Greek heritage and not as part of the geographical entity that is now the Republic of Macedonia.

Maps from Roman, Byzantine, Ottoman and Yugoslavian times have included the geographical area of the Republic of Macedonia firmly under the label 'Macedonia'.

Greek nationalist history, however, does not include the geographical area of the Republic of Macedonia in its view of Macedonia.

History aside, what is most in dispute is the use of the word 'Macedonia' in naming the country. When Yugoslavia named Vardar Macedonia the 'Socialist Republic of Macedonia' after World War II, the Hellenic Republic protested and asked Tito to rename the republic 'Vardar Macedonia' or 'Skopje Macedonia'. This was not accepted and Greece had enough to do fighting its own civil war and keeping out communism to worry too much about the name of its neighbour. But, internally, Greece continued its policy, followed since the end of World War I, of moving ethnic Greeks and Greek-speakers into Aegean Macedonia and moving Macedonians out whilst suppressing the use of their language and traditions. In this way Greece could at least control from its side any irredentist tendencies that Aegean Macedonia might have towards the SRM.

However, when the Republic of Macedonia claimed itself as the independent 'nation state of the Macedonian people' writ large in its new constitution of 1991, this was too much for the Greeks. Some Macedonian politicians started to call for reunification with Aegean Macedonia, and Athens feared an uprising in Aegean Macedonia and a desire by the two sides to rekindle long-lost dreams of the ancient royal dynasty of the Macedons. Newly independent Macedonia did not help matters by adopting the star of Vergina, formerly the flag of the ancient Macedonian kingdom, as their flag and stamping the star on their coins. Greece slammed a unilateral economic boycott on the fledgling state.

Fearing more troubles in the Balkans the international community worked hard for a solution. The interim title 'Former Yugoslav Republic of Macedonia', or 'FYROM' for short, has been agreed for international official use while diplomats work harder for something less contentious. Especially since the final demise of the Federal Republic of Yugoslavia in 2003, the name 'FYROM' is as unsuitable today as giving the Hellenic Republic the name of 'Former Ottoman Protectorate of Greece' or FOPOG for short.

In a spirit of compromise in 1995, the flag was changed to its present amended form and the coins were reissued without the star of Vergina. The boycott was lifted and relations between the two states have slowly started to improve. An interim accord was brokered that allowed Macedonia to use its constitutional name in bilateral relations with other countries, but use Former Yugoslav Republic of Macedonia in international organisations until another name was agreed on by both countries. In addition, the interim accord agreed that Greece would not block Macedonia's entry to any international organisation on account of the name dispute. As of 2003 and for the first time since World War II, Greece has begun to issue visas to Macedonians who had previously lived or had family on the Greek side of the border. Tearful reunions on Aegean soil have abounded.

The dispute over the name gave way to Greece becoming one of the top three investors in the country. Macedonia is working hard to have countries recognise it under its constitutional name, or even simply as Macedonia. As more and more countries bilaterally recognise Macedonia under its constitutional name, Greece has once again become more vociferous on the issue and many in Greece still refer to the state as simply Skopje. In addition, Greece refuses to officially recognise Macedonians in Greece as an ethnic minority in their own right, but recognises them as Bulgarian.

Although the returning VMRO-DPMNE government in Macedonia has dropped its original irredentist claims towards Aegean Macedonia, Prime Minister Gruevski has blatantly riled Greece by naming the country's international airport

Alexander the Great (confusing the matter even further with Greece's Macedonia Airport at Thessaloniki), and announcing that Macedonia will seek compensation for Macedonians who were forced out of Greece and thus lost land after World War II and the Greek civil war. The government's lavish spree on historical statues, particularly in the centre of Skopje (see page 125) has further aggravated animosity between the two countries. Prime Minister Gruevski's family, incidentally, hail from Aegean Macedonia.

International patience with this dispute is growing thin, especially since the EU revealed late in 2004 that Greece had been under-reporting its economic figures in order to get into the euro zone in 2000, and by 2011 was subject to a €109bn EU bailout of its national debt, which stands at 180% of its GDP. Greece's blockade of Macedonia into NATO, and most likely into the EU, breaks the 1995 interim accord between both countries. As a result Macedonia has taken Greece to the International Court of Justice. A verdict is due in 2012.

GOVERNMENT AND POLITICS

The governing system in Macedonia is a parliamentary democracy. Due to the infancy of Macedonia's democracy, political parties, and therefore government, are still very new to the political, economic and legal intricacies of successfully governing the country. As a result, and as a remnant from communist times, government institutions are not particularly transparent, and engender little public faith. Macedonia's fledgling civil society has a long way to go to achieve full participation in local and national governance, and a paucity of dialogue between government and civil society does not help.

In addition, political parties, electoral practices and the parliamentary system are in a fairly regular state of flux. Recent wide-reaching changes to the electoral system have been successful in ensuring fairer and more transparent elections, but there are still many problems especially regarding the elimination of family and proxy voting, and tacit intimidation. The most recent parliamentary elections of 2011 were declared fair and free from violence by the EU, and there were indeed no major official complaints of election fraud. Yet anecdotal evidence indicates that many citizens still felt pressured to vote for the incumbent government if they wanted to keep their state-run job.

HEAD OF STATE The current head of state, President Gjorge Ivanov, was elected in March 2009, succeeding Branko Crvenkovski, who was elected after the previous president, Boris Trajkovski, died tragically in a plane crash in February 2004. As Macedonia is a parliamentary democracy, the president holds little real power and the post is largely ceremonial. In Macedonia's volatile ethnic environment, however, the president can, and does, play an important role in inter-ethnic and inter-party relations. The next presidential election is due in 2014.

LEGISLATURE Parliament is a unicameral Assembly (*sobranje* in Macedonian), which consists of 123 seats. Parliamentary elections are held every four years based on six-district party-list proportional representation. There is no election threshold. Registered parties or coalitions put forward closed candidate lists in one round of votes. The six districts are a new innovation as a result of the Ohrid Framework Agreement in an attempt to more fairly represent minority communities. Professionalisation of the electoral boards (previously run by mixed party appointees) has also helped to eliminate intimidation and collusion in fraud.

Since 2011 three additional parliament seats have been allocated to diaspora representation in each of Australasia, Eurafrica, and the Americas.

In 2011, early parliamentary elections re-elected VMRO-DPMNE and its coalition for a third time since it lost power after the conflict of 2001. VMRO-DPMNE has been somewhat reformed since it ruled in 2001, and this has largely come about with the break-off of its more nationalist element in 2004 into the new VMRO-Narodna (VMRO People's Party under the continued effective leadership of former prime minister Ljupčo Georgievski). Although VMRO-DPMNE lost seats overall, it did win the three diaspora seats.

As of June 2011, the number of Assembly seats by party are as follows:

- 56 VMRO-DPMNE, coalition
- 42 Socialist Democratic Party of Macedonia (SDSM in Macedonian), coalition
- 15 Democratic Union of Integration
- 8 Democratic Party of Albanians
- 2 National Democratic Revival

EXECUTIVE The head of government is currently Prime Minister Nikola Gruevski; the prime minister is elected by majority vote by the Assembly, as is his cabinet, the Council of Ministers. Of the 19 cabinet posts, five are held by Albanians: Environment, Economy, Local Self Government, and for the first time ever both Justice and Defence. Two of the four deputy prime minister posts are also held by ethnic Albanians. In addition, ethnic Albanians occupy a number of deputy minister posts, but these hold little real authority, as it is the state secretary of each ministry who actually has the most authority, after the minister.

JUDICIARY Constitutional and supreme court judges are appointed by the Assembly. Lower (first-instance) and appellate (second-instance) court judges are appointed by the State Judicial Council, whose 15 members are elected by a mixture of judicial election, Assembly appointment, presidential appointment and ex-officio posts. Although the court system in Macedonia is designed to be independent of politics, there is in fact still much overlap and low self-regulation. This is not helped by the fact that there is no independent protection for judges who want to go against the political line. A national strategy for reform of the judiciary was adopted in 2004, but the full benefits of these reforms have yet to materialise. Unfortunately, Macedonian courts and law enforcement mechanisms tend to shy away from responsibility, not least because criminal pressures to do so are high. As a result the confidence of national citizens and international investors in the legal system in Macedonia is low. Progress in closing the chasm between legal reform and implemented reality is glacial.

ECONOMY

Macedonia's economy has been slow to improve. Already the poorhouse of Yugoslavia, Macedonia's economy deteriorated even further in the early 1990s through the sanctions imposed on Serbia, a unilateral economic boycott levied against Macedonia by Greece, inimical relations with Bulgaria and minuscule trade relations with even poorer Albania. Although all these areas of trade relations have improved, the conflict of 2001 did not help to alleviate the situation and like many post-communist countries, Macedonia is experiencing the brain drain so familiar when the country's young and educated, needed to revitalise the economy, leave for more lucrative jobs abroad.

In 2010 the estimated official unemployment figure for Macedonia was 33.1% of the working population, although surveys show that half of these do have part-time work of some nature, or work on the black market. With the world in economic decline, an increasing number, now 31% of the population, lives below the national poverty line, with 5.3% living on less than US$2 per day. Total public debt is 34% of GDP (see page 2), and while GDP growth fell to 0.7% in 2010, it bounced back up to 5% in the first half of 2011. Macedonia has relative financial stability in the world market, in large part because of its stringent lending criteria, and its currency, the denar, has remained fairly stable as it has been pegged to the euro since 1998. Inflation in 2010 was 1.6%.

Macedonia exports a number of raw materials such as iron and zinc, but it has very few exports from skilled labour or light industry, never mind anything high tech. Textile manufacturing had been developed during the 20th century but, although Macedonia continues to export some clothing, it has proved difficult to compete against the likes of China and India. Macedonia imports over 50% more in dollar value as it exports.

Macedonia's natural metallic resources have included copper, gold, iron ore, manganese, nickel, tungsten, lead, silver and zinc, but these resources are dwindling. For the building industry it also has abundant granite, gypsum, lignite, siliceous and quartz sands, as well as marble for which there is a large quarry and factory near Prilep.

Being located so far south in Europe but with ample rivers and water resources, Macedonia also grows large quantities of corn, grapes, peppers, rice, tobacco, tomatoes and wheat. Unfortunately, without suitable cooling houses to store this produce out of season, Macedonia's agricultural industry remains tied to the seasons. It has to sell far too cheaply in the summer and has little to sell in the winter. In order to join the EU Macedonia will also have to start regulating produce size and quality, which will require expensive changes to agricultural practices and probably put small farms out of business.

Tobacco has been one of Macedonia's main exports, and during the summer harvests you can see it drying almost everywhere, but especially in Prilep where Macedonia's main tobacco factory is located. In recent years though, with the trend towards producing less harmful cigarettes, Macedonia's heavy-tar tobacco has become less popular.

Grapes on the other hand are on the rise as Macedonia's wines and liquors become more popular. The wine industry is poised to take off, and so now is a good time to get in if you want to try Macedonian wines while they are still inexpensive and unadulterated. For more information on Macedonia's wines, including wine tours, see page 357.

Much of Macedonia's farming is still done by hand, and although the industry is slowly becoming more mechanised, you can also often see animals used for ploughing the fields and hauling crops. Land is terraced in many of the mountain areas and families and neighbours pool labour during intensive planting and harvesting times. Macedonia is full of contrasts like that – one week you will see snow on the mountaintops, and the next week families are planting rice in paddy fields.

PEOPLE

The French call the Macedonian people a 'mixed salad', *une salade macedoine*. In fact anything mixed up is *macedoine*. Macedonia is arguably the most ethnically diverse country in the Balkans, if not in the whole of Europe and a quick look at Macedonia's history will show you why. Macedonia has been anything but a homogeneous nation. Aside from various settlers in the Neolithic, Bronze and Iron ages, Macedonia has been invaded, starting with the Romans, by over a dozen tribes, races and empires. And those are the ones that didn't stay. Then there are those who made a home in Macedonia.

This has largely to do with the fact that Macedonia lies on two important trading routes across Europe. The Via Egnatia linked the sea port of Durres in Albania with Constantinople in Byzantium and brought Romans, Albanians, Gauls, Crusaders, Byzantines, Turks, Bulgarians, Roma and Greek tribes. The Diagonal Way linked northern Europe with Greece and brought Vlachs, numerous Slav tribes, Goths, Huns, Avars, more Serbs and more Greeks.

The disputed question of Macedonian identity is one that numerous academics have written about, and there are many books on the subject. If you want a lively discussion in Macedonia, then inquire of a person's origins, and you'll find that your interlocutor will furnish you with a complicated family tree as long as your arm, and each person's background will be different.

If Macedonians and their overlapping neighbours cannot agree on who Macedonians are then I could not possibly hope to write an accurate account of such a topic. Nevertheless, from a lay perspective, which is often at least simple, I shall give an overview of some of the aspects which have contributed to Macedonian identity, and some of the arguments which are out there at the beginning of the 21st century, some 7,000 years after humankind is believed to have first settled in Macedonia.

Neolithic settlers came into Macedonia from 5000 to 2500 BC and are believed to have spoken a Proto-Indo-European language. According to Herodotus, the Dorian tribe moved up into southwest Macedonia sometime before the Trojan War, around 1200 BC. There they became known as *Makedoni*, which is derived from the ancient Greek word *makedonos* meaning tall, probably at the time referring to highlanders. Some in Macedonia think the word *Makedonci* might be derived from *majka* in reference to the matriarchal society of the Neolithic settlers (see page 16).

The royal house of Macedon, which ruled in the millennium before Christ, has legendary origins from the Greek god of thunder, Zeus. In reality, they are likely to have been a tribe who migrated up from beyond the Greek islands. In the 7th century BC the Makedoni started to mix with the non-Greek-speaking tribes of Paeonia and Pelagonia. Descriptions of these people from the classics of Thucydides, Herodotus and Tacitus show that the Paeons were mostly mountain people, strong and quick, who also influenced the language spoken by the Macedonians. As Professor Nicholas Hammond, the leading authority on ancient Macedonia, says, ancient Macedonian 'contained words of early Greek origin but was not intelligible to contemporary Greeks. The Macedonians in general did not consider themselves Greeks, nor were they considered Greeks by their neighbours.' The royal house on the other hand 'being of foreign extraction and divine descent' (Hammond) were confirmed as Greek in the 5th century BC when they were allowed to compete in the Olympics.

When the Romans invaded in the 2nd century BC, they most certainly left their seed in Macedonia. The invaders from the north, however, Goths, Huns and Avars, seem to have left nothing behind, not even a village or a crop, but razed everything in their way.

The next most influential invasion was by the Slavic tribes from beyond the Carpathian Mountains. There are many of these tribes, tall and hardy, but those thought to have settled in northern Macedonia were the Mijaks in the Debar and Galičnik region west of the Vardar and the Bryzaks to the east of the Vardar.

They came as pagans and were gradually Christianised by the indigenous folk of Macedonia. They were allegedly also quite different Slavs from the Slavic tribes of Serbia and those of Bulgaria, although they all spoke a commonly rooted language.

The creation in AD862 by the monks Cyril and Methodius of a script for the Slavic language (Glagolitic, which was later superseded by Cyrillic) helped them to convert many Slavs to Christianity, and helped to formalise the language of numerous Slav tribes. Bulgarian and Macedonian tribes spoke a very similar language due to the influence of the Bulgarian Empire over Macedonia.

Slav origins remain the base of the Macedonians today, despite Ottoman rule over Macedonia from 1392 to 1912. Although many Slavs converted to Islam they continued to speak Macedonian (now known as the Torbeši – see page 44). It wasn't until the Serb annexation of northern Macedonia to the Kingdom of Serbs, Croats and Slovenes at the end of the second Balkan War of 1913 that the Serb people and language started to gain a serious foothold in northern Macedonia. This was continued during communist Yugoslavia with the Serbification of the Macedonian language under Blaže Koneski, and the prominent influx of pro-Serb Yugoslav partisans into positions of power in the government.

A growing number of Macedonians prefer to see themselves and their country as a heterogeneous mix of the rich tapestry that makes up this crossroads in the Balkans. As a result some prefer not to be called 'Slav' Macedonian as they are no longer purely Slav. Foreigners have always travelled through the land, some bringing products and prosperity, others bringing domination and destruction. New Macedonia wants peace, prosperity and freedom from persecution in a civic-based society rather than to get hung up on ethnic terminology.

MACEDONIAN MINORITIES NEXT DOOR The Hellenisation of Aegean Macedonia, the Serbification of Vardar Macedonia and the Bulgarisation of Pirin Macedonia are topics of continued dispute. Macedonians are not officially recognised as an ethnicity in either Bulgaria or Greece. Both countries recognise Macedonians as Bulgarians. This goes back to the historical quest for influence over, and division of, Macedonia between these two countries and, later, Serbia.

In Bulgaria, some Macedonians are trying to be recognised as an ethnicity and to gain greater autonomy for their culture and self-government. The Bulgarian court judgement banning the formation in Bulgaria of a Macedonian association under the name OMO Ilinden states that 'there is no Macedonian minority in Bulgaria. There are no historical, religious, linguistic, or ethnical grounds for such an assertion.' This judgement banning the formation of OMO Ilinden has been deemed contrary to the right of association under the European Convention of Human Rights, and Bulgaria was ordered (again) in 2006 to repeal the judgement. The EU is applying plenty of pressure on Bulgaria to have the party recognised but, at the time of writing, OMO Ilinden is still waiting to be allowed to register.

In Greece, slavophone Macedonians who were exiled and lost property in the civil war just after the end of World War II are also trying to seek recognition from the Republic of Greece, including a return of their property. The plight of slavophone Macedonians in Greece is well described in Anastasia Karakasidou's 1997 book *Fields of Wheat, Hills of Blood* (see *Appendix 4*, page 360). In 1994, slavophone Macedonians in Greece formed the political party Rainbow (*www.vinozito.org*) to campaign for recognition of their culture and language as a minority ethnicity in Greece. The official Greek position is still that there is no Bulgarian or Macedonian minority in Greece. In 1999, the Greek office of Helsinki Monitor estimated that there are some 10,000–30,000 slavophone Macedonians in Greece. If you travel in

Aegean Macedonia (northern Greece) you can still find people in their sixties and older who speak Macedonian.

In 2004, the Union of Serbia and Montenegro agreed with Macedonia to recognise each other's ethnicities as a minority in their respective countries. This was generally not a bone of contention. However, there are pockets of Macedonian-speaking Muslims in southern Kosovo and adjoining areas of Albania who are known as Gorani. In Kosovo, the Gorani have claimed that they were persecuted by the Kosovo Liberation Army after the Yugoslav army retreated under NATO bombing in 1999, and that they have since been marginalised further by the redrawing of municipal boundaries in Kosovo.

Macedonians have been recognised as an ethnicity in Albania since World War II, but figures are disputed and range from 5,000 to 350,000. The disagreement over figures, recognition and rights to land is largely a mutual recognition issue as well as a fear of the break-up of sovereignty and territorial integrity. These issues are typical of the Balkans and while they are progressing towards stability, they are some way from being settled. The issue over Albanian rights in Macedonia is still very current.

MINORITIES IN MACEDONIA TODAY Ethnic minorities in Macedonia are numerous. Their numbers have varied over the years and in Yugoslavia they often claimed different nationalities in order to avoid persecution. So the number of Turks, Albanians or any other ethnic or religious group fell or rose according to who was most in or out of favour with the authorities in the year of the census. Sadly this phenomenon has continued in the years since the independence of Macedonia.

Albanians Albanians have bordered on the northwest of Macedonia for millennia. Whether they are descendants of Illyrian tribes is disputed, but they have a unique language which, although it has adopted many words over the centuries from Greek, Latin, Turkish and Italian, remains for the most part grammatically distinct and one of the oldest branches of the Indo-European linguistic tree.

Albanians started to make serious inroads into northwest Macedonia and Kosovo, however, only in the 17th century when Ottoman persecution of the native Slav population emptied these areas of their inhabitants. After the fall of the empire of Gjergj Skenderbey (see box, page 253), the Albanians were largely loyal to the Ottoman *beys* (chieftains, lords). Most converted to Islam and were rewarded with new lands bordering Albania. Many also learnt the Ottoman elite language and were schooled in Anatolia, later becoming *beys* in their own right.

However, when the Turkish nationalism of the Young Turks emerged at the beginning of the 20th century, Albanians in Macedonia, fearing repression from the encroaching Serbs, rallied for their own cause. In 1912 at the end of the first Balkan War, Albania became an independent state and with it went a small slice of Macedonia that lay south and north of Debar.

Much of Macedonia's 'Albanian question' is linked with the rise of nationalism in neighbouring Kosovo in the face of Serbian persecution, rather than with any significant desire to join Albania. Communist Macedonia did not help this perception and Albanians were almost as badly persecuted in Macedonia as they were in Kosovo. Fortunately, Serbian/Yugoslav persecution of ethnic Albanians in Macedonia does not go back the centuries that it does in Kosovo, and so there is hope yet that a civic-based state (incorporating EU-preferred rules of subsidiarity or local self-government) might work out for the Albanians in Macedonia.

Unfortunately, however, new Macedonia has inherited the discriminatory leftovers of the Socialist Republic of Macedonia (SRM), which have been compounded by the sudden curb on movement instigated by the erection of borders between the formerly borderless communist republics. So whereas ethnic Albanians used to be able to go to university in Priština in Kosovo to receive teaching in Albanian, suddenly they had no access to teaching in their own language. The number of schools where children could receive instruction in Albanian was also heavily reduced. Less than 5% of the police force was Albanian in a country where Albanians claimed they made up more than a third of the population, yet over 80% of prison inmates were from the Albanian community. Moreover, the 1991 constitution stressed the nationality of the Macedonians, with Albanians as equals, rather than that the new Macedonia was a home for a mix of ethnicities as it had been for many centuries.

Furthermore, disenfranchised from the emerging political process in the new pluralist republic, ethnic Albanians refused to take part in the referendum on independence. They also refused the census of 1991 that would have established their numbers, fearing that the manipulation of the figures by the government would be used against them. Instead the Albanian community carried out their own census of their population in 1992, and it is starting from this time that other Muslim groups in Macedonia, such as the Turks and the Torbeši (see below), have alleged that the Albanian community has pressured them to count themselves among the Albanian community in order to swell the numbers for their census.

The Ohrid Framework Agreement of August 2001 (see box, page 34) established significant civic rights for the Albanian community, and the ensuing census of 2002, which numbered the Albanian community at 25%, settled previous disagreements about population numbers. The tangible lure of EU membership in the years to come is a further stabilising factor.

OTTOMAN TURKISH VERSUS TURKISH

It is important to note that the rulers of the Ottoman Empire were not necessarily Turkish. They were a ruling elite made up first and foremost of Muslims, and secondly of those who spoke Ottoman Turkish. As a result, Albanians such as Skenderbey (see box, page 253), and the Christian boys taken by the dervish orders of Islam under the *devširme* tax (see page 25) would become a part of the Ottoman elite who ruled the empire on learning Ottoman Turkish and converting to Islam.

Turks on the other hand were considered by the elite to be the uneducated masses of peasant Anatolia. It is from these masses that Atatürk rose up against the Ottoman sultans and pashas to bring about modern Turkey. The masses spoke a different Turkish from that of the Ottomans of the Osmanli elite, which acted as a class barrier in everyday life.

Ottoman Turkish, however, was a language of convoluted court phrases, with words and grammar borrowed from Persian and Arabic for which the Arabic script was used. Arabic words stress the order of consonants as their distinguishing framework, and have little representation for short vowels. This does not suit other languages very well, such as the Turkish of the masses, Macedonian or Albanian. As a result, towns like Debar could be transliterated back out of Arabic script as any variety of spellings such as Diber, Dibrah or Debar, so long as d, b and r were in the same order. The Arabic script seen today above many mosque doorways and windows is therefore the script of Ottoman Turkish, and not related to the modern Latin-script-based Turkish.

Turks After the demise of the Ottoman Empire and the withdrawal of the Ottoman elite, many Turks fled back to Turkey in the wake of widespread retaliation by the Serbs who replaced the Ottoman leaders. This policy of encouraging what can only be described as 'cleansing' was continued under communist Yugoslavia in the 1950s and 1960s through handshake deals with Turkey whereby anywhere between 80,000 and 150,000 'Turks' left Yugoslavia via Macedonia and Bulgaria for Turkey. Many were not in fact Turks at all nor did they speak Turkish, but were Albanians or Macedonian Muslims (Torbeši – see opposite) who took advantage of the offer to escape further persecution in Yugoslavia. At the last census of 2002, less than 4% of Macedonians declared themselves to be of Turkish descent. This 4% are spread throughout the municipalities of Čair, Vrapčiste, Gostivar, Plašnica, Radoviš and Centar Župa.

The true ethnic Turks of Macedonia are the Yoruks (see box, page 46). Yoruk villages are found in the Radoviš area, Vrapčiste and Gostivar.

Torbeši Some of the 'Turks' mentioned above, such as the majority of the population of Plašnica, are in fact ethnically Macedonian Muslims. They cast themselves as Turks in the census because they do not speak Albanian, are not Orthodox Macedonian, but by religion are closer to the Turkish community.

These Muslim Macedonians are sometimes called *Torbeši*, although this is often seen as a derogatory term, and applies to Muslim Macedonians in Macedonia as well as those in Albania. The Albanians sometimes refer to Muslim Macedonians as *Pomaks* even though Macedonians might argue that this is a term reserved for Muslim Bulgarians who come from the Rhodope mountain region. Albanians have historically seen the Bulgarians and Macedonians as one and the same.

Roma The Roma, along with their Sinti cousins, total almost 14 million throughout Europe. They migrated from northwestern India between the 11th and 14th centuries as travelling labourers, and although most have settled, many still live transient lives. Sadly, the 20th century brought considerable misfortune to the Roma, and the wars throughout the former Yugoslavia in the 1990s caused the most significant Roma population movements since the end of World War II. Poorly portrayed in the Western mass media, the Roma have arguably been the most severely affected in the long term by the harsh consequences of war. This is in large part because of their lack of representation in modern-day governing institutions and interest groups: no politician, soldier, businessperson or cleric has come forward to defend them locally.

The Roma's origins in northwestern India are very obvious from their facial features and elaborate traditional dress. They are mostly dark skinned, speak their own language originating from Sanskrit and have distinctive customs and traditions. The main ethnic division of Roma can be further subdivided into Arli, Kovaci/Burgudji, Djambazi, Baruci, Juzari, Pristevaci, Gilanli and Topanli. All subdivisions speak a dialect of the Roma language (for more on the Romani language, see textbox, page 164). In addition to sub-ethnic divisions, in Macedonia Romani identity is largely split into those of Muslim faith (Xoraxane Roma) or Christian faith (Dasikane Roma). Faith as a means of identity has changed over time and, as ever, is fickle.

According to the last national census of 2002 (based on official citizenship), the number of Roma in Macedonia is 53,879 or 2.66% of the total population. Field research indicates, however, that actual numbers are much closer to 150,000. In the biggest built-up settlement of Roma in the world, some 13,300 people have their home in Šuto Orizari, north of Skopje (see page 162). They mix very little with the remainder of the Macedonian community and inter-ethnic marriages are extremely rare. Part of the reason that they have not mixed with their host communities has traditionally been because of their transient lifestyles.

In Macedonia in recent decades, however, many Roma have settled permanently all over the country. Now, it is discrimination and a significant difference in lifestyle and outlook that keep the Roma from acceptance by, and even wanting to integrate fully into, their place of settlement. Traditionally, the Roma have been skilled labourers in carpentry, copper and blacksmithing, leather upholstery, basket weaving, repairs and more. They are also renowned as skilled musicians and dancers. Their tendency towards a life on the move has not led them to put much emphasis on formal education, and so as the 20th century moved away from a product-based economy towards a service- and technology-based economy, the Roma and their skills were somewhat left behind. The move towards a throwaway society has not helped either, and so the Roma are largely left to manual labour and menial jobs; many have taken to begging.

In Skopje, especially in the municipality of Šuto Orizari, there is quite a significant class difference among the Roma. Some have gone abroad, earned good money visible by their small, well-kept houses, and have qualified in recognised trade skills. Within Macedonia, from a mere handful in tertiary education in the early 1990s there are now some 200 Roma studying at university level. Most of them are pursuing careers in human and social sciences and are actively taking part in various academic training modules, organised by Romaversitas (*www.romaversitas.edu.mk*, only in Macedonian at the time of writing; see also *Stuff your rucksack* on page 118 to find out how you can help Romaversitas directly). It is hoped that these students will be the driving forces behind reorganising and modernising their communities.

At the other end of the spectrum, there are those who live in slums, such as on the outskirts of Bitola or Prilep, or the 1,700-plus remaining refugees from the conflict in Kosovo who mostly beg or wash windscreens at the traffic lights in Skopje. You will also see many of the Roma hawking clothes, hats and alarm clocks on the Stone Bridge, or plying the street with their boxes of cigarettes, tissues and chewing gum. Often you can also see a matriarchal figure order children to beg from potential clients as they come along the street. Although these children are forced to beg, they can still appear happy, laughing and playing as children do even if they have been on their feet all day. Occasionally, if they receive no alms they will get angry, not exactly a good sales technique, but understandable when they are likely to receive a clip around the ear from mum or dad for not returning with cash. Then they will return to playing a game of tag or jumping in the water fountain. It is questionable how much of the money they receive from begging ends up in their pockets or is taxed from a cartel that 'runs' the area.

The spiral of poverty that the Roma have found themselves in has lead to international efforts to try to stop discrimination against them and to bring them back up above the breadline. The OSCE's Office for Democratic Institutions and Human Rights, based in Warsaw, does significant work in this regard throughout Europe, and a number of non-governmental international Roma networks have started up as the Roma try to lift themselves out of poverty. Macedonia has signed up to the Roma Decade of Inclusion 2005–2015 (*www.romadecade.org*), in which the government has pledged to tackle improvements for Roma in basic services, health, education, housing and employment. Improvements are not easy: the Roma themselves are not keen to adopt the trappings of conventional Western lifestyles, whilst developing (and especially former socialist) economies struggle to harness the potential of entrepreneurship for self-employment and small businesses.

For more on the Roma in Skopje see page 162 and for their background throughout Europe see www.romani.org. A good website on the human rights and legal struggles of the Roma is that of the European Roma Rights Centre (*www.errc. org*). In Macedonia there are several charities – for more information see *Travelling positively* on page 117. Donating to a charity that has long-term goals for the community as a whole has proved to be far more effective in reducing long-term poverty than putting money directly into a bottomless pit. Unfortunately, like most of those living on the breadline or below, many Roma see little use for training in

YORUKS – AN ETHNIC TURKISH COMMUNITY IN MACEDONIA

Abridged, with permission, from Yoruks *by Elizabeta Koneska, Museum of Macedonia, 2004*

In the eastern part of Macedonia lives the Turkish Yoruk ethnic population, concentrated mostly in the mountainous areas of the Dojran-Valandovo and Radoviš-Štip region. In the historic sources the Yoruks are referred to as nomadic tribes of Turkmen origin who had emigrated from the steppes of central Asia to Anatolia, and from there settled in the eastern part of the Balkans from the 14th to the 16th century.

The migration of the Yoruks was probably the most successful colonising strategy of the Ottoman authorities in the Balkans compared with their attempts at colonising other central Asian tribes. The reasons for their settling in the Balkans were of a socio-economic and military-strategic character. Some researchers suggest that the favourable climate and rich grazing pastures of Macedonia were the crucial motive for the Yoruk migration. In favour of this, some researchers argue that they settled in the areas of rich pastures abandoned by Vlach farmers.

The Yoruk population was tribally well organised and as such fitted easily into the Ottoman army, which led to organising special units for different military, semi-military and other duties (dragging cannons, transporting materials, working in mines, maintaining and securing fortresses, etc). The Yoruks had a privileged status and in order to be motivated for their duties they were exempted from certain state taxes. They were thus treated as 'children of the conquerors'.

In order to get some benefits, substantial parts of the Islamised population joined the Yoruks. The census records from the early 16th century registered the phenomenon of some Islamised Christians joining the Yoruks in the Prilep region, Ovčepole and Tikveš, after the Yoruks crossed from the left to the right bank of the River Vardar. One of the mitigating circumstances for adopting Islam through the Yoruks was the fact that they were organised in *tarikats* – dervish orders that were religiously more tolerant. In this regard, bear in mind that the religious rituals of both populations included numerous pre-Christian and pre-Islamic pagan shaman elements, which brought them closer together.

The Yoruk community transformed from a nomadic to a stationary way of life in the 15th and 16th centuries. As a result, the state passed laws ordering those who hadn't changed their abode for more than ten years to be deprived of the right of Yoruk status, which meant they had to fulfil their duties of paying taxes to the state.

As an individual Turkish ethnic group in Macedonia the Yoruks are distinguished by their language, customs and folkloric particularities and, considering contemporary times, their rather closed social community. The Yoruks of the computers and sewing when this may not get them jobs in the current climate and their immediate needs are for food and housing. Trying, therefore, to get past the initial stumbling block of 'teaching a man to fish rather than giving him the fish' is still proving difficult.

Aromanians/Vlachs The Aromanians (known as Vlachs in Macedonian) arrived in Macedonia in Roman times from the 2nd century BC onwards. They are not related to the Romanians of Romania in language or ethnicity, although many did

Background Information PEOPLE

Radoviš-Štip region who live in the foothills of the Plačkovica Mountain, however, differ with their own particularities, not only from the other Turkish populations, but also from Turks living in the lowland villages in the same region. That's why the villages of Alikoč, Kodjalija, Kaluzlija, Supurge and Prnalija from the Radoviš district are particularly interesting.

The contradiction between the traditional and the contemporary way of life is reflected in the contrast between male and female Yoruks. The women wear their colourful and archaic traditional gowns, and their means of communication is limited, mostly due to the language barrier (the female population, almost without exception, speaks only Turkish). The men, meanwhile, have already adopted modern behaviour, dress and mobile phones.

The unfavourable conditions and living standards in the Yoruk villages in the past decades gave rise to emigration, mainly to Turkey and to some western European countries. The Yoruks from Macedonia were not involved in the great migrations of the Turkish population typical for the period after the fall of the Ottoman Empire. The first massive emigration of the Yoruks from these villages occurred in the 1950s, together with the emigration of a considerable part of the Turkish population from Macedonia. The second emigration wave took place at the beginning of the 1990s, following the dissolution of Yugoslavia, and was motivated by economic conditions as well as the actual political events. Since the end of the 1990s emigration has slowed.

The present language of the Yoruks is a conserved, archaic, specific Turkish dialect that has endured thanks to the considerable isolation of this population and the minimal external influences. The folkloric particularities of the Yoruks are most impressively reflected through the colourful traditional gowns worn by the female population of all ages. The Yoruk women make all the parts of the gowns, through weaving to sewing and embroidering. From the period of adolescence to marriage, girls are constantly preparing their dowry. For everyday use women and girls usually wear colourful dresses of ready-made fabric.

According to the old tradition, on Bajram or for weddings the Yoruks organise wrestling (*pehlivan*) contests, stone-throwing (*tašitmak*) contests and horse or donkey races. The wedding customs are certainly the most impressive. Marriages between blood relatives are avoided, but it often happens that two brothers marry two sisters (a kind of an 'exchange' of a sister and a brother for another brother and a sister, which saves money).

Elizabeta Koneska is Macedonia's leading ethnologist on the Yoruk community and works at the Museum of Macedonia. She can be contacted at e ekoneska@freemail. org.mk.

emigrate there over time. They have always spoken a Latin-based language and refer to themselves as Armčnji. There are a number of names for them, however: the word *vlach* comes from the Greek and, along with other derivatives, has a mostly derogatory meaning centred around 'idiot' or 'bleat'. The Greeks in fact call them Koutzovlachs (*koutzos* meaning 'lame') – connected to a story that the Aromanians refused to participate in the Greek wars by claiming to be lame in one leg! They are called Ulah in Turkish, Tschobani in Albanian and Cincari by the Serbs. *Cincari* denotes 'stingy' and is often confused with the Aromanian and Romanian word for 'five'.

The Vlachs have always been in the business of trade. Many did well out of sheep farming, and it is not difficult to suppose that they may have followed the Roman legions who needed supplies. Certainly the main Vlach settlements in Macedonia are along the Via Egnatia, and their traditional villages, such as Malovište, show a once wealthy standard of living. Although the Vlachs today are well integrated into Macedonian society, and now mostly live in the towns rather than in their old villages, many can still be found to the fore of prosperous local businesses and hotels. They remain well educated, often speaking a number of languages and have a knack for figuring out good market niches.

Due to their relatively recent assimilation into Macedonian life it is difficult to assess the exact numbers of Vlachs, not least because many Vlach descendants may no longer consider themselves Vlach, but prefer in these times of possible ethnic segregation to call themselves simply 'Macedonian'. The 2002 census numbered Vlachs at less than 0.5% of the population.

Other minorities There are lots of other very small ethnic groups in Macedonia. The next most significant group are the Serbs who were encouraged to settle in

THE MIJAKS OF WESTERN MACEDONIA *Mimoza Gligorovska*

The Mijaks have lived in western Macedonia for at least five centuries. The Mijak region, Mijachija or the Reka region, is named after the Radika River and its tributary the Mala River. Broadly speaking the area is bound by the Šar Planina to the north; the Korab, Dešat and Krčin mountains to the west; Bistra and Stogovo to the east; and the Debar Valley to the south. Within this area, the Mijaks are pocketed into four smaller regions. The Gorna (Upper) Reka region, from the village Brodec to the village Volkovija is mostly abandoned today but, in the past, was inhabited by Albanian-speaking Macedonians, called Shkreti. The Dolna (Lower) Reka, from the village Žirovnica to the village Skudrinje, and the Golema (Big) Reka, from the confluence of Mala Reka into the Radika to the confluence of the Radika into Lake Debar, are barely much more populated. Only the Mala (Small) Reka from the village of Galičnik to the village of Gari is seeing a small revival of seasonal tourism.

Over the course of time, the Mijaks have become a mix of Orthodox and Islamic religions. Their Islamisation started in the 16th century but was not widespread, rather individual, and lasted for a long period of time. Some authors note cases where half of the family was Orthodox and the other half Muslim. The conversion to Islam divided the Mijaks into Mijaks (Orthodox Macedonians) and Torbeši (Muslim Macedonians).

Their main occupation was and still is cattle breeding, and some records from before World War II note that they also used to herd more than 2.5 million sheep and 150,000 horses. They are known as the best woodcarvers and icon painters

Macedonia when Vardar Macedonia became a part of the Kingdom of Serbs, Croats and Slovenes after World War I. Serbs made up 1.8% of the population in the 2002 census, but they do not form a particularly homogeneous group as they are scattered throughout the country and are completely assimilated into Macedonian life. Nevertheless, the Serbs have their own political party, as do most of the ethnicities in the country, reflecting a politics divided along ethnic lines rather than along any real differentiation in political platform. There are also significant groups of Croats and Montenegrins from Yugoslav days; Greeks from the 19th century when the Orthodox Church was governed from Athens; Armenians who immigrated during the Middle Ages; and Ashkali Egyptians who immigrated along with the Indian Roma. The Ashkali Egyptians, and many of the poor Turks who were left in Macedonia after the demise of the Ottoman Empire (eg: parts of Strumica), are often discriminated against as Roma.

The Mijak (see box below) are the next most well-known minority. They were not officially counted in the census and so their numbers are unknown.

LANGUAGE

There are two official languages in Macedonia: the Slavic-rooted Macedonian spoken by most of the population; and Albanian, which has equal status alongside Macedonian in municipal and government affairs where Albanian speakers make up 20% or more of the citizens in a particular municipality. For basic phrases in both Macedonian and Albanian see *Appendix 1*.

The **Macedonian** language is firmly based in the Slavic family of languages. Traditionally written in Cyrillic, it is occasionally found in Latin script especially

in Macedonia. Petar Filipovski-Garka, his brother Marko Filipovski and Makarie Frčkovski, all from the village of Gari, are the sculptors of the iconostasis in the Sv Spas Church in Skopje, the Sv Gavril Lesnovski Church near Kratovo and the Sv Jovan Bigorski Monastery near Debar. Another famous artist, icon and fresco painter Dimitrie Krstev (1819–72), known as Dičo Zograf, came from the village of Tresonče. He painted more than 1,500 artefacts all over the Balkans, and his work is still exhibited today as an example of a then very unique style of combining harsh post-Byzantine symbolism with Baroque ornamentation.

The Mijaks speak the Mijak dialect, part of the western Macedonian dialects. Some of the main differences from standard Macedonian are the use of the consonant group 'šč' instead of 'št' – *ščo* and not *što* (meaning what); the replacement of consonant 'a' with 'o' in many words – *zobi* instead of *zabi* (teeth), *kode* instead of *kade* (where), *roka* instead of *raka* (arm); and the transformation of 'lj' into the palatal 'l'.

Finally, the Mijaks have a most intriguing flag, one of the oldest in Macedonia. It is white with a red and yellow border and a yellow cross inside a red and yellow circle. The yellow segments of the circle represent the rays of the sun and, of course, is not unlike the symbolism of Macedonia's star of Vergina. The cross divides the letters ИС ХР (IS HR standing for Jesus Christ) and НИ КА (NI KA meaning victory). Four symbols standing in each corner of the flag are the ancient Macedonian lion, the Byzantine double-headed eagle, the Bogomil star and prostrate half-moon, and a Celtic dragon.

in advertising. In past centuries it was closely related to Bulgarian and remains very similar in certain aspects of grammar and some vocabulary. Macedonians and Bulgarians can usually understand each other even if they can't speak the other's language. During both world wars Bulgaria's short rule over Macedonia saw an attempt to sway the Macedonian language back towards Bulgarian. When communist Yugoslavia won Macedonia, it set about reversing this and Serbifying the language. Today, the Macedonian alphabet is more similar to Serbian but has 31 letters instead of Serbian's 30 and four differing letters. Macedonian grammar, however, remains closely linked to Bulgarian. Serbia is also now increasingly using the Latin script rather than Cyrillic.

The Macedonian brother-saints Kiril and Metodi (Cyril and Methodius), followed by saints Clement and Naum, invented and spread Cyrillic throughout Slavic-speaking countries (see *Religion*, below) from the 9th century onwards. Old Church Slavonic is still the language and script used in sermon books today in Macedonia.

Albanian belongs to the Indo-European family of languages, but its roots, going back to the ancient language of the Illyrians, are some of the oldest and as a result its basic grammar and vocabulary resemble no other in the same family. Since its evolution in Albania, however, it has come under the influence particularly of Greek, Latin and Italian, therefore you will find a lot of words which are similar to these neighbouring languages. There are also some Slav and Turkish words.

There are two main dialects in the Albanian language: Gheg, spoken in the north of Albania, Kosovo and northwestern Macedonia, and Tosk, spoken in southern Albania. Up to the 19th century, Albanian could still be written in five different alphabets. This made communication and learning difficult, and in 1908 at the Conference of Monastir (Bitola) the decision was made to try to unify the language under one alphabet and literary standard. The Latin alphabet was chosen to provide 36 letters.

It was not until the 1960s and 1970s that a standard literary form of Albanian was finally formalised. This standard form, which is taught throughout the Albanian-speaking world, consists mostly of the Tosk dialect and grammar, with some Gheg additions. The Albanian given here is the standard literary form.

Most Macedonians below the age of 45 will speak at least a smattering of English and some are fluent. Among older Macedonians and especially in the Albanian communities German is more likely to be the second language of choice. On the odd occasion when you will find explanatory literature at a historic site or church, it will probably be in French rather than English.

RELIGION

Today, most of Macedonia is either Orthodox Christian or Sunni Muslim. There are some Roman Catholics, Bektaši and Methodists, as well as a good smattering of agnostics and atheists. Despite Yugoslavia's efforts to keep the states secular and to discourage religious life, the downfall of communism has brought about a revival in religion that is now proving to be both a unifier within a community, and a separator of those communities within the state.

Many Macedonians have rallied around the Orthodox Church as a means of expressing their hard-won national identity, a trend that was inadvertently encouraged through the Ottoman millet system (see box, page 52). The rise of the Orthodox Church is most obvious by the increasing number of huge metal crosses lit up across the country, and the number of new churches being built despite the terrible state of the economy (a lot of this money comes from the Macedonian diaspora). Monasticism has also been injected with a new lease of life as of 1995, with the revival and refurbishment of a great many monasteries in Macedonia.

Muslim Albanians have expressed their distress at the use of the Orthodox Church as a symbol of the Macedonian nation, and whilst this has fuelled the conflict between the Albanian community and the Macedonian authorities, Muslim Albanians have also retaliated with the construction of many new mosques. This has not helped matters, especially as non-Albanian Muslim numbers have been used to justify the need for new mosques, yet services are often only held in Albanian.

Both sides in the conflict of 2001 desecrated churches and mosques, which is a war crime under the Geneva Convention, and sadly reflects a history of such practices in the region. Many churches were destroyed or built over by the Ottomans during their time in Macedonia. Of note was Sv Sofia in Ohrid (see page 183) – photographs of it as a mosque can still be found. Even more mosques were destroyed by the Macedonians when the Ottomans finally left in 1912.

HISTORY OF THE ORTHODOX CHURCH IN MACEDONIA
Jesus's disciple Paul was called upon by the vision of the 'man of Macedonia' to spread the word of God along the River Vardar. His journey in the middle of the 1st century is detailed in Acts 16:10–17:15, and many believe he made it as far as northern Macedonia. Timothy and Silas stayed on in Macedonia after Paul left, and they may have made greater inroads into the wilds of the upper Vardar. But by the 4th century, Macedonia had an established Christian Church under the Metropolitan of Skopje. Aside from written records elsewhere, early evidence of Christianity in northern Macedonia can be seen by the remains of numerous Christian basilica across the country.

When the Slav tribes came in the 7th century, they too were converted to Christianity. These newcomers brought with them the problem of how to teach the Scriptures through a foreign language such as Greek or Latin. To alleviate this problem the Byzantine emperor Michael III summoned the monks Cyril and Methodius (Kiril and Metodi in Macedonian), who were natives of Macedonia, to go forth and teach the Scriptures to the many Slav speakers in their native language. This they did in the year 862, travelling along the River Bregalnica and to do so they created the Glagolitic and Cyrillic scripts, variations of which we are familiar with today.

Thus Byzantium increased its influence over the region by using what is now known as 'Old Slavonic' to win over the local slavophone population. Shortly afterwards, as Byzantium began to fall and Bulgaria was first made a state, Bulgaria continued this practice of exerting influence through the Church by establishing the Bulgarian Patriarchate, with its sphere of influence away from the Greek Orthodox Church and the influence of Byzantium.

The Bulgarian prince Boris ordained Clement in 893 as the first Macedonian Slav Bishop of the Bishopric of Velika (believed to be around the River Treška). Clement had been a disciple of Kiril and Metodi during their travels in Macedonia, and so had much influence in the land. His seat was at Ohrid, and he brought his fellow disciple from those travelling days, Father Naum, with him to Ohrid. There they set up the first Slavic monastery and school.

Later in 976, Tsar Samoil (see box, page 22), who had rebelled against Bulgarian authority and founded his own empire, also founded his own church, the autocephalous Ohrid Archdiocese, in order to bolster his own empire. But with the fall of Samoil in 1014, the Byzantine emperor Basilius reduced the new archdiocese to a mere archbishopric.

Thus the Archbishopric of Ohrid remained for seven and a half centuries until in 1767 the Turkish sultan Mustapha III gave in to Greek pressure and allowed

The Ottoman millet system, whereby people were classed according to religion rather than race, allowed Christianity to live effectively alongside Islam. For the Ottomans an elite ruling class was important, and so the Church's influence over its subjects was just as much an integral part of their rule over the empire as the Islamic faith was over its respective followers. Within each millet system (the word millet comes from the Arabic word *millah* and literally means 'nation'), the Ottomans were just as likely to inflict havoc on the lower echelons of the Christian millet as they were on the Muslim millet or the Jewish millet. The corollary of this millet system was that several religion-based 'nation-states' grew up alongside each other. In addition, political in-fighting within each millet system caused even further rivalry in the power vacuum left by the Ottomans following their demise, as played out in the desire of various factions of the Orthodox Church and their national leaders to 'rule' over Macedonia in the Balkan wars of 1912 and 1913.

Whereas the Jews were deported en masse during World War II to concentration camps and gas chambers such as those in Treblinka in Poland, many Muslims remained, and some believe even today that they should still be allowed free rein over their followers as in the millet days. The Orthodox Church, already disunited by national factions, more easily made the transition to the Westphalian nation-state system, which upholds sovereignty and non-interference in internal affairs as the key pillars of government and international relations. Unfortunately, the Westphalian nation-state system does not sit alongside the millet system so well, as a nation-state must have complete jurisdiction over a geographical area, whereas the millet system allows for several separate jurisdictions to apply to different people within the same geographical area.

the Archbishopric of Ohrid to be dissolved, and even the eparchy of Ohrid was reshuffled to have its seat at Durres in present-day Albania, thereafter known as the Eparchy of Albania. Along with the reshuffle, Greece bargained the right to administer the Orthodox Christian faith in upper Macedonia. New churches built in Macedonia during this period of the late 18th century and the 19th show a lot of Greek influence and engravings, as do older churches that were renovated or refurbished during this time, and many of them were refurbished purely in order to illustrate the authority of the Greek Church.

During the Russo–Turkish wars of the late 19th and early 20th centuries, Russia granted Bulgaria its wish for orthodox influence over northern Macedonia. Bulgaria then lost out to the Serbs at the end of the second Balkan War of 1913 and northern Macedonia fell under the influence of the Serbian Orthodox Church, long since separate from the Greek Orthodox Church.

It was not until March 1945 that the Archdiocese of Ohrid put forward a resolution to create an autonomous Macedonian Orthodox Church. The Serbian Orthodox Church, of course, refused. Thirteen more years of discussions ensued until finally, in 1958, the Serbian Orthodox Church gave in and in the following year the Macedonian Orthodox Church gained its autonomy, although still under the patriarch and canonical unity of the Serbian Orthodox Church.

The Macedonian Church was still not happy, however, and after more heated debate, the Holy Synod of the Macedonian Orthodox Church proclaimed itself autocephalous and completely independent of the Serbian Orthodox Church on 19 July 1967, exactly two centuries after the Archbishopric of Ohrid had been dissolved by the Ottomans. The legality of this move under the respective constitutions of both the Macedonian and Serbian Orthodox churches is still a bone of contention between the two churches, and the Serbian Orthodox Church still doesn't recognise the independence of the Macedonian Orthodox Church. For more about the Macedonian Orthodox Church visit their website (*www.mpc.org.mk*), which has information in English as well as some beautiful photographs, the Church calendar, and information about the lives of saints celebrated in the Orthodox calendar.

Whether you are a believer or not, the churches, mosques and monasteries in Macedonia are amazing treasures which deserve to be kept for posterity. Although monastic life and the Church have received a new boost since the independence of Macedonia, many of the churches and monasteries do not receive much funding. It is obvious which ones receive fewer donations by the state of disrepair that the churches and inns are in. The more remote and less well-known monasteries are particularly badly off. Well-wishers usually leave 10 or 50MKD at the church altars, and you might want to consider giving more generously to some. If you would like to make a larger donation by banker's draft or international money order, the residing father or sister will be able to furnish you with suitable details.

THE ISLAMIC RELIGIOUS COMMUNITY IN MACEDONIA Of the two main Islamic groups of believers, Sunni and Shi'a, most Muslims (about one-third of the population) in Macedonia are **Sunnis**. Not all of these are Albanian or Turkish, but many are ethnic Macedonian Muslims (Torbeši, see page 44), Roma or other ethnicities.

In addition, there are also a small number of **dervish** believers of different *tarikat* (subdivisions or orders of the dervish Muslim faith) such as the Halveti, Bektaši, Nakshi-Bandi, Kadiri, Melami, Rufa'i or Sinani. Officially, there are no Shi'a followers in Macedonia, but some of the orders, especially Bektaši, contain some Shi'a doctrinal elements. The connection stops there, however, and there is no contemporary hierarchical connection with the Shi'a in Iran.

During Ottoman rule over Macedonia, there was no separation of 'Church' and state, and the millet system (see box opposite) was used by the Ottoman sultans to rule over the different religious communities. At that time, the sultan was the highest Muslim religious authority. From 1918 to 1927, the Islamic community in Macedonia came under the authority of the Great Mufti of Belgrade, after which the Islamic believers of all Yugoslavia were unified under the Great Mufti of Sarajevo.

When Yugoslavia was formed in 1944, the Islamic Religious Community (IRC) in Macedonia registered in its own right with the Socialist Yugoslav Republic of Macedonia as the sole representative of the Muslim faith. The IRC is built on the doctrinal foundations of Sunni Islam, and has about 450 registered mosques and some 500 clerics.

There is only one Islamic school in Macedonia, the Isa Bej Medrese in Kondovo. Originally established in the 15th century, and revived in the 1930s as a rival private school to the Royal Yugoslav state-run Big Medrese of King Aleksander set up in Skopje, the Isa Bej Medrese was re-opened in 1979 in Kondovo after a period of closure during early communist times. By then many believers had gone abroad (and still do) to receive their religious education before taking up religious leadership positions at home. Due, of course, to the strong influence of the Ottoman period and continued links with Turkey, most receive their religious education in Turkey. The Turkish school of Islam teaches a modern secular version of the Muslim faith and these teachings continue to dominate in Macedonia. As in many other countries in the region, however, reactionary leanings in the Islamic community have led some to seek more traditional schooling in Egypt, while others have gone to Syria and Saudi Arabia, which offered scholarships to students from abroad. Some students returning from Saudi Arabia have brought back the experience and preaching of Wahabi and Salafi Islam, both of which teach relatively radical views and practices. Wahabi and Salafi preaching in Macedonia is weak although Wahabi- and Salafi-linked NGOs continue to try to further their influence through their work in poor communities and in building new mosques. Most mosques, especially in major towns, such as the Motley Mosque in Tetovo, are of the Turkish school, and open and friendly to (appropriately clad) visitors, including women.

The only other Islamic organisation in Macedonia that has tried to register itself separately from the IRC is the Bektaši dervish community. Macedonia's law on religion, however, stipulates that only one representative of each major faith is allowed to register. Whilst this arbitrary provision has allowed for Orthodox, Catholic and various Protestant branches of Christianity to register, only one organisation is allowed to represent the Muslim faith. This serves the IRC (and the Macedonian Orthodox Church) well as this way it has better control of the influence of various sects of Islam (and the considerable funding that can go with them). It clashes, however, with the European Convention on Human Rights and will probably have to change in due course if Macedonia wants to get into the EU (although Greece still has an equally restrictive law on religion).

The head of the IRC in Macedonia today is the Reis-ul-Ulema (president). He governs the Riyaset, which is an executive body responsible for religious and spiritual activities and which is answerable to the Meshihat (the Assembly of the Islamic Community consisting of 51 members). Below the Riyaset and Meshihat, mosque communities are divided into 13 religious committees, each of which is headed by a mufti.

EDUCATION

The Macedonian Constitution mandates free and compulsory primary and secondary education. Children begin schooling at the age of six, enrolling in primary school, which lasts nine years. Secondary school lasts a further three or four years, depending on the type of school, which only became compulsory in 2006. There are 1,034 primary schools, 44 of which are for children with special needs, and 115 secondary schools, of which 11 are private and four are special needs. In addition to teaching in Macedonian, teaching is also available in Albanian, Turkish and Serbian in some schools. In the past few years, certain public high schools have also begun teaching classes in English or French.

Skopje has two international schools, the American school NOVA (*www.nova.edu. mk*), and QSI International (*www.skopje.qsischool.org*). Both offer pre-kindergarten through to high school. In addition, the British Children's Academy (*www.tbcadacemy. com*) offers nursery care from six months to six year olds. Their website offers a very useful nursery checklist on what to look for when choosing a nursery.

Post-secondary education can be obtained at one of the five state universities. These are located in Skopje (*www.ukim.edu.mk*), Bitola (*www.uklo.edu.mk*), Tetovo (*www.unite.edu.mk*), Štip (*www.ugd.edu.mk*) and Ohrid (*www.uist.edu.mk*). Annually, on average, there are 6,000 students in the Goce Delčev University in Štip, 15,000 students enrolled in the University of Bitola, 7,000 in the University of Tetovo, and 37,000 in the University of Kiril i Metodi in Skopje. There are also many accredited private institutions like the New York University (*www.nyus.edu.*

mk), American College (*www.uacs.edu.mk*), MIT University (*www.mit.edu.mk*), FON University (*www.fon.edu.mk*), Euro College Kumanovo (*www.eurocollege. edu.mk*) and the South Eastern European University (*www.seeu.edu.mk*), which is a private–public non-profit initiative. All universities have adopted the European Credit Transfer and Accumulation System (ECTS) and courses at most of them last for three years for a Bachelor's degree and an additional two for a Master's.

Macedonia's education system suffers from low salaries, poor facilities and old-style teaching based on rote learning rather than developing analytical skills. There is an excess of law and economics graduates and a dearth from technical sciences. Professors rarely keep to exam timetables or office hours and students feel that they should pay bribes in order to pass an exam and get their diploma. A study conducted in 2011 by the UN Office on Drugs and Crime (UNODC) placed Macedonia highest in the region for bribery, with doctors, police and teachers most subject to it.

However, over the past few years the government, supported by international organisations, has slowly started reforming the education system. Free books for elementary and high schools as well as a number of scholarships for the best university students have been introduced. Schools are being renovated all over the country, and computers installed for every pupil. The government project to translate 1,000 prominent technical textbooks is near completion.

The literacy rate in Macedonia is around 97%. The dropout figures are highest for Roma and Muslim girls in both primary and secondary school.

CULTURE

Macedonia's potentially most important and unique contribution to world art is its little-known and unverified claim that 12th-century Renaissance art originated in its secluded monasteries (see box, pages 160–1). Religious art is certainly making a comeback in Macedonia. On other fronts, while there are no big, famous museums, art galleries or world-renowned festivals, there are always plenty of smaller events going on, in Skopje year-round and all over the country during the summer festival season. Venues and playlists are usually announced only a few days before the event, so you need to keep your eyes peeled for the information or log on to www.culture.in.mk regularly. Festivals and saints' days also have a big following in Macedonia. A list with approximate dates is covered on page 102. Skopje, and some of the other larger towns in Macedonia, have a small but thriving classical arts scene in music, ballet, opera and drama, as well as modern drama in Macedonian and minority languages.

HANDICRAFTS Macedonia has a long tradition of indigenous handicrafts mostly developed around religious art (see below). In addition, there are manmade Ohrid pearls (page 185), silver filigree jewellery, iron and copper work, carpets, embroidery, and local musical instruments (page 58) to be found here. See *Shopping* on page 104 for where to purchase most of these items.

RELIGIOUS ART The arts in Macedonia, like its nationhood and politics, are fractured. During Ottoman times still-life was banished and so depictions of such retreated to Macedonia's many monasteries. These took the form of frescoes, icons and woodcarvings of which there are a great many in Macedonia that are literally priceless and uninsurable.

Makarije Frčkovski and the Mijak brothers Marko and Petar Filipovski from Gari were famous in the early 19th century for their iconostasis carvings. In total

55

they carved four iconostases during their lifetime. Three can still be admired at Sv Spas Church in Skopje, the Monastery of Sv Jovan Bigorski near Debar, and Sv Gavril Lesnovski near Kratovo. A fourth in Sv Nikola Church in Kruševo was destroyed when the church was razed during the Ilinden Uprising in 1903. In 1999, a tourist is alleged to have offered the head priest at Sv Jovan Bigorski a blank cheque for the church's iconostasis. Aside from the fact that dedications to God cannot be bought at any price, the piece is irreplaceable and so it remains there today and hopefully forever.

Icons up until the 10th century were made of terracotta, such as those found in Vinica (see page 273) and many are now on view at the National Museum of Macedonia in Skopje. Thereafter they were generally paintings inlaid with silver and sometimes gold from the gold mine outside Radoviš. Most of these are still in their original churches, but some of the more important icons and frescoes, rescued from centuries of neglect during the Ottoman Empire, have been put on display in Skopje's and Ohrid's galleries.

The influence of Macedonian Byzantine church frescoes on the Renaissance is described in the box on page 160. The best three examples of these are at Sv Pantelejmon near Skopje (page 162), Sv Sofia in Ohrid (page 183) and Sv Gjorgi near Kurbinovo (page 193). A good website with more information on many of the monasteries is www.preminportal.com.mk, which has a specific section on monastery tourism and on religious art in some of the monasteries.

MODERN ART Modern art has taken hold of Macedonian artists in a big way, as if trying to catch up with centuries of artistic deprivation. The Museum of Contemporary Art, which was set up in 1964 after the disastrous earthquake in Skopje the year before, houses a permanent collection of modern art as well as frequent travelling exhibitions. Many pieces were donated to the museum as a result of the earthquake, including a piece by Van Gogh, which is usually stored down in the basement, but can be viewed on request.

The Museum of the City of Skopje (the old railway station) and the national galleries of Čifte Amam and Daud Pasha Amam, both former Turkish baths, also hold travelling exhibitions. Those living in Skopje will not have failed to notice the amount of modern art, alongside the compulsory icon or two, that adorns the walls of modern Skopje apartments. Today, the works of Macedonians such as Iskra Dimitrova, Omer Kaleši and Ibrahim Bedi are beginning to travel the world.

Since Yugoslav times, and especially since independence, Macedonia has encouraged artist colonies to grow and flourish. Ohrid is home to many Macedonian artists and you will frequently see budding artists trying their hand at representations of city life. The monasteries have also encouraged art, where the tranquillity of monastic life is often conducive to artistic development. Several art colonies take place in Macedonia during the month of August, including those at the Monastery of Sv Joakim Osogovski near Kriva Palanka, the Mijak village of Galičnik, the Monastery of Sv Petka in Velgošti near Ohrid, and the village of Kneževo near Kratovo.

FILM AND PHOTOGRAPHY Photography and photojournalism have strong pioneering roots in Macedonia going back to the early 19th-century days of the Manaki brothers (see page 205). Today, exhibitions of the works of Alexander Kondev or Samir Ljuma can be found around Macedonia, and the works of Rumen Kamilov and Marko Georgievski can be seen in numerous magazines and articles about Macedonia.

The Manaki brothers also experimented with film back in the early 1900s, and Macedonia had a vibrant film-making industry during Yugoslav times. This has continued since independence with Milčo Mančevski's 1995 release *Before the Rain*. Others have followed, such as *Dust* (Mančevski, 2001), *The Great Water* (Ivo Trajkov, 2004, based on the book of the same title by Živko Cingo), *Soul Hunter* (Oliver Romevski, 2004), *Secret Book* (Vlado Cvetanovski, 2004), *How I Killed a Saint* (Teona Mitevska, 2004), *Bal-Can-Can* (Darko Mitrevski, 2005), *Shadows* (Mančevski, 2007), *Mothers* (Mančevski, 2009), *Punk's Not Dead* (Darko Popov, 2011) and *The Third Half* (Mitrevski, 2012).

For an interesting and thought-provoking insight into the undercurrents of the 2001 conflict (especially as it was made seven years before the conflict broke out), *Before the Rain* is an excellent introduction. *Dust* gives a view of early 20th-century Macedonia under the Ottoman Empire, while *Bal-Can-Can* portrays through black comedy the continued mêlée of relations in the Balkans a century later. *Punk's Not Dead* is a very up-to-date road-movie-style depiction of ever-present tensions in the Balkans and a thorough indictment of nationalist trends emerging in Macedonia. *The Peacemaker*, featuring George Clooney, is a Hollywood blockbuster that draws on the recent difficulties and porous nature of Macedonia's borders as an excuse for excessive violence beyond anything ever seen here in reality.

Fortunately for English-speakers visiting Macedonia, foreign films are usually given Macedonian subtitles rather than dubbed, so going to the cinema needn't be hard work if you don't speak Macedonian, and it is one of the reasons why so many young Macedonians speak such good English.

MUSIC The soundtrack for these films has also injected life into Macedonian musical compositions by bands that combine traditional music with modern sounds such as Anastasia (*Before the Rain*) and Olivier Samouillan and Project Zlust (*How I Killed a Saint*). Other popular artists on the scene are Kiril Dzajkovski (*Dust, The Great Water*); Trifun Kostovski (Macedonian soul); Toše Proeski (modern pop and fusion – sadly, Proeski was killed in a car accident in Croatia in 2007); Kaliope (a long-time favourite of the Macedonians); Synthesis, who use traditional Macedonian instruments and vocal tones (see box, page 58); Tung Tung, an Albanian ethno jazz group (recent albums *Red Grapes*, 2003, and *Gold Coin*, 2005); and Adrian Gadja (modern Albanian).

One of the easiest introductions to the Macedonian modern/traditional music mix is the album *Treta Majka* (Third Mother) by the famous Serbian Leb I Sol lead guitarist Vlatko Stefanovski, the Macedonian guitarist Miroslav Tadic and the Bulgarian *kaval* player Theodosii Spasov. Equally good is the album *The Path in the Sun* by the Dragan Dautovski Quartet.

Unless you look out for these new sounds, however, you will find an overwhelming amount of traditional Macedonian music played in restaurants and at family gatherings all over Macedonia. This is an acquired taste and a must for traditional ceremonies where Macedonia's national dance, the *oro* (*kola* in Serbian), is compulsory for all participants. The *oro*, a circle of dancers holding hands, proceeds in an anticlockwise circle getting gradually faster. There are a number of different versions of the steps to the dance, the most basic being a three steps forward, one step backward arrangement. The *oro* generally comes across as quite a serious affair, although allegedly they are having fun.

Even more serious is *chalgia* music from the 18th and 19th centuries. Chalgia mixes secular Byzantine music with classical Turkish music from earlier centuries. It comes across as generally sober and its lyrics frequently tell of loss and yearning.

Like its people, Macedonia's musical instruments have a mixed origin. Many were brought to this land with the various invaders passing through over the centuries, while others are home grown. Playing traditional instruments is seeing a small revival in fusion music and in the revival of ethnic festivities. It is a rare wedding, holiday or religious event that doesn't bring out one of these traditional instruments – or perhaps an entire band of them. To give you an idea of what they are and how they sound, below is a snapshot of the most common ones.

KAVAL Traditionally a shepherd's instrument, the *kaval* resembles a flute. It is made of one piece of wood about 70cm long, usually ash, open at both ends and ornately decorated throughout. It produces a lovely warm sound, almost melancholic. You can hear the kaval frequently played in pairs, with the first leading a melody and the second one droning along with a slightly lower key.

GAJDA Macedonia's version of the bagpipe – its origins are in Macedonia's mountain villages. *Gajdas* have four main parts: the chanter (*gajdarka*), a wooden tube with seven finger-holes in front and a thumb-hole at the back; the drone (*brchalo*) producing the constant sound; the duvalo, a wooden pipe attached to the bag where the musician blows air in; and of course the bag itself (*mev*), made of tanned sheep or goat skin. The Gajda is usually accompanied by a kaval or two, a tambura, and perhaps a percussion instrument like the tapanče, daire or tarabuka.

ZURLA Typically played at weddings, social occasions and Turkish wrestling matches (*pelivan*), the *zurla* has a distinct piercing sound that is usually heard well above the drum (*tapan*) that accompanies it. It is a wooden (walnut or plum) two-part, wind instrument, the body of which is a conical pipe. A beak (*slavec*) is inserted into the upper, narrow part. Zurlas originated in the Middle East and were brought to Macedonia either by the Turks or the Roma, the latter of whom most often play it today. The larger (male) zurla is usually found in Skopje, Tetovo,

Chalgia was played on traditional Macedonian musical instruments such as the *canoon*, *kemane*, *oud*, tambourine and *tarabuka* (see box). A six-CD anthology was brought out in 2006, and can be bought from Jugoton in Skopje. If you don't fancy the six-CD set, there is an interesting, more modern rendition of chalgia in the album *Kaldrma* (referring to an old type of road construction from the Ottoman period) by the pop/modern jazz Macedonian group String Forces and the traditional Macedonian Pece Atanasovski Ensemble (see page 103). Chalgia is played live every Wednesday at Vinoteka Temov (see page 137) in Skopje old town.

A CD of Macedonian church music by the monks of Jovan Bigorski is available at Jugoton if you don't make it to the monastery for the 05.30 liturgy.

Many of the bands hired for traditional functions and festivities are Roma bands, and one of the songs almost invariably played is 'Mjesečina', meaning 'moonlight', by Goran Bregovič, made famous in the Yugoslav film *Underground* (Emir Kusturica, 1995). The Roma have a strong history of music making, immortalised in the songs of Esma Redžepova-Teodosievska, the queen of Roma music.

LITERATURE Macedonian literary history is also split into two sections. The spread of the Cyrillic and Slavic languages is very much connected to the saints

Veles, Prilep, Bitola and Kratovo, while the smaller (female) zurla is played around Gostivar and Kumanovo.

SUPELKA A shepherd's instrument that looks and sounds like a recorder.

DUDUK A blocked-end flute that can be found in two lengths: 70cm like the kaval, and 25cm.

TAMBURA Brought to Macedonia in the 14th and 15th centuries via the Turks from the Middle East, the tambura is a long-necked string instrument with a pear-shaped body, made of walnut. It produces a metallic, tingling sound, and is played both solo and as part of an ensemble.

TAPAN This is a good-sized drum. What sets it apart is that the musicians of Macedonia play it with two specially designed drumsticks – known as a *kukuda* and a *pračka*. The kukuda is a narrow pipe made of wood, while the pračka is more like a thin switch. Each one strikes a different side of the drum and the difference in sound is remarkable; together they produce an impression that something big is about to happen. The *tapan* is the traditional accompaniment for most folk bands playing at special occasions. You'll find it at the Galičnik wedding, for instance (see page 249).

DAIRE Essentially a tambourine.

TARABUKA An hourglass-shaped drum, medium size, made of wood and animal skin. Its origins are uncertain, but it has been variously connected with Greece, the Middle East and India. It is quite often used as accompaniment to the tambura.

KEMANE An instrument similar to the violin or viola.

Kiril, Metodi, Clement and Naum (see page 171) and the development of the Archbishopric of Ohrid. Ohrid's Museum of Slavonic Literacy is dedicated to the historiography of its development.

Whilst much of Europe underwent a great literary phase during the Renaissance, Macedonia was firmly under Ottoman and Greek influence, which did not encourage indigenous writings. The 19th-century Miladinov brothers (see page 195) went a long way to cast off this dark period in Macedonian song, poetry, literature and literacy. A whole slew of authors and poets have appeared since then, most recently Živko Cingo, Radovan Pavlovski and Petre M Andreevski. The works of Božin Pavlovski, now living in Australia, are also available in English (see *Appendix 4* for titles).

ARCHITECTURE Macedonian architecture goes back a long way, the earliest discoveries of which date back to the Bronze and Iron ages. The ancient Paeons built fortresses out of huge limestone blocks, using a technique called Cyclopean masonry. No mortar was used, but the precise joints of the rocks and their huge size kept these constructions together for thousands of years. Very little of this architecture is visible today, although some remains can be found at Prosek above Demir Kapija, Mariovo and Vajtos (see page 311).

Thereafter, Macedonian architecture is centred largely round the development of the Church, until the arrival of the Ottomans at the end of the 14th century when Turkish inns, baths, mosques and clock towers influenced the skylines of towns like Skopje and Bitola. During the 18th century the development of what has become known as the 'old style of Ohrid, with extended eaves, spacious and splendid, with two entrances' (Pavlovski, *The Red Hypocrite*) became common among the rich and influential, such as the Ottoman lords, monastery inns and wealthy traders. One of the finest examples of this type of house is the Robev residence, now the National Museum of Ohrid, but they can be seen all over Macedonia in various states of disrepair, desperate for renovation. Some excellent architectural drawings of this type of architecture are on display at the Museum of Bitola.

Sadly, the renovation of traditional houses is costly, and therefore largely left undone. In addition, many of the beautiful 19th-century buildings of the grand European style, which used to adorn most of central Skopje, collapsed during the earthquake of 1963. In the aftermath, the money donated by hundreds of international donors to rebuild Skopje was used to bring in the latest competitive craze in concrete creations, both communist and international, which is still to be seen today. A fine example of this is the main post office in Skopje next to the Stone Bridge.

In 2010, the government revealed its plans, named Skopje 2014, to transform the centre of the capital. Some of the old buildings which were destroyed by the 1963 earthquake (such as the National Theatre, and the Officers House, which is to become the Museum of the Macedonian Struggle) are being rebuilt (if in a slightly different location). They are joined by endless statues, a prominent Archaeological Museum sporting Corinthian columns, a new Ministry of Foreign Affairs and headquarters of the Financial Police, and a new bridge. Despite its name, the project aims to be ready in 2013 to mark the 50th anniversary since the 1963 earthquake. For more on the controversy behind the €100 million project, see page 125.

2

Practical Information

... for one does not come to Macedonia every day, and time and opportunity are not to be thrown away.

Journals of a Landscape Painter in Greece & Albania, Edward Lear, 1848

WHEN TO VISIT

Located so far south in Europe, Macedonia is great to visit most of the year round. It is particularly welcoming during spring and autumn, outside the high tourist seasons and when the weather is at its most pleasant. It can be warm and sunny during the day from as early as March and as late as November. Skiing is usually available from December through to early April. July and August can be very hot, getting sometimes up to 40°C during the day in Skopje and along the Vardar Valley. This can be particularly unpleasant if taking lengthy journeys by public transport where there is no air conditioning and the local population fears getting ill from a breeze from an open window. The mountains remain pleasantly cool, however, and even Ohrid is relatively quiet mid-week in the summer.

HIGHLIGHTS

SCENIC OUTDOORS The lake and town of Ohrid (see *Chapter 5*) are seen as the jewel of Macedonia's crown. And it is not without reason that Ohrid's medieval architecture and pristine natural setting are preserved by UNESCO as a place of historic, cultural and scenic significance. Outside the height of the summer season it remains a wonderful little getaway spot, and should not be missed on any trip to Macedonia. The back route from Skopje through Debar to Struga and on to Ohrid is worth the extra time.

All three of Macedonia's **national parks** – Pelister, Mavrovo and Galičica – offer many marked hiking trails, and beautiful scenic drives on improving roads. The one **hike** not to miss is the 10km hike from Mount Vodno just outside Skopje down to Lake Matka (see page 155), which also offers rock climbing, caving, camping, kayaking and yet more scenic hikes to local monasteries and beyond. There are also many beautiful hikes to waterfalls, glacial lakes and other scenic spots (see *Chapter 10*), and along the Via Egnatia (see page 6). If you'd like to tandem paraglide or learn for yourself, this is one of the cheapest places in Europe. Mountain biking, horseriding or a hot air balloon are also great ways to experience Macedonia (see page 105).

WINE AND *RAKIJA* TASTING Macedonia has a very old history of wine making going back to Philip II, and there are some indigenous grapes in the country that make a very quaffable vino. It's difficult to find Macedonian wines outside the Balkans so make the most of trying them here (see page 357 for more on Macedonia's wine varieties). Macedonia's *eau de vie* is *rakija*. For most, *rakija* is *rakija* is *rakija*, but Alchemist is leading the way in producing *rakija* differentiated by grape, such as their very smooth Black Muscat (see more on *rakija* on page 100). In Skopje visit Skovin wine cellars (page 305), or the *rakija* bars, wine bar and Old City Brewery in Čaršija. If you get the chance though, go to Tikveš Wine Cellars (see page 306) in Kavadarci, the home of Macedonian wine, or take the opportunity to stay at Popova Kula vineyard. Two wine festivals not to miss are Sv Trifun on 14 February (page 308) and the harvest festival in September, both in Negotino.

ARCHITECTURE AND ARCHAEOLOGY Don't miss out on the 16th-century villages of the Macedonian minorities. **Galičnik** village of the Mijaks hangs on the edge of a deep ravine and every July holds the biggest wedding party you'll ever go to (page 249).

Malovište village, located in Pelister National Park, is an old Vlach village, formerly housing rich Vlach traders. It is now being renovated to preserve its heritage and is a beautiful example of the rich variety of Macedonian culture. There are hundreds of other fine old villages off the beaten track that have yet to be fully discovered and you'll find that taking a trip away from your main route will always reap a reward.

Macedonia's Turkish history is well worth looking into, and is best preserved in Skopje's old town, **Čaršija**. See *Chapter 3* for details of the old trading inns of Suli An, Kapan An and Kuršumli An, the bathhouses of Čifte Amam and Daud Pasha Amam, and the mosques of Mustafa Pasha and Sultan Murat.

Macedonia is literally buried in archaeological ruins, which are becoming more accessible every year: Neolithic villages on Lake Ohrid and in Skopje; Cyclopean fortresses at Prosek and Mariovo; Roman towns at Heraklea and Stobi; World War I battlefields at Doiran and outside Bitola. It's also possible to take part in archaeological digs through the Balkan Heritage Field School (page 15).

SPIRITUAL INNS

Orthodox A trip to Macedonia would be incomplete without at least visiting one monastery. They are renowned for their intricate woodwork and delicate architecture and for some of their remote but beautiful locations. The country boasted over a thousand churches and monasteries at the zenith of Orthodox ministry in the region during the 14th to 16th centuries. Ohrid was the centre of the Orthodox Church at the time and still has over 200 churches and monasteries overlooking its shores. Some of the most spectacular working monasteries to visit are Sv Joakim Osogovski (page 281) near Kriva Palanki; Sv Jovan Bigorski (page 253) near Debar; the World Monuments Fund-listed Treskavec Monastery (page 226) near Prilep; Sv Gavril Lesnovski (page 287) near Kratovo; Kališta Monastery (page 196) for its nearby cave churches looking over Lake Ohrid; and Zrze Monastery (page 228) set high on a cliff.

All these spiritual sites are covered in greater detail in the relevant chapters of this guidebook. For those who want to make churches and monasteries the theme of their visit, here are some further suggestions: the Monastery of Sv Naum (page 187) on Lake Ohrid; the women's monastery of Jankovec (page 220) near Resen; the Monastery of Sv Leonthius (page 301) near Vodoča village; the women's Monastery of Eleusa (page 302) in Veljusa village; the Monastery of the Archangel Michael (page 267) in Varoš, Prilep; the women's Monastery of Sv Gjorgi (page 254) in Debar; the Church of Sv Spas (page 145) in Skopje; the Church of Sv Gjorgi (page 221) in Kurbinovo for examples of 12th-century Renaissance art; the cave Church of Archangel Michael (page 194) in Radožda on Lake Ohrid; the Christian basilicas in Heraklea (page 213); Plaošnik (page 183) for its early Christian mosaics; and of course all the churches listed in the chapter on Ohrid (page 169).

Muslim/dervish True to the religious variety of Macedonia, there are also some beautiful mosques and dervish *teke* worth seeing. Marvel at the Motley Mosque in Tetovo, beautifully painted like a house of cards outside and like a tea tray inside (page 241), or admire the blue artwork of the Mustafa Pasha Mosque in Skopje. Also in Tetovo is the best preserved dervish Baba Arabati Teke (page 241), and in Struga the best preserved Halveti *teke* (page 193).

A DOZEN MORE HIGHLIGHTS

- Ascend to the towers of King Marko in Prilep for a 360° view of the Pelagonia plains and visit Prilep Tobacco Museum, catch the Prilep Beer Festival in July (page 221)
- Visit the town of Kratovo, situated around an old volcanic crater, for its rock art and volcanic droplets (page 284)
- See where Atatürk went to school in Bitola (page 205)
- Visit Kruševo (page 229), the capital of the ten-day Republic of Kruševo in 1903 where one of the most successful Macedonian revolutions against the Ottoman Empire took place, to see some of the best-preserved architecture from the 18th and 19th centuries, and a re-enactment of events on 2 August
- Bathe in the renovated local hot springs at Katlanovska Banja (page 159), communist style at Banjište (page 253) and visit the progressing renovation of the Roman baths in Bansko (page 302)
- Ski at Popova Šapka, Mavrovo, Kožuf, Kruševo or Pelister, and relax afterwards with a massage and a choice of local grills
- Ride the cable car to the top of Vodno Mountain outside Skopje (page 154)
- Learn of Macedonia's tragic Jewish history at the new Holocaust Museum (page 143)
- Watch the solstice on the Palaeolithic throne of Cocev Kamen sacrificial and megalithic ancient observatory (page 287)
- Safari in Mavrovo National Park to try and catch a rare sighting of the Balkan lynx or endangered vultures (page 248)
- Scuba dive in Lake Ohrid (page 169)

SUGGESTED ITINERARIES

ONE WEEK More than likely you will land in Skopje, so take two days to visit (see page 121). Then hire a car to take the back road to Ohrid, lunching at Hotel Tutto in Janče on the way, or take the early bus there direct. Spend two days in Ohrid, one to see the town, the second to hike in the Galičica National Park, tandem paraglide or take the boat to Sv Naum, swim and sunbathe. Finally drive over to Galičica National Park to hike up to Two Lake viewpoint, and down to Lake Prespa. Stop in Bitola for a late lunch on the fashionable Širok Sokok, then journey on to Prilep to visit Treskavec Monastery (page 226, or take the bus there direct). Treat yourself to a night at Popova Kula winery and hotel to sample their wines before returning back to Skopje the next day.

TWO WEEKS After three days in Skopje (page 121), including one when you visit nearby Lake Matka (page 155) and Katlanovska Banja (page 159), travel to Ohrid via Tetovo to see the Motley Mosque, Baba Arbata Teke and the Tetovo Kale (page 233). After two days in Ohrid (see above), make your way to Bitola. Spend one full day here to see the Roman ruins of Heraklea, visit Attatürk's former military school and museum, and the best ethno museum in Macedonia at Krklino (page 212). Stay in the Hotel Millenium Palace or Villa Dihovo. Take a day to visit Prilep (see above) and pop over to Kruševo, home of the Ilinden Uprising and pop star Tošе Proeski (page 230). Overnight in Popova Kula winery and hotel (page 310). Take the next day to hike up to Prosek (page 311) and visit the tiny Demir Kapija Museum. Move on to Strumica and then Berovo to stay at the gorgeous Aurora Resort and Spa, or at Hotel Manastir. While you're there, take a day to hike in the area and breathe in the pristine air. Then make your way to Kratovo to visit the stone towers, see the nearby Stone Dolls, and hike up to Gorni Kratovo to see volcanic bombs (page 286). Return to Skopje via the Devil's Wall near Sv Nikole (page 289).

TOUR OPERATORS

Operators outside Macedonia who can book your ticket and hotel and make up an itinerary for you are few, but increasing:

VISITING CHURCHES AND MONASTERIES
Sally Broughton Micova

Macedonia is full of amazing churches and monasteries. Although many of them date back to Byzantine times, they are most often still working churches or inhabited monasteries. Therefore it is good to know a bit about their decorum in order to avoid feeling uncomfortable and to understand some of what is going on.

There is a difference between parish churches and monasteries. It is important to remember that when entering a monastery complex you are entering the place where the sisters or brothers of that community live. Most monasteries have members of their community dedicated to dealing with visitors, and will often have signs out front explaining what is expected, such as respecting the dress code, not making too much noise, and don't go nosing around the living quarters unaccompanied.

In both parish churches and monasteries, men and women should wear tops that cover their shoulders and are not too revealing. Men should wear trousers that come below the knee at least and women should have skirts below the knee. Often a box of skirts for covering legs and shawls for shoulders can be found at the entrance of the monastery. However, women regularly visit churches and attend services in trousers, so there will be no box of skirts at the entrance of a church. Unlike in many other Orthodox countries it is not necessary for women to cover their heads when entering churches in Macedonia.

Most of the time you will be entering the monastery to see the church inside, but there will often be members of the community at the entrance or inside the church welcoming visitors, so feel free to ask about the residences, called *konaci*, as some might also have areas open to the public. Some of the larger monasteries even take in overnight guests. They do not charge officially, but it is customary to leave a few hundred denars as a donation and or a packet of coffee or box of cookies. Monastic communities do not eat meat and live simply, but they often have guests who they provide with coffee and cookies so such gifts are always appreciated.

AUSTRALIA

Tucan Travel 217 Alison Rd, Randwick, Sydney, NSW 2031; ☎ 02 9326 6633, 1300 769 249; f 02 9326 5993; e ozsales@tucantravel.com; www. tucantravel.com; ⏰ 09.00–17.30 Mon–Fri (exc 10.00–17.30 Thu), 09.00–13.00 Sat (phone calls only). Offers 12- to 40-day tours through the Balkans with 1 or 2 days in Ohrid. They have extended phone hours & call centres in other countries so it is worth looking at the contact page on their website to see if they have a telephone number for your country.

CANADA

Adventures Abroad 2148-20800 Westminster Highway, Richmond, BC, V6V 2W3; ☎ 604 303 1099; e online form: www.adventures-abroad. com. Offers custom walking, culture & family tours of the Balkans for up to 1 month.

UK

Andante Travel The Old Barn, Old Rd, Alderbury, Salisbury, Wilts SP5 3AR; ☎ 01722 713 800; f 01722 711 966; e tours@andantetravels.co.uk; www. andantetravel.co.uk; ⏰ 09.00–17.00 Mon–Fri. Specialising in archaeology & the ancient world, Andante has espied the potential in Macedonia by offering a tour of the best of the country's Roman ruins, medieval churches & Ottoman architecture. Might not do tours including Macedonia every year, so keep checking.

Explore! Nelson Hse, 55 Victoria Rd, Farnborough, Hants GU14 7PA; ☎ 0845 867 9491; e res@explore.co.uk; www.explore.co.uk; ⏰ 08.00–18.30 Mon–Fri, 09.00–16.30 Sat & bank holidays. Explore! runs several interesting tours through Bulgaria, Macedonia & Greece, focusing on ancient Macedonia & Europe's last frontier.

Monasteries in Macedonia often close their doors in the evening, but churches are always open unless they are in remote areas in which case you may have to look around for a key tucked somewhere outside or find someone in a nearby village who has the key.

People come in and out of Macedonian churches all the time, just to light a candle or leave an offering or spend a bit of time reflecting. There is usually a small window where someone sells candles, small icons, prayer bracelets, etc. In village churches or remote locations often there is just a pile of candles on a table or window ledge and people leave money, usually 5–10MKD per candle. There may be special stands for candles or boxes with sand. People light candles in the upper parts of the stand for the living and in the under part of the stand for the dead. Smaller churches might have a separate box placed lower or to the side.

Most churches, except for very small ones, will have an icon placed on a stand in the middle. This will be either the patron saint of the church or the saint relevant to the day in the calendar. People will usually cross themselves at the entrance and then go to that icon, cross themselves and kiss the icon. They usually leave small change, bills or other offerings on the central icons and on other icons around the church. However, this practice is actually discouraged by the church and it is more appropriate to place any offerings in the slots or boxes next to the icons.

You will notice that there are no pews or rows of chairs in Macedonian churches. There may be a few around for those who need to sit, but the congregation stands for the service. It is not uncommon for people to come and go during the service, especially those with small children, so don't feel like you have to stay outside if you happen upon a service when visiting a Macedonian church. Feel free to enter and spend a bit of time listening to the choir and watching the service. Just be careful not to make too much noise or be disruptive.

If you specifically want to attend a service, they usually start at 07.30 or 08.30 on Sundays, though in monasteries they may start earlier.

Newex The Old Rectory, Cyffylliog, Ruthin, North Wales LL15 2DW; ☎ 01824 710 320; f 0845 280 1921; e contact@newex.co.uk; www.newex. co.uk. The 1st tour operator outside Macedonia to provide walking holidays exclusively in Macedonia. Their 2011, 1-week hotel to hotel treks in the Shar, Mavrovo and Galičica mountains will be guided, but future treks offered may include self-guided itineraries.

Reality & Beyond Quenington Old Rectory, Cirencester, Glos GL7 5BN; ☎ 01285 750 888; f 01285 750 540; e lucy@realityandbeyond. co.uk; www.realityandbeyond.co.uk. Historian & art historian Lucy Abel Smith provides high-quality individually tailored tours for the discerning, providing exclusive insight into the architecture, culture & history of Macedonia.

Regent Holidays Mezzanine Suite, Froomsgate Hse, Rupert St, Bristol BS1 2QJ; ☎ 0845 277 3317; f 0117 925 4866; e regent@regent-holidays. co.uk; www.regent-holidays.co.uk; ⊕ 09.00–17.30 Mon–Fri, 10.00–14.00 Sat. The 1st UK tour operator to branch into the region, Regent Holidays can book you accommodation in Macedonia, book you on 1 of their special group tours or provide you with an individual tour package tailored to your wishes.

Tucan Travel 316 Uxbridge Rd, Acton, London W3 9QP; ☎ 020 8896 1600; f 020 8896 1400; e uksales@tucantravel.com; www.tucantravel.com; ⊕ 09.00–17.30 Mon–Fri (exc 10.00–17.30 Wed), 09.00–13.00 Sat (phone calls only). The UK head office of the operator of the same name in Australia (see above). Extended phone hours in the evening.

USA

Adventures Abroad 1124 Fir Av #101, Blaine, WA 98230; ☎ 360 755 9926; e online form: www. adventures-abroad.com. Offers custom walking, culture & family tours to the Balkans.

Kutrubes Travel Agency 328 Tremont St, Boston, MA 02116; ☎ 800 878 8566, 617 426 5668; f 617 426 3196; e adventures@ kutrubestravel.com; www.kutrubestravel.com. Has recently started tours including Macedonia & can provide individually tailored packages, as well as just accommodation bookings.

Serious Traveler 5500 Bucks Bar Rd, Placerville, CA 95667; ☎ 800 762 4216, 530 621 3007; f 530 621 3017; e info@serioustraveler. com; www.serioustraveler.com. Does a 6-day extension in Macedonia added onto their Albania & Bulgaria trips, including visiting Treskavec by jeep & Tetovo's Motley Mosque.

LOCAL TOUR OPERATORS Macedonia's **National Tourism Portal** (*www. exploringmacedonia.com*) offers thousands of ideas, links and contacts for visiting the country, including local tour operators specialising in Macedonia. A complementary site linking much more about Macedonia is **www.macedonia-timeless.com**, with the introductory CNN advert filmed by Macedonia's internationally acclaimed film director Milčo Mančevski (see page 57).

In addition to the tour operators listed below, the **Association of Tourist Guides** (*Dimitrie Cupovski 12, Skopje;* ☎ *02 3290 425;* m *078 205 505;* f *02 3225 833;* e *ztvmk.official@gmail.com*) can also help with guides. To arrange outdoor sports activities, see more specific details listed on pages 105–12.

Bike Macedonia Petar Poparsov 23/14, Skopje; ☎ 075 341 131; e contact@ride.mk; www.ride. mk. Offers regular 8-day scheduled mountain-biking tours across Macedonia for €899 pp with full vehicle support & including hotels (bike rent is separate at €20/day), or flexible non-scheduled tours if your dates don't coincide with the scheduled tours. Family bike tours available, as well as 'high octane' tours over 2,000m for the superfit. An awesome way to see Macedonia.

Cycle Macedonia e info@cyclemacedonia. com; www.cyclemacedonia.com. Offers 8-day

road cycling tours around Macedonia, covering 35–60km per day. Includes bike rental, food, accommodation & full vehicle support for US$1,400. Proving very popular.

Go Macedonia Ankarska 29A, Skopje; ☎f 02 3071 265; e gomacedonia@t-home.mk; www. gomacedonia.com. Go Macedonia cater almost exclusively for foreign tourists. They offer a themed tour of the month, which concentrates on a different part of Macedonia over a w/end & which individuals can sign up to. They can also arrange group tours, make individual arrangements, & are the only Macedonian specialists in family holidays. Bike tours also available.

Macedonia Travel Orce Nikolov 109/3, Skopje; ☎ 02 3112 408; m 078 337 336; e info@macedoniatravel.com; www.macedoniatravel.com. Conveniently located in the popular eating district of Debar Maalo, this company specialises in travel within Macedonia, & particularly hiking & adventure in the northwest & centre of the country. Also offers car rental.

Macedonia Vision Savana, Skopska 9a, Skopje; ☎ 02 3115 826; f 02 3114 206; e info@macedoniavision.com; www.macedoniavision.com. Macedonia Vision is particulary good at wine, spa & monastery tourism & can book your accommodation in a monastery.

No Limit Office 7, 1st Floor, Paloma Bjanka Business Centre, Dame Gruev bb, Skopje; ☎ 02 324 6099; e info@nolimit.mk; www.nolimit.mk, www.balkanexperience.com. A young new company with good connections in the region, &

experience of getting Macedonian hiking maps. Good for outdoor & adventure sports.

Simonium Travel Podgrage 76, Čaršija, Skopje; ☎ 02 5511 366; f 02 5511 367; m 070 319 301; e contact@simoniumtravel.com.mk; www.simoniumtravel.com.mk; ⊕ 09.00–17.00 Mon–Sat. Specialises in discreet travel for the discerning within Macedonia, especially Byzantine art tours. Located in the heart of Čaršija, old town Skopje, it is also a good little souvenir shop.

Turist Bitola Krali Marko 16, 7000 Bitola; ☎ 047 202 777; f 047 202 776; e turist@turist.com.mk; www.turist.com.mk. Has extensive experience working with foreign tour groups & agents. Can find you accommodation throughout Macedonia as well as arrange trips to sites.

Visit Macedonia Njudeliška 4/1, Skopje; ☎ 02 3071 614; e info@visitmacedonia.mk; www.vm.com.mk; ⊕ 08.00–17.00 Mon–Fri. Good website with useful links page to help plan what you want to do in Macedonia.

RED TAPE

Nationals from neighbouring countries, Australia, the EU, Iceland, Israel, New Zealand, Norway, Switzerland and the US, among others, do not need visas at present for stays of less than 90 days within a six-month period starting from the day you first enter the country. Nationals of Japan, Montenegro and Turkey can enter visa-free for up to 60 days in a six-month period. For an up-to-date check on which nationals do require visas, visit http://macedonia.visahq.co.uk. Visa requirements tend to change with a change of government, so keep this in mind. Your passport will need to be valid for at least three months beyond the end of your visa. If you wish to change your status in the country from one of short business trip or holiday to one of temporary residence, this can only be done back in your home country through your country's Macedonian embassy. The US Embassy in Macedonia has a good webpage on the requirements of foreign stay in Macedonia (see listing on page 69).

POLICE REGISTRATION The Law on Foreigners (at time of writing only available in English at www.iomskopje.org.mk/Legal/Law_on_Foreigners_ENG.pdf and on UNHCR's website) governs the stay of foreigners in the country. It is essentially based on the old Yugoslav law and is similar in all the former Yugoslav republics. Under Article 139 (amended in 2010 to double the time allowed to register) a foreigner must be registered with the police at the latest within 48 hours of arriving in Macedonia. If you are staying in a hotel or other licensed accommodation, then the hotelier will do this for you and must register you within 24 hours of your arrival at the hotel. The hotel will fill out the necessary *potvrda* (certificate) for you and you need do nothing except provide your passport for your identification details. You are entitled to keep your section of the *potvrda* (normally returned with your passport at the end of your stay) and it is advisable to make sure you keep your copy, because if you can't prove your official registration for any part of your stay in Macedonia then you could be subject to deportation.

2

If you are staying in private accommodation then your host must register you at the nearest police station within 48 hours of you arriving at their house. The necessary *potvrda* should be available at the local police station and must be signed by your host. If your host is unavailable for any reason, then you will need a letter of invitation to stay at their house, accompanied by a copy of their identification papers, and if they are not Macedonian, then a copy of their legal basis for residency in the country (work or residency permit, diplomatic status, etc).

Until a few years ago, the police did not check up on this system stringently. The political atmosphere in Macedonia is changing, however. If you are not registered, the police have every right to deport you, even if you do plead the innocent tourist. Most unregistered tourists will probably get away with a warning, especially as the law is not widely or easily available, nor is an official tourist bureau system in place as in other former Yugoslav countries such as Slovenia and Croatia to deal with these issues easily and in extended office hours. In today's climate in Macedonia, if you register late, or not at all, and your host is not openly connected with the current ruling political party, then the chances of your host being fined (possibly substantially) are increased.

CUSTOMS You can bring in as much personal luggage as you like, although expensive items such as laptops, cameras, musical instruments, sporting equipment, radios and jewellery should be declared on entry if you want to leave with them without any hassles. You must declare if you bring in over €10,000 in cash (or travellers' cheques). You will need to ask for a customs declaration form to fill out, as they are not automatically given out as they are in the USA.

You may leave with more than you entered, providing you can prove that it was bought with legally exchanged money, so make sure you keep any bank or ATM receipts. Antiques and icons require a certificate of approval from the Ministry of the Interior before they can be exported.

Duty free allowances are 1 litre of spirits; 200 cigarettes or 50 cigars or 250g of tobacco; perfume for personal use.

EMBASSIES

For a full and up-to-date list of Macedonian embassies abroad and embassies in Skopje see www.mfa.gov.mk

MACEDONIAN EMBASSIES ABROAD.

ⓔ Albania Rr Kavajes, nr 116, Tirana; ☎+355 4 230 909, 274 765; f +355 4 232 514; e tirana@mfa.gov.mk; www.missions.gov.mk/tirana

ⓔ Australia 74 Banks St, Yarralumla, Canberra, ACT 2600; ☎+612 6282 6220; f +612 6282 6229; e info@macedonianemb.org.au; www.missions.gov.mk/canberra

ⓔ Austria Kinderspitalgasse 5/2, A-1090 Wien; ☎+43 1 524 8756; f +43 1 524 8753. Visa section: ☎+43 1 524 8757; f +43 1 524 8754; e vienna@mfa.gov.mk, botschaft@makedonien.co.at

ⓔ Bulgaria Frederic Joliot-Curie 17, Block 2, Floor 3, Suite 5, 1113 Sofia; ☎+359 2 870 /5098; f +359 2 971 28 32; e sofia@mfa.gov.mk; www.missions.gov.mk/sofia

ⓔ Canada 130 Albert St, Suite 1006, Ottawa, ON K1P 5G4; ☎+1 613 234 3882; f +1 613 233 1852; e emb.macedonia.ottawa@sympatico.ca; www.missions.gov.mk/ottawa/

ⓔ Greece Liaison Office, Papadiamanti 4, P Psychico, 154 52 Athens; ☎+301 67 49 585; f +301 67 49 572; e athens@mfa.gov.mk. Consulate in Thessaloniki: Tsimiski 43, Thessaloniki; ☎+30 2310 277 347; f +30 2310 278 598; e solun@mfa.gov.mk

ⓔ Kosovo Ul 24 Maj br 121, Priština; ☎+381 38 247 462; f +381 38 247 463; e prishtina@mfa.gov.mk; www.missions.gov.mk/prishtina

ⓔ Netherlands Laan van Meerdevoort 50–C, 2517 Am Den Haag; ☎+ 31 70 427 44 64–5;

f +31 70 427 44 69; e hague@mfa.gov.mk;
www.missions.gov.mk/hague
E Serbia Gospodar Jevremova 34, 11 000
Belgrade; ☎+381 11 328 49 24; f +381 11 328
50 76; e belgrade@mfa.gov.mk; www.missions.
gov.mk/serbia
E Switzerland Kirchenfeldstrasse 30, 3005
Bern; ☎+41 31 352 0028; f +41 31 352 0037;
e bern@mfa.gov.mk; www.missions.gov.mk/bern
E Turkey Karaca sokak 24/5-6,
Gaziosmanpasha, Ankara; ☎+903 12 439

9204/8; f +903 12 439 0206; e ankara@mfa.gov.
mk; www.missions.gov.mk/ankara
E UK Suites 2.1 & 2.2, Buckingham Court,
75–83 Buckingham Gate, London SW1E 6PE;
☎020 7976 0535–8; f 020 7976 0539; e london@
mfa.gov.mk; www.missions.gov.mk/london
E US 2129 Wyoming Av, NW Washington, DC
20008; ☎+1 202 667 0501; f +1 202 667 2131;
e washington@mfa.gov.mk; www.missions.gov.
mk/Washington

FOREIGN EMBASSIES AND CONSULATES IN MACEDONIA
Embassies in Skopje

E Albania Slavej Planina 2; ☎02 3246 726;
f 02 3246 727; e embassy.skopje@mfa.gov.al;
www.albanianembassy.org.mk
E Austria Mile Pop Jordanov 8; ☎02 3083 400;
f 02 3083 350; e skopje-ob@bmeia.gv.at
E Bosnia & Herzegovina Mile Pop Jordanov
56; ☎02 3086 216; f 02 3086 221; e emb.bih@
neotel.net.mk
E Bulgaria Zlatko Šnajder 3; ☎02 3116 320;
f 02 3116 139; e secretary@bgemb.org.mk
E China, People's Republic of 474 Ulica br
20; ☎02 3213 163; f 02 3212 500; chinaembmk@
mfa.gov.cn
E Croatia Mitroplit Teodosij Gologanov 44;
☎02 3248 170; f 02 3248 004; e croemb.skopje@
mvpei.hr; www.mvpei.hr
E Greece Borka Talevski 6; ☎02 3130 198; f 02
3115 718; e grfyrom@mfa.gr
E Hungary Mirka Ginova 27; ☎02 3063 423;
f 02 3063 070; e mission.skp@kum.hu
E Italy 8-ma Udarna Brigada 22; ☎02 3236
500; f 02 3236 505; e segreteria.skopje@esteri.it;
www.ambaskopje.esteri.it
E Netherlands Leninova 69–71; ☎02 3129
319; f 02 3129 309; e sko@minbuza.nl; www.
nlembassy.org.mk
E Norway 8-ma Udarna Brigada 2; ☎02 3129
165; f 02 3111 138; e embskp@mfa.no; www.
norway.org.mk

E Poland Djuro Djakovic 50; ☎02 3112 647;
f 02 3119 744; e skopje.amb.sekretariatt@msz.
gov.pl; www.skopje.polemb.net
E Romania Rajko Zinzifov 42; ☎02 3228 055;
f 02 3228 036; e romanamb@cabletel.net.mk
E Russian Federation Pirinska 44; ☎02 3117
160; f 02 3117 808; e embassy@russia.org.mk;
www.russia.org.mk
E Slovenia Vodnjanska 42; ☎02 3176 663;
f 02 3176 631; e vsk@gov.si
E Spain 27 Mart, 7; ☎02 3231 002; f 02 3220
612; e emb.skopje@maec.es; www.maec.es
E Sweden 8-ma Udarna Brigada 2; ☎02 3297
880; f 02 3112 065; e ambassaden.skopje@
foreign.ministry.se; www.swedenabroad.se
E Switzerland Maksim Gorki 19; ☎02 3128
300; f 02 3116 201; e sko.vertretung@eda.
admin.ch; www.eda.admin.ch/skopje
E Turkey Slavej Planina bb; ☎02 3113 270;
f 02 3117 024; e turkemb.skopje@mfa.gov.tr
E UK Salvador Aljende 73; ☎02 3299 299;
f 02 3179 726; e britishembassyskopje@fco.gov.
uk; www.ukinmacedonia.fco.gov.uk. Passport
renewal only available in Düsseldorf!
E US Samoilova 21; ☎02 3102 000; f 02 3102
499; e EmbSkoWebM@t-home.mk; http://skopje.
usembassy.gov

Consulates in Skopje

E Australia Londonska 11b; ☎02 3061 114;
f 02 3061 834; e austcon@mt.net.mk
E Belgium Koco Racin 14/4–3 9; ☎02 2043
314; f 02 2043 314
E Canada Praska bb; ☎02 3225 630; f 02 3220
596; e honcon@unet.com.mk

E Denmark Aleksandar Makedonski 12; ☎02 3104
001; f 02 3104 004; e dan.cons@alkaloid.com.mk
E Japan Bd Partizanski Odredi 15a; ☎02 3118
063; f 02 3117 440
E Slovakia Budimpeštanka 39; ☎02 3090 360;
f 02 3090 367; e emb.skopje@mzv.sk

Consulates in Bitola

The City of Consuls, as Bitola was also known, still has 11 consulates. A full list is at www.bitolatourist.info.

ⓔ Bulgaria Bulevar 1 Mai 53; ☎047 202 893/894; f 047 202 947; e bgconsulate@t-home.mk
ⓔ Greece Tomaki Dimitrovski 43; ☎047 237 350; f 047 220 310; e grofficebitola@mfa.gr

ⓔ Slovenia 29 Noemvri 4/2; ☎070 207 959; f 047 254 138; e miskomojsov@yahoo.com
ⓔ Turkey Maršal Tito 154-26; ☎047 222 693.
ⓔ UK Maršal Tito 42; ☎/f 047 228 765; m 070 350 819

GETTING THERE AND AWAY

Low-cost airlines are starting to serve Skopje, but mostly during the summer and only on certain days of the week. Most regional public transport users travel by the frequent and cheap buses to Macedonia as the train is slow and decrepit. Aside from the car option, and if you are thinking of walking in, make sure you enter at a designated border crossing (see *Security and safety*, page 86).

BY AIR For daily flight times in and out of Macedonia see www.airports.com.mk. At the time of writing, Wizzair and Pegasus are the only budget operators flying to Skopje, from London Luton and London Stansted respectively, as well as from a growing number of other airports including Venice, Istanbul and Izmir. Various other airlines fly direct from continental Europe, and with Skopje's Alexander the Great Airport opening up a new international terminal building late in 2011, new operators are likely to start using Skopje as a regional hub. In the summer a few airlines also fly direct to Ohrid's St Paul the Apostle Airport (see page 172), including from Tel Aviv and Moscow. A Wizzair flight from London can cost as little as £20 one-way.

The alternative to expensive flights into Skopje is to look at neighbouring airports such as Priština, Sofia or Thessaloniki for cheap deals and then take the bus. Try the following agents for cheap flights:

✈ Bravofly www.bravofly.com. Online bookings only.
✈ Dial-a-flight ☎0844 811 4444; www.dialaflight.com
✈ Pegasus Airlines www.flypgs.com. See website for local call centres. Local call charges apply.

✈ STA Travel www.statravel.com. Many offices around the world.
✈ Trailfinders www.trailfinders.com. Many branches throughout the UK.
✈ Travelbag ☎0870 890 1456; www.travelbag.co.uk
✈ Wizzair www.wizzair.com. See website for local numbers, but high call charges apply.

Skopje Airport Skopje's airport is tiny with only two gates, so arriving 45 minutes before departure is usually sufficient. When the overseas Macedonians return for holidays in the summer months you might want to arrive a whole hour in advance for flights to Austria, Germany and Switzerland. There is a small shop selling souvenirs and Macedonian newspapers in the check-in area, as well as a coffee bar, a post office counter and two cash machines. Skopje Airport is not yet set up for email-ticketing, so these are not available for purchase inside Macedonia. In addition, you will often have to collect your onward boarding card on a multi-leg trip at the transit desk of your transit airport as Skopje Airport might not be able to issue these. This can be somewhat harrowing if you have a very short stopover and don't know the transit airport, but it usually works. There is a small duty free section inside the departure lounge (no newspapers, and only limited Tikveš and Bovin wines on sale).

Unfortunately, there is still no mass public transport to and from Skopje. Therefore, the only way to travel the 25km into Skopje town is to take a taxi. Taxis picked up outside the airport charge an extortionate €25 or 1,500MKD to go into Skopje. Some hotels pick up and drop off guests for free if you book in advance. Alternatively book a taxi online with Lotus (*www.lotustransport.com. mk*) who will take you from the airport into Skopje for 900MKD (€15). This is the same price as a taxi flagged down on the street going to the airport. When taking a taxi to the airport and if you are unlucky enough to get a driver who does not speak much English, make sure you ask for the '*aerodrom vo Petrovec*', not to be confused with a part of Skopje city which is also called *Aerodrom* after the old airport!

BY RAIL (♁ *02 2449 212;* e *mztransportad@t-home.mk; www.mzi.mk*) There are only two international trains entering Macedonia. The daily service from Belgrade takes nine hours, which is ludicrously slow and you would be much better taking the four-hour bus service. The daily service from Priština leaves Skopje mid-afternoon and departs Priština early in the morning. The 2½-hour journey spends 40 minutes at the border changing engines. The train is well used on the Kosovo side, but few use it on the 35-minute Macedonian passage. If you get stuck at Blace border on the way to Skopje, then it is only a 20-minute walk to the road crossing where you can pick up a taxi to Skopje for 900MKD.

The domestic timetable is online at http://mz-rail.atwebpages.com/pdf/ timetable_MZ_2011-12.pdf in Macedonian and for the 2012 timetable in English see box, pages 72–5. Online train bookings are not possible at the time of writing.

BY BUS Due to the lack of cheap flights and frequent comfortable trains, Macedonia is well served by international-standard coaches, especially to and from Germany and Switzerland. See www.sas.com.mk for complete bus listings. Destinations to and from Skopje (one-way ticket) include:

🚌 **Belgrade** 12 a day (6hrs; 1,420MKD)
🚌 **Frankfurt** 3 a day (departing Skopje at 08.00, 09.30, 11.45; 24hrs; 6,900MKD)
🚌 **Istanbul** Once a day (departing Skopje at 16.00; 14hrs; 2,560MKD)
🚌 **Podgorica** Twice a week (departing Skopje at 18.00 Wed & Sat only; 10hrs; 1,950MKD)
🚌 **Priština** 3 a day (departing Skopje at 09.00, 11.30, 15.00; 3hrs; 340MKD)

🚌 **Sofia** 7 a day (departing Skopje at 06.30, 08.30, 15.00, 16.00, 22.00, 23.00, 24.00; 5hrs; 1,550MKD)
🚌 **Thessaloniki** 3 a week (departing Skopje at 07.00 Mon, Wed & Fri only; 5hrs; 1,280MKD)
🚌 **Tirana** Once a day (departing Skopje at 19.00; 7hrs; 1,370MKD)
🚌 **Zagreb** Twice a day (departing Skopje at 13.00, 17.00; 15hrs; 3,200MKD)

International coaches also serve other locations in Macedonia, especially between Germany and the northwestern towns of Gostivar and Tetovo. For bus station details in Macedonia see individual chapters. Timetables and price information from some countries to Macedonian are available at www.eurolines.com. At the time of writing Macedonia had yet to put its international coach services on the Eurolines website. There is a left luggage service at Skopje Bus Station.

BY CAR The easiest and most convenient way to get around Macedonia is still by car (a 4x4 if you plan to go anywhere off the beaten track). But driving to Macedonia from the further reaches of Europe, especially places like Britain and Finland, is an extremely long journey – at least three days.

If you do intend to drive from Britain, for instance, a recommended route would be to cross at Calais for a cheap, short ferry journey, drive along the roads of France, which are usually fairly empty although there are road tolls to pay (German roads are toll-free, but packed, and speed restrictions are becoming more widespread), cross the Alps at the Simplon Pass and head for Venice. From here take the overnight car ferry to Durres in Albania, or Igoumenitsa in Greece. Either journey from these ports to Skopje is arduous mountain driving (six hours from Durres via Ohrid, or ten hours via Bitola from Igoumenitsa), but the scenery is fantastic. The drive down through Italy, whilst making the ferry journey shorter, is packed with other drivers,

TRAIN DEPARTURE TIMES FROM SKOPJE AND BITOLA

TRAIN DEPARTURE TIMES FROM SKOPJE

651　02.25　Dračevo 02.37, Zelenikovo 02.49, Veles 03.15, Ovče Pole 04.02, Štip 04.21, Balvan 04.32, Bančo Prkje 04.41, Sokolarci 04.50, Obleševo 04.55, Kočani 05.10

660　02.50　Skopje North 02.58, Gjorče Petrov 03.06, Tetovo 03.47, Gostivar 04.11, Kičevo 04.45

611　06.05　Lisiče 06.11, Dračevo 06.16, Orešani 06.22, Zelenikovo Novo 06.25, Zelenikovo 06.28, Smesnica 06.32, Kadina Reka 06.35, Pčinja 06.40, Rajko Žinzifov 06.46, Veles 06.56, Zgropolci 07.11, Nogaevci 07.16, Gradsko 07.22, Stobi 07.26, Kukuričani 07.32, Crveni Bregovi 07.36, Krivolak 07.42, Negotino Vardar 07.47, Dubravo 07.53, Demir Kapija 08.03, Klisura 08.11, Miravci 08.23, Miletkovo 08.27, Smokvica Nova 08.31, Smokvica 08.35, Prdejci 08.37, Gevgelija 08.43

600　06.20　Madžari 06.26, Ilinden 06.35, Miladinovci 06.43, Deljadrovci 06.47, Agino Celo 06.51, Romanovci 06.59, Prevoj 07.03, Kumanovo 07.09, Karpoš 07.14, Tabanovci 07.20

641　06.48　Lisiče 06.54, Dračevo 07.00, Jane Sandanski 07.10, Orešani 07.12, Zelenikovo Novo 07.15, Zelenikovo 07.19, Smesnica 07.23, Rajko Žinzifov 07.39, Veles 07.53, Toploka 08.02, Čaška 08.12, Stari Grad 08.22, Martolci 08.28, Vasil Antevski 08.35, Teovo 08.39, Sogle 08.42, Bogomila 08.50, Oreše 08.58, Gostiražni 09.09, Slenče 09.16, Brailovo 09.23, Senokos 09.28, Prilep 09.39, Galičani 09.46, Bakarno Gumno 09.52, Trojkrsti 09.57, Novoselani 10.01, Loznani 10.05, Dame Gruev 10.12, Bitola 10.27

662　08.05　Železarnica 08.09, Skopje Sever 08.14, Gjorče Petrov 08.23, Saraj 08.29, Sulari 08.35, Raduša 08.44, Orašje 08.48, Jegunovce 08.54, Jegunovci F-ka 08.57, Rataje 09.04, Tetovo 09.11, Žerovjani 09.20, Vranovci 09.26, Gostivar 09.33, Lakavica 09.340, Padalište 09.51, Zajas 09.58, Štrogomište 10.01, Dlapkin Dol 10.04, Kičevo 10.12

336　08.20　Kumanovo 08.51, Tabanovci 09.23, Preševo 10.00, Vranje 10.51, Leskovac 12.20, Niš 13.20, Stalakj 14.24, Lapovo 15.25, Mala Krsna 16.23, Belgrade 17.58

613　09.00　Lisiče 09.06, Dračevo 09.12, Orešani 09.19, Zelenikovo Novo 09.22, Zelenikovo 09.26, Smesnica 09.32, Rajko Žinzifov 09.41, Veles 09.52, Zgropolci 10.07, Nogaevci 10.12, Gradsko 10.18, Stobi 10.22, Kukuričani 10.28. Crveni Bregovi 10.32, Krivolac 10.38, Negotino Vardar 10.43, Dubravo 10.49, Demir Kapija 10.59, Klisura 11.07, Miravci 11.19, Miletkovo 11.23, Smokvica Nova 11.27, Smokvica 11.31, Prdejci 11.33, Gevgelija 11.39

2081　13.20　Lisiče 13.26, Dračevo 13.32, Jane Sandanski 13.37, Orešani 13.39, Zelenikovo Novo 13.42, Zelenikovo 13.46, Kadina Reka 13.52, Pčinja 13.56, Rajko Žinzifov 14.01, Veles 14.10

643　14.30　Lisiče 14.36, Dračevo 14.42, Orešani 14.48, Zelenikovo Novo 14.51, Zelenikovo 14.55, Smesnica 15.00, Rajko Žinzifov 15.14, Veles 15.26, Toploka 15.35, Čaška 15.45, Stari Grad 15.55, Martolci 16.01, Vasil Antevski 16.06, Teovo 16.12, Sogle 16.15, Bogomila 16.23, Oreše 16.31, Gostiražni 16.42, Slepče 16.49, Brailovo 16.56. Senokos 17.01, Prilep 17.12, Galičani 17.19, Bakarno Gumno 17.26, Trojkrsti 17.31, Novoselani 17.35, Loznani 17.39, Dame Gruev 17.45, Bitola 18.00

often resulting in traffic jams in motorway scenery. For times and prices of ferries between Italy and the Balkans see www.cemar.it.

If you're hitchhiking around the Balkans, a good place to find lifts is www.gorivo.com.

MAPS AND TOURIST INFORMATION

Tourist information centres are beginning to appear in major towns in Macedonia now, although some are an outlet for local souvenirs rather than useful maps and

563 15.20 Lisiče 15.25, Dračevo 15.31, Jane Sandanski 15.36, Orešani 15.38, Zelenikovo Novo 15.41, Zelenikovo 15.45, Kadina Reka 15.49, Rajko Žinzifov 16.03, Veles 16.14, Košulčevi 16.21, Jazla 16.29, Tošo Arsov 17.37, Orce 16.43, Ovče Pole 16.57, Štip 17.17, Balvan 17.28, Bančo Prkje 17.36, Zletovnica 17.41, Sokolarci 17.47, Obleševo 17.52, Kočani 18.07

220 16.30 Madžari 16.35, Ilinden 16.44, Miladinovci 16.52, Deljadrovci 16.56, Agino Selo 17.00, Romanovci 17.04, Prevoj 17.08, Kumanovo 17.18, Karpoš 17.23, Tabanovci 17.29

892 16.35 Skopje Sever 16.44, Gjorče Petrov 16.52, Volkovo 17.00, Gj. Jankovic 18.00, Uroševac 18.39, K. Polje 19.01, Priština 19.37

631 16.50 Lisiče 16.56, Dračevo 17.02, Jane Sandanski 17.07, Orešani 17.09, Zelenikovo Novo 17.12, Zelenikovo 17.15, Smesnica 17.19, Kadina Reka 17.21, Pčinja 17.26, Rajko Žinzifov 17.31, Veles 17.41, Zgropolci 17.55, Nogaevci 18.00, Gradsko 18.05, Stobi 18.09, Kukuričani 18.15. Crveni Bregovi 18.20, Krivolac 18.25, Negotino Vardar 18.29, Dubravo 18.35, Demir Kapija 18.45, Klisura 18.53, Miravci 19.03, Miletkovo 19.07, Smokvica Nova 19.11, Smokvica 19.15, Prdejci 19.17, Gevgelija 19.23

664 16.50 Zelezarnica 16.54, Skopje Sever 16.58, Gjorče Petrov 17.06, Saraj 17.11, Supari 17.17, Raduša 17.20, Orašje 17.31, Jegunovce 17.37, Jegunovce F-ka 17.39, Rataje 17.46, Tetovo 17.53, Bresnica 17.55, Želovjani 1802, Vranovci 18.08, Gostivar 18.15, Lakavica 18.22, Padalište 18.33, Zajas 18.40, Strogomište 18.43, Dlakin Dol 18.46, Kičevo 18.54

541 17.10 Veles 17.52, Bogomila 18.35, Prilep 19.26, Bitola 20.00

2022 19.00 Madžari 19.06, Ilinden 19.15, Miladinovci 19.23, Deljadrovci 19.27, Agino Selo 19.31, Romanovci 19.35, Prevoj 19.39, Kumanovo 19.45, Karpoš 19.50, Tabanovci 19.56

645 18.30 Lisiče 19.38, Dračevo 19.42, Jane Sandanski 19.50, Orešani 19.52, Zelenikovo Novo 19.55, Zelenikovo 19.58, Smesnica 19.02, Rajko Žinzifov 20.14, Veles 20.27, Toploka 20.37, Čaška 20.59, Stari Grad 21.09, Martolci 21.15, Vasil Antevski 21.22, Teovo 21.26, Sogle 21.30, Bogomila 21.38, Oreše 21.46, Gostiražni 21.57, Slepče 22.04, Brailovo 22.10, Senokos 22.15, Prilep 22.25, Galičani 22.32, Bakarno Gumno 22.38, Trojkrsti 22.41, Novoselani 22.47, Loznani 22.51, Dame Gruev 22.56, Bitola 23.13

334 20.10 Kumanovo 20.41, Tabanovci 21.23, Preševo 22.05, Vranje 22.58, Leskovac 00.16, Niš 01.20, Stalak 02.20, Lapovo 03.20, Mala Krsna 04.44, Belgrade 05.43

2083 22.40 Lisiče 22.46, Dračevo 22.52, Jane Sandanski 22.56, Orešani 22.59, Zelenikovo Novo 23.02, Zelenikovo 23.06, Smesnica 23.09, Rajko Žinzifov 23.21, Veles 23.30

2024 23.00 Madžari 23.05, Ilinden 23.13, Miladinovci 23.19, Deljadrovci 23.23, Agino Selo 23.27, Romanovci 23.31, Prevoj 23.35, Kumanovo 04.27, Tabanovci 04.37

TRAIN DEPARTURES FROM BITOLA

2040 06.50 Dame Gruev 07.06, Loznani 07.11, Novoselani 07.14, Trojkrsti 07.18, Bakarno Gumno 07.24, Galičani 07.31, Prilep 07.38

2042 16.21 Dame Gruev 16.36, Loznani 16.41, Novoselani 16.44, Trojkrsti 16.48, Bakarno Gumno 16.53, Galičani 16.59, Prilep 17.06

TRAIN ARRIVAL TIMES IN SKOPJE

From	Arrival time
611 Tabanovce 05.03, Karpoš 05.08, Kumanovo 05.14, Prevoj 05.19, Romanovci 05.23, Agino Selo 05.27, Deljadrovci 05.31, Miladinovci 05.35, Ilinden 05.42, Madžari 05.50	05.55
600 Veles 05.11, Rajko Žinzifov 05.22, Pčinja 05.27, Kadina Reka 05.33, Smesnica 05.35, Zelenikovo 05.40, Novo Zelenikovo 05.43, Orešani 05.45, Jane Sandanski 05.47, Dračevo 05.52, Lisiče 05.58	06.03
640 Bitola 03.10, Loznani 03.30, Novoselani 03.33, Prilep 03.49, Senokos 03.58, Brailovo 04.03, Slepče 04.08, Gostiražni 04.17, Oreše 04.27, Bogomila 04.36, Sogle 04.43, Teovo 04.46, Vasil Antevski 04.52, Martolci 04.59, Stari Grad 05.06, Čaška 05.16, Toploka 05.28, Veles 05.40, Rajko Žinzifov, 05.51, Smesnica 06.04, Zelenikovo 06.09, Novo Zelenikovo 06.11, Orešani 06.14, Jane Sandanski 06.21, Dračevo 06.27, Lisiče 06.33	06.38
335 Belgrade 21.50, Mladenovac 23.15, Palanka 23.45, Lapovo 03.13, Stalakj 01.13, Niš 02.50, Leskovac 03.27, Vranje 04.43, Preševo 06.05, Tabanovce 06.40, Kumanovo 06.52	07.22
630 Gevgelija 04.49, Prdejci 04.55, Smokvica 04.77, Smokvica Nova 05.01, Miletkovo 05.05, Miravci 05.10, Klisura 05.21, Demir Kapija 05.29, Dubrovo 05.39, Negotino Vardar 05.45, Krivolak 05.48, Crveni Bregovi 05.52, Kukuričani 05.57, Stobi 06.02, Gradsko 06.06, Nogaevci 06.12, Zgropolci 06.17, Veles 06.33, Rajko Žinzifov 06.47, Pčinja 06.52, Smesnica 06.59, Zelenikovo 07.04, Zelenikovo Novo 07.06, Orešani 07.08, Dračevo 07.15, Lisiče 07.21	07.26
661 Kičevo 05.33, Dlapkin Dol 05.39, Strogomиšte 05.44, Zajas 05.49, Padalište 05.56, Lakavica 06.03, Gostivar 06.10, Vranovci 06.16, Žerovjani 06.23, Breznica 06.30, Tetovo 06.33, Rataje 06.39, Jegunovce F-ka 06.49, Jegunovce 06.52, Oraše 06.58, Raduša 07.02, Sulari 07.09, Saraj 07.15, Gjorče Petrov 07.19, Skopje Sever 07.27, Železnarica 07.31	07.35
540 Bitola 05.30, Prilep 06.10, Bogomila 06.47, Veles 07.30	08.11
650 Kočani 05.50, Obleševo 06.303, Sokolarci 06.07, Zletovica 06.12, Vančo Prkje 06.18, Balvan 06.26, Štip 06.39, Ovče Pole 06.58, Orče 07.12, Tošo Arsov 07.18, Jazla 07.26, Košulčevi 07.34, Veles 07.50, Rajko Žinzifov 08.00, Zelenikovo 08.16, Zelenikovo Novo 08.19, Orešani 08.21, Jane Sandanski 08.23, Dračevo 08.29, Lisiče 08.36	08.40
613 Tabanovci 07.47, Karpoš 07.52, Kumanovo 07.58, Prevoj 08.03, Romanovci 08.07, Agino Selo 08.11, Deljadrovci 08.15, Miladinovci 08.20, Ilinden 08.31, Madžari 08.40	08.45
891 Priština 07.10, Kosovo Polje 07.015, Uroševac 07.54, Gj.Jankovic 09.00, Volkovo 09.29, Gj.Petrov 09.36, Skopje Sever 09.44	09.51
632 Gevgelija 09.56, Prdejci 10.02, Smokvica 10.04, Smokvica Nova 10.08, Milekovo 10.12, Miravci 10.17, Klisura 10.28, Demir Kapija 10.36, Dubrovo 10.50, Negotino Vardar 10.57, Krivolak 11.02, Crveni Bregovi 11.06, Kukuričani 11.12, Stobi 11.17, Gradsko 11.22, Nogaevci 11.28, Zgroploci 11.34, Veles 11.50, Rajko Žinzifov 12.00, Pčinja 12.05, Smesnica 12.12, Zelenikovo 12.17, Zelenikovo Novo 12.20, Orešani 12.23, Dračevo 12.30, Lisiče 12.35	12.40
663 Kičevo 12.18, Dlapkin Dol 12.24, Strogomišta 12.29, Zajas 12.34, Padalište 12.41, Lakavica 12.48, Gostivar 12.55, Vranovci 13.01, Žerovjane 13.08 Tetovo 13.19, Rataje 13.25, Jegunovce F-ka 13.35, Jegunovce 13.38, Oraše 13.43, Raduša 13.47, Sulari 13.54, Saraj 14.01, Gjorče Petrov 14.06, Skopje Sever 14.14, Železnarnica 14.18	14.22

information. In some cases you might be much better off going to a travel agency for information, especially in towns outside Skopje.

MAPS
Street, regional and country maps Maps of Macedonia are becoming available in a variety of formats from most bookshops and big supermarkets,

From	Arrival time
2080 Veles 14.23, Rajko Žinzifov 14.34, Pčinja 14.39, Kadina Reka 14.45, Smesnica 14.47, Zelenikovo 14.56, Novo Zelenikovo 14.59, Orešani 15.01, Jane Sandanski 15.03, Dračevo 15.08, Lisiče 15.14	15.19
642 Bitola 12.45, Dame Gruev 13.01, Loznani 13.06, Novoselani 13.09, Trojkrsti 13.13, Bakarno Gumno 13.19, Galičani 13.25, Prilep 13.35, Senokos 13.44, Brailovo 13.49, Slepče 13.54, Gostiražni 14.03, Oreše 14.13, Bogomila 14.22, Sogle 14.29, Teovo 14.32, Vasil Antevski 14.36, Martolci 14.43, Stari Grad 14.49, Časka 15.00, Toploka 15.10, Veles 15.27, Rajko Žinzifov 15.38, Kadina Reka 15.53, Smesnica 15.55, Zelenikovo 16.00, Novo Zelenikovo 16.03, Orešani 16.05, Dračevo 16.13, Lisiče 16.20	16.25
337 Belgrade 07.50, Mladinovac 09.15, Palanka 09.45, Lapovo 10.13, Stalakj 11.11, Niš 13.05, Leskovac 13.45, Vranje 15.12, Preševo 16.30, Tabanovci 17.05, Kumanovo 17.17	17.47
2021 Tabanovci 17.45, Karpoš 17.51, Kumanovo 17.57, Prevoj 18.01, Romanovci 18.05, Agino Selo 13.09, Deljadrovci 18.13, Miladinovci 18.18, Ilinden 18.25, Madžari 18.34	18.40
634 Gevgelija 17.28, Prdejci 17.34, Smokvica 17.36, Smokvica Nova 17.40, Milekovo 17.44, Miravci 17.49, Klisura 18.01, Demir Kapija 18.10, Dubrovo 18.19, Negotino Vardar 18.30, Krivolak 18.35, Crveni Bregovi 18.39, Kukuričani 18.44, Stobi 18.48, Gradsko 18.51, Nogaevci 18.56, Zgroploci 19.01, Veles 19.15, Rajko Žinzifov 19.24, Pčinja 19.29, Smesnica 19.36, Zelenikovo 19.40, Zelenikovo Novo 19.44, Orešani 19.47, Dračevo 19.54, Lisiče 20.00	20.05
2023 Tabanovci 20.11, Karpoš 20.17, Kumanovo 20.23, Prevoj 20.27, Romanovci 20.35, Agino Selo 20.38, Deljadrovci 20.42, Miladinovci 20.47, Ilinden 20.54, Madžari 21.03	21.08
652 Kočani 18.23, Obleševo18.36, Sokolarci 18.41, Zletovica 18.47, Vančo Prkje 18.52, Balvan 19.00, Štip 19.11, Ovče Pole 19.29, Orče 19.43, Tošo Arsov 19.49, Jazla 19.57, Košulčevi 20.05, Veles 20.25, Zelenikovo 20.51, Dračevo 21.04, Lisiče 21.10	21.15
665 Kičevo 19.15, Dlapkin Dol 19.23, Strogomište 19.28, Zajas 19.33, Padalište 19.40, Lakavica 19.47, Gostivar 19.56, Vranovci 20.00, Žerovjane 20.07, Brezovnica 20.14, Tetovo 20.18, Rataje 20.24, Jegunovce F-ka 20.33, Jegunovce 20.36, Oraše 20.41, Raduša 20.45, Sulari 20.52, Saraj 20.58, Gjorče Petrov 21.03, Skopje Sever 21.11, Železarnica 21.15	21.19
644 Bitola 18.35, Dame Gruev 18.50, Loznani 18.55, Novoselani 18.59, Trojkrsti 19.03, Bakarno Gumno 19.09, Galičani 19.15, Prilep 19.24, Senokos 19.33, Brailovo 19.39, Slepče 19.45, Gostiražni 19.53, Oreše 20.03, Bogomila 20.13, Sogle 20.20, Teovo 20.24, Vasil Antevski 20.29, Martolci 20.37, Stari Grad 20.44, Časka 20.54, Toploka 21.04, Veles 21.15, Rajko Žinzifov 21.24, Zelenikovo 21.40, Orešani 21.45, Dračevo 21.53, Lisiče 22.00	22.05

TRAIN ARRIVAL TIMES IN BITOLA

2041 Prilep 05.30, Galičani 05.37, Bakarno Gumno 06.00, Trojkrsti 06.05, Novoselani 06.09, Loznani 06.13, Dame Gruev 06.20	06.36
2043 Prilep 07.50, Galičani 07.57, Bakarno Gumno 08.03, Trojkrsti 08.08, Novoselani 08.12, Loznani 08.16, Dame Gruev 08.23	08.38

such as Vero, Ramstore or Tinex. Town maps of Tetovo, Struga, Skopje, Prilep, Ohrid, Makedonski Brod, Kruševo, Dojran, Demir Kapija and Berovo, and made by Trimaks (*www.trimaks.com.mk*), are available throughout Macedonia. Maps to more towns are becoming available and many can also be bought for download from Trimaks. Locally made maps of Bitola, Kratovo and Strumica are available in those places only.

Street names in Macedonia can make your stay a bit like playing hide and seek. Many streets don't have a name, but simply a number. In addition, some street names have changed at least twice since independence and the name given on the map may not correspond to the name actually signposted and used by the locals. Maršal Tito Street in Skopje, the main pedestrian street, is a case in point. On the Trimaks map of the city it is named Makedonija. On the street itself it retains its old name and that is still what people call it.

This guide follows Macedonian common usage as much as possible and street names are in their Macedonian spelling followed by the house number. If it is a numbered street then it is given as, for example, *Ulica 000*, followed by the house number (*broj*) *br0*. Many streets are named after dates in history, so house number 60 on the street of First of May is written here as '1st Maj 60'. As if all this is not confusing enough, some buildings, especially large factories or institutions, do not have numbers at all, in which case the street name is followed by *bb*, indicating *bez broj* meaning 'without number'.

Note that some streets have been renumbered several times due to new building work; as a result several buildings have the same number or have their old number still showing!

Hiking maps Since topographical mapping was de-classified, new 1:25,000 hiking maps of Macedonia (map information as at 2004) have been available for 250MKD each. Note that these maps do not use the WGS84 military grid referencing system (MGRS), but the old Yugoslav Croatian-based referencing using the Gaus-Krüger (Krigerova) ellipsoid. The grid co-ordinates used in this guidebook are based on the old Yugoslav Croatian-based grid referencing system currently used by the new Macedonian maps. Eventually the maps will be available with WGS84 MGRS. For those of you who require a conversion, visit the webpage given in the box opposite.

The new maps are meant to be available at some point over the counter in shops and hotels but this was not the case yet at time of writing. They are available directly from SAGW head office (*Trifun Hadži Janev 4;* ✆ *02 3170 114/120;* f *02 3171 668;* e *prodazba@katastar.gov.mk; www.katastar.gov.mk;* ⏰ *09.00–16.30 Mon–Fri*). Known locally as the *katastar*, the head office is in Avtokomanda district (not in Karpoš, which is the local municipal office for Skopje only), and its entrance is actually on Jani Lukrovski where there is a statue of Atlas opposite a primary school. You can check which maps you wish to order online by navigating from their home page to 'Maps' and then to 'Useful information'. Navigate to 'How to obtain' and you'll be able to download an order form. The form was in Macedonian at time

---

GRID REFERENCES USED IN THIS EDITION

Please note that contrary to the first edition, which gave grid references in what is slowly becoming the world standard (WGS84 Military Grid Reference System or MGRS as used on NATO mapping), this edition has all its co-ordinates in the Croatian map datum (ellipsoid used) and Macedonian position format. This is so that they can be used directly with the new Macedonian 1:25,000 maps currently being released. For the few who have access to the NATO military mapping of the country, please see the Macedonia page at www. bradtguides.com/guidebook-updates for the WGS84 MGRS grids and how to convert between both systems. The page also gives instructions on how to set your GPS for use with Macedonian maps.

of writing, even on the English webpages, but an English version is available on the Macedonia page at www.bradtguides.com/guidebook-updates. Payment for the maps needs to be made through the post office. This can seem a bit daunting, but is in fact very easy. At SAGW, when you go to get the maps, their English-speaking staff will furnish you with a photocopy of a payment slip with all the details that you require. At the tiny post office five minutes by foot further down the street on Jani Lukrovski, the friendly staff will often help you fill out the real form, and all you have to do is provide your name and address and passport number. Pay in cash and take your receipt back to SAGW, who will then give you your maps.

OSM Garmin maps are available for download for free from www.ggbs.org/index.php/maps.html, and via the link on the Bradt Macedonia update blog.

HEALTH *with Dr Felicity Nicholson*

IMPORTANT PHONE NUMBERS
Ambulance ✎ 194
Fire service ✎193
Police ✎192

(A new combined number 112 should come into use soon.)

Make sure you get **health insurance** that is valid for Macedonia before arrival, unless you are prepared to pay for any mishaps yourself. Macedonian doctors and hospitals expect to be paid in cash on the spot by foreigners seeking treatment, and once furnished with your receipt, appropriately translated, you can reclaim your money back from your insurer. Most travel agents abroad will be able to sort you out with the appropriate health insurance, and some give a good deal, combining health and travel insurance with insurance against theft.

It is usually a good idea to get any treatment that you need before you go travelling. Compared with some countries, **medical treatment** is cheaper in Macedonia than in, say, the US, and standards can be as good as at home. Most doctors speak English. Nevertheless, it is always more comforting to get treatment at home.

Common illnesses can be treated in Macedonia by the pharmacists in any local pharmacy (*apteka*). Many have English-speaking staff, and they can also advise you of the nearest family practitioner if you are in need of a doctor. If you need hospitalisation, this is best left till you get home, unless it is an emergency, in which case either call ✎194, or it may be quicker to get a taxi to take you to the nearest hospital (*bolnica*). In Skopje, City Hospital (Gradska Bolnica), the red-brick building on 11th Oktomvri opposite the parliament, deals with all emergencies requiring anaesthesia. The emergency outpatients' entrance is around the back. There are several 24-hour pharmacies in big towns. In Skopje there is one on Dimitri Čupovski between McDonald's and the traffic lights.

VACCINATIONS There are no vaccinations that are legally required for entry into Macedonia, but health care practitioners will advise the following to be on the safe side: tetanus, diphtheria and polio (this comes as an all-in-one injection – Revaxis – and lasts for ten years), and hepatitis A. It is wise to visit your doctor or a travel health clinic about four to six weeks before travel. If you are going to be in the country for a long time (four weeks or more), are dealing with refugees or children or are working in a medical setting then immunisation against hepatitis B and meningitis is worth having. For hepatitis B ideally three doses of vaccine should be taken before travel. These can be given at 0, 1 and 6 months; 0, 1 and 2 months; or if time is short at 0, 7 and 21–8 days if you are 16 or over. Only Engerix B is currently licensed for the last schedule. Rabies vaccine would also be recommended as Macedonia is classified as a high risk country. This means that potentially all mammals can carry the disease. Treatment is not always available if you have not had three doses of vaccine taken over ideally 28 days before a potential exposure.

Tick-borne encephalitis (TBE) This potentially fatal disease is spread by bites from infected ticks. Vaccination would be recommended if you are intending to walk through forests, or are likely to be a long-term resident in rural areas. Three doses of vaccine are ideal but two doses can be given as little as two weeks apart if time is short. A third dose is then given five months or more later, if there is continued risk. In the UK the vaccine used is Ticovac, and there is also a junior version for those under 16.

Always wear long-sleeved clothing, trousers tucked into boots and a hat. Ticks can drop from overhanging branches onto your head and this is particularly a problem with children. Ticks should ideally be removed as soon as possible, as leaving ticks on the body increases the chance of infection. They should be removed with special tick tweezers that can be bought in good travel shops. Failing that you can use your fingernails by grasping the tick as close to your body as possible and pulling steadily and firmly away at right angles to your skin. The tick will then come away complete as long as you do not jerk or twist. If possible douse the wound with alcohol (any spirit will do) or iodine. Irritants (eg: Olbas oil) or lit cigarettes are to be discouraged since they can cause the ticks to regurgitate and therefore increase the risk of disease. It is best to get a travelling companion to check you for ticks and if you are travelling with small children remember to check their heads, and particularly behind the ears. If you have not had the vaccine and think or know you have been bitten by a tick you should go straight to medical help as there is a preformed antibody (Tick immunoglobulin) which should be administered as soon as possible after exposure.

Spreading redness around the bite and/or fever and/or aching joints after a tick bite imply that you have an infection that requires antibiotic treatment, so seek medical advice.

Tuberculosis Experts differ over whether a BCG vaccination against tuberculosis (TB) is useful in adults; discuss with your travel clinic. However, it may be recommended for children who have not yet been vaccinated especially if they are likely to be mixing closely with the local population. This is more important for longer-stay trips. Tuberculosis is spread through close respiratory contact and occasionally through infected milk or milk products.

Rabies Rabies is carried by all warm blooded mammals. It is not commonly reported, but Macedonia is classified as a high risk country. It can be passed on to humans through a bite, scratch or a lick over an open wound and also through saliva getting into the eyes, nose or mouth. You must always assume any animal is rabid and seek medical help as soon as possible. Remember there is a ten-day incubation period where the animal can appear well but is infectious. Scrub the wound with soap and under a running tap or pouring water from a jug. Find a reasonably clear-looking source of water but at this stage the quality of the water is not important; then pour on a strong iodine or alcohol solution or gin, whisky or rum. This helps stop the rabies virus entering the body and will guard against wound infections, including tetanus.

Pre-exposure vaccinations for rabies are ideally advised for everyone, but are particularly important if you intend to have contact with animals and/or are likely to be more than 24 hours away from medical help. Ideally three doses should be taken over four weeks, though three weeks will do if time is short. Contrary to popular belief these vaccinations are relatively painless.

If you are bitten, scratched or licked over an open wound by a sick animal, then post-exposure prophylaxis should be given as soon as possible, though it is never too late to seek help, as the incubation period for rabies can be very long. Those who have not been immunised will need a full course of injections. The vast majority of travel health advisors including WHO recommend rabies immunoglobulin (RIG), but this product is expensive (around US$800) and is often hard to come by – another reason why pre-exposure vaccination should be encouraged, as if you have had all three pre-exposure doses then you will no longer need RIG, but just two further doses of cell-derived vaccine three days apart.

Tell the doctor if you have had pre-exposure vaccine, as this will change the treatment you receive. And remember that, if you do contract rabies, mortality is 100% and death from rabies is probably one of the worst ways to go.

TRAVEL CLINICS AND HEALTH INFORMATION A full list of current travel clinic websites worldwide is available on www.istm.org/. For other journey preparation information, consult www.nathnac.org/ds/map_world.aspx. Information about various medications may be found on www.netdoctor.co.uk/travel.

UK

Berkeley Travel Clinic 32 Berkeley St, London W1J 8EL (near Green Park tube station); ℡020 7629 6233; ⌚ 10.00–18.00 Mon–Fri, 10.00–15.00 Sat

Cambridge Travel Clinic 41 Hills Rd, Cambridge CB2 1NT; ℡01223 367362; f 01223 368021; e enquiries@travelcliniccambridge.co.uk; www.travelcliniccambridge.co.uk; ⌚ 10.00–16.00 Mon, Tue & Sat, 12.00–19.00 Wed & Thu, 11.00–18.00 Fri

Edinburgh Travel Health Clinic 14 East Preston St, Newington, Edinburgh EH8 9QA; ℡0131 667 1030; www. edinburghtravelhealthclinic.co.uk; ⌚ 09.00–19.00 Mon–Wed, 9.00–18.00 Thu & Fri. Travel vaccinations & advice on all aspects of malaria prevention. All current UK prescribed anti-malaria tablets in stock.

Fleet Street Travel Clinic 29 Fleet St, London EC4Y 1AA; ℡020 7353 5678; www. fleetstreetclinic.com; ⌚ 08.45–17.30 Mon–Fri. Injections, travel products & latest advice.

Hospital for Tropical Diseases Travel Clinic Mortimer Market Centre, 2nd Floor, Capper St (off Tottenham Ct Rd), London WC1E 6AU; ℡020 7388 9600; www.thehtd.org; ⌚ 09.00–16.00 Mon–Fri. Offers consultations for travellers with complex health needs & is by appointment on Wed & Fri only. Runs a healthline (℡020 7950

7799) for country-specific information & health hazards. Also stocks nets, water purification equipment & personal protection measures. Travellers who have returned from the tropics & are unwell, with fever or bloody diarrhoea, can attend the walk-in emergency clinic at the hospital without an appointment.

InterHealth Travel Clinic 111 Westminster Bridge Rd, London SE1 7HR; ℡020 7902 9000; e info@interhealth.org.uk; www.interhealth. org.uk; ⌚ 08.30–17.30 Mon–Fri. Competitively priced, 1-stop travel health service by appointment only.

MASTA (Medical Advisory Service for Travellers Abroad) London School of Hygiene & Tropical Medicine, Keppel St, London WC1 7HT; ℡09068 224100; e enquiries@masta.org; www. masta-travel-health.com. This is a premium-line number, charged at 60p/min. For a fee, they will provide an individually tailored health brief, with up-to-date information on how to stay healthy, inoculations & what to take.

MASTA pre-travel clinics ℡01276 685040. Call or check www.masta-travel-health.com/travel-clinic.aspx for the nearest; there are currently 30 in Britain. They also sell malaria prophylaxis, memory cards, treatment kits, bednets, net treatment kits, etc.

NHS travel website www.fitfortravel.nhs. uk. Provides country-by-country advice on

Elisaveta Barabanovska (e barabanovska@gmail.com) and Aubrey Harris (e aharrisjr@gmail.com)

Baba lekovi, literally 'grandmother cures', are traditional folk remedies in the Republic of Macedonia that provide a window into understanding some common and current medical practices among the ethnic Macedonians, especially among those who live in the villages. With an unemployment rate perpetually hovering around 30%, many ethnic Macedonians cannot afford basic medical care, and specialised care even less so. Accompanying the poverty of this beautiful Balkan jewel is a 30% high school dropout rate. Thus, these grandmother cures are the default choice for many people who are either too poor to pay for medical services or uneducated and/or ignorant of modern medical practices, or both.

For centuries, traditional cures have been passed down the generations by word of mouth to treat anything from a bad cough, the common cold or more serious illnesses such as breast cancer. These grandmother cures may be natural: a type of rakija made from chestnuts is used to treat a bad cough and bronchitis; *majčina dušica* ('mother's spirit') tea is made from the herb thyme and is used to treat the common cold; raw cabbage leaves applied directly to the breast are used to treat breast cancer. But while many cures are derived from natural ingredients, not all are. If a person has back pain, cotton may be soaked in gasoline, and then applied directly to the skin. Some of these cures seem to have their merits, others may be quite ineffective or even do harm.

Will usage of *baba lekovi* continue? Macedonia is a country in transition. Given its aspirations to enter the European Union, and the greater development aid that will come with this entry, it is perhaps certain that some traditional remedies will be discarded in favour of the new. One television advertisement for an over-the-counter cold medication features a traditional Macedonian grandmother insistent upon curing her grandchild with traditional folk remedies, but only to be gently rebuffed by her daughter with a more modern solution. This will not be the last

immunisation & malaria prevention, plus details of recent developments, & a list of relevant health organisations.

Nomad Travel Stores Flagship store 3–4 Wellington Terr, Turnpike La, London N8 0PX; ☎020 8889 7014; f 020 8889 9528; e turnpike@ nomadtravel.co.uk; www.nomadtravel.co.uk; walk in or appointments ⊕ 09.15–17.00 daily, late night Thu. 6 stores in total countrywide: 3 in London plus Bristol, Southampton, Manchester. As well as dispensing health advice, Nomad stocks mosquito nets & other anti-bug devices & an excellent range of adventure travel gear.

Trailfinders Immunisation Centre 194 Kensington High St, London W8 7RG; ☎020 7938 3999; www.trailfinders.com/travelessentials/ travelclinic.htm; ⊕ 09.00–17.00 Mon, Tue, Wed & Fri, 09.00–18.00 Thu, 10.00–17.15 Sat. No appointment necessary.

Travelpharm *www.travelpharm.com*. The Travelpharm website offers up-to-date guidance on travel-related health & has a range of medications available through its online mini-pharmacy.

Irish Republic

Tropical Medical Bureau Grafton St Medical Centre, Grafton Bldgs, 34 Grafton St, Dublin 2; ☎1 671 9200; www.tmb.ie. Useful website specific to tropical destinations.

USA

Centers for Disease Control 1600 Clifton Rd, Atlanta, GA 30333; ☎(800) 232 4636, (800) 232 6348; e cdcinfo@cdc.gov; www.cdc.gov/travel.

advertisement on Macedonian television promoting a new, brighter, hipper and more modern European way in preference to the traditional folk remedy. Recorded here for posterity are a sample of *baba lekovi* showing a snapshot of Macedonian tradition and history.

Illness to be treated	Ingredients and tools	How to apply
High fever	Socks, vinegar and rakija	Soak the socks in vinegar and rakija, and allow the person to wear until the fever comes down (usually worn overnight while the person is sleeping).
Extreme cold or slight fever	Gasoline, warmed pork fat	The pork fat is warmed in a cooking dish over a stove. Then, in a separate container away from direct heat or flame, gasoline is mixed into the pork fat. This mixture is usually rubbed into the back, shoulders, neck, and maybe the legs.
Kidney stones	Spring water high in sulfur (usually from a local mountain spring)	Drunk to destroy, not prevent, kidney stones.
Swollen joints, and broken bones while being transported to a doctor	Bread, sugar, red wine and a bandage	Take a handful of bread, a handful of sugar, and form into a ball. On top of this bread-sugar ball, pour red wine. Then, using a bandage, apply and secure this to the swollen joint. This may also be used on areas of a suspected broken bone while on the way to the doctor.
Difficulty breathing due to a cold	Water, vinegar, black ground pepper and rakija	All ingredients are heated to a soft boil in the room where the sick person lies, and remain boiling until symptoms disappear.

The central source of travel information in the USA. Each summer they publish the invaluable Health Information for International Travel.
IAMAT (International Association for Medical Assistance to Travelers) 1623 Military Rd, 279 Niagara Falls, NY 14304-1745; ☎716 754 4883; e info@iamat.org; www. iamat.org. A non-profit organisation with free membership that provides lists of English-speaking doctors abroad.

Canada
IAMAT (International Association for Medical Assistance to Travellers) Suite 1, 1287 St Clair Av W, Toronto, ON M6E 1B8; ☎416 652 0137; www.iamat.org
TMVC Suite 314, 1030 W Georgia St, Vancouver, BC V6E 2Y3; ☎905 648 1112; e info@tmvc.com;

www.tmvc.com. 1-stop medical clinic for all your international travel medicine & vaccination needs.

Australia, New Zealand, Thailand
IAMAT PO Box 5049, Christchurch 5, New Zealand; www.iamat.org
TMVC (Travel Doctors Group) ☎1300 65 88 44; www.tmvc.com.au. 22 clinics in Australia, New Zealand & Thailand, including *Auckland* Canterbury Arcade, 170 Queen St, Auckland; ☎9 373 3531; *Brisbane* 75a Astor Terr, Spring Hill, Brisbane, QLD 4000; ☎(07) 3815 6900; e brisbane@traveldoctor.com.au; *Melbourne* Dr Sonny Lau, 393 Little Bourke St, 2nd Floor, Melbourne, VIC 3000; ☎(03) 9935 8100; e melbourne@traveldoctor.com.au; *Sydney* Dr Mandy Hu, Dymocks Bldg, 7th Floor, 428 George

St, Sydney, NSW 2000; ☎ 2 9221 7133; f 2 9221 8401

South Africa
SAA-Netcare Travel Clinics e travelinfo@netcare.co.za; www.travelclinic.co.za. 12 clinics throughout South Africa.
TMVC NHC Health Centre, cnr Beyers Naude & Waugh Northcliff; ☎ 0 11 214 9030;

e traveldoctor@wtmconline.com; www.traveldoctor.co.za. Consult the website for details of clinics.

Switzerland
IAMAT (Internationl Association for Medical Assistance to Travellers) 57 Chemin des Voirets, 1212 Grand-Lancy, Geneva; e info@iamat.org; www.iamat.org

COMMON PROBLEMS To state the absolutely obvious, it is a good idea to be fit and healthy before going on holiday! Many of us, though, have usually just raced through a work or college deadline before leaving and the time to unwind and relax is just when the common cold or stomach flu takes hold. Food hygiene standards and tap drinking water in Macedonia are safe for the average traveller. If you have never allowed your stomach to harden to foreign bacteria, then drink the ubiquitous bottled water, and avoid drinking from mountain streams and water fountains. Water fountains in towns are usually from the same source as tap water and therefore safe.

Diarrhoea Unless you are a seasoned world traveller and have a stomach like cast iron, you may get a small bout of the trots on coming into contact with new foods, water and cooking. In Macedonia this is unlikely to turn into full-blown diarrhoea requiring antibiotics to clear it up. If it does, the pharmacy can sort you out, or, if you are prone to a bit of Delhi belly, bring some suitable medication with you from home. There is good evidence that a single 500mg of ciprofloxacin (assuming that it is not contraindicated for you) and a couple of stopping agents such as Imodium will stop about 80% of travellers' diarrhoea very quickly. It is worth discussing options with your GP, or travel health advisor.

You should always ensure that you drink bottled, boiled or filtered water and clean your teeth with the same to minimise upset stomachs. It is also wise to stay away from dairy products as they may not be pasteurised and therefore can put you at risk of TB and tick-borne encephalitis. If you do get travellers' diarrhoea then it is important to replace not only the fluids that you have lost but also the salts. See the box, page 84.

Mosquitoes These are not prevalent in most of Macedonia as the country is so mountainous, but in the low-lying areas around Skopje and south along the Vardar, you might find one or two. You'll find many more to the north and south of Macedonia in Serbia and Greece. Malaria in Macedonia was last seen in World War I, so it is no longer necessary to take anti-malarial tablets.

FIRST-AID KIT As with any travels away from your medicine cabinet at home, it is a good idea to have a small first-aid pack with you. You can buy these ready-made from any good pharmacy at home, such as Boots in the UK, or Walgreens in the US, or you can just make up a small kit yourself from the following items:

- plasters/Band-Aids
- painkillers such as aspirin, paracetamol or Tylenol
- lipsalve
- sunscreen
- antiseptic cream (diluted tea-tree oil works well)

- mosquito bite cream (this should ideally contain DEET or a natural-based insect repellent containing citronella or eucalyptus)
- spare contact lenses if you are a contact lens wearer

WOMEN'S HEALTH If as a female traveller you find yourself, expectedly or unexpectedly, with health problems peculiar to the fairer sex, you will be glad to know that there are some good English-speaking gynaecologists in the capital. A private practitioner is Dr Biljana Davčeva (*101 Orče Nikola;* \ *02 311 0113;* ⏰ *09.00–17.00 Mon–Fri*).

Common remedies for cystitis, such as cranberry juice or Emergen-C, are hard to find. Uve-Mix herbal tea, available in most supermarkets, is the local solution. It tastes horrible, but mixed with dried basil (*basilikum*) and St John's wort (*kantarion*) is quite effective. Your first remedy should be 48 hours of heavy drinking (of water and Uve-Mix herbal tea), with absolute abstinence from caffeine and tannin (for another week). Avoid long journeys where you can't get to the toilet frequently. If you still have problems after a 48-hour concerted effort, then you will almost certainly need antibiotics. Amoxicillin, a form of penicillin good for waterworks and intestinal problems, is available over the counter cheaply.

Condoms are readily available in Macedonia, but tampons with applicators are not. OB tampons without applicators and regular sanitary towels are ubiquitous.

HEALTH AND SAFETY IN THE MOUNTAINS In the mountains, health and safety go hand in hand. Although Macedonia's mountains are not very big, they are sufficiently remote, and trails sufficiently obscure, that without a good hiking map (preferably 1:25,000, 1cm = 0.25km) it's very easy to get lost. Make sure you are a proficient hiker before venturing for long hikes into the mountains here, otherwise a two-hour walk in the park could turn into an eight-hour mountaineering ordeal. Alternatively, and preferably, go with a guide. The tour operators on page 66, or the clubs in *Chapter 10*, page 320, will be able to find a guide for you.

Know the potential dangers of mountaineering and how to deal with them before you venture out on a hike, and preferably be first-aid proficient. If you've no idea what you are getting into and have come to Macedonia for the mountains, then there are safer playing grounds than these for an introduction to mountaineering, but the list of health and safety considerations below will give you an idea of what you are up against. If you get into trouble, call \ 192 for the police who will be able to get the mountain rescue service out.

Your medical pack for any extended hiking trip (more than two hours) should contain at least the following:

- large plasters/Band-Aids and surgical gauze
- antiseptic cream and wipes
- painkillers
- crêpe bandages x 2
- surgical tape and zinc-oxide tape
- Compeed for blisters
- iodine-based water purification tablets (available from any good mountaineering shop, but hard to find in Macedonia)
- emergency blanket and inflatable splint if you are going on a long trip

Dehydration In these untamed mountainous regions, the going can get tough, and like all mountains, water can sometimes be hard to find when you need it. Bring plenty

TREATING TRAVELLERS' DIARRHOEA
Dr Jane Wilson-Howarth

It is dehydration that makes you feel awful during a bout of diarrhoea and the most important part of treatment is drinking lots of clear fluids. Sachets of oral rehydration salts give the perfect biochemical mix to replace all that is pouring out of your bottom but other recipes taste nicer. Any dilute mixture of sugar and salt in water will do you good: try Coke or orange squash with a three-finger pinch of salt added to each glass (if you are salt-depleted you won't taste the salt). Otherwise make a solution of a four-finger scoop of sugar with a three-finger pinch of salt in a 500ml glass of clean water. Or add eight level teaspoons of sugar (18g) and one level teaspoon of salt (3g) to one litre (five cups) of safe water. A squeeze of lemon or orange juice improves the taste and adds potassium, which is also lost in diarrhoea. Drink two large glasses after every bowel action, and more if you are thirsty. These solutions are still absorbed well if you are vomiting, but you will need to take sips at a time. If you are not eating you need to drink three litres a day plus whatever is pouring into the toilet. If you feel like eating, take a bland, high carbohydrate diet. Heavy greasy foods will probably give you cramps.

If the diarrhoea is bad, or you are passing blood or slime, or you have a fever, you will probably need antibiotics in addition to fluid replacement. A dose of ciprofloxacin or norfloxacin repeated twice a day until better may also be appropriate (if you are planning to take an antibiotic with you). Note that both norfloxacin and ciprofloxacin are only available on prescription in the UK. If the diarrhoea is greasy and bulky and is accompanied by sulphurous (eggy) burps, one likely cause is giardia. This is best treated with tinidazole (four x 500mg in one dose, repeated seven days later if symptoms persist).

of water with you, at least a litre per hour of uphill in the summer, and especially if you don't know where your next water source will be. It is very arid here and the lack of overhead cover can cause excess sweating. Dehydration will make you tired and prone to injury, and makes some people's vision blur. If you find yourself short of water, try to conserve what you have left, and take small sips every now and again. Don't over-exert yourself, and breathe through your nose rather than your mouth to stop excess moisture escaping. Keep covered to prevent excess moisture being lost in sweat.

Injury Injuries are usually caused when you are tired and/or hiking beyond your limit. It is, therefore, important to know what your limits are, and those of your travelling partners, and to recognise when it is time for a rest. Come properly equipped for the task at hand, with good hiking boots and an appropriate overcoat as a minimum. Many Macedonians wander around in flimsy, inappropriate shoes. This may suffice for a hike to a popular monument, but will get you into trouble further afield. If you do sustain an injury that would normally require stitching, then bind the wound with a large plaster or surgical tape and then secure it laterally with zinc-oxide tape.

Sunburn Do wear a hat, sunglasses and plenty of sunscreen (available in the pharmacies). The sun here is stronger than in northern Europe and it is easy to forget that point until it is too late. If you do get badly burnt, apply an after-sun cream or calamine lotion, cover up and don't go back out in the sun without a total sunblock. A cold wet teabag also works well for sunburn.

Sunstroke After the onset of dehydration and sunburn you are heading for heat exhaustion and then sun/heatstroke. While heatstroke can be fatal, if you recognise the early-stage symptoms soon enough you should never get that far. It is usually more difficult to tell in oneself than in others, so watch your hiking partner carefully. The easiest signs to look for are muscle cramps or numbness, dimmed or blurred vision, weakness, irritability, dizziness and confusion. If any of your hiking partners are talking utter drivel (more than normal anyway), are not able to have a logical conversation with you, and particularly if they say they don't need water or to get out of the sun, then sit them down in the shade immediately, loosen any tight clothing, sprinkle water on them and fan them to cool them down. They should take regular sips of water, but not drink a pint down flat. If your hiking partner shows the above signs, and feels sick, and particularly if their skin feels hot and dry, then the body has gone into shutdown mode. They may soon fall unconscious and medical attention is required quickly. Phone ⟍194 for help.

Altitude sickness You are unlikely to suffer from altitude sickness in Macedonia, as it is difficult to gain enough height to do so. Nevertheless, altitude sickness does not discriminate, and should you decide to climb Mount Korab or Titov Vrv in one day from Skopje, no matter how young you are or how much mountaineering you have done sometime in the past, it may still hit you. The best way to avoid altitude sickness is to acclimatise. If you don't have that option open to you, and you start to feel dizzy, sick and overly short of breath, then the next best thing to do is to stop and rest. If this doesn't help then descend slowly to a lower level (500m is usually enough), and consider doing something else for the day. Sadly, there is no coca tea in Macedonia to help with altitude sickness.

Hypothermia Hypothermia occurs when the body loses heat quicker than it can make it. This is most likely to happen when the body is wet and cold, inactive, hungry and tired. Uncontrollable shivering, drowsiness and confusion are telltale first signs. If the person has stopped shivering, is physically stiff, and indifferent to their surroundings, then the body is already in shutdown mode. The person's body temperature must be raised immediately with plenty of warm, dry clothing, shelter and warm sweet drinks to increase the blood sugar level. Exercise will not help. At severe levels, skin contact with another warm body, preferably in a sleeping bag, might be required. At this point the medical services should be brought in. Do not heat the person with anything hotter than body temperature or immerse the person in hot water as this might simply cook outer extremities. Do not rub or massage the person, but warm the core of the body first.

WILD AND DEADLY NASTIES Some poisonous snakes and spiders do exist in Macedonia, such as black and brown widow spiders, and some adders and vipers. However, they do not seek out humans, so you are extremely unlikely to come across any.

You are less likely to get bitten if you wear stout shoes and long trousers when in the bush. Most snakes are harmless and even venomous species will dispense venom in only about half of their bites. If bitten, then, you are unlikely to have received venom; keeping this fact in mind may help you to stay calm. Many so-called first-aid techniques do more harm than good: cutting into the wound is harmful; tourniquets are dangerous; suction and electrical inactivation devices do not work. The only treatment is anti-venom. In case of a bite that you fear may have been from a venomous snake:

- Try to keep calm – it is likely that no venom has been dispensed
- Prevent movement of the bitten limb by applying a splint
- Keep the bitten limb BELOW heart height to slow the spread of any venom
- If you have a crêpe bandage, wrap it around the whole limb (eg: all the way from the toes to the thigh), as tight as you would for a sprained ankle or a muscle pull

And remember:

- NEVER give aspirin; you may take paracetamol, which is safe
- NEVER cut or suck the wound
- DO NOT apply ice packs
- DO NOT apply potassium permanganate

If the offending snake can be captured without risk of someone else being bitten, take this to show the doctor – but beware since even a decapitated head is able to bite.

FURTHER READING
Wilson-Howarth, Dr Jane, and Ellis, Dr Matthew *Your Child Abroad: A Travel Health Guide* Bradt Travel Guides, 2005
Wilson-Howarth, Dr Jane *Bugs, Bites & Bowels* Cadogan, 2006

DENTAL TOURISM Dental work in Macedonia is of a very high standard and often less than half the price of private dental treatment at home. Most dentists speak English and have trained in Europe or the US. With the advent of low-cost flights to Macedonia, some dental practices are working together with tour operators to provide you not only with excellent affordable dental care but a fantastic and unique holiday experience with it. Whilst information available in English is still limited (use Google Chrome to help translate web pages if they're not available in English), more is coming online. Try the following websites: www.dentalmacedonia.com and www.qlio.org.mk, or contact Picasso Dental (*Bul Jane Sandanski 109/1-2, Skopje;* \ *02 6090 979;* m *078 707 007;* e *info@picassodental.mk; www.picassodental.mk*).

SECURITY AND SAFETY

The security situation in Macedonia has calmed down significantly since the end of the hostilities of 2001 (see page 32) and foreigners have never been a target. In fact, you are undoubtedly safer in Macedonia than you are in most major Western cities, from both theft and terrorism.

To be on the safe side, avoid areas known to be unsafe and large public demonstrations which may get heated. The website of your embassy in Macedonia will usually carry the most up-to-date information on the security situation, and the US embassy site also has comprehensive security and safety advice on their Consular Information Sheets at www.travel.state.gov. Many embassies advise their citizens to register at the embassy if they intend to stay in the country for any length of time, and to phone for the latest security advice on a particular area if they are going off the beaten track. To register with the UK embassy (anywhere in the world) go to https://www.locate.fco.gov.uk/locateportal/.

INTERNATIONAL TRAFFICKING OF WEAPONS, DRUGS AND PEOPLE While national crime levels are relatively low (see *Personal safety* below), international trafficking of humans more than makes up for the deficit. The porous, forested mountain borders of Macedonia are easy trafficking routes and have long been a route for heroin and opium from Afghanistan to Europe.

Poor border controls and high taxes make smuggling cigarettes and other goods in and out of Kosovo a profitable business for people in a country where unemployment is around 40%. Illegal wood-cutting is also a problem (and to animal habitat) especially when Kosovo continues to have an abysmal supply of electricity. If you are hiking up in the border areas, the chances of you stumbling across illegal trade are very slim. Always bring ID with you, however, just in case, and looking very obviously like a hiker will ensure that any smugglers will keep out of your way.

Illegal trade in weapons is much less of a problem here than trafficking in people. The government has done a lot over the past ten years to combat trafficking, and in 2011 Macedonia regained its Tier 1 grading by the US government in its annual Trafficking in Persons (TIP) report (*www.state.gov/g/tip*). Tier 1 means the country acknowledges the existence of trafficking in persons, complies with minimum standards to combat trafficking and continues to improve efforts to combat trafficking. Macedonia is both a transit country and an end user of trafficked people. Most are women who come from countries even poorer than Macedonia and, tempted by the lure of easy money abroad waitressing or as a domestic help, they are often beaten, raped and forced into prostitution and modern slavery. Victims include minors who believe they are going for better schooling, and the 2011 TIP report for Macedonia acknowledges that Roma children are also forced into begging. While numbers of foreign women trafficked to or through Macedonia seem to have decreased, numbers of Macedonian women who are trafficked internally within Macedonia is on the increase. In January 2003, MSNBC carried a very good article on this very issue in Macedonia, which can be found at www.msnbc.com/news/sexslaves_front.asp. *Gone Without Trace* (Orion Books, 2007), a thriller by C J Carver based on extensive research and plenty of truth, centres around the trafficking of women through the northwest of Macedonia and Kosovo.

Due to the difficulty in policing this issue, foreign visitors who bring their children with them are advised to bring the appropriate documents proving the legal relationship of parent and child. A passport may suffice, especially if the child is on your passport, but if you have separate passports with different names then you may want to bring additional proof. Although traffickers don't usually take children so blatantly over an established border crossing, border police may suspect the worst. The same goes for young couples entering Macedonia. If you would like to help with the anti-trafficking effort here in Macedonia see the *Travelling positively* section at the end of this chapter, page 118.

PERSONAL SAFETY In many respects crime is lower in Macedonia than in many countries in western Europe or in America. Nevertheless, you should take the usual precautions: this is not a country where you can leave your house unlocked when you are out, and you should keep your valuables close if you are going through a crowded place or travelling by public transport.

If you come to live in Macedonia as part of the international community then, as with a move into any new property, you may want to make sure the locks are changed in case former tenants have a key that falls into the wrong hands. Car theft is generally not a problem in Macedonia.

If you get stopped or detained by the police, for any reason whatsoever, remember to stay calm and polite. In any nation, smart-alec wisecracks, sarcasm, anger and lack of co-operation are seen as suspicious behaviour. You do have the right to ask why you have been stopped or detained, however, and, of course, the right to legal representation once you have been charged. You can be detained for up to 24 hours without being charged, by which time your embassy or consulate should have been informed of your detention. You also have the right to be spoken to in a language that you understand, so you might be better off waiting for an interpreter or a policeman who speaks your language rather than digging yourself into a bigger hole. The interpreter may take a while getting to you!

DRIVING AND ROAD SAFETY Speed restrictions are enforced here. Speed limits are posted and are generally 50km/h in built-up areas, 80km/h outside built-up areas, 100km/h on dual carriageways and 120km/h on motorways. Seat belts must be worn in the front and back seats of a car if fitted. Children under the age of 12 are not allowed in the front of cars, but there is no requirement for child seats in the back. The blood alcohol limit is 0.05% (0% for newly licensed drivers, who may not drive between 23.00 and 05.00 unless accompanied by a driver older than 25). Visibly drunk people may not travel in the front of a vehicle. Dipped headlights during the day are compulsory. Crash helmets are compulsory for motorcyclists. For more on Macedonian driving regulations see www.theaa.com/motoring_ advice/touring_tips/macedonia.pdf.

Macedonian lane discipline and driving etiquette has improved over its poor record a decade ago. Nonetheless, you would do well to be wary. Don't be surprised to find vehicles without headlights at night, extremely little use of indicators, lorries backing down the road when they have missed their exit, parking on the pavement and two cars stopped in the middle of the road for a chat. As a pedestrian, you'll also have to keep your wits about you when crossing the road, as drivers pay scant attention to zebra crossings.

If you get into an accident or breakdown, the AutoMobile Association of Macedonia (℡ 196; www.amsm.com.mk) can assist. AMSM Services (℡ 02 15 555; www.amsmspi.mk) also gives good information on road works and traffic congestion, including at the border crossings.

If you are fined by the police, remember to make sure you are given a ticket/ receipt for your fine so that you can be certain the money is going into the government coffers not the policeman's pocket. Fines can be paid at a post office or bank and are reduced by 50% if paid within eight days.

PERSONAL HARASSMENT Don't expect to always be left alone as you wander around Macedonia looking at antique treasures and antiquated institutions. You will probably come across two situations where you will wish that you could be left in peace. The first form of harassment will come from begging Roma (see page 44) who may follow you around for up to 15 minutes quietly begging for money, and may even get angry, though rarely physically violent, if you don't give them money. Macedonians get this treatment too, and the best thing to do is not to give them any (giving money tends to encourage more begging); you can try what most Macedonians do, which is to say sternly 'begaj, odmah', meaning 'scram, immediately'. If this does not succeed then dive into a café where the waiter will take care of the little beggar for you.

The second form is really just an uncomfortable invasion of personal space, usually from teenage boys who are bewildered and defensive about what on earth you think you are doing on their turf. Trying to engage them in friendly conversation with a winning smile (which often works, see page 117) may only raise their defences as a battle of hormones, pride and stubbornness ensues. This is how fights start, and no matter how much you might want to push them away or punch them in the face for getting too close to you, your belongings or your car, you are, after all, a guest in their home town or street, so back off confidently, and remember that locals at home probably aren't too friendly either; the difference is that you don't usually wander into that part of town.

DOGS There are a lot of stray dogs in Macedonia, and while they don't tend to be savage, or even a nuisance, some of them do carry disease and infections, so don't approach them, or take them in. Rabies is not common here, but leishmaniasis is more prevalent. Leishmaniasis is transferred by sandflies from host to new prey, and can be deadly if left untreated. Dogs with a mangy appearance and losing clumps of hair could have leishmaniasis.

If you do take in a stray dog, take it to the vet immediately for a check-up and all the necessary injections. There is no animal home here in Macedonia, and most dogs are not treated too well, so you probably have more to fear from a kept dog than a stray dog. The big shepherding dogs here, the *šarplaninec*, are well trained to guard their flock, so don't approach them or the flock, no matter how docile they may appear from several metres away. You may not return with your hand, and the dog won't be put down.

WOMEN TRAVELLERS

Sexual harassment is not usually a problem in Macedonia, and women here dress as skimpily as in the West. Macedonians think it is a bit strange, however, to travel on your own, especially as a woman; and keeping in mind the high level of trafficking in women which has gone on in Macedonia in the past (see page 56), you'd better have your wits about you if you travel alone as a woman in out-of-the-way places after dark. There are no obvious red-light districts in Macedonia, as prostitution is illegal, but there are bars and hotels and parts of towns that service this trade.

As with anywhere in the rest of the world, if you are a single female driver and an unmarked police car indicates that you should pull over, you should turn on your hazard lights and drive slowly to a public area such as a petrol station before stopping. You could also phone the police on ✆ 192 to check if the police car is genuine.

GAY TRAVELLERS

The gay and lesbian scene is very limited in Macedonia and it would be considered most strange if not offensive for same-sex couples to walk hand in hand down the street, never mind kiss in public. Booking into a hotel would not be considered so strange unless you insisted on a *'francuski krevet'* (double bed), as double rooms normally come with twin beds.

When being gay was decriminalised in 1996, the gay community in Macedonia cautiously took steps to promote greater acceptance. That trend has ground to a halt over the last five years. Egal (*Kole Nedelkovski 12a/2, 1000 Skopje;* ✆ *02 3220 851; www.egal.org.mk*) is currently the only organisation in Skopje working on gay and lesbian issues, by focusing on sexual. There are currently no venues openly welcoming gays and lesbians in Macedonia, although private parties in some public venues do take place.

DISABLED TRAVELLERS

Disabled travel in Macedonia is very challenging. Pavements are uneven and often completely blocked by parked cars. Wheelchair accessibility is poor even in Skopje. Most big shopping malls, museums and many government buildings have wheelchair ramps. Some buses in Skopje operate wheelchair lifts, but at the time of writing it's not known whether such buses will be available in other towns around the country. Local municipalities are working hard, however, to catch up to ensure better access for wheelchair users. The Holiday Inn and Aleksandar Palace in Skopje, and the Ramada Plaza outside Gevgelija offer rooms equipped for wheelchair accessibility.

For the visually impaired, most of the traffic lights are accompanied by a fast beep for red and slower beep for green. Don't be afraid to ask for help – many Macedonians, at least in Skopje, speak English. The staff in some SP (СП) food stores are trained in sign language but, of course, this won't be helpful if you're not familiar with Macedonian sign language.

TRAVELLING WITH CHILDREN *Gerard and Sonja McGurk*

Visitors to Macedonia will quickly realise that the country is very accommodating towards children. Macedonian attitudes towards children are tolerant and relaxed and Macedonians themselves are exceptionally welcoming to families with children. Safety standards will not be up to US litigious culture, but costs are low, making a family holiday less of a shock to your wallet.

EATING OUT Most restaurants and cafés are happy for children to run around unsupervised. Don't be surprised! Some restaurants with larger space have dedicated play areas for children outside, and some inside, especially in family-run hotel restaurants. Cafés located along Skopje's riverside quay (*kejot* in Macedonian) have small play areas for children, allowing parents and guardians a relaxing respite. Overall, there is an ever-increasing range of outlets for families with children to enjoy.

IGROTEKA This is the Macedonian for children's play areas. There are a good number of these across the country and they're available for private party bookings or to simply take your younger children to run off their excess energies. In Skopje, some such places are Habyland (see page 152), Kids Land in the Ramstore Mall (located in the first floor beside McDonald's, good for soft play) and on the first floor of the Vero Centre.

BREASTFEEDING There is traditionally a positive attitude in Macedonia towards breastfeeding. While it's not too common in public, it is not discouraged or frowned upon. You may prefer, therefore, to be discreet, and cover up with a light scarf.

BABY CHANGING FACILITIES Skopje has an increasing number of locations that cater for children of young ages. Public toilets with baby changing facilities are non-existent and should generally be avoided for their lack of hygiene. It is perfectly acceptable, in extremis, to make use of nearby restaurants or cafés, which in larger towns will have clean toilet facilities. The further you go from Skopje, the less likely you will be to find bespoke child changing facilities (nor will they be advertised). Check on arrival if you need to make use of such facilities.

SUPPLIES Most of the larger, more well-known supermarkets (Vero, Ramstore or Tinex) and pharmacies across Macedonia will have well-stocked supplies of kid-friendly products, milk formula, creams, wipes, nappies (including pull-ups) and medicines for young children. Some of the products' names may not be the same as at home.

GETTING ABOUT Transporting children around Macedonia can still be a challenge. Access ramps for buggies are rare. The arrival of new, modern buses (made in Ukraine and China) in Skopje (and later to be rolled out to the rest of the country) should in theory make it easier for families travelling with buggies to move around the capital city. Taxi drivers can be found in most towns and cities and will usually help with putting buggies in the car – as ever it depends on their general mood at the time.

HOTELS Many of the smaller family-run hotels listed here have three- or four-bed rooms. Ask at the time of booking whether an extra bed can be added for the duration of your stay. Some hotels will make every effort to help out by putting a small camp bed into a room if given some notice. Larger hotels usually have suites with pull-out sofas. Children under five can often stay free if using your bed, and under 12s might be half price. It's worth checking the hotel website for these offers or to ask in advance.

RECOMMENDED SITES AND ACTIVITIES Whilst most of these things are based in or around Skopje, some are further afield. Check the pages shown in brackets for further details.

Skopje: Habyland (152); Cherry Orchard restaurant and riding stables (153); Skopje Zoo (152); Gradski and Kamen Most beaches (151); Vodno cable car (156).

Elsewhere: Aquapark at Proboštip (288); Ethno Selo and Ginovci Park near Kriva Palanka (283); Ohrid Luna Park (187); Berovo for easy hiking and outdoor activities (276).

WHAT TO TAKE

CLOTHING Unless you know you are staying only in Skopje and Ohrid in the summer, then bring an overcoat or jacket, and it is cold enough for a fleece in the mountains no matter what time of year. Casual dress is the norm on the streets. Businessmen tend to wear short-sleeved shirts in the summer, and you may wish to pack such a shirt or polo shirt if you intend to go to one of the nicer restaurants in Skopje. Nightclubs here don't have a dress code, but some churches and mosques do (see page 116). In spring and autumn it may be very warm during the day, but in the evening it can also get quite cold, and some state-run hotels may have not yet turned on or already turned off the central heating, so bring warm enough clothes.

PLUGS, ADAPTORS AND CONVERTERS Macedonia's electricity is 220 volts and uses two types of plug, both with the same two round pins commonly used in northern Europe. Plug casings come in the round-case variant as well as the six-sided flat-case variant.

There are a number of great travel adaptors available now that take a multiple choice of plugs and give multiple options in pins. If you are coming from North America and wish to bring American electrical appliances with you, then you can also purchase a power voltage converter which will convert the 220 volts of European electricity into 110 volts for your appliance.

Bring a universal sink plug, especially if staying in lower-end accommodation.

TOILETRIES AND MEDICINES You can buy all the basics in Macedonia, although if you are coming here to live for a while you may wish to bring your favourite face cream or aftershave lotion. Contact lens solutions are expensive here, and contact lenses can take a while to order, so bring plenty with you. Always bring spare glasses if you wear them; it is a nightmare anywhere in the world if you break your only pair.

Bring clothes washing powder (unless you want to buy a large tub in the supermarket here) as launderettes are almost impossible to find, although there are dry cleaners. The Western four- and five-star hotels have a laundry service. A basic first-aid pack as mentioned under *Health* (see page 82) is also useful.

DOCUMENTS Obviously a passport, with visa if required, ticket and money (see opposite) are essential. If you are travelling with children then some sort of proof that you are their legal guardian is advisable to stop a potentially harrowing ordeal at the border when police might think you are trafficking children. If you are bringing your own car, then make sure you have the right insurance. The international blue or green card insurance, which does not have Macedonia (MK) or any other countries you want to visit or travel through struck off, is valid here. A photo ID driving licence is required here, for both hiring and driving a car.

GIFTS It is always a good idea to bring family photographs and postcards of your home town with you on holiday. They make good talking points and you can give the postcards out as a small gift. If you are invited into a Macedonian home, you may be given sweet syruped preserved fruits as a welcome. It is also a good idea to give something in return, and sweets from your home country are an ideal gift. Note that Macedonians can get all the German chocolates and many others besides, and anyway chocolate is not a good thing to bring in the summer as it will melt. More permanent small souvenirs are ideal.

For an idea of gifts to bring back from Macedonia see *Culture* (page 55).

SPORTS GEAR Light sports shoes or open-toed hiking sandals like Tevas are fine for walking around or a short hike to a popular monument, but anything more arduous requires suitable hiking boots. A long pair of hiking trousers is useful, as the paths here are often overgrown and prickly, thorny or full of nettles. Dock leaves can be a remedy for nettle stings but unlike in the UK they rarely grow next to nettles here. A hiking pole (or a stick picked up at the beginning of your hike) is a useful nettle and bramble whacker and helps to scare away snakes and dogs. Hiking without a stick is bound to elicit the comment from locals who meet you on your hike that you should have one. It is easier to get sports and hiking gear here than it used to be (but it will be more expensive than the outlets at home). It does get very hot in the summer, so bring enough changes of clothing so that you can swap out of your sweaty T-shirt when you get to the top of your hike. This helps to prevent you from getting a chill, which can easily happen when you reach the colder climes of the summit.

Bring a good daypack and your favourite water container: wide-mouthed Nalgene bottles are far easier to fill from a mountain stream than reused plastic water bottles. The Camelbak (*www.camelbak.com*) is very useful in this arid climate. You'll need to bring your own climbing boots if you intend to do any rock climbing, but the rest you can hire here from one of the clubs. Ski hire, including carving skis, is reasonable, but tele skis, ski de randonée or cross-country skis are seldom available to hire.

CAMPING There are no dedicated basecamp stores here, so you'll need to bring outdoor accessories with you. There is only one type of bottled stove fuel here, and it is not the butane/propane self-sealing screw-on Coleman type, so you'll either need to bring plenty of canisters (and most airlines won't let you bring them any more) or buy one of the local stoves, which you can find in any outdoor market. Alternatively, bring an all-purpose fuel stove and buy petrol.

MONEY

The Macedonian denar has been pegged to the euro since 1998, and is therefore very stable. There is no smaller division of the denar. MKD is the international three-letter currency code, which is also used when Latin rather than Cyrillic script is used.

The denar comes in 10, 50, 100, 500, 1,000 and 5,000 notes, although you'll often find the 1,000 denar note hard to change. The 5,000MKD note usually stays firmly on the cashier's side of the bank counter. Macedonian shops never seem to have much change, so hoard your small notes, and change large notes whenever you can. Coins come in one, two, five, ten and 50 denar.

There are no money changers on the street here, so money is either changed in banks or in the many legal money-changing booths in the main towns. Travellers' cheques are good for back-up funds, but if you have a debit card or credit card then you'll find lots of cash machines available all over Macedonia. Not all ATMs take international credit cards, so look out for the Visa/MasterCard and other labels indicating that they can do international transactions. You can change money at the airport both before you exit the arrivals lounge and in the departure hall. Remember to phone your bank to let them know where you are travelling and when, so that they don't block your bank card the first time you use it abroad!

Euros are the foreign currency of choice here. All the main hotels, restaurants and even a lot of the bed and breakfasts, especially in Skopje and Ohrid, will accept euros, although they may not always be able to give you all the right change in euros.

BUDGETING

On the most meagre of budgets, staying in local rooms, at monasteries, mountain huts and campsites, buying from the market or *kebapci* stalls, and using public transport, you could manage on around €15 a day, excluding your ticket to Macedonia. Trains are cheaper than buses, but there are few trains. Most museums in Skopje and a lot of the churches in Ohrid charge a 100MKD entrance fee, but many things are also free. Hiking in Macedonia's beautiful mountains and national parks doesn't yet require an entrance fee, but wild camping is forbidden.

Some €25 a day would just about bring you into the bed and breakfast bracket and it is hard to pay more than €10 for a meal, except in Skopje. At the other end of the scale you would be hard pressed to spend €350 a day here even if you were staying at the Aleksandar Palace Hotel in Skopje for your entire trip and hiring a 4x4 vehicle. Macedonia's local gifts (woodcarvings, Ohrid pearls, filigree, embroidered linen) are not all that cheap by comparison, and buying these items could deprive you of several hundred more euros.

At the time of writing these are shop prices for:

1.5 litres water	25MKD	street snack	60MKD	T-shirt	250MKD
½ litre beer	34MKD	Mars bar	25MKD	camera film	250MKD
loaf of bread	30MKD	postcard	50MKD	litre of petrol	66MKD

GETTING AROUND

In the summer, some Jat Airways flights connect Ohrid and Skopje. Check with a travel agent for times. Most people travel around by bus or car, although train, bicycle and walking are also options. Macedonians do hitchhike, but usually only locally, so you can get a ride.

BY TRAIN There are fairly limited options available for travel by train. There is a line from Skopje to Kičevo through the northwest of the country, which will take you to Tetovo and Gostivar, but not to Mavrovo and Debar. The line to Bitola via Veles and Prilep is a pretty ride, and certainly a recommended route to Prilep. The line to Gevegelia is also pretty, and it's worth a stop at Demir Kapija for some hiking and lunch at Popova Kula. The lines to Kumanovo and Kočani don't hold much attraction and you would be better off taking buses direct to places further

DISTANCES BETWEEN TOWNS AND BORDER CROSSINGS IN MACEDONIA

Blace
70 **Tabanovce**
187 166 **Delčevo**
188 183 142 **Dojran**
179 174 150 38 **Bogorodica**
208 204 259 198 189 **Medzitilija**
202 237 330 268 259 111 **Kafasan**
178 155 44 98 106 248 318 **Berovo**
183 181 239 177 168 16 92 227 **Bitola**
156 177 243 181 170 91 99 226 78 **M.Brod**
175 171 146 34 4 185 258 102 166 166 **Gevgelia**
86 117 246 248 229 138 119 240 124 75 225 **Gostivar**
150 183 312 291 282 150 65 300 134 115 278 68 **Debar**
178 155 11 131 239 248 319 35 228 232 137 230 297 **Delčevo**
122 118 161 94 79 110 183 138 90 86 75 167 202 150 **Kavadarci**
131 162 263 209 191 91 73 255 78 25 187 46 89 252 111 **Kičevo**
132 102 64 146 149 196 278 52 178 178 145 180 245 53 90 222 **Kočani**
121 70 162 205 212 262 286 151 241 227 208 166 234 151 172 211 99
115 63 118 168 174 212 280 107 196 197 170 160 224 107 137 205 55
178 173 230 174 165 65 166 218 52 55 161 140 154 219 81 62 174
62 10 156 176 170 189 227 139 176 162 166 107 172 145 113 152 92
111 107 143 82 68 121 195 127 100 98 64 156 214 132 10 201 80
193 224 305 249 194 79 28 293 56 86 190 107 66 294 155 61 250
142 140 199 143 128 61 134 187 41 37 125 108 153 188 49 62 141
142 112 124 80 94 166 244 82 147 147 90 177 253 113 49 232 66
218 213 267 214 232 44 63 255 30 108 228 142 102 256 120 96 215
102 54 118 138 147 162 267 107 149 149 143 147 210 107 82 192 49
22 49 179 171 162 182 187 163 176 137 160 67 134 168 105 112 115
193 224 317 264 249 92 13 305 79 86 245 106 52 306 170 60 265
171 141 95 51 55 188 268 54 175 173 51 216 281 85 82 261 98
61 92 221 223 204 162 145 217 149 99 200 24 94 210 147 70 157
70 65 120 124 110 133 203 111 120 116 106 110 184 109 52 155 63
108 75 94 109 122 163 243 83 150 155 118 157 219 83 63 181 32

afield like Kriva Palanka or Berovo. The maximum one could pay for a train ride anywhere in Macedonia at the time of writing was 435MKD for a Skopje–Bitola return ticket. See page 71 for information on timetables.

BY BUS Buses are the preferred mode of transport for Macedonians because they're frequent and cheap. Buses are not air conditioned and do sometimes break down; few of them have on-board toilet facilities either, so you may have to wait for the toilet break along the road. There is no bus service from the airport. For more on bus times and prices, see individual towns in the following chapters.

BY CAR Macedonia's roads are currently undergoing a facelift and driving around the country is now a joy, and in fact highly recommended. If you love driving and yearn for the open road with uncluttered vistas and little in your way except for the odd turtle/tortoise or a few goats, then Macedonia is the place to drive. See the

> **CAR-HIRE AGENCIES**
> **Avis** ☏02 3222 046; www.avis.com.mk
> **Budget** ☏02 3290 222; wwww.budget.com.mk
> **Europcar** ☏02 307 6425; www.europcar.com
> **Setkom** ☏02 3298 392
> **Sixt** ☏02 306 4666; www.sixt.com

K.Palanka
44	Kratovo
220	190	Kruševo
60	53	162	Kumanovo
157	103	93	97	Negotino
273	266	138	214	167	Ohrid
195	160	32	130	61	106	Prilep
132	88	141	102	37	211	110	Radoviš
256	231	103	206	132	35	71	181	Resen
103	57	144	44	73	213	112	58	183	Sv.Nikola
99	93	159	39	95	174	131	125	198	80	Skopje
273	267	153	214	182	15	121	231	50	254	174	Struga
156	117	166	131	75	237	134	29	205	87	149	255	Strumica
141	135	164	82	136	132	132	167	184	122	44	132	196	Tetovo
116	86	111	55	41	180	79	77	145	33	50	190	113	85	Veles
90	52	151	66	51	215	119	37	180	25	86	230	66	128	40	Štip

section on *Driving and road safety* for tips on driving in Macedonia, especially if you are not used to driving on the right-hand side of the road.

There are many places to hire clean, reliable, modern cars in Skopje and other big cities, as well as at the airport. **Setkom** (↳ *02 311 3755;* e *1990@t-home.mk*), in the Hotel Continental in Skopje rents out a Kia Picanto for as little as €25 per day for a two-week period. This makes them the cheapest place in Macedonia for car hire and 4x4 vehicles are also available. A local company, you won't find them on the internet, but they have friendly and reliable service, as well as good prices. For road distances and listings of other car-hire agencies, see page 95. You'll pay about 75MKD per litre for unleaded petrol in Macedonia, and about 66MKD per litre for diesel.

Road tolls (*Peage, Патарина*) Tolls operate on the highways, of which there are currently only two in Macedonia: north–south between Blace to Gevgelija (minus the single-lane carriageway through Demir Kapija); and east–west between Kumanovo and Tetovo. Prices are posted at the entrance to the toll, and range from between 30MKD (eg: from the airport to Skopje) up to 120MKD (for the longest section of road) for a car without a trailer. Payment is only accepted in cash in denar, and it's rare for a toll both to be able to change 1,000MKD, so make sure you have plenty of small change on you.

BY TAXI All taxi fares now have a flagfall of 40MKD (50MKD in Ohrid) with a 30MKD/km and 5MKD/minute tariff (40MKD/km and 5MKD/minute in Skopje). It is difficult to take even a short taxi ride in Skopje now for less than 100MKD. Outside Skopje, taxis are still a quick and cheap way to get around town and to places further afield. All official taxis should be metered and carry a taxi sign on the roof of the car. When phoning for a taxi from a mobile phone always add the local prefix before the four- or five-digit taxi number (eg: ↳ 02 15157 to call Lotus Transport in Skopje).

Most of the longer journeys outside of the main town have a fixed price and drivers will often refer to a printed list provided by their company. Make sure you agree the price before taking a longer journey so that you run less risk of being overcharged. For instance, the posted price for a trip from Skopje Airport to the centre of town is 1,200MKD, but most drivers charge 1,500MKD. If you book with a taxi firm in advance (such as Lotus, see below, or Naše Taxi (↳ *02 15152*), both of whom have English phone operators) they can send a taxi to the airport to bring you into the centre for only 900MKD. They will usually run the meter, then stop the car at the 900MKD point to turn off the meter and continue the journey unmetered.

If you are going to a remote part of town, there's quite a high chance that the taxi driver taking you there will not know where it is, so you may wish to ask a few drivers until you get one who knows, or make him (there are extremely few female taxi drivers) phone into his radio centre so that they can give him directions. Otherwise they may drive around for a while and charge you the extra time and fuel.

A good, clean and reliable taxi firm, based in Skopje, who can drive you or transport personal items (including pets) on your behalf anywhere in Macedonia is **Lotus Transport** (↳ *02 15157 for taxis in Skopje or* ↳ *02 3109 116 for other services;* f *02 3122 174;* e *contact@lotustransport.com; www.lotustransport.com*). If a taxi number becomes defunct, check www.infotaxi.org for the most up-to-date information.

BY BICYCLE Biking tours are a great way to get around Macedonia, but you do need to be fit, as it is a hilly little country. For some web accounts of unguided cycle tours through Macedonia see *Web resources* in *Appendix 4*, page 361.

To hire a bike, join or arrange a bike tour in Macedonia, see Bike Macedonia and Cycle Macedonia on page 66, and the biking section on page 106.

ACCOMMODATION

Accommodation in Macedonia is generally inexpensive, but the standard you receive for the price you pay is a bit of a lottery.

HOTELS Generally speaking, state-run hotels built before the 1990s are basic, shoddy and overpriced even if they have been fairly recently renovated. In addition, and irritatingly, they tend to charge foreigners more than they charge Macedonians. On the few occasions that such hotels have been included in this guide, the price discrimination is indicated. Many state-run hotels are now being privatised and with that will hopefully come some improvements. Between late spring and early autumn (15 April to 15 October), state-run hotels may get a bit cold as the heating is turned off during this period.

Family-run or boutique hotels are excellent value for money and are increasing in number. Many petrol stations have small motels on the side and as most of them have been built fairly recently they are usually clean and tidy if basic, but reasonably priced. Hotel prices usually include breakfast, although only the top-notch hotels will manage to serve a buffet breakfast or provide room service.

In this guide, unless otherwise stated, all rooms come with an en-suite bathroom, free Wi-Fi and breakfast, and all prices are per room per night. If you ask for a room for two people you will usually get a twin room with two single beds. To get a room with a double bed in, you must ask for '*soba co eden krevet za dvojica*' (a room with one bed for two people), sometimes called a '*francuski krevet*' meaning 'French bed'. Even if you ask for this, don't be surprised in cheaper and older accommodation if you end up with a twin room in which the hotel staff expect you to simply push the beds together. Or they may give you the *apartman* which is the Macedonian equivalent of the honeymoon suite and usually much more expensive. Rooms with three single beds are also quite common.

Top 10 The following is a list of recommended 'boutique-type' hotels, chosen in part for their strategic locations around the country so that you can visit all of Macedonia in comfortable value-for-money accommodation, but also in part for their peculiarities. Anticlockwise around the country starting in the capital, they are:

Rose Diplomatique, Skopje Small, beautiful, near the centre of town. Page 135.

Bistra, Mavrovo A fireside over the lake, by the ski resort. Page 230.

Hotel Kalin, Lazaropole Beautifully refurbished, beautiful setting. Page 252.

Kutmičevica, Vevčani Small & quaint in the Republic of Vevčani. Page 199.

Villa Jovan, Ohrid A genuine Ohrid-style house. Page 177.

Hotel Millenium Palace, Bitola Right on Širok Sokok. Page 97.

Podgorski An, Strumica Out of the way but worth the stay. Page 307.

Aurora Resort & Spa, Berovo Luxury in the wild east. Page 276.

Etno Selo Timčevski, Kumanovo Traditional yet modern. Page 278.

Popova Kula, Demir Kapija Fine wine & dining overlooking the vineyards. Page 312.

BED AND BREAKFASTS In days gone by there was a whole bed and breakfast world in Macedonia. The collapse of the Yugoslav economy and the 2001 conflict in

Macedonia all but killed off this industry, but it is beginning to make a comeback, even outside Ohrid. Travel agents will say they'll try to find bed and breakfast options for you, but will probably cajole you into a hotel as they don't make much money off the bed and breakfast trade. The nascent tourist industry in Macedonia, however, is trying to encourage this sector. Sometimes the bed comes without breakfast, so make sure you ask what your options are. Bed and breakfast usually starts at about €10–15 per night.

SELF-CATERING ACCOMMODATION There is actually quite a lot of this in Macedonia as it is popular with Macedonians, but the properties are not well advertised in English. Some private accommodation (ie: self-catering) is listed at hotels.exploringmacedonia.com and local tour operators listed in each chapter in this book will also have some contacts.

MONASTERIES Monasteries are excellent value for money, even if you are not on a shoestring budget. As most of them were revived only 15 years ago, accommodation in their new inns is generally better than in most state-run hotels and half the price. Prices range from about 300MKD for a bed in the old quarters with shared bathroom, to 800MKD for a bed in an en-suite room in the new quarters. The monasteries don't usually have a restaurant attached but, as they are remote, they usually have cooking facilities available to guests.

The catch with staying in the monasteries is that they are not always very convenient to book into and as they are popular with Macedonians they are often booked up quite early. Very few of the staff/monks/nuns in them speak any English so you may need to get a Macedonian friend to help you, or a tour operator. If you can't get a tour operator to help you book in (eg: Go Macedonia, see page 66) or opt to do so yourself, try to phone during normal working hours. If you want to try turning up without a booking, then at least try to get there before 17.00 otherwise the inn staff may have gone home already, as they usually only stay around until all the pre-booked guests have arrived. Finally, soon after you arrive, you will need to get a registration card from the inn staff and go and register yourself at the local police station. Unlike in hotels, the inn staff will not do this for you. Some monasteries expect you to attend a church service if you are staying the night.

CAMPING Yugoslav-style camping is not always public transport friendly. People usually come in their car, hence they are called *autocamp*, and they are not, therefore, necessarily close to public transport. They are often large, full of old caravans, and not always scrupulously clean. Facilities and amenities, such as showering blocks and shops are also not good or nearby. They are cheap, however, and 500MKD will usually get you a tent space for four plus your car. Tourism tax is an additional 40MKD per person.

Strictly speaking, wild camping is illegal but many Macedonians do it, especially at a local festival or event. If you are going to camp wild, then please take away all your rubbish and leave the place in a good condition.

MOUNTAIN HUTS Most of the 30 mountain huts in Macedonia are covered in *Chapter 10*, page 321. They cost about 300MKD for a bed with bedding. It is best to phone ahead (Macedonian usually required) as most of the huts are not permanently staffed, or go with one of the many hiking and mountaineering clubs. The huts rarely provide food, so you will need to bring all your provisions, but there is always plenty of water.

YOUTH HOSTELS The Macedonia Youth Hostel Association (✆ 02 3216 434; f 02 3165 209; e hostelsfm@hotmail.com; www.macedonia-yha.org) is based in the Skopje youth hostel, the Ferialen Dom (page 135), close to the bus and train station. It is no cheaper than some of the bed and breakfasts, but if you are a YHA member then it is the cheapest accommodation in Skopje. Their site now lists six other MYHA locations. Some are proper hotels, some are summer camps which can only be booked through the YHA, and few are close to public transport. The official Hostelling International website lists the same hostels although you can't book most of them on line there either (*www.hihostels.com/dba/country-MK.en.htm*).

A variety of former state-run hotels, family guesthouses and hotels have cottoned on to the hostel website networks, however, and advertise on such sites as youth hostels (where you can get your discount) or as independent hostels, although many of them are in fact mid-to-expensive hotels. A couple of the sites advertising the more budget end of the spectrum are www.hostelsweb.com and www.hostelworld. com/countries/macedoniahostels.html, the latter including a price comparison.

HOSPITALITY CLUB The Hospitality Club is a worldwide network, whose members are ordinary private citizens offering a place to stay in their home for free. You have to be a member of HC and agree to abide by the network's rules in order to use their services, which are run on an honesty basis. For more information and a list of hundreds of places to stay in Macedonia for free, visit http://secure.hospitalityclub. org/hc/hcworld.php?country=118.

✖ EATING AND DRINKING

Macedonian cuisine combines simple, healthy, Mediterranean cooking with centuries of spicy Ottoman influence. It is a celebration of fresh, organic, small-scale produce, and its wine is traditionally made with no sulphites. Summer markets teem with good local fruit and vegetables, whilst the winter holds crisp pickles (*turšija*) and jars of tasty red pepper spreads. Restaurants are getting better at offering some of the delicious *domašni* (home-style) dishes, but outside the main towns simple restaurants might only serve grilled chicken breast or pork chops and a few basic side dishes. Like most of continental Europe, Macedonians have a tradition of going out to eat, and with their children. So you'll find many places (fewer in Skopje) are very child friendly.

Macedonian **meze** (from the Turkish, and ultimately Persian *maze*; also known as *ordever*, literally 'hors d'oeuvre') is the best-kept secret of Macedonian cuisine. Usually served at the start of a banquet, *meze* is so tasty and varied that it can make a whole meal on its own. The Macedonian *meze* are a variety of cold 'creamed' vegetable spreads, initially cooked till soft and then hand blended with herbs and spices, onions and garlic, and doused with not too much oil. The most common are *ajvar* (see below), *pindžur* (roasted aubergine and peppers), *tarator* (yoghurt, cucumber, walnuts and garlic), *kajmak* (a type of clotted cream, often mixed with hot chillis and potatoes), egg and mushroom, and sweet grilled red peppers doused in garlic and oil (the latter usually only available in late summer). Eaten with pitta bread, *sarma* (stuffed vine leaves), local cured ham, Parmesan and a strong local drink like *mastika* or *rakija*, it is a real treat.

The most famous of these *meze* is **ajvar**. This is made every autumn when red peppers are at their most abundant. The best, of course, is homemade (*domašni*). To be invited into a Macedonian home to make *ajvar* is quite a privilege, and will give you an idea of the meticulous preparation that must go into preparing this Macedonian speciality. Some say that to be invited to make *ajvar* is like being offered the possibility of citizenship.

Without giving away the secret recipe, in essence the peppers must be softened to remove their skins and then simmered for hours, whilst stirred constantly, so that the peppers plus other added ingredients become a rough paste. The prepared *ajvar* is then sealed in jars for use throughout the coming year till the next pepper harvest. Macedonians will make *ajvar* by the vat load, and family members will often come home from distant lands in order to partake in the occasion.

The main fare of any Macedonian meal is either meat or freshwater fish. **Lamb** is the most expensive and therefore not often served in cheaper restaurants. It comes roasted either in the oven or on a spit, and served in a big chunk on your plate, usually without rosemary, never mind mint. Otherwise the staple meat dish for most Macedonians is **skara**. This is plain grilled pork or chicken, usually salted and basted. *Skara* is so popular that you can buy it from street stalls by the kilo! Veal (*teleško meso*), beef, eel (*jagula*), stroganoff, thinly sliced garlic liver (*džigr*), schnitzel, fresh pork ribs (*svježe rebra*), pork chops (*kremenadle*) and skewered kebabs (*ražnič*) are also prolific. *Kebapči* are an extremely popular form of *skara*. They are a Balkan speciality of small sausage-shaped burger meat, well seasoned and very tasty with a beer and some good bread. Other popular traditional meat dishes are stuffed peppers, pork knee joint and *selsko meso* (village meat), which is a stew of different meats and sausages in an earthenware pot. *Makedonsko meso* is a variation of this with Macedonia's famous capsicum peppers.

Freshwater fish, either trout or carp (*krap* in Macedonian), is abundant in Macedonia. Ohrid is most famous for its *letnica* and *belvica* trout, and Dojran for its native carp. These particular fish varieties are peculiar to the lakes and cannot be found outside Macedonia, and for this reason (among others) Ohrid is protected

RESTAURANT PRICE CODES

Based on the average price of a main course.

Expensive	$$$$$	€15+; £13+; US$20+; 1,000+MKD
Above average	$$$$	€8–15; £7–13; US$10–20; 500–1,000MKD
Mid range	$$$	€4–8; £3.50–7; US$5.50–10; 250–500MKD
Cheap & cheerful	$$	€2–4; £1.75–3.50; US$2.75–5.50; 120–250MKD
Rock bottom	$	<€2; <£1.75; <US$2.75; <120MKD

under UNESCO. Ohrid trout, which has been caught in the past at over 20kg in weight, has been over-fished and this is not helped on the Albanian side of the border by lakeside boys selling trout by the bucketful. You may, therefore, want to think twice before partaking too often of this famous and increasingly rare Ohrid dish. It is now illegal to fish for Ohrid trout (see page 11).

If you are ever invited into a family home it is likely you will be offered syruped and candied fruits and a glass of homemade *liker* or *rakija* (see box, page 306) made from grapes. Macedonia's particular speciality is *žolta* (meaning literally 'yellow'), which is *rakija* yellowed by the addition of extra wheat at a secondary fermenting stage. It is usually very strong, but often sipped rather than thrown back in one as *rakija* is in many other Balkan countries. *Mastika* is another Macedonian speciality liquor, which is remarkably similar to ouzo. If you stay to eat, the meal will start with salad, followed by a hearty soup, the main course and then a dessert.

Fresh **salads** in Macedonia, especially outside Skopje, are not very inventive. Your four main choices are a green salad (lettuce); a mixed salad (cucumber, tomato, grated cabbage and carrot); a Šopska salad (cucumber, tomato and grated white goat's cheese); and Greek salad (cucumber, tomato, cubes of feta cheese and maybe some olives). Vinaigrettes and salad dressings are almost unheard of, so don't expect a choice of thousand island dressing, blue cheese or ranch, or even salad cream. There is usually olive oil and vinegar served alongside and balsamic vinegar available in Skopje.

Other Macedonian specialities include *tavče gravče*, butter beans stewed in an earthenware pot; *pastrmajlija*, a famous bread dough, pork and egg dish from Strumica which seems to be the Macedonian equivalent of pizza; *turlitava*, a vegetarian baked mix of local vegetables; and *'piti'*, usually translated as 'pies'. These are not pies in the English sense with a shortcrust top and bottom and fruit or stewed meat in the middle, but a *burek*-type affair consisting of layers of filo flaky pastry or pancake interlaced with egg and cheese, or sometimes meat and the odd spring onion.

There are also plenty of other Macedonian dishes that are usually cooked at home rather than served in restaurants, as they are more labour intensive. These include *juvki*, a semolina-based pancake which is allowed to dry crisp before being broken and re-cooked with milk and water for breakfast or lunch; *sirden*, which is the Macedonian equivalent of haggis; *pača* (brawn), made from the boiled meat of a pig's head or knuckles, fried with onions and herbs, and served cold in slices; *mantiji*, a seasoned meat pasty; and *mezelek*, offal stew.

Macedonian **desserts** – if you still have room by the time you have eaten your *meze*, hearty soup (*čorba*), *skara* by the kilo served with fried chips and several glasses of Macedonian wine – are few and mostly borrowed from other cultures, such as pancakes, *baklava*, *sutljaš* (rice pudding cake), fresh fruit and ice cream. *Ravanija* and *gurabii* are two types of syrupy cake, which you may be served in a Macedonian home, but rarely in a restaurant. Mouth-wateringly delicious, dark red forest honey (*šumski med*) can be bought at roadside stalls on the way to the Ohrid – some of the best are at the stalls south of Kičevo.

The art of **breakfast** is slowly coming to Macedonia. Kaj Maršal Tito on Ohrid Klimentski, Trend café on the Ploštad and Mečo's on Leninova in Skopje serve breakfast from 08.00 every day. Mečo's even has three cooked choices with drinks and bread for 99MKD before midday. Tivoli's in Tetovo also serves omelettes first thing in the morning. Breakfast for Macedonians traditionally consists of a strong coffee before work possibly with bread and cheese or jam, and at the weekends *juvki* or *tarama* (a cereal-based baked dish), then a break at around ten for a *gevrek* or *kifla* (sesame bread ring) and plain drinking yoghurt or *ajran* before settling down for a long lunch around 14.00. In Skopje, bakeries serving delicious pastries are becoming common, but outside Skopje it is wise to make sure you have breakfast included in your hotel bill, or buy something in, as you'll find few places on the streets that will serve you anything to eat. In Ohrid you can get sweet and savoury muffins, including *proja* (corn muffin with spinach) at Dva Biseri café from 08.00 in the morning. And beware the hot chocolate – it is often a filling warm chocolate mousse served in a cup!

Otherwise the preferred **drink** in Macedonia is coffee, either the strong Turkish variety which is a challenge to drink without sugar, served in espresso-size cups, or the usual cappucinos, machiattos and espressos. Turkish tea, served in small glasses, is popular in Albanian areas, and you'll sometimes see servers on bicycles or rollerblades carrying trays of them through the streets to customers. Fruit tea is usually considered a drink for the sick, but don't be deterred! Macedonia has lots of fruit teas (*ovošen čaj*) and mint tea (*čaj od nane*), and their mountain tea (*planinski čaj*) is a refreshing drink served in all the mountain huts and many restaurants. *Majčina dušica* (mother's little soul) tea is also a very popular tea of wild thyme. *Salep*, a drink made of ground wild orchid root and hot milk, is of Turkish origin and usually served with a sprinkling of ground cinnamon. You won't find it everywhere, but it's very tasty and warming on a cold winter's day. Another Turkish drink plentiful in B vitamins and carbohydrates is *boza*, a thick tart drink made from slightly fermented wheat (4% alcohol content). Its origins go back to Mesopotamia and it came to Macedonia with the Ottoman Empire. Available in ice-cream parlours and sweet shops, it is also good mixed with blueberry juice (*borovnica*). For more on Macedonian wines, see page 359.

If you're a vegetarian, travelling in Macedonia need not be too difficult although you'll probably have had enough of *meze*, *turlitava*, *tavče gravče* and *pohovani kromid* (breaded onions) by the end of your stay. If you're a coeliac, then your time might be more difficult. Rice dishes are usually served everywhere, and chips. You might want to make sure you ask for everything *bez leb* in order to avoid the waste of ubiquitous bread.

PUBLIC HOLIDAYS AND FESTIVALS

Macedonian national holidays are as follows:

1–2 January	New Year
7 January	Orthodox Christmas
April (usually)	Easter
1–2 May	Labour 'Day', when everybody goes picnicking
2 August	Ilinden (see page 104)
8 September	Referendum Day
11 October	National Day

A variety of other celebrations are observed in Macedonia, but are not national holidays. These include Eid-al-Fitr and Kurban Bayran (moveable dates according to the Muslim calender) and others are:

13 August	Ohrid Framework Agreement
22 November	Albanian flag day

SAINTS' DAYS Every saint has his or her festival day and these are celebrated by the locals at the church dedicated to the named saint. Usually, the villagers gather at the church or monastery with pot luck food dishes, drink and music, and make merry. Some of the bigger monasteries such as Sv Joakim Osogovski attract thousands of visitors on these days, and donations to the church funds are usually generous.

As the Macedonian Orthodox Church runs on the amended Gregorian calendar first adopted by the Eastern Orthodox Church in 1923, some of the saints' and holy days that western Europeans might know are celebrated in Macedonia 13 days later. Some have a completely different celebration day. Below are a few of the Orthodox saints' days with their western Gregorian dates, followed in brackets by the page number reference to the church where you can see the celebrations in action. For the full Macedonian Orthodox calendar see www.mpc.org.mk. The Macedonian for Saint is Sveti/a (Sv).

28 January	Sv Gavril Lesnovski (page 289)
14 February	Sv Trifun (page 310)
22 March	Sv Leonti (Leonthius) (page 303)
6 April	Sv Metodi
6 May	Sv Gjorgi (George, Gjurgjovden) (pages 223, 282)
24 May	Sv Kiril and Metodi of Solun (Thessaloniki)
14–15 June	Sv Erasmus of Ohrid (page 191)
2–3 July	Sv Naum of Ohrid (page 189)
2 August	Sv Ilija
7–8 August	Sv Petka (Peter, or Paraškjevija in Vlach) (pages 201, 216)
9 August	Sv Kliment Ohridski (page 149) and Sv Pantelejmon (pages 167, 268)
14 August	Sv Stefan (celebrated on 26 December in the UK) (page 190)
28 August	Sv Bogorodica (the Virgin Mary) (pages 191, 220, 228, 234, 245, 262, 275, 285)
29 August	The 15 martyrs of Tiberiopolis (Strumica) (page 301)
10 September	Sv Jovan Krstitel (John the Baptist) (page 259)
8 November	Sv Dimitri
21 November	Sv Archangel Michael (pages 196, 237, 271)
4 December	Sv Bogorodica Prečista (page 262)
19 December	Sv Nikola (known to many of us as Father Christmas)

FESTIVALS There are many festivals throughout the year, but most take place in the summer. The year kicks in with an Orthodox New Year festival, also known as the **Twelfthtide Carnival**, in the village of Vevčani (see page 200) on 13 and 14 January. It is a colourful two-day event attracting several thousand visitors who dress up in fancy dress and masks. The 19 January is **Epiphany**, when Bishop Naum throws a golden cross into Lake Ohrid in honour of John the Baptist and thereby blesses the lake. The practice is repeated all over Macedonia at local lakes and rivers, where men dive in after the cross purely for the honour of retrieving it.

Sv Trifun Day, for the patron saint of wines, is on 14 February. This is becoming an increasingly popular festival to celebrate Macedonia's wines. During the first three days of Orthodox Lent (usually the same time as the Catholic/Protestant Easter) is the **Strumica Carnival** (page 303), followed a few weeks later by **Orthodox Easter**. On the Saturday evening of Easter weekend, people go up to their local churches shortly before midnight with a coloured boiled egg and, when the bells of midnight have struck, a competition ensues to see whose egg survives when cracked against another. Fancy dress is the way to celebrate **1 April**, which, however, has nothing to do with fools.

After Easter is the summer-long season of festivals. Bitola kicks off with its **Monodrama Festival** in early May. On 22–23 May every year is the Pece Atanasovski **Musical Folk Instrument Festival** (page 103) in Dolneni, near Prilep. For more on what some of Macedonia's native musical instruments are see the box on page 58. Next come **Makedox** (*www.makedox.mk*) which showcases contemporary documentaries in Kuršumli An. Then it's time for the **Buskerfest** (*www.buskerfestmakedonija*) when Skopje's main square and other venues around Skopje are the stage for busker performances.

Throughout July and August, Skopje, Ohrid and Bitola hold their summer festivals, when blues concerts, plays, ballet and opera fill historical venues and open-air theatres. In Skopje these finish in early August when the government goes on holiday, but they continue in Ohrid, which also holds a **Folklore Festival**, the Green Beach music festival and Salsa Dance festival in July, and the **International Swimming Marathon**, a 30km course from Sveti Naum to the town of Ohrid, in August.

The **Prilep Pivofest Beer Festival** takes place in early July (page 228) where you can sup Macedonia's local brews with *čevapi*, peppers and other local as well as more international accompaniments to beer (sausage and mustard). The second weekend in July is the very popular **Galičnik Wedding Festival** (see page 251), which attracts many thousands of visitors and it is well worth the visit up to this pretty mountain village. For Macedonians, one of the most important events of the year is **Ilinden** on 2 August (see page 26), when the people of Macedonia stood up against the Ottoman Empire and brought in the ten-day Kruševo Republic. The **Ilinden Sailing Regatta** is held on the first three days in August on Lake Ohrid.

There are numerous **artists' colonies** throughout the summer including the International Pottery Workshop in Resen in early August, the Traditional Costumes Exhibition on the first weekend after 2 August in Struga, and the Painters' Colony in Kneževo. The Monastery of Sv Joakim Osogovski holds a Young Artists' Convention in the last week of August, which is also when its very popular saint's day falls. At the end of August the **Struga Poetry Evenings** (see page 195) take place over the bridge where Lake Ohrid empties into the River Drim in Struga.

In September Bitola holds the **International Film Camera Festival** in honour of the Manaki brothers. Štip holds its popular **Makfest of International Music** in October (page 269), while Bitola holds its classical music festival **Interfest**. Skopje holds its **International Film Festival** in October along with the **Skopje Jazz Festival**, which usually puts on some excellent artists. September and October are also very good months for wine tours (see page 309).

December finishes up the year with **Christmas markets** selling local crafts and mulled wine. **New Year's Eve** sees fireworks over the River Vardar in Skopje and equally colourful celebrations in many other towns across Macedonia.

Hooked or hankering once you get home, here are a couple of Macedonian festivals that take place outside Macedonia: Victoria, Austrialia (*www.mccvic.org*) and Rochester, New York (*www.macedonianfest.com*).

SHOPPING

Local handicraft in Macedonia is plentiful, but in the past has been hard to find and generally over-priced. Prices are coming down, but are still not low. Indigenous handicrafts include ceramics, stained glass and terracotta as well as traditional icons, manmade pearls, earthenware, traditional blankets, hand-embroidered linen, leather goods, paintings, silver filigree jewellery, iron and copper work, carpets, embroidery, local musical instruments, woodwork and museum reproductions.

The best place to purchase handicrafts is still Ohrid, although a number of hotels are now beginning to offer items. The Christmas handicraft fair at Čifte Amam in Skopje is becoming a popular event for making timely and original Christmas purchases and there are sometimes stands in the Ramstore. Makedoniko (*www.macedoniko.com*) offers mail order delivery around the world. See *Skopje, Chapter 3*, page 123, for details of where to buy souvenirs and handicrafts in Čaršija. Skopje's Roma part of town (see page 164) is the best place to order their hand-embroidered costumes, but traditional Macedonian costumes, like you might see at Galičnik or Ilinden, are harder to find.

For those living and working in Skopje, *Chapter 3* covers more of the items that you may be looking for while living away from home. English books can be found at Ikona, Matica and the English Learning Centre. Skopje is a good place to get handmade suits (see page 143), and Štip has a number of clothes and shoe outlets (see page 269) who supply Marks & Spencer and other European shops.

If you get hooked on the Macedonian starter *ajvar*, a delicious dish consisting of stewed red pepper and herbs, you can buy this in jars in the supermarket. However, the best *ajvar* would be homemade so try to buy it locally in places like Brajčino, where you can also buy local *rakija*, *liker*, jams, wild mushrooms and excellent homemade *baklava* if you eat in a local home (see page 219). The best *mastika* (aniseed liqueur) is bought at monasteries such as Sv Jovan Bigorski.

For more on local wines see page 359, and on *rakija* see the box on page 306.

ARTS AND ENTERTAINMENT

Skopje is the best place for most arts and entertainment in Macedonia, although Ohrid (*Chapter 5*), Bitola (*Chapter 6*) and Štip (*Chapter 8*) do have some events that rival, if not better, what is available in the capital. With a population of only 500,000 Skopje cannot offer endless variety, but it does have a few drama theatres, its own philharmonic orchestra and a number of art galleries. For more information on all of these see *Chapter 3*, page 123. For more details on Macedonian arts and culture see *Chapter 1, Culture*, page 55.

Summer festivals there are aplenty (see page 102) and most towns do something. You won't find the latest blockbusters in the cinemas, but the films won't be dubbed so you will be able to hear them in their original language.

Macedonia's national football team, nicknamed the Red Lions, plays in Skopje throughout the football season, and the most popular match is the match against England, whenever that occurs.

OUTDOOR PURSUITS

Macedonia is a haven for the outdoor sports enthusiast. Its mountains and waterways and lack of paved roads make it a pleasure to hike and bike in, and offer countless opportunities for paragliding, climbing, caving and kayaking. Many Macedonians themselves are keen outdoors people too. The country is starting to offer commercial trips and ready-made outdoor package holidays, and there are plenty of clubs that welcome outside interest if you are staying longer term. Most sports in Macedonia are regulated by a federation, where you can get further information, including applicable laws and permit requirements, and find out about local clubs. Contact details for most federations and some clubs are given below. The Macedonian Sport Climbing Federation (MSCF), the Macedonian Mountain Sport Federation (MMSF) and the Macedonian Speleological Foundation (MSF) are all co-located at Bd 11 Oktomvri 42a, 1000 Skopje. Respective phone, email and web addresses are listed separately below. Information on how to get to the locations mentioned below is given in the individual chapters in Part Two of this guidebook.

BIKING Mountain biking is a growing sport in Macedonia, where there are literally thousands of off-road and dirt tracks. **Energi Cycling Club** (affiliated with Bikestop shop (see below) *Bd Ilinden 38a, 1000 Skopje;* \ *02 3231 772;* m *075 475 188;* e *info@energi-cycling.com; www.energi-cycling.com*) rents out bicycles and organises regional mountain-bike tours and smaller local tours. As a club they also promote developing biking trails in Macedonia as well as local sustainable tourism to historical and natural sites of interest. **Cycle Macedonia** and **Bike Macedonia** (see *Tour operators*, page 64) organises one- to two-week cycling holidays. **Go Macedonia** (see page 66) rents bikes for 700MKD per day.

Bikestop, owned by Ljubiša Kondev (*Orče Nikolov 101/6, Skopje;* \ *02 3231 772; www.bikestop.com.mk (only in Macedonian);* ⊕ *10.00–20.00 Mon–Fri, 09.00–15.00 Sat*) is all you'll need for parts, service or a whole bike. Their website also has a mountain-biking map for Macedonia which can be downloaded for free.

FISHING Fishing in Macedonia is widely done, but only marginally successful. Despite boasting the first recorded instance of fly fishing (see *www.flyfishinghistory. com*), Macedonian rivers today tend to suffer from one of two conditions: being overgrown or over-fished. Trees, shrubs and heavy overgrowth crowd riverbanks in many of the valleys, making casting nearly impossible and even if you do manage, odds are you'll lose your gear on a snag. Over-fishing is so rampant in the open areas that 'keepers' are rare indeed. Lax enforcement of regulations and licensing mean that every kind of bait is used, limits aren't respected (or imposed), and few buy a licence. Moves are afoot to make fishing more sustainable in Macedonia, but efforts are slow.

For the avid fisherman, Macedonia has trout, carp, bream and other freshwater species native to its streams, rivers and lakes. The Radika (see page 64), running from Mavrovo Lake to Debar and beyond, is a classic, albeit over-fished trout river. Running between craggy, forested mountains, it's got plenty of water and its deep holes hide some big fish – despite the proximity of the road along its entire length. The Crni Drim, running from Ohrid Lake to Debar, offers a number of choice spots, despite most of the river being inaccessible due to heavy overgrowth. The Treška, from Makedonski Brod north is accessible in several places, and therefore heavily fished. But fishing where it empties into the reservoir, or by boat on the reservoir itself, has brought considerable success. Finally, the Pčinja, starting just east of Kumanovo and emptying into the Vardar near Veles, has several accessible parts, including a glorious valley north from the village of Pčinja itself.

Lake fishing in Macedonia is subject to a prohibition on trout fishing in Lake Ohrid (see page 171). Still, the country has several bountiful lakes that offer decent sport fishing. Among the best are Debar, Dojran, Matka, Prespa and Mavrovo.

For more information contact the **Sport Fishing Federation Združenija na Sportski Ribolovci na Makedonija** (*Kočo Racin 75, Skopje;* \ *02 3164 539*). There you can get a licence for waters in the Vardar region of Skopje for 800MKD, or a nationwide licence for 1,690MKD. Licences last for one year and are available to foreigners who can show a passport. Various discounts exist for the young and the elderly, and licences for women are free.

Note that many waterways will have additional fees, ranging from 200–400MKD, which are levied in one of two ways: on site (*na lica mesto*) or by purchasing a sticker at the federation to attach to your licence. On-site fees appear to be paid only if the warden finds you. At the time of writing, catch limits were 3kg of fish of all varieties, with the exception of trout, which carries a limit of two fish only, each of 30cm or longer. A good website on fishing in Macedonia is www.ribar.com.mk.

HIKING AND MOUNTAINEERING These are by far the most popular outdoor sports in Macedonia. For more information on hiking clubs, huts and trails see *Chapter 10*.

HORSERIDING There are two riding schools outside Skopje (see page 123) and numerous stables around the country. Horseriding club **Bistra Galičnik (m** *077 648 679, 078 649 001;* e *hcbistragalicnik@gmail.com; www.hcbistragalicnik.com. mk*) offers single- and multi-day tours on horseback to Vodno, through Mavrovo National Park and elsewhere. Local tour operators can arrange horserides outside Skopje and guided donkey rides to local sites are becoming increasingly available: see individual chapters for more.

KAYAKING Once a big sport in Macedonia, kayaking appears to be on the decline, perhaps due to the expense of equipment and the upkeep of courses. Nevertheless, Macedonia offers numerous white-water rapids and a number of competition courses including those on the River Vardar in Skopje itself and at Lake Matka just outside Skopje. For more information contact the **Association of Kayaking on Wild Waters Fans of Macedonia** (*Rabotnički Sport Hall, 1000 Skopje;* \ *02 322 5234*). The Rabotnički Sports Hall also houses the **Swimming Association of Macedonia** (\ *02 323 6223*).

PARAGLIDING Paragliding is a very popular and awesome experience in Macedonia, which is crammed with great accessible take-off sites, such as Mount Vodno outside Skopje, Popova Šapka above Tetovo, Galičica Mountain above Lake Ohrid, as well as sites in Kruševo, Strumica and Prilep. The interconnectivity of mountains, valleys, ridges and ravines here makes it possible to fly for several hours and up to 30km in one direction. It is also relatively cheap to learn to fly here compared with club rates in western Europe. Paragliding is overseen by the **Aeronautical Society of Macedonia** (*www.vfm.org.mk*). The best commercial paragliding club in Macedonia offering courses and tandem flights is:

Vertigo Sv Mihail Cekov No 7-1/11, Skopje; m 075 281 090 (club president Sašo Smilevski), 078 440 449 (club secretary Karolina Smilevska); e info@paraglidingohrid.com; www. paraglidingohrid.com. Offers the full range of beginners, intermediate & advanced courses as well as tandem flights. All the instructors are nationally certified. A 5-day beginner's course costs €450 including loaning out equipment for you to learn to fly. Club members can usually be found at MKC Club Restaurant in the Macedonian Youth Centre in Skopje when not in the air. They also sell equipment.

ROAD RALLY RACING Mount Vodno is the location each year in mid-May (just as you might want to go out for your first hike of the year) for the Macedonian

Hill Climb Championship. Hundreds of souped-up and stripped-down cars, including the odd Zastava or two, race up the winding road to the top. If you want a quiet hike or bike in the hills, this event makes for a thoroughly terrible day, otherwise it is quite exciting. For more information contact Velibor Kaevski (✆ 075 894 577).

ROCK CLIMBING *Kačuvačka* as it is called in Macedonian is a fast-growing sport, and there are some excellent climbs to be had at Lake Matka near Skopje (traditional, multi-pitch), Kaneo at Ohrid (bolted), Pilav Tepe (also known as Ploca) near Radoviš and Demir Kapija (bolted) right off the main road to Greece, amongst other places. The **MSCF** (✆ *02 3165 540;* e *contact@climbing.org.mk; www.climbing.mk*) is very active and their website lists a number of affiliated clubs and a guide to climbing routes. For climbs specific to Pilav Tepe see below. Try also www.alpinizam.org for general information on other rock climbing areas. Rock climbing gear has yet to make it to Macedonia, so you'll have to bring your own. The nearest place to buy gear is in Sofia, Bulgaria, at Stenata (*www.stenata. com*). Active clubs include:

Bolder Crux Ploča Climbing Club Pilav Tepe, 17km west of Radoviš on the road to Štip & Skopje; e alpinistzm@yahoo.com (club president Zoran Majstorski); www. plocaclimbing.com. The rock climbing park at Pilav Tepe, known as Ploča (Macedonian for slab or tile), is the most developed & most accessible climbing site in Macedonia. Golem Ploča features 12 bolted, multi-pitch routes. Mala Ploča has bolted & traditional routes. There are also 7 boulders below the big wall featuring bolted routes & bouldering problems. All the different sections are connected by maintained trails with signs & are a mere 10min walk from the Climbing Hut Ploča. The climbing hut complete with kitchen, bathroom (with hot water for showering) & 2 dorm-style bedrooms with a total of 12 beds is available for use by all. There are also opportunities for camping, hiking & mountain biking on marked trails around Lake Mantovo, the village of Brest & the Monastery of Sv Pantelejmon. The restaurant

Pilav Tepe is located a stone's throw from the hut, offering traditional Macedonian cuisine & a great view of the rock & its climbers. The club meets every Tue & Thu 19.30–21.00 at the Sportska Sala, Radoviš, where they have an indoor climbing wall.
Everest Climbing Club Radovan Kovačevik 9, 1480 Gevgelija; ✆ 034 213 743; m 070 218 811; e alpiclubeverest@yahoo.com; www.clubeverest. mk. Club secretary Živko Murdžev.
Matka Climbing Club Franklin-Ruzevelt 68 1/2, Skopje; ✆ 02 2670 058; m 070 34 28 28; on Facebook as Alpinistički Klub Matka. Offer experienced guides for all of Macedonia & Bulgaria as well as rock climbing lessons at all levels of experience. The club can provide most of the necessary equipment such as ropes, helmets & other safety devices, but you will have to provide your own footwear. Prices vary from €20–80 depending upon the duration & location of climbs & the amount of equipment hired.

Other indoor walls can be found at:

OU 'Toso Arsov' Borko Talev bb, Štip; ✆ 070 527 586
Sport Hall 'Mladost' Negotino; ✆ 075 615 931

Sport Hall 'Nikola Karev' Negotino; ✆ 070 781 685

SAILING There is only one lake really worth sailing on in Macedonia, and that is of course Lake Ohrid. **AMAC SP-BOFOR Boat Club** (*Kaj Maršal Tito bb, 6000 Ohrid;* ✆ *046 256 386;* e *stevco@amacsp-bofor.com.mk; www.amacsp-bofor.com.mk*) has been sailing on the lake since 1937 when it was established under the club's original name 'Strmec', a fast regional wind. They offer a variety of small to medium sail boats for hire at around 4,000MKD per day as well as reasonably priced sailing lessons. They also organise the annual Ilinden Sailing Regatta on Lake Ohrid on Macedonia's national day, Ilinden, on 2 August every year.

SCUBA DIVING If you fancy exploring the tectonic edges of Lake Ohrid then **Amfora Dive Centre** (*Lazo Trposki 35, 6000 Ohrid;* \046 254 900; m *070 700 865;* e *sekuloski@ yahoo.com; www.amfora.com.mk*) can take you; in the summer they also have a desk at Hotel Granit in Ohrid (\ *046 207 100*). Lake Ohrid has a dramatic drop-off at its tectonic shelf, which is worth exploring, and there is also a Neolithic stilt village (Bay of Bones, see page 188), which can be accessed with special permission.

SKIING There are three main ski resorts in Macedonia: Mavrovo, Popova Šapka and Kožuf. **Mavrovo** (*www.skimavrovo.com*; see page 250) is the most popular by far, with a day pass costing 1,200MKD. It is the best-equipped in terms of facilities, hotels, restaurants and bars, but it is also the lowest of the three ski resorts, going up to only 1,860m (from a base lift of 1,255m). **Popova Šapka** (*near Tetovo; www. popovasapka.com*; see page 245) and Kožuf (near Gevgelia and on the border with Greece; see page 315) both offer more exciting terrain, but are also prone to high winds. Popova Šapka ski resort, set between 1,708m and 2,510m, has been long in need of funds, and charges 800MKD for a day pass. **Kožuf** (*www.skikozuf. com*), having only opened in 2007, is still in the process of being completed. It lies between 1,480m and 2,150m and charged 800MKD for a day ski pass in 2011. Children under eight years old and adults over 65 go free. There is also some skiing on Pelister, Kruševo and Galičica.

SPELUNKING/POTHOLING/CAVING Macedonia is probably most well known outside the country for its speleology or caving. The karst formations of so much of Macedonia's ground structure make it ideal for caves. There are over 500 caves (*peštera* in Macedonian) in the country, only 300 of which have been explored. Only four are protected: Pešna, Ubavica, Mlečnik and Gorna Slatinska. This number does not, however, reflect the amount of spectacular caves. Some of the caves have underground rivers, lakes, multiple caverns and of course stalagmites and stalactites. Many are home to rare underground life forms as well as prehistoric fossils. Most caves have not been made tourist-friendly yet and so most are really accessible only with the correct equipment, experience and preferably a guide. The only cave open daily to tourists (300MKD entrance fee) is Vrela at Lake Matka (see page 157 for more on the caves there).

For clubs and potential expeditions, the **MMSF** can be contacted at the address on page 321 (m *070 449 182;* e *speleomacedonia@yahoo.com; www.speleomacedonia. org.mk*). By area the most well-known caves are at:

Gostivar The longest cave in Macedonia, at 1.2km, is Gonovica south of Gostivar, which has an underground river and the highest underground waterfall of 7m. Near here is also Ubavica cave, almost 1km in length, also with a waterfall.

Karadžica and Sopište The deepest cave in Macedonia is Solunska 4, just below Solunska Glava on Mount Karadžica. It is 450m in depth, with a single shaft of 250m in depth and contains the only ice cave formations yet known in Macedonia. Spela Bobguni near Patiška Reka is one of the more speleologically difficult and rewarding caves. There are about 50 other caves in the Sopište karst region.

2

Kavadarci Named the most beautiful cave in Macedonia is the 120m-long Gališka cave near Tikveš Lake. Its entrance at 10m high is easily accessible and its numerous water cascades and high humidity show off the colours of the various minerals inside. Bela Voda cave, 955m in length, with a lake at the end is near Demir Kapija.

Kičevo Slatinksi Izvor (meaning Slatino Springs) is near the village of Slatino south-southeast of Kičevo. It is over 1km in length and was considered significant enough in caving terms (stalagmites, stalactites, river and lake features) to be submitted to UNESCO in 2004 for consideration as a World Heritage Site.

Makedonski Brod Pešna cave (page 231) near Makedonski Brod is the most accessible of caves, with a large entrance and the ruins of a medieval fortress. The Slatino caves are also near here, as well as Golubarnik, Momiček and Laprnik caves

PHOTOGRAPHIC TIPS   *Ariadne Van Zandbergen*

EQUIPMENT Although with some thought and an eye for composition you can take reasonable photos with a 'point and shoot' camera, you need an SLR camera with one or more lenses if you are at all serious about photography. The most important component in a digital SLR is the sensor. There are two types of sensor: DX and FX. The FX is a full-size sensor identical to the old film size (36mm). The DX sensor is half size and produces less quality. Your choice of lenses will be determined whether you have a DX or FX sensor in your camera as the DX sensor introduces a 0.5x multiplication to the focal length. So a 300mm lens becomes in effect a 450mm lens. FX ('full frame') sensors are the future, so I will further refer to focal lengths appropriate to the FX sensor.

Always buy the best lens you can afford. Fixed fast lenses are ideal, but very costly. Zoom lenses make it easier to change composition without changing lenses the whole time. If you carry only one lens a 24–70mm or similar zoom should be ideal. For a second lens, a lightweight 80–200mm or 70–300mm or similar will be excellent for candid shots and varying your composition. Wildlife photography will be very frustrating if you don't have at least a 300mm lens. For a small loss of quality, teleconverters are a cheap and compact way to increase magnification: a 300 lens with a 1.4x converter becomes 420mm, and with a 2x it becomes 600mm. NB 1.4x and 2x teleconverters reduce the speed of your lens by 1.4 and 2 stops respectively.

The resolution of digital cameras is improving the whole time. For ordinary prints a 6-megapixel camera is fine. For better results and the possibility to enlarge images and for professional reproduction, higher resolution is available up to 21 megapixels.

It is important to have enough memory space when photographing on your holiday. The number of pictures you can fit on a card depends on the quality you choose. You should calculate how many pictures you can fit on a card and either take enough cards or take a storage drive onto which you can download the cards' content. You can obviously take a laptop which gives the advantage that you can see your pictures properly at the end of each day and edit those you want to keep and delete rejects. If you don't want the extra bulk and weight you can buy a storage device that can read memory cards. These drives come in different capacities.

Keep in mind that digital camera batteries, computers and other storage devices need charging. Make sure you have all the chargers, cables and converters with you. Most hotels/lodges have charging points, but it will be best to enquire about this in advance. When camping you might have to rely on charging from the car battery.

near the village of Gorna Belica. In Golubarnik (meaning pigeon roost) have been found ancient human skulls and the largest (2m) cave pearl in Macedonia.

Other areas There are numerous other caves along Matka Dam, in Galičica National Park and around Lesnovo. Zemjovec cave near Krapa, Kumanovo, allegedly emits healing waters. The small cave of Alilica near Tresonče marks the start of the Biljana waterfall series along the River Tresončka. Some of the largest caves in the country include Dolna Duka and Krštelna.

WILDLIFE SAFARIS Game hunting is popular in Macedonia and the Jasen Forestry Reserve is still an exclusive wildlife range, once the preserve of the military and the president. The last president, Branko Crvenkovski, elected in 2004, dropped the annual diplomatic hunt, and took up tree-planting instead.

DUST AND HEAT Dust and heat are often a problem. Keep your equipment in a sealed bag, and avoid exposing equipment to the sun when possible. Digital cameras are prone to collecting dust particles on the sensor, which results in spots on the image. The dirt mostly enters the camera when changing lenses, so you should be careful when doing this. To some extent photos can be 'cleaned' up afterwards in Photoshop, but this is time-consuming. You can have your camera sensor professionally cleaned, or you can do this yourself with special brushes and swabs made for this purpose, but note that touching the sensor might cause damage and should only be done with the greatest care.

LIGHT The most striking outdoor photographs are often taken during the hour or two of 'golden light' after dawn and before sunset. Shooting in low light may enforce the use of very low shutter speeds, in which case a tripod/beanbag will be required to avoid camera shake. The most advanced digital SLRs have very little loss of quality on higher ISO settings, which allows you to shoot at lower light conditions. It is still recommended not to increase the ISO unless necessary.

With careful handling, side lighting and back lighting can produce stunning effects, especially in soft light and at sunrise or sunset. Generally, however, it is best to shoot with the sun behind you. When photographing animals or people in the harsh midday sun, images taken in light but even shade are likely to look better than those taken in direct sunlight or patchy shade, since the latter conditions create too much contrast.

PROTOCOL In some countries, it is unacceptable to photograph local people without permission, and many people will refuse to pose or will ask for a donation. In such circumstances, don't try to sneak photographs, as you might get yourself into trouble. Even the most willing subject, however, will often pose stiffly when a camera is pointed at them; relax them by making a joke, and take a few shots in quick succession to improve the odds of capturing a natural pose.

Ariadne Van Zandbergen is a professional travel and wildlife photographer specialising in Africa. She runs The Africa Image Library. For photo requests, visit the website www. africaimagelibrary.co.za or contact her direct at e ariadne@hixnet.co.za.

At time of writing it is not known whether the new president Gjorgi Ivanov will resume the sport. Hunting and wildlife safaris can be arranged through local hotels, such as the Bistra in Mavrovo (see page 250) and the Molika on Pelister Mountain (see page 216). See page 211 for more on the types of wildlife to look out for on a wildlife safari.

PHOTOGRAPHY

It is forbidden to take photographs in churches, restricted military areas, and of military installations. Most people do not mind if you take their photograph, but you should always ask first, and if they say no, do not insist. In the more remote villages, farmers may also not agree to you taking photographs of their animals. They believe that if you take a photograph even of only one animal it will take a part of the animal's soul and this will affect the whole flock.

Negative film is easy to get, and development costs around 350MKD. Slide film is more difficult to get and can cost up to 500MKD just for the development. There are photo development stores co-located with all the bigger Vero stores, which will also do professional passport photographs too. Stanimir Nedelkovski (✆ 070 217 975) develops very high-quality colour, and black-and-white slide film. Developing black-and-white slide film costs €4, and colour is €10. He will also let you use his laboratory to develop your own film. And he can produce high-quality digital photographic prints.

For more top tips on photography, see box on pages 110–11.

MEDIA AND COMMUNICATIONS

NEWS OUTLETS The current centre-right government has recently hit hard on the media, to the extent that international organisations, European governments and freedom of speech NGOs have all spoken out. The government has supposedly cracked down on tax evasion but appears to have targeted only media outlets that are critical of the government. As a result A1 Television, which had been the most reputable television station to give relatively balanced news, has practically had to shut down since its offices were first raided in November 2010. A1 was raided in connection with alleged money laundering through Plus Produkcija, who own the three most widely read newspapers in the country, *Vreme*, *Špic* and *Koha e Re*, who have also been forced to close.

In order to silence other democratic mechanisms that might counter this, the government has changed the composition of the Broadcasting Council so that it is effectively run by the government. The changes were rushed through parliament in an emergency procedure in July 2011, thus circumscribing public or stakeholder debate. Then in August 2011 the Macedonia state television, MTV, fired its entire board of governors, contravening the country's broadcasting law, and has fired labour union members who are journalists critical of the government. This has affected the independence of another leading newspaper *Utrinski Vesnik*, and the television station Alsat-M. For more on the issue see Reporters Without Borders (*www.en.rsf.org/Macedonia*).

What's left? – Kanal 5, Alfa, Sitel, Skynet and Telma – and other more local channels. MTV2 broadcasts purely in Albanian, and MTV3 broadcasts all the parliamentary sessions. Macedonian Radio and Channel 77 are the two main news-heavy radio stations broadcasting in the Macedonian language, but there are dozens of local radio stations. Some of the most popular radio stations that a lot of the restaurants tune into are Antenna 5 (95.5) and City Radio (94.7). BBC World Service is available on 104.7 between 22.00 and 08.00 with on-the-hour news.

The daily newspapers produced in Cyrillic are *Dnevnik*, *Večer*, *Nova Makedonija*, *Makedonija Denes*, *Vest*, *Vreme*, and *Utrinski Vesnik*, which is the most serious of them all. There are three weekly Macedonian-language news magazines: *Denes*, *Aktuel* and *Start*. *Forum* is a bi-weekly politics and life magazine which caters to a politically more analytical sector of Macedonians, and which critiques without necessarily being critical. *Forum* also has an interesting quarterly magazine.

The two main Macedonian-language news agencies are MIA (*www.mia.com.mk*) and Makfax (*www.makfax.com.mk*), both of which have very good news in English that is updated several times a day. MIA requires paid registration for expanded news articles, while Makfax does not.

MIA, A1 and Sitel provide mobile phone news updates.

On the Albanian side the news agencies include Balkanweb, Kosova Press, Kosova Live, Kosovo Information Centre and Albanews. There are two main daily newspapers, *Fakti* and *Lajm* and one weekly, *Lobi*.

There are also Roma and Turkish media stations and papers produced in-country, as well as most of the major international newspapers and magazines available in Skopje after 19.00 every evening.

POST The post in Macedonia is relatively reliable for low-value items, although not very fast. It usually takes between one and two weeks for letters to be delivered between Europe or America and Macedonia by standard post. Stamps can be bought only at the post office, although there is a philatelic bureau at the Ploštad end of the Trgovski Centar in Skopje if you are looking for commemorative stamps.

Most packages are opened on arrival in the country and items of value may be stolen. As a result, high-value items, and even books, should be sent by FedEx or DHL. FedEx (*www.fedex.com.mk*) services in Skopje can be found at Boulevard Partizanski Odredi 17 (⬆ *02 3137 233*; e *macedonia@fedex.com.mk*) opposite the cathedral; DHL (*www.dhl.com.mk*) has offices in most main towns (see website) and in Skopje can be found at the Holiday Inn and at City Travel on the ground floor of Paloma Bjanka business centre (⬆ *02 3212 203/4*; e *city@t-home.mk*).

If you want post sent to you whilst travelling, have it addressed to you at Name, Poste Restante, Pošta, Town Name. You will be able to pick it up at the town's main post office. Make sure that your surname is printed clearly in capitals and underlined, and bring some identification with you when you go to pick up your mail.

TELEPHONE Phone booths accepting coins, credit cards and pre-paid phone cards are also available all over the country. Pre-paid phone cards can be bought at newsagents and are easily visible by the big phone-card advertising boards in the shape of a telephone.

Mobile phone providers are T-Mobile, Vip and One, where you can purchase a local SIM card with an initial few hundred minutes for as little as 250MKD. Monthly contracts are also available. The main T-Mobile outlet is on the ground floor of Skopje's Trgovski Centar. T-Mobile and One both have outlets in Ramstore. Make sure you bring ID (or at least know your passport number). Top-ups are sold in 200, 300, 590 and 1,000 impulses (and cost that many MKD respectively). Your phone can be topped-up for you electronically at the point of sale.

If you are thinking of using your own mobile phone from home with a local SIM card, make sure that your phone is unlocked and enabled for use abroad and with non-service provider SIM cards. This is usually done for free now by your home service provider, but it may need to be sent away (recorded delivery) for a few days before you leave home.

Using internet telephony, eg: Skype (*www.skype.com*), is a cheap way to 'phone' home from internet cafés. An increasing number of travel agents and hotels in Macedonia now list their Skype username on their website. A useful telephone directory website is imenik.telecom.mk. The local telephone directory is the local dialling code followed by 188.

INTERNET Internet cafés are increasingly difficult to find, not least because Wi-Fi is open and free throughout most of Macedonia. Most hotels also have free Wi-Fi. The Contact Café on the top floor of the Trgovski Centar in Skopje charges 120MKD per hour and has printing and fax services.

T-Mobile (*www.t-home.mk*) can provide internet to your home for those moving to Macedonia.

As with writing to any person in anything other than their mother tongue, Macedonians are unlikely to answer an email that is not in Macedonian. So don't expect a reply too quickly, or at all, unless you have already established contact with them by phone or in person (see *Business*, below).

BUSINESS   *Ray Power, CEO of the British Business Group Macedonia*

Business hours in Macedonia are generally adhered to in Skopje but a little less obviously in some of the smaller towns. Opening times vary from 06.30 (post offices), 07.00 (banks), 08.00 (supermarkets and green markets), 09.00 (some shops) to 10.00 (other shops). Some places shut for lunch, especially in the summer when the day is hot, and some travel agents outside Skopje for instance will close from 11.00 to 17.00 and then open again till 20.00. Closing times also vary from 15.00 (some museums and repair stores, even if their stated closing time is in fact 16.00) to 16.00 (government and media offices) to anything between 17.00 and 22.00. Bars and restaurants are required by law to be closed from midnight on weekdays and from 01.00 at the weekends although licensed nightclubs can remain open until 04.00 on weekends. If you are trying to get hold of government officials it is best to do so between 10.00–12.00 and 14.00–15.00. Most shops are closed on Sunday.

If you have not done business in the Balkans before, and especially if you come from a time-driven and impersonal business culture like the US, UK, Germany or Switzerland, you'll probably find doing business in Macedonia requires a slight change of pace. Firstly, Macedonians value their relationships highly and like to engage on a personal rather than exclusively professional level. This can be a little disconcerting for some Western 'go-getters' where the focus is on getting the job done. It's often taken for granted that deadlines are flexible so when planning meetings or 'back-to-back' agendas be prepared for reworking it on the fly. In that sense, Macedonia is very Mediterranean.

Secondly, seeing that Macedonia is a country of only two million it's not unusual to find that people choose relatives and friends to execute services. Whilst this can be helpful it does pay to shop around a bit and build your own network of less direct relationships as Macedonia does have a culture where favours are a form of capital. This is not necessarily a bad thing and functions well for those who have a sensitivity and consideration for long-term business relationships.

Thirdly, as with many eastern European countries, there is not necessarily a long tradition of customer service so you will still find some older companies and state-run organisations, such as the post office, leaving you a little frustrated at the rather blunt attitude of staff. That being said, a smile and some consideration for their relatively uncomfortable working environment and typically low wages will win friends and a level of service that no trained staff will ever match. Top tip in Macedonia: the relationship is always the priority.

Finally, as a result of the historically centralised communist economy, entrepreneurialism is a relatively new skill so whilst you will meet some brilliant business people you can still find those people who expect opportunities to be handed to them on a platter. In cases of the latter you will be able to discern them by the excessive lunch and dinner meetings with no follow up or next steps. If you are in a position where you are stuck with such business associates best results are achieved by closely managing the process and insisting on office-based meetings and emphasising deliverables.

With the vast majority of younger people (below 45) speaking English, Macedonia is a business-friendly country that has undergone a tremendous amount of change in the last 15 years. Much of the change in recent years has been focused on creating a better business environment so, for example, setting up a company now takes just a couple of days compared with the six weeks it used to take. Please note, however, that setting up your company is only the first step. There may be a number of industry regulatory procedures which your new company may need to hurdle before it can become operational. This can take considerably longer, so it is worth researching these before going ahead with setting up in Macedonia.

Macedonia is very proud of its wine industry, which has been growing steadily during the last ten years; but it also has a lot to offer in the wider context of agriculture with large amounts of unused arable land. The more recent focus on the IT industry also makes Macedonia a suitable choice for outsourcing and and it's fair to say they are very well suited to agile development work. With its free economic zones Macedonia is also attracting major manufacturing companies who require a competitive workforce within Europe.

On the whole, business activities are still very personal and ensuring that introductions and relationships are managed accordingly will minimise delays and maximise productivity. For more on setting up a business in Macedonia, see the *Web resources* in *Appendix 4*.

BUYING PROPERTY

Buying property in Macedonia as an individual (rather than a company) became possible in 2008. Foreigners can purchase from any estate agent, although few will speak English. Property prices in the capital are high considering where Macedonia is on its path to EU accession (2015 maybe?). Outside Skopje and Ohrid lakeside, prices are much lower, but attractive properties are in much need of renovation. A small fixer-upper in Stenje on the beach of Lake Prespa can cost as little as €5,000. Macedonians claim they are some of the best builders in the world, and that does not mean cheap, but there is relatively little substantial corroboratory evidence. Buying property in Macedonia can be very long-winded (over a year from initial offer to completion), and if you don't speak Macedonian, then you will need to pay out for the translation of key documents, even if you do use a local lawyer who speaks English. Make sure that the title of the property is verified independently in case there is an ownership dispute on the property. One website listing properties for sale in Macedonia is www.homeonsale.co.uk > Europe > Macedonia. For a guide on buying property in Macedonia see www.globalpropertyguide.com/Europe/Macedonia.

CULTURAL ETIQUETTE

DRESS For the most part modesty is not an issue in Macedonia. That said, you'll find many Muslim women here of all ages dressed from head to foot in a long overcoat and headscarf no matter what time of day or year, and as a woman you may find it uncomfortable to wander around strongly Muslim areas in a crop top and low-cut shorts. Nudism is unheard of on the lake beaches.

DRUGS As everywhere in the world, there is a drugs scene in Macedonia, although it is small. Drugs are also illegal, even marijuana, so don't use/deal unless you want to risk ending up in a Macedonian jail. Dealing in drugs carries a hefty penalty, doubly so if you are caught taking them over a border crossing. Finally, make sure you keep an eye on your bags at all times while travelling into Macedonia so that no-one can stuff anything illegal in there without you knowing.

RELIGIOUS ETIQUETTE You should certainly be modestly dressed to enter a mosque and its grounds, and while most churches don't seem to mind what you wear, there are a few that require decent dress, such as Treskavec, Lesnovo and Marko's Monastery. Decent dress means covered shoulders, torso and legs. It is forbidden to take photographs inside churches.

Although many Macedonians are atheist as a leftover from communist days, increasing numbers have retaken to the Macedonian Orthodox Church with renewed vigour. Aside from in tourist-frequented Ohrid, Macedonians might find it odd if you don't cross yourself three times before entering the church and light a candle immediately on entering it. Practising Macedonians believe that you will not enter through the gates of heaven if you do not bring oil or wax with which to burn the light of God.

TIPPING Tipping is not a necessity here, where most Macedonians can hardly afford more than a coffee in a bar. However, it is greatly appreciated by waiting staff, and as a foreigner if you can afford it, it's certainly a small boost to the economy, morale and attitudes towards tourists. An extra 10 or 20 denar is suitable on smaller sums of money up to 500MKD, usually rounded up to the nearest 50 or 100, and on larger sums, up to 10% is appropriate.

INTERACTING WITH LOCAL PEOPLE

MACEDONIAN HOSPITALITY Macedonian hospitality is extensive and often overpowering. Especially outside Skopje and Ohrid, where people are not used to contact with foreigners, Macedonians whom you meet will go out of their way to show you a site or monument and then insist on giving you a cup of thick, black, sweet Turkish coffee and a gift from their garden, or some other memento. They will do this, even if you speak no Macedonian at all and they do not speak your language, which can make the conversation somewhat one-sided! They are not looking for a passport to your home country or even any other favour, and if you exchange addresses they will not usually follow up on it unless you do.

Macedonians would simply consider it too rude not to answer a request to the fullest extent and offer you a coffee in their home, and of course they are inquisitive to know who you are, where you come from and how you live in your own country. Trying to say no is extremely difficult without being rude, unless you have some handy pressing excuse, like 'I will turn into a pumpkin at midnight if I don't leave right now' or 'We left my mother in the car and she needs to go to the hospital for brain surgery.' In other words, no excuse will be satisfactory and especially the lame excuse that you do not have enough time, for the one thing that Macedonians do have a lot of is time, and they know that if there's five minutes' leeway in the schedule somewhere then you can fit in a half-hour coffee, and if there isn't five minutes in the schedule then you wouldn't be visiting their remote village anyway.

My advice is to make the most of this laid-back way of life. It probably won't be around for much longer, as the fast pace and impersonal attitudes of modern-day life catch up with Macedonia. You may have to reschedule your cramped itinerary and knock something else off the list in order to fit in that coffee, but an invitation into the tenth house is still a privilege and will give you a momentary snapshot of how Macedonians live today.

A SMILE As you travel around Macedonia, especially off the beaten track, you may be greeted at first with a cold, hard stare. Some communities are not often visited by outsiders and so the locals will be suspicious and inquisitive if not bewildered by your intentions to sightsee around their home. Even other Macedonians from a far-away town get this treatment. A smile, a wave and a greeting like 'Zdravo', or 'Tungjatjeta' in Albanian regions, or even just 'Hello' will miraculously make your intentions to the locals clear, and their hostile glare will instantly dissolve into a winning smile and a greeting in reply. Initiate a conversation and the obligatory coffee is bound to follow along with a personal tour of their home and town.

CULTURAL QUIRKS Every society has its little idioms and beliefs – here are a few from Macedonia. *Promaja* is the Macedonian word for 'draught', not as in beer, but as in the wind/breeze that blows in through an open door or window. Many (particularly older) Macedonians, like a lot of people in the Balkans, believe that *promaja* is the root of all illness, so don't be surprised if you are asked to close a window or door even on a blistering hot day. *Le le* is an exclamation which Macedonians say all the time to add emphasis to a sentence. It's not directly translatable into anything in English, but other languages use similar expressions, like *ahh yoaaaa* in some Chinese dialects. *Ajde* is another frequent exclamation. It means 'let's go' or 'come on' or 'you're kidding'. You'll hear these two exclamations in the Macedonian language all over the place.

POLITICS AND HISTORY Macedonians are painfully aware of their history and politics, and are extremely interested in the slightest rumour of political intrigue. Macedonians will happily talk politics and history with you, but beware that you may not get them off the topic once started, no matter how many times you've heard the same tale of oppression and inequality. This phenomenon is particularly Balkan, but in Macedonia it is exaggerated by the fact that Macedonia's national neighbours mostly do not believe (largely for political reasons) that there is such a thing as an ethnic Macedonian, and as a result some question whether Macedonia should even be a sovereign state. As a foreigner, you'll never be right, and whatever you read in *Chapters 1* and *3* of this book is bound to offend someone, be they Macedonian, Serb, Albanian, Turk, Bulgarian, Greek, Orthodox or Muslim. So take what you hear with a small pinch of salt and debate politics with great caution, even if you were a top scorer in the debating society at college.

There is a Macedonian proverb that goes 'If my cow dies, may my neighbour's cow die too.' This, sadly, does sum up a lot of the attitude of people here. But, as Mahatma Gandhi said, 'An eye for an eye makes the whole world blind.'

TRAVELLING POSITIVELY

The interaction of the outside world with Macedonia can have a variety of effects. Hopefully, your visit to Macedonia will have a positive impact on the tourist industry and, indirectly, on the economy and the people. If you have room in your rucksack or suitcase on your way out or have a load of stuff to get rid of when you leave Macedonia, then try bringing some things to the organisations listed on the Macedonian page of www.stuffyourrucksack.com (see box below). These organisations are in dire need of some basics, like books, shoes, pens and other small items you might have lying around your house. If you would like to get more personally involved with charities and institutions in the country then here are a few to start you off. For environmental protection organisations see page 13.

ANTI-TRAFFICKING The trafficking of women through and into Macedonia is a particularly entrenched problem (see page 56), not helped on the Macedonian side by a weak policing and judicial system, and on the international side by the difficulty that the international community has in classing it as a crime separate from slavery, abduction, rape, torture, theft and prostitution. The whole issue is driven by huge financial profits and made easy for traffickers by the lack of public awareness.

Open Gate (*Otvorena Porta-La Strada Macedonia, PO Box 110, 1000 Skopje;* \ *02 2700 107/367;* e *lastrada@lastrada.org.mk; www.lastrada.org.mk*) campaigns on anti-trafficking. Their work has helped to set up a safe house and helpline for trafficked women in Macedonia.

CIVIL SOCIETY The role that civil society plays in any country is an important contribution to self-governance and to providing checks and balances on government and people's hard-earned taxes. In Macedonia civil society is weak by European and American standards. International funding is trying to develop the role that parliamentarians should play as the elected representatives of the people, as well as the role that non-governmental organisations can play. Sadly, the NGO scene is still largely supply driven by the amount of donor funding available rather than demand driven by the confidence that citizens can make a difference. What are sorely missing are skills and competent local stakeholders (and a responsive government). If you have the skills, the funding or the time to help with civil society development in Macedonia it will make a difference. **Volunteer Centre Skopje**

STUFF YOUR RUCKSACK – AND MAKE A DIFFERENCE

www.stuffyourrucksack.com is a website set up by TV's Kate Humble which enables travellers to give direct help to small charities, schools or other organisations in the country they are visiting. Maybe a local school needs books, a map or pencils, or an orphanage needs children's clothes or toys – all things that can easily be 'stuffed in a rucksack' before departure. The charities get exactly what they need and travellers have the chance to meet local people and see how and where their gifts will be used.

The website describes organisations that need your help and lists the items they most need. Check what's needed in Macedonia, contact the organisation to say you're coming and bring not only the much-needed goods but an extra dimension to your travels and the knowledge that in a small way you have made a difference.

(Emil Zola 3-2/3, Skopje; ✆ *02 2772 095;* e *vcs_contact@yahoo.com; www. vcs.org. mk)* places volunteers in a variety of projects across the country depending on their skills. US citizens might also want to look into two-year placements with the **Peace Corps** *(www.peacecorps.gov).*

ROMA To read more about the Roma see page 44. There are a number of organisations that are trying to serve their needs and bring the very poor back out of poverty and into education and jobs. **ARKA** in Kumanovo has been instrumental in this regard. Contact the president Feat Kamberovski *(Karaorman 6, 1300 Kumanovo;* ✆ *031 421 362, 070 629 105;* e *arka@arka.org.mk, arka_ku@ yahoo.com; www.arka.org.mk).*

Part Two

THE GUIDE

3

Skopje

Telephone code 02

> The Turkish residue was thick in Skopje. Men in white skullcaps played backgam-
> mon and drank rose-hip tea from small hour-glass-shaped receptacles … I crossed
> the flagstone bridge over the Vardar River, built on Roman foundations that had
> withstood major earthquakes in AD518, 1535 and 1963 … Ahead of me was 'new'
> Skopje …
>
> Robert D Kaplan, *Balkan Ghosts*, 1993

The up-and-coming town of Skopje is divided by the River Vardar into the
predominantly Muslim half to the north of the river, and the predominantly
Orthodox Christian half to the south. Most government offices, main shopping
centres and the main railway station are found on the southern side of town,
although the old Turkish side of town, known as **Čaršija**, remains the main tourist
attraction, with a large daily bazaar, a variety of interesting old buildings and cafés,
the remnants of the Kale fortress and a small but buzzing nightlife.

Skopje is a city of many cultures and is worth at least a couple of days itself. It
is currently going through a massive urban renewal programme, so there is lots
of controversy to see and experience around town. Don't miss out on the **cable
car** up to Vodno Mountain, the Jewish **Holocaust Museum**, **Kale Fortress**, and a
taste of Čaršija **old town**. Further just outside Skopje (see *Chapter 4*), Katlanovska
Banja **hot springs** is worth a visit, as is the Church of Sv Pantelejmon for its rare
Byzantine frescoes.

HISTORY

Nestled in the valley of the Vardar River, Skopje has been a welcome respite
from the surrounding mountains since Neolithic times. It first became a major
settlement around 500BC when it formed part of the outer reaches of the Illyrian
nation now known as Albania. As Rome moved its empire eastward, the settlement
became known as Skupi, and later came under Byzantine rule upon the division of
the Roman Empire. Thereafter Slavs, Greeks, Bulgarians, Austro-Hungarians, Serbs
and Turks all ruled the city.

In 1392 began 520 years of Ottoman rule when the city became known as
Üsküb, and it essentially languished as a backwater trade stop compared with
fashionable Monastir (now Bitola). After further swaps among regional powers
during and between both world wars, it was finally incorporated in 1944 into
Federal Yugoslavia and made the capital of the autonomous Republic of
Macedonia. It has been the capital of the independent Republic of Macedonia
since 1991 when the fledgling state broke free from the Federation during the
collapse of Yugoslavia.

CHRONOLOGY

6500BC	Neolithic tribes inhabited the Skopje region at Madžari and Govrlevo
700–500BC	Illyrians founded a settlement at present-day Zlokučani and a fort at Kale
148BC	Skupi made the seat of the Roman district government of Dardania as part of the larger province of Moesia superior
AD395	Under the division of the Roman Empire, Skupi became part of the Byzantine Empire ruled from Constantinople
AD518	Skupi almost completely destroyed by earthquake. Emperor Justinian rebuilt the town a few kilometres further south
AD695	Skupi taken over by Slavs
10th century	Known as Skoplje under the Macedonian-Bulgarian Empire
1189	Became part of the Serbian Empire before reverting to Byzantine rule
1282	Conquered by the Serbian king Milutin II
1346	Milutin's grandson, Stefan Dušan, claimed Skopje as his capital and proclaimed himself Tsar
1392	Beginning of Ottoman rule over the Balkans for the next 520 years. Town known to the Turks as Üsküb
15th century	Many Jews fled to Üsküb from Spain
1555	Earthquake destroyed much of the centre of Üsküb
1689	Occupied by the Austrian general Piccolomini. Plague infested the city and, on leaving, Piccolomini burnt it down.
1873	Üsküb to Saloniki railway line built
1910	Mother Teresa – Gondza Bojadziu – born in Skopje
1912–13	First and second Balkan wars
1914	Skopje ruled by Bulgaria
1918	Came under the rule of the Kingdom of Serbs, Croats and Slovenes
1920	Ruled for six months by the Yugoslav Communist Party
1941	Ruled again by Bulgaria
1944	Became the capital of the Federal Yugoslav Socialist Republic of Macedonia
1963	Earthquake razed much of Skopje
1991	Skopje became the capital of the independent Republic of Macedonia

THE ANCIENT SITES OF SKUPI AND KALE

Kale, the Ottoman fortress that overlooks Skopje and the Vardar Valley, housed human settlements from as early as Neolithic times c3500BC. Geographic evidence shows that such prehistoric settlements would have been on the edge of a marsh, but the rise of the mountains surrounding Skopje turned the area into the fertile plains of the River Vardar. It became a natural route of passage between greater cities further east and west, between the Aegean Sea in the south at Thessaloniki (earlier known as Saloniki and today still called Solun in Macedonian) and any travels further north.

In the 7th and 6th centuries BC many Greeks, tempted by trade and lands elsewhere, travelled and settled further north. The Illyrians settled in what is now known as Albania, and the outer reaches of their nation covered the source of the River Vardar all the way down to the foothills of the Vodno and the Skopska Crna Gore. They built the first fort at Kale, and others on Gradište above the present-day district of Dolno Nerezi, and later founded the town of Skupi in the area of the present-day Zlokučani village to the northwest of the town centre.

While other ancient cities of today's Macedonia, such as Hereaclea near Bitola and Stobi near Gradsko, came under the rule of the Macedonian Empire of Aleksandar III of Macedon, Skupi remained part of the Thracian earldom of Dardania until the 2nd century BC. Roman expansion east brought Skupi under Roman rule in 148BC when it became the seat of local government for the district of Dardania as part of the province of Moesia superior.

A PART OF THE BYZANTINE EMPIRE When the Roman Empire was divided into eastern and western halves in AD395, Skupi came under Byzantine rule from Constantinople (today's Istanbul) and became an important trading and garrison town for the region. When Skupi was almost completely destroyed by an earthquake in 518, the Byzantine emperor Justinian (born in Tauresium 20km southeast of present-day Skopje, see page 168) built a new town at the fertile entry point of the River Lepenec into the Vardar. The town was known during his reign as Justiniana Prima.

By the end of the 6th century, Skupi had declined in prestige, although newer settlements were emerging on the northern slopes of Mount Vodno. These were destroyed, however, by invading Slav troops in 695, who fortified Kale and the northern side of the Vardar.

The region soon came back under Byzantine rule. The town prospered and expanded, whilst many churches and monasteries were established in the tranquillity and remoteness of the surrounding hills.

MEDIEVAL SKOPLJE By the 10th century, Byzantine rule of Skupi was waning and the town was known as Skoplje under the Macedonian-Bulgarian Empire. In 996 it fell within the breakaway state of Tsar Samoil (see box, page 22). Although Skoplje was not made capital of the new state, the town retained its strategic trading importance until Tsar Samoil's death in 1014, when Skoplje withered again into decline, aided by another earthquake levelling the town at the end of the 11th century.

The Byzantine Empire took advantage of the decline in Skoplje during the 12th century to regain influence in the area, and some fine examples of Byzantine frescoes were painted during this time. Byzantium lost control of Skupi again in 1282 to Serbian king Milutin II. Milutin's grandson, Stefan Dušan, made Skopje his capital, from which he proclaimed himself Tsar in 1346.

FIVE HUNDRED YEARS OF OTTOMAN RULE Rolling back Byzantine rule across much of the Balkans, the Ottoman Turks finally conquered Skopje in 1392 beginning 520 years of Ottoman rule. The Turks named the town Üsküb. At first the Ottomans divided the greater Macedonian region into four *vilayets*, or districts – Üsküb, Kjustendil, Monastir and Saloniki – and as the northernmost of these, Üsküb was strategically important for further forays into northern Europe. Later Kjustendil was given back to Bulgaria, Janina to Greece and Shkodra went to Albania.

Under Ottoman rule the town moved further towards the entry point of the River Serava into the Vardar. It also became predominantly Muslim and the architecture of the town changed accordingly. During the 15th century, many travellers' inns were established in the town, such as Kapan An and Suli An, which still exist today. The city's famous Stone Bridge – Kameni Most – was also reconstructed during this period and the famous Daud Pasha baths (the largest in the Balkans and now a modern art gallery) was built at the end of the 15th century. At this time numerous Jews driven out of Spain settled in Üsküb, adding to the cultural mix of the town and enhancing the town's trading reputation.

At the beginning of Ottoman rule, several mosques quickly sprang up in the city and church lands were often seized and given to ex-soldiers, while many churches themselves were converted over time into mosques. The most impressive mosques erected during this early period include the Sultan Murat or Hjunkar Mosque, Aladža Mosque and the Mustafa Pasha Mosque.

In 1555, another earthquake hit the town, destroying much of the centre. The outskirts survived and the town continued, nonetheless, to prosper with traders and travellers. Travel reports from the era number Üsküb's population anywhere between 30,000 and 60,000 inhabitants.

For a very short period in 1689, Üsküb was occupied by the Austrian general Piccolomini. He and his troops did not stay for long, however, as the town was quickly engulfed by the plague. On retreating from the town Piccolomini's troops set fire to Üsküb, perhaps in order to stamp out the plague, although some would say this was done in order to avenge the 1683 Ottoman invasion of Vienna.

For the next two centuries Üsküb's prestige waned and by the 19th century its population had dwindled to a mere 10,000. In 1873, however, the completion of the Üsküb–Saloniki (now Skopje–Thessaloniki) railway brought many more travellers and traders to the town, so that by the turn of the century Üsküb had regained its former numbers of around 30,000.

Towards the end of the Ottoman Empire, Üsküb, along with other towns in Macedonia – Kruševo and Monastir (now Bitola) – became main hubs of rebellious movements against Ottoman rule. Üsküb was a key player in the Ilinden Uprising of August 1903 when native Macedonians of the region declared the emergence of the Republic of Kruševo. While the Kruševo Republic lasted only ten days before being quelled by the Ottomans, it was a sign of the beginning of the end. After 500 years of rule in the area the Ottomans were finally ousted in 1912 during the devastating first Balkan War (see box on page 28 for an eyewitness account).

THE BALKAN WARS AND THE WORLD WARS As the administrative centre of the region, Üsküb also administered the *vilayet* of Kosovo under Ottoman rule. This did not go down well with the increasingly Albanian population of Kosovo, who preferred to be ruled by Albanians rather than the ethnic Slav and Turkish mix of Üsküb. Albanians had started to intensify their harassment of Serbs in the area over the past decade, culminating on 12 August 1912 when 15,000 Albanians marched on Üsküb in a bid to take over the city. The Turks, already weak from other battles against the Balkan League of Greece, Serbia, Montenegro and Bulgaria during the first Balkan War, started to flee. When Serb reinforcements arrived some weeks later, the 23 October Battle of Kumanovo (50km northeast of Skopje) proved decisive in driving out the Ottomans from all of Macedonia.

Skopje remained under Serbian rule during the second Balkan War of 1913 when the Balkan League countries started to fight amongst themselves. Then World War I gave Bulgaria the opportunity to retake Skopje in 1914.

By 1918, however, it belonged to the Kingdom of Serbs, Croats and Slovenes, and remained so until 1939, apart from a brief period of six months in 1920 when Skopje was controlled by the Yugoslav Communist Party. The inter-war period of Royalist Yugoslavia saw significant immigration of ethnic Serbs into the region. An ethnic Serb ruling elite dominated over Turkish, Albanian and Macedonian cultures, continuing the repression wrought by previous Turkish rulers.

During World War II, Skopje came under German fascist occupation and was later taken over by Bulgarian fascist forces. March 1941 saw huge anti-Nazi demonstrations throughout the streets of the town, as Yugoslavia was dragged into the war. But Nazi war crimes were not to be stopped and on 11 March 1943, Skopje's entire Jewish population of 3,286 was deported to the gas chambers of Treblinka concentration camp in Poland. Another year and a half later, on 13 November 1944, Skopje was liberated by the partisans, who wrested control after a bitter two-day battle.

THE FEDERAL YUGOSLAV SOCIALIST REPUBLIC OF MACEDONIA From 1944 until 1991 Skopje was the capital of the Federal Yugoslav Socialist Republic of Macedonia. The city expanded and the population grew during this period from just over 150,000 in 1945 to almost 600,000 in the early 1990s. Continuing to be prone to natural disasters the city was flooded by the Vardar in 1962 and then suffered considerable damage from a severe earthquake on 26 July 1963. Over 1,000 people were killed as a result of the earthquake, almost 3,000 injured, and over 100,000 were made homeless.

Nearly all of the city's beautiful 18th- and 19th-century buildings were destroyed in the earthquake, including the National Theatre and many government buildings, as well as most of the Kale Fortress. Fortunately, though, as with previous earthquakes, much of the old Turkish side of town survived. International financial aid poured into Skopje in order to help rebuild the city. The Japanese architect Kenzo Tange headed the mixed Japanese–Yugolav team which laid the plans for Skopje's reconstruction, and the result was the many concrete creations of 1960s communism that can still be seen today. Even Mother Teresa's house was razed to make way for a modern shopping centre (the Trgovski Centar).

INDEPENDENCE Skopje made the transition easily from the capital of the Federal Yugoslav Socialist Republic of Macedonia to the capital of today's Republic of Macedonia. The city livened up considerably when Skopje housed the headquarters of the NATO intervention into Kosovo in 1998 and 1999, but saw some of its own rioting during 2001 when internal conflict between the Albanian community and the Macedonian majority erupted over the lack of Albanian representation in government and other social institutions. This effectively killed off business in the old town, Čaršija, which would no longer be frequented by ethnic Macedonians from the south side of the river. It took almost ten years to reverse this trend, and Čaršija is now alive and kicking again, and *the* place to go out at night.

This upturn in business for Čaršija, some say, is just one concession gained by the minorities in the massive and overtly ethnic Macedonian urban renewal programme on the south side of the river that got under way in 2011. Skopje 2014, as it is known, is costing the country almost €100 million to build new public buildings and over 120 statues which, aside from the massive cost and lack of public consultation, are also antagonising the country's relationship with Greece (see page 148). For an individual write-up on each of the main buildings and monuments see National Theatre (page 140), *Museums and galleries* (page 144) and *Monuments and statues* (page 148). The lack of public consultation has also neatly sidestepped any debate on the geological suitability of building so many large public buildings in the centre of Skopje. The 1963 earthquake destroyed most of central Skopje and, in line with geological studies done at the time, it is the reason why Kenzo Tange did not simply rebuild the old centre.

Much has been written in the news and online about the controversy of the programme. Tim Judah's musings in *The Economist*'s blog 'Eastern Approaches' is one such source.

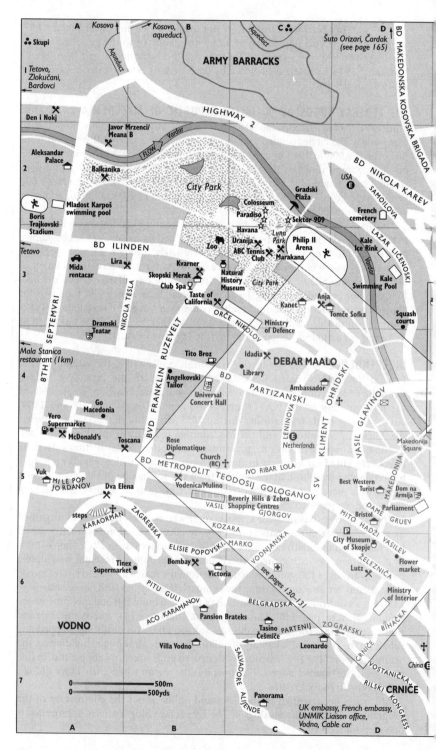

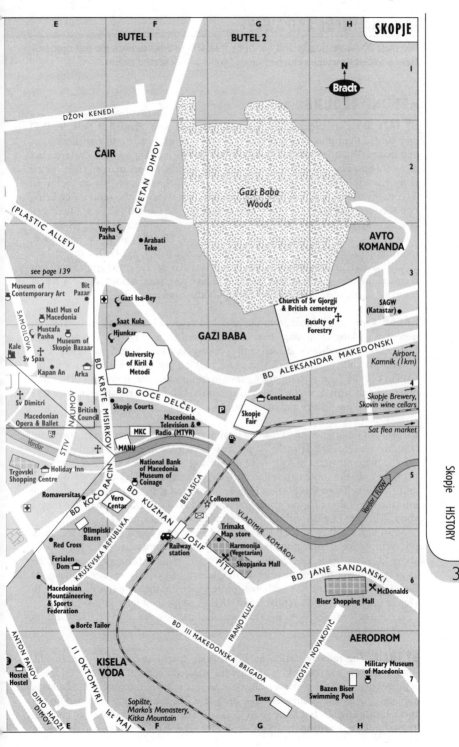

GETTING THERE AND AWAY

See page 70 for getting in and out of Skopje, where links to both the full domestic train and bus timetables can be found. Skopje is well served by bus.

GETTING AROUND

BY TAXI Taxis are plentiful but increasingly expensive. Flagfall is now 40MKD and 40MKD/km plus 5MKD/minute. Taxis come in a variety of four-door sizes and makes. You might find a few old Skodas and former Yugoslavian Zastavas, but most are now new, clean and air-conditioned models. All are marked with lighted taxi signs on the roof, and you can flag them down almost anywhere on the street. Taxi ranks can be found at the main intersections of town, the central one being opposite McDonald's on Dimitri Čupovski near the Ploštad [133 E4]. Taxis can also be ordered from any of the following telephone numbers: ⤷15152 (Naše Taxi – all yellow cabs; *www.nasetaxi.com.mk*), ⤷15157 (Lotus – all white cabs; *www.lotustransport.com*), ⤷15177, 15190, 15192, 15193, 15194, 15195. The dispatchers at⤷15157 and⤷15177 speak English. Many taxi drivers also speak good English or German, and those who do will be quick to give you their business card for repeat business. Remember to prefix with 02 if phoning from a mobile.

BY CAR Cars can be hired from the rental companies listed on page 95. You can now pay parking from your mobile phone credit via SMS (*www.parknow.mk*). Instructions are indicated at each of the parking zone boards and pay meters. Type in the zone code (eg: A3) then space and your car registration number. Send the SMS to 144144. To end your parking session, simply text the letter S to 144144. You don't need to register online to use this service, but online registration does give you your parking history and other options.

BY BUS These can get very crowded during rush hour, but they are frequent and cover a wide area. The Trimaks Skopje map has a good inset of the city bus routes. See the map on page 158 for routes to outlying villages. City bus timetables and maps for both the inner city and to outlying villages are available at www.jsp.com.mk. The **Inter Town Bus Station** [129 F6] is located at the train station where the information desk staff speak good English (⤷2466 011/313). And they also have a good website in English with all the bus timetables and prices.

Main times for key direct buses are listed in the box opposite. Not all the buses run at the weekend, and Sunday is particularly poorly serviced, so check the website above for exact times. Out-of-the-way places will require a change of buses at the local main town; for instance, buses to Oteševo or Brajčino require a change at Resen. Prices are quite low (although more expensive than the train). A single to Dojran is 410MKD and a return is 590MKD. A single to Stobi is 210MKD.

For buses from Skopje to international destinations, see page 71. There are no direct buses to Greece.

BY TRAIN The **railway station** on Bd Kuzman Josef Pitu [129 F6] (⤷3116 733, 0121 079; www. mz.com.mk) is 15 minutes' walk southeast of the Stone Bridge. It is probably one of the sorriest main stations you will come across in the Balkans, although it is as safe as anywhere else in Skopje. The information desk staff do not speak much English, but fairly good German. There are two trains a day going to Thessaloniki, one early in the morning and the other late afternoon, and there is an afternoon train to Priština (Kosovo) returning early in the morning. For train times see the tables on pages 72–3 and 74–5.

TOURIST INFORMATION

The Skopje Tourist Information Office is at Vasil Agilarski bb [133 H3] (*next to Restoran Nacional;* ☏ *3223 644;* ⊕ *08.30–16.30 daily*. Tour operators specialising in Skopje are listed on page 66. Good maps of Skopje abound, and the Trimaks map includes all the bus routes.

BUS DEPARTURES FROM SKOPJE

Berovo via Delčevo	07.30, 08.15, 12.30, 16.15
Berovo via Vinica	08.45, 09.30, 13.20, 14.15, 15.15, 16.30, 18.00
Bitola	04.15, 06.00, 09.00, 11.00, 12.30, 13.30, 14.30, 15.00, 15.30, 16.30, 17.00, 17.30, 19.00, 21.00
Debar	09.20, 12.00, 14.00, 15.15, 17.00
Delčevo	07.30, 08.15, 12.30, 15.30, 16.15, 17.15, 18.05
Dojran	08.30, 14.00, 16.00 (Nov Dojran only)
Demir Kapija	08.30, 11.00, 14.00, 15.00, 16.00, 17.30
Gevgelija	08.30, 11.00, 14.00, 16.00, 17.30, 18.00
Gostivar	At least every half hour from 05.30 until 21.30
Katlanovo Spa (Bus 53)	05.05, 06.05, 07.00, 07.30, 08.25, 09.15, 09.55, 11.00, 11.35, 12.25, 13.40, 14.15, 15.20, 15.55, 16.35, 17.40, 18.25, 19.15, 20.20
Kavadarci (Negotino)	06.00, 12.00, 13.45, 15.00, 18.00, 19.30
Kavadarci (Rosoman)	09.00, 13.00, 15.45, 17.00, 20.15
Kočani	07.30, 08.15, 08.45, 09.30, 12.30, 13.30, 14.30, 15.00, 15.45, 16.30, 18.00, 18.30, 19.30
Kratovo	07.30, 13.00, 15.30, 16.00, 16.40
Kriva Palanka	06.00, 09.00, 10.30, 11.30, 12.30, 13.20, 14.00, 15.00, 16.00, 17.00, 17.30, 18.00
Kruševo	07.45, 16.15, 16.45
Kumanovo	Every half hour from 06.00 until 21.30
Negotino	08.30, 11.00, 12.00, 14.00, 15.00, 16.00, 17.00, 17.30, 19.30
Ohrid (Kičevo)	05.30, 06.00, 06.55, 07.00, 08.00, 08.30, 09.00, 10.00, 11.00, 14.00, 14.45, 15.30, 16.00, 16.30, 17.30, 18.30, 19.00
Prilep	04.15, 06.00, 07.45, 08.30, 09.00, 11.00, 12.30, 13.30, 14.00, 14.30, 15.00, 15.30, 16.15, 16.30, 16.45, 17.00, 17.30, 18.00, 19.00, 21.00
Radoviš	06.00, 08.05, 10.00, 12.05, 13.00, 14.00, 15.00, 15.30, 16.00, 17.00, 17.30, 18.00, 19.00, 20.37
Resen	06.00, 11.00, 12.30, 13.30, 15.30, 16.30, 17.30
Štip	06.00, 07.30, 08.15, 08.50, 09.30, 10.00, 11.30, 12.05, 12.30, 13.00, 14.30, 15.00, 15.15, 16.00, 16.30, 17.00, 18.00, 19.00, 19.30
Stobi	08.30, 11.00, 14.00, 16.00, 17.30
Struga	05.30, 07.00, 08.00, 09.30, 11.00, 12.30, 12.50, 13.15, 14.00, 14.30, 14.45, 16.00, 16.10, 17.30, 19.10, 20.00
Strumica (Radoviš)	Same as Radoviš (plus 14.30, except 17.30)
Sv Nikole	11.30, 12.30, 14.30, 15.00
Tetovo	At least every half hour from 05.30 until 21.30
Veles	At least every half hour from 04.15 until 21.00

3

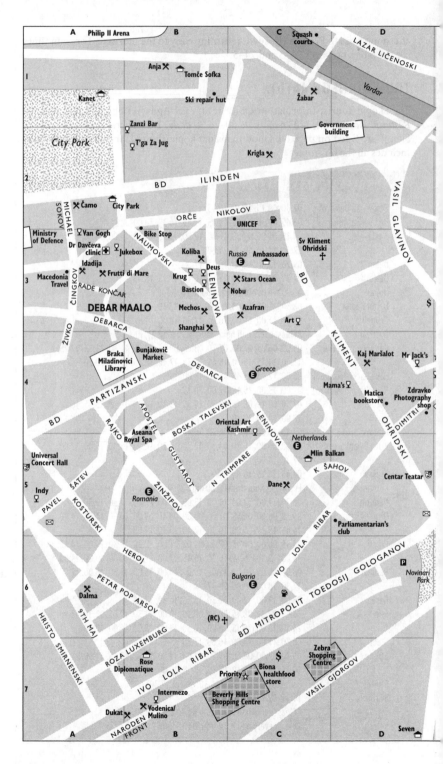

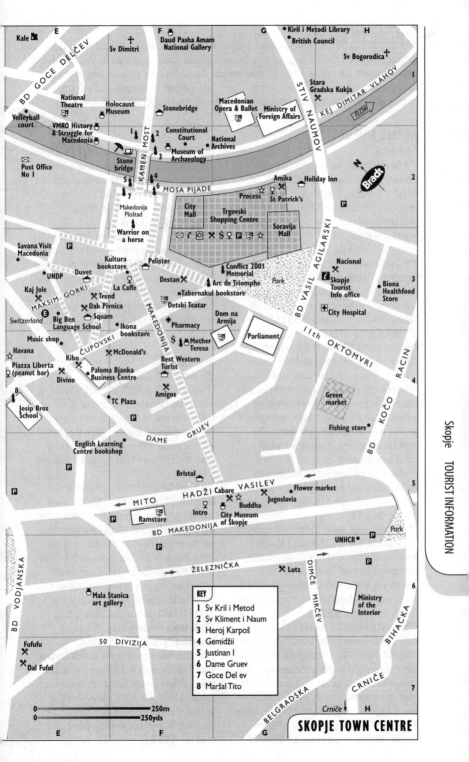

KEY

1 Sv Kril i Metod
2 Sv Kliment i Naum
3 Heroj Karpoš
4 Gemidžii
5 Justinan I
6 Dame Gruev
7 Goce Del ev
8 Maršal Tito

SKOPJE TOWN CENTRE

Skopje offers a whole range of hotels and private rooms, as well as youth hostels, and summer camping sites. If you would like to book online and no website address or email is offered below then try under 'accommodation' on www. exploringmacedonia.com, where most of these hotels offer online booking.

HOTELS AND HOSTELS
Top end

🏠 **Best Western Hotel Turist** [133 F4] (85 rooms) Gjuro Sturgar 11; ☎ 3289 111; f 3289 100; e turist@bestwestern.at; www. bestwestern-ce.com/turist. The hotel's coffee shop entrance is on the busy pedestrian street Makedonija in the centre of the city. Western 4-star standards. $$$$$

🏠 **Continental** [129 G4] (230 rooms) Bd Aleksandar Makedonski bb; ☎ 3116 599; f 3222 221; www.hotelcontinental.com.mk. A 4-star tower-block hotel. It has good conference facilities & a decent restaurant. $$$$$

🏠 **Holiday Inn** [133 G2] (178 rooms) Mosa Pijade 2; ☎ 3292 929; f 3115 503; e hiskopje@ holiday-inn.com.mk; www.holiday-inn.com/ skopje. Another 4-star hotel conveniently located near the centre of town. It is next to the Trgovski shopping centre so is very close to amenities such as restaurants, supermarkets, underground parking, pubs & the Millennium Cinema. The hotel has an excellent fitness centre, which is not open to the public. Reserve a room well in advance as the hotel is often booked with international conferences. During Aug prices can drop by up to 50% when Skopje empties for the summer. $$$$$

🏠 **Stonebridge Hotel** [133 F1] (41 rooms) Kej Dimitar Vlahov 1; ☎ 3244 900; f 3244 901; www.stonebridge-hotel.com. Opened in 2006, this top-quality hotel has an unrivalled view over the city & River Vardar from the top-floor dining room. Small pool, fitness room & very nice Turkish steam room. $$$$$

🏠 **Hotel Aleksandar Palace** [128 A2] (135 rooms) Bd Oktomvriska Revolucija; ☎ 3092 392/ 3092 200; f 309 2152; e info@aleksandarpalace. com.mk; www.aleksandarpalace.com.mk. Located by the river, on the western outskirts of town. Its restaurant is good value, has reasonable food & is open to non-residents. Its fitness centre is also open to non-residents at 380MKD per session (800MKD inc use of sauna & lukewarm

jacuzzi) & is the best available, although its layout is not the best for privacy. There is no swimming pool, but there is an Olympic-size pool next door to the Aleksandar Palace. $$$$

🏠 **Hotel Arka** [141 D4] (26 rooms) Bitpazarska 90/2; ☎ 3230 603; f 3238 781; e info@hotel-arka.com.mk; www.hotel-arka. com.mk. Modern, well maintained with good facilities for the price. Small pool on the 7th floor (also the dining area), Wi-Fi in rooms. Setting in the old town is a little bit tatty. Can be hard to find, but is signposted from Bd Krste Misirkov, or turn behind the small fountain on Bitpazarska. $$$$

Mid range

🏠 **Hotel Ambassador** [132 C3] (35 rooms) Pirinska 38; ☎ 3121 383; f 3215 729; e info@hotelambasador-sk.com.mk; www. hotelambasador-sk.com.mk. In the courtyard next to the Russian Embassy. This is the hotel with the statue of liberty on top & a couple of other Roman figures. Close to bars & restaurants. $$$$

🏠 **Hotel Bristol** [133 F5] (33 rooms) Makedonija 1; ☎ 3114 883; f 3236 556; www. makedonijaturist.com.mk. A 3-star hotel at the end of Maršal Tito with an older feel to it, this was the original meeting place for the Skopje International Rotary Club starting in 1924 (now held in the Hotel Aleksandar Palace). Owned by the same company as the Jadran below, it is one of the original old-time hotels of Skopje, & slightly better kept than the Jadran. $$$$

🏠 **Kamnik Hunting Lodg** (15 rooms) Kamnik bb; ☎ 2523 522; f 2580 540; e info@kamnik.com.mk; www.kamnik.com.mk. A great restaurant (if you like game) & modern rooms. Shooting range downstairs, tennis courts outside, fitness gym, & it is also the meeting location of the Wine Knights! For more on the restaurant & directions see under *Where to eat* on page 137. $$$$

🏠 **Hotel Pelister** [133 F3] (6 rooms) Above the restaurant of the same name in the town square; 📞3239 584; e contact@pelisterhotel. com.mk; www.pelisterhotel.com.mk. Well furnished, with prime views of the Warrior on the Horse. **$$$$**

🏠 **Rose Diplomatique** [132 B7] (8 rooms) Roza Luxemburg; 📞3135 469; f 3129 058; e info@rosediplomatique.com.mk; www. rosediplomatique.com.mk. A very nice small hotel with an attractive interior & a good restaurant (for residents only). Buffet b/fast. The hotel is often full so book well in advance. **$$$$**

🏠 **Victoria** [128 B6] (11 rooms) Slave Delovski 18; 📞3107 600; f 3107 610; e hotelvictoriaskopje@yahoo.com; www. hotelvictoria.com.mk. Nicely furnished new hotel in the quiet foothills of Vodno. Free transfer to & from the airport. **$$$$**

🏠 **Villa Vodno** [128 B7] (12 rooms) Partenij Zografski 79a; 🗸f 3177 711; e villavodno@ t-home.mk; www.villavodno.com.mk. An immaculate house with spacious apts in the foothills of Vodno. Fireplace downstairs, fitness machines available; airport pick-up & drop-off for €15. **$$$$**

🏠 **Leonardo** [128 C7] (9 rooms) Partenij Zografski 19; 📞3177 517; e info@hotel-leonardo. com.mk; www.hotel-leonardo.com.mk. Small hotel in the quiet foothills of Vodno. Small garden, buffet b/fast. **$$$**

🏠 **Tomče Sofka** [132 B1] (17 rooms) Jordan Hadžikonstantinov Džinot 14, City Park, near the stadium; 📞3117 250, 3127 293; e contact@ tomcesofka.com.mk; www.tomcesofka.com.mk. Set on a bustling strip of cafés & restaurants near the river. **$$$**

Budget

🏠 **Ferialen Dom** [129 E6] (26 rooms) Prolet 25; 📞3114 849; f 3235 029; e hotelfsm@ hotmail.com; www.macedonian-yha.org. The only true youth hostel in Skopje offering discounts to Hostelling International members. Not far from the train station or the centre of town. Clean, tidy en-suite rooms. A lively restaurant downstairs. **$$$**

🏠 **Kanet** [132 A1] (13 rooms) Jordan Hadžikonstantinov Džinot 20; 🗸f 3238 353; e contact@hotelkanet.com.mk; www. hotelkanet.com.mk. This clean basic hotel is located on the edge of the city park near the river, bars & restaurants. **$$$**

🏠 **Hotel Kapištec** (11 rooms) Mile Pop Jordanov 3; 📞3081 424/425; e kapystec@ t-home.mk; www.hotel-kapistec.com.mk. Clean & quiet. **$$$**

🏠 **Hotel Seven** [132 D7] (9 rooms) Vodjanska 28; 📞3176 905; e contact@hotel7.com.mk; www.hotel7.com.mk. Basic rooms, directly opposite the entrance to the main hospital. Secure parking available. B/fast can be brought up from Žužu bakery downstairs. **$$$**

🏠 **Hotel Square** [133 E3] (8 rooms) Nikola Vapcarov 2, 6th Floor (take the lift to the 5th & walk the final floor); 📞3225 090; f 3225 077; e hotelsquare@mt.net.mk; www.hotelsquare. com.mk. Nicely furnished small rooms with a good view over the square. **$$$**

🏠 **Hotel Tasino Češmiče** [128 C6] (59 rooms) Belgradska 28; 📞3177 333; f 3176 736; e tascinocesmice@t-home.mk; www.tasino.com. mk. A 3-star hotel at the foot of Vodno Mountain, looking more like a train station than a hotel. Quiet setting. **$$$**

🏠 **Hostel Hostel** [129 E7] (4 rooms & 4 dorms) Anton Popov 18; 📞3222 321; e hostel@ hostel.com.mk; www.hostel.com.mk. Cheap & cheerful, including free tea & coffee. LGBT friendly. **$$**

🏠 **Hotel RM** [141 C4] (10 rooms) Jorgandžiska 12/14; 📞3117 133, 3131 288; f 3131 239; m 070 252 751; e contact@hotelrm. mk; www.hotelrm.mk. Right in the old town next to the *bezisten* old covered market. Small, old & tidy. **$$**

PRIVATE ROOMS AND PANSIONS If you would prefer to stay in a private room in order to get a more Balkan feel to your visit then this can be arranged through the Skopje Tourist Information Office (page 131). Make sure you ask for something near the centre of the city otherwise you may have a long walk. Private rooms start at 1,200MKD or €10 per person per night, excluding breakfast, and usually offer shared bathrooms.

Bed and breakfast-type lodges or *pansions* include:

🏠 **Mlin Balkan** [132 G5] (4 rooms) Leninova 79; ✆02 3110 635. A 10min walk from the centre. Fully renovated. **$$$**

🏠 **Pansion Brateks** [128 B6] (3 rooms) Aco Karamanov 3a; ✆3176 606; m 070 243 232; www.brateks.com.mk. Popular & therefore often full. A 20min walk from the centre & set at the

foot of Mt Vodno among the houses of the rich & the diplomats, giving it an airy upmarket feel. German is spoken & only a little English. **$$$**

🏠 **Vuk Skopje** [128 A5] Mile Pop Jordanov 1; ✆02 3081 426/427. A 20min walk from the centre. Clean & basic. **$$$**

CAMPING
⛺ **Autocamp Bellevue** At the Hotel Belleview, site is 5km east of Skopje on the way to the airport; Ul 32, br24; ✆2572 277; f 2572 276;

e bellevue-skopje@bestwestern.at; www. bellevue.com.mk. **$**

✖ WHERE TO EAT

Traditional food abounds in the city and, slowly, there is some variety moving in too, including Japanese, Chinese and Indian, as well as Italian, Greek and Turkish. For an overview of Macedonian cuisine see *Eating and drinking* on page 99.

Eating out is still quite cheap, with a lunch dish often as little as 150–200MKD, and evening meals going up to 1,000MKD or more if you eat on the expensive side. Almost any menu in Skopje will appear in English as well as Macedonian. All restaurants are now non-smoking indoors, and in the summer there is an abundance of outdoor seating. With its concentration of eating establishments and proximity to the centre, Debar Maalo is the place to eat out, although Čaršija is fast catching up.

Most restaurants (unless otherwise stated) open at 12.00 and stay open until midnight. Some restaurants open at 08.00 for breakfast, especially of the cooked variety, such as at **Mecho's**, **Trend**, and **Pivnica** (all detailed below). Turkish cuisine can be found mostly in Čaršija, the old Turkish side of town. *Kebapci* at any of these restaurants is very good especially if accompanied with grilled red peppers and a beer. Unless otherwise listed, all restaurants are open seven days a week.

ČARŠIJA
✖ **New Orleans Fish & Jazz** [141 C4] Čaršija bb (opposite Turist); ✆3224 560. Better at jazz than fish, the jazz being live every Fri, Sat & Sun evening. There's not just fish on the menu, & it's certainly a welcome & varied offer in the old town. Great setting with a cosy upstairs for the winter. **$$$**

✖ **Pivnica An** [141 B5] Inside the old Turkish inn of Kapan in the old town; ✆3212 111. An atmospheric setting; offers a few vegetarian dishes. **$$$**

✖ **Turist** [141 C4] At the north entrance to Kapan An, where the bread is always grilled with smotherings of *kepabci* dripping & plenty of *vegeta* seasoning. **$**

DEBAR MAALO
✖ **Koliba** [132 B3] Naum Naumovski 62; ✆3101 017; www.koliba.mk. A steakhouse. Done well or rare, as you wish. **$$$$**

✖ **Nobu** [132 C3] Leninova 29; ✆3121 123. Sushi lovers can only hope that this place will stay open & expand its menu. Sake & salmon abound, but *tobiko, uni* & other rarer delicacies might take some years to tempt the Macedonian palate. Also serves some good stir-fries. **$$$$**

✖ **Shanghai** [132 B3] Leninova 36; ✆3228 100. Serves excellent Shanghainese food. Most of the rest of the food is imported from China, & the tofu is exquisitely fresh & made on the premises. Take-away service available. Try their salt & pepper fried prawns, fish or pork for something truly Chinese. **$$$$**

✘ **Azafran** [132 C3] Naum Naumovski Borče 33a; ☏3221 907; www.azafranmk.com; ⊕ 11.00–24.00 Mon–Sat, 12.00–24.00 Sun. A welcome & authentic change, serving tapas, paella & other favourites. $$$

✘ **Frutti di Mare** [132 A3] Rade Končar 5; ☏3132 145; ⊕ Mon–Sat. Specialises in Dalmatian & Mediterranean seafood dishes. $$$

✘ **Taste of California** [128 B3] Orce Nikolov 134; ☏3214 008; ⊕ 12.00–24.00 Mon–Sat. From Californian chefs, a great mix of Tex-Mex & fusion. Very good salads, with a variety of real dressings, & to-die-for desserts. Just like in California. Also one of the few places you can get Alchemist *rakija* (see pages 306–7). $$$

✘ **Čamo** [132 A2] Mihail Sokov 6a, down a small garden path to the right of Van Gogh; ☏02 316 1130. Čamo is an unassuming place that is so popular you may need a reservation during peak lunchtimes. Try their *sarma*, braised tongue & *pavlaka* (sour cream cheese). $$

✘ **Dane** [132 C5] Božin Stijkov bb, opposite the Dutch Embassy; ☏3229 457. Dane serves very good *pleckavica* (hamburger patties) & *meso vo salamura* (pork preserved in salt vats). $$

✘ **Mechos** [132 B3] Leninova 38 (next to the Chinese restaurant); ☏3166 659. Good pizzas & cooked b/fasts. The rest of the menu is average. $$

REST OF SKOPJE

✘ **Dalma** [132 A6] 227 Ulica (cnr with Petar Poparsov); ☏3246 616; www.dalma.com.mk; ⊕ 10.00–24.00 Mon–Sat, 13.00–24.00 Sun. Very good Dalmatian dishes in a small exclusive atmosphere. Superb fresh octopus (best eaten with truffle oil), lamb chops & salt baked fish. $$$$

✘ **Kvarner** [128 B3] Andon Dukov 27; ☏3090 752. Excellent Istrian seafood flown in fresh. Try their fish carpaccio, sea bass & Malvazia white wine. $$$$

✘ **Mulino** [132 B7] Ivo Lola Ribar bb; ☏3232 877. Vodenica in Macedonian, this restaurant sports a decorative waterwheel & fishpond. Very popular with government & ambassadors. If you want to eat during the popular eating hours after 20.00 you may need to phone in advance to reserve a table. $$$$

✘ **Toscana** [128 A5] Ivo Lola Ribar 72a; ☏307 9994. By far the best Italian cuisine in town as recommended by Italians. Small & personable.

The head Italian-trained chef & owner, Vlado, will recommend his freshest pasta of the day & latest culinary delights, & they also do a mean tagliata à la rosmarin. $$$$

✘ **Amigos** [133 F4] Maršal Tito/Makedonija 11; ☏3228 699. Less authentic Mexican, but a wide variety of cocktails for a very good price in a popular location. Also has a stall upstairs in Ramstore. $$$

✘ **Amika** [133 G2] Above the Irish Pub; ☏3113 488. Serves good quiche Lorraine, tagliatelle pesto Genovese & French onion soup. $$$

✘ **Anja** [132 B1] ☏3161 377; www.anja.com.mk. Less traditional, more pizza-pasta. Popular place in the park. $$$

✘ **Balkanika** [128 A2] Oktomvriska Revolucija 24 (as if heading for the Aleksandar Palace but in the park); ☏3073 712. Nice outdoor seating. Best *pastrmalija* in town. $$$

✘ **Dab Pivnica** [133 E3] Maksim Gorki 1; ☏3221 173; e info@pivnica.com.mk; ⊕ 08.00–24.00. Just off the main square & would be easy to miss if you were not to look for the 2 huge dark brown wooden doors. Don't miss a mixed platter of their cold creamed starters (*meze*), Parma ham & chunks of Parmesan cheese, with a side basket of their delicious sesame-seed pizza-bread strips. This is often enough for a meal on its own, but they have lots of other excellent dishes including aubergine & mozzarella pizza, mixed grills & an excellent rack of lamb ribs. $$$

✘ **Dukat** [132 B7] Teodosij Gologanov 79; ☏3211 011. Specialises in local fish & traditional dishes. $$$

✘ **Dva Elena (Two Deers)** [128 A5] Zagrebska 31; ☏3082 382. An excellent steakhouse, replete with stuffed bear. $$$

✘ **Kamnik** Kamnik bb; ☏2523 522; www.kamnik.com.mk. Hidden in Avtokomanda district; turn immediately before the Lukoil petrol station on the way from the airport into town. Lots of stuffed animal trophies deck the walls. Serves wild boar sausages, Macedonian venison, rabbit bechamel stew & more. Try their cold cut sausages, salamis & hams for a range of game choices. Also has a wide choice of Macedonian & foreign wines. $$$

✘ **Lira** [128 A3] Nikola Tesla 11; ☏3061 726; www.lyra.com.mk. Excellent traditional live music every evening. Fireplace & patio. Good lamb in a cream sauce. $$$

✖ **Makedonska Kukja**   Bd Mitropolit
Teodosij Golaginov bb, opposite the Alumina
factory; ☎3296 415; m 070 208 519; www.
makedonskakuka.com. Traditional Macedonian
décor & food; live music in the evenings. $$$

✖ **Stara Gradska Kukja (Old City
House)**   [133 H1] Pajko Maalo 14, opposite the
east side of the Macedonian National Theatre;
☎3131 376. This beautifully renovated old-style
Macedonian house from 1836 is atmospheric,
complete with intricate wooden ceiling &
traditional food. $$$

✖ **Stars Ocean**   [132 C3] Pirinska 35; ☎3228
337. Authentic Chinese food, very reasonably
priced & fairly popular. $$$

✖ **Tomče Sofka**   [132 B1] ☎3117 250. Good
traditional food & a small hotel upstairs. $$$

✖ **Aladin**   [133 G2] Trgovski Centar, 2nd
Floor; ☎3232 002; ⊕ 10.00–24.00 Mon–Sat,
14.00–24.00 Sun. This is the favourite Um Zina
of old. Excellent Arabic dishes in an Aladinesque
setting. $$

✖ **Da Gino's**   [133 G2] Trgovski Centar, 2nd
Floor, next door to Aladin; ☎3121 109. This place
offers the best pizzas, made in true Italian style.
Impressive fresh seafood platter, squid ink pasta
& very good beef carpaccio. $$

✖ **Divino**   [133 E4] Dame Gruev 7; ☎3296
588. Buffet style & reasonable quality for a
decent price. Serves mostly traditional foods,
sandwiches, soup, desserts & drinks. Nice seating
area. Conveniently located. $$

✖ **Javor Mrzenci**   [128 A2] Signposted as
Meana B on Bd Oktomvriski Revolucija, near the
Aleksandar Palace; ☎3097 070. Small & local.
Very good lamb chops. $$

✖ **Kaj Jole**   [133 E3] Maksim Gorki bb;
☎3220 529. This is the hangout of the
Macedonian Writers' Association. Its basic décor
& unassuming signage (Jole is written in Cyrillic
above the entrance at the street, then take the
2nd door on the left down the corridor) belie its
good, traditional food. $$

✖ **Kaj Maršalot**   [132 D4] Bd Kliment Ohridski;
☎3223 829. Decked out in true Yugonostalgia
with busts of Tito & waiters in red pioneer
scarves. Traditional music & food add to the
atmosphere. Great full cooked b/fasts. $$

✖ **Kibo**   [133 E4] Vasil Glavinov bb, Paloma
Bjanka business centre, 2nd Floor; ☎3133 535.
Good salad bar, hearty soups, fried squid, apple

strudel & fresh sweet beetroot juice (*džus od
cvekot*). $$

✖ **Krigla**   [132 C2] Ohridski Kliment 8, cnr of
Ilinden; ☎3117 869. National restaurant. Nice
atmosphere. $$

✖ **Lutz**   [133 G6] Železnička bb (noticeable
by the smoke & steam pouring out of the coke-
stove chimney by the front door); ☎3110 306.
It serves particularly impressive *ražnič* (skewered
meats & vegetables) on a small sword, which takes
about 40mins to cook, so make sure you order a
starter to stave off the hunger while wafts of your
sizzling *ražnič* tantalise your taste buds. Also to be
recommended is their thinly sliced *džigr* (liver).
Fried to perfection in local herbs & seasonings, it is
like liver you will never have eaten in an English-
speaking country! No frills, but the real McCoy. $$

✖ **Mala Stanica**   [128 A4] Moskovska 26;
☎3061 024. Run by the chefs of Macedonia's 1st
president, the food here is exceptionally good,
especially for the price. Richard Gere ate here when
filming for *Hunting Party*, & his photo is on the wall
as you enter. Try *tikvica meze* (courgette spread) to
start, & *sutljaš* (rice pudding cake) for dessert. $$

✖ **McDonald's**   [133 F4] Dimitri Čupovski 13;
☎3130 131. Also on Jane Sandanski at Aerodrom
& on Bd Metropolit Teodisij Gologanov next to
the Vero hypermarket. If you're desperate there's
always the familiar double cheeseburger with
large fries & Coke. Ivo Ribar Lola has a kids' play
area & a drive-in. $$

✖ **Nacional**   [133 H3] Vasil Agilarski, opposite
the park by the Trgovski Centar; ☎3214 200.
Has excellent pizza bread served as a big domed
spaceship accompanied by live elevator music.
Lovely outdoor patio. $$

✖ **Pelister**   [133 F3] On the main square;
☎3112 482. Lots of outside seating from which
to observe the square & even in the winter the
glass-fronted restaurant offers lots of sunlit
areas as well as upper seating in a more cosy
atmosphere. Has an excellent salad bar of some
of the best Italian antipasti. The owner has 2
other restaurants, Dal Fufol [133 E7] & a fast-food
version Fufufu [133 E7], both on Vodnjanska St.
$$

✖ **St Patrick's**   [133 G2] Trgovski Centar, ground
floor (facing the river); ☎3220 431. Aside from
Guinness, this 1st of the Irish pubs to come to
Skopje, has a surprisingly large menu of non-
Balkan dishes, including stir-fries & curries. $$

✗ **Trend** [133 E3] Ploštad Makedonija, Nikola Vapčarov 2; ✆3132 425; ⊕ 08.00–04.00. As its name suggests, this is one of *the* places to be seen. Modern menu, 3 b/fast choices & lots of cocktails. $$

✗ **Žabar (Frog)** [133 C1] Kej 13 Noemvri bb; ✆3132 411. The only restaurant actually overlooking the Vardar River. Good spare ribs (*rebra*). No frog! $$

✗ **Destan** [133 F3] 11th Oktomvri bb, next to the Triumphal Arch. Only serves *kebapci*, which nonetheless are acclaimed for their adherence to a special family recipe handed down over several generations. $

VEGETARIAN Only **Harmonija** [133 G6] is dedicated to vegetarian food in Skopje. Some places, such as **Pelister** [133 F3], **Kibo** [133 E4], **Divino** [133 E4] and **Dab Pivnica** [133 E3], also have good salad bars and vegetarian dishes. **Pivnica An** [141 B5] in Čaršija offer a few vegetarian plates, and most *meze* choices will be vegetarian. A lot of Italian places will have non-meat pizzas and pastas.

✗ **Harmonija** [133 G6] Skopjanka Mall 37; ✆2460 985; ⊕ Mon–Sat. Offers a feast of macrobiotic meals. The owner & cook, Tanja, earned her degree in macrobiotic cuisine in the US & is able to give you a dietary consultation on appointment. $$$

CAFÉ BARS, WINE BARS, COFFEE SHOPS AND TEA HOUSES Skopje's most popular place now is Čaršija old town, which surpasses the still popular strip from the old railway station and current Museum of Skopje [133 G5] along Makedonija pedestrian area to the café bars on the riverside ground floor of the Trgovski Centar [133 G2]. The cafés along the pedestrian area often sport large comfortable armchairs outside under big shady umbrellas to help you while away a summer afternoon.

♀ **Mr Jack's** [132 D4] Partizanska Odredi 3; ✆3231 999. A true Irish bar, as even the Irish in Skopje would claim, but hard to find back off the main road at the bottom of a high-rise complex. Pleasant, relaxing & welcoming.

♀ **Oriental Art Kashmir** [132 C4] Cnr of Nicola Trimpare & Leninova. A bohemian theme with intimate seating cubicles facing a small fountain in the middle of the bar.

♀ **Orient House** [141 C4] Podgrage bb. Old town bohemian, very relaxed. Good *salep* (wild orchid root drink) sprinkled with chocolate.

♀ **Piazza Liberta** [133 E4] Dimitri Čupovski 24; ⊕ 08.00–24.00. Also known as Kikiriki, meaning 'peanut', due to the free peanuts served with your drinks, the shells of which are simply thrown on the floor. Old reading-room atmosphere with shelves filled with books & big upstairs windows that look out onto the street. Named after the square that used to be here before the 1963 earthquake.

♀ **Tito Broz** [128 B4] Partizanska bb, opposite the Universala Sala. Nothing Yugonostalgic about this place, which styles itself on a Starbucks-type atmosphere & menu with long flavoured coffees, hot chocolate (not the pudding type), cookies & cakes. Wi-Fi available for the addicted.

♀ **Vinoteka Temov** [141 B4] Gradište 1a, Stara Čaršija; ✆3212 779; ⊕ 11.00–01.00. At last a quaint wine bar in the old town, serving a wide variety of Macedonia's own finest wines as well as an extensive range of wines from abroad. Live music is played most evenings, including traditional *chalgia* on Thu.

ENTERTAINMENT AND NIGHTLIFE

Despite its small size, but being the capital, Skopje has a choice of theatre, dance, concerts and cinema, as well as pubs and nightclubs. The Skopje Tourist Information booklet, available free every month from many travel agencies and hotels, lists a full calendar of events in the city, as well as many useful addresses and telephone numbers.

THEATRES AND CONCERT HALLS

🎭 **Detski Teatr** [133 F3] Dimitri Čupovski 4; ✆3222 619

🎭 **Dom na Armija (Army Hall)** [133 G4] Makedonija bb; ✆3118 450. Holds classical concerts once a week on Thu at 20.00 except in Jul, Aug & Sep.

🎭 **Dramski Teatar** [128 A4] Šekspirova 15; ✆3063 453; www.dramskiteatar.com.mk

🎭 **Macedonian National Theatre** [133 E1] Centar Teatar, Kliment Ohridski; ✆3164 667; e contact@mnt.com.mk; www.mnt.com.mk. Hosts modern drama & plays. The theatre is due to move into the new reconstruction of the old Officers Club, which is being built on Evrejsko Maalo opposite the Holocaust Museum.

🎭 **Macedonian Opera Ballet** [133 G1] Quay Dimitar Vlahov; ✆3118 451; e biletara@mob. com.mk; www.mob.com.mk. Stages opera & ballet.

🎭 **Theatre of National Minorities** Nikola Martinoski 41, Čaršija; ✆3296 583. Holds plays in Albanian & Turkish.

🎭 **Univerzalna Sala** [132 A5] Partizanski Odredi bb; ✆3245 615; e info@univerzalna.com. mk; www.univerzalna.com.mk. Holds concerts 2 or 3 times a week, both classical & modern jazz/ rock. Skopje's jazz festival is held here for a week every Oct.

CINEMAS Skopje has several small cinemas.

🎬 **Dom na Armija** [133 G4] Maršal Tito bb; ✆3118 450. Shows films on a projector screen in a large auditorium. All films are screened in their original language & tend to come out a few months after their release in their country of origin.

🎬 **Frosina Cinema** Youth Culture Centre, Quay Dimitar Vlahov; ✆3115 805. Often shows art or foreign movies, usually a different one every evening at 20.00.

🎬 **Millennium** [133 G2] Trgovski Centar, 1st Floor; ✆3120 389; www.kinomilenium.mk. The biggest & best at 150MKD.

🎬 **Ramstore** [133 F5] Mito Hadzi Vasilev; ✆3178 030. Has 2 small new screens also at 150MKD.

NIGHTLIFE

Bars Many of the café bars mentioned above are popular all through the evening and into the small hours. Other tried and tested bars that draw a faithful crowd are:

🍸 **Bastion** [132 B3] Pirinska 43; ✆3223 636; ⊕ 08.00–24.00 Mon–Thu, 08.00–01.00 Fri & Sat, 10.00–24.00 Sun. Opposite Nobu sushi bar. Popular place & sometimes the hangout of the film director Milčo Mančevski.

🍸 **Café Art** [132 C3] Partizanski; ⊕ 20.00–01.00. Has laid-back music & old hits accompanying interesting artistic installations by the owner Malinski.

🍸 **Damar** [141 B4] Gradište bb, Čaršija old town. Next to Vinoteka Temov, this laid-back hip café bar opens late & has a tiny little enclosed 'garden' at the back.

☆ **Havana Club** [133 E4] ⊕ 20.00–03.00. In the city park. Very popular in the summer with large outdoor area.

🍸 **Jukebox** [132 A3] Orče Nikolov 99; ⊕ 20.00–03.00. Small & cosy with live jazz on Thu night, & dedicated DJs most nights. Named after the original 1940s jukebox still to be found there.

☆ **La Kanja** [141 B5] 50 Divizija 33, Čaršija old town; ⊕ 21.00–02.00. Holds live gigs most nights.

🍸 **Mama's** [132 B4] Kliment Ohridski 60; ✆3239 120; ⊕ 10.00–24.00 Sun–Thu, 10.00–01.00 Fri & Sat. Wonderful blues & jazz bar with comfortable seating & live piano or jazz trios providing an atmosphere in which you can still (just about) talk to accompanying friends.

🍸 **Marakana** [128 C3] City Park; ⊕ 21.00–04.00, restaurant downstairs ⊕ 08.00–24.00. Live jazz upstairs every evening after 22.00.

🍸 **Pasha** [141 B4] Gradište bb, Čaršija old town; ✆3224 914; ⊕ 12.00–02.00. Plays Salsa on Sat. Very popular & spills out onto the street. Great cocktails.

🍸 **Van Gogh** [132 A3] Michel Sokov 74; ⊕ 09.00–24.00 Sun–Thu, 09.00–01.00 Fri &

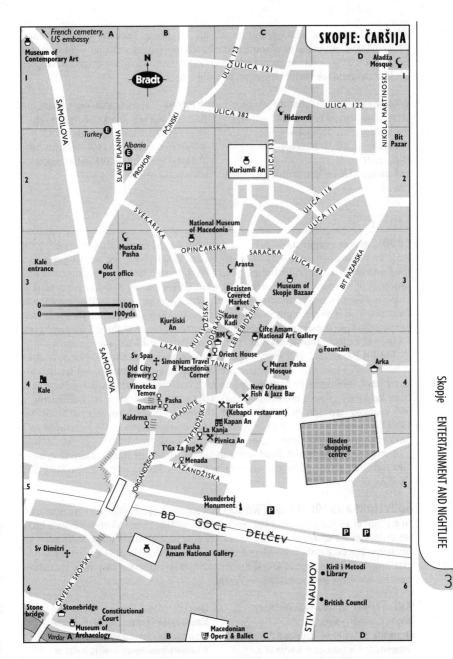

French cemetery, US embassy
Museum of Contemporary Art
SAMOILOVA
N
Bradt
ULICA 123
ULICA 121
ULICA 382
Hidaverdi
Aladža Mosque
ULICA 122
NIKOLA MARTINOSKI
Bit Pazar
Turkey
SLAVE PLANINA
PROHOR
PČINSKI
Albania
Kuršumli An
ULICA 133
ULICA 116
ULICA 111
SVEKARSKA
National Museum of Macedonia
Mustafa Pasha
OPINČARSKA
SARAČKA
ULICA 183
BIT PAZARSKA
Kale entrance
Old post office
Arasta
Bezisten Covered Market
Museum of Skopje Bazaar
0   100m
0   100yds
Kjuršiski An
MUTAVDŽISKA
PODGRAGJE
Kose Kadi
LEB LEBIDŽISKA
Čifte Amam
National Art Gallery
RM
Orient House
Fountain
LAZAR
TANEV
Arka
Sv Spas
Simonium Travel & Macedonia Corner
Murat Pasha Mosque
SAMOILOVA
Old City Brewery
Vinoteka Temov
New Orleans Fish & Jazz Bar
Kale
Damar
Pasha
GRADIŠTE
Turist (Kebapci restaurant)
Kaldrma
Kapan An
La Kanja
TAFTADŽISKA
Pivnica An
Ilinden shopping centre
T'Ga Za Jug
Menada
KAZANDŽISKA
JORGANDŽISKA
Skenderbej Monument
P
BD GOCE DELČEV
P
P
Sv Dimitri
Daud Pasha Amam National Gallery
CRVENA SKOPSKA
Kiril i Metodi Library
STIV NAUMOV
British Council
Stone bridge
Stonebridge
Constitutional Court
Museum of Archaeology
Vardar
Macedonian Opera & Ballet

Skopje ENTERTAINMENT AND NIGHTLIFE

3

Sat. Another bar frequented by Mančevski when he is in town. Offers salsa on Wed & mixed/gay nights on Sun. Quiet setting spilling out onto the cobblestone road.

Clubs Some of the bigger clubs listed below move outdoors to the city park in the summer. Colosseum, Havana and Paradiso are inside the Luna Park, and Sektor 909 is behind the Gradski Plaža river beach. Unless listed, the clubs did not have a website at time of writing, but are all on Facebook. They are generally open 22.30–04.00 daily. For a list of some of the bands touring see www.password.mk; for tickets to tour concerts see www.mktickets.mk. For more information on Skopje's lively club scene see skclubbing.com, or clubbersguide.mk.

☆ **Colosseum** [128 C2] Behind the post office at the railway station. It's the longest-running club in Skopje, & is a huge space.

☆ **Havana** [128 C3] Dimitri Čupovski near Piazza Liberta

☆ **Paradiso** [128 C2] Maksim Gorki above Trend Café

☆ **Process** [133 G3] Gradski Centar, ground floor, next door to St Patrick's pub; ℡ 3215 476; m 075 414 004; e contact@process.com.mk; www.process.com.mk; ⊕ 23.00–04.00 Tue–Sun

☆ **Sektor 909** [128 C2] Bd Kliment Ohridski; www.secktor909.com

SHOPPING

FOOD The **Vero supermarket** chain (at the huge Vero Centre shopping mall [128 A5]) and **Ramstore** [133 F5] on Mito Hadzi Vasilev have the widest ranges of food available in Skopje, including ginger, basil, fresh limes, mint and horseradish sauce, fresh seafood (from Greece), and Jamie Oliver sauces. Another supermarket chain is **Tinex** [129 G7], which along with Vero, takes all major credit cards. Local fresh produce is best bought from the big fresh markets either at the Bit Pazar (see below), the **Green market** [133 H4] on the western corner of Kočo Racin and 11th Oktomvri, or **Bunjakovač market** [132 B4] on Partizanski just after Leninova.

The **Bit Pazar** [141 D2] is the biggest outdoor market in Skopje. Not only does it have fresh vegetables, fruit, meat products, fish, spices, pulses and tea, it also has a large ironmongery section and, in fact, you can buy almost anything there. Now held every day, it used to be held on Tuesdays and Fridays only, following a 600-year-old tradition, being first held by the monks of the Monastery of Sv Gjorgi Gorga. The monastery no longer exists but the market is still in the same spot and has expanded over the former grounds of the monastery.

There are several **health food** stores in Skopje under the Biona chain. One is on Gradski Zid (℡ 3166 309), and another in Beverly Hills shopping centre [132 C7] (℡ 3223 327).

SOUVENIRS AND LOCAL CRAFTWARE Conveniently, many souvenirs are now sold in a number of shops around the town, although these are still sometimes a little obscure. Čaršija is the best place to get genuine locally made handicrafts such as leather slippers, hand-embroidered cloths, musical instruments and ethnic-style clothing. Šutka (see page 164) is the place to order lavish Roma costumes. Ramstore has two souvenir stores, Ikona and Vivaldi.

Balkan Corner Ul 106 no 42. Handmade filigree & jewellery shop.

Dzambaz Ul 106 no 34. Traditional shoes & souvenirs from wood, copper & terracotta.

Dzelo Stara Čaršija 39 (Gold St). Handmade filigree & silver jewellery.

Hemboj Debarska 3. Wool & cotton carpets & traditional clothes.

Kvalitet Gradishte 19, opposite Murat Pasa Mosque. *Opinci* – traditional shoes.

Lisec Ul 106 no 2. *Opinci*.

Macedonian Corner [141 B4] Podgrade 76; www.macedoniancorner.mk. Traditional & handmade souvenirs, T-shirts, books on Macedonia & Macedonian films & music.

Sonce Gradiste 28 (opposite Kapan An entrance). Traditional souvenirs.

CLOTHES Skopje is awash with shoe shops and there are also plenty of clothes shops. Most of these products are mass produced in China and imported. The **Trgovski Centar** [133 G2], **City Mall** [133 F2], **Soravia**, **Ramstore** [133 F5] and the pedestrian area linking these main shopping malls offer the likes of Benetton, Wolfords, Hugo Boss and Mango. Newer shopping malls have opened at **Vero Centre** [128 A5] (which has an enormous Jumbo Land full of kids stuff) and **Zebra** [132 C7], and are to be followed soon by even more. Local **tailors** in the old town are still cheap especially for repairs and copying, although the choice of materials from which to make clothes is not the best. For a top-class men's **tailor** used by the diplomatic community try **Borče** on 11 Oktomvri in Kisela Voda [129 F6] (✆ *3133 065;* m *075 230 061, 070 278 585;* e *apostolovzoran@yahoo.com*). He offers prompt service and a wide choice of materials. You can expect to pay €100–140 for a two- or three-piece suit. Women's suits are also available. Angelkovski [128 B4], used by the first president of Macedonia, pays good attention to detail and is slightly more expensive, although his choice of materials is not as wide as Borče's.

BOOKS The largest bookshop chain in Macedonia is **Ikona Books**. There are three stores in Skopje, on the ground floor of the Ramstore [133 F5], the Biser shopping centre beyond the train station and at Dimitri Čupovski 22 opposite McDonald's [133 F4]. They carry an extensive range of English books, as well as Bradt and other travel guides.

OTHER PRACTICALITIES

TELEPHONE The telephone centre located in the main post office, Post Office No 1 [133 E2] (*Orce Nikolov bb;* ✆ *3105 105;* e *contact@posta.com.mk;* ⊕ *07.00– 17.30 Mon–Sat, 07.00–14.30 Sun; www.posta.com.mk*), is open 24 hours. Calls at the post office or at telephone kiosks on the street need to be made either with tokens or using a pre-paid phone card. Both can be purchased from post offices and newspaper stands. Mobile phone cards are 250MKD, including several hundred minutes and can be bought at T-Mobile or One in the Ramstore.

INTERNET Internet cafés are a dying breed, but your hotel may have a computer and internet you can access. Contact Café on the top floor of the Trgovski shopping centre [133 G2] charges 120MKD for one hour. Wi-Fi is available in most cafés.

WHAT TO SEE

SUGGESTED ONE-DAY TOURS If you are in Skopje for just one day and do not have your own transport, the following itinerary will give you a good overview: Kale early in the morning before it gets too hot – Sveti Spas – Mustafa Pasha Mosque – Turkish tea in the old town – Čifte Amam Gallery – Suli An – Kuršumli An – Bit Pazar – *kebapci* lunch outside Kapan An – one of the new museums (Museum of Archaeology, Museum of the Macedonian Struggle or the Jewish Holocaust Museum) when they're completed and open to the public – cable car up to Vodno for a view of the city – dinner at Dab Pivnica or Pivnica An.

If you have a car, or can afford a taxi or guided tour, then a trip on to the Monastery of Sv Pantelejmon and back via Lake Matka in the morning is well worth the extra effort for a taste of the beautiful mountainous scenery of Macedonia (see *Chapter 4* for information on these places). The afternoon should take in at least Kale and Čaršija.

MUSEUMS AND GALLERIES

Museum Complex of the Macedonia Struggle [133 E2] (*11 Mart bb;* ⊕ *09.00–17.00 daily; entry 100MKD*) Opened on Independence Day, 8 September 2011, this is part of the Skopje 2014 urban renewal programme and the move by the current government to hallow and materialise Macedonian ethnicity and culture. Its original title of VMRO Museum and the Museum of the Victims of Communism really does signify the perspective of the exhibition, and there has been some criticism that the museum doesn't fairly represent some of the positive benefits which also came with communism and socialism. For more on the formation and struggles of VMRO and on the communist years, see page 26.

This museum literally is history in the making and is intended to show a different perspective from that of the Museum of the Macedonian Struggle in Thessaloniki, which looks at the issue from a Greek perspective. For your entry fee you'll get a 90-minute guided tour of the museum in one of several languages, including English. The museum's huge artistic depictions are mostly by Russian or Ukrainian painters, as Macedonia does not have a strong heritage in still-life painting. Be warned: the many life-size wax figures in the museum will fool the innocent, and as such the exhibition is not recommended for children under the age of ten or those who might be sensitive to seeing depictions of torture, death and the execution by hanging of a wax figure.

City Museum of Skopje [133 G5] (*Mito Hadzivasilev Jasmin;* \ *3114 742; www.mgs.org.mk;* ⊕ *09.30–17.00 Mon–Sat, 09.30–13.00 Sun; entry 100MKD*) The museum is housed in the old railway station on the southern end of Makedonija. The original Skopje–Thessaloniki railway started from this station in 1873, but the present building was built in 1940–41. The earthquake of 26 July 1963 destroyed a large portion of the building and station, leaving the station clock fixed at 05.17 when the earthquake hit. The clock hands have remained at this time ever since and the building became the city museum soon after. The new railway station is now 20 minutes' walk away further east. The museum exhibits a permanent history of the city through the centuries (although the 20th-century section has been closed for years) as well as temporary exhibitions of local artists, architects and designers. A small brochure in English can be obtained at the front desk.

Daud Pasha Amam Gallery [133 F1] (*Kruševska 1a;* \ *3133 102, 3124 219; www.nationalgallery.mk;* ⊕ *10.00–18.00 Tue–Fri, same hours at w/ends of special exhibitions only; entry 100MKD*) This is the obvious copper cupola building to your right as you enter the old town from the Stone Bridge. It is well worth a visit just for the building itself. Built in the 15th century as a bathhouse while Skopje was under Turkish rule, it was then one of the most magnificent of its kind, boasting 13 different-sized copper cupolas and varying degrees of hot steam rooms and cold baths separated for men and women. Nowadays only the beautiful roof and ceiling architecture remain. The gallery houses mostly contemporary art, although there are a few older pieces, one dating back to the 13th century. The art is an added bonus to the building if you like modern art, although a good working Turkish steam bath in Skopje is sorely missed.

Čifte Amam National Art Gallery [141 C4] (*Bitpazarska bb;* \ *3109 566, 3126 856; www.nationalgallery.mk;* ⊕ *10.00–18.00 Tue–Fri, same hours at w/ends of special exhibitions only; entry 50MKD*) This is another former Turkish bathhouse, the second largest in Skopje, built at the beginning of the 16th century under the orders of Isa Bey, the son of Isak Bey. It now houses various travelling exhibitions and lies immediately south of Suli An. Another old bathhouse in Čaršija is **Šengul Amam** (also known as Gurciler Amam) next to Kuršumli Han. Like Čifte Amam, it was badly damaged in the 1963 earthquake, but this bathhouse has not been repaired.

Jewish Holocaust Museum [133 E1] (*11 Mart bb;* ✆ *3122 697;* e *info@ holocaustfund.org.mk; www.holocaustfund.org;* ⊕ *08.00–16.00 Mon–Fri; entry free*)
The museum opened in 2011 and was made possible from funds received when Macedonia's denationalisation law took effect in 2000. This law returned property which had been nationalised during the communist era back to its original owners. In the case of the more than 3,000 Jews from Macedonia who were victims of the Holocaust during World War II, their property was sold and the money received was put into the Holocaust Fund for the museum. The museum is a vivid and sobering memorial, and a very worthwhile visit.

Museum of Contemporary Art [141 A1] (*Muzej na Sovrjeme Uumetnost, Samoilova bb, PO Box 482;* ✆ *3117 734; www.msuskopje.org.mk;* ⊕ *09.00–16.00 Tue–Sun; entry 50MKD*) The museum lies to the west of Kale on top of the hill. A large, airy building, it holds 4,360 prominent international as well as national exhibits. Many of the exhibits are donations given to Macedonia after the 1963 earthquake when the 1963 New York convention of the International Association of the Plastic Arts called upon the artists of the world to support the city's reconstruction through associated artwork. The custom-built museum opened in 1970 with a remarkable collection of international donations created especially for it. Such pieces include a canvas named *Head of a Woman* (1963) by Picasso, which is usually stored in the basement, but can be viewed upon request. The piece was stolen from the museum in 1995 but intercepted at the border and returned.

National Museum of Macedonia [141 B3] (*Čurčiska bb;* ✆ *3116 044; www. musmk.org.mk;* ⊕ *08.00–16.00 Tue–Fri, 09.00–15.00 Sat, 09.00–13.00 Sun; entry 100KD*) The museum lies between Mustafa Pasha Mosque and Kuršumli An in Čaršija. It is not marked up as the 'Museum of Macedonia' from the outside and the entrance is merely a break in the red railings on the southernmost side of the complex. If you haven't got much time to visit ancient sites in Macedonia, then the museum is a good way to get an overview of all the civilisations that have passed along the River Vardar. Many of the best iconostases in the country are also housed here, and there are some excellent exhibits of the world wars, including weaponry and ammunition. Many of the exhibits are being revised and the number of texts in English is increasing.

Some of the archaeological exhibitions are held in **Kuršumli An**, access to which can only be gained through the main museum. Originally a tavern and then for a long time a political prison (see below for a history of the inn), Kuršumli An is open Monday to Friday.

Museum of Skopje Bazaar [141 C3] (✆ *3114 742;* ⊕ *10.00–14.00 Tue–Fri; entry free*) Suli An, another old trading inn, houses the Museum of the Skopje Bazaar which holds an interesting exhibition on trading life in Skopje during the Ottoman Empire. The museum and exhibits are in need of repair and all the text is in Macedonian. The museum itself is upstairs, and downstairs is the university's Department of Applied Arts. You can walk around the courtyard to see the students working in the downstairs rooms and the department's entrance hall has several

modern art paintings. Exhibitions and public lectures are advertised in Macedonian on the front door. Suli An lies in the centre of the old bazaar area and the front entrance to the inn often looks closed, but it is usually in fact open.

Military Museum of Macedonia [129 H7] (*Military Academy in Aerodrom;* ☏ *3283 624;* ⊕ *Mon–Fri 09.00–15.00 Mon–Fri; entry free*) The museum covers Macedonian military history in the broadest sense of the term, starting with the campaigns of Aleksandar the Great up until World War II.

Macedonian Museum of Natural History [128 B3] (*Ilinden 86;* ☏ *3117 669;* ⊕ *09.00–16.00 Tue–Sun; entry 30MKD*) There is not much to see in the museum and all the text is in Macedonian, but there are some impressive remains of prehistoric animals found in Negotino and other areas of Macedonia, and lots of stuffed eagles and vultures as well as other animals of the region. Make sure you have small change as the ticket attendant does not.

Museum of Coinage [129 F5] (*National Bank of the Republic of Macedonia, Bd Kuzman Josifovski Pitu 1;* ☏ *3108 108;* ⊕ *09.00–15.00 Mon–Fri; entry free*) A truly amazing collection which will take you through the history of coinage right from Paeonian times. Literature available in English. Bring ID in order to get through the main bank entrance.

Memorial House of Mother Teresa [133 F4] (*Makedonija bb, nr Dom na Armija;* ☏ *3290 674;* e *info@memorialhouseofmotherteresa.org; www. memorialhouseofmotherteresa.org;* ⊕ *09.00–20.00 Mon–Fri, 09.00–14.00 Sat–Sun; entry free*) On 27 August 1910, Gonxha Bojaxhiu, of Albanian descent, was born in Skopje. A devout Catholic, she went on to be known to the world as Mother Teresa. Her memorial house in Skopje was opened in 2009. It is not a replica of her actual house, which was just in front of today's Trgovski shopping centre, but it is designed to give an idea of how she might have lived in a similar house (although considerably enlarged for visitors). The museum also has a glass chapel at the top and a conference hall in the basement. The memorial house was deliberately built on the site of what used to be the old Catholic church where she was baptised, received communion and sang in the church choir. The exhibition there on her life is first class. Outside is a larger than life statue of her, which was put up shortly after her original house. The site of her former house is marked with a small plaque at the western entrance to the Trgovski Centar.

Museum of Archeology [133 F3] (*Kej Dimitar Vlahov bb*) Due to open in 2012, this imposing building replete with Corinthian columns is also the new seat of the Supreme Court, and the new home of the National Archives.

HISTORICAL SITES
Kale Fortress [133 E1] (*www.skopskokale.com.mk*) The present-day site has seen some sort of occupation since 4000BC and has been a working fortress since the 6th century AD. It served as a barracks to the Turkish army during Ottoman rule, and then to the JNA (Jugoslav National Army) until the 1963 earthquake razed most of the fortress. Much of it is only now being restored. Continuing excavations have revealed artefacts dating back to the Thracian era of 200BC when the Dardanians fought from Kale to defend the surrounding area from the invading Romans. In May 2010, archaeologists discovered the largest find of coins from the Byzantine

era ever unearthed in Macedonia. Some of the current visible structure dates from the 10th-century enlargement of the fort under Tsar Samoil. The ramp was partly built of stones from the ancient town of Skupi, which was destroyed in 518.

At time of writing the Kale was closed until further notice because of demonstrations, which erupted there over the attempt to rebuild a church in the grounds. Once it opens again, the main gateway of Kale can be approached just after the flyover entering Čaršija, or a more scenic route is to follow the cobbled street up Gradište past all the bars, then up the steps to the forecourt of the Monastery of Sv Spas. The main entrance is opposite the old post office.

Kamen Most [133 F2] The 214m Stone Bridge, which joins the old Turkish town to what has now become the centre of the city south of the river, was first built in the late 15th century under the orders of Sultan Mehmet II the Conqueror. By then the population of the city was increasing so rapidly, due to the draw of merchants to this important trading town, that people were already living beyond the original town walls. The only bridge across the river was many miles away further west, so a new bridge here, close to the main hub of the town, helped with the problem of overcrowding on the north side of the river as well as easing the arduous trading route into the town from the south.

The original stonework of 13 arches of travertine stone still stands, although the top of the bridge has been changed a number of times since it was built. Originally at a width of 6.33m, it was widened to 9.8m in 1909, and then returned to its original width in 1992. During the conflict of 2001 the bridge was badly damaged, and due to the bad relations between the communities, it took almost ten years to add the final piece to a replica of the old lookout post.

The bridge was originally built with stone pillar railings, used by the Ottoman rulers of Skopje to spike the heads of traitors and criminals. The bridge became a public execution place and, amongst many others, the Ottomans sentenced Karpoš, the 'King of Kumanovo', to death by impalement on the bridge in 1689.

Saat Kula [129 F3] The dark red-brick clock tower near Hjunkar Mosque (Sultan Murat Mosque) the last remaining portion of the old city walls. Erected in the mid 16th century, the top half of the clock tower was originally made of wood and housed a clock brought over from Hungary. In 1904 the wooden structure was replaced with stone and a new clock was procured. That clock was then destroyed in the earthquake of 1963 and has not been replaced since.

Bezisten [141 C3] The covered marketplace of the old bazaar area is a courtyard-type building with more stores built inside the courtyard itself. It is located behind Čifte Amam to the northwest. Originally built in the 15th century for trading cloth and material, the store soon spilt outside the original structure, forming narrow little cobbled lanes between the one- and two-storey shops, which leaned onto each other. The old bazaar quickly became 18 different trading houses – goldsmiths, cobblers, ironmongers, corn exchange, etc – and the remnants of these can still be seen today. The Bezisten of today is a 19th-century structure, housing some non-governmental organisations, and occasionally a café bar.

Turkish trading inns Čaršija has a number of Turkish trading inns, which are well worth a visit, including Kuršumli An belonging to the Ragusan merchants, Suli An and Kapan An. These inns usually have one or two entrances but no windows on the outside. The entrances lead into a large courtyard, which is surrounded on all four sides on the first floor by wooden-balconied guest rooms looking out onto the courtyard. Underneath these, on the ground floor, were the stabling and storage quarters. There was often a well in the centre of the courtyard where guests would usually gather to while away the evening.

As you go past the old bazaar area of Čaršija from the Stone Bridge the first inn you will come to is **Kapan An** [141 C4]. Its walls now house several restaurants and bars both inside the inn and outside.

Further down the street towards Bitpazar is **Suli An** [141 C3], which is now the Museum of the Old Skopje Bazaar (see page 145).

Kuršumli An [141 C2], meaning Bullet or Lead Inn, to the northwest of Bitpazar is probably one of the most impressive inns of its period. At the time it was designed to stable up to 100 horses, and house their traders and owners. Some of the rooms even had their own fireplace, which was deemed quite a luxury in those times. In 1878 the building became the town prison. It now holds archaeological exhibitions as part of the Museum of Macedonia next door.

MONUMENTS AND STATUES Unlike many former communist cities, Skopje does not display the usual array of statues to communist heroes, although there are still plenty of communist/late 1960s–1970s-style buildings to be seen, such as the main government building [132 D2], main post office [133 E2] and the Macedonian Opera and Ballet [133 C1]. There is a larger-than-life-size statue of Mother Teresa on Makedonija [133 F4] outside her Memorial House (see page 146).

After considerable controversy, a statue of **Skenderbey** [141 C5] (see box, page 255, for more about him) was erected on 28 November 2006 (Albanian Flag Day) in front of Ilinden shopping centre. An Albanian national hero, and a Catholic who stood up in the mid 15th century against the Ottoman colonisation of the area, the erection of his statue was controversial for three reasons. For many ethnic Macedonians, admitting the statue of an Albanian hero into Skopje touches upon a sore point regarding ethnic Albanian encroachment on ethnic Macedonian land, rights and nationhood. For the Turkish community (who once built the old town) Skenderbey is seen as the enemy. For the Islamic community, Skenderbey's reconversion back to Catholicism is seen as treachery. On the purely aesthetic side, the statue does a lot to enhance this modern concrete edge of the old town.

In 2010, the centre-right government revealed its plans for Skopje 2014, an urban renewal programme for the beautification of the centre of the city. Aside from a number of significant new buildings (some mentioned already, and also a new Ministry of Foreign Affairs, Agency for Electrocommunications and a Department of Financial Police) at least 18 new statues have also been erected. Almost all bolster the ethnic Macedonian side of the country's history. The most controversial of them all has been the **Warrior on a Horse** in the centre of Ploštad. The 24m-high statue in a fountain is decorated with bronze reliefs of the life of the warrior. Despite its official name, it is clear that the warrior is Alexander the Great on Bucephalus. Its obscure title is in deference to the ongoing dispute with Greece over Macedonian history.

CHURCHES, MONASTERIES AND CEMETERIES
Monastery of Sveti Spas (Holy Salvation) [141 B4] (*Makarije Frckovski 8;* ✎ *3163 812, 3109 401*) This is the only remaining monastery in the centre of Skopje and houses one of its most beautiful churches. Some of the foundations of the monastery date back to the 14th century, before Ottoman times. Under Ottoman rule it became illegal for a church to be taller than a mosque, so the church was

mostly rebuilt from below ground in order to accommodate the height of the original church bell tower.

The present three-naved church dates from rebuilding in the 18th and 19th centuries. Three of the most famous woodcarvers of the time, Makarije Frckovski of Galičnik and the brothers Marko and Petar Filipovski from the Mijak village of Gari, worked for five years from 1819 to 1824 to create the 10m-wide, 6m-high **iconostasis** (the intricate woodwork divider between the nave and the main part of the church). The iconostasis is cut from the wood of walnut trees, and is made up of two rows of partly gold-inlaid icons depicting scenes from the Old and the New Testaments. Many of the scenes have been carved to reflect Macedonian traditions and folklore, such as the figure of Salome, who is dressed in traditional Macedonian garb. Among their more famous works, Frckovski and the Filipovski brothers carved even more stunning iconostases for the Monastery of Sv Jovan Bigorski in Mavrovo National Park and the Monastery of Sv Gavril in Lesnovo.

In the monastery courtyard is the marble sarcophagus of the revolutionary **Goce Delčev**, leader of the Independence for Macedonia Revolutionary Organisation (IMRO – to which the present-day government VMRO-DPMNE traces its roots), until he was shot in 1903 by Ottoman soldiers at Banica (Karié in Greece). His remains were exhumed during the Bulgarian occupation of Banica during World War I and moved to Sofia, when Tsar Ferdinand I of Bulgaria awarded his father a life pension in recognition of the price three of his sons paid with their lives to further the freedom of Macedonia. When Bulgaria occupied Banica again during World War II, his grave near Banica was restored (but not his remains). As part of a policy to recognise Macedonian consciousness, Delčev's remains were finally moved to Skopje in 1946 and interred at Sv Spas. His ethnicity remains a bone of contention between Macedonians and Bulgarians, many of whom say he is Bulgarian (and that there is no such ethnicity as Macedonian). A small exhibition on his life is inside the inns of the monastery, and his statue is on the south side of the Stone Bridge.

Church of Sv Dimitri [141 A6] Also north of the river, the church is just west of the Stone Bridge. The original church was built in the 14th century and in typical Macedonian fashion the bell tower is separate from the main building. The present structure dates from the 19th century.

Cathedral of Sv Kliment of Ohrid [132 C3] (*Cnr Partizanski & Ohridski*) A 20th-century building shaped interestingly in the form of a dome with a smaller dome at each corner, making it easily mistaken for a modern mosque at a quick glance.

Church of Sv Gjorgi and British Cemetery [129 H3] (*1st left off 16 Makedonska Brigada*) The cemetery houses over 100 graves of British servicemen who died during the two world wars. A service is held by the British Embassy here each November.

French Cemetery [128 D2] (*Samoilova bb, after the Museum of Contemporary Arts*) The cemetery houses the graves of almost 1,500 French servicemen who died in World War I. A tiny museum at the entrance displays documents and photographs of the period.

MOSQUES The Čair and Čaršija districts of the old town have over 30 mosques. In the mid 17th century Evlija Čelebi, a famous Turkish travel writer of the time, noted 120 mosques in Skopje. Most were burnt down in the fire of 1689 started by the Austrian general Piccolomini in order to rid the town of a rampaging plague. A few of the mosques from that time remain.

Mustafa Pasha Mosque [141 B3] (*Samoilova, opposite the main entrance to Kale*) The largest and most decorated of all the mosques in Skopje was built in 1492 at the order of Mustafa Pasha while he was Vizier of Skopje under Sultan Selim I. The entrance to the mosque is through a four-column porch, which is crowned with three cupolas and a 124-step white minaret rises from its western end. Inside, the pulpit and prayer recess are made from intricately worked marble and the walls are of a beautiful blue pattern work. The five windows in each wall are staggered, rising up the walls of the mosque to create a pyramid effect. Despite having stood the test of time well, the mosque did have to undergo major restoration after the earthquake of 1963 and was refurbished again through Turkish funding over a five-year period ending in 2011. In the grounds of the mosque are Mustafa Pasha's mausoleum and his daughter Umi's sarcophagus.

Hjunkar Mosque [129 F4] (*Bd Krste Misirkov*) Also known as the Sultan Murat Mosque, it pre-dates the Mustafa Pasha Mosque by some 50 years. It was built next to the Monastery of Sv Georgi Gorga near the present-day university of Sv Cyril and Methodius. At the time, the monastery was one of the most important monastic centres in the Balkans, but when Isak Bey, then commander of the Turkish army, built the **Aladža Mosque** [141 D1], the Pasha Bey Mausoleum (still visible in the grounds of the Aladža Mosque) and a *medresa* (school for teaching the Koran) on the actual grounds of the monastery, he effectively destroyed life at the monastery. The *medresa* no longer exists, nor the monastery, but both mosques remain on either side of Bd Krste Misirkov. The mausoleums of Sultan Beyhan and of Ali Pasha of Dagestan lie in the grounds of the Hjunkar Mosque.

Yayha Pasha Mosque [129 F3] (*Bd Krste Misirkov*) Further north on Bd Krste Misirkov, this mosque was built in 1504 for Yayha Pasha, the son-in-law of Sultan Bayazit II. Notable for its modern four-sided roof, it is the imposing mosque visible as you come off the highway from the airport into the centre of town. Originally, the prayer area was roofed with one large and five small domes, but these were destroyed in the last earthquake of 1963.

Murat Pasha Mosque [141 C4] (*Opposite Čifte Amam*) This modern square-roofed mosque was built in 1802. The original 15th-century structure was burnt down when General Piccolomini set Skopje alight in 1689.

Kose Kadi Mosque [141 C4] (*Bezisten*) At the western end of Bezisten (the covered market) above a passageway of shops, this 17th-century mosque was last renovated in 1993.

Hidaverdi Mosque [141 C1] (*Between Kuršumli An and the Theatre for Minorities*) This looks more like a half-renovated shopfront than a 16th-century mosque, despite having been restored in 1995. It lacks the usual distinguishing minaret.

Gazi Isa-Bey Mosque [129 F3] (*Čairska*) Once held as one of the first libraries in Skopje. In the mosque grounds is a 560-year-old plane tree (*Platinus orientalis*).

ACTIVITIES

Skopje offers a host of sports facilities and outdoor pursuits. For **volleyball** courts see below. For more on **outdoor pursuits** such as biking, tandem paragliding, hot-air ballooning, rock climbing and others, see pages 105–12. For **horseriding** and the **Vodno cable car** see *Chapter 4*.

VARDAR ESPLANADE The southern bank of the River Vardar to the west of the Stone Bridge is paved all the way to the Aleksandar Palace Hotel and another 3km beyond. With views onto the surrounding mountains, the 6km stretch makes a wonderful walking, rollerblading, cycling or running route, and is a great place to see the locals taking a stroll, too. It is lit at night most of the way. A paved riverside walk extends several kilometres also along the opposite southeastern half of the river. Two sand beaches with café bars at Gradski Plaža are near the City Park and at Kamen Most Plaža (⊕ 09.00–22.00). At the northern end of Kamen Most Plaža is a large sanded volleyball and handball court, which is available for free with prior booking in person at the court.

SPORTS HALLS
Boris Trajkovski Stadium [128 A2] (*Bd 8th Septemvri;* \ *3089 600;* e *info@scboristrajkovski.gov.mk; www.salaboristrajkovski.gov.mk*) Named after the late president, who died in a plane crash in 2004, the stadium opened in 2008. Home of the Macedonian national basketball, handball and volleyball teams, it can hold up to 10,000 spectators. It has an ice hockey rink, bowling hall, carting circuit, fitness gym, table tennis and aerobics. There are also four restaurants, sports clothing outlets and a large sports bar. Carting is open 09.00–24.00 and costs 450MKD for 10 circuits or 800 MKD for 20 circuits. Their Olympic-size pool is in the building next door on the east side (⊕ *10.00–16.30 & 20.30–24.00 daily; entry 200MKD*). Check the website for other times and prices.

Philip II Arena [128 C3] (*City Park*) Home of the Macedonian national football team they are most often seen practising and playing there. Tickets for matches can be purchased at the stadium box office or from the **Football Association of Macedonia** (*8th Udarna Brigada 31a;* \ *3235 448, 3229 042*). For more on Macedonian football see www.macedonianfootball.com.

Kale Sports Complex [128 D3] (*Lazar Ličenoski 316;* \ *3118 711;* e *contact@cdklubmaki.mk; www.cdklubmaki.mk;* ⊕ *09.00–22.00 Mon–Thu, 09.00–24.00 Fri–Sun*) Another big sports complex, including an outdoor swimming pool and an ice-skating rink in the winter.

SWIMMING There are two other pools in addition to the Boris Trajkovski pool and Kale pools above.

Olympiski Bazen [129 E5] (*Kočo Racin bb* \ *3162 958;* ⊕ *20.00–24.00 Tue–Fri, 10.00–16.00 & 20.00–24.00 Sat & Sun*). The pool complex also offers a fitness centre open every day 09.00–23.00, although it is not as pleasant to work out in as the fitness centre at the Aleksandar Palace Hotel (open to the public, see page 134).

Bazen Biser [129 H7] (*Just off Kosta Novakovič in the Aerodrom part of town;* ⊕ *10.00–18.00 & 21.30–01.00 daily; entry 100MKD*) This 25m outdoor pool has a grass area and a smaller children's pool. Serves drinks and snacks. It's packed after midday so go early or in the evening.

TENNIS Clubs are plentiful in Skopje, and private lessons cost 700–1000MKD per hour. Courts are an additional 300–450MKD per hour, with lighting adding another 100MKD. Try one of the following:

ABC [128 C3] Ilindenska; ☎3063 622. Also has a popular café & drinks bar.
As Bd Avnoj, Aerodrom; ☎2403 114. A big fitness complex with 10 courts.
Evroset Skupi; ☎3095 385. Nice viewing area & café looking down on the courts.

Forca Londonska; ☎3060 333; www.forza.com. mk. 2 outdoor courts. Pleasant atmosphere.
Hipodrom ☎2521 444. Outdoor courts, summer only, near Avtokomanda.
Jug City Park; ☎3118 530
Kamnik Kamnik bb (see page 137 for directions); ☎2523 522. Excellent restaurant.

SQUASH
Squash Club [132 C1] Lazar Ličenoski 31; ☎3227 077. Nice café with a view onto the courts.

SPAS After a day of sports or hiking, opportunities to relax and pamper yourself, especially if you can't get as far as Katlanovska hot springs (page 161) include:

Aseana Royal Spa [132 B4] Sv Apostol Guslarot 12; ☎3246 442; www.aseana.mk; ⊕ 10.00–22.00 Tue–Fri, 12.00–20.00 Sat–Sun. Treatments include Balinese body massage, facials, body toning & pedicures. Prices range from 400MKD for a foot massage to 4,200MD for an exotic flower bath.

TCC Plaza Spa Vasil Glavinov 12; ☎3111 807; www.tccplaza.com. This is a membership-only spa, but has an excellent value monthly half-day membership for €25. Includes hot stone loungers, massage, a gym & a very nice bijou pool.

CHILDREN'S ACTIVITIES For more ideas on children-friendly activities in Skopje see page 90.

Habyland [128 A2] Boris Trajkovski Centre, see page 151; ☎3120 275; e habyland@yahoo.com; www.habyland.mk; ⊕ 10.00–22.00 daily; entry before 13.00 100MKD, after 13.00 150MKD Mon–Fri, 200MKD Sat. For children up to the age of 12, this centre is the best value for money in Skopje by far. Has a massive indoor jungle gym, a ball pit, games area, outdoor jungle gym & a child-friendly carting rink. The indoor has limited air conditioning due to the doors opening out onto the patio café. The café, overlooking the outdoor activities (which are not in the shade), serves snacks, small pizzas, ice cream & the usual range of drinks. Caters for parties with advance booking.

Skopje Zoo [128 B3] Ilinden 88; ☎3220 578; e info@zooskopje.com.mk; www.zooskopje.com. mk; ⊕ 09.00 daily until dark (16.00 in winter, 19.00 in summer); entry 50MKD. This small zoo has seen a resurgence of popular interest in the last 2 years, with significant investments being made to the infrastructure & services. Well-kept animals include lions, tigers, cheetahs, monkeys, zebras, dromedaries, ostriches, deers & alligators. There's a jungle gym & horseriding for younger children, & a welcome outdoor café in the shade.

right The village of Kaneo has been home to fishermen for over 500 years (SS) page 183

below Statue of Sv Kliment, a missionary who came to Ohrid and was involved in setting up the first monasteries that taught in Slavic (TE) page 173

bottom The 2,000-year-old Roman theatre in Ohrid is once again being used for outdoor concerts and performances (SS) page 184

left Mavrovo National Park makes an ideal base for hikers and skiers, while it is also home to culturally unique and isolated Mijak villages (SS) page 250

below Stone doll natural rock formations near the village of Kuklica — legend says the figures are the result of a petrified wedding (KS) page 290

bottom The Šar Mountains offer a host of hiking trails and are home to 49 glacial lakes (BJ) page 226

right   Tsar Samoil's Fortress in Ohrid dates only from the end of the 10th century, but there is evidence that a fortress has stood on the top of Ohrid Hill since at least the 3rd century BC (KS) page 184

below   At 2,753m, Mount Golem Korab is the highest peak in Macedonia and shares the border with Albania (BJ) page 342

bottom   The megalithic observatory at Kokino dominates the surrounding area at a height of 1,013m above sea level (BJ) page 279

above left The Roman site of Stobi was first discovered in 1861, and even today only a fraction of the city has been uncovered (BJ) page 311

above right The village cave church high on the cliffs above Radožda contains frescoes dating back to the 13th century (JC) page 196

below The remote Monastery of Treskavec has a beautiful setting under the summit of the impressive Zlatovrv (BJ) page 208

bottom The Vlach town of Kruševo is the highest in Macedonia, at 1,250m (KS) page 231

above   The fully working monastery of Sv Jovan Bigorski is famous for its architecture, ornate iconostases and relics (SS) page 259

right   The Mijak village of Galičnik hosts the famous Wedding Festival every year, featuring rituals, costumes, folk dances, traditional music and the Orthodox wedding ceremony itself (WC) page 251

below   Macedonia's second city, Bitola, has maintained much of the 18th- and 19th-century architecture in its centre (SS) page 207

above The eastern part of Macedonia is home to the Turkish Yoruk ethnic population, who are distinguished by their language, customs and bright traditional dress (KS) page 46

left The *tapan* is played with two specially designed drumsticks known as a *kukuda* and a *pračka* (BJ) page 58

below Pelivan wrestling: in each round two men, smothered in sunflower oil and wearing only leather breeches, compete to tussle the other to the ground (SL) page 251

right Easter Sunday service at Sv Sofia in Ohrid; the major festivals of the Orthodox calendar are still celebrated with much pageantry (B/A) page 50

below Traditional Macedonian folk dancing is performed at festivals up and down the country, such as here at Velestovo (JC) page 196

bottom Macedonian cuisine is a celebration of fresh, organic produce (SS) page 99

above **Wolf** (J&CS/FLPA) page 10
left **Dalmatian pelican** (MS/FLPA) page 12

POPOVA KULA

Temple of wine

Popova Kula Winery offers a unique opportunity to enjoy excellent wines and traditional Macedonian food but also to undertake different recreational activities or just to relax in a quite atmosphere surrounded by magnificent landscapes. Within the winery we have a hotel with 7 fully equipped rooms and 4 apartments, a restaurant, wine tasting room and meeting room. We organize winery tours and wine tastings every day. On request we organize: sightseeing, vineyard promenades, archeological sites tours, hiking, biking, hunting, fishing, bird watching.

We are located only 80 km south from the Skopje Airport just 2Km from the highway E-75 in a quiet area near the lovely town Demir Kapija.

Cheers

For more info visit: www.popovakula.com.mk
For reservation write to us at: reservation@popovakula.com.mk

POPOVA
KULA
WINERY

4

Outside Skopje

Telephone code 02

> After a ten-mile drive from Skopje we arrived at the little monastery which is called Matka, or the Mother, because it is so kind to barren women … on a broad ledge under dripping cliffs, here hung with purple flowers, among wind-swept trees that leaned laterally over the abyss …
>
> Rebecca West, *Black Lamb and Grey Falcon*, 1941

Most of Macedonia is accessible from Skopje in one day if you have a car, depending on how long you want to spend at a place, and whether you're prepared to return after dark. Here, however, are a few suggested day trips closer to Skopje, which need not be reliant on the convenience of your own vehicle.

✗ WHERE TO EAT

Outside Skopje are several great traditional restaurants. Although they can be difficult to find and certainly quicker and more convenient to get to by car/taxi than by public transport, they are all set in beautiful scenery, where a hike in the local hills and woods is rewarding and helps to work up an appetite.

✗ **Klet** (see page 164) $$$

✗ **Čardak** Sv Ilija Monastery, 5km north of Skopje; m 070 410 919; www.restorancardak. com; ⊕ 10.00–24.00 daily. A good place to eat if you have been out walking in the Skopska Crnagore. In the grounds are a small fish pond, a 300-year-old Aspen tree & a kids' play area. In summer, seating is outside under the trees, & in winter in the large balconied (*čardak*) traditional inn. To get there take the road through Butel & turn left before Radišani village & head towards Mirkovci. The restaurant & monastery are signposted (just keep your eyes peeled). To get there by bus, the #61 (towards Pobožje), #71 (towards Banjani) & #81 (towards Blace) all go past the turn-off to Čardak. Ask the driver to let you off at Restoran Čardak Sveti Ilija. $$

✗ **Cherry Orchard** Volkovo; \ 2055 195; m 070 225 642; ⊕ 09.00–21.00 Tue–Sun. Set in the grounds of the El Kabon riding stables, which have a well-manicured terrace & lawns overlooking the exercise paddocks & a delightful children's play area. The restaurant building itself was used in the Macedonian movie *Dust* by Milčo Mančevski, & was reconstructed as the stables (whose horses were used in the movie) at the end of filming. The well-groomed interior offers fireside seating in winter, but is sadly not well frequented, not least because it is complicated to get there by car. The #22 bus from anywhere on Partizanski ends its journey 700m from the restaurant where it is signposted for the stables.

By car follow ring-road signs towards Pristina then take the (1st exit) turn-off for Orman, driving under the bridge following signs for Volkovo. Follow the newly laid tarmac road & take the 1st right after the bus station, following signs for the stables. $$

✗ **Planinski Dom Matka** (see page 160) $$

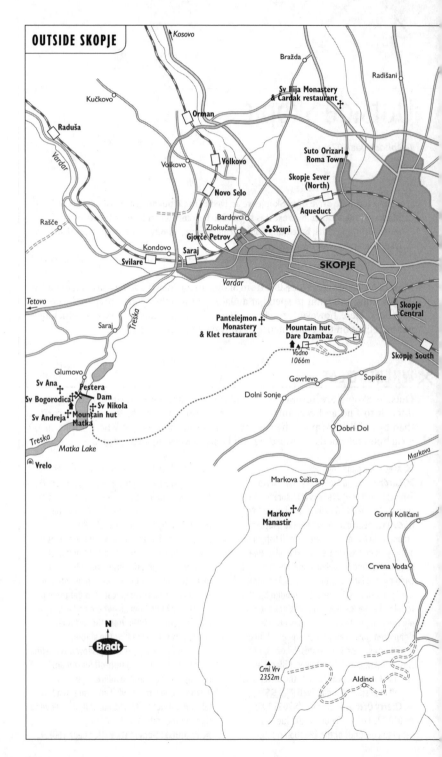

Kosovo

Bražda

Radišani

Kučkovo

Sv Ilija Monastery
& Cardak restaurant

Orman

Raduša

Suto Orizari
Roma Town

Vardar

Volkovo

Volkovo

Skopje Sever
(North)

Novo Selo

Aqueduct

Rašče

Bardovci

Zlokučani

Skupi

Kondovo

Gjorče Petrov

Svilare

Saraj

SKOPJE

Tetovo

Vardar

Saraj

Treska

Pantelejmon
Monastery
& Klet restaurant

Mountain hut
Dare Dzambaz

Skopje
Central

Vodno
1066m

Skopje South

Glumovo

Govrlevo

Sopište

Sv Ana

Pestera
Dam

Dolni Sonje

Sv Bogorodica

Sv Nikola

Sv Andreja

Mountain hut
Matka

Dobri Dol

Treska

Markova

Matka Lake

Vrelo

Markova Sušica

Gorni Količani

Markov
Manastir

Crvena Voda

N

Bradt

Crni Vrv
2352m

Aldinci

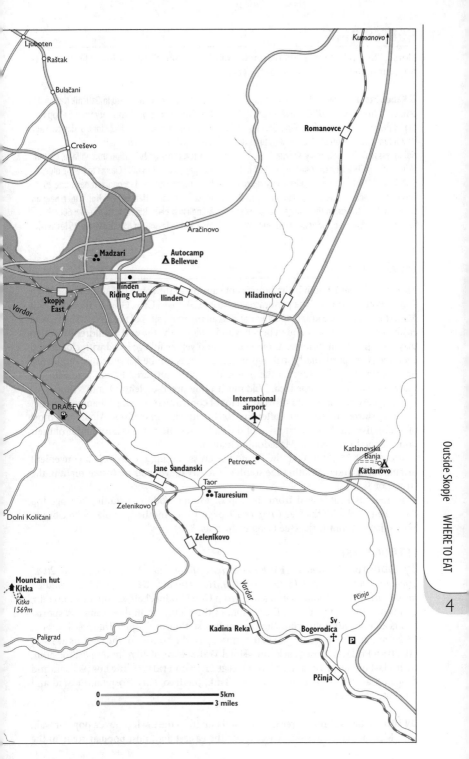

HORSERIDING

Horseriding is becoming increasingly popular around Skopje. Riding fees are c€10 for 40 minutes, or €100 per month. Try:

El Kabon Stables Cherry Orchard in Volkovo district; ☎ 2055 195; m 070 225 642. To get to El Kabon see the details for Cherry Orchard Restaurant above. A great place for kids to have riding lessons while you enjoy a meal.

Horseriding Club Bistra Galičnik; m 077 648 679, 078 649 001; e hcbistragalicnik@gmail.com. This club provides horses for the famous Galičnik wedding. They can bring their horses up to Skopje for rides up to Vodno by prior arrangement (all

year), or you can take a trip in Galičnik National Park (Jun–Oct only). Prices vary from €17 pp for a 3hr guided ride, up to €122 for a 3-day package overnighting in tents & hotels.

Ilinden Riding Club Hipodrom village, east of Skopje; m 070 338 002. Claims to be the oldest horseriding club in Macedonia. It has some 20 horses, including Hanoverian, Holsteiner, Belgian & English breeds. Riding lessons only: 600MKD for a 45min lesson, or 6,000MKD for 15 lessons.

MOUNT VODNO

Mount Vodno at 1,066m is the prominent summit to the south of Skopje topped by a 75m yellow steel cross. The panorama of Skopje, Skopska Crna Gore to the north and Mount Kitka to the south is spectacular and all the main sites of the city can be viewed easily. There are lots of wooden benches and tables at the top and a children's wooden play area. In late autumn vistas of vivid red and yellow foliage laced with clouds and evergreens are particularly striking. Sweet chestnuts can be harvested in abundance on an early morning walk up the mountain, but be prepared to compete with the many locals with the same idea. Wild mushrooms are also plentiful at this time.

The steel cross at the top provoked a lot of controversy among Albanians when it was first started in 2002, just after the 2001 conflict. Some ethnic Albanians, most of whom live on the opposite side of the valley, see the cross as a reminder of their domination by the ethnic Macedonian majority.

It costs 100MKD to take the lift up the cross. Lit up, the cross is a convenient orientation marker denoting the south of the city if ever you are lost at night in the streets of Skopje.

Numerous routes lead from the top of Mount Vodno, including a ridge-top day hike to Lake Matka (see *Chapter 10*, page 157). Another popular hike close to Skopje is to Mount Kitka (see *Chapter 10*, page 340).

GETTING THERE

By cable car (☎ 0800 15115; *http://zicnica.jsp.com.mk*; ☺ Apr–Sep 09.00–20.45 Tue–Sun, Oct–Mar until 16.30; entry 100MKD rtn, over 64s free with ID, children under 6 free) The 1,600m *žičnica* leaves from Hotel Vodno, halfway up the mountain, and is due to be extended to the bottom of the mountain in due course. A special bus goes once an hour from the central bus station in Skopje. The first bus is at 08.20, and further buses leave at 20 minutes past the hour until the last bus at 18.20 (19.20 on Fridays). Buses back from Hotel Vodno leave at 40 minutes past the hour, with a last bus at 20.10 (and an extra bus at 21.15 on Fridays). The bus picks up and drops off at the Macedonian National Bank, Jugdrvo, City Hospital, Ploštad and the State Hospital.

By foot It takes almost three hours to walk up from the town centre, a popular walk with Macedonians on a sunny weekend. The easiest and most popular route to the summit is from the entrance to Vodno National Park on Ulica Salvadore Aljende. The westernmost road opposite the turn-off to the Hotel Panorama takes you over a couple of small bridges, up past a modern apartment block to your left, and then past some lovely old farmhouses. This quickly leads up into the woods above the town, and the main path is easy to follow. There are numerous diversions off the main path, and almost all diversions heading upwards will pop out at the summit eventually. The main path is marked with red and white stripes painted on trees, and joins the road again just before the entrance to Hotel Vodno and the turn-off to Sv Pantelejmon Monastery. It's also possible to take the bus (see page 324) to here.

From Hotel Vodno many people simply walk along the tarmac road and there are numerous tracks from the road where people veer off to gather chestnuts. The dedicated hiking path through the woods, however, actually starts to the left of the restaurant and mountain hut Skopje 63 above the barrier on the tarmac road. It is marked with yellow and green stripes painted on the trees. The path joins the road again about 1,200m from the road's end at the mountain hut and cross.

By horse Horseriding Club Bistra (see page 107) provides guided horse rides to the top of Vodno by prior arrangement.

WHERE TO STAY AND EAT A restaurant is due to open at the top of the cross, as well as another at the bottom, but was a long way from completion at the time of writing.

Dare Djambaz (50 beds) 3234 365, 3143 236. The mountain hut at the summit offers beds, basic food, a collegial atmosphere & welcome shelter if the weather has turned foul on the way up the mountain. It's well worth the visit just for the numerous photos of Macedonians who have climbed mountains around the world to proudly fly their flag, & also for the hot sweet mountain tea (*planinski čaj*) at 20MKD per cup.

Hotel Vodno (28 rooms) Sredno Vodno; 3177 027; f 3178 866; www.makedoijaturist. com.mk. The only hotel at the bottom of the cable car has a mediocre restaurant & standard rooms. $$$

LAKE MATKA AND CAVES

Lake Matka is the beloved quick getaway retreat of most Skopjites. There is hiking, boating, restaurants, churches, monasteries, caves and a small hotel. The lake itself was manmade by damming the River Treška and before the river was dammed, Sv Andreja Church and the old mountain hut, which is now a café and restaurant with rooms, used to stand 20m above the river. The steep-sided ravine is quite awesome and the cliffs are popular with the climbing crowd, who can often be viewed at their sport from the café terrace.

GETTING THERE It is a mere half-hour **drive** from the city. **Bus** 60 from anywhere on Bd Partizanski goes there hourly for 60MKD, Monday–Saturday. The last bus returns from Matka at 23.00. On Sunday there is a reduced service, and you'll need to take bus 5 from anywhere on Partizanski to its last stop at Deksion and then take the 60 from there. The last bus on Sundays is at 21.00. A taxi from the centre of Skopje costs 600MKD, or 200MKD from Saraj if you take bus 12 or 22 there. Once at Matka bus stop and car park it is a ten-minute walk along the River Treška from the parking area and bus stop to the foot of the dam, and then another ten minutes up past the dam where the path opens up to the grounds of the Matka Hotel and Restaurant and the Church of Sveta Andreja.

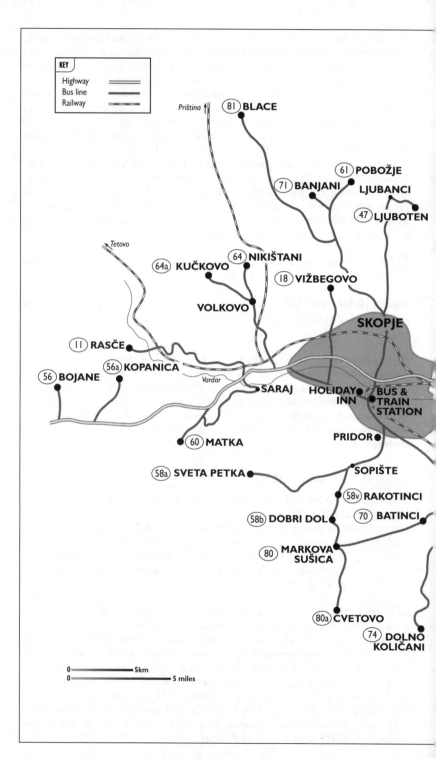

WHERE TO STAY AND EAT

Planinski Dom Matka (5 rooms) ↘3052 655, 3022 922; **m** 070 217 900; **e** contact@canyonmatka.com; www.canyonmatka.com. Now with a proper restaurant, as well as the lakeside café. All rooms en suite with Wi-Fi, large flat-screen TVs, & all mod cons. Excellent value for money. **$$/$$**

✗ Restoran Peštera Just before the dam; ↘2052 512. Also known as the Bear Cave, & has a nice outdoor patio & a small indoor restaurant set into the rock walls, making it rather cool inside. The food is traditional Macedonian including a good house stew & allegedly you can eat bear steak here too. **$$$**

WHAT TO SEE AND DO Small **boats** from outside Dom Matka café will take you down the lake for €10 a boat.

There are several impressive **caves** around Matka. The main ones are Ubava, Vrelo, Podvrelo and Krstalna. Vrelo, accessible by boat only, is open to the public for 300MKD (per person, including a 30-minute boat trip, and 30 minutes back). A small landing dock between the entrance information centre and Dom Matka runs the boats for the lake, and a boat leaves once five or more people are queued up. Podvrelo is almost completely underwater: with a depth of well over 500m, it may be the deepest known underwater cave in the world, and so is for the accomplished cave diver only. Ubava (meaning beautiful) has the most stalagmites and stalactites, waterfalls and colours, and archaeological findings in the cave indicate that it may have been used as a shelter during Palaeolithic (Old Stone Age) times almost 10,000 years ago. For more about the caves see Dom Matka's website (*www.canyonmatka.com*).

There is a lot of **hiking** in the surrounding hills, which are home to over 50 species of protected butterflies and moths. Various paths lead to over a dozen churches and monasteries, some long abandoned, some in full working order.

Next door to Dom Matka is **Sv Andreja Church**, built in the 14th century by another Andreja (not the saint), the brother of King Marko (see page 202).

Near Restoran Peštera the bridge over the river takes you to a path leading up to the **Church of Sv Nikola**, which has an excellent view onto the hotel and café. Above the Restoran Peštera is the **Monastery of Sveta Bogorodica**. It is a working monastery with inns, which are not open to the public, and a small church. Above the entrance to the church is an inscription reading:

> By the will of the Father, the Son and the Holy Ghost and the divine temple of the Mother of God came Lady Milica. She found this church unroofed, built a roof for it, painted its frescoes and built a wall around it. Mention, Lord, that this took place in 1497.

To the left of the entrance to the monastery is a path marked red which leads up to the churches of Sv Spas (80 minutes) and Sv Trojica (85 minutes) and the ruined Monastery of Sv Nedela (95 minutes). The walk to these churches is beautiful, although the trail is steep and badly marked so patience is required to get there. **Sv Spas** was built in the 14th century on the foundations of an earlier church, and renovated in 1968. To the right of the church as you approach it (ie: to the northeast) are the large and overgrown limestone blocks of an ancient fortress. The site continued to be populated into Ottoman times when it was known as Markov Grad (Marko's Town). It was also a hideout for Macedonian revolutionaries, until it was discovered by the Ottomans and ransacked.

An alternative rendition to the end of this fortress comes in the form of a love story. Allegedly, an Ottoman *bey* fell in love with the beautiful Bojana from Marko's Town, and when she refused his overtures, the *bey* decided to take her against her will. The citizens of the fortress helped her and killed almost a hundred Turk soldiers before Bojana realised her fate was sealed and threw herself to her death from the steep cliffs of the canyon into the River Treška. The soldiers took revenge by razing the fortress to the ground. The only building still left standing (just about) is the **Church of Sv Nedela** (Sv Sunday) with its ruined archway and old fresco of the saint. Take care going up to this church, as it stands on precariously steep ground.

There are two paths from here back down to the lake at Sv Andreja. The longer path marked yellow goes via Matkin Dol. It is very steep and should be walked with care. The name Matkin Dol means Torture Valley, which might give you an idea of how difficult it is. There are a few small caves along this path where monks retreated in order to find union with God.

To the left of Dom Matka are several boards showing the walks, animals and sites in the area, as well as a guide board with the climbing routes on the large rock face on the opposite side of the lake. For those wishing to do some serious climbing or extended hiking and mountaineering in Matka or anywhere else in Macedonia or Bulgaria, **Matka Climbing Club** (page 108) offers experienced guides as well as rock-climbing lessons.

The path along the river continues after the monastery, past a huge memorial of a carabiner hung on a piton stuck into the rock. The memorial was put up to commemorate the lives of climbers lost in a climbing accident at that spot in the early 1990s. The rest of the path along the lake is mostly good, but in some places it is crumbling and requires a bit of careful footwork. Again, it's not a walk for those with severe vertigo.

Eventually, the hike comes to the end of the lake and continues up the River Treška. Parts of the river cliffs are quarried for rock, so you may not be able to walk more than the first 3km, as the cliffs become unsafe. The middle reaches of the Treška between Makedonski Brod and Lake Matka are meant to be good fishing, and these can be reached more quickly by driving around via Sopište.

KATLANOVSKA BANJA

Katlanovska Banja **hot springs** (*banja* is Macedonian for 'thermal baths'), 30km outside Skopje near the airport, is the only Western-standard spa in the country (❨ *2581 002;* f *2581 032;* e *katlanovskaspa@katlanovskaspa.com; www.katlanovskaspa. com;* ⊕ *07.00–21.00; entry: main pool €4/hr; private pool for 2 €15/hr*). It is the only hot springs in Macedonia open to both sexes at the same time. Some excellent spa packages are available, including the full range of massage, body mudpacks and facials, as well as monthly special offers. See their website for specific details. The spa has a restaurant, and there is a small shop for snacks and small supplies.

Since the area was essentially trashed after housing refugees and internally displaced people from the conflicts in Kosovo and in Macedonia, it has been cleaned up, but still has a way to go to become the popular place it once was for a picnic, a walk in the countryside or a fishing trip, and the main sanatorium is still in need of much renovation. Nevertheless, many locals come to collect the medicinal waters of the natural springs coming from the rock faces on the approach to the baths.

There are a couple of old picnic gazebos in the grounds.

GETTING THERE Bus 53 goes to the baths from Skopje (see timetable, page 131). Return buses to Skopje run at 04.45, 05.20, 06.00, 07.10, 08.00, 08.45, 09.45, 10.25, 11.20, 12.55, 13.50, 14.45, 15.25, 16.25, 17.05, 17.40, 19.00, 19.35, 20.30, 21.15, with a reduced service on Sundays. An up-to-date timetable is also available on the spa website.

To get there by **car** there are two approaches, one from the north side when coming from Kumanovo and one from the south. To get to the south side, go east out of Skopje, past the airport as if going to Greece, and then take the Katlanovska Banja exit on the right. Keep following the signs and when you run out of signs, follow the river. If you get disoriented or lose the river on your right, just open the window and follow the faint sulphur smell.

THE OLD STONE AQUEDUCT

The 55-arch aqueduct is a hidden gem. Some sources say it dates back to first century AD Roman times when it brought water 9km from Lavovec to Skupi. Others say it was built by Justinian I (see page 169) when he rebuilt Skupi after

BYZANTINE ART ORIGINS OF THE RENAISSANCE

Lucy Abel Smith, director of art tour specialists, Reality & Beyond

The Byzantine Empire became consciously and seamlessly the heir of the Romans, the Late Antique world and Christianity after Constantine split the Western Empire from the Eastern in 330. Naming Constantinople after himself he declared it his empire's capital, and the New Rome. It comes as no surprise that intellectual thought and art patronage followed the new emperor, court and church in one.

All over the region from Albania to Macedonia and beyond, this continuity is palpable especially in the great basilicas and baptisteries of the 6th century and onwards, frequently on the foundations of Greek, Roman or earlier. Heraclea is an obvious example. Modern-day nationalism has slowed the study of early Christian sites, when the trade routes were so important for the spread of ideas and objects. Back then, the latest ideas travelled in the form of ivories, enamels or even sketches. Rivers and seas were the easiest routes and it was scholars, monks and pilgrims who disseminated the new ideas and the forms to express them.

The West, meanwhile, found itself under constant threat from waves of non-Christian Huns, Vandals and Goths, etc, during the so-called Dark Ages. Any religious and indeed artistic continuity was difficult. It was in Byzantium that the human form, based on antiquity, made real the message of Christianity and developed its iconography. All this was in the hands of the monastic scriptoria in Ohrid and other centres and in the Court in Constantinople. (There was a short interval in the 9th century when a period of iconoclasm mirroring that in the Islamic world, meant that the depiction of the human figure was disallowed.) The fact is, however, that it was the world of Byzantium and some Western monasticism that held the ring. The sack of Constantinople in 1453 by the Turks, makes it difficult to follow exact developments. Artists dispersed to regions such as Macedonia, Kosovo and Serbia, where the scriptoria and architects in places like Ohrid were pivotal in progressing their field both artistically and geographically.

For two vital periods, the art and iconography of Byzantium became used as a rich mine by the West. First in the Renaissance of the 12th century, and again during the period of the early Italian Renaissance in the 14th.

The 12th-century Renaissance (c1165–c1210) was a time of energetic intellectual activity in the West taking on ideas from the Court in Byzantium and the earthquake of 518. Still others say the Ottoman lord Isa Bey built it in the 16th century to supply the many amams, such as Čifte, Gurciler and Daut Pasha Amam. When the English traveller Dr Edward Brown wrote about it on a 1673 visit, he counted around 200 arches.

It is now in disrepair and completely unprotected, although attempts have been made in the past to keep it from falling down completely. Despite this it is one of the three largest and best preserved in the former Yugoslavia (the others are Diocletian's aqueduct near Split in Croatia, and the Bar aqueduct in Montenegro).

To get there on foot, cross the river at the Aleksandar Palace Hotel and join the E65 highway going north to Kosovo. Just over 300m after turning onto the E65, the road crosses a small stream/ditch. The stream is marked on the Trimaks maps of Skopje, but the aqueduct is not (nor is the huge army barracks)! Turn right immediately after the stream onto a dirt track. Follow this alongside the stream for 500m until you reach the gates of the army barracks at a crossroads. From the

from classical antiquity itself. Increasing emphasis was placed on the individual and their faith. Artists strived to portray emotion such as in the Church of Sv Pantelejmon in Nerezi, where the late Roman 'damp fold', which conveyed three-dimensionality, was used to great effect in the *Lamentation of Christ* in the naos. Experimenting with light and shade, a few years later, created the monumental classical figures of Studenica, in Serbia. These developments are paralleled in frescoes, sculpture, metalwork, ivories and enamels in Germany, Italy, France and England. This new approach to the human figure transformed the fear-inducing God and Judge of the early Romanesque period to the forgiving Christ with Mary, his Mother, as intercessor for mankind.

When it comes to the next Renaissance, the better-known Italian Renaissance, there is no doubt that Byzantium held the key both in the range of story telling and the sense of placing a credible human form in credible space. The backgrounds of gold or blue are infinite but the architecture and landscape within them experiment with perspective. Many of the painterly techniques, iconography and forms of the precursors of the early Renaissance in Italy, such as Cimabue or Cavalini, were those of the artists of Byzantium. The two seminal masters of the early Renaissance, Giotto and Duccio, took liberally from the tradition. Although 1453 was a disaster for Constantinople, the style and quality from this period can still be enjoyed in many of the churches of Macedonia.

Meanwhile the Italian Renaissance returned once more to the exploring and experimenting classical antiquity and broke free from its links with Byzantium. These ideas developed into the High Renaissance and the arts of Bramante, Raphael, Michelangelo and Leonardo. The Orthodox Church meanwhile chose to retain its traditional forms and techniques, veering little from the ideas laid down under the Comenian dynasty (1081–1185).

This subject is complex with much cross-fertilisation, but as Ernst Kitzinger pointed out in his *Art of Byzantium and the Medieval West:*

> It is a fascinating field encompassing as it does the whole problem of the Greek and the Western world in their estrangement as well as in their kinship … [My purpose] will have been accomplished if I have been able to show that during a crucial period of its artistic development the West received from Byzantium vital help in finding itself.

barracks gates it is a 500m walk past a few cottages to the aqueduct, which is visible from the barracks. You may not be allowed to take photographs of the aqueduct with the barracks in the background, so position yourself with the barracks behind you to take your shots.

PANTELEJMON MONASTERY

In the village of Gorni Nezeri, halfway up Mount Vodno, is the Monastery of Pantelejmon. The 12th-century church dedicated to Sv Pantelejmon, the patron saint of physicians, was built in 1164 on a Roman cult site by Aleksij (Angelus) Komnen, the grandson of Byzantine Emperor Alexios Komenos I. The **frescoes** inside are some of the few surviving in Macedonia as part of the body of Byzantine art that is believed to have influenced and ushered in the Renaissance (see box, page 162). The fresco of the Lamentation of Christ unusually shows Mary cradling Jesus between her legs, again in keeping with the increasing realism of the artistic style of the time. The church is often closed in the evening, so go early if you intend to stay on to eat at the restaurant there.

The church is surrounded by inns (see below) and a restaurant, **Klet** (↘ *3081 255; $$$*), offering traditional Macedonian fare. The restaurant has excellent views of the Vardar Valley, with a long outdoor patio area for sunset on a summer evening.

GETTING THERE It takes about 20 minutes by **taxi** to the monastery from the centre of Skopje, which should cost in the region of 700MKD. There are two routes to Pantelejmon Monastery from Skopje: the easiest route is to take the road just below Hotel Vodno around the mountain; the shorter route is to take Kozle Street all the way to the end past the long blue factory on the right, and at the end of the factory complex take a left turn marked Gorni Nezeri all the way up to the monastery.

WHERE TO STAY
⌂ **Hotel Pantelejmon** (12 rooms) ↘3081 255. Expensive simplicity. **$$$**

ŠUTO ORIZARI ROMA SETTLEMENT AND MARKET

Šuto Orizari, or Šutka for short, is the home of the sizeable Roma minority (see page 44) who live in Skopje. It is a part of Skopje that is little visited by tourists, and most Macedonians would think you were a bit crazy to want to go there. Nonetheless, the daily market is super-cheap (and filled with a lot of junk) and it's where you can get some of the hand-sewn and embroidered Roma clothing and shoes.

More interesting than a wander through the market (where even the Roma will tell you to keep a tight hold on your wallet) is a walk around some of the side streets off the northern end of Vietnamska. This area of their settlement will give you a feel of how the Roma live and love a carefree and artistic life. The closely packed one- or two-storey houses are usually immaculately whitewashed with a decorative fence of moulded concrete or ironwork, topped with whitewashed lions and Pekinese dogs pawing a ball. Wooden caravan wheels, harking back to the nomadic days of the Roma, adorn the walls and fences. Many of these lovely homes are not built from money earned here in Macedonia, but are the result of years away working in Germany and Austria.

The atmosphere and surroundings are not unlike a Chinese or Indian neighbourhood in Malaysia or some other southeast Asian country. Children

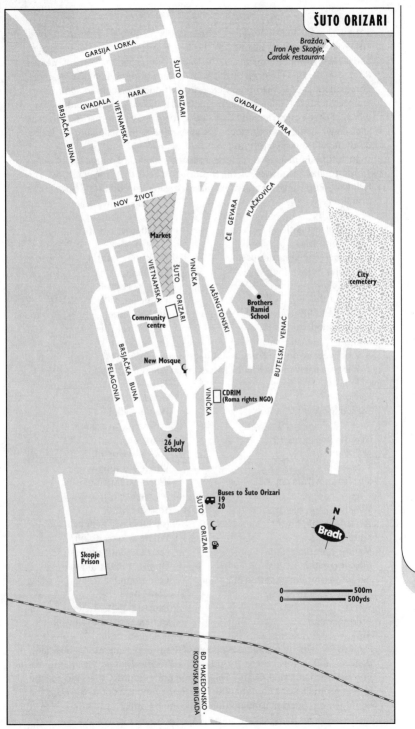

ŠUTO ORIZARI

Bražda,
Iron Age Skopje,
Čardak restaurant

GARSIJA LORKA

ŠUTO

ORIZARI

GVADALA

HARA

GVADALA

HARA

BRSJAČKA BUNA

VIETNAMSKA

NOV ŽIVOT

PLAČKOVICA

ČE GEVARA

Market

VIETNAMSKA

ŠUTO

VINIČKA

ORIZARI

VAŠINGTONSKI

**Brothers
Ramid
School**

City
cemetery

**Community
centre**

BUTELSKI VENAC

BRSJAČKA BUNA

PELAGONIA

New Mosque ☪

VINIČKA

☐ **CDRIM**
(Roma rights NGO)

● **26 July
School**

Buses to Šuto Orizari
🚐 **19**
20

ŠUTO

N ↑

ORIZARI

☪

Bradt

🚌

**Skopje
Prison**

| 0 | | 500m |
| 0 | | 500yds |

BD MAKEDONSKO -
KOSOVSKA BRIGADA

4

DID YOU KNOW? ROMANI LANGUAGE AND FAMOUS ROMA PEOPLE

The Romani language belongs to the North Indo-Aryan (Indic) languages and is close to Hindi, Punjabi and the Dardic languages. There are numerous Romani dialects, influenced by the Roma's place of settlement. For example, Romani words of Iranian origin include *baxt* (luck, fortune), *ambrol* (pear), *khangeri* (church), *angustri* (ring), *ruv* (wolf) and *vurdon* (wagon). Romani words of Greek origin include *drom* (path, road), *isviri* (hammer), *karfin* (nail), *klidi* (key), *kokalo* (bone), *papin* (goose), *petalos* (horseshoe), *tsox* (skirt), *amoni* (anvil) and *zumi* (soup).

In return Romani has also contributed significant numbers of slang words to the languages of the countries where they have settled. The following English slang words (standard meaning in brackets) have come from Romani:

Bamboozle (cheat)	Dad (father)
Bosh (nonsense)	Lolly (money)
Bungalow (one-storey house)	Nark (informant)
Busk (play music)	Pal (friend)
Char (clean)	Posh (classy)
Chav (youth)	Rogue (rascal)
Corker (tell a lie)	Rum (strange)
Cushty (good)	

A good website on the Romani language is www.rroma.org.

Here are a few phrases in the Macedonian Romani language:

Lacho dive	Good day/Hello
Sar san?/So keres?	How are you?/ What are you doing?
Ov sasto (m)/ov sasci (f)	Thank you
Naj pala soste!	You're welcome!
Katar aves?	Where are you from?
Sar si to anav?/Mo anav si ...	What's your name?/ My name is ...
Va/Na	Yes/No
Tjiri familija si vi tusa?	Is your family with you?
Kaj djas?	Where are you going?
Na haljovava tut	I don't understand you
Haljoveja man?	Do you understand me?
Av mansa (sing)/aven mansa (pl)	Come with me
Ava kari	Come here
Roma	People
Achov devlesar	God be with you/Farewell

Famous Roma people or famous people of Roma origin are mostly musicians, dancers and actors. These include Elvis Presley, Django Reinhardt, Yul Brynner, Michael Caine, Charlie Chaplin and Bob Hoskins. Others include the former footballer Eric Cantona. The new Roma Ambassador to the EU is the world-famous Spanish flamenco dancer Joaquin Cortes.

laugh and play in the streets and this is a world away from the Roma who beg on the streets with their babies and who have been trafficked to beg. But behind the laughter of children, the concerns of adults are not difficult to find.

In a community where education is not always highly valued, it is difficult enough to get the really poor of the Roma community to attend school. It is even more difficult when the main school in Šutka, Brakja Ramiz i Hamid, is filled three times over capacity and has few facilities and insufficient teaching staff. The school gymnasium has no heating in winter and most of the windows are broken. Water runs down the walls of the changing rooms and many of the corridors in the school.

On the bright side, the Roma are outstandingly talented in music and dance. The school has a few musical instruments of its own, but most of the children bring their parents' instruments into school, the very instruments that their parents earn their living from by playing in bands for hire at parties and festivals. In recent years, despite the poor teaching conditions and the other overwhelming concerns of poverty, Brakja Ramiz i Hamid has repeatedly won the first prize in the annual Skopje school choir and school orchestra competitions.

To find out more about the Roma see page 44, or to help Brakja Ramiz i Hamid directly see www.stuffyourrucksack.com.

GETTING THERE To get to Šutka take the 19 or 20 bus heading north from Dame Gruev outside the main post office, or take the ten-minute **taxi** ride for less than 350MKD. Ask to be dropped off at the Šutka Pazar, which is on the main street through Šutka.

ARCHAEOLOGICAL SITES AROUND SKOPJE

NEOLITHIC SKOPJE – GOVRLEVO AND MADŽARI
The history of greater Skopje spans more than 7,000 years. The oldest habitation in the area dates to the Neolithic or New Stone Age (5000–3000BC). Archaeological evidence from the sites of Tumba in Madžari and Cerje in Govrlevo suggests a society of some sophistication with dwellings built of mud brick and/or wood.

The people of these sites venerated the earth, as the sustainer and ultimate repository of all human life, represented by the 'Venus' figurine or Golemata Majka (Great Mother) found at Madžari in 1981. Copies of the figurine feature in all the craft and souvenir shops around the country. Part of a figurine of an inhaling male torso was found at Govrlevo as well as a manuscript seal. Both items show advanced use of pottery and the Govrlevo seal suggests a literate and administratively well-organised civilisation some 7,000 years ago. The male figurine has been named Adam of Macedonia, and is considered by some archaeologists to be one of the ten most important archaeological discoveries in the world.

A reconstruction of the Neolithic village in Madzari is open to the public (e *donco.naumovski@tumbamadzari.org.mk; www.tumbamadzari.org.mk;* ⊕ *08.00–14.00 Tue–Fri, 10.30–17.30 Sat & Sun; entry free*). To get there take bus 65 and get off at Tumba Madžari.

IRON AGE SKOPJE – BRAŽDA
Some 10km north of Skopje, at the foot of the Skopska Crna Gora Mountain, lies the village of Bražda. The picturesque surroundings of this village host the Iron Age or proto-historic and early antique (800–300BC) antecedent to Skopje, which is situated on the top of a small hill covering some 4.5ha and is reputed to be the capital of the Agriani tribe. Details of the settlement morphology are rather poor and little is visible, but one monumental building,

probably the tomb of a noble or a king, is extant. The Agriani, an ethnic community that lived in the northeastern part of modern-day Macedonia around Skopje, are frequently mentioned in inscriptions from the 4th century BC. Renowned for their fighting prowess they were one of the elite units in the Macedonian army of Alexander the Great. Čardak Restaurant near here is listed on page 153. To get there, take **bus** 61 (towards Pobožje), 71 (towards Banjani) or 81 (towards Blace), all of which go through Bražda along the bumpy cobbled road.

ROMAN SKOPJE – SKUPI Skupi became the administrative, cultural, economic and religious centre of the entire region following the Roman victory over Perseus in the third Macedonian war of 168BC and the foundation of the Roman province of Dardania. In the year AD313, following the Edict of Milan, it became the seat of the episcopate. Skupi was razed by the earthquake in 518, during the reign of Emperor Justinian (see page 169) but did witness low level squatter re-occupation.

The extent of the Roman colony of Skupi is largely unknown, even after significant archaeological excavation, the most recent being in 2008 when a church was discovered. The buildings visible within the excavations are a hall reputed to be the civil basilica, the centre of civil administration of the town, with its mosaic floors; a small Roman bath; a north–south aligned street (or *cardo*), possibly the Cardo Maximus; a theatre; remnants of part of the city wall; and the ground plan of a church or basilica.

Recent excavations by the Museum of Skopje have uncovered part of the city wall and have identified that the limit of the urban area (though still unknown) was greater than suspected. A basilica was also discovered along with a complete and rather beautiful statue of Venus Pudica associated with a possible bath building. The statue is 1.7m high, white marble and has a dolphin tattooed on the left leg. It is the only complete sculpture to be found on Macedonian soil yet and dates to the 3rd century.

By far the most remarkable discovery relating to Skupi, by dint of its preservation, is the standing Roman gravestones or *stele* some 150m further up the road towards Bardovci. What makes these gravestones unique is that they were found *in situ*, preserved by being buried under a later mound. This level of preservation of Roman monuments is unparalleled in the Roman world.

The archaeological site is located next to the road to the village of Bardovci and has an obvious access. A newly constructed path leads the visitor around the excavations and along which a number of noticeboards explain a little of what you are looking at. The site is 1.5km from the Aleksandar Palace Hotel. To get there take the bridge north over the river and turn left at the traffic lights 200m after the river. Take the second right turn 1km down the road to go towards Bardovci, and the ruins are on the right after another 100m.

TAURESIUM

On the northeast side of the village of Taor are the excavations for the town of Tauresium. The oldest section of the excavation has revealed the foundations of a four-towered castle, which was known as Tetrpirgia, built in the 4th century AD. The Ostrogoth Theodahad was born there around AD480. After he arrested Queen Amalaswintha, he went on to become king of the Ostrogoths for a short period from 534 to 536. He ruled the Kingdom of Italy, which was formed by the Ostrogoths after the collapse of the Western Roman Empire, and which was in turn defeated in the Gothic Wars of 535–554 by another man born in Tauresium. That man was the

Byzantine emperor Justinian I. He was born in AD483 and ruled Byzantium 527–65. Justianian rebuilt Skupi in its current location after the Roman town was destroyed in the earthquake of 518.

The site was first excavated by the famous British archaeologist Sir Arthur Evans. He wrote about his discoveries in the 1880s in his book *Ancient Illyria: An Archaeological Exploration*, which covers extensive observations on the wider Illyria region. For more on the excavation site see www.tauresium.info.

The village of Taor is 25km southeast of Skopje, on the River Vardar. To get there, you can either **drive** the old road via Dračevo, and cross the river at Orešani, or go to Katlanovo and head for Orešani and Zelenkivo. By public transport you can take the **train** to Zelenikovo and then cross the Vardar at the bridge behind the station (don't head into Zelenikovo village) and take the 3km track north over the hills or along the river to Taor. The track over the hills leads you past an old cross at the 454m trig point and then past the excavation site itself. From here it is another 7km to Katlanovska Banja hot springs, where you can take the #53 bus back (see page 161).

MARKOV MONASTIR

Tucked in the foothills of Jakupica Mountains, south of Vodno Mountain, is the village of Marko Sušica, at the southwestern end of which is King Marko's Monastery. The monastery church dedicated to Sv Dimitri was started by Marko's father, King Volkašin, in the mid 14th century, and then finished by Marko after his father's death in 1371. This may have been as close as Marko's kingdom got to Skopje, and from here the border probably went through his brother's monastery of Sv Andreja at Matka and on to the Šar Mountains.

The monastery has **frescoes** of the king himself, as well as an interesting fresco of the Three Wise Men visiting baby Jesus, and one of Sv Clement, the first archbishop of Ohrid. Although Ohrid was never a part of Marko's kingdom, the archbishopric was always behind the fledgling kingdom, and the absence of Serbian saints and church figureheads in Marko's monastery is seen as a good indicator that Marko adhered to the Church of Ohrid rather than the new Church of Serbia.

GETTING THERE Bus 80 goes to the village of Markova Sušica. To **drive** or **bike** yourself, take Ulica 11th Oktomvri southeast out of town and keep on this road as it becomes Ulica Sava Kovačevič and leads on to the village of Sopište. Take care to keep going straight on Sava Kovačevič and do not follow the main road around to the left when it turns into 1st Maj Street. After Sopište bear left towards Dobri Dol and Markova Sušica (signposted). At the crossroads just before the village, go straight on over the bridge and into the village until you reach the monastery on the other side. You will require shoulder and leg coverings to enter the church itself.

The small stream running below the monastery is a popular picnic site.

SV BOGORODICA MONASTERY NEAR KOŽLE

On the drive to Veles from Skopje, the road south follows the River Pčinja from Katlanovska Banja until it joins the Vardar. The road winds around the sides of a steep gorge making interesting driving and offering fantastic scenery. Fortunately, at this section there are (or at least should be) no oncoming cars as the road north takes a completely separate route further east. On this southerly road, a couple of kilometres before the River Pčinja joins the Vardar, there is a spacious stopping place on the right-hand side of the road with a couple of holy roadside shrines and a water fountain. This place also marks the stop for the Monastery of Sv Bogorodica, which can be seen across the river from the roadside.

The 500m hike starts through a metal entrance to the left of the fountain, goes across a small wooden bridge crossing the river, and ends up in the courtyard of the monastery. It is no longer a working monastery, but is kept by two wardens who live there. They might join you at this juncture to explain the place.

The site was originally just a shrine in the rocks and, like many rock shrines in Macedonia, it eventually became a cave church. This one was built using old train rails from 1918 to help support the roof, but by the 1930s it was completely abandoned. It took another 40 years for the church to be rebuilt in 1976, thereby saving some of the original roof frescoes, and replacing the old iconostasis.

If you spy the monastery on the way down south, but don't manage to stop, remember you won't be able to see it on the way back north as the north road does not pass that way.

5

Lake Ohrid and Galičica National Park

Telephone code 046

> The waters, limpid as the crystal of the rock, from which property the lake perhaps
> acquired its Greek name (for lychnis signified transparent), discover a bottom of clear
> sand, at even a depth of from nine to fourteen English fathoms.
>
> F C H L Pouqueville, *Travels in Epirus, Albania, Macedonia and Thessaly*, 1820

Lake Ohrid is the jewel of the Macedonian crown. Both the lake and Ohrid town are under the protection of UNESCO as a site of rare environmental, scientific and cultural significance. And not without due reason: the lake itself is an ancient one, and one of the oldest in the world, belonging in the ranks of Lake Baikal in Russia, Lake Tanganyika in Tanzania and Lake Titicaca in Peru/Bolivia. It is the oldest continuously existing lake in Europe, some three to five million years. It has also been proposed by some scientists that it may be the most diverse lake in the world for its size.

The town has roots going back to Neolithic times. Many of these historical remains are still being excavated and some can be seen in the museum or in the form of churches, castles and other architecture. Aside from these attractions, Macedonians love Ohrid because it is their seaside: the crystal clear waters beckon in the long hot days of summer, followed by a cocktail at one of the waterfront cafés. Then there is **Ohrid Festival**, attracting world-renowned artists to perform in the **Roman theatre**, **medieval fortress** and many other lakeside venues. The two main towns situated on the lake are Ohrid and little-visited, but quaint, Struga.

And once you have partaken of the festivals and seen the sites of the town – Tsar Samoil's Fortress, Sv Sophia's Church and the Robevi House to name a few – there are plenty of things outside the town too: the **lake springs** at Sv Naum; **cave churches** at Kališta and Radožda; caving, hiking and paragliding in **Galičica National Park**, including to a panoramic point to see both Ohrid and Prespa lakes; diving in and sailing on the lake; the **Twelfthtide Carnival** in the Republic of Vevčani; and day trips by jeep, donkey or foot to nearby **mountain villages**.

OHRID

HISTORY The shores of one of the oldest lakes in the world have been inhabited since prehistoric times. The earliest signs of humankind in the area have been found in Dolno Trnovo, to the north of the main town, and at the Bay of Bones at Gradište, dating from the late Bronze Age (around 12,000–7000BC). Although there is nothing of the graves left to see at Dolno Trnovo, the Bay of Bones stilt village has been reconstructed, and some of the related artefacts are on display in the Ohrid Museum.

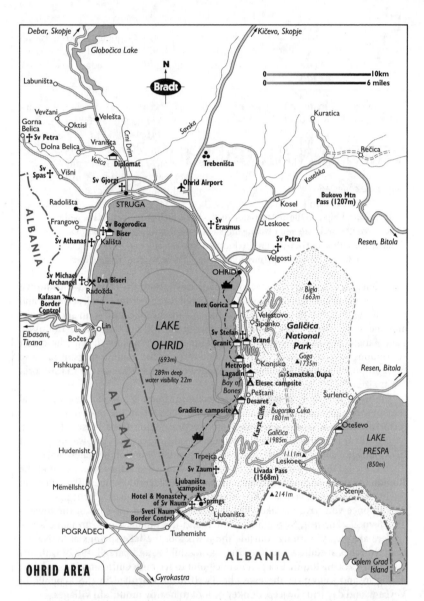

OHRID AREA

Debar, Skopje

Globočica Lake

N
Bradt

Kičevo, Skopje

Labuništa

0 ————— 10km
0 ————— 6 miles

Kuratica

Vevčani

Rečica

Velešta

Savska

Gorna Belica
Oktisi

✝ Sv Petra

Dolna Belica

Vraništa

Crni Drim

Velica

Diplomát

Trebeništa

Ohrid Airport

Sv Spas ✝ Višni

Bukovo Mtn Pass (1207m)

Sv Gjorgi ✝

Kosel

Radolišta

STRUGA

✝ Sv Erasmus

Leskoec

Resen, Bitola

Frangovo

Sv Bogorodica ✝ Biser

Sv Petra ✝

Sv Athanas ✝ Kališta

Velgosti

OHRID

Sv Michael Archangel ✝ Dva Biseri
Radožda

Kafasan Border Control

Inex Gorica

Velestovo

Bigla 1663m

Elbasani, Tirana

Lin

Bočes

LAKE OHRID

(693m)

Šiponko

Galičica National Park

Sv Stefan
Granit

Brand

Pishkupat

289m deep
water visibility 22m

Metropol
Lagadin

Konjsko

Goga 1735m

Samatska Dupa

Resen, Bitola

A L B A N I A

Bay of Bones

Elesec campsite
Peštani

Desaret

Šurlenci

Gradište campsite

Bugarska Čuka 1801m

Galičica 1985m

Hudenisht

Trpejca

Karst Cliffs

1111m

Oteševo

LAKE PRESPA

(850m)

Sv Zaum ✝

Leskoec

▲2141m

Stenje

Mëmëllsht

Ljubaništa campsite

Livada Pass (1568m)

Hotel & Monastery of Sv Naum ✝ Springs

Sveti Naum Border Control

Ljubaništa

POGRADECI

Tushemisht

A L B A N I A

Golem Grad Island

Gyrokastra

Later, tribes known as the Brigians, Ohrygians and Enhelians settled in the area. These tribes neighboured the Illyrians, who at that time had moved through Ohrid into areas further west (now Albania). They were displaced by the Desaretes (also of Illyrian descent), and it is as the capital of Desaretia that Lychnidos (present-day Ohrid) is first mentioned.

Lychnidos was founded and named by Cadmus the Phoenician (from Canaanite lands in today's Middle East). After he founded Thebes in the 14th century BC, he abdicated in favour of his grandson and travelled further north to fight for the Enhelians. There are two possible meanings to Lychnidos. In ancient Greek the name means 'town of lamps' (*lychnis* = lamp, *dos* = town). In Phoenician, however, *lihnis* means 'water reeds'. Lake Ohrid has gone through periods of partial desiccation when the water level has varied. When Cadmus founded Lychnidos, the lake may have been much smaller with significant reeds along its edges, just as parts of Lake Prespa are today.

By the 4th century BC, the town was conquered by the Macedonians of Philip II, and then the Romans in the late 2nd century BC. The town was developed further during Roman times by traders travelling along the Via Egnatia (see page 6), which passed through Radožda and Lychnidos. A Roman fort also existed further around the lake at Gradište (the first 0.5m of the outer wall of which has now been rebuilt for visitors to view). With these travellers came preachers of Christianity.

By the 5th century AD, the first early basilicas were being built in Lychnidos. Twelve are believed to have been built in total, although only six have been found so far. The largest and most significant of these is at the site of today's Monastery of Sv Kliment at Plaošnik. The large size of the basilica indicates the importance of this church and of the bishops who resided here, whose work grew with the arrival of pagan Slav tribes in the 6th century. Other basilicas found around Lake Ohrid are at Sv Sophia, Sv Erasmus and another in the hills above Biljana Springs.

By 879, the town was no longer called Lychnidos but was referred to by the Slavs as Ohrid, possibly from the Slav words *vo hrid*, meaning 'on a hill' as the ancient town of Lychnidos was at the top of Ohrid Hill.

A few years later, the missionaries Kliment and Naum came to Ohrid and set up the first monasteries that taught in Slavic (see box below). This strengthened the already strong religious tradition in the town, and a century later, when Tsar Samoil

THE FIRST UNIVERSITIES OF KLIMENT AND NAUM

Kliment (Clement, AD840–916) and Naum (AD835–910), like the brothers Kiril and Metodi, were native Macedonians. Both had been disciples of the brothers and travelled with them on their pioneering journey to Moravia in Hungary, to teach the Slavs in their own language, which brought about the invention of the Glagolitic and Cyrillic scripts. The diaries of both men have been passed on through the ages, the best known of which are the Extensive Hagiography and the Short Hagiography of Sv Kliment.

Kliment would have been 22 when he accompanied Kiril and Metodi to Moravia, and 46 by the time he came to the Ohrid region to teach the Scriptures there. In 893 at the age of 53 he was appointed Bishop of Velika, a large swathe of land reaching up to the River Treška around Kičevo, by Tsar Simeon of the new Bulgarian state recently freed from Byzantium. As a result of his new duties he had to move from his original monastery up in the wilds, north of Ohrid, into Ohrid itself where he founded a new monastery, the Monastery of Sv Kliment, and asked for his former fellow disciple, Naum, to join him in order to help teach the Scriptures to their ever increasing congregation. They mostly taught in the Glagolitic script, which only fully died out to be replaced by the dominant Cyrillic script in the 12th century.

The diaries record that over 3,500 pupils attended the Monastery of Sv Kliment, and numbers became so demanding that Naum set up the Monastery of Sv Naum in 900 at the other end of the lake. When he died in 910, he was buried in the vaults of the church, and it is believed that if you stand over his crypt and put your ear to the wall, you will hear Naum's heart beating even today.

Lake Ohrid and Galičica National Park   OHRID

5

(see box, page 22) moved the capital of his empire to Ohrid, he also made Ohrid the head of its own autocephalous patriarchate

Tsar Samoil's fortress city at Ohrid is still visible today, although parts of it were destroyed when Samoil was defeated by the Byzantine emperor Basilius II in 1014. Ohrid then became a part of the Byzantine Empire again and the patriarchate of Ohrid was reduced to an archbishopric. But it remained an influential archbishopric nonetheless, whose reach extended from the Adriatic in the west as far as Thessaloniki to the south and all along the River Danube in the north to the Black Sea, and the Archbishop of Ohrid was always a powerful political appointee.

The Archbishopric of Ohrid, although nominally under the patriarch of Constantinople, went from strength to strength as well as growing in geographical influence even under the Ottoman Empire (see box, page 52). By the end of the 16th century the jurisdiction of the Archbishopric of Ohrid went as far as the Orthodox communities in Dalmati and Venice in mainland Italy, as well as to Malta and Sicily.

Ohrid's privileged position within the Ottoman Empire through its seat as the archbishopric was rarely challenged, although in 1466 this was jeopardised when the citizens of Ohrid sided with the Albanian Lord Skenderbey (see box, page 255) against their Ottoman rulers. Several high-ranking Church officials and the archbishop were jailed as a result and died in prison, and the Church of St Sophia, which was the seat of the Ohrid archbishopric, was converted into a mosque.

When the Archbishopric of Ohrid was abolished in 1767 at the behest of the Greek patriarchate, Greek influence on Ohrid's religious life became pronounced, much to the dislike of the locals. It took just over a century for the locals to then convince the Ottomans to shut down Greek teaching in Ohrid in 1869. Thereafter, Ohrid's history follows a very similar pattern to the rest of northern Macedonia. VMRO's branch in Ohrid rose up on Ilinden in 1903 like the rest of the land, and was brutally put down again afterwards. Under Yugoslavia, Ohrid saw development in tourism, and Tito even had a summer residence on the lake, now reserved for Macedonia's government.

Tourism is picking up again now in Ohrid, so many of the socialist-style hotels are being completely renovated and many smaller family-run hotels and new apartments are springing up along the lake. The Macedonian parliament enacted zoning laws in 2010, and so most of the old town is protected in keeping with its status as an UNESCO heritage town. Enforcing the law is another matter, and you will still see a few new builds. Jet skis are now banned from the lake between 08.00 and 19.00 in July and August, but legislation has yet to catch up with speedboat use and the mix of raucous bars in the predominantly residential old town. Outside the peak season of July and August, it is quieter and cheaper, as are weekdays any time of the year.

GETTING THERE AND AWAY The railway line to Ohrid closed down in 1966 when the decision was taken not to upgrade the 60cm gauge line to the current 143.5cm gauge. Although trains and lines are to be upgraded in Macedonia, the Kicevo to Ohrid line is unlikely to receive funding. An excellent webpage on the old 17-hour steam journey is at www.penmorfa.com/JZ/ohrid.html. Otherwise you may travel as follows:

By air Macedonia's only other international airport, aside from Skopje, is Ohrid's St Paul the Apostle Airport (♦ 262 503, 252 830; f 252 840; e llohrid@airports.com. mk). It is 14km north of the town, and closer to Struga than it is to Ohrid itself. There are only a few flights a day in and out of the airport, mostly in the summer from Amsterdam, Belgrade, Düsseldorf, Ljubljana, Tel Aviv, Vienna, Moskow and

Zurich. At the time of writing the only flight from Skopje to Ohrid was with Jat Airways (originating in Belgrade). Full flight details for Ohrid Airport can be viewed at ohd.airports.com.mk.

By bus The inter-town bus station Pitu Guli 4 is 2km north of the centre (\ *260 339*). There are frequent buses to Ohrid from all over Macedonia with more frequent services in the summer. Buses leave at least every two hours from Skopje and cost 450–520MKD one-way. The frequent buses towards Sveti Naum and Struga also ply Turistička Bd and can be picked up from there. A taxi ride to the bus station from the centre of town costs 100MKD. Up-to-date bus times can be found in Macedonian at www.ohrid.gov.mk/index.asp?novostiID=112 (on the Macedonian version only). For the main bus times see the box below.

By car If you are driving to Ohrid from Skopje (around 2½hrs), you should consider taking the back road through Mavrovo National Park via Debar (3hrs 15mins). The dramatic tour through the mountains winds past four dams (Mavrovo, Debar, Golema and Mala Globočica) and close to the border with Albania. It is especially worthwhile in the autumn when the trees turn colour.

GETTING AROUND
By taxi The old town is small enough to walk around (but hilly) and driving is restricted. Taxis have a minimum fare of 50MKD plus a per kilometre charge of 30MKD. Taxi ranks can be found at either end of Makedonski Prosvetiteli street, or call one of the following numbers (prefixed 046 from a mobile phone): \ 1580, 1583, 1591, 1592, 1585, 1588, 1595, 1599.

By boat A good way to get around the lake is by boat. During June to September a daily boat service runs from the main boat quay in Ohrid to Sv Naum and returns in the late afternoon. Most hotels post the boat times. The approximate times can also be found in the box on page 175.

There are lots of boat taxis that will take one or a whole boatload of passengers for a ride for a minimum of €10. You'll see many a boat-taxi driver along the harbour and wandering the streets, often wearing a sea captain's hat, and they will

BUS DEPARTURES	
FROM OHRID INTER-TOWN BUS STATION	
Belgrade, Serbia	15.30 & 17.30 daily
Sofia, Bulgaria	19.00 daily
Frankfurt/Dortmund, Germany	05.30 Wed & Sat
Kičevo–Skopje	04.30 (summer only), 05.30, 07.30, 10.45, 12.45, 15.00
Bitola–Skopje	10.00, Bitola 07.00, 13.15
Kočani	06.00
FROM OHRID TURISTIČKA	
Struga	05.30–22.30 every 15mins
Elsani	13 buses every day 05.30–1930
Peštani/Desaret	16 buses every day 05.50–21.30
Trpejca/Sv Naum	05.00, 06.00, 12.15, 15.30, 18.30

Lake Ohrid and Galičica National Park   OHRID

5

	Out	Return
Ohrid quay	10.00	17.15
Hotel Park	10.10	17.05
Hotel Granit	10.20	16.55
Hotel Metropol	10.25	16.50
Hotel Desaret	10.35	16.40
Sv Naum	10.45	16.30

probably ask you if you want a ride long before you have got around to asking them. An extended tour around the harbour will cost you €20, €30 will take you to Struga, Kališta or Radožda where the view of the cave church from the water is quite striking (at least one hour's boat journey), and €45 will take you on the two-hour journey to Sveti Naum.

For larger boats contact tour guide Dzingis Patel (see contact details under *Tour operators* below) who can arrange hiring a boat for the day or half day. A 30-passenger boat, for instance, including lunch on board with drinks, works out at about €50 per person.

Town maps Free town maps are available in some of the big hotels. A 1:6,000 map of Ohrid can be bought in most supermarkets and bookstalls, both in Skopje and in Ohrid itself. The Trimaks map also includes a 1:65,000 map of the lake on the back of the city map, as well as some useful information on sites, telephone numbers and street names.

TOUR OPERATORS/TOURIST INFORMATION For help with bookings, tours and further information once in Ohrid, contact:

Dea Tours Kej Maršal Tito 40; ☎ 265 251; f 230 648; e info@deatours.com.mk; www.deatours.com.mk; ⊕ 09.00–20.00 daily. Friendly multilingual staff with a wealth of knowledge about the region. They can arrange various tours including ethno-tourism, donkey rides, adventure tours, mountaineering & other possibilities. Can also help with finding accommodation in all price ranges.

Džingis Patel m 070 331 232; e dzingispatel@gmail.com. Tour guide extraordinaire, personable & sensitive of the local environment, fluent in English & Turkish. Very knowledgeable on the living lake that is Ohrid as well as on the region. Can guide around Ohrid as well as the surrounding villages.

General Tourist 2000 Partizanska 6; ☎ 260 423; f 262 516; e gen2000@t-home.mk; www.generalturist2000-ohrid.com.mk; ⊕ 09.00–20.00 daily. Aside from tours in the region they also offer all the usual travel agency services.

Vis-poj Tourist Information Centre, Makedonski Prosvetiteli 7; ☎ 255 605; f 255 602; e info@vispoj.com.mk; www.vispoj.com.mk; ⊕ 09.00–20.00 daily. Conveniently located on the main street into the centre of town, with a larger office also at Turistička 50. Good link on their website to private accommodation.

WHERE TO STAY
Old town

Hotel Aleksandrija (15 rooms) Kosta Abraš bb; ☎ 258 860; e info@hotelaleksandrija.com; www.hotelaleksandrija.com. Overlooking the lake at the entrance to the old town, offers 2 deluxe apts with jacuzzi, & the remainder are all dbl-bed rooms. $$$

Hotel Toni (25 rooms) Abas Emin 3 (behind the old town); ☎ 250 001/002; e hoteltoni@t-home.mk; www.hoteltoni.mk. Modern hotel.

Rooms have cable TV, AC, bathroom & internet hook-up. **$$$**

🏠 **Villa Forum** (4 rooms) Kuzman Kapidan 1, Gorna Porta; 📞 251 340; **m** 070 819 713; **e** villaforumohrid@yahoo.com; www. villaforumohrid.com.mk. At the top of the old town overlooking the amphitheatre & lake. 1 twin, 2 dbls & 1 suite, all with an extra fold-out armchair-bed. **$$$**

🏠 **Villa Germanoff** (3 rooms) Tsar Samoil 57; 📞 266 831, 262 048; **e** germanoff@visitohrid. com.mk; www.visitohrid.com.mk/germanoff. The Piano Room with a view onto the lake is one of the nicest rooms in Ohrid. Say in advance if you want b/fast included. Electric kettle & drinks in each room. **$$$**

🏠 **Villa Jovan** (9 rooms) Tsar Samoil 44; **m** 075 377 644; **e** vilajovan@gmail.com; www. booking.com/Villa-Jovan. Beautifully restored old town house, complete with stone sinks, even if en-suite bathrooms are small. Deluxe on the top floor has view of the lake & a jacuzzi bath looking out on the stars. Well worth booking in advance. **$$$**

🏠 **Villa Sveta Sofia** (5 rooms) Kosta Abraš 64; 📞 254 370; **f** 254 363; **e** info@vilasofija. com; www.vilasofija.com. Of traditional Macedonian architecture in the old town with its own restaurant & private bar. Exquisite service accompanies every room. **$$$**

🏠 **Lucija's** (7 rooms) Kosta Abraš 29; 📞 265 608; **m** 070 352 804; **f** 266 396; **e** lucija@ t-home.com.mk; www.vilalucija.com.mk. Excellent value for money for its location. The patio is right on the water so you can go for a quick swim before b/fast, & the house is right opposite the Jazz Inn, so you don't have far to stumble in the evening either! **$$**

🏠 **Villa Kaneo** (4 rooms & 2 apts) 📞 265 583; **m** 070 353 999; **e** maslova@ohrid.com. mk; www.ohridaccommodation.com.mk. Nice tasteful rooms in 2 houses, 1 in Kaneo overlooking the lake & another in the centre of town, Villa Dudan. Private bathroom but not en suite. **$$**

🏠 **Villa Rustika** (5 apts) Hristo Uzunov 1; 📞 265 511; **m** 070 212 114; **e** villaoh@yahoo. com; www.villarustica.com.mk. Fantastic 270° view of the lake from the top suite & a beautiful garden, below a massive kiwi tree, for b/fast in the morning or a nightcap. **$$**

🏠 **Dimče Kanevče** (3 rooms) Kočo Racin 39, Kaneo; 📞 262 928; **m** 070 800 760; **e** dkanevce@ hotmail.com. Very nice rooms, simple & clean, right on the lake with a private jetty to swim from. Shared bathroom. **$**

🏠 **Stefan Kanevče** (9 rooms in various houses) Kaneo; 📞 260 350; **m** 070 212 352; **e** stefan_ kanevce@yahoo.co.uk (see box, page 183). **$**

Along the quay (*in order of cost, not as they are found along the quay*).

🏠 **Riviera** (36 rooms) Kej Maršal Tito 6; 📞 268 735, 251 912; **f** 254 155; **e** contact@rivierahotel. com.mk; www.rivierahotel.com.mk. The hotel also has a restaurant with patio seating, a piano bar & mini-shop. Buffet b/fast. **$$$**

🏠 **Hotel Tino** (18 rooms) Kej Maršal Tito 55; 📞 230 450; **f** 261 665; **e** hoteltino@mt.net.mk; www.hoteltino.com.mk. Standard clean rooms with AC & bathroom. **$$$**

🏠 **Millenium Palace** (25 rooms) Kej Maršal Tito 110; 📞 267 010, 265 414; **f** 263 361; **e** info@milleniumpalace.com.mk; www. milleniumpalace.com.mk. Standard smart hotel. Also has its own sauna, fitness centre & restaurant. A great buffet b/fast is 300MKD for non-residents. **$$$**

🏠 **Villa Biljana (5 rooms)** Kej Maršal Tito 111; 📞 266 444; **m** 070 833 130; **e** reservations@ vilabiljana.com.mk. Sandwiched between the Millenium & the Lebed, these rooms offer the view & location of the other hotels without the extra hotel trimmings. **$$$**

🏠 **Hotel Lebed (12 rooms)** Kej Maršal Tito 112; 📞 250 004; **f** 046 263 607; **e** tani@t-home. com.mk; www.hotellebed.com.mk. The last accommodation at the quiet end of the quay, this recently renovated hotel offers private parking with 24hr surveillance. Prices vary according to whether rooms have a lake view. **$$$**

🏠 **Villa Dea** (10 rooms) Kej Maršal Tito 40; 📞 265 251; **e** info@deatours.com.mk; www. deatours.com.mk. Excellent value & location for the price. Rooms have balcony & view over the lake. B/fast available at Hotel Royal next door. **$$**

🏠 **Apartmani Argiroski** (8 apts) Kej Maršal Tito 26; 📞 262 844; **m** 070 743 576; **e** argiroski_ apartments@yahoo.com; www.argiroski.com. Set down the little alley on the way to the Catholic church, these apts are clean, modern & some have a view of the lake from the balcony. **$$**

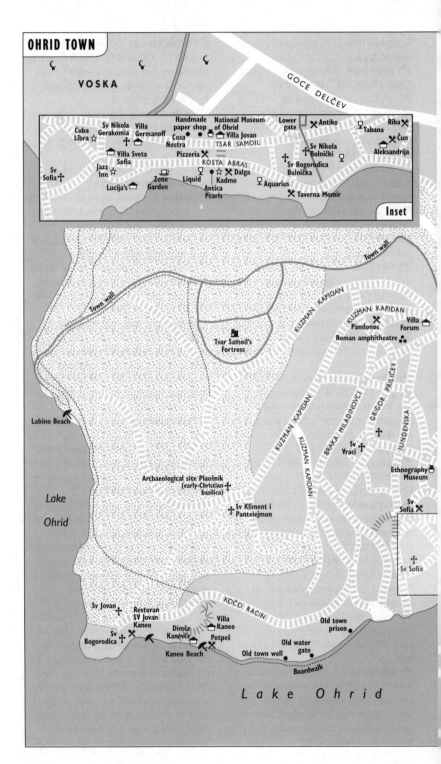

OHRID TOWN

VOSKA

GOCE DELČEV

Inset

Cuba Libra ☆

Sv Nikola Gerakomia

Villa Germanoff

Handmade paper shop

National Museum of Ohrid

Villa Jovan

Lower gate

Antiko

Tabana

Riba

Čun

Cosa Nostra

TSAR SAMOIL

Sv Nikola Bolnički

Aleksandrija

Villa Sveta Sofia

Pizzeria

KOSTA ABRAS

Sv Bogorodica Bolnička

Sv Sofia

Jazz Inn

Lucija's

Zone Garden

Liquid

Antica Pearls

Kadmo

Dalga

Aquarius

Taverna Momir

Inset

Town wall

Town wall

KUZMAN KAPIDAN

KUZMAN KAPIDAN

Pandonos

Villa Forum

Roman amphitheatre

Tsar Samoil's Fortress

KUZMAN KAPIDAN

KUZMAN KAPIDAN

BRAKA MILADINOVCI

GRIGOR PRILIČEV

ILINDENSKA

Labino Beach

Sv Vraci

Ethnography Museum

Archaeological site Plaošnik (early-Christian basilica)

Sv Sofia

Lake

Ohrid

Sv Kliment i Pantelejmon

Sv Sofia

Sv Jovan

Restoran SV Jovan Kaneo

Villa Kaneo

KOČO RACIN

Sv Bogorodica

Dimče Kanevče

Potpeš

Old town prison

Kaneo Beach

Old water gate

Old town well

Boardwalk

Lake Ohrid

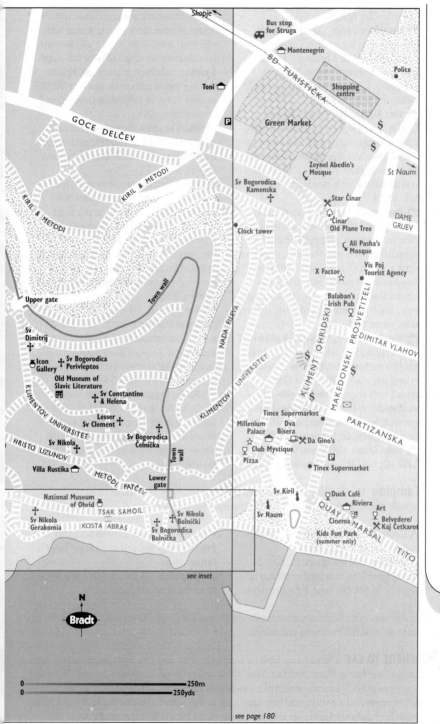

Skopje

Bus stop
for Struga

Montenegrin

Police

BD TURISTIČKA

Toni

Shopping
centre

P

GOCE DELČEV

Green Market

$

$

KIRIL & METODI

Zeynel Abedin's
Mosque

St Naum

KIRIL & METODI

Sv Bogorodica
Kamenska

Star Činar

DAME
GRUEV

Clock tower

'Činar'
Old Plane Tree

Ali Pasha's
Mosque

Town wall

X Factor

Vis Poj
Tourist Agency

Upper gate

Balaban's
Irish Pub

Sv
Dimitrij

KLIMENT OHRIDSKI

MAKEDONSKI PROSVETITELI

DIMITAR VLAHOV

Icon
Gallery

Sv Bogorodica
Perivleptos

NADA FILEVA

$

Old Museum of
Slavic Literature

Sv Constantine
& Helena

KLIMENTOV UNIVERSITET

$

KLIMENTOV UNIVERSITET

$

Lesser
Sv Clement

Tinex Supermarket

PARTIZANSKA

HRISTO UZUNOV

Sv Nikola

Sv Bogorodica
Čelnička

Millenium
Palace

Dva
Bisera

Da Gino's

Villa Rustika

METODI PATČEV

Town
wall

Club Mystique

Pizza

Lower
gate

Tinex Supermarket

P

Sv Kiril

Duck Café

Riviera

National Museum
of Ohrid

Sv Naum

QUAY MARŠAL TITO

Art

Sv Nikola
Gerakomia

TSAR SAMOIL

Sv Nikola
Bolnički

Cinema

Belvedere/
Kaj Četkarot

KOSTA ABRAS

Sv Bogorodica
Bolnička

Kids Fun Park
(summer only)

see inset

N

Bradt

0 ————— 250m
0 ————— 250yds

see page 180

Around the lake

🏠 **Hotel Inex Gorica** (125 rooms) In the same complex as the president's summer residence; ☎277 522; e bookings@inexgorica.com; www.inexgorica.com.mk. Pleasant & high quality. Access to 3 small beaches & a café pavilion on the water. **$$$$**

🏠 **Villa Aleksandar** (12 apts) Naselba Rača bb; ☎261 644; f 257 089; e reception@aleksandarvilla.com.mk; www.aleksandarvilla.com.mk. Colonial in style, this luxurious hotel complex is 3km from the centre of Ohrid, 100m from the water, & backs onto Galičica National Park. **$$$$**

🏠 **Apartments Lagadin** (4 apts) ☎254 200; m 070 307 460; e tkanevce@hotmail.com; www.visitohrid.com.mk/lagadin. Spacious & tastefully furnished, including all the usual hotel extras as well as a lounge & small kitchenette. View & sounds of the lake from the balcony. Lagadin Beach, a shop & restaurants are a few mins away. Prices exclude b/fast & vary according to the season. **$$$**

🏠 **Hotel Desaret** (252 rooms & 9 villas) Near Peštani; ☎285 951; f 285 915; e e-makedonija@tlen.pl; www.hoteldesaret.com.mk. Despite its large size, a nice facility with a wide beach & more privacy in the little villa-type accommodation. Good sports facilities & has its own disco. For those hankering after well-kept communist décor, this is the place. **$$$**

🏠 **Hotel Granit** (233 rooms) Sv Stefan bb; ☎207 100; f 207 141; e reservations@hotelgranit.com.mk; www.hotelgranit.com.mk. Despite its name, this is a pleasant, large hotel with direct access to the lake & a jetty for boats. Lakeside rooms are subjected to the café music & evening conferences or events spilling onto the lawn. Paddle boats on the beach are 200MKD per hour. Suites are better value for money for 2 people sharing. **$$$**

🏠 **Hotel Lagadin** (10 rooms) ☎285 227; m 070 261 448; e dance@hotellagadin.com.mk; www.hotellagadin.com.mk. Basic rooms above the restaurant. **$$$**

🏠 **Hotel Sveti Naum** (30 rooms) ☎283 080; e info@hotel-stnaum.com.mk; www.hotel-stnaum.com.mk. Your chance to stay in the holy grounds where Sv Naum himself taught & preached. Situated at the south end of the lake, the monastery is tranquil at night but can be just as busy as Ohrid during the day with visitors. The peacocks crow loudly early in the morning. **$$$**

🏠 **Hotel Brand** (26 rooms) On the hill side of the road above Hotel Granit; ☎277 220–2; e hotel@tkprilep.com.mk. A friendly hotel that benefits from the beach access & some of the facilities of the Granit without the luxury cost & loud music in the summer. **$$**

🏠 **Studio Lagadin** (2-bedroom house & 1 apt) Lagadin 14; m 075 303 084, 070 278 566; www.ohridforever.com. Set up on the hill behind the main bustle of little Lagadin, the pleasant garden & seating area offers a view of the lake. **$$**

Camping (**$**)All the sites listed here are 500MKD per tent space (maximum four people per tent space), plus 50MKD tourism tax per person.

🏕 **Elesec** (70 tent spaces) 10km on the eastern road of Lake Ohrid; ☎285 926

🏕 **Gradište** (400 tent spaces, 25 c/vans & 8 bungalows) 17km from Ohrid on the way to Sv Naum; ☎285 945/845. Huge, but with it comes a long stretch of beach & several ball courts. Conveniently located next to the Bay of Bones & Peštani village.

🏕 **Ljubaništa** (65 tent spaces) Close to the Sv Naum end of the lake; ☎283 240

If you run out of options above, private rooms are available around the lake for as little as 350MKD without breakfast.

✗ **WHERE TO EAT** Ohrid has a host of little pizzerias and fish restaurants along Tsar Samoil and Kosta Abraš, and fast-food joints and cafés galore along Kliment Ohridski. They can quickly become much of a muchness, and Ohrid is begging for some cuisine alternatives and a really good breakfast café in the centre. Despite the fact that Ohrid trout is endangered and illegal to fish, restaurants here still occasionally serve it.

✗ **Antiko** Tsar Samoil 30; \265 523; ⊕ 12.00–24.00 daily. An upmarket place to eat, with a wooden interior. Traditional Macedonian dishes take 3hrs to prepare so order ahead. **$$$**

✗ **Belvedere** Kaj Četkarot, Kaj Maršal Tito 3; \231 520; ⊕ 08.30–24.00 daily. Notable for its old wooden wagons on the lawn outside. The spoof street name *Kaj Četkarot* was coined by the owner, Klime, in reference to his father, who used to make brooms (*četke*). Serves traditional food in a national-style setting, including cooked b/fasts. **$$$**

✗ **Dalga** Kosta Abraš 3; \255 999; e dalga@ restorani.com.mk; www.dalga.restaurants.com. mk; ⊕ 10.00–24.00 Sun–Thu, 10.00–01.00 Fri & Sat. Ohrid's original lakeside fish restaurant sporting photos of all the rich & famous who have ever eaten there. **$$$**

✗ **Pandonos** Brakja Miladinovci 14 (directly overlooking the amphitheatre); \266 942; ⊕ 12.00–24.00 daily. Charming restaurant with terrace views from up high of the lake & serves traditional Macedonian food in a traditional setting with the best of Macedonia's trad/mod ethno music. **$$$**

✗ **Restoran Sv Sofia** Tsar Samoil 88; \267 403; www.restoransvetasofija.com.mk; ⊕ 08.00–24.00 daily. On the uphill side of Sv Sofia Church, has a wonderful outdoor patio overlooking the church, & good food. Try their excellent fried squid. **$$$**

✗ **Taverna Momir** Kosta Abraš 1; \262 117; e momir@restorani.com.mk; www.momir. restaurants.com.mk; ⊕ 08.00–24.00 Sun–Thu, 08.00–01.00 Fri & Sat. Nice lakeside seating with more Macedonian food. **$$$**

✗ **Da Gino's** Main square; ⊕ 08.00–24.00 Sun–Thu, 08.00–01.00 Fri & Sat. Branch of the Skopje pizzeria. Excellent pizzas with fresh mushrooms rather than tinned. **$$**

✗ **Elite Laguna** Kaj Maršal Tito; ⊕ 12.00–24.00 daily. Pleasant little place overlooking the yacht club boats on Biljana Springs estuary, although the food is nothing special. Limited menu of traditional fare & pizzas. **$$**

✗ **Potpeš** Kaneo; ⊕ summer only 09.00–01.00 daily. At the end of the boardwalk towards Kaneo, & has a further deck out on the water. Cocktails & sunloungers. **$$**

✗ **Restoran Sv Jovan Kaneo** Kaneo; m 078 203 099; ⊕ summer only 09.00–01.00 daily. Right on the water, with some comfy seats & serving basic dishes as well as cocktails. Lots of sunloungers. **$$**

✗ **Star Činar** 7 Noemvri 1; \260 890; ⊕ 12.00–24.00 daily. Local food at local prices overlooking the old plane tree. Serves extremely strong green *rakija* (*zelena rakija*). **$$**

ENTERTAINMENT AND NIGHTLIFE

Bars and cafés These stretch all the way from Restoran Kaneo Beach (see *Where to eat* above) to Cuba Libra (see *Nightclubs* below) at Biljana Springs, although it is mostly hotel fronts along the quay.

♀ **Aquarius** Kosta Abraš 30; ⊕ 10.00–01.00. Very popular place right on the lake.

♀ **Balaban's Irish Pub** Bd Makedonija Prosvotiteli; ⊕ 10.00–01.00. Just like you would expect an Irish pub abroad to be, but no draught Guinness.

♀ **Carpe Diem** Kosta Abraš 32; ⊕ 10.00–01.00. Listen to Aquarius's music in the summer but at a slightly lower volume with a slightly less trendy crowd.

♀ **The Duck Cafe** Kaj Maršal Tito 1; m 075 304 505; www.theduckcafe.com.mk; ⊕ 09.00–02.00. Plays classic blues & jazz, with a live band every night in the summer.

⌨ **Dva Bisera Café** Kliment Ohridski bb, next door to the restaurant of the same name, near Sv Kliment's statue; ⊕ 08.00–24.00. Serves a variety of sweet & savoury pastries, fresh fruit juice & the usual coffees. **$**

♀ **Liquid** Kosta Abraš 17; \258 552; www.liquid.com.mk; ⊕ 10.00–01.00. Ultra trendy on the lakefront featuring live bands at the w/ends. Serves cocoa. Has Wi-Fi.

♀ **Tabana** Tsar Samoil 11; ⊕ 10.00–01.00. Has a fantastic rooftop pub overlooking the lake.

⌨ **Zone Garden** Kosta Abraš 66. The only café to have a stretch of sand in the old town. Popular with the bronzed & beautiful.

5

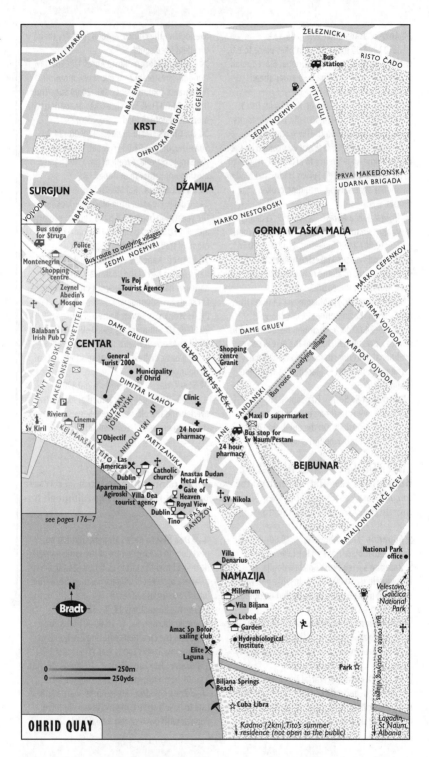

ŽELEZNICKA

RISTO ČADO

KRALI MARKO

Bus
station

ABAS EMIN

OHRIDSKA BRIGADA

EGEJSKA

SEDMI NOEMVRI

PITU GULI

KRST

DŽAMIJA

PRVA MAKEDONSKA
UDARNA BRIGADA

SURGJUN

ABAS EMIN

MARKO NESTOROSKI

GORNA VLAŠKA MALA

VOJVODA

Bus stop
for Struga

Police

Bus route to outlying villages

MARKO CEPENKOV

Montenegrin

SEDMI NOEMVRI

Shopping
centre

SIRMA VOJVODA

Zeynel
Abedin's
Mosque

Vis Poj
Tourist Agency

Balaban's
Irish Pub

DAME GRUEV

DAME GRUEV

KARPOŠ VOJVODA

CENTAR

General
Turist 2000

Shopping
centre
Granit

KLIMENT OHRIDSKI

MAKEDONSKI PROSVETITELI

Municipality
of Ohrid

DIMITAR VLAHOV

Bus route to outlying villages

Clinic

SANDANSKI

Riviera

Cinema

KUZMAN
JOSFOVSKI

24 hour
pharmacy

Maxi D supermarket

Sv Kiril

KEJ MARŠAL

NIKOLOVSKI

PARTIZANSKA

JANE

Bus stop for
Sv Naum/Pestani

Objectif

24 hour
pharmacy

BEJBUNAR

TITO

Las
Americas

Dublin

Catholic
church

Anastas Dudan
Metal Art

Apartmani
Agiroski

Villa Dea
tourist agency

Gate of
Heaven

SV Nikola

Dublin

Royal View

Tino

SPAS
BANDZOV

see pages 176–7

Villa
Denarius

National Park
office

NAMAZIJA

N

Millenium

Velestovo,
Galičica
National
Park

Bradt

Vila Biljana

Lebed

Garden

Amac Sp Bofor
sailing club

Hydrobiological
Institute

Elite
Laguna

Bus route to outlying villages

Park

0   250m
0   250yds

Biljana Springs
Beach

Cuba Libra

Lagadin,
St Naum,
Albania

OHRID QUAY

Kadmo (2km), Tito's summer
residence (not open to the public)

Nightclubs
These are abundant in Ohrid. Here are a few favourites.

☆ **Cuba Libre** Biljana Springs Beach; www.cubalibreohrid.com; ⏱ 11.00–04.00. The hottest place in town, & right on the water if you need a dip. A café bar during the day, live bands every night.

☆ **Jazz Inn** Kosta Abraš 74; ☎ 255 552; www.jazz-inn.mk; ⏱ 22.30–01.00. Good, live music Thu–Sat. Very popular.

☆ **Kadmo** Kosta Abraš 9; ☎ 258 720; www.kadmobeach com.mk; ⏱ 09.00–01.00 (till 02.00 Fri & Sat). Named after the Phoenician Cadmus (see page 172). A lakeside restaurant during the day & nightclub in the evening; also has a beach location at Biljana Springs.

☆ **X Factor** Bd Makedonija Prosvetiteli; e x-factor_oh@hotmail.com; ⏱ 22.00–03.00. Rock & techno nightclub.

WHAT TO SEE AND DO A first-time trip to Ohrid would be incomplete (and almost impossible) without seeing at least one church (even if only from the outside) and taking a walk along the lakeside boardwalk.

A suggested one-day itinerary Meander through the old town to Sv Sofia church, stopping in at the craft and handmade paper galleries on the way; from Sv Sofia church go down to the boardwalk and remember to look up at the old town watergate and cliff-face prison on the way. Take a break at Podepeš lakeside café or continue on through the houses to Restoran Sv Jovan Kaneo. Visit Sv Jovan Church and either go through the forest to Labino beach and/or up to Kale Fortress. Lunch at Pandanos overlooking the amphitheatre on the way back down into town, or at Belvedere by the old horse-drawn wagons. Take a long siesta in the hot day of summer, and then walk along the quay to Cuba Libre café to work off lunch. Dine

FIVE HUNDRED YEARS OF THE KANEVČE FAMILY AT KANEO

The Kanevče family came to Kaneo from Kičevo over 500 years ago in the late 1400s. They settled in the sheltered nook of the rocks of Kaneo still protected within the town walls, and quickly became wealthy lake fishermen after they bought the fishing rights for the northern half of the lake from Peštani to Kalište from the Ottomans. The family soon outgrew the small settlement at Kaneo and expanded into Ohrid itself where some of the early 19th-century houses still belong to the family, such as the one below Sveta Sofia Church and their older houses on Kaneo beach. Ohrid's abundant fishing and its position on a major trading route kept the Kanevče family busy up until the beginning of the 20th century.

Then with the Balkan wars, the division of Macedonia, the closed-door policies of early communism, and the negative effects of a bloated and over-centralised socialism, the luck of the Kanevče family went downhill. Stefan Kanevče, who remembers those days of good fishing with his grandfather, is still a keen fisherman and will happily take you out fishing on the lake if you want. He's also a mine of knowledge on many things in Ohrid and Macedonia. But the fishing trade isn't what it used to be, and he and his family have little money now to renovate the beautiful but crumbling houses at Kaneo. His, however, has the few rooms in Macedonia where you can actually stay in an original 19th-century house, complete with intricate wooden ceiling, closets and wardrobes. No heating and no television, only the sound of the waves of the lake to lull you to sleep at night.

at Elite Laguna or go back into town, pick up souvenirs at Anasas Dudan's metal art gallery or Ohrid pearls on Tsar Samoil. This itinerary can shortened by taking a boat across the lake between Kaneo or Labina and the harbour or Cuba Libre.

Beaches Most people come to Ohrid to go swimming in pristine waters. If you don't have access to the water from your accommodation, then popular places to take a dip are:

Zone Garden To the left and on the lake side of this café is a small pebble public beach. No changing facilities.

Podepeš At the end of the boardwalk. Sunloungers free of charge if you order a drink.

Kaneo Next to the church of Sv Bogorodica. No dedicated changing facilities aside from the restaurant toilets outside. Sunloungers for those ordering from the café.

Labino Accessed via a walk through the forest or by boat. Still quiet & out of the way at the time of writing. No facilities.

Biljana Springs Dedicated beach with lifeguards, children's play area & sand. Changing

facilities available. Close to Cuba Libre café.

Lagadin Offering a long stretch of pebble beach which practically merges into the neighbouring village of Peštani. Lots of new accommodation here as well as a few restaurants & cafés.

Trpejca Tongue in cheek, known as the St Tropez of Lake Ohrid, in a play on the similarity in spelling with the famous French beach resort. Close to Sv Zaum Church & beach (accessible by boat only), the tiny hamlet of Trpecja is 19km from Ohrid itself. Offers a couple of lakeside restaurants, a minute pebble beach & a mooring deck from which to dive into the lake.

Historical sites

Tsar Samoil's Fortress (⏱ *09.00–19.00 daily; entry 90MKD*) The fortress dates only from the end of the 10th century, but records from Livy and other ancient historians tell that a fortress has stood on the top of Ohrid Hill since at least the 3rd century BC and other findings go back even further. In 2002, a golden mask and glove similar to those found in Trebenište (see box, page 190) from the Paeonian period were found behind the fortress walls.

Today much of the 3km fortified wall which enclosed the fortress can still be seen, although the inside of the fortress itself was mostly destroyed and is still awaiting restoration. Up until the Ottomans arrived in Ohrid in 1395, the town was completely enclosed within these great city walls, and only two gates, the Upper Gate and the Lower Gate, existed by which to enter the town. With the arrival of the Ottoman Turks the town expanded beyond its walls, with the Christian population within the town walls, and the Ottoman Turkish population outside it.

Mesokastro The Turks meanwhile built up what came to be known as the Lower Town of the Mesokastro area. There you will find two working mosques, the Zeynel Abedin Mosque and Ali Pasha's Mosque, astride the **900-year-old plane tree** (*Platanus orientalis*) known locally as Činar in the middle of Kruševska Republika Square. Allegedly, this tree's hollow trunk used to house a barber's shop at sometime in its history and later a very small café. As the old Turkish town winds around the back of the town wall you can still see a few old Turkish shops which are no longer in use, but their dust-covered artefacts and tools are still on display. These may not be around for much longer as new buildings encroach.

Roman theatre The Roman theatre near the Upper Gate is just over 2,000 years old, but had been buried for centuries until, in the early 20th century, trial excavations confirmed its location. The next few decades of turmoil put the full excavation on hold, until in the 1960s the excavations finally got going again. By the 1990s the amphitheatre was fully uncovered and is now once again being used in the summer as in days of old for outdoor concerts and performances. If you manage to attend a concert there, take a close look at your seat to see if you can decipher the name of the season ticket holder who owned that seat thousands of years ago.

Museums and galleries

National Museum of Ohrid (*Tsar Samoil bb;* ☏ *267 173;* ⏺ *10.00–14.00 & 18.00–21.00 daily*) The museum was first established in 1516 in Sv Kliment's Church of Bogorodica Perivleptos as a museum to the Archbishopric of Ohrid. This must make it one of the oldest museums in the world. Now the collection is divided into the archaeological display housed in the Robevi residence and the ethnographic display housed in the Urania residence. The Robevi house on Tsar Samoil is the renovated wooden three-storey house, which is a museum piece in itself, and one of the finest examples of 19th-century Macedonian architecture in the land; well worth a visit.

Icon Gallery (☏ *251 395;* ⏺ *09.00–13.00 & 17.00–20.00 daily; entry free*) Within the grounds of Sv Bogorodica Perivelptos Church, this gallery displays a range of some of the most valuable icons of the 11th to 19th centuries saved from churches all over Macedonia.

Churches and monasteries
According to legend recorded by the Turkish chronicler Evliya Celebija in the 17th century, there were once 365 churches within the city boundaries. Whilst that is not so now, if ever it was, there are a lot of churches still within the old walls. Here are six of the most important within the town to start you off, Sv Sophia being by far the most significant. Details of many more of the lesser churches can be found in various booklets available in most of the church shops and bookshops in Ohrid. Many of the churches require an entry fee of 100MKD per person. In those few that do not charge an entry fee it is customary to leave some money at the altar or icons anyway.

Sv Sofia The church was built in the early 11th century as a cathedral church for Archbishop Leo of the Archbishopric of Ohrid. It was also built on the remains of a former basilica. It still contains a few fragments of rare 11th- and 12th-century Byzantine frescoes (see page 162). Much of the original fresco work was destroyed when the church became a mosque in 1466 (see page 174). During the Bulgarian occupation of Ohrid in the second Balkan War of 1913, the mosque was used as a warehouse, then re-converted to a church at the end of the second Balkan War.

As a mosque the inside of the cathedral had been completely whitewashed and so it took extensive work during the second half of the 20th century to retrieve the 11th-century frescoes that lay underneath. Most of these are now on display again, as well as some of those from later renovations of the church in the 12th and 14th centuries. Sv Sofia is one of only two churches in the world to display such a high number of well-preserved 11th-century frescoes. The other is Sv Sophia in Kiev.

Sv Kliment at Plaošnik Dedicated to saints Kliment (Clement) and Pantelejmon, this was completed in 2002. It stands beside the original site of Kliment's very own monastery school, started in 893. Kliment had built the original church on the ruins of the early 5th-century basilica at Plaošnik, and had even built his own tomb into the church, in which he was buried upon his death in 916. Almost 150 graves were recently found and suggest that the church was also a hospital during Kliment's time.

The church was renovated and enlarged three times in the 12th, 13th and 14th centuries, but during the time of Ottoman rule it was transformed into the Imater Mosque. Sv Kliment's relics were then hastily moved to the 10th-century church of Sveta Bogorodica Perivleptos. The mosque did not survive the end of the Ottoman Empire and after its destruction only the legend remained that Sv Kliment's monastery and his tomb used to stand at Plaošnik.

Excavations started in 1943, and it was not long before the foundations of the church, the basilica and the tomb were found. Frescoes from the renovation and enlargement periods have also been found, but none from the original 9th-century church. The foundations of the 5th-century basilica have been preserved and are on display in front of the new church. Excavations continue, and there is discussion in the town about restarting a theology university at the site.

Sv Bogorodica Perivleptos (Sv Kliment's Church of the Holy Mother of God Most Glorious)

Built in 1294/95, this church is an identical replica of the Panagia Bellas church in Boulgareli, Epirus, almost 200km to the south in Greece. It took on the Sv Kliment prefix only when Sv Kliment's relics were transferred there during the Ottoman Empire. At the same time the church became the cathedral of the archbishop when the original cathedral at Sv Sophia was converted into a mosque. By the end of the 15th century the cathedral had started to become a collection point for historical records and artefacts saved from other churches around Ohrid. In 1516 the cathedral's collection and its library became the archbishopric museum, which is now the National Museum of Ohrid housed in the Robev residence (see page 185).

In the 1950s, centuries of smoke and soot from candles and incense were carefully cleaned from the frescoes to reveal some interesting examples of late medieval painting. Look out for the fresco of the Last Supper, which is being eaten outside rather than inside, and note the use of perspective from Byzantine renaissance painting of the late 12th century as opposed to the older style still employed in many of the more traditional churches.

In the grounds of the church is the Icon Gallery, and the late 19th-century town house now housing the Office of the Protection of Ohrid (despite the fact that it itself looks run-down and inactive).

Sv Jovan Kaneo

This is the most frequently visited church in Ohrid because of its beautiful location on the cliffs directly above the lake. It was built at the end of the 13th century by an unknown benefactor, but shows signs of both Byzantine and Armenian influence. Inside, a group fresco of the 3rd-century Sv Erasmus, believed to be one of the first missionaries to the area, together with the 9th-century Sv Clement and the early 14th-century Archbishop Constantine Kavacila of Ohrid, betrays the eclectic nature of the church. Despite being built around the same time as that of Sv Clement's Church of Sv Bogorodica Perivleptos, it was painted in the older style of pre-Byzantine renaissance frescoes.

This church features visibly in Mančevski's *Before the Rain*, a must-see film about Macedonia (see page 367). Behind the church, a small path leads up to Sv Kliment's Church at Plaošnik. Tucked away in the rock below the entrance to the church grounds is also the very small cave church of Sv Bogorodica.

Sv Bogorodica Bolnička and Sv Nikola Bolnički These are to be found on either side of a small lane leading from the Lower Gate of the town wall to the lake. Both were built in the 14th century and were originally hospital churches (*bolnica* in Macedonian), separated into the women's hospital of the Virgin Mary, and the men's hospital of Sv Nikola. The men's hospital is some 70 years older than the women's and is an interesting construction of an older church inside a newer one. Both back onto the town wall, parts of which can still be found in the church grounds. Sv Nikola is usually closed, but well worth a look – ask Slavica next door at the women's hospital to open the heavy walnut doors for you.

Local artisans Ohrid is home to many painters, sculptors, woodcarvers and other artisans hidden away in narrow streets. Vangel Dereban **silver filigree** workshop is at Sveti Kliment Ohridski 40. In the lower town, Vasil Malezan **packsaddle workshop** is at Goce Delčev 40, and Milan Belevski **cobbler** is at Goce Delčev 26 for handmade shoes and repairs. Two exceptional artisans worth visiting are:

Anastas Dudan Metal Platework Jane Sandanski 14; 264 804; m 070 501 573; ⊕ 09.00–20.00 daily; e dudan1@t-home.mk; www.anastasdudan.com.mk. Anastas is a skilled & unique craftsman in producing art on metal sheets, be they copper, silver, gold or plated. His small shop offers a variety of icons, pictures, mirrors & plated books, but he can also produce work to order in 2–3 days, if you provide him with a picture of the image you want him to produce. His work has been presented to the famous & beatified, including several popes.

National Workshop for Handmade Paper Tsar Samoil 60 253 610; m 075 465 131; ⊕ 09.00–20.00 daily; e panevski@ohridpaper.com.mk; www.ohridpaper.com.mk. Fascinating little shop with 1 of only 2 replicas of the Gothenburg press. Paper is handmade, hand-printed in the press & sold in the shop.

Paintings and artwork can be found in many galleries in the old town as well as here:

Atelier Gallery Tsar Samoil 52. For the work of Živko Pejoski.
Gallery Bukefal Sv Kliment Ohridski 54

Gallery Ohridska Porta 29th November 3; 260 755; m 070 250 560. For the work of Vangel & Rubens Naumovski.
Gallery Upevče 7th November 10

Ohrid pearls made from the scales of local fish are sold in many shops along Kliment Ohridski and at:

Antica Pearls Kosta Abraš 51 & Klimentov Univerzitet 87
Gallery Marija Dame Gruev 28

Woodcarving workshops and wooden icons are available at:

Atelier Rezbar Gorna Porta (Upper Gate). Behind the shop you can also see the woodcarver at work.

Barok Tsar Samoil 24
Porta Tsar Samoil 32
Tron Tsar Samoil bb (near Villa Germanoff)

Walking along the lakeside Heading south out of Ohrid along Kej Maršal Tito is particularly pleasant in the evening when the sun is setting on the lake. Sometimes there are buskers and street performers on the quayside, and in the summer there is also a luna park with rides, trampolines, and a bouncy castle for children. At the end of the quay (1.3km from the centre's main street, Makedonija Prosvetiteli) is the yacht club Amac CP-Bofor and the **Biljana Springs** estuary. The springs are renowned for their refreshing drinking water, which is bottled and sold throughout Macedonia. For more information on the yacht club's membership, docking fees and yacht hire, see page 108.

DIVING IN LAKE OHRID

A tectonic lake almost 300m in depth with endemic plant and animal life, Ohrid offers a number of underwater attractions to the scuba diver. Arguably one of the most interesting sites is the (3,200-year-old) **Bronze Age stilt-village** Michovgrad, also known as the **Bay of Bones**, near Gradište. Discovered in 1997 and named after the diver who found it (see below), the village had been built on stilts over the marshy edges of the lake when the waters were not as high as they are today. The stumps of former stilts can still be seen sticking out of the sand under the water, as well as many pieces of broken amphora and other pottery. The best finds are on display in the small museum at the Bay of Bones. The site is a nationally protected area, and experienced divers may go there with permission.

As a geological area, the lake is interesting because of its depth and steep drop-offs. The steepest drop-off closest to the shoreline is beneath the karst cliffs over Gradište and Sv Zaum Church. Here, a 20m sheer wall shelters endemic plants, freshwater mussels and sponges. *Plašica*, *belvica* and gudgeon are plentiful to see when diving, and occasionally it is possible to see some *mrenka* and crayfish. Ohrid trout on the other hand are rarely seen as they live deep in the lake. Night diving offers the best chance to see eels as well as chub and larger fish coming up to feed.

Just south of Struga is a sunken **World War II German coastguard boat** and two **World War I tugboats**. The latter were deliberately sunk during the war to stop them getting into enemy hands. An Ottoman Empire rifle has been found in the lake (see the town museum, page 195), and on the Albanian side of the water there is believed to be a small **World War II aeroplane**. A project is also ongoing to try to find part of the Via Egnatia, which is believed to lie somewhere underwater between Struga and Ohrid around Sv Erasmus Church.

All of these sites (except the aeroplane) can be seen through **Amfora Dive Centre**, based at the Hotel Granit (❝ *207 100;* m *070 700 865;* e *sekuloski@yahoo. com; www.amfora.com.mk*). Their chief instructor and divemaster, English-speaking Micho (the discoverer of Michovgrad), has done over 5,000 dives in Lake Ohrid, and is also the Macedonian army's special forces diving instructor. As with diving anywhere, take care not to disturb the lake bed: not only is the sandy bottom very easily disturbed, causing a deterioration in visibility, but the lake's endemic species are also vulnerable. Visibility is at its best in the lake (up to 22m) during May and September. You will need to purchase a yearly dive licence before diving. Thereafter the dive fee to Michovgrad is €30; all other sites €20, including all equipment. Tank refill is €10. Amfora Dive Centre is Scuba Schools International certified and will also accept PADI, BSAC and other licensed divers. Diving courses are available on request.

Check you are satisfied with the equipment provided before diving. A diving buddy of mine who is a British army diving instructor noticed on our dive that the tanks were out of date, hence this added word of caution.

On the far side of the small bridge over the Biljana Springs estuary is the Army Water Training Centre, which has a beautiful little beach with a view onto Ohrid town, Tsar Samoil's fortress and the Church of Sv Jovan Kaneo. Cuba Libre and Kadmo café bars and nightclubs are also here. The next 1.7km along the lake goes through partially wooded grounds away from the main road to the Hotel Park. Cyclists and rollerbladers frequent the path and there are several little entry points to the lake. At Hotel Park, the path skirts around **Tito's summer residence**, which sits atop the promontory that marks the south end of Ohrid Bay. It is now used by the government of Macedonia for officials visiting the country and so is not open to visitors.

On the other side of Tito's summer residence is the four-star Hotel Inex Gorica and a number of holiday camps. A path along the rocky shore continues from inside the Inex Gorica complex for another 2km in front of other holiday camps and hotels until it meets up with the main road.

Heading north out of Ohrid old town, past the Church of Sv Jovan Kaneo is a pleasant walk for about 500m to the back of the town. There is plenty of exploring to be done among the old wall and fortress, with splendid lake views.

Festivals and events in Ohrid Summer is the big festival season for Ohrid. The programme for most of the events can be seen on the events calendar at www.ohrid. com.mk.

The season often kicks off in June with the **Ohrid International Swimming Marathon** in which, since 1962, swimmers have been invited to test their strength against the 30km course from Sv Naum to Ohrid. Over the first weekend in July is the **Balkan Festival of Folk Song and Dance**, which is part of the UNESCO association of the international council of Organisations of Folkore Festivals and Folkore Art. Despite its name, this festival includes song and dance from around the world. The following weekend sees the new and increasingly popular Ohrid Salsa Camp (*www.sportdancenova.mk*)

From mid-July to mid-August is the **Ohrid Summer Festival** (*www.ohridsummer. com.mk*) now over four decades old. Classical concerts and plays are held in historical and outdoor locations around the town, such as in the amphitheatre, basilicas, churches and Tsar Samoil's fortress. On Ilinden, 2 August, is the Ilinden Sailing Regatta. Towards the end of August is the **Ohrid Troubadour Festival** (*www. ohridfest.org.mk*) of popular and folk music, as well as the **Ohrid Choir Festival**.

OUTSIDE OHRID

SV NAUM MONASTERY The Monastery of Sv Naum is right at the other end of the lake near the border with Albania. It is a beautiful and popular site, with well-kept grounds that are home to a flock of peacocks, including an albino, and a source of the waters for Lake Ohrid. New inns built in the last decade make up the Hotel of Sv Naum (see contact details on page 180).

The actual early 10th-century Church of the Holy Archangels built by Sv Naum is in fact buried beneath the present 16th-century church, which stands in the middle of the monastery courtyards. The church had been destroyed during Ottoman rule and its remains were rediscovered only in 1955 when excavations beneath the present church floor were carried out. The original church was a typical trefoil or clover-leaf design and contained the tomb and relics of Sv Naum himself. These have been preserved and re-interred beneath the new floor of the present church, which is now marked with black and white marble to show the floor plan of the original 10th-century church.

THE GOLDEN MASKS OF MACEDONIA

North of Ohrid Airport, outside the village of Trebenište, are some of the most important and richest archaeological discoveries ever to be made in Macedonia. The unearthing of ten burial chambers in 1918 revealed the lavish ceremonies of the ancient Paeons and Macedonians of the 1st millennium BC. Four almost complete golden masks were found in the graves as well as jewellery, pottery, ceremonial clothing, shoes and part of a fifth mask. The burial chambers belonged to rich princes of the region who were cremated at death, so only the burial riches remain. Two of the masks were taken to Belgrade and are on display at the National Museum of Serbia. The other two were taken to Sofia, where they are displayed at the Archaeological Museum. Each mask is worth in the region of €18 million. Part of a sixth mask has been found at the Petilep tomb in Beranci, near Bitola, and more tombs, long since ransacked, exist all over Macedonia.

Sensationally in 2002, Pasko Kuzman made his name as Macedonia's leading archaeologist when he discovered a fifth complete golden mask during excavations at Tsar Samoil's fortress in Ohrid. As yet unseen by the general public, the mask is due to go on display in a Golden Room at the new Museum of Archaeology in Skopje in 2012. Little but age-old scars in the ground exist at the Trebenište tomb now, and Ohrid fortress is still under excavation.

The present church was enlarged in the 17th and 18th centuries, and in 1799 the tiny chapel over Sv Naum's underground tomb was built. When you enter the chapel, which is to the right as you enter the narthex, and listen very carefully above the tomb, you are said to be able to hear Sv Naum's heart still beating. Touching the stone above the tomb is also meant to make a wish come true.

BOAT TRIPS FROM NAUM A boat trip down to the springs, which feed Lake Ohrid, is available from Sv Naum. Trips and boat numbers are limited by the Galičica National Park authorities as the springs are a rare natural phenomenon and therefore it is important not to disturb the ecological balance in the waters. This doesn't stop unlicensed boatmen from trying to take surplus visitors in the busy summer months, so make sure you take a legal ride. The 45 springs, which bubble up from the bottom of the crystal clear stream bed, mostly bring water from the neighbouring lake of Prespa on the other side of Galičica National Park. Prespa lies another 157m above Lake Ohrid and so the water is effectively siphoned off through the bed of Galičica Mountains into the spring on the other lower side of the mountain.

A good boatman to go with is Nikola Pavleski. For 150MKD on your half-hour trip to the springs and back he will give a constant stream of information in English and Macedonian, as well as stops just to listen to the tranquillity and the orchestra of birds, allow for photographs and of course see the bubbling springs themselves. He tops it off with a round of *rakija* for everyone.

SV STEFAN MONASTERY AND CAVE CHURCH Just 5km outside Ohrid is the Monastery and Cave Church of Sv Stefan, hidden away above the lake a 500m hike from the lake road. The original cave church was built in the 9th century at the time of Sv Clement. Villagers from the surrounding settlements of Šiponko, Gorica and Konjsko up the hill have since built the present walls and in the 15th century the church was painted with frescoes.

To get there take the path uphill from opposite the Hotel Beton, 4.5km from the petrol station on the eastern edge of Ohrid. The path is marked with a hand-painted sign saying Sv Stefan in Cyrillic.

At the gateway into the monastery the path continues up above to the villages of Šiponko in the north and Konjsko in the south, and further hiking into Galičica National Park. Beware the Šarplaninec sheepdogs in the old and dying settlement of Šiponko, and the villagers don't like strangers wandering around on their own.

There are two more cave churches on the eastern side of the lake, one at Sv Erasmus and Sv Ekaterina between Ohrid and Struga, and one on Gradište II beach at Gradište campsite near Peštani halfway to Sv Naum. There are good views of Lake Ohrid from these churches.

STRUGA

On the northern shore of Lake Ohrid is the town of Struga. Also boasting human settlements going back to Neolithic times (3,000BC), the old name of Struga is Enchalon, the ancient Greek word for eel, which is still a popular food in the area (see page 188). The new name Struga comes from the old Slavic *straga* meaning 'cross', but some say it also comes from the word *struže* meaning 'blowing wind'. With just over 16,000 inhabitants in the town and 35,000 people in the municipality, Struga is less than half as populous as nearby Ohrid. Dwarfed in size and popularity by its neighbour, Struga is nevertheless an up-and-coming town and a delightful getaway from busy Ohrid in the height of the summer season. Its many cafés along the River Drim leading out of Lake Ohrid make a good day or night out and there are some pleasant places to stay and to visit in the vicinity.

GETTING THERE AND AROUND There are regular **buses** to Struga from all over the country. Many buses from north of Struga are on their way to Ohrid, and stop at the petrol station turn-off, where a *kombe* minibus is waiting to transport passengers for an extra 50MKD each the 15 minutes into town. It is less than half an hour's drive from Ohrid to Struga, which costs 300MKD by **taxi**. Ohrid Airport (see page 174) is only 15 minutes away by taxi. The minimum taxi fare in Struga is 40MKD flagfall and 30MKD per kilometre.

There are no town buses as such, but buses to Ohrid and to Radožda do pick up in town (see map on pages 196–7) rather than you having to trek out to the inter-town bus station (📞 780 770) at the northern outskirts of the town, which is 1.5km from the centre. There are three international bus services leaving from Struga:

BUS DEPARTURES FROM STRUGA	
Kičevo–Skopje	06.00, 08.30, 10.30, 12.00, 14.00, 16.00, 17.30
Mavrovo–Skopje	05.00, 05.45
Bitola–Skopje	07.00, Bitola 10.00
Debar	05.45, 08.00, 10.00, 11.30, 13.00, 14.30, 17.30
Ohrid	from 05.00–22.00 every 15mins
Vevčani	from 05.00–20.00 every hr
Labuništa	from 05.00–20.00 every 30mins
Oktisi	from 05.00–20.00 every 30mins
Nerezi	05.00, 15.30
Radožda	06.15, 09.00, 13.00, 15.00, 19.00

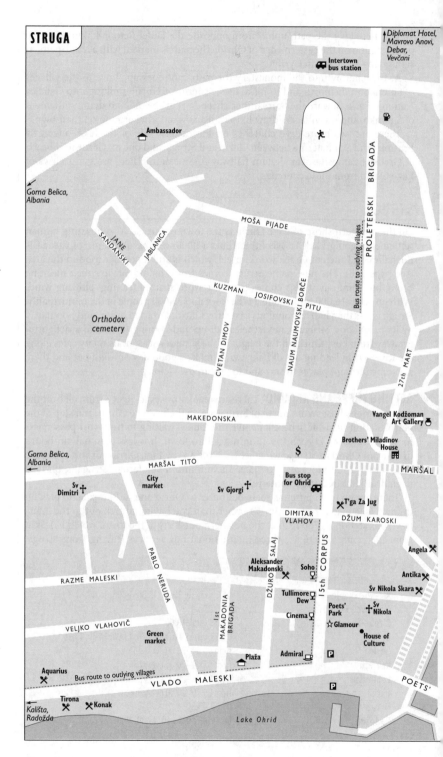

STRUGA

Diplomat Hotel, Mavrovo Anovi, Debar, Vevčani

Intertown bus station

Gorna Belica, Albania

Ambassador

MOŠA PIJADE

JANE SANDANSKI

JABLANICA

PROLETERSKI BRIGADA

Orthodox cemetery

KUZMAN JOSIFOVSKI BORČE PITU

CVETAN DIMOV

NAUM NAUMOVSKI

Bus route to outlying villages

27th MART

MAKEDONSKA

Vangel Kodžoman Art Gallery

Brothers' Miladinov House

Gorna Belica, Albania

MARŠAL TITO

MARŠAL

City market

Sv Dimitri

Sv Gjorgi

Bus stop for Ohrid

T'ga Za Jug

DŽUM KAROSKI

DIMITAR VLAHOV

15th CORPUS

Angela

PABLO NERUDA

Aleksander Makadonski

DŽURO SALAJ

Soho

Antika

Sv Nikola Skara

RAZME MALESKI

Tullimore Dew

Poets' Park

Sv Nikola

1st MAKADONIA BRIGADA

Cinema

Glamour

House of Culture

VELJKO VLAHOVIČ

Green market

Plaža

Admiral

Aquarius

Bus route to outlying villages

VLADO MALESKI

POETS'

Kališta, Radožda

Tirona

Konak

Lake Ohrid

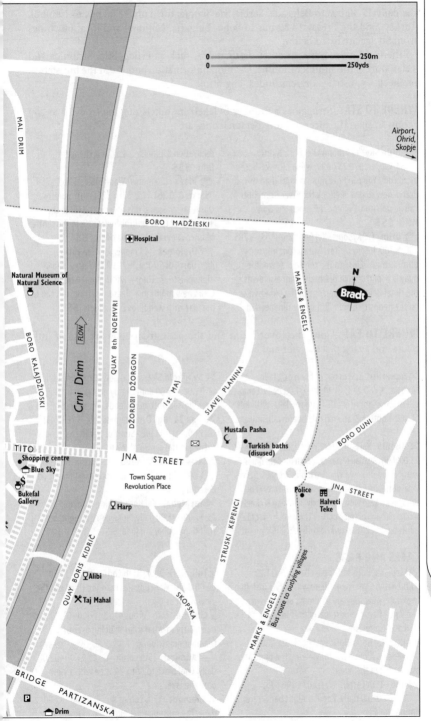

the daily 17.30 bus to Belgrade, Serbia, via Skopje; the daily 12.00 bus to Istanbul, Turkey; and the Friday 18.30 bus to Sofia, Bulgaria. National and local bus times from Struga are listed below.

There are more buses to other destinations, such as Prilep, Štip, Strumica and Veles, during the summer months. For more information enquire at the bus station or check www.struga.org/eng/index_eng.html.

WHERE TO STAY
Struga has a number of lakefront hotels ranging from 10 to 250 rooms in size. The nicer or more personal ones are:

Blue Sky (23 rooms) Kej Boris Kidrič; 784 590; m 070 757 999; www.bluesky-hotel. piczo.com. You can't get more central than this. Brand-new rooms overlook the River Drim, but can be noisy on a w/end. All mod cons & free Wi-Fi. **$$$**

Drim (205 rooms) Kej Boris Kidrič 51; 785 800: f 780 460; e contact@drim.com.mk; www. drim.com.mk. Close to the centre of town, the quay & a long stretch of beach. Drim also owns the Hotel Belgrad at the edge of the old town & on the pedestrian area. But it is in dire need of

renovation & is noisy even if it is cheaper than Drim. **$$$**

Plaža (20 rooms) Vlado Maleski bb; 783 055; m 070 261 175; f 786 126. With a pretty Ohrid-style façade, this hotel was built in the 1980s & yet to be refurbished. Close to the centre of town & overlooking the beach. **$$**

Diplomat (43 rooms) Velešta village, 4km north of Struga; 793 022/720; e info@ diplomatstruga.com; www.diplomatstruga.com. Clean new rooms in a pleasant setting, but can be popular with weddings & banquets. **$$**

WHERE TO EAT
Along the River Drim and the pedestrian zone are lots of little pizza and snack places, cafés and bars.

Aquarius 1.5km out of town on Vlado Maleski; 780 273; ⊕ 11.00–01.00 daily. For a glitzy atmosphere overlooking the lake, with lots of blue lighting & an enviable boardwalk into the lake. **$$$**

Angela Kaj Boris Kidrič west bank; ⊕ 11.00–23.00 daily. A small restaurant with modern blues music & rough-hewn wooden tables & chairs. Serves local dishes including *furnagiska* (a *pastrmalija* or pitta bread base with pork or chicken, egg & cheese), *souflaka* (bowl of spicy pork or chicken), fresh grilled mushrooms, pizzas & turkish coffee. **$$**

Sv Nikola Skara Kaj Boris Kidrič west bank; ⊕ 11.00–23.00 daily. A tiny grill joint on the river blessed with good food & friendly staff. **$$**

T'ga Za Jug Džumkarovski bb; 788 741; ⊕ 11.00–01.00 Tue–Sun. For traditional food & setting in the centre of town. **$$**

Aleksandar Makedonski Razme Maleski; ⊕ 11.00–01.00 Tue–Sun. More traditional food & setting. **$$**

Taj Mahal Kaj Boris Kidrič east bank; ⊕ 11.00–01.00 daily. Not a curry in sight, but traditional Albanian food. **$$**

CAFES AND BARS
Harp Kaj Boris Kidric east bank; ⊕ 11.00–01.00 daily. 5 years ago there was only 1 Irish pub in Skopje; now they are in almost every town. This one offers the best margaritas in town, as well as a Guinness.

Alibi Kaj Boris Kidrič east bank; ⊕ 11.00–01.00 daily. A good bar for viewing the opposite, busier side of the bank.

Soho 15th Corpus 37; m 071 396 575; ⊕ 11.00–02.00 daily. Popular night bar & café during the day.

Tullimore Dew 15th Corpus 39; ⊕ 10.30–02.00 daily. More popular than the Harp, but the view is not as good.

Cinema 15th Corpus 41; ⊕ 11.00–02.00 daily. Busy café bar prior to going over to Glamour nightclub.

Admiral 15th Corpus 43; ⊕ 11.00–02.00 daily. Cool place to drink a coffee with a view onto the lake.

☆ **Glamour** 15th Corpus 40; ⊕ 22.30–03.00 daily. The most popular nightclub in town.

Other restaurants and pizzerias such as **Konak** and **Tirona** are springing up near Aquarius.

WHAT TO SEE AND DO Struga offers a long pebble beach right in the centre of town, a lovely riverside walk from the lake through town along the Drim River, and a small, compact, pedestrian old town area. Aside from wandering around the narrow streets, here are a few noteworthy sites.

Natural Museum of Natural Science (*Boro Kalajdžioski bb;* \ *786 664;* m *070 786 644, 070 782 487;* e *info@museumstruga.mk;* ⏲ *09.00–17.00 daily; entry free*) The legacy of Dr Nikola Nezlobinski (deceased), it has over 10,000 examples of flora and fauna, local history, archaeology and ethnology from around Ohrid and Prespa. Mostly from his own collection and displayed in his original house, the collection is the best available on the region. Dr Nezlobinski, a Russian doctor who immigrated here in 1924 during Royalist Yugoslavia when Serbia encouraged many Russians to move to Macedonia, first put his collection on display in 1928. It is best to phone ahead to make sure or arrange for the museum to be open as it is often closed despite its alleged opening hours.

Vangel Kodžoman Art Gallery (*Boro Kalajdžioski bb;* m *070 786 644, 070 782 487;* ⏲ *09.00–17.00 daily; entry free*) An annexe to the Natural Science museum (see above), this gallery houses Kodžoman's paintings of old Struga. He was one of the founders of the Society of Macedonia Artists and his work has been recognised with several awards. Some of his paintings can be seen at www.museumstruga.mk/gallery.aspx.

The Brothers' Miladinov House (*Maršal Tito bb;* \ *786 270;* e *struga@svp.org.mk; open by prior appointment only*) This beautifully restored old town house (see box, page 197) hosts the **Struga Poetry Evenings Collection** (*www.svp.org.mk*) for the international festival held every year at the end of August. Always opened with Konstantin Miladinov's famous 'Longing for the South', the poetry evenings were started in 1962, exactly 100 years after the death of two of the brothers. Recitals take place throughout the town on the bridges over the Crni Drim. At the beginning of August is the festival of Kengo jeho (meaning 'Songs' Echo') **celebrating Albanian songs and dances** from Macedonia and the region. **Lake Day** is celebrated on 21 June with kayak races, music and food stalls. A festival of **Byzantine music**, the Struga Autumn of Music, takes place in the second half of autumn.

Church of Sv Gjorgi On the western outskirts of the old town, the church was built in 1835 on the grounds of an older, 16th-century church, which contains a number of icons dating back to the 13th century, including one of Sv Gjorgi from 1267.

Halveti Hayati Hasan Baba Teke (*Turistička bb, next to the police station*) This small dervish inn and mosque was built in the first half of the 18th century at the request of Hasan Baba of the Halveti order of dervishes. The Halveti sect (originating from their founder Omer Halveti from 14th-century Iran and Afghanistan) are renowned for cultivating a quiet and more introverted following than some of the other dervish sects.

Town mosque and disused Turkish baths (*Next to the post office on JNA St*) Badly in need of renovation before it is lost forever, but if other renovations in the town are anything to go by, then this could be due soon, and will most likely end up as an art gallery. Worth noting on the way to the *teke*.

Festivals and events in Struga The **Struga Poetry Evenings** (*www.svp.org.mk*) is an international festival held every year at the end of August in the beautifully restored Brothers Miladinov House (*Maršal Tito bb;* ✆ *786 270;* e *struga@svp.org. mk; open by prior appointment only*). Always opened with Konstantin Mikadinov's famous 'Longing for the South', the poetry evenings were started in 1962, exactly 100 years after the death of two of the brothers. Recitals tale place throughout the town on the bridges over the Crni Drim.

At the beginning of August is the festival of Kengo jeho (meaning 'Songs' Echo') **celebrating Albanian songs and dances** from Macedonia and the regions. **Lake Day** is celebrated on 21 June with kayak races, music and food stalls. A festival of **Byzantine music**, the Struga Autumn of Music, takes place in the second half of autumn.

GALIČICA NATIONAL PARK

Founded in 1958, Galičica National Park extends from Ohrid Lake shore immediately west of Velestovo, through Velestevo village, around the peak of Bigla at 1,663m and then down to the shores of Lake Prespa just east of the village of Šurlenci. It includes all the land south of this line to the border of Albania. The park also includes the island of Golem Grad (see page 221) in Lake Prespa.

The park offers endless hikes in pristine countryside, although few of them are well marked so be confident of your orienteering skills before you go into the park, or take a guide. The top of the range plateaus out to a beautiful wide valley with a dirt vehicle track running through it. Some old ski lifts go up to some of the peaks. The highest peak completely in the park, Bugarska Čuka (meaning 'Bulgarian peak'), so named because it was held by the Bulgarian army during World War I, lies midway through the park, and from this peak there's a **panoramic view of both Lake Ohrid and Lake Prespa**. A new rangers' hut (grid 8914 4265) has been built along the plateau road, some 2.5km from which is the small **cave of Samatska Dupa**. A mere 235m long, but high enough to walk through for the most part, it is one of the few caves in Macedonia that has electric lighting. The entrance to the cave is locked. To visit the cave with the lights turned on, arrange a tour with one of the tour agencies on page 176.

Almost 3km south of Trpejca village is the turn-off to the southern mountain pass of Livada at 1,568m. The winding asphalt road gives spectacular views of Lake Ohrid on one side and Lake Prespa on the other. From the pass, a two-hour hike south on a marked path leads to the peak of the range on the border with Albania. Both Prespa and Ohrid Lake can also be seen from this point.

On the Prespa side the road continues past the dishevelled holiday resort of Oteševo and on to Carev Dvor and Resen. The road is partly cobbled and partly badly paved.

DAY TRIPS IN THE AREA

RADOŽDA Radožda is the last village before Albania on the western side of Lake Ohrid. This sleepy fishing village right on the shore comes alive in the summer, its many restaurants are renowned for offering the very best fish from the lake. The village **cave church** high on the cliffs is dedicated to the Archangel Michael. It is a small pilgrimage in itself to ascend the many steep steps and will certainly help you work up a good appetite. Amongst the frescoes on the cave rocks is one of the archangel at the Miracle of Chonae. Some of the frescoes in this church date back to the 13th century. The door to the cave itself is usually kept locked, so ask for the key in the Dva Biseri Restaurant at the bottom of the steps before you find the door locked at the top.

Less well known is that sections of the Roman **Via Egnatia**, which followed the much older Candavian Way, can still be seen at the back of the village. As they are mostly built of blocks some 3m wide and perfectly jointed, it is easy for the visitor to appreciate what a feat of civil engineering the Via Egnatia was. This section of the road, however, is made of smaller blocks. It lies around 2km or a half-hour walk from

MILADINOV'S 'LONGING FOR THE SOUTH'

The Miladinov brothers, Dimitrija (1810–62), Naum (1817–95) and Konstantin (1830–62), were pioneers in re-establishing the supremacy of the Macedonian language in Macedonia during a time when Greek had been brought into Macedonian schools and sermons. Dimitrija was a prominent Macedonian-language teacher and struggled daily for the Ottoman authorities to recognise the Macedonian language. His brother Naum was a distinguished musician, and his youngest brother Konstantin became one of Macedonia's most famous poets with his poem 'Longing for the South' (T'ga za Jug, in Macedonian), written while studying in Russia. T'ga za Jug is now the name of a popular Macedonian wine and of numerous restaurants throughout Macedonia. Dimitrija and Konstantin both died in prison in 1862 for their efforts to bring the Macedonian language officially back to Macedonia. Their efforts were not wasted, however, and seven years later, in 1869, the Greek schools in the Ohrid region were finally shut down.

Longing for the South

If I had an eagle's wings
I would rise and fly with them
To our own shores, to our own climes,
To see Stamboul, to see Kukuš,
And to watch the sunrise: is it
Dismal there, as it is here?
If the sun still rises dimly,
If it meets me there as here,
I'll prepare for further travels,
I shall flee to other shores
Where the sunrise greets me brightly
And the sky is strewn with stars.
It is dark here, dark surrounds me,
Dark fog covers all the earth;
Here are frosts and snows and ashes,
Blizzards and harsh winds abound.
Fog everywhere, the earth is ice,

And in the breast are cold, dark thoughts.
No, I cannot stay here, no,
I cannot look upon these frosts.
Give me wings and I will don them;
I will fly to our own shores,
Go once more to our own places,
Go to Ohrid and to Struga.
There the sunrise warms the soul,
The sunset glows on wooded heights;
There are gifts in great profusion
Richly spread by nature's power.
Watch the clear lake stretching white
Or bluely darkened by the wind,
Look upon the plains or mountains:
Beauty's everywhere divine.
To pipe there to my heart's content!
Ah! let the sun set, let me die.

Konstantin Miladinov (1830–62). Translated by Graham W Reid.

5

the centre of the village. After the Dva Bisera Restaurant, at the first village shop, turn right up the hill to a small church where the tarmac runs out. A pleasant hike along a stone-walled road through the woods goes past a section of stone road and a small church dedicated to Sv Bogorodica. Until here the path follows a contour around the mountain and then rises for another ten minutes to the flagstones of the Via Egnatia. The exact lie of the road beyond this section has still not been uncovered, but part of it is now believed to be underwater below Sv Erasmus between Struga and Ohrid. To get to see the road ask for the *kaldrma* (meaning 'flagstone'). For more on the Via Egnatia see www.viaegnatiafoundation.eu.

Where to stay and eat

There are a number of small restaurants along the Radožda shore road. Listed from east to west:

✕ Dva Biseri On the village square; ✆787 118; ⏲ 08.00–24.00 Sun–Thu, 08.00–01.00 Fri & Sat. The 2 old ladies who cook here hold the secrets of their fresh-cooked lake trout close to their heart. It really is the most divine trout you'll ever taste, as good as if you had caught it yourself & whisked it straight onto the barbecue. $$

✕ Albatross ✆787 021; ⏲ 11.00–24.00. $$

✕ Letnica (Little Diver) m 070 232 699; ⏲ 11.00–24.00 Sun–Thu, 11.00–01.00 Fri & Sat. Has a spacious glasshouse upper deck for a good view of the lake. $$

✕ Aleksandrija ✆782 752; m 070 212 613; ⏲ 11.00–24.00 Sun–Thu, 11.00–01.00 Fri & Sat. $$

🏠 Vila Marij Blaž (4 rooms) ✆787 056; m 071 616 627; e j.jovanoska@yahoo.com. This small hostel offers b/fast outside right on the shorefront. The extensive restaurant offers a wide variety of the lake fish including Struga's famous baked eel. There is also a small swimming deck & a pontoon inviting you for a dip before your meal. $$

✕ Ezerski Raj (Paradise Lake) ✆787 193; ⏲ 11.00–24.00 Sun–Thu, 11.00–01.00 Fri & Sat. The last restaurant before the entrance to the campsite & the footpath to Albania, it has a beautiful wooden deck overlooking the lake as well as views onto the Albanian peninsula of Lin village. Serves the local specialities of *gjomlezec* & *vitkalnici*. $$

KALIŠTA On the way to Radožda, 5km from Struga, is the small settlement and monastery complex of Kališta, located right on the shores of the lake and next to the Hotel Biser. The monastery is the summer residence of Archbishop Naum, the highest church official in the Holy Synod of the Macedonian Orthodox Church. Within the monastery complex is the **cave church of Sv Bogorodica**, whose frescoes date back as far as the 15th century. Access to the church is often closed, so ask at the Hotel Biser (see below) if they can open it for you.

A 500m walk south of the monastery along the shore is the tiny **cave church of Sv Atanas** set high in the cliffs. The steps up to the church are not for those who suffer from severe vertigo, and one would be hard pushed to deliver a service inside the church to a congregation of more than half-a-dozen people.

Where to stay

🏠 Hotel Biser (230 beds) On the lakefront; ✆785 700; f 780 404; e info@ hotelbiser. com.mk; www.hotelbiser.com.mk. Built as a traditional Macedonian house, but much bigger. Open all year & recently refurbished, it is a tranquil place with a wide beachfront, a restaurant set into the rock wall, & a small pizzeria near the beach. $$$

Getting to Radožda and Kališta Both villages can be reached by **car** from the turn-off at Frangovo on the E850, or by taking the coastal road from Struga through Kališta. By far the most picturesque way to get there though is by **boat taxi** from

Ohrid, as it is quite impressive to see the cliffs and church loom up over the village. A boat taxi will cost you €30 round trip whether there is one passenger or six, but the boat will wait for you and your party to finish your half day around Radožda to take you back to Ohrid. **Buses** to the villages leave from Struga bus station at 06.15, 09.00, 13.00, 15.00 and 19.00.

OKTISI, VAJTOS AND THE REPUBLIC OF VEVČANI Less than half an hour north of Struga are the villages of Oktisi and Vevčani. The pretty old village of **Oktisi** lies along a tributary of the Crni Drim and has a number of old watermills hidden along its banks. On the outskirts of the village is a 5th-century Christian basilica with some excellent examples of late Roman mosaics. Above the village in the hills is also an overgrown site called **Vajtos Kale** where a castle is alleged to have stood from Paeonian times. Some say that Vajtos is the eighth stopping place on the Via Egnatia, and the last stop before Ohrid, but it is much more likely that this was a stop on the Crni Drim road to northern Albania. The rock outcrop shows little sign of having been a castle, but the vantage point is pretty and it is easy to imagine that the wide road up to Vajtos might have been the Via Egnatia. For a circular route description to Vajtos and Vevčani with a sketch map, see page 330.

Turning right before the mosque in Oktisi, go over the bridge to get to the next village of **Vevčani**. Allegedly the villagers of Vevčani held their own referendum during the break-up of Yugoslavia for their very own republic. Although they didn't manage to gain independence, they nevertheless created their own coat of arms, passports and even printed specimen currency, replicas of which can be bought in the local shops (but not to be used as legal tender). The village is beautiful, with babbling brooks, old-style houses and proud people. Here there are a number of old *babas* and *tatkos* in traditional dress who will be happy to have their photograph taken. The spring at the back of the village erupts from the rock and the area has been maintained with a small bridge, walkways and benches for all to enjoy. Buses go to Vevčani from Struga every hour from 05.00 until 20.00.

🏠 Where to stay and eat

🏠 **Premier** (10 rooms) On the way up to the church; ☎790 620; m 071 380 295; e hotelpremiermk@yahoo.com; www. hotelpremier.com.mk. Modern rooms, bar & b/fast room. Wi-Fi, all mod cons. **$$$**

🏠 **Domakjinska Kukja** (4 rooms) Behind Sv Nikola Church; ☎790 505; m 070 366 855; e gliso_kompani@t-home.mk; www.

hoteldomacinskakuca.com.mk. The 1st traditional inn to revive in the village, its restaurant has a fireside atmosphere, beer-barrel tables upstairs & good food. **$$**

✗ **Kutmičevica** (2 rooms) Nr Sv Nikola Church; ☎798 399/626; m 070 249 197. Predominantly a traditional restaurant with indoor & outside seating, & 2 small rooms with fireplaces. **$$**

GORNA BELICA Another good day trip away from the lake is up to the village of Gorna Belica, 16km northwest of Struga. The village is now mostly the weekend residence of Strugites, but it has a fine Vlach church, a high view onto Lake Ohrid, proximity to the Via Egnatia and good hiking up to a glacial lake and a cave church. The village first became a settlement in 1769, when the Aromanians (Vlachs) of Moskopole, southern Albania, were driven out of that town by the destruction wrought by the local Ottoman *bey*, and moved up here with all their animals, belongings and families. They chose this spot along the River Belica, where villagers believe that the old crumbling **Church of Sv Clement** is no less than his actual 9th-century summer monastery from before he moved to Ohrid permanently as bishop.

The Aromanians built their own church, **Sv Petka**, or Paraschevia, in Vlach, up above Sv Clement's Church, and it is a fine example of an early 19th-century Vlach church. By that time, 1829, the Greek influence on the old Ohrid archbishopric was all pervasive and so all the original inscriptions on the church are in Greek. The church is cared for by the Dunoskis and if they are around they will be happy to tell you more about it. Look out for the **wooden hawk** above the central lantern in front of the iconostasis. This original pulley system still flaps the wings of the hawk as the lantern is pulled up and down, making a loud clapping noise.

The village celebrates two festivals in honour of both patron saints, Sv Petka on 8 August and Sv Clement on 9 August. This double whammy fills the village up with visitors on those two days and it is well worth a visit if you can make it. Other patron saint festivals exist for neighbouring churches and holy sites, one of the most interesting being the dedication to the **Church of the Perumba**.

The tiny cave church was built in 1998 in honour of a local legend about a girl who, several centuries ago, was being chased by the local Ottoman thugs. The girl ran up against the steep cliff rocks where the church is now and fell to the ground

THE TWELFTHTIDE CARNIVAL

Vevčani has held a Twelfthtide carnival on 13 and 14 January every year since the middle of the 6th century. The 12 days after Christmas, which in the Orthodox calendar is on 7 January, are meant to be a time when evil spirits are at their most active with regards to wreaking havoc on the coming year. On New Year's Eve (13 January in the Orthodox calendar), the villagers start a two-day event designed to banish evil spirits from entering into the new year. People dress up in costumes and masks representing all things evil and unlucky in the hope that if evil is faced with its own reality this will scare it away. The costumes and disguises are a testament to what Macedonians find evil or unlucky. Typical costumes include policemen, soldiers, pregnant brides, an old groom, a funeral procession as well as ghoulish monsters of all varieties. Local politicians and international organisations are ridiculed, and the Ottoman times are also caricatured. A procession of floats starts at midday on the 14th when all sorts of ingenious horror stories are depicted and include tables of human heads, bird flu inspectors (including live chickens) and giant condoms. The procession ends in the village square in the late afternoon with a lot of parading around a fire in which all the costumes are ritually burned.

Concentrating on the banishment of evil as a serious business rather than on the celebration of the end of fasting, this festival has some sinister overtones mixed with alcohol. A fight or two usually breaks out between inhabitants of the upper village and the lower village and it is allegedly the time to punish dogs! Nevertheless, the carnival has started to become a popular national event, attracting over 2,000 visitors every year. When you arrive in the village on the carnival days, you will be stopped by masked men in camouflage uniforms who will ask to see your passport before letting you into the village. The correct passport to show is, of course, the Republic of Vevčani passport, which can be purchased from the masked 'police' for 200MKD. Grill and drink stands provide revellers with sustenance through the small hours, and if you have not managed to book yourself (well in advance) a room in the village, then try the Hotel Diplomat outside Struga (see page 194).

exhausted, knowing that there was nowhere for her to escape. She prayed to God for deliverance and just as the thugs were catching up with her, they saw her fragile body fly up into the air as a pure white dove (*perumba*). The dove flew away and locals have honoured the place as a holy site ever since.

The locals walk up to the site once a year on the first weekend in June. Due to the proximity of the site to the Albanian border, the hike takes place only with the accompaniment of local Macedonian soldiers. For more information on how to join the hike, ask in Gorna Belica or contact **Alpinistički Klub Patagonia** (*Dimitar Vlahov 52, Ohrid;* ✆ *263 699;* e *carboris@t-home.mk*). Any other hikes west of Gorna Belica and up to the glacial lake in the north are also best accompanied by a professional guide or other Macedonian who knows the area. The tracks are not well marked and encounters at the border could become difficult.

Getting there To get to Gorna Belica take the main road west out of Struga for about 2km and take the turning to the right signposted Zagračani. After 1.5km you will come to a T-junction immediately after a very small bridge. Turn right and then almost immediately left along an unmarked road. This road leads first of all up to the village of Visni. After the village follow the asphalt road around to the right and continue on another 5km to the village of Gorna Belica.

REČICA More as an aside on the way between Ohrid and Resen, if you want to see some natural, 100% ecologically sound **washing machines**, go to the tiny hamlet of Rečica. Called *valavica* or *valajca* for short in Macedonian, they are also sometimes referred to as *virovčanka* (whirlpools). Essentially a local stream is siphoned off via a small wooden canal and allowed to drop a few metres into a huge wooden, lined bowl set in the ground. The rush of water swirls around in the bowl into which the blankets, rugs and some modern-day washing liquid are added. After the time taken to have a small picnic with *rakija* and a good chat, the rugs and blankets are hung up to dry on wooden poles in a nearby field and collected in a few days when the items are dry. This was once a centre for traditional blanket and rug making, and local people still come here to have their old rugs and blankets washed. Sadly, traditionally made rugs and blankets are not for sale here, although local honey is.

Getting there To get to Rečica, take the road towards Resen. After 15km take the turning left towards Kuratica, and after 1km take the turning right through the working quarry. Less than 3km along this dirt track will take you to the *valavica* area just before the village. The village itself has a small church and several old watermills further upstream.

AROUND THE LAKE INTO ALBANIA A good half-day trip in the area if you have a car and car insurance to cover you in Albania (most hire cars from Macedonia aren't covered for Albania) is to drive around the lake. It is not uncommon for many countries to become 'blurred' at the edges, a little neglected by central administration and adopting some of the characteristics of the country next door.

The border crossing itself is straightforward. Once on the other side the full effect of former communist Albania's paranoia about foreign influence and invasion comes into plain view. The countryside is strewn with concrete dome lookouts and troop defences, which appear like giant molehills from a mole gone mad all over the hills. These defensive positions complete with rifle lookouts do not cease until you are back in Macedonia on the other side of the lake. Most have now fallen into disrepair, and some have even fallen into the lake.

5

After the death of Serbian Tsar Dušan in 1355, a mere ten years after he had been crowned king in Skopje, the Serb kingdom started to fall apart at the seams. Tsar Uroš took over, helped by the Mrnjavčevič brothers, Volkačin and Uglečа. They headed feudal kingdoms within the empire and in 1365 Volkačin proclaimed himself co-tsar and ruler of the western side of the empire with its seat of power at Prilep.

Volkačin had four sons and several daughters by his wife Elena. Marko, the eldest, was born in 1335. Thirty-six years later in 1371, when Volkačin and his brother were killed fighting against the Ottomans in Thrace, Greece, the crown of the empire passed to Marko, as neither Tsar Uroš nor Volkašin's brother Ugleša had any heirs. Even though he was of Serb origin, King Marko is often viewed by the Macedonians as the stepping stone for Macedonian nationhood between Tsar Samoil (967–1014) and the ten-day Kruševo Republic of 1903.

Prilep was centrally placed within Marko's kingdom, which reached from the Šar Mountains in the northwest down the western bank of the River Vardar to Kastoria (in present-day Greece) in the south. Rarely did his kingdom include Skopje or Ohrid, and eventually Prilep fell to the Ottomans in 1394. A year later King Marko was killed in Romania while forced to fight for the Ottomans against the Vlachs.

Along the lake in summer, boys will hold up strings of fresh trout caught from the lake, and a number of nice-looking lakeside restaurants on the way around will serve freshly caught fish and local vegetables.

At the southern end of the lake is **Pogradec**, which has a few shops and buffet bars along its main street and a lot of money changers who will buy your euros and dollars from you. On your way out of Pogradec, back to Macedonia make sure you head towards the lakeside road shortly after the centre of town before you go veering off on the main road into the wilds of central Albania. There are a couple of nice restaurants set in a park just before you get to the Sv Naum border.

It doesn't matter which way round you go, although the anticlockwise direction can appear more of an eye-opener than the other way around.

Alternatively, for the fit and keen, a bike ride around the lake is 90km, including some serious hills. One day for the super-fit; two or three days for a more leisurely ride. Bikes can be hired along the quay in Ohrid or ask at Cycle Macedonia, Sunny Land Tourism or Vis-poj.

6

Pelagonia, Prespa and Pelister

Telephone code for Bitola 047   Rest of Pelagonia 048

This is the story of Kruševo:
> Just after midnight on the morning of August 2, 1903 (this was the day that the general uprising was proclaimed), a rattle of rifles and a prolonged hurrahing broke the quiet of the peaceful mountain town. Some three hundred insurgents under 'Peto-the-Vlach' and four other leaders had taken the town by surprise.
>
> Frederick Moore, *The Balkan Trail*, 1906

This southeastern corner of Macedonia, known as Pelagonia in ancient times, is rich in history both natural and manmade. The **Via Egnatia**, a monumentally long Roman road linking the Adriatic crossing at Durres with Constantinople (now Istanbul in Turkey), traverses Pelagonia, which has traditionally been rich in trading towns. **Pelister National Park**, on the Baba mountain range, is the oldest national park in Macedonia. It conserves some rare glacial lakes, the Pelister Eyes, and is a haven of hiking and hidden Vlach villages. From up in its hills you can see both major and minor **Prespa lakes** (the latter lies in Greece and Albania), as well as the mountain range of Galičica National Park on the other side of the lake. When Ohrid is heaving with tourists in the summer, genteel Lake Prespa beckons with its deserted sandy beaches at Stenje, Konsko and Nakolec.

If you visit nowhere else in this region, spend at least a couple of days in Prilep to see the ruined **Towers of King Marko** and the remote **Monastery of Treskavec**. The scenery at these two sites is magnificent and is the setting of the films *Before the Rain* and *Dust* by Macedonia's most famous film director, Milčo Mančevski. Prilep's Beer Festival in mid-July is also quickly becoming the most popular festival in Macedonia.

HISTORY OF THE REGION

It is believed that a tribe known by the name of Linkestris were the first to inhabit the area south of Bitola around 4500BC. Just over 4,000 years later the first major town to be established in the rich Pelagonia Valley was the ancient Macedonian town of Heraklea Lyncestis. It was founded by Philip II of Macedon (the father of Aleksandar III of Macedon) in the middle of the 4th century and named in honour of Hercules, with whom the Macedonian royal dynasty of the Argeads identified. The additional name 'Lyncestis' in turn honours the ancient tribe of Linkestris. Although Philip lived there for some time, his son was eventually born in Pella over the present-day border in Greece.

With the fall of the ancient kingdom of Macedonia, Heraklea came under Roman rule in the 2nd century BC and continued to grow as an important trading town. By this time the Via Egnatia passed through Heraklea where it crossed the Diagonal

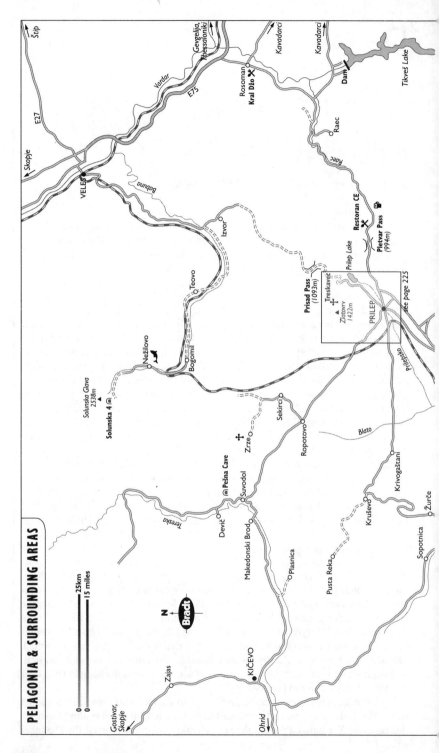

PELAGONIA & SURROUNDING AREAS

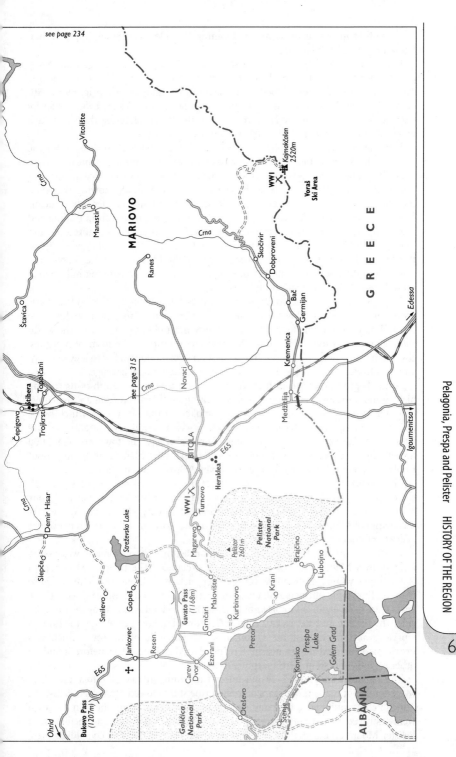

see page 234

see page 315

Vitolište

Crna

MARIOVO

Manastir

Štavica

Crna

Ranes

Crna

Skočivir

Dobproveni

Bač

Germijan

Kremenica

Kajmakčalan
2520m

WWI

Voraš
Ski Area

GREECE

Edessa

Topolčani

Stibera

Čepigova

Trojkrsti

Demir Hisar

Novaci

Crna

BITOLA

E65

Heraklea

WWI

Turnovo

Slepče

Smilevo

Gopeš

Streževsko Lake

Magarevo

Grnčari

Malovište

Kurbinovo

Pelister
2601m

Pelister
National
Park

Brajčino

Krani

Ljubojno

Medižitlija

WWI

Igoumenitsa

Bukovo Pass
(1207m)

Ohrid

E65

Jankovec

Resen

Carev
Dvor

Ezerani

Gavato Pass
(1168m)

Pretor

Konjsko

Prespa
Lake

Golem Grad

Oteševo

Stenje

Galičica
National
Park

ALBANIA

Way, another major north–south road joining Heraklea with Stobi, Štip and then Kustendil (now in Bulgaria).

Julius Caesar used Heraklea as a supply depot during his campaigns and many of his veterans settled there. Later, during the time of early Christianity in the 4th century, Heraklea developed as the seat of the regional bishopric. By the 5th century, Roman rule was in decline and Heraklea was ransacked several times by marauding Avars, Goths and Huns from the north. When a large earthquake struck in AD518, the inhabitants of Heraklea abandoned the city.

Later, in the 7th century the Dragovites, a Slavic tribe pushed down from the north by the Avars, settled in the valley and gave the river its present name of Dragor. Eventually a new town was established immediately north of Heraklea, mentioned under the name Obitel in one of the charters of Tsar Samoil, showing that even then the town was closely associated with churches and monasteries (*obitel* means family chamber of a monastery). The town continued to prosper from trading and eventually became the third largest city in the Balkans after Constantinople and Thessaloniki. The surrounding area also thrived as a centre of Christian worship, so that by the time the Ottomans came at the end of the 14th century they named the town Monastir due to the number of monasteries in the surrounding hills, which served the monks of the 500 churches in the region.

Soon, Monastir became so important that the French set up a consulate there. Eleven other countries followed suit. The influx of 18th- and 19th-century architecture can still be seen in Bitola today, despite artillery fire and bombing during the world wars. Mixed with the influence of Ottoman architecture in the form of mosques, covered markets and bathhouses, Bitola has a very cosmopolitan feel to it even today, and its inhabitants still pride themselves on their international heritage.

At the beginning of the 19th century, Monastir was at the zenith of its trading history and the railway even came to town, linking southern Macedonia with Skopje, Belgrade and beyond. French was widely spoken in the town, which included a number of foreign and international schools as well as a military academy that was attended by Turkey's pro-reform leader, Kemal Atatürk. The town boasted 2,000 households, and every second one owned a piano, on which many a song about Bitola was composed. Allegedly there are over 200 songs about Bitola.

The Manaki brothers (see box opposite), famous for their pioneering work with the camera, opened their studio of art photography in Bitola in 1905. In honour of their work in photography and later cinematography, Bitola started the first international Manaki Film Camera Festival in the world in 1979, which continues every September.

At the end of the 19th century, revolution against the Ottomans was taking hold all over Macedonia, and Bitola was no exception. The Internal Macedonian Revolutionary Organisation (IMRO) was very active in Bitola and there are those who say that some of the guerilla warfare tactics developed in Bitola during those years were even exported to other nations such as Ireland rising up against foreign rule. The Ilinden Festival every 2 August (a national holiday) celebrates the Ilinden Uprising of 1903 against the Ottomans. The Republic of Kruševo which was proclaimed the next day in nearby Kruševo lasted only ten days before it and all other regions of dissent were sharply put down.

The Balkan wars of 1912–13 put an end to Ottoman rule in Bitola and all of Macedonia, but many more years of foreign rule still followed. Reprisals against the Turkish community were high and over 40 of the 60 Turkish mosques in the town were destroyed. Beautiful Bitola was practically demolished by German shelling from Pelister Mountain during World War I, in which over 13,000 French soldiers died, almost as many Germans, and an unrecorded numbers of Serbs and Macedonians. In addition, Nazi occupation in the early 1940s annihilated Bitola's thriving Jewish scene when 3,011 Jews were deported on 11 March 1943 to Treblinka in Poland. Today, Macedonia's entire Jewish community is only around 1,000.

While Bitola has languished in Balkan obscurity during the 20th century, modern lines of communication and transport have bypassed the once important trading centre. To add insult to injury, the provincial town of Skopje was made capital of the Federal Yugoslav Socialist Republic of Macedonia. Since then, Bitola, far from the heart of Yugoslavia, has only ever been given secondary consideration. It has little chance now of regaining its importance in trade, but it may still become a prime cultural destination.

BITOLA

The main town of the region and once a major trading town, Bitola is currently the second largest city in Macedonia with over 80,000 people, and is the seat of Macedonia's second university. It has managed to maintain its pretty 18th- and 19th-century architecture in the centre of town, and these buildings tell of the former glory of Bitola when every major European country had a consulate here due to the amount of trading and business conducted in the town. The River Dragor divides the old Turkish town from the 18th-century town and conjures up a beautiful tree-lined canal effect, drawing in the cool air of the Baba Mountains. Despite being further south than Skopje, Bitola is usually cooler year round, sometimes up to 12–15°C cooler – lovely in the summer when Skopje can get up to the high 30°Cs, but bring an extra sweater in the winter.

GETTING THERE AND AROUND There are only four **trains** a day to Bitola from Skopje and four back out (see box, page 72). The train is slow and decrepit, but the journey at least between Prilep and Skopje is scenic. The average train journey time from Skopje to Bitola is 3½ hours, for 420MKD return. There were no trains between Bitola and Greece at the time of writing.

YANAKI (1878–1960) AND MILTON (1882–1964) MANAKI

The Manaki brothers were born in the Vlach village of Avdela, near Grevena in present-day Greece, where they first got into photography and opened their first studio. Wanting to expand their work, however, they moved to Bitola in 1904, then the centre of the western Macedonian region. After opening their new studio in 1905 they went on to win the gold medal in the Big World exhibition in Sinaia, Romania, became the court photographers for King Karol of Romania, and started to travel Europe widely on photographic assignments. In 1907 they brought back the 300th Bioscope cine camera from London, allowing them to start making films in the Balkans. Thus began their historical recording of the tumultuous events in Macedonia in the lead-up to and during the Balkan wars and the two world wars. Unfortunately, there is no museum dedicated to their work, but their photographs can be seen in every museum in Macedonia, depicting the life and times of events such as the Ilinden Uprising, the Turkish reprisals and state visits by kings and ambassadors, as well as the simple life in villages and of everyday people. For more information on the Manaki brothers go to www.manaki.com.mk.

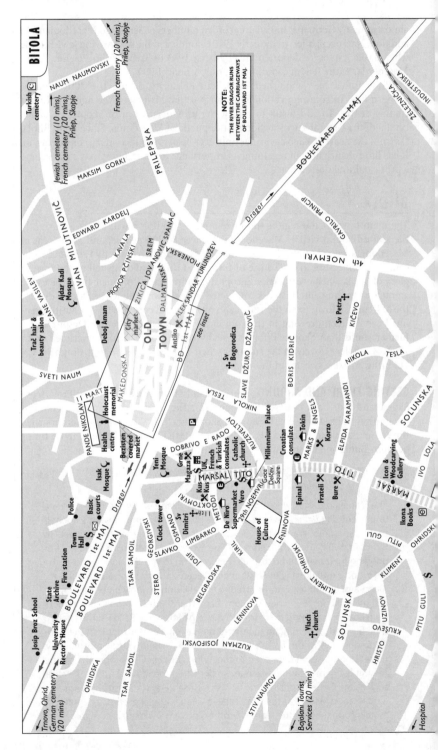

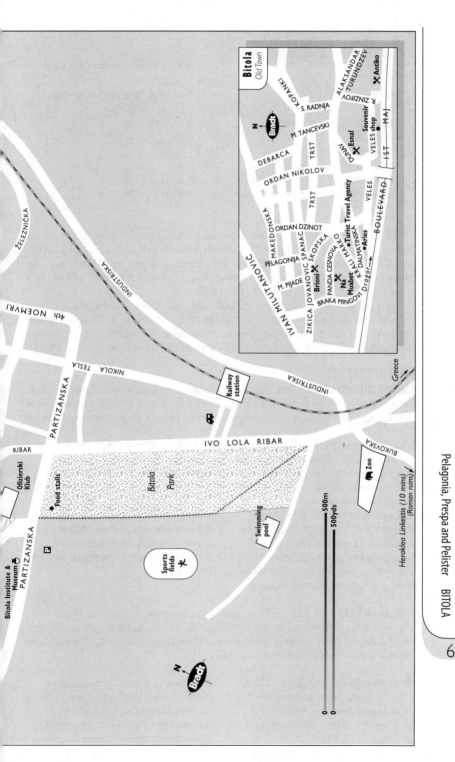

Bitola *Old Town*

ALAKSANDAR TURUNDZEV
R. ZINZIFOV
✗ Antiko
S. RADNJA
Souvenir shop
Esnaf ✗
DUNAV
M. TANCEVSKI
VELES shop ●
KOPANKI
DEBARCA
TRST
1ST MAJ
ORDAN NIKOLOV
TRST
VELES
BOULEVARD
Turist Travel Agency
ALI MARKO
Na ✗
Muabet
KRALINSKA
Aries ●
PELAGONIJA SPANAC
ORDAN DZINOT
SKOPSKA
Dragor
MAKEDONSKA
PANDA CESNOVA
BRAKA MINGOVI
M. PIJADE
Brioni ✗
ZIKICA JOVANOVIC
IVAN MILUTINOVIC

ŽELEZNIČKA
INDUSTRISKA
4th NOEMVRI
NIKOLA TESLA
PARTIZANSKA
Railway station
INDUSTRISKA
Greece
RIBAR
Ofizierski Klub
● Food stalls
Bitola Park
IVO LOLA RIBAR
BUKOVSKA
🐘 Zoo
Bitola Institute & Museum
PARTIZANSKA
🅿
Swimming pool
Sports fields
500m
500yds
Heraklea Linkestis (10 mins) (Roman ruins)

Skopje	05.00, 05.45, 06.30, 07.30, 09.00, 11.00, 11.50, 14.30, 16.30, 17.15
Ohrid	06.30, 09.00, 09.30, 13.15, 15.00, 16.00, 18.30, 19.30
Kičevo, Gostivar and Tetovo	05.00, 10.00, 14.00, 16.00
Strumica	07.00, 14.15
Gevgelija	15.00
Prilep, Negotino and Radoviš	14.00
Resen	06.30, 09.00, 12.00, 13.15
(connecting bus from Resen to Brajčino)	09.00, 11.30, 14.30, 16.00

The **bus** station (✆ *231 420; http://transkop-bitola.tripod.com*) on Ulica Nikola Tesla is opposite the train station (✆ *237 110*). Bitola is well connected by bus to the rest of the country and a typical ticket from Bitola to Skopje is 450MKD one-way (three hours) or 590MKD return. There are four city buses: #1, #4, #5 and #6. Two buses serve surrounding villages: #11 and #12.

Taxis are abundant. Flagfall is 40MKD, and then 30MKD per kilometre, with set prices for destinations further outside the town. A taxi to Krklino or Dihovo is 150MKD, a taxi to Magarevo, Trnovo or Nižepole is 200MKD. Taxi operators include those on ✆ 1577, 1591, 1592 (prefix with 047 if calling from a mobile phone).

TOUR OPERATORS
Tourist information Sadly, the tourist information bureau was closed in 2011, but it did leave behind the most up-to-date website available on Bitola at the time of writing (*www.bitolatourist.info*). Otherwise contact one of the tour operators above.

Aries Dalmatinska 6; ✆ 224 155; e info@aries. com.mk; www.aries.com.mk. Located in the old town, their website has a very good range of self-catering accommodation & small villas in Pelister National Park. Rents cars.
Balojani Tourist Services 111d Solunska (difficult to find); ✆ 220 204; f 220 205; e info@ balojani.com.mk; www.balojani.com.mk. Exceptionally good service, especially for hiking in all 3 national parks & visiting the eco-villages, as well as for wider ranging tours combining

neighbouring countries in the region. Very well connected in the local area.
Turist Krali Marko 16; ✆ 202 777; f 202 776; e predrag@turist.com.mk; www.turist.com.mk. Located in the old town, has extensive experience working with foreign tour groups & agents. Can find you accommodation throughout Macedonia as well as arranging trips to sites. Friendly, English-speaking staff, & have maps of Bitola for sale for 100MKD.

WHERE TO STAY Bed and breakfast stays can be arranged through Turist and Aries tour operators (see above) or try the hotels below. There are several more very nice hotels and villas less than 10km away in the villages of Dihovo, Magarevo and Trnovo in Pelister National Park (see page 215).

De Niro (18 rooms & 2 apts) Kiril i Metodij 5; ✆ 229 656; f 207 233; e hotel-deniro@t-home. mk; www.hotel-deniro.com. In the centre of town. Nice bar & restaurant downstairs. Beautiful rooms if a bit small. **$$$**

Epinal (175 rooms) On the cross of the pedestrian zone Maršal Tito & Leninova; ✆ 224 777; e reservation@hotelepinal.com; www. hotelepinal.com. Popular with tour groups of Greek visitors, it offers full comfort, including a gym, pool, sauna, jacuzzi & casino. Sometimes has some very good deals as low as €20 pp. **$$$**

🏠 **Millenium Palace** (26 rooms) Maršal Tito 48; 📞 241 001; **f** 226 882; **e** h.milenium@ t-home.mk; www.milleniumpalace.com.mk. Accessed from the front through an indiscernible door among the throng of cafés on Širok Sokok, you'll step through the narrow Balkan-style double doors as if into another world of nostalgic calm when travel was a privilege & a pleasure. Beautifully restored to its former 19th-century

glory (but with all mod cons), narrow cabinets line the corridors with artefacts from a bygone year. You can't beat the location. Also has a beautiful restaurant & bar upstairs with buffet breakfast, & its own pizzeria downstairs at the back. **$$$**

🏠 **Apartments Tokin** (8 rooms) Marks & Engels 7; 📞 232 309; **m** 070 250 272; **e** tokinhouse@yahoo.com; www.tokin-house. com. A beautiful 1915 Austrian exterior, with an additional sunny b/fast room & grape-vine shaded yard. Standard-style rooms. **$$**

✖ **WHERE TO EAT AND DRINK** The main pedestrian area, **Maršal Tito**, hosts numerous café bars and restaurants. There is a small **Vero supermarket** at the north end of Maršal Tito if you want to buy provisions for a day out or simply a snack and drinks. The big Vero superstore is on Partizanski, 2km west of the centre. In order of price try also:

✖ **Antiko** Bulevar 1st Maj 243, on the left bank of the river next to the old town; 📞 239 660; ⊕ 12.00– 24.00 Sun–Thu, 12.00–01.00 Fri & Sat. Traditional restaurant with live music & good food. **$$**

✖ **De Niro** Kiril i Metodij 5; 📞 229 656; **f** 207 233; **e** hotel-deniro@t-home.mk; www.hotel-deniro.com; ⊕ from 08.00 for b/fast. Serves traditional Macedonian food throughout the day, & has a nice patio at the back. **$$**

✖ **Grne** Maršal Tito 37; 📞 237 800; **e** toskoskibt@yahoo.com; ⊕ 11.00–24.00 Sun–Thu, 12.00–01.00 Fri & Sat. Overlooking the statue of Philip II, this is a classic-style national restaurant. **$$**

✖ **Kus-Kus** Kiril i Metodij 2a; 📞 222 603; www. kuskus.mk; ⊕ 12.00–24.00 Sun–Thu, 12.00–

01.00 Fri/Sat. Opposite Hotel De Niro, more of a pizzeria than the French restaurant it claims to be. Boasts a wide range of salads. **$$**

✖ **Bure** Maršal Tito 82–88; 📞 236 519; ⊕ 11.00–24.00 Sun–Thu, 11.00–01.00 Fri & Sat. Quaint décor & serves very good pizzas. **$**

✖ **Esnaf** Dunav 1 (in the old Turkish inn); 📞 225 318; ⊕ 08.00–21.00 daily. Lacking any nostalgia or touristic regard, this tiny practical eatery with wooden benches & tables is a hidden oasis in the old town predominantly serving local vendors their lunch or a coffee. **$**

✖ **Frateli** Maršal Tito 64; **m** 078 456 012; ⊕ 08.00–24.00 daily. Offers b/fast deals, as well as snack meals through out the day. **$**

OTHER PRACTICALITIES

Post and communications The main post office is at Bd 1st Mai – the actual service counter is outside. Stationary can be bought at the *knigoteka* on the other side of the boulevard where you see the Фотокопир sign. Free Wi-Fi internet is available along the whole of Širok Sokok. With ubiquitous smart phones, internet cafés are increasingly difficult to find.

24-hour newsagent **Together** (part of the Together and Tobacco chain of newsagents), on Maršal Tito 37, sells phone top-ups, No international newspapers or maps of Bitola (yet).

Medical emergency and pharmacy **Clinical Hospital Bitola** on Partizanska bb (📞 *251 211*).

24-hour health centre Find this at Pande Nikolov bb (📞 *194*). **Feniks Apoteka** is a 24/7 pharmacy (📞 *242 575*) in the same building.

ATMs and money exchange These are abundant, especially along Maršal Tito.

Beauty salon English-speaking and international award-winning make-up artist Igor Gorko and his staff can spruce you back to form after a hard day of sightseeing at their little salon **Trač** (*Cane Vasilev 15;* \ *520 444;* m *071 519 934*). Facials start from 400MKD; wash, cut and blow dry from 250MKD.

WHAT TO SEE AND DO Bitola is a pretty town to walk around. The pedestrian street Maršal Tito, known locally as **Širok Sokak** (Turkish for wide alley), is lined with 18th- and 19th-century protected buildings. It's easy to get absorbed by the cafés and restaurants along the street so don't forget to look up at the architecture as you wander along. The street runs from the old Ottoman bazaar at the northern end down past the House of Culture, the now disused Dom na Armija officers' club, the town museum and then on to the town park, which has some children's fun rides, small food stalls, and lots of busts of famous Bitolans lining its leafy avenues. A new statue of Philip II on his horse rearing in front of a fountain surrounded by Macedonia shields was erected at the northern end in 2011 in the frenzy of beautifying Macedonia that has accompanied 'Skopje 2014' (see page 60). The tree-lined **Boulevard 1st Maj** runs the length of the **River Dragor** and dissects the old Ottoman bazaar. Along the boulevard going west out of town are a number of the old consular residences. The present consulates of the United Kingdom, France and Turkey are on the corner of Maršal Tito and Kiril i Metodi.

Ottoman bazaar and old town This was the once the centre of trade with over 900 shops grouped according to craft. You'll still see a few of the old storefronts at the cobblers and the furriers but the intense trading of old has gone to out of town shopping centres like Vero. On the west of the old bazaar is the covered **Bezisten**, which still houses one of Bitola's markets and whose gates are still locked at night. On the northern side is the old Turkish baths, **Deboj Amam**, which now serves as the large kitchen of a bakery. Surrounding the old town are several mosques: the **Isak Mosque**, built in 1506; the **Yeni Mosque**, built in 1559 over three older churches dating from as early as the 11th century, as revealed by archaeological excavation in 2010–11; and the **Ajdar-Kadi Mosque**, built in 1562 by Kodja Sinan, a prominent Ottoman architect. Opposite Yeni Mosque is the **clock tower** built in the 1830s, and whose bells and musical mechanisms have been renewed several times, mostly notably in 1936 by the then German government as a gift of gratitude for the cemetery for German soldiers killed in World War I (see opposite). Finally, to the south of the old town is the **Magaza** (⊕ *10.00–20.00*), which used to operate like a corn exchange (it is the Turkish word for 'shop'), where all sorts of goods, not just corn, were bartered and traded in the large hall. Today the Magaza is a gallery for travelling exhibitions from all over the world

Dom na Kultura (*Maršal Tito bb*) This is the modern concrete and glass structure on the corner of Širok Sokok and Leninova, opposite the Hotel Epinal. It houses the National Theatre Bitola (\ *232 340;* e *teatarbt@yahoo.com; www.teatarbt.org.mk*) and the American Corner, which has a wide range of books by American authors available to borrow.

Bitola Institute and Museum (*Kliment Ohridski bb;* \ *233 187;* e *bitolamuseum@gmail.com; www.bitolamuseum.org;* ⊕ *10.00–18.00 Tue–Sun; entry 100MKD, plus 500MKD to take photos, 1,000MKD to take video*) The museum building itself was once one of two buildings housing a local Ottoman military academy. It is famous for being the military academy that Attatürk attended from 1896 to 1899 prior to him going on to become commander-in-chief of the Turkish military and then the first president of Turkey. One wing of the museum is dedicated to an excellent exhibition in English, Macedonian and Turkish about Atatürk, rivalling even the one at Gallipoli. Most interestingly, don't miss the love letter from Atatürk's only true love, the Bitola-born Vlach girl Eleni Karinte, which is translated onto a big poster in the entrance of the exhibition. Of the two buildings, known as the Red Building and the White Building, only this the White Building still exists. The Red Building was destroyed in World War I.

The other wing of the museum has an equally excellent exhibition dedicated to the history of Bitola and artefacts found in its surroundings. Some enormous mammoth teeth are on display, and then further historical finds through to World War II. Notably on display is the 'Bitola inscription' stone of Jovan Vladislav (Ioan the Autocrator). This stone marks the building of a fortress in Bitola by Jovan Vladislav in 1015. The inscription reads that Jovan was Bulgarian by birth and related to Samoil whose army was defeated by the Byzantine tsar Vaslius II in 1014. This statement contradicts the Macedonian theory that Tsar Samoil was Macedonian rather than Bulgarian. Some say, on the other hand, that the stone is a fake. The exhibition also includes displays of local architecture, Bitola's partisan movement, and the status of Bitola as the fashion centre of the region in the 19th century, when anybody who wanted to be dressed in the latest European fashion would come to a renowned Bitola tailor for *à la fanga* fashion.

Jewish memorials
The Bitola Museum has a new dedication to the 3,011 Jews of Bitola who were gassed at Treblinka in Poland. The dedication includes a list of those deported and an urn of ashes. A memorial to the victims stands in front of the health centre on Pande Nikolov. Little remains of Jewish life in Bitola which had the second largest Jewish population in the region after Thessaloniki in the 19th century. Only the **Jewish cemetery** on Ilindenska (behind the Makpetrol station at the entrance to Bitola from Skopje) still exists, with a display room in the memorial house there showing photos, letters and other documents. A room at the Ethno Museum Krklino (see page 214) is also dedicated to Jewish life and artefacts from the 19th century. For more on the Jewish history of Bitola visit www.cassorla.net/Monastir

Cemeteries
In addition to the Jewish cemetery mentioned above, Bitola has several other noteworthy cemeteries. The **French memorial cemetery** to the fallen of World War I is sandwiched between the corner of Dolni Orizari and Novački Pat, 2km east from the centre of town. The main entrance is on Novački Pat, and another entrance on Dolni Orizari is by the side of the memorial house, which holds the list of those interred at the cemetery, a small photographic exhibition and the guest books (*livre d'or, zlatna kniga*) for signing. The cemetery holds the graves of 6,230 named French soldiers of Christian and Muslim faith, as well as a monument dedicated to a further 7,000 unknown French soldiers. The groundsman, who can open the memorial house for you, took over tending the graves from his father. He speaks some French (but no English),

The **German memorial cemetery** to the fallen of World War I is 1.5km west from the town centre. After crossing the last bridge north over the Dragor River, follow the main street called Deveani uphill for almost 1km. The cemetery does not contain the thousands of graves that the French cemetery has, but there is an impressive and solemn monument and an excellent view of the valley. (The **British memorial cemetery** is in Greece behind the village of Doiran, further to the east.)

The **Turkish cemetery** is on Ilindenska, behind the Makoil petrol station, next to the Jewish cemetery. Sadly, it has not been maintained and is an eerie reminder of the Ottoman period when the Turkish community was a majority.

Ethno museum Krklino (286 666; m 070 312 146; e info@muzejkrklino.mk; www.muzejkrklino.mk; ⊕ by appointment (or chance – the family live next door); entry 100MKD). At the back of the village of Krklino, 5km northeast of Bitola, is by far the best ethno museum in all of Macedonia: the private collection of the

IN SEARCH OF A WORLD WAR I PILOT

Abridged from text by Eric Allart, history teacher, former professional archaeologist. Translation by M Marc.

On 5 April 1918, Brigadier (Corporal) Pilot Léopold Michel Montoya was reported missing in action when his plane – a Nieuport 24 – was shot down by the German ace Gerhard Fieseler behind the Bulgarian lines, south of Caniste. (Fieseler, who later became an aerobatics champion, aircraft designer and manufacturer, was awarded the Golden Military Merit Cross and the Iron Cross, first and second class, for 19 aerial victories he won over Macedonia during World War I.) On 21 April 1920, the French court of Bordeaux officially declared Brigadier Montoya killed in action, and his family were informed by the German Red Cross. Although Montoya's wife died in childbirth, her daughter, Audette, survived her and was brought up by her grandparents. In-between the two world wars, the family attempted in vain to have Léopold's burial place located.

In 2005, whilst off duty, Captain Fief, of the French gendarmerie, came across Montoya's identity disc at an antique dealer's shop in Skopje. On inquiring around the battlefield site where the disc had come from, a shepherd from Kruševica confirmed to him that his father had been requisitioned to bury 'both pilots' killed on the ground by Bulgarians in 1918. Another shepherd on the plateau south of Caniste was able to point out a bush commonly known as the location of the pilot's burial place. The topography of the site hardly allows an emergency landing and the plane is likely to have been seriously damaged before Montoya was killed on the ground by Bulgarian troops.

Back in France, Captain Fief found the pilot's grand-nephew, Christophe Montoya, who confirmed that Léopold's daughter was still alive. With the help of a war veterans' society, the Montoya family re-contacted the French Ministry of Defence and the French Embassy in Skopje to ask for the location and repatriation of Léopold's body. The family have been trying to uncover, positively identify and repatriate Brigadier Montoya's body since 2009, but seeking funding and battling through government red tape is hindering progress. Ongoing archaeological and regressive mapping work with the aid of photos of the area taken in 1918 by an anonymous pilot of the 504th Squadron based in Bac, northeast of Bitola, which was Montoya's squadron, will help to solve much of the contradictory data surrounding the circumstances of the death of Brigadier Léopold Michel Montoya, killed in action, 'mort pour la France'.

Tanevski family. Boris has dedicated an entire two-storey building to housing the rich collection of motorbikes, cars, household goods and clothing from over the last century. The collection has motorbikes from World War II, a 'Wanted' poster for Tito, old gramophones and some of the very few Jewish household items from Bitola not destroyed by the Bulgarians, among many other things. Boris also sells homemade wine and *rakija*. A taxi from Bitola costs 150MKD.

Heraklea Linkestis (*Entry 150MKD, permission to photograph another 500MKD*; see *History of the region*, page 203) This is a 20-minute walk from the end of the park. This significant Roman town, founded by Philip II, is only 12% uncovered, so visits in future years should prove ever more fruitful, especially as historical records show that there are still a number of houses and tombs of the rich and famous at the time to be found. Several important relics and buildings have already been uncovered including the amphitheatre, baths, basilicas and some impressive mosaics, only some of which are on show in the summer. There is a small museum, a snack and drink shop, and a souvenir shop with books on the site in English available for sale. Most of the more important statues are on display in the town museum or in the National Museum in Skopje. Considerable archaeological work continues there every year, and for those who wish to take part, the Balkan Heritage School (*www.bhfieldschool.org*) organises volunteer workshop here most years.

Churches There are a number of churches in Bitola, the most significant being that of **Sv Dimitri**, renowned for being one of the biggest churches in the Balkans. It was built in 1830 during Ottoman times when churches were not allowed to be ornate or ostentatious on the outside. As a result, the builders lavished the inside of the church, which has been well preserved to this day. The opulence of the church is captured in the opening scenes of *The Peacemaker* (1997) starring George Clooney, which were filmed in Sv Dimitri. The Catholic **Church of the Holy Heart of Jesus** on Širok Sokok was first founded in Easter 1857. The current neo-Gothic-style structure dates from 1909 after the earlier Baroque-style church caught fire and was destroyed.

Festivals Several festivals take place in Bitola every year. **Bit Fest** is the largest and takes place from the last week in June to the third week in August (see *www.bitola.gov.mk* for a programme). It comprises a variety of events ranging from musical to theatre to comedy in several venues across the town. **Interfest** is an international festival of classical music, held in August. **Heraklea Evenings** are a series of outdoor theatre and musical events held over the summer in places like the amphitheatre in Heraklea as well as other outdoor venues. Over the summer there is also the **International Graphics Convention**, the **International Children's Festival**, the **Small Monmartre**, and others.

PELISTER NATIONAL PARK AND ECOTOURISM

Opened in 1948, Pelister National Park is the smallest (12,500ha) but oldest national park, located on the southwest border of Macedonia. It is famous for its ancient Molika pine trees (*Pinus peuce*), as well as rare lynx, bearded eagle, gentian plants and many other different types of flora and fauna. Mount Pelister, at 2,601m, is the summit of the Baba Mountains, which are in fact a part of the Rhodope range of mountains of Bulgaria. There are several ways to access the park — see individual entries below for how to get there.

WHERE TO STAY AND EAT

Šumski Feneri (8 rooms, inc 5-bed apts) Near Trnovo; ☏ 293 030; f 293 131; e sfeneri@t-home.mk; www.sumskifeneri.com.mk. Set around a cosy foyer & landings laden with well-kept plants & flowers. The hotel also has conference facilities for 40 & restaurant seating for 140. The Vlach family Musulanov have run the hotel for many years now & their daughter, Ljubica, speaks good English & will give guided tours of Bitola & Malovište on request. To get to the hotel, head west out of Bitola along the river & turn left at the battered sign for Pelister Park, & then right onto a cobbled road for 1km. The hotel is on the left. **$$$**

Molika (56 rooms) Pelister National Park, at the top of the mountain road; ☏ 229 406; e hmolika@mt.net.mk; www.hotelmolika.com.mk. This hotel, commanding amazing views, is almost ski-in ski-out. All rooms are en suite with TV & central heating. **$$**

Villa Balojani (3 rooms) Magarevo; ☏ 220 204; m 075 207 273; e info@balojani.com.mk. A quaint little family-run villa. **$$**

Villa Dihovo (3 rooms) Dihovo, 5km outside Bitola; ☏ 293 040; m 070 544 744; e contact@villadihovo.com; www.villadihovo.com. A beautifully renovated traditional house in the village of Dihovo in the foothills of Pelister with very pleasant lawns, fruit trees & excellent food. All rooms sleep up to 4. A small kitchen is available to guests. Small shared shower room only. A taxi to the villa from Bitola costs 140MKD. Villa Dihovo does not have a set price for rooms & food, but asks you to pay what you think your stay is worth. Alcohol does have a set price, & their homemade wines, beers & *rakija* are well worth tasting, especially the beer. There are also a couple of restaurants in the village & a shop. **$$** – at your discretion.

Mountain huts on the Baba Mountains are listed on page 323.

WHAT TO SEE AND DO Skiing is the favourite winter pastime in Pelister. To get to the ski lifts from Bitola, drive west and turn off for the park after about 3km towards Trnovo. Keep driving through Trnovo and Magarevo until you get to the end of the road. Unfortunately, there is no public transport to the ski lifts, other than a taxi. Make sure you fix the price of the journey before you set off.

Hiking is the popular summer sport. The walk from Hotel Šumski Feneri in Trnovo village to Magarevo further up the mountain takes you along part of the Via Egnatia. Parts of the road still have the cobbles laid down by French troops fighting in the area during World War I.

Malovište A Vlach settlement that is well worth a visit and is a real museum piece is Malovište. It was once a rich trading village, and it is not difficult to see that some of the houses were very stylish in their time. Most are now in various states of decay. The **Church of Sv Petka** is usually open and, unusually for most churches in Macedonia, its exonarthex is on the left of the entrance rather than on the right. The church sometimes allows stranded travellers to stay overnight in a couple of makeshift beds in the upper gallery. Behind the church is a graveyard containing some gravestones as old as the church itself. Forty minutes' hike from the village is the **Monastery of Sv Ana,** which houses guests for the moderate price of 200MKD per night per person.

Malovište has had some funding from the EU to spruce itself up and put out some advertising. There is a small information room just where the tarmac runs out (ask in the village to be let in) where you can buy a well laid-out book on the village (also available from Hotel Šumski Feneri). In the absence of a village shop there are drinking fountains near the church.

Getting there To get to Malovište from Bitola take the highway towards Resen for almost 20km and take the exit marked Kazani. At the crossroads turn left and

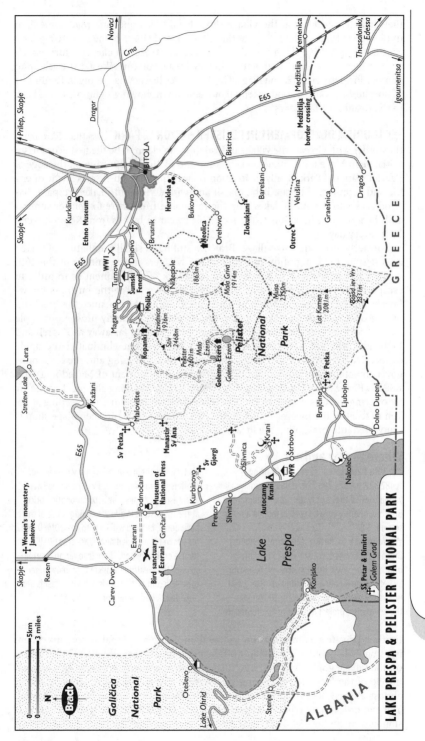

LAKE PRESPA & PELISTER NATIONAL PARK

then take the next left at the village shop. Follow this one-lane road some 5km until you get to the village. Back at the crossroads, if you take the road straight on north, you will drive along the River Šemnica to **Streževo Lake**, and turning left at the village of Lera and then left again at Sviništa, you can take a dirt track up to another formerly rich Vlach village, **Gopeš**. Gopeš has not had as much funding as Malovište, but is also a good potential museum town showing a glimpse of life back in the wealthier Vlach days.

ECOTOURISM DEVELOPMENT IN PELISTER NATIONAL PARK
Less than 5km from the border with Greece, the village of **Brajčino** can claim to be the first ecotourism initiative in Macedonia. Brajčino is pristine and picturesque, sitting on the edge of Pelister National Park. Its idyllic location is away from the hustle and bustle of city life and is protected by the Baba massif and with a view onto Lake Prespa. It has good access to the glacial lakes atop the range and from there to Pelister summit and the mountain huts. It is easily accessible by car or by bus from Resen (several buses every day).

Formerly a rich trading village, Brajčino still has a small population of mixed ages despite the emigration of many of the villagers in the middle of the 20th century to Canada and Scandinavia due to a lack of employment or in order to escape communist persecution. The departure of most of the business know-how from the village has left it in hard times, even more so since the break-up of Yugoslavia which has taken its toll on the village's formerly prosperous apple trade. Previously, apples from the area would be sold as far away as Zagreb and Ljubljana, whereas new borders and taxes have all but eliminated the apple export. Now the villagers, through the help of Swiss funding and the local non-governmental organisations of DEM (Ecological Movement of Macedonia) and BSPM (Bird Society Protection of Macedonia), are reviving the local economy by offering visitors access to their pristine lifestyle in return for keeping it so. Ten percent of the income of the guides, accommodation and the village shop is reinvested into preserving the local area.

Where to stay and eat
Vila Raskrsnica (2 rooms) Brajčino; 482 322; m 075 796 796; e Vila_Raskrsnica@yahoo.com. With the only full-time restaurant in Brajčino, offering very tasty local food in a rustic setting. **$$**

Manastir Sv Petka (24 dormitory beds) Brajčino; 482 444; m 070 497 751; e info@brajcino.com; www.brajcino.com.mk. Manastir Sv Petka is no longer a working monastery, but was renovated by the villagers in 2003 under the ecotourism project in order to accommodate visitors. It is set in a meadow above the village & offers utter tranquillity, a view onto Pelister & a fantastic night sky. The accommodation price at the monastery includes bedding & use of the bathrooms, but you will have to pay 30MKD extra for a towel if you need one, & another 60MKD for use of the kitchen. There is so far no heating, so once the weather turns cold you may prefer to seek accommodation elsewhere. B/fast is not provided. A bed in the dorm is 350MKD. **$**

Further, **private accommodation** can be found at www.prespalive.com.mk. There is a small village shop and café just off the main square that also offers information on the village guides and tours. A village lunch or evening meal can be arranged in one of the local houses, giving you that extra special local experience, eating almost entirely locally grown and produced food (see *Eating at home* below). You can order three types of menu: a basic menu for 350MKD (three courses), a standard menu for 450MKD (four courses) and a special menu for 550MKD (for special occasions). Children aged between five and 12 years pay half price, younger than five years free. Wine with your meal is not included in this cost. See contact details above for Manastir Sv Petka, or Balojani Tourist Services (see page 210) can organise everything for you.

What to see and do The village has done a lot of work to tidy up local hiking trails and to keep them well marked and signposted. Hiking guides can be arranged

EATING AT HOME

Brajčino offers the chance to eat with the locals. Some friends and I ordered a day ahead for the special set menu to be served at 19.00 upon our arrival in the village. There is no à la carte menu, but vegetarian food or other dietary requests can be included, if the order is placed in advance.

We arrived in good time and walked up the narrow winding roads of the village to Jadranka's little farm at house number 144 (the village is so small that there are no street names). The family were waiting for us and ushered us into their tiny Sunday room, the one reserved for guests and special occasions.

Sitting at the neatly laid table we were offered a shot of *rakija* or *liker* as an aperitif to welcome us to their home. I chose the *liker* made of a *rakija* base re-distilled with blueberries and sugar. Fortunately, the Macedonians take their time over their liqueurs, and this one was well worth savouring; accompanied by salad fresh from their garden, I could have drunk two or three glasses, but saved myself for the homemade wine which was to come with the main course.

We moved on to a country veal soup, so delicious that I asked the origin of the calf. 'Yes, it is our calf,' Jadranka replied. Feeling slightly guilty that I was eating from their larder, I continued the conversation enquiring if the calf had had a name. 'Rusa,' came the reply. 'Ah yes, well Rusa is indeed most delicious,' I added in my best Macedonian. Everyone burst out laughing at this point, probably at my attempt to speak Macedonian.

The next course included more of Rusa's melt-in-the-mouth offerings, accompanied by sweet roasted peppers and sautéed potatoes. Their homemade wine was fruity and mild, quaffable by the jugful, although we restrained ourselves to fit in some of their homemade peach juice, while we chatted away with the family about each other's lives. Formerly the area had lived well from sheep farming, but now Macedonia's depressed economy could not support the high price of sheep. With so little work in the locality, Jadranka and Jonce were glad to receive the extra income that ecotourism might bring their way. Jonce can be hired as a mountain guide by the day or half day (1,500/800MKD) and, in addition to set meals, Jadranka sells dried boletus mushroom, *liker*, *rakija* and other homemade products such as jam, juice and wine.

We finished the meal with some homemade marble cake, cherries from their garden and a cup of coffee or mountain tea. Fully satiated, we then meandered back down the hill to our beds for an exquisite night's sleep.

The next evening we ate at Milka's house (now Vila & Restoran Raskrsnica). We were greeted with the Macedonian tradition of candied fruits (locally grown and produced, of course) and shots of mint or cherry *liker*. More homemade courses followed, ending with a delicious *baklava* made of walnuts and poppy seed.

for 800–1,200MKD for a half day or 1,500–3,600MKD for a full day (depending on the number of people) to take you on less well-trodden trails and to give you an insight into local flora, fauna and history. It's a five- to six-hour hike to the mountain hut of Golemo Ezero at one of the 'Eyes of Pelister', and then another three-hour hike from there to the summit of Pelister.

Brajčino village itself is pretty to walk around and an ideal setting for walks with children. There are many animals to be seen in the village farmyards and a number of buildings are marked with information plates on the usage, architecture and previous owners of the building. Much of this information is from the book *Brajčino Stories* by Meto Jovanovski from Brajčino, a former chairperson of the Macedonian Pen Club. The **bey's house** (*Begot Kukja*), the house of the last Ottoman commander for the area from the end of the 19th century, can be viewed inside if you ask for the key in the neighbouring houses or at the village shop.

There are six churches near the village dating from medieval times through to the beginning of the 20th century. The medieval churches are those dedicated to Sv Petka, Sv Bogorodica and Sv Atanas. It's not known exactly when these churches were built or even in what order, but all contain frescoes of the same era and, like so many churches in Macedonia, are in various stages of disrepair.

The **Church of Sv Petka** lies in the grounds of the old monastery 15 minutes' walk outside the village. Sv Petka's holy day is 8 August, when up to 600 of the local villagers gather in the monastery with food and drink to celebrate.

The small **Church of Sv Bogorodica** leans against a cliff above the village. The cliff can be seen from the village and, although the church itself is obscured by trees, the rock face is marked out with a cross at the top of the cliff. Set into the cliff are a number of 'cells' where local monks used to stay overnight in days of old.

The medieval church 15 minutes' walk to the south of the village is dedicated to **Sv Atanas**. It is mostly in ruins but the grounds still house some graves.

The church closest to the village and still used by its inhabitants is the **Church of Sv Nikola**. Built in 1871, it is in a pretty location with a good view onto Lake Prespa. The main nave of the church is usually locked, although you may be able to access the glass-fronted exonarthex. Ask in the village for the key. The bell tower is a recent addition, made of a simple metal frame but in the traditional Macedonian style of being separate from the church itself.

The churches of **Sv Ilija** (1915) and **Sv Archangel** (1919) are located outside the village and are very simple and rarely used.

Further down the valley is the larger village of **Ljubojno**. It is made up of houses similar in style to Brajčino's, although a few 19th-century town houses have also made it into the village square. Clearly seen above the village are the two churches of **Sv Petka** and **Sv Pavle**, which vigilantly watch over Ljubojno.

LAKE PRESPA

Lake Prespa, on the other side of Galičica Mountains from Lake Ohrid, offers a peaceful, cooler and cheaper alternative to Lake Ohrid, and is well worth a visit in July and August when even Ohrid can get blisteringly hot and the festivities can be too much. Combined with Pelister Mountain, which is exactly 800m higher than the Galičica Mountains, the area offers a lot for those who love the outdoors. Most people access Lake Prespa via Bitola, but if you're coming from Ohrid by car, then a trip over the southern end of the Galičica mountain range offers fantastic views and the opportunity to hike up to Two Lakes Viewpoint (see page 332).

The lake is situated 850m above sea level, and the surroundings are refreshingly cooled by the mountain air. Due to the relatively shallow depth of Prespa, only just over 50m, the lake itself can get quite warm, up to 25°C in the summer. A shallow sandy shoreline allows children to play and swim safely where their feet can still touch the bottom.

Sharing its borders with Greece and Albania, the lake lies close on the Greek side to a smaller lake of the same name situated between Greece and Albania. The two lakes are separated only by a narrow strip of land in Greece, and in centuries gone by the two lakes used to be one. During that time, the name Prespa, meaning blizzard, came about because of the illusion created of an almighty bli€ard when the lakes would freeze over; covered in snow, the lakes would appear like a white-out to anyone looking in their direction. Other legends abound as to how the lake came into existence (see box, page 223).

WHERE TO STAY There is a lack of good places to stay on the lake itself, in part because it is not as good a lake to swim in as Ohrid. Most Macedonians tend to stay in Pelister National Park (see page 215) or in little villages like Brajčino (see page 218). Further private accommodation can be found at www.prespalive.com. mk. Ezerani bird sanctuary also offers basic accommodation (see page 222), or try:

Hotel MVR (56 rooms) Krani; ☎483 247. This is arguably the safest hotel in Macedonia as it belongs to the Ministry of the Interior & is reserved primarily for use by the police. It is rarely anywhere near full, however, & it has a good location on the lake. With a small exclusive beach for hotel customers, it's good value for money. Rooms are basic in that very 'socialist' style, all en suite but no TV or AC (it rarely gets that hot there anyway). The hotel has a restaurant that seats over 100 guests & is sometimes booked up for weddings, but usually you will have the terrace to yourself. The hotel also has about 20 hook-ups for c/vans & camping, with block showers & toilets. To get to the hotel turn towards the lake (signposted Ezero) from the main lake road where it is also signposted Krani in the opposite direction. This road will also take you to **Autocamp Krani** (which is not as nice as the hotel but is cheaper) but turn off left before you reach the gated entrance of the *autocamp*. **$**

WHAT TO SEE AND DO Aside from swimming in the lake and enjoying the cooler temperatures of Pelister Mountain, the must-do thing at Lake Prespa is to visit the **island of Golem Grad**, sometimes known as Snake Island for all the water snakes that live around its shores. The island is now uninhabited and is part of the nature reserve of Galičica National Park. It contains endemic flora and fauna protected by the island's lack of contact with the rest of the world, so if you do get the chance to go, be sure to leave no trace.

The island had been inhabited over the centuries going back to Neolithic times. It is believed that Tsar Samoil was crowned tsar on the island in AD976, and the remains of two 14th-century churches, dedicated to Sv Petka and to Sv Dimitri, are built on the foundations of 6th-century early Christian basilicas. Other ruins of an old village can also be found there.

If you can't find a local to take you out to the island, then boat trips can be arranged by Go Macedonia or Macedonia Travel in Skopje (see *Tour operators* on page 66). On the trip you will see a variety of birdlife much of which gathers on the island. When you go back to your boat, look out also for all the water snakes, which may have gathered around the boat. As soon as you step into the water or move the boat, they will disappear and are perfectly harmless. Make sure you visit the island in the morning and return very soon after an early lunch at the latest, as the winds on the lake can pick up in the early afternoon. In 2011, two tourists had to be rescued by helicopter from the island in the afternoon when a storm brewed up. In the morning when they left for the island there had not been a cloud in the sky.

If you are approaching the lake from Ohrid via the E65 then it is worth a look into the **women's monastery of Jankovec**, a few kilometres before the town of Resen. This was the first women's monastery to be brought back to life after several decades of neglect during communist times. Sister Kirana, who heads the best group of fresco painters alive today in Macedonia, brought the nuns to the run-down 16th-century monastery in 1998. They have done a lot of work to it since then and their skills as fresco artists are in high demand throughout Macedonia. They also weave, and sometimes you can purchase their handicrafts at the monastery.

There are a number of access points to the shores of Lake Prespa where there are small beaches and resorts. The largest of these is at **Oteševo** on the northwestern side of the lake. Oteševo also houses the national centre for respiratory illnesses, due to the superb quality of the air at Lake Prespa.

There are smaller beaches at Konjsko, Asamati, Pretor, Krani, Nakolec and Dolni Dupeni right on the border with Greece (the border crossing here was still closed at the time of writing). Oteševo and Pretor also offer hotels and beach-style bungalows in an original and ageing communist style.

Konjsko is on the western side of the lake near the border with Albania. It has a lovely little public beach, which is quite secluded, and the village itself is the site of an ancient settlement which is largely intact and now protected as part of Macedonia's cultural heritage. A small cave church dedicated to Sv Elias can also be found near the village. The asphalt road does not go all the way, so be prepared for a hike or take a 4x4.

Krani has a lovely small private beach available to those staying at the Hotel MVR (see *Where to stay*, page 221), whereas the beach at **Dolno Dupeni** is larger and public, and has a small food and drinks hut.

The beach at **Nakolec** has the added attraction of being next to this small mixed-ethnicity village, one of the few in the area along with Krani, Grnčari and Arvati. The **Church of Sv Atanas** on the shore of Nakolec used to stand practically in the water, but now lies some way off due to the water loss from the lake. The receding shoreline has allowed for some excavation, however, which has revealed the foundations of buildings further into the lake. As measures are now being taken to refill the lake, these excavations will undoubtedly be covered over once again but hopefully not before the research on them has been finished. Nakolec also used to have a number of wooden houses on stilts, but these are no longer standing. The old Bektaši *teke* in the village is being rebuilt.

At the northern end of the lake the village of Podmočani has a small **museum of national dress** (✆ *489 260*; m *075 985 313*) and artefacts in a small house on the main road. Still the private collection of a local farmer, Jone Eftimoski, it is open to public viewing for a small entry fee. There are over 140 costumes from all over Macedonia along with jewellery, weapons and coins. Just as you get to the start of the cobbled part of the road there is a small green sign marked 'museum' pointing to the house on the right of the main road. It may not look open, but there is usually someone around in the front garden who will let you in and give you a guided tour.

Further along the lakeside road is the **bird sanctuary of Ezerani**. As with any birdwatching it is best to go early during the day or in the evening, otherwise you may find only a herd of cows among the rushes, eating discarded apples.

Legend has it that a town once stood in place of the great Lake Prespa. While walking through the local woods one day, the son of the king of the town chanced upon a wood nymph whose beauty surpassed that of any girl he had hitherto laid eyes upon. On asking her name, she replied in an enchanting voice 'Nereida'. The king's son fell immediately in love with the nymph and came to the woods many times to woo her and take her hand in marriage, offering her all the riches of his father's land and a place by his side as the queen of the kingdom. But the nymph turned down his generous offer, saying that she could not marry a mortal without sinister consequences befalling the groom and his homeland. Unable to imagine a deed so awful and unable to suppress his love for the nymph, he chose one night to have her kidnapped and kept her in confinement until she accepted his offer of marriage. Upon their pronouncement as husband and wife, however, the heavens opened and a downpour of rain ensued. The rain did not stop until the whole town was underwater and every citizen had drowned. The result is the present-day Lake Prespa. The moral of the story is that when a woman says 'no' she really does mean it.

The bird sanctuary is home to over 115 different species of bird, including wild geese, pelicans and local moorhens. It is a part of the University of Skopje and internationally protected by EURONATUR. University members can stay at the sanctuary for a discounted price, but non-members pay €15 per night for bed and breakfast. The rooms and facilities are in great need of attention.

The next turn-off on the left leads to the village of **Kurbinovo**. This is a typical working local village along a pot-holed tarmac road crowded with meandering sheep, goats and cows. At the second house on the left, a two-storey white building with a railed front lawn, ask for the key to the **Church of Sv Gjorgi** (*kluč za Sveti Gjorgi*), and continue on up the road. At the crest of the hill in the village turn right through a narrow row of houses and continue another couple of kilometres until you turn into a large tarmacked parking area, obviously out of keeping with the surroundings. Above the car park is the 12th-century Church of St George. There are a number of medieval frescoes inside dating from when the church was first built in 1191. Some in Macedonia believe that the style of these frescoes was the seed of the **Renaissance arts** in Italy (see box, page 162). Unfortunately, of the many frescoes depicting the life of St George, few can be seen now.

PRILEP *Telephone code 048*

If you are venturing beyond Skopje and Ohrid and are wondering where to go next, and/or want a compact representation of Macedonian life through the ages, then go to Prilep. The town is situated under the Towers of Marko, a ruined medieval fortress, and has two worthwhile monasteries in the vicinity. The town also has a well-preserved, if small, old Turkish town and a pedestrian area where it is simply nice to drink coffee and relax. The area is so symbolic of Macedonian culture that it has been used twice by Macedonian film director Milčo Mančevski, as the setting for a couple of his films. The name of the city itself derives from the ancient tribe of the Pelazgi. Macedonia's fledgling beer festival takes over in mid-July and attracts over 300,000 people.

Belgrade	07.30, 09.40, 18.00
Sofia	05.40, 20.30
Skopje	14 buses a day from 05.30–17.15; 320MKD sgl, 500MKD return.
Bitola	14 buses a day from 05.30–23.00; 100MKD sgl.
Ohrid	08.15, 09.40, 12.30, 16.30, 17.00, 18.40; 300MKD sgl, 500MKD return.
Strumica	06.45, 07.40, 15.15
Veles	05.30, 06.30, 06.40, 15.00, 15.15
Kičevo	05.30, 07.00, 09.00, 14.15, 16.00
Kočani	08.30, 15.40
Resen	10.00, 14.35, 18.35

And once a day to Brajčino 13.20; Gevgelija 15.40; Radoviš 14.40; Kavadarci 14.00; Probištip 16.00; Oteševo 16.00; and Struga 18.00.

GETTING THERE AND AROUND

By bus There are frequent buses to Prilep from all main cities. The bus station (✆ 425 555) is on Kuzman Josifovski. See box above for times.

By car The drive to Prilep between the Babuna and Dren mountains is also very pretty, although the road is often only one way in each direction and blocked with tractors, lorries or expansion work. The pass at Pletvar lies at 994m above sea level. For the back road from Veles to Prilep, see page 268. If you are travelling from Prilep to Veles, take the lake road out of town and at the marble statue of a cannon above the lake take the right-hand fork onto a dirt track.

By taxi Once in Prilep, the best form of transport if you get tired of walking through the small town is one of the numerous taxis. Contact **Prilep Taxi Service** (✆ 15188; m 077 731 333). Flagfall is 50MKD, plus 30MKD/km thereafter.

By train Prilep train station (✆ 412 660) is 500m to the west of the centre of town. Four trains travel to/from Skopje every day (see times on pages 72–3 and 74–5). If you don't manage any other train journey in Macedonia, this is the one to do, as it takes you through some great mountain scenery. The section from Veles to Prilep is in parts not even accessible by road and midway between the towns of Sogle and Bogomila offers a fantastic view of the Solunska Glava Mountain with its 800m drop from the summit. The Skopje–Prilep return costs 350MKD and takes approximately two hours each way.

TOUR OPERATORS

Info Tours Kuzman Josifovski 11; ✆ 419 418; m 075 259 000; e contact@infotours.mk; www. infotours.mk; ⊕ 08.30–13.30 & 17.00–19.30 Mon, Tue, Thu & Fri, 08.30–15.00 Wed & Sat, Sun closed. Conveniently located near the bus station.

⌂ WHERE TO STAY

⌂ **Kristal Palas** (22 rooms) Lenin 184; ✆ 418 000; f 400 060; e info@kristalpalas.com. mk; www.kp.com.mk. Near the railway station. Modern & the best place to stay in town. Has a lovely if small, warm, indoor rooftop swimming pool with a 270° panorama of the town. Popular with wedding receptions, which can get a bit noisy in the evening. **$$$**

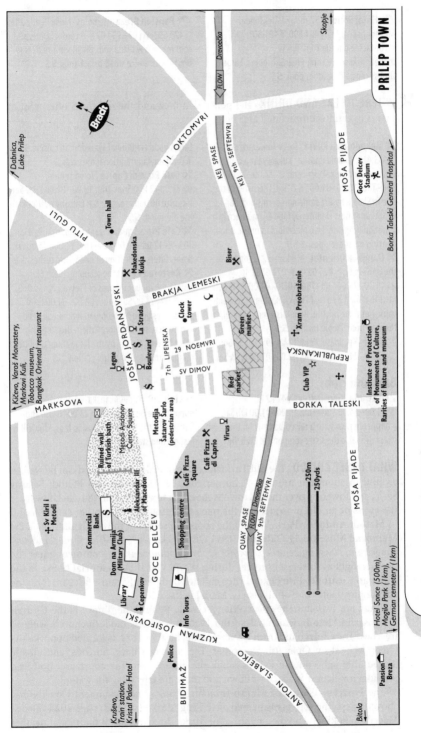

6

225

PRILEP TOWN

Skopje

FLOW Drevečka

11 OKTOMVRI

KEJ SPASE

KEJ 9th SEPTEMVRI

MOŠA PIJADE

Goce Delcev Stadium

Borka Taleski General Hospital

Dabnica, Lake Prilep

PITU GULI

Town hall

Makedonska Kukja

BRAKJA LEMESKI

Biser

Clock tower

Xram Preobraženie

REPUBLIKANSKA

Green market

Club VIP

Institute of Protection of Monuments of Culture, Rarities of Nature and museum

Kičevo, Varoš Monastery, Markovi Kuli, Tobacco museum, Bangkok Oriental restaurant

MARKSOVA

JOŠKA JORDANOVSKI

Legne

La Strada

Boulevard

29 NOEMVRI

7th LIPENSKA

SV DIMOV

Red market

BORKA TALESKI

Ruined wall of Turkish bath

Metodi Andonov Cento Square

Aleksandar III of Macedon

Sv Kiril i Metodi

Commercial Bank

Metodija Šatarov Šarlo (pedestrian area)

Café Pizza Square

Café Pizza di Caprio

Virus

MOŠA PIJADE

Dom na Armija (Military Club)

Library

Cepenkov

GOCE DELČEV

Shopping centre

Info Tours

KUZMAN JOSIFOVSKI

QUAY SPASE

FLOW Drevečka

QUAY 9th SEPTEMVRI

250m

250yds

0

0

ANTON SLABEJKO

BIDIMAŽ

Police

Kruševo, Train station, Kristal Palas Hotel

Hotel Sonce (500m), Mogila Park (1km), German cemetery (1km)

Pansion Breza

Bitola

N

Bradt

🏠 **Hotel Sonce** (52 rooms) Aleksandar Makedonski 4/3a; ☎ 401 800; f 401 801; e contact@soncega.com; www. makedonskosonce.com. Pleasant rooms. Large fitness centre & outdoor pool. **$$**

🏠 **Pansion Breza** (9 rooms) Moša Pijade 24a; ☎ 423 683; m 071 214 071; e contact@breza. com.mk; www.breza.com.mk. Rooms in a large house with a nice small b/fast area. **$$**

✗ **WHERE TO EAT AND DRINK** The pedestrian area and the old town offer a lot of places to eat. Recommended are:

✗ **Makedonska Kukja** Joska Jordanovski 4; ☎ 433 419; e makedonska_kuka@yahoo.com; www.makedonskakuka.com; ⏰ 12.00–24.00 Sun–Thu, 12.00–01.00 Fri & Sat. The sister of the one in Skopje by the same name, this popular restaurant offers traditional food & ambience in a traditional setting. Live Macedonian music & folk dancing most evenings. **$$$**

✗ **Bangkok Oriental** Marksova 212, opposite the university; ☎ 425 027; m 071 656 746; ⏰ 10.30–24.00 Sun–Thu, 10.30–01.00 Fri & Sat. Real Thai food by a real Thai chef, Shen. Excellent value not to be missed. Regulars even come all the way from Skopje for this. **$$**

✗ **Biser** Kej Spase, Kej 1st Maj 29; ☎ 415 366; ⏰ 12.00–24.00 Sun–Thu, 12.00–01.00 Fri & Sat.

Offers good traditional Macedonian cuisine & accompanying traditional music. **$$**

✗ **Café Pizza di Caprio** Town square; ⏰ 12.00–24.00 Sun–Thu, 12.00–01.00 Fri & Sat. Has nice upstairs seating & a balcony overlooking the old town. **$$**

✗ **Café Pizza Square** Jane Sandanski; ☎ 415 301; ⏰ 12.00–24.00 Sun–Thu, 12.00–01.00 Fri & Sat. Offers a selection of hot & cold dishes. **$$**

✗ **Restoran Ce** At the stopping place 5km before the mountain pass of Pletvar; ☎ 450 050; ⏰ 08.00–24.00 Sun–Thu, 08.00–01.00 Fri & Sat. Serves good Macedonian food if you need somewhere to eat before Prilep. The stopping place is recognisable by the large shining white marble cross & new petrol station. **$$**

Bars and clubs

🍸 **La Strada** Goce Delčev; ☎ 414 212; ⏰ 11.00–24.00 Sun–Thu, 10.00–01.00 Fri/Sat. A happening bar with a raised balcony off the street. It is also the sister company of Club VIP.

☆ **Club VIP** Republikanska, Kej 9th December, opposite the bus station; ⏰ 23.00–04.30 Thu–Sun. When the beer fest is losing legs, Club VIP is just getting started.

WHAT TO SEE AND DO The **old Turkish centre** of Prilep is small and can be walked around in about ten minutes. It borders on the pedestrian area Metodi Šatarov Šarlo, and towering over the old town is the **clock tower**. Next to the clock tower are the **ruins of an old mosque**, and the one remaining wall of another can be found in **Metodi Andonov Park**. West of the shopping centre in the centre of town is the **Memorial Museum 11 Oktomvri 1941** (Ilindenska bb; ☎ 434 011; e muzejprilep@ yahoo.com; www.muzejprilep.org.mk; ⏰ by appointment). It commemorates the partisan fight against fascist forces during World War II. A **memorial house to the Kuzman Kosifoski-Pitu** (a key Prilep agitator in the fight against fascism) is on the street named after one of his sisters, Mara Josifoski 20.

There are two churches near Prilep's centre. Behind the library is the **Church of Sv Kiril i Metodi**, which dates from 1926. It is a fairly modern church, with no frescoes. The **Church of Xram Preobraženie**, built in 1871, is located opposite the Green Market on Quay 9th December. The church is dark, no frills, and mostly locked although you can look through the glass doors. The courtyard, however, provides a welcome place to sit down and there are taps there for water.

The **Fortress Towers of Marko** (*Markovi Kuli*) stand prominently on the hill above Prilep. The fortress is named after King Marko (see box, page 202), the last Macedonian king, who died fighting the Turks. Archaeological findings show that parts of the fortress date back to the Iron Age, the 3rd and 4th centuries BC and later periods during the Ottoman Empire. Most of what remains to be seen today is from medieval times. It is mostly in ruins, but still well worth the hike, and the views from the top over the ruins and beyond are magnificent.

To get there from the centre of town take Ulica Markovska uphill and turn off to the right after about 1km where the road levels off, just after a small pharmacy and a car mechanic shop, opposite some conference halls. Keep going uphill until you get to the back of the houses that will lead you to the gravel road to the towers. The road passes the famous stone called Slon, meaning the elephant, which marks the beginning of the Markovi Kuli site and continues in a blaze of white crushed marble (Prilep is also a marble-mining town) around the back of the hill. This is the easy route up, suitable for a high-clearance vehicle, although whether you will find parking space at the top on a busy weekend is another thing.

Alternatively, you could take on a frontal assault of the towers and go straight up the middle of the rocks. A path eventually forms itself if you bear right of the entrance. It must have been suicidal as a foot soldier, even with armour and weapons, to attack the towers from this direction: hard work all the way up and raining arrows. Bring plenty of water with you, at least half a litre per person on a hot day, as there is none at the top and thirst would spoil an otherwise lovely gambol among the rocks.

The frontal assault and parts of the towers are steep, require some scrambling and have no handrails, so this is not advisable for those who are prone to vertigo. A watchtower has been recreated at the eastern end of the rocks using concrete, and it looks decidedly out of place. The highest part of the rock formation is marked by a metal-girder cross, similar to the one in Skopje but smaller.

From the top it is also possible to hike 8km north to Zlatovrv, where the monastery of Treskavec lies (see page 228 and *Chapter 10*).

Prilep's memorial to the fallen of World War II is at **Mogila Park**, a kilometre southwest from the centre of town. Whilst the arrangement of 1m-high modern-art fists is nothing spectacular, the park itself is pretty and relatively clean.

A ruined **German cemetery** is at Penka Koteska Street, behind what is known as the old cemetery (*stari grobišta*). The cemetery contains the graves of 1,683 German soldiers from World War I, 156 other foreign soldiers from World War I and almost 50 German soldiers from World War II.

On the southeastern edge of the Marko Towers' rock feature, in a part of Prilep called **Varoš**, is the **Monastery of Sv Michael the Archangel**. It is perched between the rocks looking out to the Pelagonia plains and now houses five nuns. As you enter the monastery take note of the 15th-century iron doorway. Little remains of the original church, built in the early 12th century, but two partial remains of frescoes and some of the original walls can be seen in the church vaults.

The church now standing in the monastery courtyard is made up of two parts built during medieval times and of three classical period marble columns, which were found by the monks who built the monastery. The second oldest Cyrillic inscription to be found in Macedonia is carved at eye level into the far right pillar as you stand in the exonarthex (the oldest inscription is the epitaph dedicated to Tsar Samoil's mother and father). The remaining housing for the nuns was erected in the 19th century. Underneath the main inn is a deep well that is entered via a small doorway.

Allegedly there were once 77 churches in the Prilep area, but only six were left standing after the Ottoman Empire moved in. The **Church of Sv Atanas**, which no longer has a roof, can be seen on the road to Sv Michael's Monastery.

To get to Varoš take Gorče Petrov out of town past the turning to Markovi Kuli. At this point the road turns into Orle čopela, and very quickly you'll come to a bust of Orle Čopela on the right at the top of the rise in the road. Take the right turn just before this monument onto Borke Dopačot (in typical Macedonian fashion this is not marked as such at the turning!). Follow this asphalt road all the way to the monastery.

The **Prilep Beer Festival** (*Pivofest*) is fast becoming the biggest event in Macedonia, attracting up to 100,000 people on the last night. Music groups from all over the region play every night of the four-day event, and it is thus starting to rival similar events in the rest of the Balkans. It usually takes place on the second weekend in July and it will prompt the only time when the trains to Prilep will be full. Although wild camping is technically illegal in Macedonia, it is the only way in which Prilep can cope with the overload of people. For more information see www. pivofest.info.

OUTSIDE PRILEP

PRILEP TOBACCO MUSEUM (*Kruševsko Đadeč bb;* \ *401 090;* m *075 288 636;* e *muzejzatutun@mail.com.mk;* ⊕ *by appointment only during the week*) Housed in the grounds of the Tutun Tobacco Institute, the Prilep Tobacco Museum was opened in 1973 to celebrate 100 years of the tobacco factory that now houses both the institute and museum. Especially for the occasion, Tito ordered the purchase of over 750 items for display in the museum ranging from German tobacco pots, Chinese cigarette cases, Russian snuffboxes and Ottoman pipes, to intriguing cigar cutters and ornate *nargilehs* (water pipes) for both scented tobacco and opium. The room housing the exhibits seems an anti-climax on first entry, but a closer look at the carved faces and scenes on the artefacts reveals an exquisite craftsmanship that is fascinating and compelling, even if you don't agree with smoking (and smoking had been banned in 1634 by a decree from the Ottoman sultan). Artefacts made from a variety of woods, bone, ivory, silver, gold inlay, pearl lacquer, silver filigree, silver nitrate inlay, semi-precious stone and glazed enamels are all on display. Sadly, very little information is available in Macedonian or English. However, many of the stories behind the pieces can be told by the museum curator Aleksandar Tretkoski if he is available.

TRESKAVEC MONASTERY The remote Monastery of Treskavec is 8km outside Prilep under the summit of the impressive Zlatovrv. It is a magnificent old complex of significant historical and cultural value that is in urgent need of renovation. The site is of such worth that it made the World Monument Fund's 2006 top 100 most endangered sites. In addition to the value of the site itself, its remote setting is beautiful and earned itself a central role in Mančevski's film *Before the Rain*.

The monastery is built on the ancient town of Kolobaise, which existed from the 3rd century BC until the 7th century AD. The name of the town is written in a long inscription cut into a stone used as the base of the cross on top of the central dome of the church. There are also other inscriptions around the church that date back to the 1st century BC, when a temple to Apollo and Artemis was first built on this site.

Further remnants of the town under Roman rule can be found in the present 14th-century **Church of Sv Bogorodica**, which was built on the foundations of the original 6th-century basilica. There is a baptism font on the left of the narthex as you enter, and the walls of the narthex have a number of stone carvings and sculptures. As there are few lights in the church, it is a good idea to bring a torch with you or a lighter for the candles so that you can see the artefacts. The narthex goes around to the right, covering two sides of the church, at the end of which is a separate confessional room. This room is interesting for its fresco depicting the donors who paid to have the church built: the two old men dedicated their life to God and are shown, as is typical of frescoes of the original church donors, holding the church between them.

There is a secondary narthex before entering the nave, and from this narthex are some steps on the right that lead into a small chamber. Inside the cupola there is one of the few frescoes of Christ as a young boy (there is another in the Monastery of Sv Eleusa, also in the right-hand chamber). The church has a number of 16th-century frescoes with the typical greenish sheen on the face of the figures that was the hallmark of Macedonian rather than Greek artists. Also in the nave is a casket of the skulls of seven monks from the monastery who were executed, along with almost 200 other monks who lived there at the time, by the Ottomans.

To the right of the entrance into the monastery is the old dining hall. It contains the old stone tables and Roman jars and vats, but it is in a terrible state of repair, and the last fresco at the end of the hall is in dire need of help if it is to remain intact on the wall. The chips in it show that it is an older fresco that was deliberately chipped in order to apply plaster for a new one, which has long since gone.

Despite its former glory in the early Ottoman period, only one monk currently runs the monastery. Father Kališt, who speaks very good English, welcomes visitors and especially to the Sunday service held at 11.00. It is forbidden to enter the monastery scantily clad, so make sure you bring coverings for shoulders and legs before you get all the way there only to find you are improperly dressed and refused entry.

Outside the monastery are ancient graves cut into the rock. Water wells are encased in the stone wall to the left of the monastery main gate which leads to the ancient graves. There are also caves and monks' cells up on Zlatovrv. The stone outcrops and the views are intriguing and there are thought to be 77 animal and human forms that one can find in the rocks, such as lions, people talking to each other, a sphinx, a frog and eagles.

Father Kališt has a meagre income from this remote monastery with which to do much needed renovation work, and he charges nothing to stay in the inns, so maybe give generously at the altar when you visit the church. State-run excavation work is ongoing around the monastery, after which Father Kališt hopes to start with renovation. For route descriptions and a map of the three routes to the monastery see *Chapter 10*, page 321.

Like many modern monasteries these days, Treskavec (⟍ *800 160;* e *treskavec@ gmail.com*) has internet access and excellent mobile phone coverage.

MARIOVO To the southeast of Prilep towards the border with Greece is the region of Mariovo. This rugged, beautiful area straddles the River Crna, which is flooded to the north (forming the manmade Tikveš Lake), and to the south comes from Pelister National Park through Bitola and the ancient Paeonian city of Lynk, whose exact location is still not known. The river must have been an important one to the ancient Paeons, for outside the small village of Monastir is one of the finest examples of what little remains of their ancient cities. Built out of finely cut limestone blocks using what has become known as Cyclopean masonry (ie: a masonry technique which uses no mortar, but precision cuts and the size of the blocks to keep a construction together), these fortified cities date back to Aneolithic times.

Evidence of other such cities have been found at Prosek in Demir Kapija, Vajtos near Ohrid, Debar, Tetovo, Prilep and Skopje amongst other places, usually in high locations that are easy to defend. The site at Mariovo is unusual for being in the river valley, and archaeologists are still researching the site to see if they can find clues as to why it was located there.

To get to the site, take the road south out of Prilep towards Bitola and turn off southeast towards the town of Vitolište (signposted). After 5km the road passes **Stavica**, a picturesque village used by Mančevski in *Before the Rain*. Another 25km later the road crosses the River Crna at the new bridge that replaced the old Ottoman bridge of Hasin Bey. The river crossing is popular with picnickers and fishermen, and parts of the old bridge can still be seen. After another kilometre the old road to Monastir village is signposted from the opposite direction. Turn south to follow the dirt track (4x4 only or walk) upstream for 4km towards the village of **Monastir**. The site of large old limestone blocks can be seen from this track. At the village the site is known as *stari grad* (old town) *arxeološko naogjalište* (archaeological site), and although the two very old men who live here know about the site they are past the age being able to take you there. It is admittedly just a site of old limestone blocks, but if you want to see for yourself the closest thing you'll get to Cyclopean masonry built by the Paeons, then let your imagination build the rest of the city for you. The new road to Monastir, 4km from the bridge, does not allow a vantage point onto this site.

STIBERA RUINS
West of the highway between Prilep and Bitola, between the villages of Trojkrsti and čepigovo, are the barely uncovered ruins of the Roman town of Stibera. It was once a prominent urban centre in ancient Macedonia, and the last Macedonian king, Perseus, had his military headquarters there, from where he conducted his campaigns against the Romans in 169BC. The Greek historian and geographer Strabo writing in the 1st century BC refers to Stibera by its ancient name of Stymbara as being one of three cities located along the River Erigon (today's Crna), in the ancient Paeonian region of Derriopos and Pelagonia. The archaeological remains in Stibera range in date from the 3rd century BC to the 3rd century AD. Among the remarkable finds are more than 30 marble statues and busts, many exquisitely carved, and about 20 pediments and inscriptions. Barely cordoned off, overlooking the confluence of the Blato and Crna rivers, are the Temple of Tyche (the Greek goddess of fortune) and the town school.

AROUND MAKEDONSKI BROD
Another interesting monastery, halfway between Prilep and Kičevo, is the **Monastery of Zrze**, near the village of the same name. Quite spectacular to see from the approach, it is set into the cliffside as if it hangs there only by the will of God. The monks' cells are built precariously into the cliff walls under the monastery. The monastery inns and church are built at the site of an earlier Christian basilica, whose foundations can still be seen, along with a number of marble pillars and other artefacts.

The church dedicated to **Saints Petar and Pavle** contains frescoes from the 14th century and an additional nave, known as the Shepherd's Church, to the left of the main nave. The main church is famous for its icons, which show the Virgin Mary in profile rather than face on and on the right of Jesus rather than the left. Legend says that when the icons first came to the church they were placed, as is usual, with Mary on the left of Jesus. Every morning, however, the church's monks would come for morning prayers to find the icons reversed. Bewildered by this phenomenon the father prayed to Mary for enlightenment on the issue. She apparently told him that she had to be placed on the right of Jesus because otherwise her profile depiction would turn her back rather than her face to her son, which she would never do. The depiction of Mary in profile is unusual in Macedonia, but common in Russia.

There are also the graves of two Russian nuns in the grounds of the monastery (recognisable by the Russian Orthodox-style gravestones), and so it is believed that these icons originally came from Russia with the nuns.

To get there, turn off the road to Kičevo from Prilep at the village of Ropotovo. The turn-off is signposted for Peštalevo. Go through these next two villages until you reach the first left turn in the village of Kostinci at what appears to be the mayor's house. There is a hand water pump at this corner. Here the road turns into a dirt track and leads only to the village of Zrze and straight on to the monastery which you'll be able to see long before you come to the village. The last turn before the monastery is very rutted, so park at the corner unless you have a 4x4.

Just before Makedonski Brod is the turn-off to **Modrište**. This area of Macedonia, like Matka and Lesnovo, is riddled with caves and underground tunnels. At the end of the road at Belica are Golubarnik, Momiček and Laprnik **caves**. Near Slatina are several more caves accessible only with equipment. However, very visible on the way to Lokvica is the entrance to Pesna Cave, where the medieval ruins of former residents still exist. The cave goes back a long way through the mouth of a small tunnel at the back of the main cavernous entrance.

In Makedonski Brod itself there is the **Church of Sv Nikola**, which used to be a Bektaši *teke* (monastery of the Muslim order of the Bektaši), and some pleasant walks along the river.

Where to stay and eat In nearby **Plasnica**, an ethnic Turkish village, the local restaurant is renowned for its excellent fish dishes straight from the River Treška. On the outskirts of the village of Devič is **Mak Viking** (✆ *045 275 606;* m *071 371 169;* e *makviking@t-home.mk; www.makviking.com*). Owner of a small ostrich ranch, the restaurant serves ostrich steak and omelettes (among other dishes), and offers seven rooms at €25 for a double. Unfortunately, the ostriches themselves are not kept near the hotel. It's a 20-minute walk from the hotel to Devna Kula, an old ruined fortress which used to house the sister of Kralj Marko (see page 202).

KRUŠEVO *Telephone code 048*

Macedonians rave about Kruševo. Aside from being the place of Macedonian uprising against the Ottoman Empire in 1903, it is a very quaint Vlach town and thoroughly pleasant, with a population of 5,330. It is also the home town of Toše Proeski, Macedonia's once very promising and still very popular pop singer who died in a car crash on 16 October 2007, aged 26. At 1,250m, the town is the highest in the entire Balkans, and is a ski town in its own right, with a double-chair ski lift connecting the western side of the town to the surrounding slopes and three more lifts from there.

On 2 August 1903, the holy day of Sv Ilija, the Internal Macedonian Revolutionary Organisation (VMRO) rose up all over Macedonia to fight for independence from the Ottoman Empire. This day is known as Ilinden, literally *Ilija den* or 'Ilija's day'. After fierce fighting, Kruševo succeeded in wresting power from the Ottomans and on 3 August the new government of Dinu Vangeli announced the independence of the Republic of Kruševo to a population of 14,000 (today there are only 10,000 in the municipality of Kruševo). Nikola Karaev was made president.

It lasted, however, only ten days before the Ottomans brought the new government to its knees and the Republic of Kruševo was no more. In 2003, the celebrations commemorating the centenary of independence (even though Macedonia has been shackled for most of the intervening years) were of the utmost national and cultural significance. For the Macedonians, 2 August is like 4 July for the Americans or 14 July for the French, although much more solemn. A re-enactment of the uprising now takes place every 2 August, and is a massive attraction.

GETTING THERE AND AWAY Kruševo is located almost equidistant between Kičevo, Bitola and Prilep and can be accessed from all three towns in less than one hour. The fastest way to get there by car from Skopje is via Prilep, which takes about 2½ hours. The main **bus** station (\ 477 102) is on the far side of town on the road out to Demir Kapija. There are several buses a day to Skopje for 350MKD.

WHERE TO STAY AND EAT Family-run accommodation in Kruševo is increasing, and some of these can be found at www.booking-macedonia.com under the search term Kruševo. Most new places are located in the dedicated hotel zone at the top of Pitu Guli Street. Eating options are limited, choices being your hotel, the main dilapidated *restoran* in the centre, some new pizza parlours or a few *skara na kilo* places.

Hotel Montana (83 rooms) Pitu Guli bb; \ 477 121; f 447 680; e montanapalas@gmail.com; www.montanapalas.com.mk. Towers over the town & is well signposted: head left when the main road through town forks just after the centre. Rooms in the recently refurbished part of the hotel include b/fast & jacuzzi bath. **$$$**

Vila/Casa La Kola (9/3 rooms) Niko Doaga 21 / 70; m 075 318 778–9; e vilalakola@yahoo.com; www.lakola.com.mk. Refurbished old houses in the heart of the town. Vila La Kola

is more downmarket & cheaper but still has a traditional seating nook & b/fast area downstairs with some stone exposed wall. Casa La Kola is more upmarket, renovated with lots of traditional dark wood & a fireplace. **$$**

Vila Gora (12 rooms) Pitu Guli 53a; m 075 841 253; e info@vilagora.com; www.vilagora.com. A new build in the hotel zone, well equipped rooms & apts, including a dedicated children's playroom. **$$**

WHAT TO SEE AND DO Even if you do not make it here for the main event of the re-enactment of the Ilinden Uprising, Kruševo has plenty to visit on all the other days of the year. Aside from taking in the architectural beauty of the old houses, the main attraction for Macedonians is the **Ilinden Uprising Monument** containing the tomb of Nikola Karaev. It's easy to find: just head for the large white concrete monument on the northern hill of the town. The **house of Nikola Karaev** is now preserved as a museum, and is well worth a look inside for the rich decoration of the era. Like most of the intellectuals who made up VMRO, Nikola was obviously not from a poor background. Two more museums in the town are the **Museum of the Ilinden Uprising** (*Taka Berber 44a;* \ *477 177, 476 756*) and the **Museum of the National Liberation War** (*Nikola Karev 62;* \ *477 126*). There is also an art gallery of the paintings of the **local painter Nikola Martinoski**. The **memorial house to Toše Proeski** (*Pitu Guli bb;* ⊕ *09.00–19.00 Tue–Sun*) shows the life of this once very promising and dedicated young singer. Even by the age of 26 he was an ambassador for UNICEF and had started an annual concert, the money from which went to the poor of Macedonia and to improving education. He also funded the reconstruction of the **Church of Sv Preobrazenie** at Bušava, 7km northwest of Kruševo.

An hour's hike uphill from the Hotel Montana is **Mečkin Kamen**, the site of one of the battles for independence. There is a large statue there of a fighter throwing an extremely large boulder. This is where Macedonians gather on 2 August every year to pay homage to the early revolutionaries.

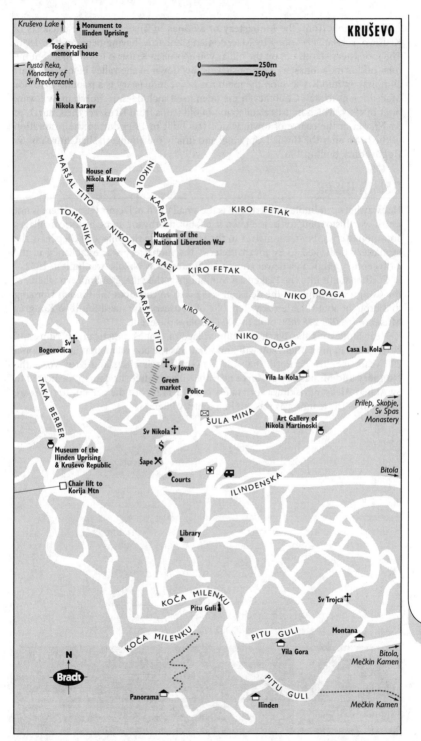

KRUŠEVO

Kruševo Lake ↑
Monument to Ilinden Uprising
Toše Proeski memorial house
Pusta Reka, Monastery of Sv Preobrazenie
Nikola Karaev

0 ———— 250m
0 ———— 250yds

House of Nikola Karaev
MARŠAL TITO
TOME NIKLE
NIKOLA KARAEV
NIKOLA KARAEV
KIRO FETAK
Museum of the National Liberation War
KIRO FETAK
NIKO DOAGA
MARŠAL TITO
KIRO FETAK
NIKO DOAGA
Casa la Kola
Sv Bogorodica
Vila la Kola
Sv Jovan
Green market
Police
TAKA BERBER
Prilep, Skopje, Sv Spas Monastery
ŠULA MINA
Art Gallery of Nikola Martinoski
Museum of the Ilinden Uprising & Kruševo Republic
Sv Nikola
Bitola
Šape
Courts
ILINDENSKA
Chair lift to Korija Mtn
Library

KOČA MILENKU
Pitu Guli
Sv Trojca
KOČA MILENKU
PITU GULI
Montana
N
Vila Gora
Bitola, Mečkin Kamen
Bradt
PITU GULI
Panorama
Ilinden
Mečkin Kamen

On the holy front, the **Monastery of Sv Spas** in Trstenik, on the outskirts of Kruševo, is relatively young by Macedonian standards, having been built in 1836. The monastery stands out on the hill as you approach Kruševo from Prilep, but the turn-off for the monastery (signposted) is low down in the valley before you start climbing up into Kruševo on the main road. The monastery is a popular place for Macedonians to stay. Churches in the town itself include the **Church of Sv Jovan**, built in 1904, which houses a collection of old icons from Kruševo; the **Church of Sv Nikola** in the centre of town, which was built in 1905 during the restoration of the town after the Ilinden Uprising; and finally the youngest, the **Church of Sv Bogorodica**, built in 1967.

DEMIR HISAR

Halfway between Bitola and Kruševo is the small town of Demir Hisar. There is not much worth stopping for in the town itself, but nearby are some historical villages and monasteries. Four kilometres to the west, outside the village of **Slepče**, is the monastery dedicated to Sv Jovan Preteča. The monastery was established in the 14th century although a newer church, dedicated to Sv Nikola, was built in 1672.

Further south into the Plakenska Mountains is the village of **Smilevo** where, at the Congress of Smilevo, the decision was taken to carry out the Ilinden Uprising that brought about the ten-day Republic of Kruševo. The small **Smilevo Kongres Museum** (m *075 298 688*) built in 2004 displays the event.

Near Smilevo is the Vlach museum village of **Gopeš**, practically in ruins and barely lived in now. There you will find what was the biggest church in Macedonia 200 years ago. To the north, halfway between Demir Hisar and Kruševo, is the **Nunnery and Monastery of Zurče** near the village Zurče. Its church, dedicated to Sv Atanas Aleksandriski, was originally built in 1121, but the current frescoes are from 1671. The iconostasis was put in a century later.

7

Polog and Mavrovo

> ... every inch of the [Šarena] mosque inside was painted with fripperies in this amusing and self-consciously amused style. There was a frieze of tiny little views, of palaces on the Bosporus with ships neatly placed around the sound, of walled gardens with playing fountains ... it was like being inside a building made of a lot of enormous tea-trays ...
>
> Rebecca West, *Black Lamb Grey Falcon*, 1941

The northwest of Macedonia along the upper reaches of the Vardar is known as Polog. It is edged by the **Šar mountain range** bordering Kosovo. Further south the **Korab** and **Dešat mountains** border Albania. The main towns of Tetovo, Gostivar and Debar are predominantly Albanian, with significant pockets of Turks in Vrapčista, Centar Župa, Plašnica and Vraneštica. If you don't speak any Albanian, you'll be more warmly welcomed among most of the Albanian community if you speak German as it is more widely spoken here than English as a second language.

Mavrovo National Park and **Jasen Forestry Reserve** are home to some stunning mountain scenery, waterfalls and wildlife. **Skiing** is available at Popova Šapka near Tetovo, and at Mavrovo, and in the summer the **wedding festival** of Galičnik takes place every July. The back road to Ohrid from Gostivar goes past Mavrovo Lake and down the Radika River into the manmade dammed valley of Debar Lake. From there it follows the Crni Drim River past the dammed Globočica Valley on to Struga. In the autumn it is probably one of the prettiest routes in Macedonia, when the densely wooded mountainside becomes a riot of red, orange and yellow. This is the area of Macedonia that could earn itself the name of 'Little Switzerland'.

TETOVO   *Telephone code 044*

With a population of 70,000, Tetovo is the gateway to the Šar Mountains and to the popular Popova Šapka ski resort. Towering above the town, covered in snow until July and as early as September, is Macedonia's second highest mountain, Titov Vrv (Tito's Summit, 2,748m). This is in fact the highest mountain that lies completely in Macedonia (and was also the highest in the whole of Yugoslavia, thus earning it its name). The higher peak of Mount Korab (2,764m) lies further to the south above Lake Mavrovo on the border with Albania.

Nestled close to Kosovo and Albania, Tetovo is the de facto capital of Macedonia's significantly sized Albanian minority. It is also the headquarters of the main Albanian-centred political parties, the Democratic Union of Integration and the Democratic Party of Albanians. Just outside Tetovo is the South East European University, Macedonia's third largest university after Skopje and Bitola.

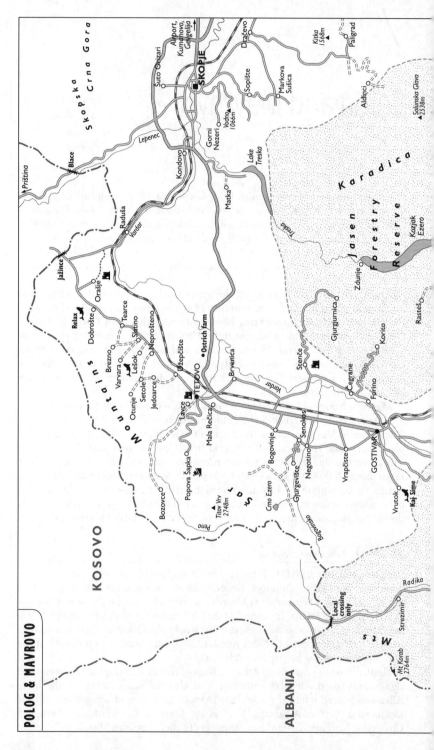

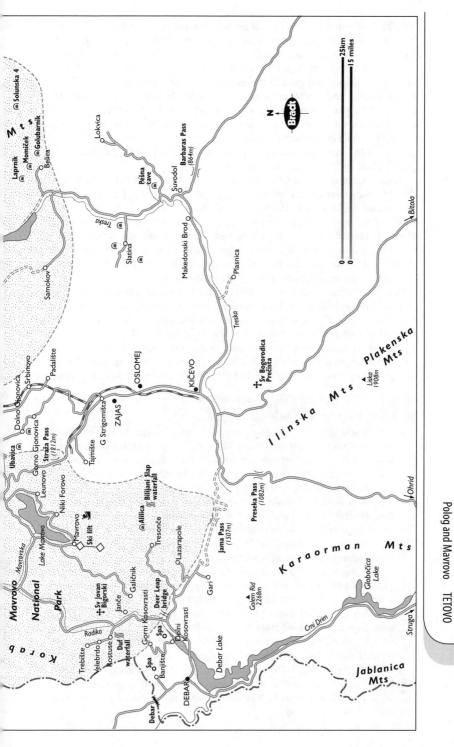

HISTORY Tetovo is a relatively new town by Macedonian standards, although there have been archaeological discoveries near the town which date back to the Bronze Age (2200–1200BC). Macedonia's oldest artefact, a Mycenae sword from this period, was found outside Tetovo. It is now on show in the Museum of Macedonia in Skopje. Copper and gold in the local streams first attracted Greek settlers but during Roman and early Slav times there were few inhabitants here. The first signs of a significant settlement appeared as a small rural village served by the Church of Sv Bogorodica during the 13th and 14th centuries. At that time the village was called Htetovo. Legend says that the village got its name after a local hero, Hteto, succeeded in banishing snakes from the village. Thereafter it became known as Hteto's Place or, in Macedonian, Htetovo.

Tetovo remained under Ottoman control from the end of the 14th century until the Ottomans were ousted from Macedonia in 1912. During that period the town was named Kalkandelen, which means 'shield penetrator', in honour of the local smithies' weapon making. Their superior craftsmanship extended to the advent of small firearms and cannons, which were traded all over the Balkans. The small hill above the town, near the present-day village of Lavce, has been fortified since Paeonian times and the Ottomans also built a substantial fortress there, the remains of which are some of the better preserved in Macedonia.

A number of mosques were built in the town, the most beautiful of which is the Šarena Mosque, built in the 16th century, which fortunately escaped the fire of the mid 17th century that destroyed most of the town. In the 16th century, the Bektaši order also settled in Tetovo, where they remain at the Bektaši *teke*.

During Turkish times Tetovo came under the *vilayet* of Kosovo and was strongly orientated towards its Albanian brothers and the Albanian struggle for independence from Ottoman rule. But the Serb victory in the Balkan wars of 1912

LEARNING IN ONE'S OWN LANGUAGE

In the early 1990s, the Albanian community tried to start the first university in the country to offer courses in Albanian. The government disapproved, repeating that Macedonian was the only official language allowed under the then constitution (the writing of which the Albanians had not participated in), and with that the struggle for the right to learn in one's own mother tongue ensued. Eventually, after intense mediation from the OSCE's High Commissioner for National Minorities, Max van der Stoel, both sides agreed on a compromise in the form of the South East European University (SEEU, also known as the Van der Stoel University; www.seeu.org.mk) offering courses taught in Albanian, Macedonian and English.

In many ways SEEU was set up to be independent of the government by being a fee-paying establishment built with international money. In the academic year of 2004/05, SEEU enrolled 3,886 students, of whom 78% spoke Albanian as their first language. SEEU has the potential to be a role model for education among mixed ethnicities around the world, and could make for a valuable exchange year for students of Balkan history and language.

With the rights enshrined in the Ohrid Framework Agreement, the Albanian community finally won their struggle for state funding for Albanian-language tertiary education with the legal recognition of Tetovo University in 2003. The following year, 1,550 students enrolled. For more on education in Macedonia, see page 54.

and 1913 left the entire *vilayet* of Kosovo, including Tetovo, Gostivar and Debar, under the control of Royalist Yugoslavia. The resulting crackdown on Islam forced many Muslims from Tetovo to emigrate to the US and Canada, while thousands of Serbs were encouraged to move into the town to develop the mining and hydroelectric industries.

The town prospered: orthodox churches were built, skiing and pony trekking started in the Šar Mountains, and White Russian settlers arrived. The 1930s were good for the new Slav settlers of Tetovo; and then came World War II and Tetovo became a part of fascist Albania. In resistance, some of the new Serb settlers set up the Macedonian Communist Party, founded on 19 March 1943 in Tetovo, but by then the Albanian Communist Party was also fighting for the town.

Eventually, the town fell to Tito under the Socialist Republic of Macedonia (SRM), and Albanians in Tetovo were subject to much the same repression as the Albanians of Kosovo in Yugoslavia. More Muslims emigrated and those who remained demonstrated periodically but violently against the communist regime, notably in the Yucel Incident of 1957 and the Kalkandelen Incident of 1968. When the troubles in neighbouring Kosovo began in 1981, Tetovo had to be put under the control of paramilitary police due to the rioting and show of sympathy with the Kosovar Albanians. The same happened again in 1989.

When it became obvious in 1990 that Yugoslavia was about to fall, over 2,000 ethnic Albanians marched through Tetovo demanding secession from the Socialist Republic of Macedonia and unity with Albania. Self-determination of an ethnic minority within a state was not a right under the SRM constitution and, protesting their lack of representation under the constitution of a new Republic of Macedonia (RM), the Albanians of Macedonia boycotted the referendum on independence from Yugoslavia and were thus excluded from almost any representation in the new government. Tetovo became the headquarters of the new Albanian political parties, which were regarded as unconstitutional by the new RM. Tensions worsened, and were fuelled by increasing lawlessness in neighbouring Kosovo. Prior to the NATO bombing of Serb forces in Kosovo, Tetovo became the rear supply base for the Kosovo Liberation Army, and then later home to thousands of Kosovo refugees.

In 1997, Ajladin Demiri, the mayor of Tetovo, was jailed for raising the double-headed eagle flag of Albania from Tetovo Town Hall, and by 2000 the outbreak of hostilities in Tanuševci, north of Skopje on the border with Kosovo, had spilled into the towns of Tetovo and Gostivar. Even after hostilities had ceased and a peace deal had been brokered by the international community, there was still inter-ethnic tension in the area. The old Tetovo–Gostivar–Debar highway (now the back road through Bogovinje and Vrapčiste), linking these predominantly Albanian towns, was the scene of many armed blockades in 2001–02.

Today, although some tensions remain, they are either inter-gang disputes, which are not aimed at the innocent tourist, or are purely of a political nature. Since the recent formation of two universities in the town (see box opposite), Tetovo has become a young and vibrant place that is welcoming and interesting.

GETTING THERE, AWAY AND AROUND Tetovo is a 40-minute **drive** from Skopje on the E65 highway (Motorway 2). There is also a **railway** service to the town three times a day from Skopje and from Kičevo (see train timetable on page 72). It costs 80MKD to Skopje and 82MKD to Kičevo. The train station (✆ 336 660) is on Ulica B Kidrič, almost 1km to the southeast of the town centre.

Tetovo bus station (✆ 336 331, 339 130; www.avtobuskastanicatetovo.com.mk) is next to the train station, although most **buses** also stop and pick up in the centre

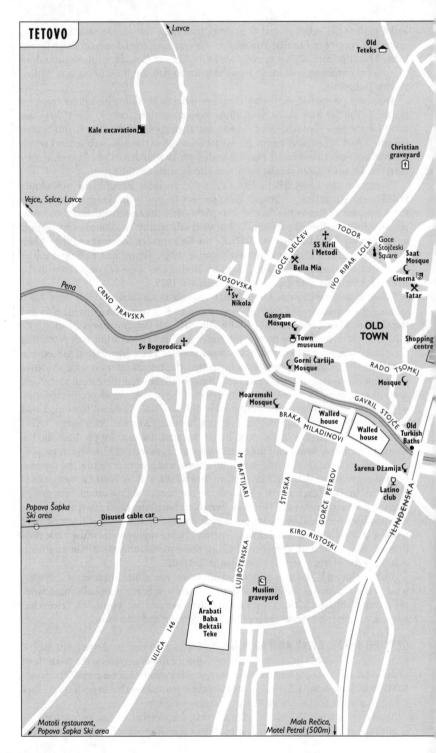

TETOVO

Lavce

Old Teteks

Kale excavation

Christian graveyard

Vejce, Selce, Lavce

TODOR

SS Kiril i Metodi

Goce Stojčeski Square

Saat Mosque

GOCE DELČEV

Bella Mia

IVO RIBAR LOLA

Cinema

KOSOVSKA

Tatar

Pena

CRNO TRAVSKA

Sv Nikola

Gamgam Mosque

Town museum

OLD TOWN

Sv Bogorodica

Gorni Čaršija Mosque

Shopping centre

RADO TSOMKJ

Mosque

Moaremshi Mosque

GAVRIL STOJČE

BRAKA MILADINOVI

Walled house

Walled house

Old Turkish Baths

Popova Šapka Ski area

Disused cable car

M BAFTIJARI

ŠTIPSKA

GORČE PETROV

Šarena Džamija

Latino club

I. HINDENSKA

KIRO RISTOSKI

LJUBOTENSKA

Muslim graveyard

Arabati Baba Bektaši Teke

ULICA 146

Matoši restaurant, Popova Šapka Ski area

Mala Rečica, Motel Petrol (500m)

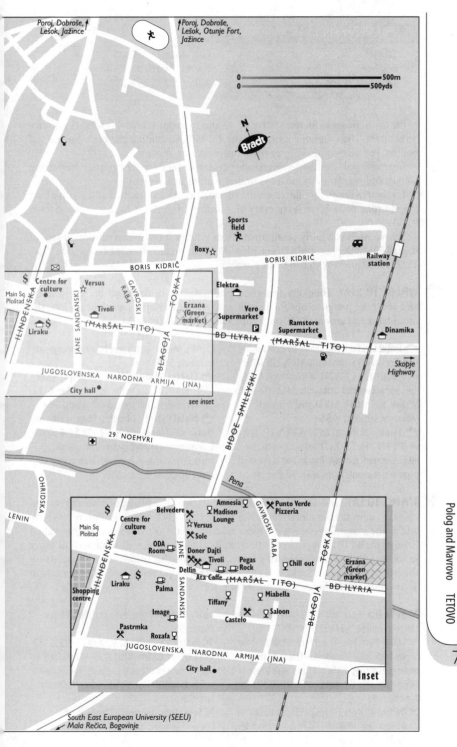

BUS DEPARTURES FROM TETOVO

Skopje	Every 45mins 06.00–20.15
Gostivar	Every half hour 06.00–20.00
Struga via Kičevo	06.15, 13.20, 15.20, 18.15

of the town. Buses to Skopje start at 05.45 and run approximately every 45 minutes until 20.00. The one-hour journey costs 150MKD including the price for the toll booths. For times of main inter-town buses see box above.

International destinations include Belgrade (eight-hour journey departing 20.00); and regular daily journeys to destinations in Germany.

Local area buses to villages on the old road north to Vratnica and south along the old road to Debreše leave every 15 minutes from Potok in the centre of town 05.50–20.00.

Tetovo itself is a fairly small town. **Taxis** run for a combined minimum fare of flagfall 50MKD, plus 30MKD/km, plus 5MKD/minute. Taxi numbers include 1560, 1577, 1590 (prefix with 046 from a mobile).

WHERE TO STAY There are few good places to stay in the town of Tetovo itself, and you may prefer to opt for Skopje only an hour away, or go right up into the mountains and stay at the Popova Šapka ski resort (see page 245).

Hotel Liraku (also known by its old name, Makedonija) (39 rooms) Ilyrija bb; 338 578; m 070 209 030; f 338 741; e info@hotel-lirak. com.mk; www.hotel-liraku.com.mk. In the centre of town, this hotel is well located & recently renovated, but noisy. **$$$**

Tivoli (30 rooms) Bd Ilyria 19; 352 370; m 071 389 213; f 352 371; e tivoli@tivoli.com. mk; www.tivoli.com.mk. Run by one of the most popular restaurants in the town. All mod cons; friendly, helpful staff; buffet b/fast & oranges at reception. **$$$**

Elektra (5 rooms) Ulica 120, Broj 2; 339 190; f 339 455. Close to the centre of town & in a quiet area. Basic, but clean & tidy rooms. **$$**

Motel Petrol (14 rooms) Studena Voda bb, 3km south of the centre; 378 090; f 378 100; e petrolcompany@petrolcompany.com.mk; www.petrolcompany.com.mk. Clean rooms above the petrol station. **$$**

WHERE TO EAT The main thoroughfare, Bd Ilyria, offers plenty of places to eat and drink, as does the parallel street to the south, Ulica JNA, which is slightly less busy and so the atmosphere along it is more relaxing. Tetovo's main green market, called Erzana, on Bd Ilyria is packed with fresh local produce as well as all sorts of other knick-knacks and cheap clothing items. There are also some nice restaurants on the way up to Popova Šapka and some at the Šapka ski resort itself. Restaurants in Tetovo include the following in order of price:

Bella Mia Goce Delcev 108 (just west of Kiril i Metodi Church); 331 332; m 070 224 922; ⏰ 12.00–24.00 Sun–Thu, 12.00–01.00 Fri & Sat. Serves traditional Macedonian fare in a pretty, traditional setting in the old town with a nice čardak (patio) in the summer. Good Bela Mia tava & pindžur. **$$**

Delfin Bd Ilyria 17; 339 125; ⏰ 10.00– 24.00 Sun–Thu, 10.00–01.00 Fri & Sat. Much less trendy than Tivoli next door; popular with the literati. **$$**

Pastrmka Pastrmka Ulica JNA 3; 335 633; ⏰ 12.00–24.00 Sun–Thu, 12.00–01.00 Fri & Sat. As the name (trout) suggests, specialises in fish as well as Macedonia's other traditional fare. **$$**

Sole Jane Sandanski 98 (opposite the House of Culture); 333 238; ⏰ 12.00–24.00

Sun–Thu, 12.00–01.00 Fri & Sat. Popular with businessmen, artists & local politicians. Delicious pasta & seafood. The focaccia with garlic is especially tasty but do not leave without trying the homemade crème caramel. $$
✗ **Tatar** 114th Ulica 2; ✆333 430;
⏰ 12.00–24.00 Sun–Thu, 12.00–01.00 Fri & Sat. A nice family restaurant, with good cold starters & rolled lamb. $$

✗ **Tivoli** Bd Ilyria 19; ✆352 370; m 071 389 312; ⏰ 08.00–24.00 Sun–Thu, 08.00–01.00 Fri & Sat. A very popular place on the main boulevard. Serves a range of good salads, risottos & excellent b/fast omelettes. Pleasant atmosphere & fine service. $$
✗ **Punto Verde** Boris Kidrič bb; ✆337 498. A pizzeria & a popular bar with a huge terrace, normally packed on summer afternoons. $

ENTERTAINMENT AND NIGHTLIFE Contrary to what you might think, Tetovo offers a great variety of places for entertainment, especially from Thursdays to Sundays.

🖳**Ata Caffe** Bd Ilyria. New & popular, near Tivoli restaurant & hotel.
🖳**Image** Jane Sandanski. Attracts a slightly older ethnic Macedonian crowd.
🖳**Palma** Bd Ilyria. A small cafeteria decorated in Rococo style.
🖳**Pegas Rock Café** Also near Tivoli.
♀**Madison Lounge** Boris Kidrič; ✆335 126. One of the entertainment icons of the town. Offers excellent music & a nice atmosphere, mainly frequented by people in their 30s.

☆**Roxy** An outdoor summer discotheque.
♀**Rozafa** Similar ambience to Tiffany.
♀**Tiffany** Bd Ilyria. A fun place popular with the trendy ethnic Albanian youth.
☆**Versus** Jane Sandanski, next door to Sole restaurant. Frequented by a young ethnic Macedonian clientele. Offers live music during summer w/ends.

WHAT TO SEE AND DO The **Šarena Džamija** (meaning coloured or painted mosque and often called the Motley Mosque by English-speakers) is known locally as Pasha Djamija (Prince's Mosque). Its colourful exterior makes the building look like it is clad in a deck of playing cards. Over 30,000 eggs were used to manufacture the paint and glaze. The site used to include an inn as well as a bathhouse on the other side of the river (currently being renovated). The grounds of the mosque contain an octagonal *turbe* (grave) of Hurshida and Mensure, the two women who paid to have the mosque built in 1459.

Other mosques in Tetovo include the **Saat Mosque**, which as its name implies used to have a clock in its minaret; the **Gorni Čaršija Mosque**, so called for its proximity to the upper bazaar area; and the **Gamgam Mosque**. Churches in town include the **Church of Sv Bogorodica** near the river, the **Church of Sv Nikola** above the river and on the way to Lavce and the fortress remains, and the **Church of Kiril i Metodi**.

The **Arabati Baba Bektaši** *Teke* is one of the prettiest sites in the town, with well-kept gardens, old-style inns and meditation platforms. A *teke* is the Sufi or dervish equivalent of a monastery belonging to one of the 12 orders of dervishes (Muslim mystics). Sufism is derived from the Sunni branch of Islam.

With the departure of the Ottoman rulers from the area in 1912 the dervishes were no longer welcome and most fled to neighbouring Albania or elsewhere. This *teke* in Tetovo was built at the end of the 18th century and remained the seat of the Bektaši until 1912 when the Ottomans were driven out of Macedonia. Although the *teke* saw a small revival between 1941 and 1945, the lands were taken as state property during Yugoslav times and made into a hotel and museum. In recent years, however, the Bektašii order has regained access to the *teke* and the site is being slowly refurbished. Although in considerable disrepair it is still the largest and most well-preserved *teke* in the western Balkans.

The prayer room and library are open to visitors if accompanied by the *baba* (priest), who will welcome any library donations of Islamic books to replace the many burnt in 1948 when partisan forces set the library alight.

Next to the *baba*'s courtyard is the *meydan*, which used to be the main place of worship for the Bektaši. Now it has been converted into a Sunni mosque (much to the annoyance of the dervishes who would like to see their *teke* completely returned to the Sufi order).

ALI SERSEM BABA AND THE ARABATI BABA *TEKE*

Ali Baba (not Ali Baba of the *Arabian Nights*) was the brother-in-law of Sultan Suleijman the Magnificent, and had been a high-ranking *baba* in the important Dimotika *Teke* (now in Greece) when his sister (who was one of the sultan's wives) fell into disfavour with her husband. As a result, Ali Baba was banished to Tetovo at the outer fringes of the Ottoman Empire where he started his own *teke*.

Another version of the story goes that Ali Baba was an official of the Ottoman Empire who gave up his position in order to live the simple life of a Bektaši monk. The sultan, angered by the departure of one of his favourite officials, yelled after Ali as he departed Constantinople, 'If you will be a fool, then go.' *Sersem*, the old Turkish for 'fool', became Ali Baba's nickname thereafter.

Whichever is the true story (the Turks favour the first one), Sersem travelled the vast empire of Turkey until he came upon the River Pena in the tranquil mountains of Tetovo. There he settled until his death in 1538, quietly practising the 'way' of the Bektaši order. After his death, his only pupil to survive him, Arabati Baba, founded a monastery in Tetovo to commemorate Sersem's life.

The present-day buildings were built at the end of the 18th century by Rexhep Pasha, also a dervish, whose tomb lies next to Sersem's in the *teke* mausoleum. Not all the buildings are still standing today: in the courtyard can be seen the foundations of what might formerly have been the *teke* stables; a fountain, meditation platform and a watchtower are also original. Some say that the blue painted tower next to the *baba*'s private courtyard was originally built to house the sick daughter of Abdulrahram Pasha. The reception inn is still in disrepair, although the library is being refurbished. One of the buildings has been turned into a Sunni mosque, but the inns around the Bektaši graveyard have been preserved for the *baba*.

Many Sufi/dervish orders include a ceremony or dance ritual called *zikr*. This involves swaying movements in time to music and/or the repetition of Islamic texts by the lead dervish or *zakir*. The ceremony requires a lot of control and concentration in order to empty the mind of all but God, and can appear to result in an almost trance-like state. The *zikr* is performed on a meditation platform like the one at the Bektaši Arabati Baba *Teke*. (For the Rufa'i dervish order, renowned for their feats of walking on hot coals and swallowing swords, the *zikr* often appears quite frantic and it is from this order of *zikr* that the phrase 'whirling dervish' comes.)

At the Arabati Baba *Teke* another ceremony takes place once a year in recognition of the martyrdom of the Shia Imam Hussein family, who were stabbed to death in Kerbela, Iraq, for their religious beliefs. As in other Shi'a communities, worshippers beat themselves to relive the martyrdom of the Imam and his family.

Around Tetovo Just above the small village of Lavce, above Tetovo, are the ruins of an **Ottoman fortress** or *kale*. The *kale* and its accompanying mosque were destroyed in the 1912 and 1913 Balkan wars. Although no longer the glorious fortress it once was, it remains one of the better-preserved remnants after Tsar Samoil's fortress in Ohrid and the *kale* in Skopje. It has also been undergoing considerable excavation work in recent years, and it is likely to be rebuilt to its former glory.

In its heyday it was quite the construction with a series of tunnels from all the main Ottoman houses in the town leading to the fortress. The thinking behind the tunnel system was to enable the defenders of the fortress to escape behind enemy lines if the fortress was besieged, allowing the besiegers themselves to be encircled. The last tunnel collapsed in the 1960s and since excavation started, two of the tunnels, to Selce and Lavce, have been found.

While the *kale* can't be seen from Tetovo, floodlights at night can be, and the views of Tetovo and the River Vardar from the *kale* are magnificent. The site remains strategically important and was used in the last conflict of 2001, as was the Pena Valley behind, for shoring up troops and supplies. In World War II the Pena Valley was bombed repeatedly by the Germans.

The paths up the River Pena lead to a number of mountain villages and past the **Iron Cave**, a large underground system popular with cavers and pot-holers. There are also attractive villages along the Tetovo road to Prizren in Kosovo. Orašje, close to the Kosovo border, has the remains of another once strategic **castle** guarding the Pena Valley. In villages such as Brezno and Varvara, you can still see good examples of traditional village architecture – wattle-and-daub houses with stone roofs. Some villages, such as Jedoarce, Setole and Otunje, are former weekend house retreats that were damaged during the conflict and are now slowly being rebuilt. While you are unlikely to come across many people, there are wonderful views over the Polog (Vardar) Valley, as well as several mountain walks through mature beech and sweet chestnut forests onto the top of the Šar range.

In the village of **Lešok**, 8km to the northeast of Tetovo, is a monastery of the same name housing the two 14th-century churches: **Sv Bogorodica** (the Holy Virgin Mary, built in 1326) and **Sv Atanas** (mid 14th century). The Church of the Holy Virgin contains frescoes from three different dates: the time of construction, the 17th century and lastly 1879. The original iconostasis and several marble columns from the original church are now on show in the city museum. The monastery was one of several in the area favoured by the 19th-century Pasha Abdulrahman, who donated money to their upkeep. Later, he attempted an uprising against the sultan and failed (it wasn't just the locals who were unhappy with the Ottoman elite) and was packed off to fight in the Crimea, where he died. Unfortunately, during the conflict of 2001, the Church of Sv Atanas was severely damaged by a bomb. It is now being reconstructed with international financing and work on new frescoes started in 2004. In the yard of the Monastery of Lešok is the tomb of the educator Kiril Pejchinovik, who was born in 1770. In his honour, the monastery hosts an International Meeting of Literary Translators every year. There is a fish farm and restaurant **Trofta** (\ *044 335 633*) as you approach the monastery.

POPOVA ŠAPKA SKI RESORT AND MOUNTAIN RANGE

Popova Šapka lies to the west of Tetovo 1,000m above the town. In days gone by it was the most successful ski resort in Macedonia, but it suffered during the conflict years for being in the heart of the predominantly Albanian region of the country and local economic renewal has been sporadic at best. The continued closure of the cable car from Tetovo town centre to Popova Šapka illustrates the problems at the local government level, while the arrival of cat-ski opportunities for off-piste skiers does at least show room for entrepreneurship. Overall, facilities are improving and it remains cheap.

GETTING THERE The road to Popova Šapka is well paved if long and zigzaggy and the snow at the top and the views of Kopilica Mountain on the way up are well worth the **drive**, although parking is at a premium. During the winter there is a **minibus** that goes up at 08.00 and comes down at 15.00. It's hard to pin down as it picks up from various differing places depending on clients, so ask through your hotel. Alternatively, a **taxi** ride from Tetovo to Popova Šapka is 900MKD. For the journey back down, ask a restaurant or café on the slopes to send up a taxi for you. A map of Popova Šapka is on the Titov Vrv map on page 339.

WHERE TO STAY

Bora (24 rooms) Signposted from the trail board by the cone-shaped ski-rental shack; 361 106; f 361 107. Right at the top of Popova Šapka settlement, it has the great advantage of being ski-in & ski-out. Recently renovated, friendly & frequented by the fit Nordic & Swiss off-piste skiers taking the cat-ski which is based there. Sunny restaurant overlooks the slopes. **$$$**

Popova Šapka (53 rooms) At the end of the tarmac road & parking; 361 020. This state-run monstrosity has the advantage of always having rooms available. Ski-rental available in the lobby. **$$**

Slavija (39 rooms) On the way up to Bora; 361 030. In need of upkeep, but boasts a swimming pool. **$$**

Kaj Dule (4 rooms, inc one 8-bed room) Just below Bora; m 070 934 309. Basic, cheap & friendly. Shared bathrooms. **$**

Konak Šara Ski Planinski Dom (mountain hut, 4 rooms totalling 14 beds) Blagoja Toska 41/14; m 070 329 898; e contact@saraski.com.mk; www.saraski.com.mk. Bijou & basic, with shared bathroom & kitchen, but based right on the slopes at the popular little café next to the new church. **$**

Smreka Planinski Dom (mountain hut, 100 beds) The pink building beyond Hotel Slavija; 02 322 5958 for the hut warden Duško Boskovski in Skopje. **$**

WHERE TO EAT AND DRINK

Bačilo Once you're in the village, take the first right & follow the road about a third of the way up; 361 001; ⊕ 11.00–23.00 daily. A very popular local restaurant with good views over the ski slope. Book a table in advance if you want to be guaranteed a place on a busy w/end. **$$**

Casa Leone Two-thirds of the way up the same road as Bačilo; 361 002; ⊕ 12.00–23.00 daily. A delightful pizzeria with a sunny dining room & narrow balcony offering even better views of the slopes. Also does a very tasty *džigr al Venezia* (liver in red wine). **$$**

Matoši Halfway up the 18km road to Popova Šapka; m 070 618 664; ⊕ 12.00–23.00 daily. This rustic restaurant offers a wide terrace & good views. **$$**

D Haus Popular café next to the Teteks Hotel at the bottom of the ski runs; ⊕ 09.00–23.00 daily. Accessible from the slopes, it is the perfect place to while away a hot chocolate or mulled wine while viewing the skiers below. **$**

We Have Snow Ski Café At the Konak Šara Ski mountain hut, by the church; m 070 329 898; ⊕ until 1hr after the closure of the ski lifts. One of the few ski-in ski-out cafés offering basic but hearty snacks. Extremely popular. **$**

WHAT TO SEE AND DO Even if you don't ski or snow-shoe, the views of the Vardar Valley from the drive up to Popova Šapka are outstanding. At the top is the new Church of Sv Naum Ohridski Čudotvorec.

For **skiing**, the resort (*www.popva-sapka.mk*) offers 20km of groomed ski runs and over 35km² of terrain for off-piste skiers. A day ski pass costs 800MKD. Carving skis and snowboards are available for renting for as little as 400MKD including boots and poles (bring ID to leave at the ski rental hut) at either the orange 'cone'-shaped hut just before Hotel Popova Šapka, or from the shop in Hotel Popova Šapka's lobby. For the **off-piste** skier, Eskimo Freeride (m *071 361 639;* e *info@eskimo-freeride.com; www.eskimo-freeride.com*) offer a day package on their two snowcats (including accommodation and food) for €159–179. **Ski lessons** are available for 700MKD per hour from Zemri Beluli at Ski School Profi (m *070 981 395;* e *atomic_180@hotmail.com*). **Snow-shoeing** and **winter mountaineering** guides are available through Ljuboten Planinarski Klub (see page 322).

In the summer, the Šar Mountains offer a host of **hiking** trails, which have all recently been re-marked, maintained and signed. An excellent trail map is available in English from Ljuboten Planinarski Klub (see page 322), as well as mountain guides ranging from €15 per hour to €125 for the weekend. Sadly, 1:25,000 hiking maps need to be ordered in advance from the Katastar in Skopje (see page 76). The area has 49 **glacial lakes**, such as Golemo Ezero, Belo Ezero, Bogovinsko Ezero and Crno Ezero; several **waterfalls** at Lešnica and Kriva Šija (see *Chapter 10*, page 338) and there are also **rock-climbing** sections at Crnen Kamen, Kobilica and below Mount Plat. For most, though, the attraction is to reach the top of **Titov Vrv** at 2,747m (see *Chapter 10*, page 338). For those seeking a greater challenge there is the 80km ridge hike all the way from Ljuboten peak to Mount Korab near Debar.

GOSTIVAR *Telephone code 042*

Today, Gostivar municipality has over 81,000 inhabitants. The town itself, while offering few renowned tourist sites, is pleasant, multi-cultural and a frequent location for seminars and conferences and a convenient stopping point on the way south. With the source of the River Vardar a mere 5km from Gostivar, the river is clean and rapid as it courses through the town. For these reasons and more, Gostivar is slowly becoming more popular.

HISTORY Habitation of the Gostivar area and the Polog Valley go back to the 7th century BC. In 170BC, the town of Draudak was built near Gostivar. The Roman historian Livy mentions that the last Macedon king, Perseus (ruled 179–168BC), attacked Draudak with 10,000 men. Later, Turkic settlers started coming to the region with the Hun settlement in the area dating to AD378. Avar, Bulgar, Kuman, Oğuz, Pećenek and Vardar Turks settled here throughout the next millennium. Later, Slav tribes came to the region and the town's current name Gostivar comes from the Slavic word *gosti* meaning 'guests' and the Turkish word *dvar* meaning 'castle' or 'fort'. In the first half of the 14th century, Gostivar is mentioned in the 1313 Bath Declaration of Serbian king Milutin, as well as by Tsar Dushan at the opening ceremony of the Hagia Maria Monastery in Kalkandelen (Tetovo).

The first Ottoman attack on Gostivar was in 1336, but it wasn't until the invasion of Yildirim Bayezid in the 1390s that the Ottomans took effective rule of Gostivar and the Polog Valley. Many Turkish families moved here from Turkey during the favourable emigration policies promoted by Sultan Murat II and Sultan Mehmet the Conqueror, and so the town grew. Over the years, Gostivar flourished as a cultural centre and by the late 19th century the town boasted seven inns, five mosques, three schools, two libraries, two dervish *teke*, a bathhouse and a clock tower. Of all of

Skopje	05.30, 06.30, 07.30, 09.00, 10.30, 12.00, 13.00, 14.00, 15.00, 15.30, 17.00, 19.30
Tetovo	05.15, 06.35, 08.30, 10.00, 11.30, 13.00, 13.45, 16.00, 17.30, 19.15
Debar	07.30, 15.30
Ohrid	07.20 (seasonal only)

these, only the clock tower built in 1566 and the Beg Mahala Mosque built in 1688 remain today.

After Ottoman rule ended in Macedonia in 1912, many Turks migrated to Turkey, especially after the world wars as suppression of Turkish culture and persecution of Turks themselves became more common. The push of the Prizren Union's Megalo Idea for a Greater Albania into the Tetovo, Gostivar and Debar regions only made life more difficult for the Turks left in Macedonia. The Yucel Incident of 1947 saw a backlash from the Turkish community and more Turks emigrated to Turkey when Yugoslavia signed an agreement with Turkey in 1950 to encourage the emigration. The agreement came about when government relations with the Soviet Union were cut in 1950 and Yugoslavia looked elsewhere for international friends. It was at this time that Turkish primary schools re-opened after many years of no education in the Turkish language.

After the 1996 municipal election of an ethnic Albanian mayor in Gostivar, Turkish was forbidden as an official communication language. The following year the mayor was arrested for flying the Albanian flag over the municipal building, which resulted in a shoot-out with government security forces. When the mayor tried to take the government to the European Court of Human Rights for infringement of freedom of speech, his case was struck down, in part because of the mayor's use of guns to defend 'free' speech was seen to justify the state's use of force.

Successive mayors since then have done a lot to clean up Gostivar. Its central area is a pleasant place to while away some time, and many of the town's different ethnic communities do just that.

GETTING THERE

By bus Gostivar is well served by buses along the Skopje–Struga/Ohrid route, as well as to and from Debar. The journey from Skopje takes one hour and costs 140MKD. The bus station (\ 217 344) and train station are co-located.

By train There are three trains a day to Gostivar train station at Goce Delčev bb (\ 213 440) from Skopje at 02.50, 08.05 and 16.50 (see page 72 for full timetable). The journey takes 90 minutes and costs 110MKD.

WHERE TO STAY AND EAT

Balkan (16 rooms) Boris Kidric 165; \214 401. Decent rooms not far from the centre. **$$**

Barok (12 rooms) Goce Delčev 46l; \214 472; m 070 378 178; e barok_sera@yahoo.com. Above the furniture store of the same name. Modern décor. **$$**

Hilton (13 rooms) Goce Delčev 14; \222 600; m 075 416 626–7; f 222 900; e contact@ gchilton.com.mk; www.gchiltion.com. Near the centre. Standard rooms, some with jacuzzi baths. **$$**

Central (27 rooms) Borče Jovanoski 56; \216 226. Basic rooms & no b/fast available so try the cafés & bakeries on the main square. **$**

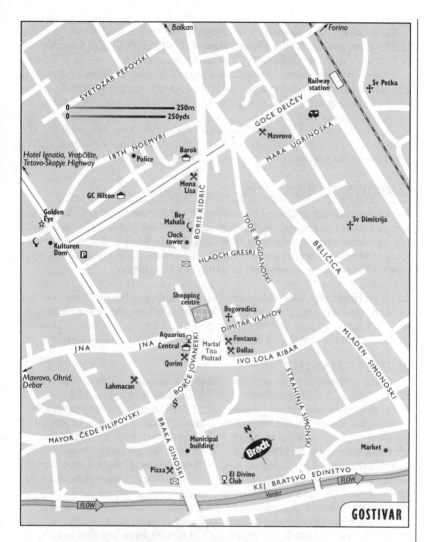

GOSTIVAR

The town centre has several pizzerias, *kebapci* diners and cafés. There are many more restaurants on the main street from the highway.

For a good trout farm restaurant outside Gostivar, try **Kaj Sime** (*Vrutok*; m *070 888 690, 070 472 311*; *$$*).

WHAT TO SEE AND DO Gostivar is largely a people-watching town. The centre, with its cafés and bars surrounding tended greens and park benches, is where local people spend the day, meet friends and drink coffee. You are much more likely to see people here in remnants of local dress than in other big towns around Macedonia, especially men in Turkish waistcoats and a variety of local hats. The *plis*, a stiff white woollen domed hat, is worn by Albanian men. The white crocheted hat is worn by Muslim men who have done the hajj pilgrimage to Mecca, while a plain or an embroidered squarish hat is worn by a lot of Roma men of the Bektaši faith.

The Ottoman **clock tower** built in 1566 is on the street behind the municipality building. Next to it is the **Bey Mahala Mosque**, built in 1688 by Ebu Bekir, the son of Kara Mustafa Pasha, and rebuilt by Ismail Aga.

A walk along the quay is pleasant and it is good to see the Vardar so clean as it enters the town. By the time the Vardar reaches Skopje it is an even murky brown colour, indicating that Macedonia still has a long way to go in waste water treatment and environmental preservation.

The nearby village of **Vrapčište** is a Yoruk Turkish village (see box, page 46). The town hall has an ethnological museum and occasionally **pelivan wrestling** matches take place in the summer.

MAVROVO NATIONAL PARK *Telephone code 042*

Ten kilometres south of Gostivar is the turn-off to Mavrovo National Park and lake. The park itself extends over the Bistra plateau across the Radika Valley and all the way up to the Dešat mountain range that forms the border with Albania. In the little town of Mavrovo there are a number of places to stay and the town makes a good base for hiking, skiing, watersports or simply as a quiet getaway.

GETTING THERE The little settlement of Mavrovi Anovi, on the road from Gostivar to Debar, is served several times a day by **bus** from Gostivar, Debar and Skopje year round. A **taxi** from here will take you over the dam for the 7km ride to Mavrovo itself for 450MKD, and during the ski season buses go all the way to Mavrovo.

WHERE TO STAY AND EAT

Radika (62 rooms) On the far side of the river; 223 300; f 223 399; e reservations@ radika.com.mk; www.radika.com.mk. The newest & most dazzling offer available near Mavrovo. Indoor & outdoor pool, spa, fireside bar. $$$$

Bistra (42 rooms) At the end of town; 489 027/219; f 489 002; e bistra@bistra. com; www.bistra.com. This is a true ski-resort hotel, with spacious lounges & reception areas, welcoming open-hearth fire, good restaurant & bar, fitness centre, pool & conferencing facilities. All the rooms are en suite with AC & TV. They also have overflow accommodation in Hotel Sport down by the lake for the same price, but it is not

nearly as luxurious even though you get to use all the facilities of the main hotel. $$$

Hotel Lodge (run by the Hotel Bistra, see above) Offers access to the Bistra facilities & is located right next to the ski lift. $$$

Srna (30 rooms) At the entrance to the village; 388 083; f 388 075; e hotelsrna@mail. net.mk; www.hotelsrnamavrovo.com. Good value for money. All mod cons. $$

Neda (25 rooms) Galičnik, 15km from Mavrovo; 046 831 307; m 070 596 114; ⊕ 1 Jul–1 Oct. Rooms are basic with no TV or AC, & aside from 4 rooms that are en suite, bathroom facilities are on the corridor. $

Mavrovo does not yet offer a wide range of places to eat, and for the price you are best off eating at the Bistra Hotel for atmosphere and quality, or at the Hotel Srna for something a little cheaper. For those determined to try something really local, the village of Trnica on the River Mavrovo just before it joins the Radika offers sour cheese and ground corn as a speciality, allegedly the best in the region. The modest restaurant is nothing to write home about, nor is the food.

ACTIVITIES IN THE PARK Mavrovo is a small but popular local **ski resort** (*www. skimavrovo.com*), offering black, blue and green runs accessible by chair lift. Oddly, the green runs are all at the top and the two black runs are the only way to ski/board down to the bottom. Unless there has been an exceptionally snowy winter, the

GALIČNIK WEDDING FESTIVAL

Nestled on a cliffside in Mavrovo National Park is the Mijak village of Galičnik. Tradition going back hundreds of years saw the travelling traders of Galičnik returning once a year in July in order to marry their sweethearts. Up to 40 weddings would take place on St Peter's Day (Petrovden), entailing a massive guest list and followed by a huge party. Village residents of Galičnik have dwindled since those giddy days, and so from 1999 onwards couples from elsewhere in Macedonia have been allowed to apply to be the privileged bride and groom for the mid-July *Galičnika svadba* (wedding). Thousands of visitors flock every year to see the rituals, costumes, folk dances, traditional music and, of course, the Orthodox wedding ceremony itself.

Preparations for the wedding start days in advance. People from surrounding villages gather for a sheep milking competition. One of the few of its kind in the Balkans, it is spectacular to see the milkmen and maids at their work. The milk is then used in a variety of local culinary specialities, including various cheeses, *kajmak* (sour clotted cream) and *sutlijaš* (sweet milk pudding).

With the gathering in the past of such a posse of men, the stag night equivalent was and continues to be a day of pelivan wrestling. In each round two men, smothered in sunflower oil and wearing only leather breeches, compete to tussle the other to the ground. The winner is he who beats all others in his weight class by keeping his opponent's back pinned to the floor for a count of three. Traditionally viewed by men only, it is increasingly drawing a female crowd.

On Saturday morning, the day before the wedding ceremony itself, the future son-in-law adorns the wedding hall with flowers and garlands. He then fires three shots to warn off any usurpers and to signal to the guests to make their way to the village. As guests arrive the future mother-in-law welcomes them with bread and water and hosts a dance in traditional dress with the closest relatives. Today, professional dancers are brought in for a colourful show of costumes and synchronisation. With the pressure mounting, the groom is then shaved in public at the village spring as a sign of the impending end of his bachelor days.

On the wedding day itself on Sunday, the day starts with the stormy arrival of the wedding party on galloping horseback to visit the bride. Reduced often to a slow trot through throngs of onlookers, the party brings a young boy with them, whom the godfather-to-be (*kum*) places with the bride's party, as a good luck charm to bring the couple a son. A bridle is then placed symbolically on the bride's head as a gesture of her devotion, faithfulness and obedience to her husband. Whilst the requirement for a son and unconditional love is no longer paramount, the tradition lingers on. The *kum* then delivers a finely adorned banner to the bride's house while she serves the guests local wine and *rakija*.

Afterwards at the village spring, mirroring the groom's ritual the day before, the bride fills jugs with water for her last time as an unwed maid. Another dance ensues at the village square, where the men dance the *teškoto*, a virile representation of the hardships of migrant workers.

Finally, clad in her finest, a Galičnik folk dress of silk and gold braid weighing almost 40kg, the bride is escorted to the central church of Sv Petar i Pavle where, in the eyes of the honoured few who can fit in the church, the wedding ceremony itself takes place in the late afternoon. Traditionally, the groom stayed until Mitrovden (8 November), but these days the groom leaves with the guests after the wedding and Galičnik returns to its sleepy self by Monday afternoon.

blacks are quickly iced up and sporting bare patches that you might prefer to leave for your best rock skis. For those who would rather not risk the narrow and icy descent, the midway station picks up skiers. Many day trippers go up just to plod around at the top, admire the view and snack at the little restaurants. A day ticket to ski in the park is 1,200MKD, a week ticket is 6,500MKD and a season ticket is 20,500MKD. Wildlife safaris can be arranged through the Hotel Bistra, which also sells fishing permits. Fishing on the lake is from 1 February to 30 October, and on the River Radika from 15 January to 30 October.

There are many hiking trails throughout the park although they are not always well marked, and for mountaineering enthusiasts Mount Korab beckons alluringly above the lake. Korab Mountaineering Club (see *Chapter 10*, page 324) organises an annual hike to Korab every September, attended by hundreds of people.

WHAT TO SEE Mavrovo National Park is not only a preservation area for the rare wildlife that lives in this most mountainous area of Macedonia, but is also renowned for its culturally unique and isolated **Mijak villages** (see box, page 48). The village of **Gari** was home to the famous iconostasis woodcarvers, the Filipovski brothers, who carved the iconostases of Sv Bigorski, Sv Spas and Sv Gavril Lesnovski churches. **Tresonče** village is the gateway to **Biljani Slap** and **Dolna Alilica Cave** (see *Chapter 10*, page 336). **Lazaropole**, formerly a hunting village, with a small ski lift, is now promoting its clean air and village tourism. There are boards in the village centre showing the local hiking trails. The beautifully refurbished **Kalin Hotel** is well worth staying in (*16 rooms;* \ *046 846 222;* e *info@kalinhotel.com.mk;* *www.kalinhotel.com.mk; $$*).

There's no public transport to the villages (oh for a Swiss postbus), and the closest you'll get by public transport is to take the Skopje/Tetovo–Debar bus and ask to be dropped off at Mavrovo Nacionalen Park. Less than 2km from the road junction into the park watch out for the 600-year-old **Deer Leap Bridge** on the left-hand side. Legend has it that the bridge was built by the local *bey* (Ottoman lord) during the 14th century to commemorate the gallant death of a deer which he and his army had been hunting. Badly wounded, nevertheless the deer continued to elude the *bey* and his army, until it reached the Garska River. The deer leapt over the river but died on the other side. To commemorate the deer's bravery, the *bey* ordered a bridge to be built in the likeness of the deer's last leap. A shaded footpath on the far side of the river makes for a pleasant hike along the Mala River.

The most famous Mijak village in Mavrovo National Park, however, is undoubtedly **Galičnik** (see box, page 251) for its nationally acclaimed annual wedding festival. The village is accessible by road only from Mavrovo town (15km) over the Bistra plateau, or by foot from Janče. The hike from Janče (see page 255 for accommodation in Janče) takes almost two hours and gives spectacular views of Mount Korab and the Radika Valley (see *Chapter 10*, page 334).

On the west side of the Radika River, opposite the Monastery of Sv Jovan Bigorski (see page 259), is a 40-minute hike from the village of Rostuše to **Duf Waterfall** (*Chapter 10*, page 334).

DEBAR

The road past Mavrovo Lake through the Mavrovo National Park snakes its way along the River Radika to the town of Debar (Diber in Albanian and also seen in older writings on the town as Dibri or Dibra). It is a fairly small town serving a municipality of 20,000 inhabitants. Although it lies in Macedonia and is only 137km from Skopje and 67km from Ohrid, its traditional cultural and economic orientation has been towards towns further afield in Albania. As a result of today's more open borders with Albania, life in Debar is reviving again, but the town is still in need of significant repair and rejuvenation. There is not much of note in the town itself, but it has a rich strategic history and lies in magnificent countryside. This is an area well worth exploring for the intrepid and is sure to be developed over time.

HISTORY The earliest recording of Debar is under the name 'Deborus' on a map drawn by the Greek astronomer and cartographer Ptolomy in the 2nd century. After Tsar Samoil was defeated in 1044 (see box, page 22) by the Byzantine emperor Basilius II, Debar was administered under the Bishopric of Bitola. In the latter half of the 14th century Debar was ruled by the Albanian Kastrioti clan, but fell under the rule of the Ottoman Empire in 1423 when the local Albanian ruler Gjon Kastrioti died shortly after his four children were taken hostage. His son, Gjergj Kastrioti Skenderbey, survived to take back his father's land and unite all of Albania in 1444. A larger-than-life-size statue of Skenderbey adorns Debar's centre, showing the fondness that the locals have for his cause (see box, page 255).

Only a few years later in 1449, Debar was overrun once again by the Turks, and became known as Dibri or Debra in Turkish. The city constantly rebelled against Turkish rule, however, not least because of the wealth of the many Turkish *bey* and *aga* who lived there off local taxes and the fat of the land. But Turkish rule also brought trade to Debar and the city centre grew and became known for its crafts industry. Much of the architecture from that period still survives and if you can get a look into some of the older houses you will find the distinctive Turkish woodcarved *dolapi* (wardrobes), *minderliki* (built-in benches), intricate ceilings and doors as well as *cardaci* (enclosed porches on the second floor).

During the Balkan wars of 1912–13 Debar was taken back by the Albanians, but was then handed over to the Kingdom of Serbs, Croats and Slovenes as a reward for helping the Allies during World War I. Thereafter many Serbs and Montenegrins were encouraged to settle in Debar, a common tactic to ensure that newly acquired land became more integrated with the motherland.

During World War II, Debar was again fiercely fought over by various partisan and fascist groups and their Great Power backers (see box, page 296) but in the end the Socialist Federal Republic of Yugoslavia won out, and Debar became part of the Socialist Republic of Macedonia in Federal Yugoslavia. Socialist Yugoslavia helped to develop the economy of the region with hydro-electric dams (Debar and Globočica lakes), local mines, quarries and tourism.

Sadly, the transition to an independent Macedonia has not helped Debar's economy in the same way the transition to communism did initially. Many minority communities left the town after the independence of Macedonia, and this trend was exacerbated by the conflict of 2001. Such high emigration has further dampened the town's chances of economic revival.

GETTING THERE AND AROUND There are two direct **buses** a day to Debar from Skopje, at 9.20, 14.00 and 17.00. The journey takes two hours and costs 630MKD. Debar is small enough to **walk** around. **Taxis** cost a minimum fare of 30MKD.

WHERE TO STAY AND EAT The old Debar Hotel has not been open for some years. These are the hotels in the area:

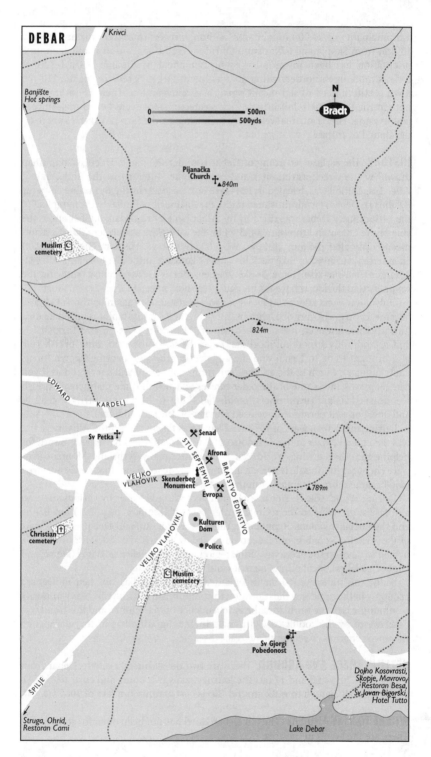

DEBAR

↗ Krivci

Banjište
Hot springs

N

Bradt

0 ————————— 500m
0 ————————— 500yds

Pijanačka
Church ✝
▲840m

Muslim Ⓒ
cemetery

▲824m

EDWARD

KARDELJ

Sv Petka ✝

✕ Senad

STU SEPTEMVRI

Afrona ✕

VELJKO
VLAHOVIK

Skenderbeg
Monument

BRATSTVO EDINSTVO

▲789m

Evropa ✕

Ⓒ

Christian ✝
cemetery

• Kulturen
Dom

VELJKO VLAHOVIKJ

• Police

Ⓒ Muslim
cemetery

ŠPILJE

Sv Gjorgi ✝
Pobedonost

↘ Struga, Ohrid,
Restoran Cami

Dolno Kosovrasti,
Skopje, Mavrovo,
Restoran Besa,
Sv Jovan Bigorski,
Hotel Tutto

Lake Debar

254

Hotel Tutto (7 rooms) \/f 472 999; e info@tutto.com.mk; www.tutto.com.mk. Built into the hillside overlooking the rest of the village, this new hotel is built to high ecological standards. The food at the restaurant is outstanding & is part of the Bitola Slow Food movement. The owner Tefik Tefikoski, nicknamed Tutto, returned from running his own construction company in Italy & is now lovingly restoring old houses across Macedonia. Original houses in Janče are due to be opened for accommodation in 2012. Child-friendly hotel with lots of play area & small tables for the small people. Old mountain footpath to Sv Bigorski Monastery goes out of the back of the hotel & takes only 25mins. **$$–$$$**

Banjište Hot Springs (75 rooms) – Banjište, 5km north of Debar; \046 832 680. Rooms at present are basic, with some converted to en suite with a TV, but as yet no AC. The hotel side of the spa is being privatised but it will take some time for the hotel to see the benefits of

this. For further details on the spa itself, see page 257. **$$**

Restoran Besa (50 rooms) Dolni Kosovrasti; \046 842 031; m 071 656 852. A basic but pleasant hotel with a nice balcony restaurant serving locally farmed trout & traditional Macedonian food. Near the Kosovrasti hot springs (see page 257). **$$**

Monastir Sveti Jovan Bigorski (35 beds) 17km north of Dolni Kosovrasti; \042 478 675. Recently & exquisitely renovated inn. By far the most beautiful place to stay in Macedonia, as long as you are inside the monastery gates by 21.00 & up for prayers at 06.00. See page 259 for more on the monastery. Bring your own food for use in the communal kitchen. **$**

Restoran Cami \046 833 721; m 070 241 205; ⏱ 11.00–23.00 daily. A place to eat offering a wonderful scenic view of Debar Lake. The turn-off to the restaurant is exactly 3km southwest of town immediately after the dam. The food is average Macedonian, but the atmosphere is pleasant. **$**

GJERGJ KASTRIOTI (SKENDERBEY)

Gjergj Kastrioti is known as the greatest hero of the Albanians for freeing and uniting all Albanians against the Turks in 1444.

Gjergj was born in Kruja, Arberia (today's Albania), to the Lord of Middle Arberia, Gjon Kastrioti, and Voisava, a princess from the Tribalda family of the Polog (Upper Vardar) Valley. Gjon had four sons, all of whom were kept hostage by the Turks in return for loyalty from the Albanian lord. When Gjon died, the Turks poisoned the four sons, but Gjergj managed to survive. He went on to convert to Islam and attend military school. He so excelled in swordsmanship and other military skills that he earned himself the title of Iskander Bey, meaning Lord Alexander. He then successfully led several Ottoman campaigns in Europe and Asia Minor, and was appointed general and then governor general of several provinces in Middle Albania.

But Gjergj missed his homeland, and in 1443, after being defeated by the Hungarians at Nišin Serbia, he deserted the Ottoman army and went back to recapture his home town of Kruja. On raising the Albanian flag – red with a double-headed black eagle, the flag that remains – Gjergj claimed, 'I have not brought you freedom, I have found it here among you.' Less than a year later, having reconverted to Christianity, he united the Albanian princes against the Turks at the Assembly of Alesio (Lezha in Albanian) with an army of a mere 20,000. He won 25 out of his 28 battles against the Turks and was supported by the Italian princes and popes across the Adriatic for staving off the Turkish assault from western Europe for 25 years.

In 1468 Gjergj died of fever, but his army kept the Turks out of Albania for another 12 years. He is the national hero of Albania and all Albanians, and his valour has been the inspiration of many national and foreign poets and writers.

WHAT TO SEE Debar is sorely missing a small museum that could tell the rich history of this strategically important town and its various rulers. But there are two orthodox churches, whose priests can tell you a lot about the town, if you want to take the time. As you come to the centre of town from the Skopje road you will be faced by the statue of **Skenderbey** (see box on page 255), also written as Skenderbeu or Skenderbeg, and not to be confused with the Skenderbeg fascist troops of World War II. This is the town's main street and continues on to Banjište, skirting the edge of the old town of Upper Debar.

Just before you exit Debar on the Skopje road is the **Nunnery of Sv Gjorgi Pobedonoset** (see box below). The nunnery was completed in 2001 and is dedicated to the church of the same name. Its grounds are small but very well kept, and hang on the edge of the cliffs of Lake Debar. If the main vehicle gate is closed, enter through the house door a little further down the nunnery outer wall. The effect of entering the door on a sunny evening accompanied by the

ST GEORGE THE VICTORIOUS

Sv Gjorgj Pobedonoset, or St George the Victorious in English, is indeed the same patron saint of England who slayed the dragon from his gallant white horse in order to save the princess. St George is a legend in many countries and it is astounding that his benevolence should reach as far as the Russian, Greek and Macedonian Orthodox churches as well as the Church of England and many other churches around the world.

George was born in AD280 in Cappadociea, now in modern-day Turkey. He joined the Roman cavalry at the age of 17 and rose to become a great swordsman and favourite of the then Roman emperor, Diocletian. George had converted to Christianity, whilst Diocletian was a firm believer in the pagan traditions. Eventually this rift in their beliefs brought George to his death. After doing his best to save Christians who had been sentenced to death by Diocletian, George was cast in prison to be tortured until he renounced his belief in Christ. Despite extreme forms of torture he did not renounce his faith and finally he was beheaded on 23 April 303 in Nicomedia near Lydda, Palestine.

He became the patron saint of the little church in Debar because that church contains the only replica of St George's original icon that stands in the Zograf Monastery at Mount Athos in Greece. When the original icon appeared miraculously in the Zograf Monastery shortly after it was built, the local monks claimed that it had been sent from Lydda by St George himself. The local bishop did not believe in the veracity of this story and so touched the icon to check for telltale signs of fresh paint. As soon as he touched the nose of the icon his finger stuck fast and eventually it had to be chopped off when all other efforts at removal failed. It is claimed that the finger remains stuck to the original icon and a bloody digit represents this on the replica icon at St George's Church in Debar.

The church frescoes reveal the life and times of St George, including his many miracles. Depictions of the terrible Emperor Diocletian show him wearing a Turkish turban, indicating the locals' views of the Turks at the time.

Many of the nuns speak English and will be able to tell you much more of the history of the church and the frescoes if you have time.

ding-a-ling-ling of the doorbell is like being transported to another world or a secret garden. The church itself is one of the best preserved in Macedonia, with all its 19th-century frescoes intact, giving it a much richer feeling than many of the churches in Macedonia which are obviously in great need of repair. Although this church dates back to only 1835, it is built on the foundations of a 16th-century church, which was destroyed by the Arnaut invasion. The 16th-century church had in turn been built on the grounds of the 11th-century castle of St George. The nuns sell a variety of handicrafts and are renowned throughout the churches of Greece and Macedonia for their excellence in making the ornate Orthodox bishops' hats.

Lake Debar, spread out magnificently below the town of Debar, is a 22km artificial lake built in 1964 as a means of producing hydro-electricity. It's a popular lake for fishing and swimming although it is little visited from outside the local area. At the southern end of the lake is the Globočica power station, which also serves Globočica Lake further upstream towards Struga. At the northern end of the lake, where the Radika River enters, is Kosovrasti spa. This is also a favourite fishing spot for the locals, as the lake fish come up to the mouth of the Radika to feed. At the time of writing it's the largest artificial lake in Macedonia (of which there are ten) and at its deepest point it is just less than 100m deep. The reservoir at Lake Treška, which is still being filled, should surpass the Debar Lake by 8km when it has been fully flooded.

OUTSIDE DEBAR

SPA CAPA DOLNI KOSOVRASTI (✆ *046 842 222;* e *info@bdcapa.com; www.bdcapa. .com*) These hot springs like all the others in Macedonia are indoors. There are separate baths for men and for women (no mixed bathing) and each bath is about 3m by 4m. One hour in the bath will cost you a mere 50MKD. The baths are open every day 08.00–21.30. Sunday evenings tend to be pretty busy. The 54-room hotel here has been completely renovated but the Banjište location of Spa Capa (see below) is a better experience.

To get here turn off the Debar–Gostivar road at the northern end of Lake Debar, and cross the bridge back over the Radika River. Follow the dirt track on the left and over the small hill for 200m back towards the lake. Over the hill are the hot springs, now inside a concrete one-storey building. Next to it is a ramshackle old Turkish house that used to cater for the hot springs, but has long since fallen into disrepair. There is a small outdoor pool available occasionally.

GORNI KOSOVRASTI VILLAGE If you follow the tarmac road straight up the side of the mountain for 20 minutes (two hours by foot), you'll come to the ethnic Albanian village of Gorni Kosovrasti. There's not much here except excellent views of the valley floor, the terraced fields on the way up and some fascinating wooden houses and barns. You'll get a real taste of mountain village life here, with cattle and goats wandering around in and out of houses and stables, and the local herdsmen riding mules and donkeys. There is a small mosque in the village.

SPA CAPA BANJIŠTE (*103 rooms;* ✆ *046 831 092;* e *info@bdcapa.com; www. bdcapa.com*) In the foothills of the Gole Krčin Mountain (2,341m), 5km outside Debar close to the Albanian border, lies this little haven of hot springs. Still more of a medical facility than a modern spa, recent renovations have rid it of the old Ottoman/communist experience. There are three springs (Nova Kaptaža, Goren

By 1943 the Axis advance into the Balkans threatened Macedonia. Albania was already held by the fascist Italian powers and the Allies were concerned that without help from special forces, the Macedonian region would also fall into fascist hands. As a result the British Special Operations Executive (SOE), a secret military branch set up by the British government in the 1940s to help defeat the enemy through sabotage and subversion, parachuted operatives into the Debar region. Their mission was to liaise with anti-Axis elements of the local resistance and the Allied forces in order to advise and see how best to help the resistance.

Major Richard Riddell, Captain Anthony Simcox, Flight Lieutenant Andy Hands and Lieutenant Reginald Hibbert were four such British SOE officers. They had been given only a few weeks' notice of their impending insertion into Debar and barely received enough language training or in-depth political background briefings, not least because their mission was to aid the resistance and not report on political developments.

The political situation there was complicated. Albania had divided into two main political factions, the pro-fascists of the puppet government under King Zog (who was living in London at the time) and the republicans, and the anti-fascist resistance of the National Liberation Movement (LNC) headed by Enver Hoxha. To complicate this otherwise clear division, there were various tribal chieftains in the hills around the Debar region who were prepared to go with either party depending on who would give them the most autonomy. And then there was the Communist Party of Albania (CPA), an offshoot of the Communist Party of Yugoslavia (CPY), which had joint control with the LNC over the Albanian National Liberation Army (ANLA), otherwise known as the Partisans. In addition, having lost the Debar, Gostivar and Tetovo regions to Royalist Yugoslavia after the Great War, many Albanians were wary of the ANLA and their political masters the CPA and LNC for their close links to the CPY. It was difficult to know in the end who would help whom.

By early 1944 Debar was firmly in the hands of the Germans and it was impossible to drop supplies into Albanian territory to help any potential pockets of resistance. Nevertheless in July 1944, Mehmet Shehu, commander of the 1st Brigade of the ANLA, now holed up north of Peshkopia in the foothills of Mount Korab, decided to march 1st Brigade into Macedonia in order to try to regain Debar from the east. The British SOE officers went with him. In four days the brigade marched over Mount Korab, down to the Gostivar–Dibra road, then up to the Bistra plateau above Mavrovo and back down to the Dibra–Kičevo road, possibly close by Tresonče, Lazaropole and Gari. Finally, marching up again towards Struga and Ohrid, the British officers heard of a supply-drop base for the Macedonia partisans only four hours' march away from their position. They convinced HQ Balkan air force to drop 'Albanian' supplies into Macedonia from where they could reinforce the ANLA with ammunition, arms and equipment. With additional help from the Royal Air Force, Debar was finally brought back into the hands of the Allies on 30 August 1944.

For a lengthier account of this operation read Sir Reginald Hibbert's piece in *The New Macedonian Question*, edited by James Pettifer (see *Appendix 4*, page 361).

and Dolen), and the baths themselves (separated for men and women) are nicely sunlit. The small lawn area outside the entrance to the baths is a pleasant place to sip a coffee and take in the magnificent view of the surrounding mountains. The baths are open 07.00–21.00 daily, and cost 50MKD to enter. Until 15.00 every day the baths are reserved for medicinal bathing and relaxing, but after 15.00 the spring is open to the public. As you approach the village you can see the run-off from the hot springs tumbling down the ditch on the side of the road, and where it burbles over the hill the water minerals have formed deposits of calcium, lime and sulphur. The smell of sulphur is strong.

MONASTERY OF SV JOVAN BIGORSKI (ST JOHN THE BAPTIST) This is a fully working monastery. It was first established in 1020 when the miraculous icon of St John the Baptist (also known as St John the Forerunner) first appeared at the spot where the church now stands. The present-day structures of the church and the surrounding monastery were built, however, in the 18th and 19th centuries. The church closely resembles those of Mount Athos in Greece, characterised by two octagonal domes, the smaller of the two near the main entrance, and the larger residing over the area of worship.

In its day this church's influence stretched over a large part of the region and into present-day Albania as far as Elbasan. Today the church is renowned for containing the final one of only four iconostases carved by the famous Makarije Frčkovski from Galičnik and the Filipovski brothers from Gari (two are in the monastery at Lesnovo – see page 289 – and the Church of the Holy Saviour in Skopje; the third in a church in Kruševo that was burnt down after the Ilinden Uprising of 1903). The iconostasis has over 500 humans and over 200 animals carved into it depicting scenes from the Old and New Testaments, and also includes a representation of the woodcarvers themselves. Many of the people depicted in the iconostasis are wearing the traditional 19th-century Macedonian costumes despite the fact that the scenes depict an era many centuries earlier. The bishop's and prior's chairs are also carved by the Filipovski brothers and Frčkovski.

The chest of relics in the church contains a fragment of bone allegedly from the right humerus of St John, as well as bone fragments of the bodies of other saints. They are apparently preserved by their holy nature. The remainder of St John's arm lies in the Cetinje Monastery in Montenegro.

The beautiful old inns, where the 1958 movie *Mis Ston* was filmed, were tragically burnt down in an electrical circuiting fire in 2010. The church was untouched, and much of the original stonework has also survived, but the dark cherry wood façades and balconies and the priceless monastery library are irrecoverable. The old inns are now undergoing reconstruction, and more of the new inns and a clock tower have been completed. To stay at the monastery, see page 255.

Church services take place at 06.00, 16.00 and 19.00 every day. The brotherhood of Jovan Bigorski pride themselves on their revival of old Eastern Orthodox ecclesiastical liturgy, which is sung according to the Byzantine tradition as opposed to the Serbian tradition brought in after the fall of the Ottoman Empire. It involves no instruments and is very melodic. The liturgy is sung by the priests at 07.00 (after an hour of prayer) and at 19.00 to start the church service, and is well worth attending. Alternatively, a double CD set of the liturgy can be bought for 600MKD at the monastery shop after the services (also available in Jugoton in the Trgovski Centar in Skopje). Monastery *mastika* (Macedonian ouzo), icons and other religious items can also be bought there.

Kičevo was known in ancient times as Uskana. It is mentioned by the Roman historian Livy when he records that the last Macedon king, Perseus, took Uskana with an army of 10,000 men during the third Macedonian War against the Romans. Kičevo became the current name of the town with the arrival of Slav settlers in the 7th century BC, although in the 11th century it was noted under the name of Kicavis in one of the documents of the Byzantine emperor Basilius II. In the 13th and 14th centuries during the reign of King Marko it was also known as Katin Grad, because this was where his sister Katina lived.

Kičevo became a part of Albania during World War II and is considered the first town in the Republic of Macedonia to be liberated by Macedonian forces when they defeated fascists here (it was retaken again later). Today the town continues to have a strong ethnic Albanian community and is the home town of Ali Ahmeti, the former National Liberation Army leader and current head of the Democratic Union of Integration. The municipality of Kičevo has just over 30,000 inhabitants.

GETTING THERE Kičevo is served by **train** (*station* \ *225 168*) and **bus** (*station* \ *223 900; e simeks-prevoz@hotmail.com*). The stations are co-located on the west side of Highway E65 less than 1km from the centre of town, which is on the east side of the highway. The last 60cm narrow gauge steam train to Ohrid sits outside the station. There are three trains a day to Kičevo from Skopje and three return. The section between Gostivar and Kičevo is the most scenic, running through close-knit mountains, numerous small tunnels, and alongside a clean pretty mountain river. A single fare Skopje to Kičevo is 182MKD. For train times see table on page 74.

Only the buses shown in the box below stop at the bus station. There are more buses, however, which pick up along the main highway between the station and the town. To get to Struga, take the bus to Ohrid and the driver will drop you off at the MakPetrol station at the junction near Struga. A minibus (*kombe*) will take you from there to anywhere in Struga from 50MKD.

Kičevo **taxis** can be called on \(045) 1544, 1991 or 1594.

WHERE TO STAY

Arabella (24 rooms) Maršal Tito bb; \ 22 552; f 222 551; www.hotelarabella.com.mk. Clean new rooms in the centre of town. **$$$**

Hotel Kičevo (23 rooms) Narodnička; \ 223 362. A basic hotel, clean & friendly, near the train station. **$$$**

Kukja na Umetnosta (20 rooms) Knežino, 6km from Kičevo; \ 262 061; m 070 793 739; e kucanaumetnost@tajmiste.com.mk. Completed in 2005 to take the strain off Knežino Monastery after the annual art colony there (Jul every year) became too secular. Beautiful surroundings. **$$**

Panorama (11 rooms) Metodija Stefanoski bb; \ 222 434. Basic accommodation between Kičevo & the village of Krušino. **$$**

Union (33 rooms) Osloboduvanje 1; \ 220 711. You can't get more central than this; location makes up for standard. **$$**

BUS DEPARTURES FROM KIČEVO	
Skopje	05.50, 07.30, 09.00
Ohrid, Bitola, Prilep	07.00, 09.00, 14.00

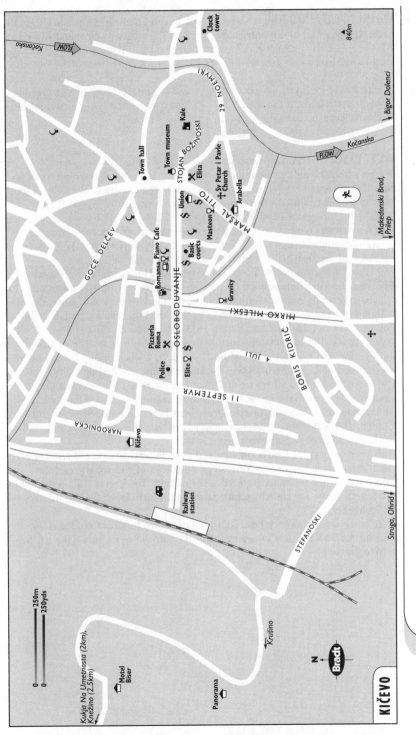

KIČEVO

Clock tower

840m

FLOW   Kočanska

Bigor Dolenci

MARŠAL TITO

Kale

Town museum

STOJAN BOŽINOSKI

Town hall

Elita

Sv Petar i Pavle Church

29

Arabella

Makedonski Brod, Prilep

Union

Masteen

Basic courts

Romansa Piano Cafe

OSLOBODUVANJE

Gravity

MIRKO MILESKI

Pizzeria Roma

Police

Elite

BORIS KIDRIČ

4 JULI

11 SEPTEMVR

NARODNICKA

Kičevo

Railway station

Struga, Ohrid

STEFANOSKI

Krušino

Kukja Na Umetnosta (2km),
Knežino (2.5km)

250m
250yds

Motel Biser

Panorama

N Bradt

KIČEVO

✗ WHERE TO EAT AND DRINK Dining out and the café culture in Kičevo are distinctly male phenomena, but not unfriendly. You'll receive a better welcome if you speak Albanian, German or English rather than Macedonian. There are lots of little *čevapi* stores in the backstreets around the town square or you can try one of the following:

✗ Elita Ploštad. The only restaurant on the town square, it offers traditional Albanian food. $

✗ Pizzeria Roma Osloboduvanje; ✆ 221 232. A new restaurant with a pleasant atmosphere. $

⎁ Romansa Osloboduvanje. A relaxed café offering sweet pastries & ice creams as well as the usual drinks.

WHAT TO SEE The town appears uneventful, although it has seen new paving, benches and refurbished buildings around the tiny town square *ploštad*. The clock tower and **Kale fortress** are all that remain of note from the Ottoman period. The Kale is a short hike up the hill behind the **town museum** on the town square (*Stojan Božinovski 1*; ✆ *222 949*; ☺ *Tue–Sun 11.00–16.00; entry free*). The building itself was used by the Partisan Army in World War II after it liberated the town, and the museum exhibition is mostly dedicated to that story. If the museum is shut when it says it should be open, try asking at the town hall, one block further north on Maršal Tito.

A few kilometres southeast of Kičevo is the **Monastery of Sv Bogorodica Prečista**, the Holy Immaculate Mother of God. Set high in the mountains, its tall majestic walls can be seen imposing over the landscape for some distance. Although the monastery originally dates back to the 14th century, it has been burnt down (on the orders of Sultan Selim in 1515) or destroyed by fire (1558 and 1843) several times. The current construction of stone is from 1848. The monastery is most renowned for Blagovestie Day on 17 April 1924, when Bishop Dositej entered the brotherhood. In 1963, Dositej became the first archbishop of the revived Ohrid Archbishopric, otherwise and now known as the Macedonian Orthodox Church. A few years later in 1967, Archbishop Dositej proclaimed the autocephaly (independence) of the Macedonian Orthodox Church from the Serbian Orthodox Church. This was without the consent of any of the other orthodox churches and has been a point of dispute ever since.

A legend of a flying icon accompanies the monastery: an icon of Mary has been taken three times to Knežino Monastery, northwest of Kičevo, and each time the icon has returned the same night via a ray of light. The icon is still on display in the church today. The church's saint's day is on the birthday of the Virgin Mary on 21 September.

To reach this monastery, head south out of Kičevo towards Ohrid and take the turn-off for Bitola. A few kilometres after the turn-off is a sign for the left-hand turn to Prečista.

The Northeast and Middle Vardar

> Some archaeological findings suggest that the site was used in the first half of the
> second millennium BC as a 'holy mountain' where probably more than one cult were
> celebrated among which the cult of the Great Mother Goddess ...
>
> Information brochure on Kokino ancient observatory, 2006

The northeast of Macedonia is little visited, although it contains rolling hills and
wide vistas from its practically empty but well-kept roads. If you like driving this
is the place where you can drive unhindered by traffic, roadworks and busy town
life. It has its fair share of churches and monasteries, hot springs and some very
interesting rock formations. In the vicinity of the extinct volcanic crater of **Kratovo**
there is **rock art**, large volcanic droplets, Stone Doll rock formations at **Kuklica**,
cave dwellings near Konjuh and a **megalithic sacrificial observatory** at Cocev
Kamen. Closer to Kumanovo is another alleged **Aneolithic observatory** near
Kokino. Near Sv Nikole is Gavolski Zid, the **Devil's Wall**.

The region's mountains rarely reach above 2,000m except in the Osogovski
mountain range, which reaches 2,252m at the border with Bulgaria. But the valleys
boast an abundance of rivers and streams, hot springs and rich paddy fields, and are
the wheat basket of Macedonia.

The main river dividing the region is the Bregalnica. Roughly running its course
was the ancient road of the Diagonal Way joining Heraklea (near Bitola) and the
valley of the River Vardar at Stobi to the valley of the River Struma near Pautalija
(now Kustendil in Bulgaria). Part of it can still be seen at Gorno Kratovo. Another
ancient route through the region was the Serres road, joining Ovče Pole in the north
to Serres (now in Greece) via Štip, Radoviš and Strumica. Both roads crossed at
Štip, making it an important trading town in times of old. Although there are fewer
uncovered Roman ruins in the north of Macedonia than in the south, a **Roman
amphitheatre** was unearthed near Klečovce in August 2003, adding to the list of
important Roman ruins already found in the region at Vinica and Bargala.

The two most visited sites in this part of the country are the **Monastery of
Sv Joakim Osogovski** outside Kriva Palanka, and the region of **Berovo** for its
lake setting and forest hiking in the cool mountains. Rarely visited, but equally
important for containing the first of four rare iconostases, is the **Monastery of
Gavril Lesnovski**. Not to be missed is **Kratovo**.

VELES *Telephone code 043*

Once an important Roman settlement going by the name of Vilazora, today this
unassuming place, and despite its former grand title as Titov Veles, is barely more
than an industrial transit town. It was known as Köprülü (written Kuprili in some

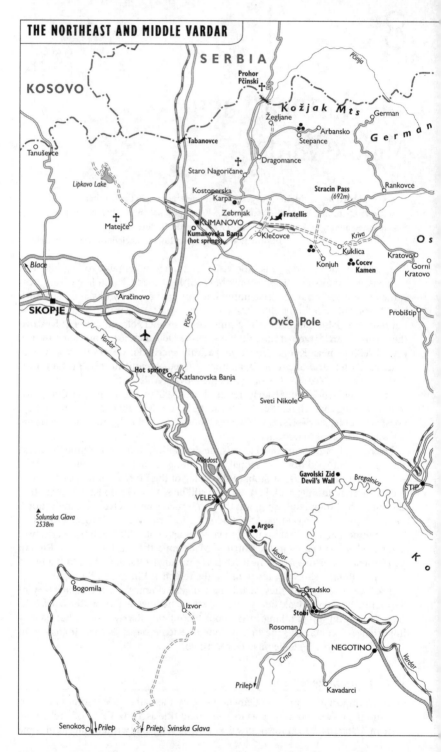

THE NORTHEAST AND MIDDLE VARDAR

S E R B I A

KOSOVO

Pčinja

Prohor
Pčinski †

Žegljane

Ko žja k Mts

German

G e r m a n

Tabanovce

Arbansko

Stepance

Tanuševce

Dragomance

Staro Nagoričane †

Lipkovo Lake

Kostoperska
Karpa

Rankovce

Stracin Pass
(692m)

Zebrnjak

Fratellis

Matejče †

KUMANOVO

Klečovce

Kriva

O s

Kumanovska Banja
(hot springs)

Kuklica

Kratovo

Konjuh

Cocev
Kamen

Gorni
Kratovo

Blace

Aračinovo

Pčinja

Ovče Pole

Probištip

SKOPJE

Vardar

Hot springs

Katlanovska Banja

Sveti Nikole

Mladost

Gavolski Zid
Devil's Wall

Bregalnica

ŠTIP

▲ *Solunska Glava*
2538m

VELES

K o

Argos

Vardar

Bogomila

Gradsko

Izvor

Stobi

Rosoman

NEGOTINO

Vardar

Crna

Prilep

Kavadarci

Senokos ○↓ *Prilep*   ↙ *Prilep, Svinska Glava*

264

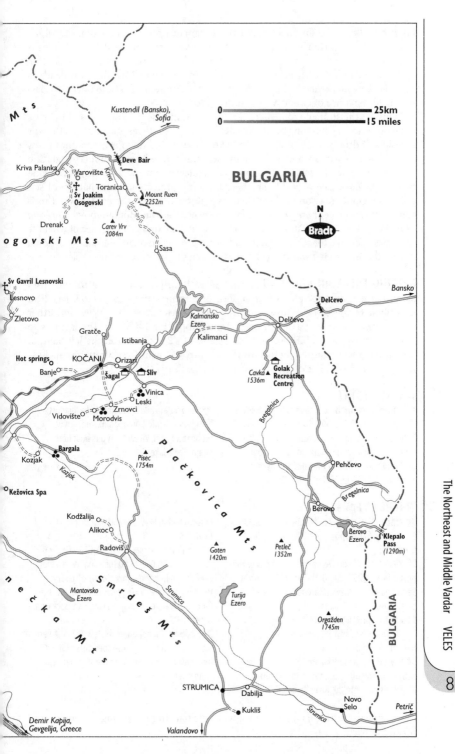

English texts) to the Ottomans, after the Albanian Köprülü noble dynasty which was started by Köprülü Mehmed Pasha, born in Veles around 1580. Köprülü means 'from Köprü', which is a village in Anatolia in Turkey. Köprülü Mehmed Pasha went on to become Grand Vizier of the Ottoman Empire from 1656 until his death in 1661. He was succeeded by his son Köprülü Fazil Ahmet Pasha (also born in Veles) who held the office of Grand Vizier until 1676.

Lying on the strategic route between the Kačanik pass (in Kosovo) and the pass of Demir Kapija, it has long been a key defence point southeast of Skopje on the way to Solun. It dropped the title *Titov* in 1996. Now, its old town is quaint, has a few cultural sites worth a wander past, and local trails have been upgraded. Pollution from the lead works outside the town is a concern, but the local environmental NGO Vila Zora (see page 13) has been running projects to remediate local soil pollution. Good news on the health side is that the industry is scaling down. This is bad news for the economy of the town, however. The Macedonian movie *I'm from Titov Veles* (Jas sum od Titov Veles) is a harrowing tale that gives an idea of what life there has been like for some, who in addition were kicked out of Aegean Macedonia during the Greek civil war in the late 1940s. Veles has moved on, albeit slowly.

GETTING THERE AND AROUND Veles has an hourly **train** service to and from Skopje (see train timetable on page 72). The train station (✆ *231 033*) is 1km northwest of the centre. **Buses** run frequently between Skopje, Veles and other parts of the country, starting at 04.15 from Skopje for 140MKD. The last bus to Veles from Skopje is at 21.00. Veles bus station (✆ *234 550*) is on the left bank of the Vardar a few hundred metres from the centre of town. **Taxi** companies include Bambi Drim (✆ *(043) 1591*) and Taksi Združenje (✆ *(043) 1593*).

🏠 WHERE TO STAY

🏠 **Hotel Romantik** (26 rooms) Lake Mladost, 9km from Veles; ✆212 999; f 212 997; e info@ hotelromantik.com.mk; www.hotelromantik. com.mk. With a good restaurant, fireside bar, pool & private beach on the lake. A daily rate is available, 09.00–17.00, for €20. **$$$**

🏠 **Brod Panini** (13 rooms) Lake Mladost; ✆211 444; e info@brodpanini.com; www. brodpanini.com. Views from this boat hotel guarantee a lake view. **$$**

🍴 WHERE TO EAT

🍴 **Amor** Maršal Tito 33; ✆233 287; ⏰ 12.00–23.00 daily. Serves pizza, pasta & *skara* (grilled meat). **$$**

🍴 **Baže Piti** Alekso Demnievski 7 (opposite the post office); ✆234 056; ⏰ 11.00–23.00 daily. Serves good pizzas, *piti* (Macedonian layered pies), *pastrmajlija* & *skara*. **$$**

🍴 **Panini** Blagoj Gorev bb; ✆233 615; ⏰ 12.00–23.00 daily. Serves pizzas & *pastrmajlija*. **$$**

🍴 **Parnak** Tito Gradska bb; ⏰ 10.00–23.00 daily. Conveniently close to the town market, its patio spills onto the River Vardar. Best *skara*

in town by far. Serves traditional Macedonian food. **$$**

🍴 **SinaSala** Maršal Tito bb; ✆613 270; m 070 393 643; ⏰ 08.00–23.00 Tue–Sun. With a view over the main bridge, this pizzeria also serves the best *pastrmajlija* in town. Order in advance for take-aways to pick up on your way back from Greece. **$$**

🍴 **Snoopy** Blagoj Gorev 67; ✆239 255. A varied menu, including the house speciality of frogs' legs. Live music outdoors in the summer. Wide wine selection. **$$**

The main street, Blagoj Gorev, is alive with café bars in the evening as people stroll up and down.

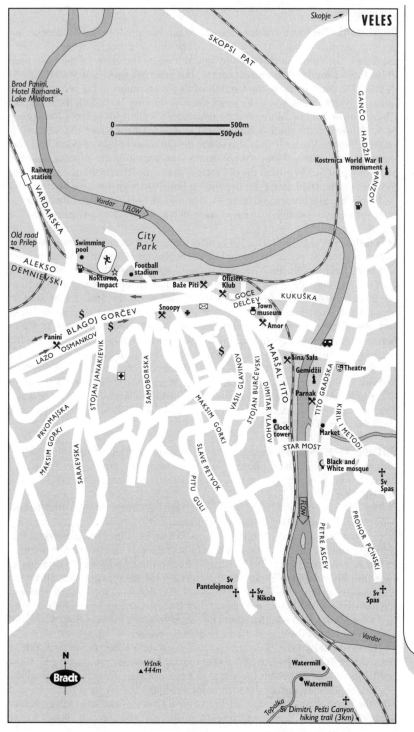

Skopje ➤

SKOPSI PAT

GANČO HADŽI PANZOV

Brod Panini,
Hotel Romantik,
Lake Mladost

Kostrnica World War II
monument

Railway
station

VARDARSKA

Vardar FLOW

Old road
to Prilep

City
Park

ALEKSO
DEMNIEVSKI

Swimming
pool

Nokturno,
Impact

Football
stadium

Baže Piti ✕

Ofizieri
Klub ✕

GOCE
DELČEV

KUKUŠKA

Town
museum

Snoopy ✕

Amor ✕

Panini ✕

BLAGOJ GORČEV

LAZO OSMANKOV

STOJAN JANAKIEVIK

SAMOBORSKA

VASIL GLAVINOV

STOJAN BURČEVSKI

DIMITAR VLAHOV

MARŠAL TITO

Sina/Sala ✕

Gemidžii

Theatre

Parnak

TITO GRADSKA

KIRIL I METODI

PRVOMAJSKA

MAKSIM GORKI

SARAEVSKA

MAKSIM GORKI

SLAVE PETVOK

PITU GULI

Clock
tower

STAR MOST

Market

Black and
White mosque

Sv
Spas

FLOW

PETRE ASCEV

PROHOR PČINSKI

N

Bradt

Vršnik
▲ 444m

Sv
Pantelejmon

Sv
Nikola

Sv
Spas

Vardar

Watermill

Watermill

Topolka

Sv Dimitri, Pešti Canyon,
hiking trail (3km)

0 ————— 500m
0 ————— 500yds

WHAT TO SEE

Right bank The town was once the site of the Paeonic fortress of Vilazora, but nothing remains to be seen now. Some of the extensive Roman ruins have been excavated. The Ottoman **clock tower** indicates where the centre of the town used to be, further south of the current centre. The **Veles Museum** is at Maršal Tito 20 (✆ 223 315). Built in 1840, the **Church of Sv Pantelejmon** in the old town rises imposingly over Veles. Just to its south towards the river is the little 14th-century **Church of Sv Nikola**. More recently refurbished is the 14th-century **Monastery of Sv Dimitri** to the south-southeast of the town past the River Topolka, which empties into the Vardar. This is also where the Ottoman Kale once stood, and now there are the remains of four old watermills scattered along the Topolka. Another 3km walk past Sv Dimitri on the old road is where the River Babuna empties into the Vardar. The trails along the Babuna up into **Pešti Canyon** have benches and multilingual panel boards indicating local fauna and flora. The 4km hike along the river and canyon is dotted with caves, some of which have churches and shrines.

Left bank The old town on the left bank of the Vardar boasts the **Kumsal Mosque** (white mosque) as well as the birthplace of the famous Macedonian revolutionary and poet, Kočo Racin. The Gemidžii statue, consisting of 12 involuted sun rays, rises up over this side of the river. The Gemidžii, made up mostly of youths from the Bulgarian High School in Veles, were also known as the Assassins of Saloniki because of the terror bombing campaign they undertook in 1903 in Solun. Their aim was to get the Great Powers to use their powers under the 1878 Treaty of Berlin to oversee Macedonia and put an end to Ottoman oppression. They didn't succeed and the ringleaders ended up in a penal colony in Libya. The bus station and the market are also on this side, as well as the town theatre and the **Church of Sv Spas**. High up, overlooking the town, is the **World War II monument** and tomb of the unknown soldier (*kosturnica*, meaning literally ossuary). This blazing white concrete structure was designed to imitate an Axis helmet struck in four. There is a small museum of the battle inside.

Outside Veles Nine kilometres north of the town is **Mladost reservoir**. This is the poor man's Ohrid, but a popular place with visitors from the region. There are a number of busy little hotels and restaurants here in the summer (see *Where to stay and eat*, page 266).

There is a very pretty back road from Veles to Prilep through the Babuna Mountains. The mountain section is not paved, and a lot of the original cobbling from over a century ago can still be seen, as well as the original mile markers. This is the old military road on which Serbian forces famously defeated Ottoman forces in the First Balkan War of 1912 and then went on to take Prilep. In speaking to Crawfurd Price, London *Times* war correspondent at the time, soldiers attributed their success against almighty odds in an uphill attack to seeing both Sv Sava and the resurrected King Marko of Prilep at their lead. It had been legend for centuries that King Marko, who was thought to be buried in a cave in the region, would rise again to lead the Serbs against their Ottoman oppressors.

The **road out of Veles** is not signposted, so can be a little hard to find. Taking the second exit into Veles from Skopje (or the third if you are approaching from the south), cross the bridge into the centre of town and take the second right off the double roundabout. Follow the road around through the north of the town, and take the next left after the sign for the hospital (*bolnica*) and the railway station (*Železnička stanica*). Keep going straight until the T-junction with Blagoj Gorev high street and then turn right. This will take you through the one-way system to pop out at the end of the high street.

The road follows the railway line to Prilep until shortly before Izvor, when the road takes a sharp turn to the left over a picturesque old bridge into Izvor itself. **Izvor**, meaning 'water spring', does indeed have a large built-up spring right next to the main road. All the locals take their drinking water from here and you might want to fill up any spare water bottles too as the water is very good. After Izvor, the road rises sharply into the Babuna Mountains and at mile marker 144, just after the water fountain and the sheep pens, is the turn-off to the monasteries of **Sv Stepanci** and **Sv Dimitri**. Watch out for turtles crossing the road here as they are not used to cars. After this, hairpin bends snake all the way around the **Pig's Head** (Svinska Glava) and just before the pass at 1,134m above sea level is the dirt track turn-off to the local mountaineering lodge. A couple of kilometres later stop at the **Monastery of Sv Gjorgi** for a good view of the descent to Prilep.

ŠTIP *Telephone code 032*

Today, Štip is still seen as the capital of the east of Macedonia, but it is a relatively sleepy town, worth a stop on the way to places further east, but not worth an overnight stay unless you are coming for the Makfest international music festival in October. The town is associated with two older names, that of Astibo from during the Kingdom of Macedonia, and Stipion from the early Byzantine era. In the 14th century, prior to the Ottoman Empire taking over the whole of Macedonia, five important churches were built in and around the town: the Church of Sv Archangel Michael, the Church of Sv Jovan, the Church of Sv Nikola, the Church of Sv Spas and the Church of Sv Basilius. In 1689 large parts of the town were burnt down during the Karpoš Uprising.

Like many Macedonian towns, Štip has claims to its own crucial role in forming a consciousness of independence in the minds of Macedonians and in so doing contributing to the struggle for that independence. Three hundred years after the town was set alight during the Karpoš Uprising, the founders of the next big uprising for Macedonian independence, Goce Delčev and Dame Gruev, both taught at schools in Štip.

The stream running through the centre of Štip brings torrents in the spring when the snow melts off the Plaškovica Mountains, but by May it is practically dry and turns into a welcome bed of green river plants. The stream is built up on either side to prevent the spring torrents flooding the town, and a pleasant walkway runs alongside. On the south side of the stream is the old cobbled road that forms part of the ancient road joining the valleys of the rivers Vardar and Struma. The centre is where Ulica Kiril i Metodi joins Ulica Vančo Prke. Legend has it that the saints Kiril (Cyril) and Metodi travelled along the River Bregalnica through Štip on their way to Moravia (now in the Czech Republic) in order to preach the Gospel to the locals in their mother tongue. For this purpose Cyril invented the Cyrillic alphabet.

GETTING THERE AND AROUND There are regular **buses** to Štip from Skopje (see box, page 13, for timetable) and the surrounding towns, and two **trains** a day from Skopje. The train station (✆ *392 904*) is about 1km out of town on the other side of the River Bregalnica. The bus station (*Partizanska bb;* ✆ *389 600/440*) is 2km from the centre. **Taxi** companies include Vani (✆ *(033) 390 860*), Radio Hit Taxi (✆ *(032) 1599*) and Asovi (✆ *(032) 1578*). A travel agent to help with accommodation and travel is: **Mediteran Travel Agency** on Vančo Prke bb (✆ *397 001; f 397 021; www.mediteran.com.mk*).

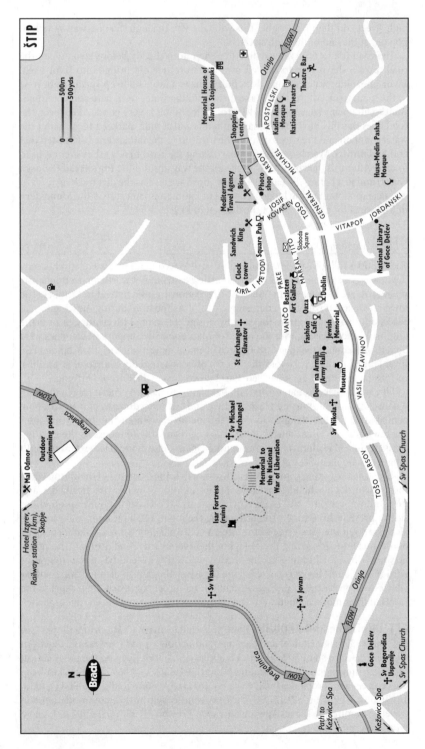

ŠTIP

0 ——— 500m
0 ——— 500yds

N

Bradt

Memorial House of
Slavco Stojmenski

Shopping
centre

APOSTOLSKI

Kadin Ana
Mosque

National Theatre

Theatre Bar

Otinja   FLOW

MICHAEL TOSO ARSOV

Husa-Medin Pasha
Mosque

GENERAL

VITAPOP JORDANSKI

National Library
of Goce Delčev

Mediterran
Travel Agency   Biser

Photo shop

JOSIF
KOVACEV

Sandwich
King   Square Pub

Clock
tower

KIRIL I METODI

MARŠAL TITO

Sloboda
Square

PRKE

VANCO
Bezisten
Art Gallery

Oaza

Dublin

Fashion
Café

Jewish
Memorial

St Archangel
Glavatov

Dom na Armija
(Army Hall)

Museum

Sv Nikola

VASIL GLAVINOV

Mal Odmor

Hotel Izgrev,
Railway station (1km),
Skopje

Outdoor
swimming pool

Bregalnica   FLOW

Sv Michael
Archangel

Memorial to
the National
War of Liberation

Isar Fortress
(ruins)

Sv Vlasie

Sv Jovan

TOŠO ARSOV

Otinja   FLOW

Sv Spas Church

Bregalnica   FLOW

Kežovica Spa

Goce Delčev

Sv Bogorodica
Uspenije

Sv Spas Church

Path to
Kežovica Spa

Skopje	first bus 05.00 (Mon–Fri), 06.00 (Sat–Sun) & every 45mins until 19.30 (270MKD)
Berovo	09.35, 10.50, 11.20; via Delčevo 10.25, 14.35; via Vinica 15.15, 17.15, 18.15, 19.35
Bitola	00.45, 13.30
Kumanovo	15.15, 18.30
Kriva Palanka	15.00
Kočani	07.15, 09.10, 11.45, 12.00, 14.10, 15.30, 18.15, 20.55, 21.30
Ohrid	07.15, 15.15
Probistip	08.45, 11.45, 16.30, 19.00
Radoviš	14.40, 17,00, 20.30
Strumica	07.30, 08.00, 11.40, 15.05, 15.40, 16.20, 17.10, 17.30, 18.45, 19.35, 20.40
Sveti Nikole	08.00, 12.30, 13.30, 15.30, 18.30

WHERE TO STAY AND EAT (See also *Kežovica Spa*, page 272.)

Hotel Oaza (37 rooms) Maršal Tito bb; \f 394 899; e info@oazahotel.com.mk; www. oazahotel.com.mk. In the centre of town, this refurbished establishment is well located & modern. Formerly called the Astibo, it also has a sauna. **$$$**

Hotel Izgrev (16 rooms) Vasil Vlahovikj 1; \394 919; f 394 918. Nicely refurbished rooms. Located 1km outside the centre on the east side of the main road into town near the railway station. It is also close to the Olympic-size outdoor pool & has its own restaurant. **$$**

Cafés and restaurants can be found in the centre of town, although much more than *skara* is difficult to find. The **Square Pub** is the main hangout, but it offers no food. **Sandwich King** over the road on Kiril i Metodi offers the standard Macedonian one-type-fits-all sandwich, or the **Biser** *skara* house on Bančo Prke offers something a little more substantial. **Mal Odmor** (*380 187*) restaurant outside town, owned by the Oaza Hotel, has patio seating, an outdoor grill and serves traditional Macedonian food. **Dublin Irish Pub** (*Maršal Tito bb;* \ *391 099;* ⊕ *08.00–24.00*) is also popular, relaxed and friendly.

WHAT TO SEE AND DO The **Isar fortress** on top of the prominent hill overlooking Štip is little more than ruins now. However, it does afford an excellent view of the modern-day town and of Novo Selo. There is ongoing work to restore some of the fortress ruins and to build a stone path up to the fortress but, unless significant restoration is carried out, one can only stand on the top of the hill, imagine the grandeur of the fortress and gaze in awe at the magnificent view that the hill still commands of the surrounding countryside.

To drive there take the obvious road up the hillside as soon as you have passed over the flyover leading from the main highway into town. This road will lead you past the little **Church of Sv Michael Archangel** built in 1332. It is set in small but beautiful grounds, but is rarely open to the public. The path then leads onto the bottom of the National War of Liberation memorial site. There is limited parking here if you come by car, and only just enough space to turn and avoid the drinking fountain. Take the steps up to the war memorial and then go on to the fortress remains. You'll get a great mobile phone signal up there, but sadly the two mobile phone towers also detract from the enchantment of the site.

8

On each of the four sides of Isar is a church built during the Middle Ages to help protect the fortress. To the south at the bottom of the hill is the **Church of Sv Nikola**, rebuilt in 1876 on the site of an older church dating back to 1341. It is the only church that is open every day, and if you ask inside, one of the priests should be able to take you to the other churches. The upper floor of the church has an extensive gallery of icons.

Opposite the church there are several sets of steps leading up past the Church of Sv Michael Archangel on the east of the fortress, which was the first of the four churches to be built. The **Church of Sv Basilius**, on the northwest side of the fortress, was built in 1337, and little remains of it today. The last church, **Sv Jovan**, was built in 1350 on the right bank of the River Otinja. Opposite it on the left bank of the River Otinja is the **Church of Sv Spas** built in 1369.

Walking along the riverbank into town from the Church of Sv Nikola, you will come to the next main building which is the renovated **memorial house to the Arsovi brothers** (✆ *392 044;* f *385 369;* ⊕ *07.00–15.00 Mon–Fri; entry free*), two local heroes renowned as revolutionaries fighting for Macedonian independence in the pre-World War II and World War II period. It was converted into the **city museum** in 1956. Outside are numerous marble Roman artefacts on display on the lawn. If you go in and speak to the museum curator, Zoran Čitkušev, he may be able to furnish you with a bilingual Macedonian–English guidebook to the town, and if you phone in advance he can also arrange a visit to the Roman ruins at Bargala.

Between the museum and the neighbouring Dom na Armija military club is a small memorial to the 561 Jewish citizens of Štip who were deported to Treblinka in Poland on 11 March 1943. Like many towns in Macedonia, Štip had a thriving Jewish community prior to the war and though the lives of these citizens are well documented, little remains to be seen of their influence now.

Behind the Oaza Hotel is the **Bezisten**, the old covered market built in the mid 17th century. It is now a modern art gallery (⊕ *09.00–12.00 & 17.00–19.00 Tue–Thu & Sat, 09.00–13.00 Fri, 10.00–12.00 Sun*). Štip's two mosques are south of the River Otinja. The **Kadin Ana Mosque**, built in the mid 19th century, is by the river next to the National Theatre (built 1924–36). It is unclear when the older **Mosque of Pasha Husa-Meda** just off Vitapop Jordanski Hill was built. Some say as early as the 14th century, others say not until the 16th. What is clear, however, is that it was built on the foundations of the much older church of Sv Ilija. Within the grounds of the mosque is the *turbeh* containing the remains of the mosque's architect.

Festivals Štip hosts a number of events and festivals throughout the year. On the **first day of spring**, Štipites walk up to Izar fortress, where they throw a pebble off the top of the hill and make a wish for the future. In July is the Štip **International Film Festival** and in October is **Makfest**, a music festival featuring a variety of world music. This is a popular event in Macedonia, so book a room early if you want to stay over for it. For more exact information on festival artists and films contact Mediteran Travel Agency (page 271).

OUTSIDE ŠTIP
Kežovica Spa (✆ *308 560*) The spa is located just off the River Bregalnica past Novo Selo. The water emerges at the L'gji spring at a temperature of 66.8°C, and is then mixed with cold water before it enters the baths. The baths themselves are separated for men and women, and are relatively pleasant and spacious. Entrance to the baths is 50MKD per person, and showers are an extra 50MKD. The baths are open 06.00–20.00 every day, except on Monday when the women's bath is

closed for cleaning until 09.00, and on Friday when the men's bath opens at 09.00. A procurement bid has gone out to modernise and partially privatise the baths, so there is hope in the next few years that it might become the long overdue modern spa attraction it could be.

Aside from 100 beds for those booked in for physical therapy and treatment, the spa also offers 40 beds in 15 rooms to those wishing to stay overnight. Although the rooms are extremely basic and cheap at 350MKD per person per night, the spa setting alongside the River Bregalnica is very tranquil, and makes a good base for those on a shoestring budget to explore other places in the region. The spa also offers limited buffet facilities, but you are better off eating in town. It's a 3km walk from the spa along the river through Novo Selo to the centre of Štip.

Remains of the ancient city of Bargala The remains can be found in the foothills of the Plačkovica Mountains near the village of Goren Kozjak, 18km northeast of Štip. The city itself was one of the major urban centres, along with the now lost cities of Kelenidin, Armonia and Zapara, of the Roman Province of Macedonia Salutaris. Though the first written references to Bargala date from late antiquity (around the 4th century BC), archaeological finds from the site suggest that the site itself was inhabited from a much earlier date. The city thrived into the 6th century AD before being overrun by the Avars. During its heyday it was enclosed in fortified walls some 300m by 150m, whose main entrance in the northwest wall can still be partly seen. Of the many antique and Roman structures to be discovered in the city, the most impressive are those of the antique bathhouse, which had a number of baths of differing temperatures as well as a sauna, and also the early Christian Church of Sv Gjorgi. The monumental tri-nave basilica and associated complex is still visible, with its impressive entrance and its eight tiers of stairs leading to a room adorned with luxurious marble columns. Such architectural grandeur reflects the importance that the city held up until the 6th century AD. The associated complex housed the bishop's palace with its wide porch and colonnaded walkways. Bargala later became a bishopric in the Byzantine Empire.

Plačkovica mountain range This offers a whole host of hiking opportunities and beautiful scenery. Take the Kozjak road from Karabinci to access the Plačkovica summit of Lisec (1,754m), Crkvište peak (1,689m) and the mountain villages of Šipkovica and Vrteška. At the latter village you can stay at the mountain hut **Vrteška** (64 beds; ℡ 384 788, 384 299). The hut warden is Marjan Ljubotenski. Beds are 350MKD per person per night.

KOČANI   *Telephone code 033*

From Štip, Highway 27 follows the River Bregalnica to Kočani. There is not much in the town itself as, until communist industrialisation, it had mostly been a farming settlement since the time of Aleksandar III of Macedon. Around 330BC, Aleksandar sent back rice from India, which was planted in these fertile fields. The ancient paddy fields in the region are still worked today, many by hand, and they provide most of Macedonia's rice. Surrounding Kočani are the archaeological sites of Morobyzdon and Vinica, and several hot springs.

GETTING THERE AND AROUND There are 13 **buses** a day to Kočani from Skopje, running 07.30–19.30, for 320MKD. The bus station (*Pavlina Belanova 11;* ℡ *272 206*) is next to the train station (℡ *274 075*). There are two trains a day from Skopje

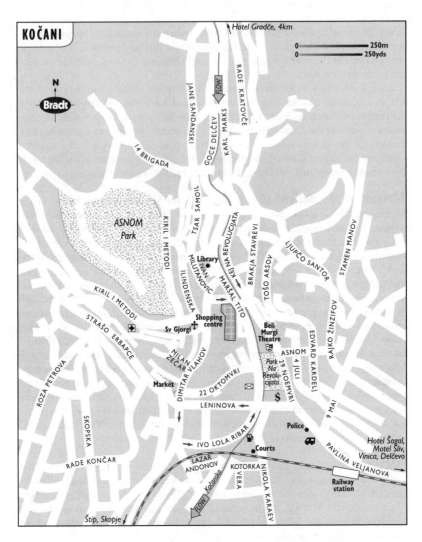

KOČANI

↑ Hotel Gradče, 4km

(see train timetable, page 72). **Taxi** companies include Radio Taxi Hit (☏ *(033) 1599)*. Flagfall is 40MKD plus 20MKD/km.

🏠 WHERE TO STAY The best places to stay are outside Kočani itself.

🏠 **Hotel Gradče** (29 rooms) 4km north of Kočani; ☏ 274 040; f 274 202; e info@ hotelgradce.com.mk; www.hotelgradce.com. mk. Well worth the winding drive for its tranquil setting in the woods & its nice rooms. **$$**

🏠 **Hotel Šagal** (16 rooms) 6km outside Kočani, before the turn-off to Vinica; ☏ 361 151/165; e sagalhotel@gmail.com; www. hotelsagal.com.mk. Completely refurbished in

2006, the hotel has indoor & outdoor restaurants, a fitness centre, sauna & tennis courts. **$$**

🏠 **Motel Sliv** (30 rooms) Less than 1km on the turn-off to Vinica from the Kočani to Delčevo road; ☏ 360 502, 362 502; e info@motelsliv.com. mk; www.motelsliv.com.mk. Nice restaurant, outdoor swimming pool & plenty of greenery. **$$**

WHAT TO SEE AND DO The more important town in the region in the 5th and 6th centuries AD was the religious complex of Morobyzdon near present-day **Morodvis**, 7km almost directly south of Kočani on the south side of the River Bregalnica. The site spans the late Roman period (4th century AD) to the 10th century AD and is one of the most significant in the Kočani region. The visible architectural remains of a monumental basilica date from the 5th and 6th centuries; it was furnished with a luxurious marble floor, massive columns and capitals. A large tomb, lavishly decorated in a multitude of colours, is incorporated into the basilica. Kočani became a bishopric in the 10th century under the Byzantine emperor Basilius the Great. Later, a small church, dating to the 13th century, was built over the earlier basilica. This town was probably on the ancient Diagonal Way, as was the neighbouring town of Vinica.

Vinica, named after its renown in Byzantine times for wine growing, is famous for the remarkable and unique **terracotta icons** found at the old fortress on the hill above the town. Archaeological finds from the fortress date to the Neolithic period. The site itself saw its heyday between the 4th and 6th centuries AD and is closely associated with the dawn of Christianity in Macedonia. The Vinica terracottas found there are ceramic tiles depicting Christian scenes in relief of traditional saints and betray an artistic style atypical of the region. The scattered pottery, stone and tile on the ground are all from the late antique settlement beneath the soil and point to the hidden city beneath your feet. The terracotta icons themselves are on display at the National Museum of Macedonia in Skopje. When the Bregalnica was dammed at Kalimansko Ezero in early communist times, Vinica gave up wine growing for rice and tobacco. From Vinica, the road east-southeast leads along the River Osojnica to Berovo.

To the west and east of Kočani are two dilapidated communist-style **hot springs**. Istibanje, 7km to the east, is generally not open. Banja, 9km to the west, is open every day 12.00–21.00. The water is allegedly good for healing stomach problems and the locals also drink the water for its general medicinal properties. The small communal baths are separated into men's and women's, costing 50MKD per visit, and a private bath cabin costs 120MKD.

DELČEVO *Telephone code 033*

Continuing along the River Bregalnica, Highway 27 passes the manmade Kalimansko Ezero. Then, 10km before the border crossing of Arnautski Grob (meaning 'grave of the Arnauts') into Bulgaria is the small town of Delčevo, named after the Macedonian revolutionary leader Goce Delčev. As a leader of the Ilinden Uprising of 1903, Goce Delčev is resoundingly honoured every year with a festival in his name on 2 August, the day of the uprising. Prior to its renaming in 1950, the town had been known by the name of Carevo Selo, meaning 'Tsar's Village' and in Ottoman times it was called Sultania.

If you need to stop to eat in Delčevo there is a fantastic kebab house called **Buffet Cinco**, on the other side of the bridge across from the centre of town. The buffet is well located with an outside terrace from which to watch the town market on Saturday afternoon, and serves the best, most succulent *ražnič* in all of Macedonia. There are frequent buses (*Delčevo bus station;* ✆ *413 684*) in and out of Delčevo on their way between Skopje and Berovo.

Three kilometres to the southeast of Delčevo are the ruins of the Byzantine village of **Vasilevo**, which was named after the Byzantine emperor Basilius II. Three kilometres to the southwest on the road to Golak is the new **Monastery of Sv Bogorodica**. The small church has bright new frescoes of all the familiar saints, but check out the new dance moves of Sts Eleuša and Ana on the right-hand side as you go in. The monastery inns have been left unfinished for years, but even if you can't overnight there, it's a great place for a picnic as the rock formations along the stream bed are a sight unto themselves and many have been converted into covered eating areas with tables and benches.

The road to Golak leads to Mount Čavka at 1,536m and the **Golak Recreation Centre** (*256 beds;* ❘ *411 733*), where there are some ski runs, plenty of hiking and several ball courts. The views of the Delčevo Valley on the way up are superb.

BEROVO *Telephone code 033*

Turning south at Delčevo, following the River Bregalnica part way, the road comes to the quaint eastern village of Berovo. Unlike most villages and towns in Macedonia, this one does not hark back to Roman, medieval or Byzantine times, but first resembled something like a village only in the late 19th century, barely 150 years ago. It got its name from the Macedonian word *bere* meaning 'to gather', probably because outsiders were so surprised that anyone would gather in a place where there wasn't already a significant settlement.

Now people come here because of the outstanding beauty of the mountains and for the cool, refreshing mountain air. At almost 900m above sea level, Berovo lies in the Maleševo Valley of the upper reaches of the Bregalnica River. Sheltered by mountains, this valley records the coldest average temperatures in winter, and it is fairly cool here in the summer too, rarely getting into the high 20°Cs. It is an excellent getaway from the scorching heat of Skopje in June, July and August, but bring an extra sweater for the evenings.

Three useful websites on Berovo are www.malesh-net.com, www.visitberovo.com.mk and the municipality website www.berovo.gov.mk.

GETTING THERE AND AROUND Considering how far away it is from the capital, Berovo is reasonably well served by **bus**. The bus station (*kej JNA bb;* ❘ *471 139*) is right in the centre of town next to 23 Avgust bridge. A journey from Berovo to Skopje is 350–450MKD one-way, and takes about 3½ hours. See timetable below.

At the **taxi** stand opposite the bus station, the taxi firms Central (❘ *1590*) and Slivka (❘ *1596*) run for a flagfall of 50MKD plus 30MKD/km.

A map of the town and of hiking in the area is available commercially in Skopje and in Berovo.

🏠 WHERE TO STAY

🏠 **Aurora Resort & Spa** (31 rooms) Berovsko Ezero; ❘ 550 965; e booking@auroraresort.mk; www.auroraresort.mk. This is the first true luxury resort in Macedonia. Aside from gorgeous rooms, view over the lake, & an outdoor pool, the resort has a small shop, travel agency, children's playground and animal farm, and organised hiking, biking and horse riding trips from the

BUS DEPARTURES FROM BEROVO	
Skopje via Vinica serving Kočani, Štip, Veles	04.20, 05.15, 07.30, 10.15, 11.30, 16.15, 17.35
Skopje via Delčevo (90mins longer than via Vinica)	07.00, 08.20, 14.30, 16.35
Struga (15 Jun–31 Aug only)	04.50
Strumica	06.00, 07.15

resort. You could easily spend a whole week here without having to even go into Berovo. **$$$**

🏠 **Hotel Monastir** (36 rooms) Kiril i Metodi 6, next to Sv Michael the Archangel Monastery; ☏279 000; f 279 037; e info@hotelmanastir. com.mk; www.hotelmanastir.com.mk. Brand-new comfortable hotel with apt-type rooms in a quaint setting. Popular restaurant, small spa, excellent value. **$$**

🏠 **Loven Dom (Hunters' Lodge)** (4 rooms) ☏470 454. This small state-run lodge has become somewhat run-down & charges double the price for foreigners. Nevertheless, it has a beautiful view of the mountains, its own tennis courts & a restaurant serving traditional Macedonian food. To get there, turn north uphill between the church in the centre of the village on the cobbled

road & the City Pub café. Keep following the road uphill for another 500m until you reach the spacious well-kept grounds of the Hunters' Lodge with its distinctive black & white, almost Tudor-style house. **$$**

🏠 **Recreation Centre Maleševo** (44 rooms) On the edge of Lake Berovo; ☏471 212, 471 555; m 070 206 850. Well designed for large groups of people & beautifully situated. It is often used for group & company retreats so ask for a discount if you are more than 10 people. **$$**

🏠 **Motel Idila** (16 rooms) 20km southeast of Pehčevo; ☏441 323; m 070 233 720. A beautiful location almost on the border with Bulgaria, this trout farm has an outdoor pool (murky) & nice rooms. Good little restaurant. **$**

For bed and breakfast options in the area phone **Atlantis Travel Agency** in Strumica (☏ 034 346 212), or search on berovobooking.com.mk. Prices are around 750MKD per person per night.

WHAT TO SEE AND DO Aside from **hiking** in the beautiful mountains, there is **skiing** in the winter from the Maleševo Recreation Centre, and **fishing** in the summer in **Lake Berovo**. The lake used to be known as Ratevo Lake, because it lies near the village of Ratevo, but now that Berovo draws more visitors it has come to be known by that village's name and the only road access to the lake is in fact from Berovo. To reach the lake take the turning downhill at the entrance to Maleševo Recreation Centre. The high road continues on to the border crossing at Klepalo. The Bulgarian side has not yet reciprocated the desire to open the border and so the road on the Macedonian side simply leads to an empty border and customs building. The lake itself is completely natural, unlike many of the reservoir lakes in Macedonia, and stays cold year round as it draws its water from the surrounding mountains.

The **Monastery of Sv Michael the Archangel** is at the eastern edge of the village, and pre-dates the village by less than half a century. The site was originally built in order to train teachers in Macedonian, away from the watchful eyes of their Ottoman rulers, who feared that the development of Macedonian language and literature would lead to revolt. A famous Macedonian literary figure, Joakim Kršovski, taught here. The monastery is surrounded by some inns where the nuns live and has a small informative museum. You will need to phone the museum keeper, Dvonko (☏ 472 733), if you want to look inside, as it is usually shut.

Nine kilometres north of Berovo is the village of **Pehčevo**. The village started out as an iron-mining town in Roman times and continued to produce iron ore throughout Ottoman rule. Remains of the mine at the foot of Mount Bukovik can still be found. Hiking in the vicinity is a popular pastime and there are a number of rooms for accommodation along the River Ravna.

KUMANOVO *Telephone code 031*

The third largest town in Macedonia after Skopje and Bitola is Kumanovo with almost 70,000 inhabitants. It is not an especially historically significant town, as it

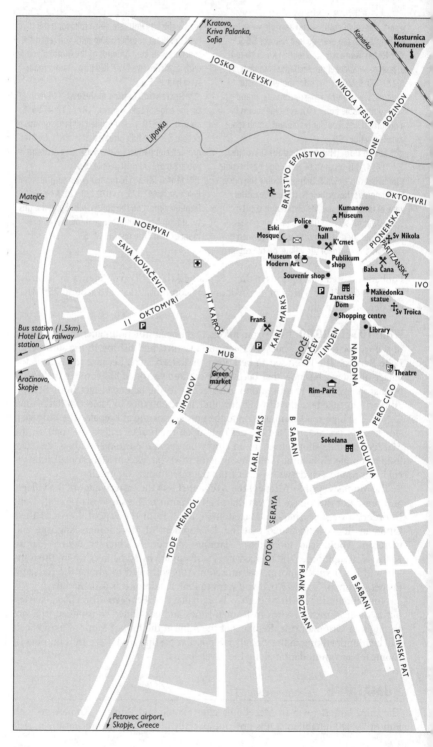

Kratovo,
Kriva Palanka,
Sofia

Kojnarka

Kosturnica
Monument

JOSKO ILIEVSKI

NIKOLA TESLA

DONE BOŽINOV

Lipovka

Matejče

BRATSTVO EPINSTVO

OKTOMVRI

II NOEMVRI

Kumanovo
Museum

Police

Town
hall

Eski
Mosque

K'cmet

PIONERSKA

PARTIZANSKA

Sv Nikola

SAVA KOVAČEVIC

Museum of
Modern Art

Publikum
shop

IVO

Souvenir shop

Baba Čana

II OKTOMVRI

Zanatski
Dom

Makedonka
statue

Sv Troica

Bus station (1.5km),
Hotel Lav, railway
station

HT KARPOŠ

Franš

KARL MARKS

Shopping centre

Library

GOČE DELČEV

ILINDEN

NARODNA

PERO CICO

Aračinovo,
Skopje

3 MUB

Theatre

S SIMONOV

Green
market

REVOLUCIJA

Rim-Pariz

KARL MARKS

B SABANI

Sokolana

TODE MENDOL

POTOK SERAYA

FRANK ROZMAN

B SABANI

PČINSKI PAT

Petrovec airport,
Skopje, Greece

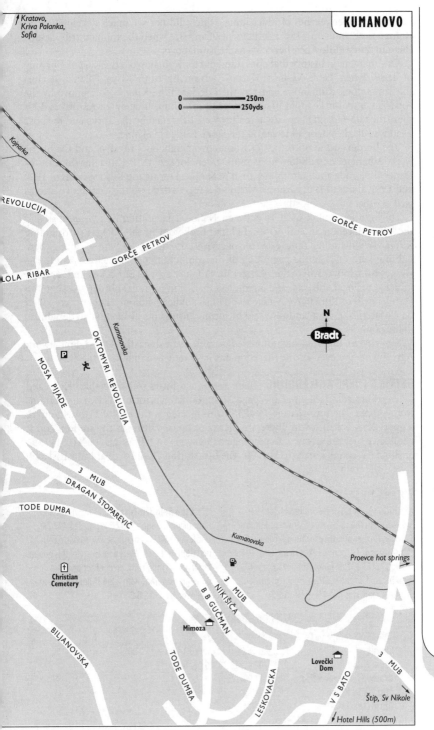

Kratovo,
Kriva Palanka,
Sofia

0 ————— 250m
0 ————— 250yds

Kojnarka

REVOLUCIJA

GORČE PETROV

GORČE PETROV

LOLA RIBAR

N

Bradt

MOSA PIJADE

OKTOMVRI REVOLUCIJA

Kumanovska

P

3 MUB

DRAGAN ŠTOPAREVIČ

TODE DUMBA

Kumanovska

Proevce hot springs

Christian
Cemetery

3 MUB

NIKIŠIČA

B B GUČMAN

Mimoza

Lovečki
Dom

BILJANOVSKA

TODE DUMBA

LESKOVACKA

V S BATO

3 MUB

Štip, Sv Nikole

Hotel Hills (500m)

lies in the upper reaches of Macedonia, which did not see much development in Roman times, and only saw a settlement of any size when the Kumani tribe settled there in the Middle Ages, hence its name Kumanovo.

One incident in history that does stand out for Kumanovo is the Karpoš Uprising of 1689, when Petre Vojnički-Karpoš, advancing from Kriva Palanka against the Turks, took Kumanovo and was then declared the King of Kumanovo by the Austrian emperor Leopold I (see box, page 24). Unfortunately for Karpoš and his men, the tale ends in Skopje, where they were beheaded by the Turks and Karpoš's head was displayed for all to see on the Stone Bridge in Skopje.

The border to the northwest of Kumanovo neighbours Kosovo, and the town's large Albanian population have more often looked to Priština in Kosovo for leadership, trade and cultural ties than to Skopje. During the Kosovo crisis of 1998 and 1999, thousands of Kosovar Albanian refugees fled into the Kumanovo area as well as other parts of northwestern Macedonia.

During the conflict of 2001 between National Liberation Army guerillas and the local Macedonian authorities, fighting broke out in the villages surrounding Kumanovo including Tanuševci (see page 239) on the border with Kosovo, where fighting here marked the beginning of the conflict of 2001; Matejče 17km to the west of Kumanovo, where the 14th-century monastery was ransacked and reprisals inflicted on local villagers; and Sopot, less than 3km from the border crossing into Serbia north of Kumanovo, where two Polish soldiers and one civilian were killed on 4 March 2003 by a landmine laid by former insurgents in an effort to destabilise the region.

Security in the area has improved significantly since the Ohrid Framework Agreement, and even ethnic Macedonians have returned to hike in the area.

GETTING THERE AND AROUND There are regular **buses** (see timetable below) and seven **trains** a day (see timetable, page 72) to Kumanovo, including two direct trains from Skopje. The train station (☏ 423 310) is located at the end of 11th Oktomvri, a good 2km out of town. There are plenty of **taxis** waiting at the station, and if perchance they are all out with passengers then you can call As Taxi on ☏ (031) 1598 or Bima Kompanija on ☏ (031) 1599. The **bus station** (☏ 423 610) at Industriska bb is near the train station.

⌂ WHERE TO STAY

⌂ **Hills** (4 rooms) Vasil Smilevski Bato 91; ☏ 452 536. In the same area of town as Mimoza but even further out. Nice location & rooms. **$$$**

⌂ **Mimoza** (8 rooms) Nikšička bb, Goce Delčev district; ☏ 413 232; e hotel_mimoza@yahoo. com. Located on the southeast edge of town off the main road, this hotel is quiet. **$$$**

⌂ **Etno Selo Timčevski** (13 rooms) Mlado Nagoričane village; ☏ 497 749; m 075 497 749; e info@etnoselo.com.mk; www.etnoselo.com. mk. Built in the old Macedonian style, this quaint hotel has all mod cons, an outdoor pool & a popular restaurant with a big children's play area. Well worth a visit. **$$**

BUS DEPARTURES FROM KUMANOVO	
Skopje	First bus 05.00 then every 30 mins until 21.00
Kriva Palanka	07.00, 09.45, 11.30, 15.00, 16.45, 19.10
Kratovo (via Probistip)	08.30, 14.00, 16.30
Štip via Sv Nikole	05.30, 12.30, 15.30
Ohrid (seasonal)	06.00

🏠 **Lav** (17 rooms) Železnički 13; ☎413 999; e hotel_lav@yahoo.com. Opposite the train station, & although a bit 1980s in style, it is at least quiet. **$$**

🏠 **Lovečki Dom** (6 rooms) 3 Mub bb, on cnr with Vasil S Bato; ☎452 773. Basic rooms. **$$**

🏠 **Rim-Pariz** (6 rooms) 3 Mub 56; ☎475 500; f 415 800; hotelrimparis@yahoo.com; www. hotelrimparis.com. Above the pizza restaurant (⏰ 08.00–24.00) of the same name. Centrally located, clean & modern but a little noisy. **$$**

✗ WHERE TO EAT AND DRINK

✗ **Baba Čana** Partizanski 3; ☎412 003; m 075 484 573; ⏰ 08.00–24.00 Mon–Sat, 12.00–24.00 Sun. A cosy Macedonian *kebapčilnica*. Plays traditional live Kumanovo folk music on Fri & Sat evenings. **$$**

✗ **Franš** Narodna Revolucija 1; ☎428 842; ⏰ 12.00–24.00. Good salads, pizza & Macedonian food. **$$**

✗ **Harp** Narodna Revolucija bb; ☎418 123; e murfo76@yahoo.com; ⏰ 08.00–24.00. 100% Irish owned Irish pub, serving good food & cheer. **$$**

✗ **K'cmet** 11 Oktomvri bb (next to town hall); ☎431 670; ⏰ 08.00–24.00 Mon–Sat. A busy little *kafana* with good traditional food. **$$**

WHAT TO SEE AND DO Kumanovo is a pleasant enough town with a bustling centre and some impressive 19th-century buildings, such as the **Zanatski Dom** and **Sokolana**. There is a small **Museum of Modern Art** opposite the town hall, and the **Museum of Kumanovo** (☎ *422 495*) just off Done Bozinov is small, but interesting if you can read Macedonian, and if you can get the curators to let you in. They are busy documenting artefacts (as most of the museums in Macedonia seem to be) and so may turn you away rather than interrupt their work to show you around.

To the east of the centre of town are two **churches** dedicated to Sv Trojica and to Sv Nikola. The Church of Sv Nikola was built in 1851 and houses icons from many other older churches in the Kumanovo region.

OUTSIDE KUMANOVO

KOKINO The archaeological site Kokino, a **megalithic observatory** often referred to as the Stonehenge of Macedonia, comprises a natural rock outcrop modified by humans. It is situated on the summit of the large neo-volcanic peak (called Taticev Kamen, grid 7906 8036 near the village of Kokino) that dominates the surrounding area at a height of 1,013m above sea level. Whilst it might look little more than an interesting rock feature, it was ranked on the NASA website in 2005 as the fourth oldest observatory in the world, although nobody from NASA has actually visited Kokino to confirm that.

The tendency of the volcanic rock to split and form geometric cracks has resulted in this remarkable natural feature; though two flat surfaces, orientated from west to east and with a difference in height of 15m, have certainly had their tops levelled by tools. The lower platform to the west preserves the traces of several stone seats (thrones), which are aligned from north to south, so that anyone seated on them would face towards the east and the rising sun.

A series of stone markers visible from the centre of the observatory mark the positions variously of the sunrise during the summer and winter solstices, the moon in its maximal and minimal declines in winter and summer, and the sun on the day of the vernal and autumn equinoxes. The use of the location as a primitive research station to track the sun through the year goes back, therefore, almost 4,000 years. Artefacts dating back to 1815BC have been found there.

The site lies about 30km outside Kumanovo. Take the Prohor Pčinski exit off the E871 (Highway 2) heading north for 7km until you get to the turning for Dragomance. Take this turn, heading northeast for another 14.6km. At the rise of a hill after Slepenče village is a sign for the observatory. Turn north onto the dirt road for 100m and the observatory is the obvious rock feature 300m to the west (unless it is foggy and then you won't see it at all, but if you keep heading uphill you will unmistakably get there).

OTHER SITES Going back to the more usual Macedonian sites, to the east of Kumanovo north of Highway 2, the **Monastery of Staro Nagoričane** in the village of the same name houses the early 14th-century **Church of Sv Gjorgi**, which was built in 1313 by the Serbian king Milutin on the foundations of an 11th-century church. The church's frescoes are almost completely intact, but the narthex has been destroyed. The monastery is surrounded by a low stone wall and has no inns. The yard, containing a few old graveyards, is unkempt and the site is usually locked. To get the key ask the police officers in the small police station opposite the church. They will contact the church warden, who should be able to come over with the key in a few minutes. Note that photography inside the church requires permission.

To get to the site, take the Prohor Pčinski exit off the E871 (Highway 2) heading north. After 100m, turn left at the T-junction and then immediately right, signposted for Prohor Pčinski. Follow this road north for 2.5km, and at the top of a small hill take the new road left to the village of Staro Nagoričane. You will come across the monastery in a few hundred metres at the edge of the village.

Before you get to the turn-off from the E871 for Prohor Pčinski is an obvious rock feature to the north called **Kostoperska Karpa**, which was also an important ritual location in the past. At the same time to the south, you will make out in the middle distance a large ruined building on top of a hill. It stands out for many miles like a nipple on the landscape. This modern ruin is what is left of the once six-storey Kosturnica **monument of Zebrnjak**, commemorating soldiers who died here fighting against the Turks in the Kumanovo battle of the first Balkan War of 1912. The monument was erected on the 25th anniversary in 1937, but blown up six years later in 1943 by the Bulgarians during their occupation of Vardar Macedonia. The 360° view from the monument across the Pčinja plain is the reason why this point was such a strategic location for occupying armies. There is no signage leading you to the monument, but you can get there by turning south off the E871 at a large white house almost 4km after the start of the E871. Turn left past the house for 1km and take the first right. This road leads straight to the monument.

Forgotten in the delta of the River Kriva near the village of Konjuh (best accessed by 4x4 or a 6km hike) are an ancient **cave village** and a **Roman rotunda** from the 6th century. The place makes for an interesting half day out and, unlike Kokino observatory, there are lots of obvious manmade rooms, waterholes, stairs and windows. To get there continue another 15.1km on Highway 2 (E871) beyond the exit to Prohor Pčinski to grid 8024 6729 where a dirt-track road heads south. At 4.8km, just after the tunnel under the yet-to-be-constructed railway, take the turning to the south across the Pčinski River. The rock formation on the left after the river is the cave settlement (grid 8016 6211). The rotunda, barely visible, is another 100m to the southwest, and the old Church of Sv George is 200m to the southeast of the settlement.

There are probably a hundred more Roman ruins in this valley, which was a route linking Skupi to Kustendil. In August 2003, a **Roman amphitheatre** was unearthed near the village of Klečevce. The **Kumanovo Hot Springs**, also popular in Roman times, are near the village of Proevce, 4km southeast of Kumanovo. There is a small outdoor pool heated by thermal waters. Entry is 50MKD.

KRIVA PALANKA   *Telephone code 031*

Kriva Palanka is now most famous for the 12th-century monastery dedicated to Sv Joakim Osogovski, 3km to the east of the town. The town is named after the river it straddles, the Kriva, which is the Slavic translation of the name first given to the town when it was founded by the Ottomans in 1633. Then it was called Egri Dere, meaning 'winding river'. The town was originally built as an important stronghold for the Ottomans on the road from Üsküb to Istanbul, but despite its supposed impregnability, it was taken by Karpoš (later given the title of King of Kumanovo, see box, page 24) during the Karpoš Uprising of 1689. When Karpoš and his men were captured and beheaded six weeks later, the town returned to Ottoman rule.

GETTING THERE AND AWAY The new **bus** station (\375 033) is north of the centre of town behind the police station. There are 11 buses a day from Skopje to Kriva Palanka for 200–250MKD, starting at 06.00 until the last bus at 18.30. Buses to Skopje via Kumanovo leave at 06.00, 07.00, 08.00, 09.30, 11.10, 13.00, 14.00, 15.30, 16.00 and 17.00. Buses to Strumica via Kratovo, Probištip and Štip leave on Monday, Wednesday and Friday at 05.30. **Taxi** companies include \(031) 1591 and 1592.

⌂ WHERE TO STAY

⌂ **Hotel Turist** (30 rooms) Maršal Tito bb; \375 209; m 071 245 063. Classic dilapidated socialist tourism right in the centre of town. Definitely a rip-off & not even a TV in the room although it is en suite. **$$**

⌂ **Villa Lulu** (3 rooms) 3km outside Kriva Palanka on the road to the border crossing to Bulgaria; \372 727; m 071 267 930; e motel@ villa-lulu.com. Infinitely preferable to the Turist above, but a stiff walk outside town. Also has a nice restaurant. **$$**

⌂ **Monastir Sveti Joakim Osogovski** (100 beds) 3km northwest of Kriva Palanka; \375

063–5. By far & away the best place to stay in the vicinity. Views from this monastery set into Mt Osogovski are beautiful. The monastery is well frequented & often full, so book a few days ahead during daylight hours as monastery life closes down after evening prayers. Ask to speak to the innkeeper, Velin, as he deals with all the bookings. Bring your own food to cook in the indoor kitchens or the outdoor grill. A small shop/café sells a few soft drinks, tea & coffee. The monastery is popular with locals as a site for Sun b/fast before church. Old inns are cheaper than the new inns. Bathroom on each floor. No TV. **$**

Also try **Dabo** in the *Where to eat* section below.

✗ WHERE TO EAT
The best places to eat are outside the centre, such as **Villa Lulu** above, or:

✗ **Dabo** Partizanska 62 (on the road towards the border); \836 126; ⊕ 10.00–22.00 daily. A fish farm & restaurant, offering (strangely enough) fish, as well as the usual Macedonian dishes. Also has a few rooms for accommodation. **$$**

✗ **Park Ginovci** Ginovci village, 18km before Kriva Palanka; \383 033; e contact@ parkginovci.com.mk; www.parkginovci.com.mk; ⊕ 10.00–24.00 daily. This traditional restaurant

is very family oriented with a playground, small petting zoo of farmed animals (inc ostriches) & little walks around a lake. Excellent food. Worth the drive. **$$**

✗ **Vodenica** Duračka Reka; \373 800; m 070 306 647; ⊕ 11.00–24.00 daily. A great family-friendly place, complete with children's playground & a small water wheel (*vodenica*) to water the fish pond. Worth the hike up. **$$**

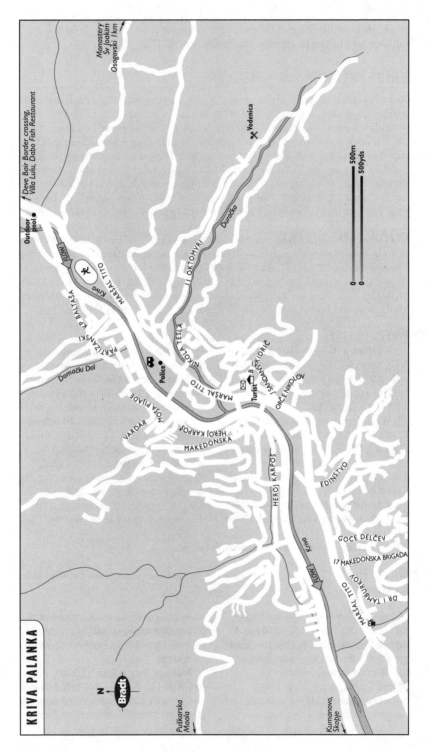

KRIVA PALANKA

Deve Bair Border crossing,
Villa Lulu, Dabo Fish Restaurant

Monastery
Sv Joakim
Osogovski 1km

Outdoor
Pool

FLOW

MARŠAL TITO

Kriva

KP BALTAŠA

PARTIZANSKI

Domaćki Dol

VARDAR

MOŠA PIJADE

HEROJ KARPOŠ

MAKEDONSKA

Police

NIKOLA TESLA

MARŠAL TITO

Turist

B ESKI DRIČ

JSANDANSKI

ORCE NIKOLOV

I OKTOMVRI

Duračka

Vodenica

HERO KARPOŠ

Kriva

FLOW

EDINSTVO

GOCE DELČEV

17 MAKEDONSKA BRIGADA

DR I TAMBURKOV

MARŠAL TITO

Puškarska
Maala

Kumanovo,
Skopje

N

Bradt

500m
500yds

0
0

284

WHAT TO SEE AND DO

Sveti Joakim Osogovski The Monastery of Sv Joakim Osogovski probably takes number one position as the most visited monastery in Macedonia. The location was first sought out as a monastery during the middle of the 12th century, and now houses two churches, the older one dedicated to the Virgin Mary (Sv Bogorodica), and the new church of the mid 19th century is dedicated to Sv Joakim Osogovski himself (see box, page 290).

The monastery was founded in the middle of the 12th century by the priest Teodor from Ovče Polje who decided to dedicate his life to God at this spot after the death of his wife. Located on a major thoroughfare to Constantinople (*Carigrad*, Town of the Tsar, in Macedonian) the monastery was frequented and honoured by Muslims as well as Christians. In 1585 the *bey* of Kriva Palanka received permission to renovate the dilapidated buildings. The old church was first converted into a mosque and then later a church. Some of the original 12th-century walls and 14th-century frescoes still exist, although most of the church is now being completely re-frescoed.

During the Austro–Ottoman War, led in Serbia and Macedonia by General Piccolomini in 1690, the monastery buildings and original church suffered extensive damage, and the Ottomans even ordered it to be destroyed as a punishment against local Macedonians who had sided with the Austrian general. Legend claims that on arrival at the monastery, the Ottomans were so overpowered by its spiritual force that they turned back, leaving the buildings undamaged. One of them, however, had taken a bone out of the tomb of Sv Joakim Osogovski, which proceeded to make the thief more nauseous the further he took it from the monastery. The thief soon realised that, for his own well-being, he needed to take the bone back to its rightful resting place, and so he returned it. The sultan was so overwhelmed by this account when he heard it that he ordered a protective marker of stone to be delivered to the monastery, which would signify to all Ottomans, Turks and Muslims that this monastery was not to be harmed in any way. The stone still stands on the wall near the new church, to the right as you enter the exonarthex, and is usually blessed by the residing Turkish ambassador to Macedonia at least once during his term in office.

The new church is an intricate complex with 12 cupolas in the main nave, two further naves and an exonarthex on two sides of the church. The 12 cupolas represent the 12 apostles, one for each containing a fresco of the apostle, and the remainder of the main nave is brimming with well-kept frescoes. Frescoes of Sv Joakim and his three brothers (see box, page 290) can be found, as well as of the church donors, and on the outside wall to the right of the main entrance are some interesting frescoes of hell and Satan. In the base of the belfry, on the western side of the new church, is the ossuary of the senior monks and priests.

Near the monastery is an ancient milk pipeline, which used to transport milk from the surrounding mountains to the monastery dairy. The pipe is no longer used, and Pop Dobri, the father of the monastery, requests that visitors refrain from visiting it as the pipeline requires some renovation to prevent further damage by careless visitors. Pop Dobri is happy to talk to visitors about the monastery although he can't always be found there as he lives in Kriva Palanka. The only monastic inhabitant is Sister Igoumina.

During the summer, the monastery holds a young artists' convention, usually in late July or early August. The church's saints' days are on 28 August, dedicated to Sv Bogorodica (the Virgin Mary), and 29 August dedicated to Sv Joakim, when the monastery is visited by several thousand visitors who come to pay their respects. Their generous offerings have allowed almost €5 million to be invested in the church since the revival of monastic life in Macedonia in 1995.

Osogovski mountain range Starting from the entrance to the monastery is the hiking path up to **Mount Carev** (2,084m). It is the highest point in this range completely in Macedonia, and has an excellent all-round view at the summit. An almost 20km hike from the monastery, it is not to be attempted in a single day, and even in two days only by the fit. For the less fit with a 4x4 the last turning before the Bulgarian border, towards Toranica village, turns into a fair-weather dirt track which comes to within 6km of the summit and then makes its way back down the other side of the mountain via the Sasa Zinc Mine and onto Highway 27 at Lake Kalimansko. The same road also comes within 4km of **Mount Ruen** (2,252m) on the border with Bulgaria. The road takes you above the treeline so the views of the surrounding mountains and into Bulgaria are extensive. It is a popular place for wild berry pickers in the summer.

If you do take this road, you may need to present identification to the mine wardens at either Toranica or Sasa where the road is gated. From Toranica gates, make sure you turn off left onto the dirt track (unsignposted) after almost 3km, just before an old building on the left and a white building on the right. For those with GPS, this is at grid 2290 7039. Do not continue on the tarmac until it becomes dirt road as this simply takes you into a logging maze. The dirt track becomes tarmac 1km before Sasa mineworks.

KRATOVO   *Telephone code 031*

Midway between the start of the E871 (Highway 2) at Kumanovo and Kriva Palanka is the turn-off for Kratovo and Probištip, which joins Highway 2 to Highway 27. On this road, deep in the belly of an ancient and burnt-out volcanic crater, is the small village of Kratovo. Nearby are Stone Age observatories at Cocev Kamen and Kokino, cave dwellings at Konjuh, volcanic droplets from the volcano that once was, and the place is littered with Stone Age rock art.

In Roman times this mining town was known as Kratiskara, meaning crater, and variations of its name, Koriton and Koritos in Byzantine times, have centred around this meaning. The crater-like hollow of the village has demanded high-arched bridges to cross the river and ingenious architecture to scale the steep ravine. The difficulty of getting to Kratovo has also left the town relatively free of communist concrete. Six defensive towers hark back to the time of King Karpoš.

GETTING THERE There are five **buses** a day from Skopje to Kratovo at 07.30, 13.00, 15.30 16.00 and 16.40 for 200MKD. Monday, Wednesday and Friday there is also a bus at 05.30 from Kriva Palanka on its way to Probištip, Štip and Strumica. Local **taxis** wait on the corner of the far side of the bridge near the Hotel Kratis. One taxi service is Džemi (Jimi) (m *071 322 502*).

WHERE TO STAY Kratovo is sorely lacking decent or affordable accommodation. Tourism is catching on, though. Ask at the **Rock Art Centre** (see page 288) to see if private bed and breakfasts have become available by the time you intend to go.

Kratis (25 rooms) Gorni Salaj bb; 481 201. The only hotel in the centre, this state-run rip-off commands a high price for what it has to offer. Much nicer accommodation is available in Kočani. **$$**

WHERE TO EAT AND DRINK Eating establishments line the village square and RUN along Ulica Partizanska. The Kratovo version of *pastrmajlija* is *pastrmajka*;

mantijas (small square meat pasties) and *mezelek* (offal casserole) are also special Kratovo dishes.

✕ Alexandria Josip Daskalov 35; ☎ 481 289; ⏱ 10.00–24.00 daily. This modern restaurant, tucked up an alleyway beneath the tower of Hadži Kosta hides one of the entrances to the old tunnel system connecting the feudal towers. The entrance is behind a closet door in the kitchen, & can be viewed for free if you dine there, or for €2 plus a free drink. Standard menu. Live bands at w/ends. **$$**

✕ Kanu Goce Delčev 20; ☎ 482 954; ⏱ 08.00–24.00 daily. Housed in an imposing factory-like building, it would be easy to pass this restaurant by. But once inside the Kratovo Academy of Science and Art (Kratovska akademija na naukite i umetnoctite: KANU for short & a tease on the real thing in Skopje) it oozes charm with its attention to detail, bygone artefacts & typical old town architecture. Good food, friendly attentive staff. **$$**

♀ Café Tea Maršal Tito 10 **m** 075 596 730. One of the original café bars before it was joined on this popular street by the summer contestors. Has a cosy inside area for the winter overlooking the old Turkish trading street. Relaxed atmosphere amid competing music in the summer.

WHAT TO SEE AND DO Several rivers run deep at the bottom of this old volcanic crater town. Three of the stone bridges across the River Tabačka – the Jokčiski, Caršiski and Gročanski – date from the early Ottoman period. A wander around the **stone streets** of the town reveals more of the Atlantic-style houses than the traditional overhanging Macedonian houses seen in Ohrid. Take to some of the streets further back from the river to get a better feel for the meanderings and steep hills. A good place to start is up the little alleyway perpendicular to the entrance to the Rock Art Centre, which will take you up to the quiet backstreets.

Of the 12 original defensive **stone towers** remaining (see box below), two are open to the public. **Saat Kula**, the clock tower, has excellent exhibitions on old life in the town, and the very top floor has been made into a small bar and drinks area, although it might not be serving. There is a precarious tiny wooden balcony here

---

TOWERS WITHOUT STAIRS

Originally there were 12 towers in Kratovo from Ottoman times. Their original use was defensive, but between times they were used by the local mine owners to store iron ore. Each of the towers is connected by underground tunnels, and it is possible to view these if you take a paid tour (enquire at the Rock Art Centre, page 288). It was the miners of Kratovo who first rallied to Karpoš's call in 1689 (see box, page 24) when he went to fight on the side of the Austrians against the Ottomans.

Now only six remain: Saat (meaning 'clock'); Simikjeva; Krsteva; Emin-beg and Zlatkovičeva; and the sixth, the Hadži Kostova tower, which was last damaged in 1929 and rebuilt in 1957. The two most impressive towers, Saat and Simikjeva, have recently been restored thanks to an EU cultural grant.

Many of the towers originally had no stairs, following an architectural trait also seen in similar defensive towers in the Caucasus, so that access to higher levels was only by ladder. If enemy forces attacked the town, then villagers could hide in the upper levels of the tower and drag the ladder up with them. If the enemy succeeded in blowing the floor of a lower level then the villagers could again ascend to a higher level, from which they would normally defend themselves by throwing projectiles, using weapons or pouring hot oil.

from which to view the town – not for vertigo sufferers. The **Simikjeva Kula** has a more sinister feel to it. The doors are tiny and the steps more foreboding, with displays of weaponry from the 19th century. The top floor has a fabulous collection of postcards from World War I. If these floors are not open, ask at the museum or the Rock Art Centre.

The **town museum** (✆ 482 015; ⊕ 09.00–16.00 Mon–Fri; entry free) is in the former *bey*'s house and later inn, Saraj, close to the old Ottoman prison. It has the usual collection of local artefacts and a display of children's art. There is no sign outside and it usually looks shut, even when the museum curator is in his office.

The Kratovo **Rock Art Centre** at Planinski 1 (✆ 481 572; e *lcfrockart@yahoo.com, stevcedonevkratovo@yahoo.com; www.rock-art.mk*; ⊕ 08.00–20.00 Mon–Sat, 09.00–16.00 Sun; entry free) explains the rock art found in the area and sells replicas and other associated items. Drop in to sample the Bitola Slow Food programme (*www.slowfood-bitola.mk*) promoting local and organic specialities, and to ask about the town. Stevče Donevski and his wife Valentina are a mine of information and thoroughly dedicated to the town, selling souvenirs, *rakija*, maps of Kratovo and postcards.

The town's only **ethno museum** is the private collection of the Donevski family from the Rock Art Centre. It is a compact collection of what were once everyday items mostly from the last 150 years, but with a few rare older pieces, ranging from kitchenware to musical instruments and World War I helmets. The collection is kept in the cellar of the Donevskis' old town house, which the family are renovating to turn into a bed and breakfast. It costs €1 to visit, including a complimentary *rakija* or homemade wine. Enquire at the Rock Art Centre nearby (see above).

Just before the last rickety metal bridge on Planinska street is a two-storey house (unfinished at time of writing) where Milaka Kocevska (m 070 754 489) hand weaves wool pile carpets and *kilims* (flat tapestry-woven rugs often used as prayer mats). It is fascinating to see her massive looms and the beautiful designs in her cramped little workshop on the edge of the town. Her work can be ordered through the Rock Art Centre.

OUTSIDE KRATOVO

GORNI KRATOVO There is a lovely hike from the centre of Kratovo up the River Kratovska to the old village of Gorni Kratovo. Taking Planinska street along the Tabačka river, after the last bridge there is a short steep section before the wide path plateaus out to a gentle hike along the middle height of the valley. In total the 3km hike takes about 50 minutes. Gorno Kratovo itself is just a few houses. The old schoolhouse is abandoned, but has a welcome spring below it. Veering off the path shortly after the old school, follow the Kratovska River into the exposed belly of the old volcano for another 700m and look out for the medicine ball-sized **volcanic droplets** wedged in the mud. Back on the main path, this continues above the village and narrows to an old Roman cobbled road above the escarpment beyond the village.

PROBOŠTIP On the edge of this tiny town is **Aquapark** (*Plavica bb;* ✆ 032 480 080; e *aquapark@aquaparkmacedonia.mk; www.aquaparkmacedonia.mk*; ⊕ 10.00–19.00 daily; entry 400MKD adults, 300MKD 2–14 years, under 2 years free). The first one of its kind in Macedonia, it exemplifies the trend that if the Macedonians can't have a seaside, they'll just bring some inland: summer only, all outdoors. A great little place to eat if you've had enough of the crowded Aquapark restaurant is **Kaj Zoki** (✆ 032 484 789; m 078 302 186; e *zoran.arsov@yahoo.com*) at the end of the market place in the centre of town. Ask for their *manastirski ručak* for a full three-course traditional meal including local aperitif, monastery wine and a coffee for only 590MKD.

COCEV KAMEN Some 15km directly east of Kratovo (grid 8211 6044 on map 682-4-4 (Pezovo)) is Cocev Kamen, a Palaeolithic (early Stone Age, some 12,000 years ago) sacrificial **megalithic observatory**. Unlike Kokino (see page 279) there are still megaliths scattered around the site, and there are very obvious signs of human use, including hewn steps, an amphitheatre, sacrificial chamber, constructed entry path, as well as the necessary seat or throne from which to divine star charts, sun and moon movements, and time of year. The site is possibly the oldest in the Balkans and had been used over many centuries. Its rock art dates possibly from the Iron Age and has the only find of a painting of a human figure on rock in Macedonia. Some say the site is on a par with Stonehenge in the UK.

The site is hotly disputed by the current government for being in competition with Kokino (which only raises the question why there can't be two sites for people to visit). As a result the panel boards previously erected with World Bank funding in 1999 have been pulled down and the site is now somewhat overgrown with brambles. It is free to visit, but bring stout walking shoes.

To get there take the road towards Kratovo from the north. At the village of Turalevo (grid 9368 6049), 5km before Kratovo, turn south before the large factory towards the village itself (signposted) and Šopsko Rudare. Follow the main road southwest for almost 10km until the village of Sekulica (grid 8769 5632). At the T-junction in the village, there is a signpost to Cocev Kamen: turn right and take the road north following a northwesterly direction for another 6km past the Dobra Voda water bottling plant until you reach a right turn (if you miss the turn you'll end up less than 1km later up a hill in a dead-end hamlet with a church). Take this and continue north another 2km (towards the villages of Donja Maala and Gornja Maala and Konjuh) until you get to a crossroads (grid 8309 6057). At the crossroads, turn right heading southwest for 1.8km to the hamlet of Šopsko Rudare. At the crossroads here turn north for 0.5km to the houses of Cocevi, after which the road becomes a dirt track continuing north towards Cocev Kamen for 0.3km before heading off west-northwest. It's a 300m walk from the dirt track over a usually dry stream bed to Cocev Kamen, which is an obvious rock formation 0.6km directly north of the village of Cocevi.

MONASTERY OF SVETI GAVRIL LESNOVSKI This monastery south of the village of Lesnovo was built in 1341 by the feudal lord Tyrant Oliver. It is one of only three to contain an **iconostasis** by the famous woodcarvers Makarije Frčkovksi and the brothers Filipovski (the other two are in the monasteries of Sv Jovan Bigorski near Debar, and the church of Sv Spas in Skopje; a fourth in Kruševo was burnt after the Ilinden Uprising. The church stands on the foundations of an earlier 11th-century church, whose mosaic floor is still the floor of the present church, and contains many interesting **frescoes** from the time it was built. The donor fresco of Tyrant Oliver holding the church is still in good condition to the left in front of the chancel, and frescoes of King Dušan, his wife and Tsar Uroš can be found on the left wall of the narthex above the baptism basin. Unfortunately, the fresco of Tsar Uroš has practically been lost. To the right on the ceiling of the narthex are frescoes of the sun and the moon and 12 animals or people seen in the night sky. Despite their amazing likeness to the zodiac signs, the friar will tell you that these are not designed to depict them.

A strict dress code is adhered to in the monastery: men must wear long trousers and women must wear ankle-length skirts. Spare clothing is provided at the door if you forget to bring such items with you.

To get here, head for Drenovo and ask there for the turning for Lesnovo. The Lesnovo road winds up the mountain and at a fork in the asphalt road follow the road to the right going up to get to the monastery rather than down to the village of Lesnovo. This road takes you past some interesting rock outcrops and the entrances to some **old rock mines** where millstones used to be cut. With a torch you can see where half-hewn millstones are still visible in the rock.

STONE DOLLS Halfway back to Highway 2 from Kratovo are the *kukla* or stone doll natural rock formations near the village of Kuklica. Formed from the weathering of porous volcanic rock, large stones teeter on top of tall columns and create imaginary animals and human forms in the rock. Several hundred stone figures are scattered over three sites. Legend says the figures are the result of a petrified wedding: once upon a time a young man from the village of Kuklica decided to marry both his sweetheart from Upper Kuklica and his sweetheart from Lower Kuklica. On the day of the wedding, when the brides saw each other, one was so jealous that she cursed the entire wedding party, turning them to stone. There is an obvious pair of stone dolls at the site, who do look indeed as if they might be going through a wedding ceremony.

The site is now well signposted, both at the E871 highway, and at the turn-off halfway to Kratovo (about 10km from either point). The stone formations (grid 870 628) cover over 1km square so have a good look around.

SVETI NIKOLE

This small town lies on top of a hill in the middle of the fertile Ovče Pole plain. Known as the 'sheep fields' the plain has been inhabited since Neolithic times and remains have been found in the vicinity of the town, mostly around the villages of **Amzibegovo** to the south of Sveti Nikole, and **Gorobinci** to the northwest on the road back to Skopje. Sveti Nikole takes its name from the church built by Serbian king Milutin in 1313. The church stands prominently on top of the hill and can be seen on the approach to the town. It is enclosed within the monastery grounds, which are often closed, so ask in the town for the key if you would like to have a look in.

THE BROTHERS OSOGOVSKI, PČINSKI, LESNOVSKI AND RILSKI

Sketchy details going back to the 10th and 11th centuries claim that the four brothers Joakim Osogovski, Prohor Pčinski, Gavril Lesnovksi and Jovan Rilski were amongst God's most dedicated monks. In order to serve God better, they all decided to follow a hermit's life and so they went the four directions of the compass, to found the monasteries named after each of them. Today, the beautifully painted Rilski Monastery is in Bulgaria, the Pčinski Monastery is in Serbia just over the border from Kumanovo, the Lesnovski Monastery containing the third iconostasis of Frčkovski and the Filipovski brothers is in the village of Lesnovo near Probištip (see above), and Osogovski Monastery is near Kriva Palanka.

Although the four are said to have been brothers, historical data show that Rilski lived at least a century earlier than the others.

Devil's Wall (*www.gavolskizid.com.mk*) is an amazing rock feature on the Bregalnica River. Over 1km long, the wall is several metres high for most of its length and is made of enormous stone blocks. Nobody is yet sure whether it is manmade or natural, and some say it was built by Alexander the Great. Its name comes from a local legend that the devil (*gavol*) made it to dam the River Bregalnica and so drown the nearby village of Bogoslovec (whose name means 'joy to God').

To get there take the road to Sv Nikole from Veles. Just before the turn-off from the highway for Sv Nikole, turn south to Bogoslovec. In the village of Bogoslovec turn right onto a dirt track heading southwest skirting around the hill Sveti Jovanski Rid. After 3km you'll round the hill and see the start of the wall. A tourist complex and hot springs are planned for the area.

The wall (grid 8440 2319) lies across two maps: 1:25,000 SAGW Map Sheets Erdželija 733-1-3 and Dobrošani 733-3-1.

9

The Southern Wine Region

> We wound our way up the mountains, past horses and carts, through a village and on to the top where we found the monastery of Veljuša with its jewel of a tiny thirteenth-century church whose foundations were seven centuries older. It stood, remarkable and unlikely as a Tardis, between a dark-furrowed vegetable patch and some recently refurbished but already tatty monastery buildings.
>
> *Why Angels Fall*, Victoria Clark, 2000

The rich Tikveš plain running from Veles along the River Vardar to Demir Kapija is renowned for its wines. Kavadarci is the **wine capital** where Macedonia's biggest vineyard, Tikveš Wines, is based, but is rivalled by neighbouring Negotino, home to the smaller vineyards. Demir Kapija is home to the old royal Yugoslav winery Elenov, as well as the imposing Popova Kula tower, a vineyard specialising in many indigenous varieties of wine. The climate is mild, the area being only 45m above sea level at the lowest point of the River Vardar at **Gevgelija** border town. Although Macedonian wines are little known, they easily rival better-known wines from the Balkans. Vineyard visits and wine tastings are a great way to get to know Macedonia's wines. For a guide to Macedonian wines, see *Appendix 3*, page 359.

The south of Macedonia was well populated by the Romans so there are lots of Roman remains, including the town of **Stobi** on the crossroads of the Axios and Diagonal ways, and the best-preserved **Roman baths** at Bansko. There are also waterfalls at Smolari and Kolešino, a tectonic lake at **Dojran**, rock climbing at the **Iron Gate** and throughout the region you'll find the usual assortment of monasteries, good hiking and pleasant swimming holes. From Dojran, through Gevgelija, and along the entire southern border, lay the **Saloniki Front of World War I**. A dedication to the fallen of 22 Division (UK) at Devil's Eye commemorates the 90th anniversary of the end of World War I. A good town to stay at to explore the region further is **Strumica**.

STRUMICA   *Telephone code 034*

Between the Belasica and Ogražden mountain ranges is the town of Strumica. It lies in a little-visited area that is teeming with history, sites and natural beauty. The town itself is one of the oldest in Macedonia to have remained in its original location and not be moved by earthquake or ransacked by marauding invaders. Neolithic remains have been found on the hill above the town, and a fortress has existed there since at least the 4th century AD. Archaeological excavation there continues and is well worth a visit.

Strumica is commonly thought to be the site of the ancient city of Doberos, mentioned by Thucydides in the 5th century BC in his tales of the exploits of King

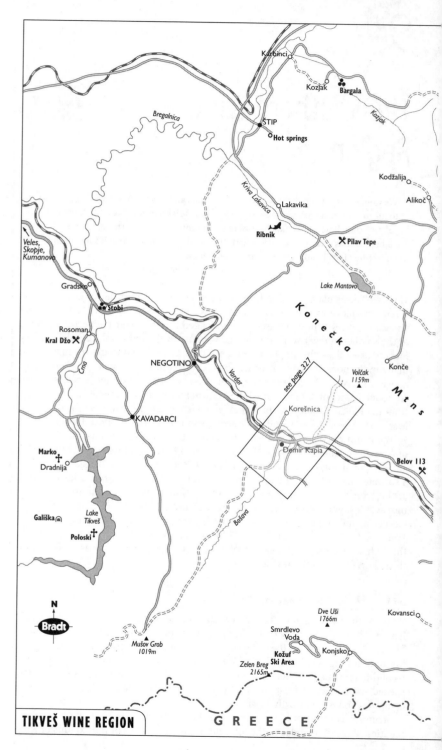

TIKVEŠ WINE REGION

GREECE

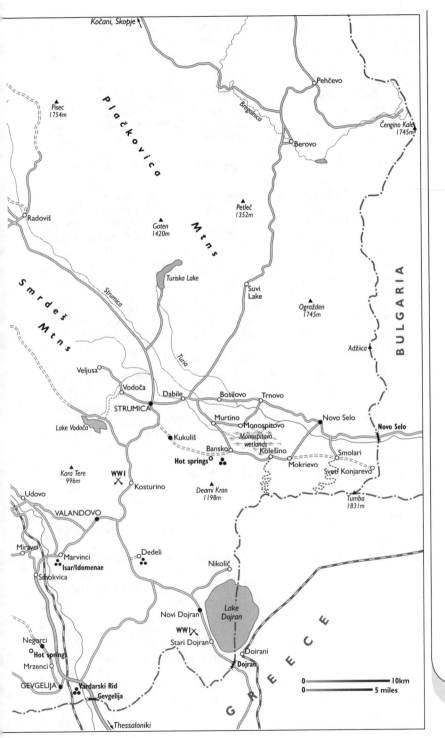

Sitalcus, an ally of the Athenians in the Peloponnesian War against the Paeonians and Macedonians. Later in the 2nd century BC, the town came under the name Astraion, meaning 'city of stars' and named after the Astrai tribe of the Strumica

AN AMERICAN HOSTAGE FREES MACEDONIA

In 1878, the Treaty of Berlin returned Macedonia to Ottoman control, thus dividing what had become Bulgaria under the Treaty of Stefano earlier that year. The people of Bulgaria tried, without success, to reunite, and many from Macedonia fled north of the border to the free municipality of Bulgaria. There they formed the Supreme Committee, with the explicit aim of reuniting the former 'Greater Bulgaria'.

Within Macedonia, a faction of the Supreme Committee was established, named the Internal Macedonian Revolutionary Organisation (today's VMRO). The poorer sibling of the Supreme Committee, it settled for the more practical aim of Macedonian independence rather than reunification with Bulgaria, as reunification clearly did not appeal to the Great Powers at the time. Money and munitions for this 'lesser' aim were not forthcoming from the Supreme Committee, however, so in 1901 the VMRO drew up a number of plans to 'raise' funds.

The idea to kidnap Miss Ellen Stone, an American missionary working in Bankso (in today's Bulgaria) came from Jane Sandanski (many streets in Macedonia are named after him). Although the local Bansko VMRO committee eventually bought into the idea, the top VMRO leadership, including Goce Delčev, did not. Sandanski went ahead nevertheless.

The act of the kidnap itself on 3 September 1901 went relatively smoothly, with nobody hurt. Sandanski was not to know at the time though, that Mrs Katerina Tsilka, taken along with Miss Stone to act as chaperone in regard to Victorian values, was pregnant with her second child.

It took five months of negotiation for the original sum of US$110,000 to be whittled down to US$63,000, raised from the American public through a huge nationwide campaign, and for the 210lb of gold bricks to be smuggled past Turkish and Bulgarian officials into the hands of the revolutionaries. In the meantime, baby Elenchie was born on 4 January 1902 in a hut near the village of Troskovo (today in Bulgaria, some 30km northeast of Berovo). After the money was 'deposited', it took another three weeks of traipsing through the mountains before Miss Stone, Mrs Tsilka, and baby Elenchie were finally left by the revolutionaries outside Strumica.

America's first modern hostage crisis had all the hallmarks of modern-day diplomacy, intelligence conundrums, public relations scandals, the terrorist versus the freedom fighter, personal advancement in the halls of power, escape and evasion. Reaching the desk of the US president Theodore Roosevelt, there was no question of setting a dangerous precedent by paying the kidnappers from state or federal funds, but every diplomatic means, including the implied threat of US warships to the Black Sea, was applied. Teresa Carpenter's excellent book, *The Miss Stone Affair*, delves into all these angles and sets the incident out in a page-turner worth reading of its own accord.

In the end, the money helped to fuel the Ilinden Uprising of 2 August 1903 (see page 26). But it was almost another 90 years before VMRO's dream of an independent Macedonia finally came to fruition.

Skopje (via Štip)	03.30, 05.00, 06.30, 08.30, 09.30,11.30,13.30,15.00, 16.00, 18.00 (400MKD)
Ohrid, Resen, Bitola, Prilep	06.00, 17.00 (350–500MKD)
Gevgelija	08.00, 10.00, 15.00, 17.00 (150MKD)
Dojran (summer only)	08.00, 10.00 (150MKD)

Valley. In Roman times the town was called Tiveriopolis after its first Roman patron, Tiberius Claudius Menon. The arrival of Slavic tribes in the 7th century gave the town its current name.

In 1902, Strumica hit world headlines when America's first international hostage incident ended with the missionary Ellen Stone walking into town (see box opposite). Later, she discovered that she had been held for some of her captivity in a house in Nivičino village, just north of Strumica.

The starry night sky above the valley is, of course, still visible today, although from Strumica's fashionable pedestrian area the only bright lights to be seen are those of the café bars.

GETTING THERE AND AROUND Strumica is served by **buses** from all over the country. The new bus station (✆ 346 030) is on Ulica Kliment Ohridski on the north side of town. See timetable above. A clean new **taxi** company in Strumica is Super Taxi (✆ 1595 (034 1595 from a mobile)), with white branded cars. Flagfall for taxis in Strumica is 50MKD plus 30MKD/km.

TOUR OPERATORS

Atlantis Dimitar Vlahov 18; ✆ 346 212; f 347 212; e strumica@atlantismk.com; www. come2macedonia.mk. Helpful friendly staff. Informative map of Strumica & the local region available.

Salonika Battlefield Tour m 078 293 573; e director@salonikabattlefieldtour.com; www.salonikabattlefieldtour.com. Provides knowledgeable English-speaking guides who, for about €100 a day, can take you around the extensive battlefield, conduct research, provide mapping & photos, arrange cemetery visits, & book your accommodation & food. Director Romeo Drobarov is a former border policeman from the area & is well informed & very helpful.

WHERE TO STAY

⌂ **Sirius** (120 rooms) Ulica Maršal Tito, near Kukliš on the Valandovo exit out of town (or left at the 1st traffic lights if you are coming from Berovo direction); ✆ 345 141; f 345 143; e sirius@t-home.mk; www.hotel-sirius.com.mk. The best hotel Strumica has to offer, although a short taxi ride from the centre. Tennis courts & a very clean outdoor swimming pool, as well as a restaurant. Nestled right against the Belasica foothills it is in a lovely setting. 5-bed dorms available. **$$$**

⌂ **Hotel 404** (11 rooms) Blagaj Jankov Mučeto 13; ✆ 345 404; e hotel404@hotmail.com. This tiny hotel at the foot of the old town is good value. **$$**

⌂ **Central** (22 rooms) Maršal Tito 1; ✆ 612 222; f 612 223; e centralhotel@t-home.mk; www.hotelcentral.mk. Located at the start of pretty Maršal Tito St, this modern hotel makes up by location what it lacks in charm. **$$**

⌂ **Ilinden** (26 rooms) Goce Delčev bb; ✆ 348 000; e info@hotelilinden.com.mk; www. hotelilinden.com.mk. Well-kept hotel that offers all the mod cons. **$$**

⌂ **Tiveriopol** (40 rooms) Bratstvo i Edinstva 20; ✆ 340 421–2. Centrally located but in a quiet backstreet, this Macedonian-standard hotel is showing signs of wear & tear despite recent refurbishment. Friendly staff. Nearby is Beauty

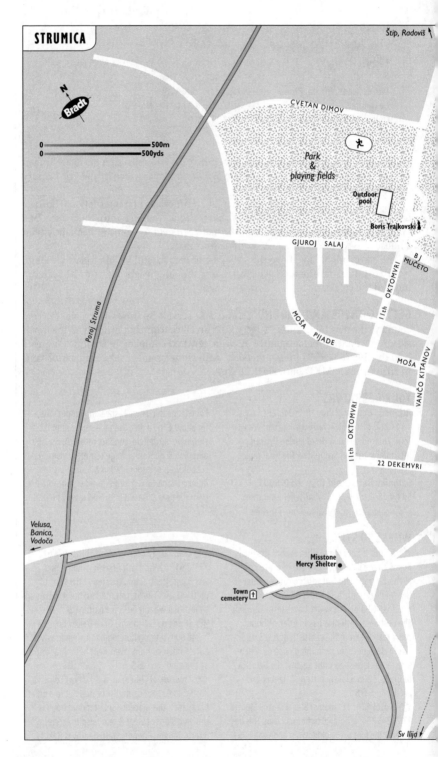

STRUMICA

Štip, Radoviš

CVETAN DIMOV

Park
&
playing fields

Outdoor
pool

Boris Trajkovski

0   500m
0   500yds

Poroj Struma

GJUROJ SALAJ

B J
MUČETO

11th OKTOMVRI

MOŠA PIJADE

MOŠA

VANČO KITANOV

11th OKTOMVRI

22 DEKEMVRI

Velusa,
Banica,
Vodoča

Misstone
Mercy Shelter

Town
cemetery

Sv Ilija

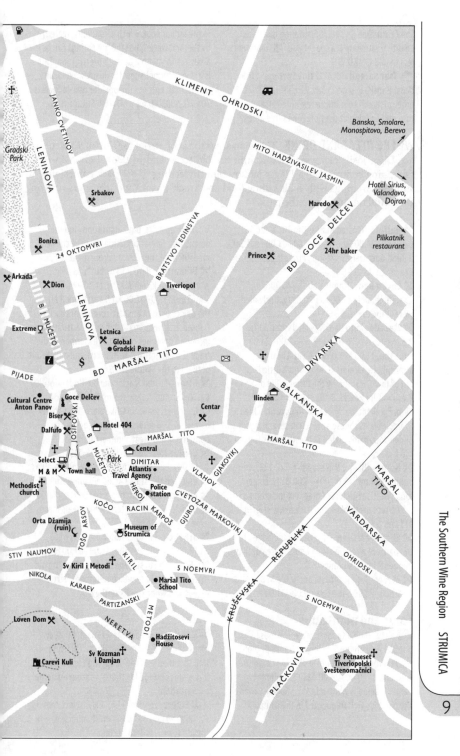

Spa Centre Tina (☎328 787) offering massage, beauty treatments & a spa jet pod. All treatments less than 840MKD. **$$**

🏠 **Tsar Samuil Hotel & Hot Springs** (165 beds) Bansko village; ☎377 210; info@hotelcarsamuil.com.mk; www.hotelcarsamuil.com.mk. Lodging at the hotel gives free access to the indoor pool, which is naturally heated by thermal waters, but the hot springs can be accessed only with a doctor's prescription. This is a classic former Yugoslav dilapidated facility. No internet. Entry to the pool for non-lodgers is 70MKD. 500MKD for a taxi into Strumica. **$**

✗ **WHERE TO EAT AND DRINK** The main areas to eat or go out for a drink in Strumica are Ulica Josif Josifovski leading into the old town and in Global Gradski Pazar (shopping centre). Ulica Blagoj Jankov Mučeto leading to the park comes alive in summer evenings with stalls selling food and knick-knacks and teenagers strutting their stuff on the way to the park.

✗ **Dalfufo** Ploštad Maršal Tito 10; ☎326 112; ⏰ 11.00–24.00 Sun–Thu, 11.00–01.00 Fri & Sat. Behind Goce Delčev's statue. Pizzas & pastas just like in Skopje. **$$$**

✗ **Loven Dom** Neretva bb; ☎345 206; ⏰ summer only 11.00–23.00 daily. Unrivalled view of the town. **$$$**

✗ **Maredo** Mito Hadživasilev Jasmin 111; ☎326 618; m 075 646 112; ⏰ 11.00–24.00 Sun–Thu, 11.00–01.00 Fri & Sat. Local atmosphere, local food. Although a little out of town, it is run by the former chef of President Trajkovski, & the standard of food is high. Excellent lamb chops & their cordon bleu (*Gordomble*) is cheese encased in several layers of delicious ham, coated in breadcrumbs & deep fried. **$$$**

✗ **Bonita** Blagoj Mučeto 54; ☎327 122; www.bonita.com.mk; ⏰ 08.00–24.00 daily. Elegant for a pizzeria with lots of greenery including a big terrace overlookingthe park. Wide selection of food. **$$**

✗ **Elizabet & Dion** Pizzerias on the edge of the park are also open long hours & are popular hangouts in the summer. **$$**

✗ **M & M** Josif Josifovski bb; ☎328 878; ⏰ 10.00–24.00 Sun–Thu, 09.00–01.00 Fri & Sat. Dark upstairs, but a light sunny lounge downstairs. Some specialities like the chicken medallions or the *fefer* steak are great. **$$**

✗ **Pilikatnik** Boro Pockov bb; ☎331 926; www.pilikatnik.com.mk; ⏰ 11.00–24.00 Sun–Thu, 11.00–01.00 Fri & Sat. Named after the device used to ensnare cormorants used by Doijran fisherman to catch fish. Nice atmosphere including paintings of Doijran fisherman at their trade. Excellent fish & fish *chorba*, but a little out of town to the southeast. **$$**

✗ **Biser** Ploštad Maršal Tito bb. Under Goce Delačev statue, follow the marble steps to an underground foodcourt-like place. Best *bourek* in town & also serves *boze*. Their gelatto is homemade & a great summertime treat. **$**

✗ **Centar** Maršal Tito 72; ☎328 425; ⏰ 11.00–23.00 daily. Good for *čevapi* as well as for enjoying the Stara Čaršija old main street. **$**

✗ **Letnica** Leninova bb; ☎344 072; ⏰ 11.00–23.00 daily. Cheap cafeteria-style meals if you need a quick bite. **$**

✗ **Srbakov** Janko Cvetinov bb; ☎327 585; ⏰ 11.00–24.00 Sun–Thu, 11.00–01.00 Fri & Sat. Serves the best *čorba* in town. Near the old market, Shukadum, which sells food every day except Sat, when it sells clothes. **$**

Cafés and nightclubs

💻 **City** Global Gradski Pazar. The most popular café on the 1st-floor entrance of Global.

🍸 **Extreme** Blagoj Mučeto bb; www.extreme.com.mk; ⏰ 10.00–24.00 daily. Despite the name, is actually quite relaxed. Midway towards the park, it's well frequented in the summer.

💻 **Inside** Global Gradski Pazar. Midway along the 1st floor of Global. The café spills out into the middle of the shopping centre where it is a quiet refuge for those wanting an actual conversation.

💻 **Select** Leniniova bb; www.select.com.mk; ⏰ 12.00–01.00 daily. The most popular café in the old town. Modern, techno.

WHAT TO SEE AND DO Strumica is a charming little town in itself and there are a whole host of things in the vicinity to keep you occupied for a good couple of weeks. The old town does not take long to get around and leads up to the restored **Loven Dom** (hunter's lodge – now a swish town-style restaurant more than a rural inn) boasting the best view over the town, for which the steep climb is also worth an expensive coffee. On the way up, Kiril i Metodi Street passes the **Church of Sv Kiril i Metodi**, completed in 1912; Maršal Tito School, built in the early 1900s; the disused court building; and the beautiful **old house of the Hadzitosevi family**, which is in dire need of preservation.

The **Museum of Strumica** (*27th Mart 2;* ✆ *345 925;* ⊕ *09.00–16.00 Mon–Fri; entry free*) is a smart new building, housing a very manageable collection of prehistoric, ancient, medieval, Ottoman period and early 20th-century artefacts gathered from around Strumica. Unique to Strumica is an early 20th-century printing press and an exhibition dedicated to America's first international hostage incident, the Miss Stone case (see box, page 296). Among the photographs of the incident is one of the house in the village of Nezilovo, north of Strumica, where she was held for a while. To get to the museum from Kiril i Metodi Street, take the steps leading down to 27th Mart Street. The museum ethnologist, Ilijas, is proud to use his English and will give you a quick tour around.

The heart of Strumica is dominated by a huge new pedestrian centre (car travel through the centre underneath it) and a larger-than-life-size **statue of Goce Delčev** for his part played in the Ilinden Uprising in 1903 against the Ottomans. To the north is the pedestrian street dedicated to the Strumica hero Blagoj Jankov Mučeto, and which is known as the Strumica **Korzo** — the place to be see and be seen. The korzo leads to the well-kept **Gradski Park** with its stadium and outdoor public pool, Aquarius. The park also has a bust of the late President Trajkovski, who was born in Strumica and died in a plane crash in 2004 over Bosnia.

From the southern end of Blagoj Jankov Mučeto is **Ulica Maršal Tito** (as opposed to the main boulevard further north) running east–west. This was the old high street and is picturesquely lined with buildings from the early 20th century. It's like a miniature Širok Sokak in Bitola, and people come to Maršal Tito Street to shop and meander. At the east end is the imposing **town hall** overlooking the **Mal Gradski Park**. Mal Park café is a relaxing place to stop in the shade and mull over the day.

On Stiv Naumov Street is the abandoned **Orta Džamija**. A national monument itself, it is plain on the inside, and is not the main point of interest here. Rather it is the **11th-century church** underneath that is of current archaeological importance. Although little is known about the true significance of the church, its size indicates a certain importance for the region, especially coupled with the medieval Carevi Kuli (see page 302) and what is likely to have been a sizeable medieval walled town at the time. The necropolis complete with skeletons is still being excavated, and some of the findings from the church are housed in the Strumica Museum.

In the very poor Turkish part of town (sadly with little Turkish architecture) is the **Church of Sv Petnaeset Tiveriopolski Sveštenomačnici** (Holy 15 Martyrs of Tiveriopol) (*Ul Slavčo Stojmenski bb*). This is where 15 Christians, who fled from Nicea (now Iznik in today's Turkey) during the persecution of Christians in the mid 4th century, are buried. Much of the lower half of the church has been uncovered, including 16 vaults, and some large mosaics, all of which can be seen. Underneath the new church, built to one side in the last century, is the **icon gallery** (⊕ *10.00–19.00 Tue–Sun; entry 100MKD*) housing some 50 icons ranging from the medieval period to the late 19th century.

On the top of the hill overlooking the town are the **Carevi Kuli** (Tsar's Towers) (*www.carevikuli.com*) of **Strumica Fortress**. Although this site has been fortified since at least Roman times, the current structure dates from Tsar Samoil's time early in the 11th century. Expansive excavation has restarted in recent years, and there are plans to rebuild the entire structure. Noticeboards in English and Macedonian dot the site. To get there, you can take a steep 20-minute hike along very narrow paths above Loven Dom. Or, for a much more enjoyable approach, hike from Sv Ilija Monastery (see next) to join the newly tarmacked road that comes around the back of the mountain through Raborci and Popčevo villages.

A nice little walk from the centre of Strumica is the one-hour hike to the small **Monastery of Sv Ilija** (2km from Loven Dom). Once at Loven Dom the trail is a wide path leading behind it along the valley. The path quickly joins and runs along the valley stream and is well maintained. A short cut up to Carevi Kuli starts halfway along the path behind some benches, but is steep and narrow. Sv Ilija Church is only open on Sundays, but outside seating and grill pits are used throughout the week in the summer, and outdoor pit toilets can be found at the start of the path behind the monastery inns. To continue to Carevi Kuli, take the path behind the monastery for 15 minutes (it descends slightly to the valley stream before rising again) to the saddle at the top of the stream. There the path joins the brand-new asphalt road from Popčevo village directly to the fortress. The asphalt road is an easy half-hour walk from the saddle. It is a steep and narrow 15-minute descent from the northern end of the fortress to Loven Dom.

For the first three days (*trimeri*) of Orthodox Lent (usually in March), Strumica holds a colourful and friendly **carnival** (*www.strumickikarneval.com*), which includes a special children's carnival as well as the main event and a masked ball.

OUTSIDE STRUMICA

VODOČA Out to the west of town through the Roma village of Banica is the very small settlement of Vodoča. This village is famous for the defeat of Tsar Samoil's army in 1014 by the army of Emperor Basilius II (see box, page 22). The 15,000 troops left of Samoil's army after their defeat on Belasica Mountain were brought here where they had their eyes gouged out. Only one man in every 100 was left with one eye to lead the remaining blinded troops back to Tsar Samoil in Prilep. The place is now called 'gouged eyes' after the Macedonian *vadi oči*.

There is no monument here explaining this piece of Macedonian history, but a monastery was built here a few years after the defeat of Tsar Samoil's empire. The present **Monastery of Sv Leonthius** is a newer construction, but right next to the church dedicated to Sv Leonthius are the ruins of the original church, which was of an early basilica style including marble columns. The columns were later moved to the Church of the Holy 15 Martyrs of Tiberiopolis, in Strumica.

An earthquake in 1931 destroyed the vaults of the church but these were finally restored in 1995 with the restoration of monastery life throughout Macedonia. Lead flashing, which can be seen on the outside of the church walls, marks where the old church walls lie. After the church was completed, the monks, who had originally been living in the Monastery of Veljusa (see page 304), moved into the inns here. The inns used to be open to travellers wishing to stay the night, but at the time of writing these were closed again.

The reconstructed church is now a wonderfully simple, high-domed affair showing the beautiful patterns of the original brickwork, with the remnants of a few frescoes. It is very unfussy compared with a lot of Macedonian churches from later periods and it instils a sense of calm. Some of the frescoes, such as those of Sv Isavrij and Sv Pantelejmon, are now on display in the National Museum of Macedonia. Still remaining in the vaults of the church, however, are believed to be the relics of the wife and son of Sv Kiril. It is very unusual for a woman to have a burial place in a church, and was especially so during those times. It is also just as unusual that Kiril's son should be buried with the mother rather than the father.

As for Sv Leonthius, to whom the church is dedicated, he was martyred in the year 320 for refusing to renounce Christianity. This imposition of the Roman emperors and their pagan gods earned him and 40 other martyrs the right to die by freezing in Lake Sebaste in eastern Turkey. By some unfathomable connection, the Day of the Newlyweds, 22 March, is dedicated to the martyrs and is also the festival day of the Church of Sv Leonthius.

A footpath along the River Vodočnica at the back of the monastery leads up to Lake Vodoča, sometimes called Lake Strumica. The 5km hike is shaded and cool and, once at the lake, gives a good view of the valley.

VELJUSA Continuing along the same road from Vodoča, the next village is Veljusa. This is quite a large village, which rises up into the hills and has two more churches as well as the church at the **Monastery of the Holy Mother of God – Eleusa**. The grounds of this monastery are extremely well kept and look out over the village and the plain of Strumica. The church was originally built in 1080 although the exonarthex was built in the 14th century. It is a small church that suffered two fires in the last century, one in 1913 and the other in 1968. Soot marks can still be seen over some of the frescoes, many of which have been destroyed over time, but some still remain, the most interesting of which is the one of Jesus at the age of 12 in the ceiling of the eastern cupola. The floor of the church shows the original mosaic construction although some of it has been renovated over the years. Some of the original marblework of the church was taken to Bulgaria during World War I and is now kept in the Archaeological Museum of Bulgaria in Sofia. Copies in marble have been made since and are now in place in the church above the entrance to the nave.

Since 1996, when the monks moved down to the Monastery of Sv Leonthius, this monastery has housed nuns.

BANSKO Bansko, 12km southeast of Strumica, is the hot springs capital of Macedonia. It may not seem much when you first arrive, but the potential is there. Aside from the rehabilitation baths for the disabled, and the medicinal baths at the Tsar Samuil Hotel, there are also the last original working Turkish baths (sadly closed in 2005) and the **ruins of a Roman bathhouse**. The Roman complex of thermo-mineral baths dates from the 3rd and 4th centuries AD. Some ten rooms, most with vaulted ceilings, are still visible covering an area of 1,000m^2, and several of these rooms are almost totally preserved. As a museum of hot spring baths throughout the ages, from Roman to Turkish to communist, all that remains to be added is a swish first-class modern outdoor complex complete with sauna, massage rooms and a restaurant serving the latest health salads and smoothies. While we wait for that to arrive, the Roman baths are being renovated.

To get to Bansko there are several buses a day from Strumica bus station, or drive out towards the Bulgarian border and turn off to Murtino and Bansko. If you have a 4x4 it is possible to drive directly from the Hotel Sirius by turning right out of the hotel through the village of Kukliš.

MONOSPITOVO WETLANDS Monospitovo Blato (see box opposite) lies between Bansko and Kolešino in the municipality of Bosilevo. To get there take the road to Bansko and Murtino, and at Murtino turn east towards Monospitovo village. The entrance to the wetlands lies to the south of the village. In the village of Bosilevo itself, a good place to eat is at **Restoran Park**, famous for its *bosilanka* deep-pan pizza. Made with pork, or with chicken and vegetables, it is served with a delicious tomato sauce on the side.

KOLEŠINO The road from Bansko continues on through the pretty villages of Kolešino, which boasts the beautiful 36m waterfall (*vodopad*), then on to Mokrievo

HOME OF THE FISH-EATING SPIDER   *Kyungah Suk*

For an authentic off-the-beaten-path experience, make a stop at the Monospitovsko Blato near Monospitovo village, itself an authentic rural village where time seems to have stood still. The Blato, as it's affectionately known by its nearby residents, is a marsh, purported to be one of the last and biggest in Macedonia. It lies sprawled at the base of Mount Belasica, 17km southeast of Strumica, and has been officially designated as an environmentally protected site, conferring upon it the status 'monument of nature'.

Currently, the Blato covers approximately 400ha. It encompassed a much greater area in the past but how much bigger depends on who you talk to. (The marsh is said to have been drained and destroyed in part during Yugoslavian times due to a malaria epidemic, which did affect World War I soldiers fighting in the area, although mysteriously there are no local hospital records of this epidemic.) Regardless, the Blato continues to be a rich haven for biodiversity with abundant vegetation and wildlife.

In 2007, the Municipality of Bosilovo applied for and received a grant from the European Union to develop the Blato as an eco-rural tourism site. The grant provided funds to develop a structure within the marsh that could be used by tourists, recreational hunters and fishermen, local village people and nature enthusiasts. The structure consists of a wooden boardwalk that extends in three directions of approximately 1km in length, in total. The boardwalk further branches out so that there are seven extensions. At the end of each extension stands a thatched wooden hut built for resting and observing the biodiversity in the Blato.

The Blato also boasts two wooden birdwatching towers from the top of which one has a breathtaking panoramic view of the marsh and the land that stretches beyond it with the majestic Mount Belasica mountain range as its backdrop. Academic and amateur nature enthusiasts have been known to spend the night at the birdwatching towers so that they can catalogue the cacophony of sounds made by the teeming wildlife in the marsh. Depending on the season, the marsh is filled with water or covered in rich vegetation.

An ecological study of the Blato was also conducted by experts from the Macedonian Ecological Society (MES) (*www.mes.org.mk/index.php?lang=eng*) as part of the project. There is a published text containing a catalogue of flora and fauna, some of them extremely rare, found in the Blato. Unfortunately, as of this writing, the text is only in Macedonian. The text catalogues over 130 species of endemic and migratory birds like little bitterns, water rails, lapwings, marsh harriers, grey heron, little egrets and many others. The marsh also contains numerous species of butterflies, fishes, lizards and other amphibians, insects and vegetation. Some of the wildlife is rare or on the endangered or protected lists, including the black stork, European otter, and the fen raft spider, which is a fish-eating carnivorous spider.

The Southern Wine Region   OUTSIDE STRUMICA

9

and Mokrino, where the asphalt road ends. Mokrino springs (Mokrinski izvori), a popular visit with locals, has been given a new lease of life with maintenance and signage making it a pleasant and easy spot to visit. A dirt track continues directly to Smolari or the asphalt road can be taken from between Mokrievo and Mokrino back up to the highway at Novo Selo, after which there is a turning down to Smolari. To get to the waterfall, head to the southwest of the town and, along the side of the village cemetery, follow the stream and footpath into the hills for 40 minutes.

RAKIJA – MACEDONIA'S ELIXIR OF LIFE   *Eric Manton,* rakija *connoisseur*

As in most Balkan countries *rakija* (pronounced 'RAK-eeyah') is the national drink of Macedonia. While rakija in the surrounding countries is made mainly from fruits such as plums (*slivovice*) or pears (*viljemovka*), Macedonian rakija is made exclusively from grapes. Macedonia's bountiful wine region, especially in the Povardarie region of the Tikveš valley, has supplied great rakija for centuries.

The term rakija applies to all distilled spirits, similar to the terms palinka or brandy. The term likely comes from the Turkish *raki*, which in turn came from the Arabic term *arak* meaning condensation. Distillation of alcohol supposedly started with alchemists originating in north Africa and the Middle East and spread to Europe in the Middle Ages through Spain, Italy and the Balkans. Alchemists used distillation for medicinal and scientific purposes in order to discover the essence of various materials. Once identified, these essences would be extracted for their curative powers. Alcohol was the preservative agent that also allowed for easier consumption. Even today in Macedonia rakija is also considered a medicine, and is called the 'elixir of life'.

In Macedonia, most people have a relative who makes their own *domašna* or homemade rakija. These private producers make their rakija the way it has been done for centuries. The fundamental ingredient is grapes; some people make rakija through the grappa method (using the leftovers from the wine-making process) or in the style of cognac (just using the juice or wine from the grapes); however, the majority of producers use the whole grape – excluding the stems, but including the juice, skins and seeds. While this type of rakija is initially slightly less smooth, the skins bring a fuller flavour.

After the grapes are crushed, they are left to ferment for three to four weeks as the natural sugars in the grapes turn into alcohol. The resulting mush is then distilled or burnt in traditional copper *kazans* or pot stills of around 100 litre capacity. Using these stills as opposed to the column stills used in large-scale commercial distilleries allows for much better quality and a more refined product since the copper pot stills extract many of the more harmful types of alcohols released during distillation. The fresh rakija is then put into glass or wood barrels for aging.

Most Macedonians prefer the *žolta* (yellow) rakija, which signifies that it has been wood aged. *Bela* rakija, or white, is less common. Aside from standard oak barrels, Macedonians also use the wood from acacia and mulberry trees. These give a different colour and flavour. For a good-quality rakija, it needs to age six to 12 months in wood, or 18 months to three years in glass. Recently some commercial producers have been slipping in syrups and extracts that add artificial aroma, colour and flavour.

This part of Macedonia clearly lies in an area influenced by Methodism. The main evangelical Methodist church is in Kolešino, but there are also lots of others around, some converted back to Orthodoxy, but they are given away by their church towers, which unlike Orthodox churches, are attached directly to the church or stand over the narthex.

A newly opened popular **national restaurant and inn** is Podgorski An on the western entry to Kolešino village (*10 rooms;* \ *034 351 100;* e *podgorski-an@ hotmail.com; www.podgorskian.com;* **$$**). Taking advantage of a local watermill, the

Another variety of rakija called *mastika* infuses the grape brandy with a combination of up to 27 herbs and spices, with the main flavours being mastic and aniseed similar to Greek ouzo. Macedonian mastika is highly regarded in former Yugoslav countries.

For many years, there were only a few brands of commercially produced rakija from the large wineries, Tikveš and Povadarie. Most of these rakijas are made of a mix of grape varieties. Their flavour mainly comes from the wood that is used to age them or from artificial flavouring. In the last seven years several specialised distilleries have appeared:

ALCHEMIST This micro-distillery has recently taken rakija lovers in Macedonia by storm. Having won two Gold medals and a Silver medal for their brandies in Belgrade Rakijafest 2010, these artisans from the Tikveš valley have introduced new ways of making rakija. Not only do they produce cuvées of a few specially selected grapes, but Alchemist also produces single-grape rakijas that highlight the distinct flavour of that variety. They also continue the original alchemical tradition of infusing the rakija with other ingredients like coffee beans, almonds or vanilla (as opposed to adding an artificial flavour at the end). Their main types of rakija are the Grand Reserve, Special Reserve, Black Muscat, Elixir, Late Harvest Vranec, Hamburg and Merlot.

ALTAN The Bahus distillery produces Altan (gold in Turkish), which is a combination of Vranec and Afus Ali grapes aged for three years in oak barrels from Kruševo. This is one of the better commercial rakijas that won a Bronze medal at the Belgrade Rakijafest 2010.

ANTIKA Divino distillery produces two ages of this quite average rakija. They also produce Muscat rakija though it is hard to discern the Muscat flavour.

BOVIN This premier winery from Negotino produces higher-class rakija with its red label Special Reserve, black label St Trifun Fine Rakija and green label St Trifun Premium Rakija (made from a cuvée of white wine grapes).

NEGOTINSKA From Negotino. Specialises in two rakijas: normal and gold. Good small family distillery.

SKOVIN The Skopje winery has been making the Markov Manastir rakija from special vineyards from around this monastery on the other side of the Vodno hill from Skopje. They recently entered on the market with a normal žolta to compete against Tikveš.

restaurant is a welcome respite and, amusingly, the restaurant chairs sport wagon wheels, making them seem a little like wheelchairs. Excellent food and setting, worth the long taxi ride from Strumica for 450MKD. Rooms are basic.

SMOLARI In a corner of Macedonia equidistant from the borders of Bulgaria and Greece is the village of Smolari, above which is the 40m drop of the **Smolari Waterfall**. It is a small site but set in beautiful surroundings and the half-hour hike to get there is along well-maintained grounds. There are a couple of makeshift cafés on the way serving *skara*, beer and soft drinks, and many people bring their own picnics.

There are several buses a day from Strumica bus station to the waterfall, or Atlantis travel agency can arrange a special bus if there is a big enough group. To drive there, head towards the Bulgarian border and after Novo Selo turn off for Smolari. Take the first right turn at the edge of the village, which is marked Vodopad (waterfall), then the next left after the village shop. This will take you to a car park. Follow the path at the side of the stream uphill for about half an hour to reach the waterfall.

VALANDOVO

The road south out of Strumica goes past the town of Valandovo and on to Lake Dojran and the border town of Gevgelija. Valandovo is renowned for its pomegranates and for a number of Roman ruins in the vicinity, such as the lost town of Idomena outside the village of Marvinci where Aleksandar III of Macedon is thought to have his burial chambers, and the necropolis at Dedeli. The town also holds Macedonia's yearly competition, the Rakijada, when local people compete in mid-October to make the best *rakija*.

Just to the west outside Valandovo is the 14th-century tower of King Marko, and to the north is the Monastery of Sv Gjorgi in the hills above Valandovo. Valandovo was also the site of fighting during World War I between the Irish 10th Regiment and the central powers of Germany and Turkey. A small graveyard to the fallen of the Irish can be found on the outskirts of the town.

Outside Valandovo, the site of the **Roman town Idomenae**, situated on a hill to the southwest of the village of Marvinci, offers splendid views towards the Valandovo and Vardar valleys.

The earliest incarnation of the city, spread over some 5,000m² within the circuit of a defensive wall, dates to the Hellenistic period (323–168BC). The visible architectural remains relate mainly to private buildings and dwellings, but there are also the remains of a pottery workshop to be seen. Although the site is not presented for the public and can be somewhat arduous to visit, several public buildings can be seen, among which is a temple dedicated to Emperor Commodus (AD180–192) in the form of the Greek god Hercules. Commodus, the son of the warrior philosopher Emperor Marcus Aurelius, called himself the Roman Hercules and famously partook in the gladiatorial arena (played by Joaquin Phoenix in the film *Gladiator*).

WINES FROM THE TIKVEŠ PLAINS

The entire course of the Vardar Valley all the way down to Thessaloniki is fertile grape-growing country, and within Macedonia the Tikveš plains between Titov Veles and Demir Kapija produce some of the best national wines. Near Demir Kapija, the ex-royal vineyard **Elenov** and the boutique vineyard **Popova Kula** are well worth a visit and a longer stay. Negotino boasts nine vineyards in its vicinity.

There are also vineyards further north around Skopje, and you'll find the local wines of smaller vineyards served in plastic bottles and cardboard cartons at local petrol station and stores.

Macedonian wines are unique amongst European wines for being made with very little, if any, additional sugar or sulphite preservatives. They are preserved, therefore, mostly by the grapes' own natural sugars and it is for this reason that almost all Macedonian wines are dry rather than sweet, and why you won't get such a big hangover the next day after drinking a bottle of T'ga za Jug (Longing for the South) or Alexandria.

A visit to one of the vineyards in September and October or around Sv Trifun day in February is always well worth the time if you'd like to try out the season's newest, or the best of last year's stock. Macedonia's wine tours are becoming more frequent. To get on the next tour see Go Macedonia (page 66). A tour, including lunch, travel and drinks, costs in the region of €35–45.

KAVADARCI *Telephone code 043*

Kavadarci was founded in the late Roman period, but most of the records of this period in its history are buried beneath **Tikveš Lake**, a manmade lake constructed in 1968 to provide irrigation and hydro-electricity to the surrounding area. To celebrate the start of the winemaking season, Kavadarci holds a **Grape Harvest Festival** on 1

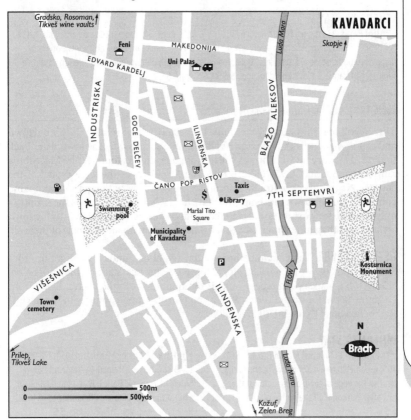

September, including grape-crushing barefoot and a masked parade. This is followed on the third Saturday of November with the **Tikveš Young Wine Festival** when the largest winery in Macedonia, Tikveš, opens its doors for people to taste the first wines of that year's harvest. If you get the opportunity, try to dine in **Tikveš wine vaults**. Situated on the main road outside Kavadarci, reservations are a must for evenings and weekends, but they might be able to serve you impromptu for lunch during the week (℡ *414 987 ext 224;* m *071 338 195;* e *aleksandar.ristovski@tikves.com.mk*).

Two interesting churches in the area are **Marko's Cave Church** in Dradnija, 4km west of the Tikveš Lake dam, and the 14th-century **Monastery of Polog** in the village of Poloski on the cliffs of Tikveš Lake. The church there, dedicated to Sv Gjorgi, is practically windowless, despite the number of window arches built into the walls, and the vaults of the church are claimed to hold the remains of Dragutin, the brother of the Serbian king Dušan. The monastery is accessible only by boat, or a 10km hike overland from the village of Pravednik. For boat trips on the lake ask at the Uni Palas hotel.

GETTING THERE There are 11 **buses** a day (fewer at weekends) to Kavadarci from Skopje, from 06.00 until 20.15, for 280MKD. The bus station (*Edward Kardelj bb;* ℡ *400 111; www.samvelcompany.com*) is near the Uni Palas hotel. Buses from Kavadarci serve Negotino, Veles, Bitola and Ohrid. **Taxi** companies include Taxi Vednas (℡ *416 001*) and Vinozito (℡ *400 400*).

⌂ WHERE TO STAY

⌂ **Uni Palas** (34 rooms) Eduard Kardelj bb; ℡419 600; e hotelunipalas@mt.net.mk; www. unipalas.com.mk. Some old, some new build; room service, gym, sauna & a lovely outdoor pool. **$$$**

⌂ **Feni** (47 rooms) Eduard Kardelj bb; ℡412 244; e info@hotelfeni.com; www.hotelfeni. com. Completely renovated; friendly attentive staff. **$$**

NEGOTINO *Telephone code 043*

Tiny Negotino is the heart of Macedonia's wineland. It has a minute Čaršija old town and can in many ways still be described as a one-horse town. The town dates back to the 3rd century BC when it was called Antigona after its founder, the Macedonia king Antigon Gonat (277–240BC). Rivalling Kavadarci as the wine capital of the country, Negotino celebrates Sv Trifun Day, 14 February, with a **parade and wine competition**. The **town museum** (*Maršal Tito 119;* ℡ *361 712*) also has the country's only **wine history exhibition**. Scattered around the outskirts and hills of the town are no fewer than nine **wineries**. See www.nagtour.com for an overview of them all.

GETTING THERE There are nine **buses** a day (eight on Sunday) to Negotino from Skopje, from 08.30 until 19.30, for 220MKD. The bus station (*Industriska bb;* ℡ *361 744; www.samvelcompany.com*) is ten minutes from the centre. Buses from Negotino serve Kavadarci, Veles, Bitola and Ohrid. A **taxi** company in the town is Radio Taxi Start (℡ *(043/070) 370 300*).

⌂ WHERE TO STAY

⌂ **Pamela** (11 rooms) Maršal Tito 4; ℡361 105; e pamelab.t@live.com; www.pamela.mk. New on the edge of town at the petrol station just after you come off the highway. **$$**

⌂ **Park** (54 rooms) Partizanski 1; ℡370 960–1; f 043 361 033; e hotelpark@t-home.mk; www. hotelpark.com.mk. Basic tidy accommodation on a hill at the edge of town. Offers wine tours to St Helen Winery. Gives YHA discounts. **$$**

STOBI

To the northwest of Negotino and just south of Gradsko, nestled into the crook of the Black River and the Vardar River, lies the ancient city of Stobi. Although many Macedonians would rate the ancient city of Heraklea (see page 215) near Bitola higher than Stobi, in my opinion Stobi is nicer to wander around. The cities were founded at the same time and both flourished under the Roman Empire, Heraklea becoming the capital of the region. With views of the surrounding mountains and riverways, it is easy to stand on the site and imagine the hustle and bustle of the ancient city, with its numerous travelling traders plying their wares and telling their tales of far-off lands. Stobi has a good little information centre and café. Entrance to the ruins costs 150MKD.

HISTORY The ancient city of Stobi was founded at the confluence of the rivers Crna (the ancient River Erigon) and Vardar (ancient Axius), at the crossing point of the Via Egnatia, the Via Axia and the Via Diagonale. The original settlement, slightly to the north of the current archaeological site, is thought to be Bronze Age in origin, dating to around 1900BC. Bronze objects from the classical and archaic periods have been found there along with pottery from the Neolithic period and the Iron Age. The later Hellenistic city was established in the 4th century BC.

Excavation in the newer, central part of the city has revealed archaeological stratigraphy dating to the 2nd and 3rd centuries BC. Its heyday, however, came following the Roman victory in the third Macedonian war in 168BC, when Macedonia was divided into four regions, and Stobi became one of the major urban centres in one of them. The Goths destroyed the town when they invaded Macedonia in AD479, and although it was rebuilt shortly afterwards, the earthquake of 518 damaged the town further. Rebuilt again, further earthquakes took their toll on the town, and by the end of the 13th century the town was completely abandoned in favour of towns like Veles further north along the Vardar, and Negotino further south.

GETTING THERE Stobi is just south of the town of Gradsko, and signposted. It is accessible right off the Skopje–Negotino highway on the east side. Travelling south take the first exit after Gradsko, some 3km, and go underneath the highway into the car park.

There is no public transport to the site, but you could take a **bus** or **train** to Gradsko or a bus to Rosoman and then a **taxi** for about 250MKD, or **walk** from Gradsko south alongside the railway for about 3km until you reach the ruins. Along the walk on the southern outskirts of Gradsko is a cemetery with German graves from World War I.

WHERE TO STAY AND EAT The café has some snacks and Gradsko has a larger shop. **Rosoman**, 7km from the ruins, has a few small places to eat, or go on to Kavadarci (see page 309) or Veles (see page 263), both of which also have hotels.

WHAT TO SEE Stobi was first discovered in 1861, but excavation did not start until 1924, and even today only a fraction of the city has been uncovered. The site is not very big and can easily be explored in a couple of hours. Aside from the ruins themselves, most of the pottery, jewellery and sculptures are in the museums of Skopje and Veles. Two of the most famous pieces, a pair of bronze satyrs, are in Belgrade's city museum.

There are numerous main buildings and town roads in Stobi. A 2nd-century amphitheatre, which was later turned into a gladiatorial ring, has the names of family holders engraved on some of the seats. There are at least five basilicae: a northern basilica, a civilian basilica, a central basilica and synagogue, an extra mural basilica, and the **Episcopal basilica**. The Episcopal basilica was built in the 5th century AD in a Hellenistic manner with an atrium, narthex (with a mosaic floor) and an exonarthex with a double apse. This was the seat of the bishop Philip. On the south of the basilica is the baptistery with a magnificent mosaic composition. There is a set of small baths (*thermae minores* or *balneum*) and a set of large baths (*thermae*), complete with three earthenware *pithoses* (vats). The **House of the Psalms** is a sumptuous urban villa or *domus* with a large reception room or *tablinium* with exceptional mosaics, as well as a collonaded peristyle/atrium and central trichlinium with an apse. Several other houses that have been identified include the House of Peristeria, the House of Parthenius and the episcopal residence. The **Palace of Theodosius** is one of the biggest buildings with a floor of marble plates, a peristilus with mosaics and marble pedestal platforms on which statues once stood. **Domus Fullonica** was a house with a fullery for treating leather or retting cloth. The roads of Stobi include the Via Axia, Via Principalis Inferior, Via Theodosia, Via Principalis Superior and Via Sacra. Finally, there is also a semicircular *plataea* (public open space), and the city well.

DEMIR KAPIJA – THE IRON GATE   Telephone code 043

From Veles via Stobi the southerly flow of the Vardar River takes it through the plains of the Tikveš region. The valley then narrows to a gap of barely 50m across where the surrounding mountains force the river through the Iron Gate mountain gorge. The Turkish term for the gorge 'Demir Kapija' means 'iron gate' and is still the name used today for the small settlement at the foot of the rocks. Beyond the Iron Gate the valley sides remain steep for another 20km. This geographical formation has forced centuries of invaders into upper Macedonia through this narrow corridor. They are effectively funnelled into a killing zone on exiting the Iron Gate into the Tikveš plain and hence the ominous name of the rock feature.

The train ride from the north through Demir Kapija to Gevgelija is pretty, although the drive is probably more so, because of the stopping place on the road between two rock towers. This stopping place, barely big enough for half-a-dozen cars, gives the appearance of being in an open-topped cave.

GETTING THERE There are six **buses** a day to Demir Kapija from Skopje leaving Skopje at 08.30, 11.00 (not weekends), 14.00, 15.00 (not weekends), 16.00 and 17.30. The 90-minute journey costs 270MKD. Demir Kapija is also a stop on the main line between Skopje and Gevgelija (see **train** times on page 72) and costs only 147MKD Skopje to Demir Kapija (*train station* ✆ 034 367 230). It is 2km to Popova Kula winery and hotel-restaurant. Taxis wait outside the train station, and Astor Taxi can be called on ✆ (043) 366 252.

⌂ WHERE TO STAY, EAT AND DRINK

⌂ **Popova Kula Winery** (11 rooms) Wine Bd 1; ✆ 367 400; f 043 367 404; e reservation@ popovakula.com.mk; www.popovakula.com.mk. In the hills behind Demir Kapija, this boutique vineyard commands an impressive view from the rooms & restaurant tower, & is worth the visit alone. Beautiful rooms, & check out their wine-tasting venue in the tower. Vineyard tours available; wine-tasting sessions take place in the restaurant tower every evening at 18.00 for

700MKD pp, including cheese & meats. Popova Kula specialises in indigenous grape varieties such as Stanushina & Žilavka, as well as the usual regional varieties. $$$$

🏠 **Elenov, the Old Royal Winery** Just outside Demir Kapija; ☎ 367 231–2; e vinarija_elenov@mt.net.mk. Dates from the days of Royalist Yugoslavia, complete with peacocks. If you can get on a tour you will see all the old wooden wine barrels still in use as well as some of the old presses (no longer in use). The former queen's house is a listed building & due to

be renovated to become a restaurant. On summer w/ends you might be able to join a lunch if they are already conducting a bigger tour. Including their wine $$$

✗ **Vodenica** ☎ 366 111; m 070 738 214; ⊕ 11.00–23.00 Tue–Sun. Serves good Macedonian food in a traditional setting. To get there turn right immediately at the end of the bridge & turn right again off the tarmac road. The track forks immediately; keep to the right-hand fork alongside the river & the restaurant is at the end of this lane. $$

WHAT TO SEE AND DO Aside from **winery visits**, there is lots of **hiking** in the hills to local caves and villages, including to the site of the **ancient fortress Prosek**, which can be seen from Popova Kula restaurant at the telecommunications tower on the hill to the east over the valley. Popova Kula can also arrange guided hikes; and see *Chapter 10* for a river hike from the Iron Gate itself and a map of the town and region, page 328.

The towering rock faces of Demir Kapija gorge (accessible from the stopping place in the middle of the tunnel through the gorge on the main road) are favourites for **rock climbing** (routes are marked, and displayed on the very informative map of Demir Kapija available in the town). If this seems a precarious access point, rest assured that plans are afoot to create another tunnel further east through the rock to continue the motorway down to Gevgelija. Don't hold your breath though.

The local **museum** (*Maršal Tito bb*; ☎ 366 502; *www.museummdk.mk*; ⊕ 09.30–16.30 *Tue–Sun; entry free*), which is opposite the train station, opened in 2011 to cater for public interest in the growing archaeological excavations in the area, and to continue the theme of Macedonia's history in wine, as other museums are doing.

GEVGELIJA *Telephone code 034*

As part of the defensive line of medieval Byzantium, and of the World War I Saloniki Front, Gevgelija is an archaeological treasure. Once a sleepy little border town, it now sports several casinos predominantly serving Greek visitors. It is also the main town serving Kožuf ski resort. The town has an interesting legend attached to its name, a small old town and a couple of large garish casinos near the highway. Allegedly the name comes from the Turkish *gel geri*, meaning 'come again', which was called to a dervish monk who had been banished by the locals. The monk had only stopped to rest overnight when he expressed his desire to stay because it was such a nice place. The locals of non-dervish religion took umbrage with the statement and made it very clear that neither he nor his religion were welcome. As he left, the locals feared that the monk's god might take vengeance on them for banishing the monk and so they called after him, '*Gel geri, gel geri.*' No-one knows if he ever did return.

GETTING THERE AND AWAY Gevgelija is probably Macedonia's busiest border crossing. Trains to Greece had stopped at the time of writing, and the only way to continue a train journey on to Thessaloniki would be to go over to the Greek town of Doirani, 25km to the east. Gevgelija train station (☎ *212 033*), is just outside town. Four **trains** a day leave for Skopje, taking almost three hours for 200MKD. For the full train timetable see page 72.

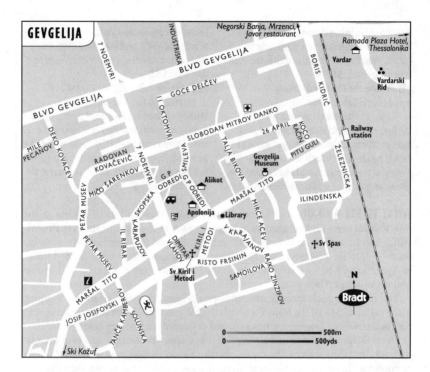

The bus station (*7th Noemvri bb;* \ 212 315) in the centre of town serves **buses** to the rest of Macedonia, but none to Greece. A timetable can be found at www. gevgelija.net.mk. **Taxis** can cross the border, however. Try Radio Taxi As (\ 213 614).

WHERE TO STAY

🏠 **Ramada Plaza** (131 rooms) Bogorodica border crossing; \ 219 500; e info@rpgevgelija. com; www.ramadaplazagevgelija.com. The first truly international-standard luxury hotel in Macedonia from a reliable & well-known chain. Expect & receive all the trimmings. Indoor pool, spa, fitness, restaurants & nightclub. You don't need to leave. **$$$$**

🏠 **Apolonija** (44 rooms) Gevgelski Partizanski Odredi 1; \ 213 222; f 213 223; e info@

apollonia.com.mk; www.apollonia.com.mk. Largely serving Greek clients of the hotel's casino. Central & recently refurbished. **$$$**

🏠 **Ašikot** (16 rooms) Gevgelski Partizanski Odredi 2; \ 212 238. A little down-at-heel, but great value for money for the centre of town. **$$**

🏠 **Vardar** (24 rooms) Round the back of Vardarski Rid archaeological site; \ 213 267; www. hotels-macedonia.com.mk/motel_vardar.html. Basic, but quiet, & friendly staff. **$$**

WHERE TO EAT
Gevgelija's best restaurants are outside the town, and if you're driving to Thessaloniki from Skopje (or vice versa), it is worth trying the following short diversions:

✗ **Javor** Village of Mrzenci; \ 212 920; ⏲ 11.00–23.00 daily. Although quite expensive by Macedonian standards, the cuisine is truly outstanding for traditional Macedonian fare. The restaurant receives a lot of Greek visitors who seem to be meeting their Macedonian cousins.

Mouth-watering spit-roast lamb & all the usual Macedonian fare. To get here turn off the main highway into Gevgelija & take the 2nd right heading north towards Negorci & Mrzenci. The restaurant stands out on the right before the small bridge, 3km outside Gevgelija. **$$$**

✗ Elita 1st Mai 13, Bogdanci; m 071 602 043, 070 881 146; e elita_ribnik@yahoo.com; ⊕ 10.00–24.00 daily. Situated on little Lake Bolovan, 2km from Nov Dojran, the setting is relaxing, the fishing good & the food delicious. **$$**

WHAT TO SEE AND DO The **Gevgelija Museum** (*Maršal Tito 26;* ✆ *213 660;* ⊕ *09.00–15.00 Tue–Sun; entry 100MKD*) mostly displays finds from Vardarski Rid as well as other local finds of pottery and money. **Vardarski Rid** is the small hill behind the city, which displays a prominent communist monument to the National War of Liberation, ie: the partisan uprising. It is the site of a Bronze Age settlement called Gortynia, which was of some standing during the 2nd millennium BC. It was only discovered as the foundations were being laid for the partisan monument.

Gortynia is first mentioned by the Greek historian Thucydides, writing in the 5th century BC. The oldest finds from the site date back to the Neolithic period but the earliest evidence of structural remains dates to the end of the Bronze Age. Occupation continued throughout the Iron Age and the town thrived between 800 and 500BC, characterised by rich finds of jewellery and the so-called 'Macedonian Bronzes' (bronze pendants with ritual and symbolic meaning associated with an as yet unknown cult).

The city played an important regional role between the 2nd and 3rd centuries BC, and numerous buildings have been discovered from this period, along with a rich hoard of over 500 coins, from the Antigonid dynasty (294–168BC). This dynasty, descended from one of Alexander's generals, Antigonese the One Eyed, ruled over the ancient Kingdom of Macedonia and the Greek city-states.

There is a nice café for coffee in the **Vardar Hotel**.

Another 1.5km along this road from Mrzenci are the hot springs of **Negorski Banji** (✆ *231 174;* e *info@negorskibanji.com.mk; www.negorskibanji.com.mk*). These baths are well kept compared with some of the other baths in the country, as they are mostly used for medicinal purposes. Male and female baths are separate, and there are additional rooms for massage and therapies as prescribed by the resident doctor. Public entry into the hot springs alone is 50MKD. A room at one of the three accommodation houses is €25 per person per day, €10 extra for full board. Recently privatised, there are plans to turn it into a Western-standard spa serving the ski resort of Kožuf.

KOŽUF SKI RESORT AND MOUNTAIN RANGE

The newest ski resort in Macedonia is at Kožuf (*Gevgelija office, Maršal Tito 124;* ✆ *034 214 441;* e *skikozuf@t-home.mk; www.skikozuf.com.mk*) on the mountain range bordering Greece. Going up to 2,200m, with a chair lift rising over 500m, and 65km of groomed runs, it boasts being the highest and best ski resort in the region, after Bankso in Bulgaria. Like Popova Šapka, its height can make it prone to wind, but the skiing opportunities are considerably greater than at Mavrovo. At the time of writing, it was still in its early days, with minimal overnight facilities, but a new asphalt road has been laid allowing for two way traffic. As a result a day pass is only 900MKD.

There are plans to re-mark the mountain trails in the range, including the 85km ridge trail from Kožuf to Kajmakčalan (near Bitola). Check the skikožuf website under 'Things to do' for more information as it becomes available.

To get to Kožuf, take the train or bus to Gevgelija and then a taxi to Smrdlevo Voda (25km, 600MKD) passing through the mountain village of Konsko on the way. At Smrdleva Voda (meaning 'smelly water' due to the sulphurous hot springs there) the

Skikožuf *kombe* (minibus) (m *070 801 801*) ferries people up the 18km to Kožuf at 08.30 (and back down at 16.00) for 100MKD each way. There are plans to tarmac the dirt road from Demir Kapija to Kožuf, but this may not materialise for a few years.

If you would prefer to stay in Smrdleva Voda, Šuklev Roman has a beautiful new house located along the stream (*4 rooms with 2 shared bathrooms;* m *071 251 433; 900MKD pp*). There is a small restaurant next door, and other rooms available throughout the village if Šuklev's is full.

LAKE DOJRAN   *Telephone code 034*

Lake Dojran was once known for its beauty, its curative reed waters (for healing skin ailments) and its very good air quality. It has become a controversy of water use. The lake is the third tectonic lake of its kind in Macedonia, after Ohrid and Prespa, having been formed from tectonic shifts in the earth's land plates four million years ago. It is the shallowest of all the lakes, being a mere 10m deep when the lake is at its fullest.

Overuse of water from the lakes and streams that feed Dojran Lake on both sides of the border had caused the lake to shrink to a third of its former size. Concerted efforts by the government have saved the lake from near extinction, although there is still some way to go to restore the biological and ecological diversity of the lake. Nonetheless, the shoreline is still teeming with wildlife, and on a sunny spring day you can see more frogs than you can shake a stick at, water snakes eating tadpoles, and a host of birds, butterflies and insects. If you are lucky, you'll also see some fish.

GETTING THERE AND AWAY Entering Macedonia from Greece via the Greek village of Doirani is a simple affair, and is in fact a shorter route from Thessaloniki than using the highway at Gevgelija, and has less traffic. The small border control station is usually very quick compared with the main Gevgelija crossing.

Two **buses** a day from Skopje (08.30 and 14.00, plus an extra service at 07.30 in the summer) serve Star Dojran and a 16.00 bus from Skopje serves Nov Dojran for 410MKD. Five more buses from Skopje serve nearby Bogdanci, from where you can take a **taxi** the remaining 18km to Nov Dojran. Ask at your hotel for returning bus times as there is no dedicated bus station at either Nov or Star Dojran. A partial timetable including to Gevgelija (from where it's easier to get to other parts of the country) is at www.dojran-info.com. A taxi to Dojran from Strumica is 900MKD.

WHERE TO STAY

Istatov (44 rooms) Entrance to Nov Dojran; 227 556; m 075 421 848; f 034 227 555; e hotel.istatov@yahoo.com; www.hotelistatov. com. Also the Istatov physical training centre, this motel is owned by Blagoj Istatov, the Belgrade Partisani football team goalkeeper in 1973, & later coach in the Netherlands & coach of the Macedonian national team. Frequented by Macedonia's football & handball teams. A little pricey for the quality, although it does have an outdoor pool, gym & restaurant (usual local fare). **$$$**

Polin (48 rooms) Maršal Tito bb; 225 770; e hotel_polin@live.com; www.hotelpolindojran.

com. This is one of the few hotels on the lake side of the main road. Has an outdoor pool as well as access to the public beachfront. Refurbished rooms. Offers lake mud spa treatments. Can be noisy in the summer due to proximity to café-bars on the beach. **$$$**

Villa Dojrana (3 rooms) Partizanska 41, Star Dojran; m 070 999 758; e villadojrana@ yahoo.com; www.villadojrana.webs.com. Self-catering apt including a tiny outdoor pool. Situated near the old clock tower high up behind the Hotel Makedonija. Views over the lake. **$$$**

🏠 **Dan Dar Apartments** (31 rooms) Maršal Tito bb; ☎ 227 339; e kontakt@aparmanidan-dar.com.mk; www.apartmanidan-dar.com.mk. Comprising an older style building & a new build, this complex just off the main road before coming into Nov Dojran has an outdoor pool & traditional restaurant. Excellent value for money. **$$**

🏠 **Hotel Makedonija** (50 rooms) Maršal Tito bb, Star Dojran; ☎ 225 003. Standard accommodation, right in the centre of the village on the main road. A common meeting place due to the large car park in front & the huge Macedonian flag marking the centre. **$$**

✗ WHERE TO EAT

The old village, Star Dojran, stretches for over 1km along the lake. Many restaurants, pizzerias, buffets and cafés line the road.

✗ **Fuktak** Maršal Tito 15, Star Dojran; ☎ 255 320; ⏱ 11.00–23.00 daily. Although this small restaurant can't boast views overlooking the lake, it is the oldest & most famous in the town (& well known across all Macedonia). The restaurant is over 120 years old, going back to the days of Macedonia's struggle to overthrow Ottoman rule. On the wall just inside the main entrance hang original photos of 8 of the founders of VMRO (Revolutionary Organisation for an Independent Macedonia). Opened just after the new train line through (now Greek) Doirani, the restaurant is named after the sound that the train engine makes: 'fuk-tak, fuk-tak, fuk-tak'. The menu offers the usual Macedonian fare, & the freshly caught carp from the lake is exquisite, extremely tender with no trace of a muddy taste at all – undoubtedly, the best carp you'll find anywhere. After 20.30 at the w/ends there is live music. **$$**

✗ **Graniko** At the far end of Star Dojran; ☎ 225 166; ⏱ 11.00–23.00 daily. With a lovely terrace overlooking the lake, offering traditional food. **$$**

✗ **Kaldrma** Just inside the road sign for Nov Dojran on the Star Dojran side of town; ☎ 277 122; ⏱ 11.00–23.00 daily. Its upstairs dining area commands great views of the lake & the mountains. Has basic local food & a variety of lake fish. If you like crunchy deep-fried fish, try the *perkija* (redfin). **$$**

WHAT TO SEE AND DO Star Dojran was largely destroyed during World War I and hence Nov Dojran sprang up. The **old clock tower** and the **Turkish baths** can still be seen in the backstreets of the Star Dojran. At the northern end of Star Dojran are the tall ruins of the **Sv Ilija Church**. Almost completely destroyed in World War I, it now has a new roof and is slowly undergoing renovation. **Dorjan Museum** (☎ 225 277; e infocentar@doijran-info.com; www.dojran-info.com), specialising in the flora, fauna and structure of Lake Dojran, is in the tiny town hall opposite the Hotel Makedonija. The lake with its **abundant wildlife** (take the *Bradt Guide to Central and Eastern European Wildlife* with you) can be enjoyed from both villages.

The World War I **Dojran battlefield** on Pip Ridge above Star Dojran is the main attraction for military buffs. Macedonia is mostly associated today with the Yugoslav conflict of the 1990s. Few now remember its part in the World War I Salonica Front, also known as the Macedonia Front, and even at the time better known as the 'forgotten front'. 'Muckydonia', as it was known in a theatre performance held by British troops in the Balkans during the war, was too small for the headline news, yet troops on the Salonika front suffered the fog of war as much as troops in Flanders, the Somme or Verdun. Casualties were born from poor communications, malaria was endemic and life behind the lines (unlike in France and Belgium) was woefully unexciting. From 1915–18, the British were held up in trenches to the southeast of Dojran whilst the Germans and Bulgarians held the northwest (see box above). In addition to almost 10,000 men dying in combat (the majority of whom were British), many men died of malaria in the much marshier conditions of a century ago.

WINNING THE DEVIL'S EYE

Abridged text from the panel boards at Kale Tepe memorial site.

The World War I Salonica Front stretched from the Gulf of Orfano in the east to Ohrid in the west, traversing variously Dojran, Strumica, Gevgelia, Prilep, Kruševo and even touching Skopje. The British offensive lay at Dojran from 1915–18, with the decisive battle of September 1918 fought by the 22 Division (UK) and the Serres Division (GR) on the Allied side. Most of 22 Division was drafted from Wales and northern England, with a few chance volunteers from elsewhere. After tragic losses, 22 Division survivors erected a memorial to their fallen comrades shortly after the war at the strong point and observation position they fought so hard to attain, which was known then as the Devil's Eye on top of Kale Tepe, or the Grand Couronne.

OPEN TO THE PUBLIC The original memorial was rediscovered among thick undergrowth and vegetation in 2007. To mark the 90th anniversary of the end of World War I, the British Embassy in Skopje, in conjunction with the Municipality of Dojran, placed a replica memorial, inspired by the original, on the site. After sweeping for unexploded ordnance by the Directorate for Protection and Rescue, the area around the memorial was cleared of undergrowth and a path and benches prepared by the Dojran Municipality. Panel boards depicting the battle at Dojran have been erected, and the original memorial can still be seen, with the new memorial above it.

The hollow in front of the 22 Division memorial represents part of a large bunker that has been demolished. Other bunkers and positions stood to the east and north, parts of which can be seen today. The bunker complex at the memorial site served a supply and command system of trenches and defences. It was known to the Bulgarians as the Ferdinand and was so named to commemorate the Bulgarian victory of 1915. Images from the time clearly show the memorial fountain, which is passed on entering the newly reopened site. Dugouts and other strong points can also be seen from there.

WHAT HAPPENED AT DOJRAN In 1914, what was later to become the territory of the Republic of Macedonia was part of Serbia and was allied to Britain and France. Austro-Hungarian and German military divisions found Serbia more difficult to conquer than they had imagined, and by early 1915 they were encouraging Bulgaria, with the promise of territorial gains, to join them. On 21 September 1915 Bulgaria mobilised its forces on the border. On 11 October 1915 the Bulgarian army began their drive towards Skopje, splitting the Serbian army in two, part of which began to retreat towards Albania and the west and part of which began to retreat towards Greece and the south.

It's a 90-minute hike to the memorial at the Grand Couronne, unless the weather is dry enough to take a jeep (which it is not most of the year, and the track is too muddy even for 4x4). Stone and rock trenches and old bunkers line the hills above the memorial, which fittingly is dotted with poppies (also Macedonia's national flower) in the summer. In addition to the UK memorial to 22 Division, there is a Bulgarian water fountain dedicated to their fallen at this site. The water is fresh, sweet and plentiful. A mountain hut has been started there, but is yet to be completed.

In order to support Serbia and try and stem the retreat, the French and British landed in Salonica (Thessaloniki) and marched north. French forces marched up the Vardar Valley as far as Veles, while the British 10 (Irish) Division marched towards Strumica forming a defensive line between Kosturino and Prstan. The amassed, well-trained Bulgarian, Austrian and German forces were unstoppable and forced the French onto the defensive to cover the retreat of the Serbs. Meanwhile, 10 Division fought fiercely in the east in a series of battles between 7 and 10 December 1915 to cover the eastern flanks of the Serbian and French withdrawal.

The Bulgarian army, in pursuit of the British and French, then occupied the southern border area and proceeded to dig in. They fortified the hills above Dojran with a well-planned system of redoubts, concrete observation positions, bunkers and machine-gun nests, the remains of which are clearly visible today.

There were two main battles in the hills above Dojran; the first in the spring of 1917 was a failure. The second battle of Dojran took place on 18 and 19 September 1918, as part of a co-ordinated assault and succeeded in tying down Bulgarian reserves so that they could not be deployed to fight the French and Serbians to the west. Following the successful breakthrough by the French and the Serbs to the west, the Bulgarian forces above Dojran retreated, leaving their positions here deserted save for British troops moving up in pursuit.

AN ICOFORT SITE There is growing international concern about the preservation and conservation of both military archaeology and what are known as 'landscapes of conflict'. In 2005 the International Council on Monuments and Sites (ICOMOS) created a subcommittee, the International Scientific Committee on Fortifications and Military Heritage (IcoFort), specifically tasked with dealing with the preservation of military archaeology and advising UNESCO. Much of what is termed military archaeology is encompassed by existing international conventions and European treaties on archaeology and heritage and in principle they are afforded the same status for preservation as would older remains, such as historic places of worship, historic buildings and other archaeological sites.

Macedonia is rich in landscapes of conflict from mid 19 century through to World War II. Dojran itself was not only a site of conflict, but also part of the physical remains of a momentous point in European and world history, one which led, ultimately, to the creation of modern Europe. It is part of a wider and very well-preserved landscape of conflict across the entire Salonica Front, with trenches and redoubts, bunkers and machine-gun nests, foxholes and shell craters all still visible in the undergrowth and largely untouched by modern-day development.

Although Dojran Municipality opened up the battlefield in 2008, it remains a difficult site to access. At the time of writing there were no signposts, and even with a 1:25,000 map (sheet 784-3-2 available from www.katastar.gov.mk) and excellent navigations skills it is easy to get lost on Pip Ridge (as many did in World War I). In addition, walking restrictions are often imposed in the summer due to the risk of wildfires (which sweep through the area most summers), and illegal loggers and their pursuant forestry patrol can cause the unannounced hiker considerable hassle. For a hassle-free and informative day, mountain guides Gele and Bingo of Salonika

Battlefield Tours (see page 297) can arrange a guided tour for approximately €25 per person (excluding travel and subsistence, and depending on any research requests you may have). Books and web resources on the Dojran battlefield are listed in *Appendix 4*.

The site is once again becoming overgrown due to lack of funding for maintenance. If you can help, please contact Salonika Battlefield Tour.

10

A Dozen Hikes

We descended to the Dibra–Gostivar road, climbed to the Bistra Plateau, descended to the Dibra–Kicevo road and climbed again in the direction of Struga and Lake Ochrid … On the 20th we camped in some beautiful high meadows with views of splendid mountains stretching in every direction …

Reginald Hibbert, *Albania, Macedonia and the British Military Missions*, 1943 and 1944 (from *The New Macedonia Question*, edited by James Pettifer, 1999)

Macedonia is brimming with beautiful countryside that makes splendid hiking for a range of fitness and experience levels. There are several multi-day hikes, including two 200km hikes from Ljuboten to Struga along the border with Albania (permit still required) and from the capital Skopje to the beautiful Lake Ohrid. There are also many shorter hikes of an hour or less to waterfalls, caves, glacial lakes, hidden monasteries, or other points of interest.

The **Macedonian Mountaineering and Sports Federation** (*MMSF, 11 Oktomvri 42a, 1000 Skopje;* \ *02 3165 540;* e *contact@fpsm.org.mk; www.fpsmf.org.mk*) are starting to put together hiking booklets and guides in English with an aim to providing western European-standard information on trails and huts. Together with brand-new 1:25,000 hiking maps being published on the whole country by the State Authority for Geodetic Works (see page 76), only a fresh coat of paint on some of the old hiking-trail markings and some much neglected trail maintenance is needed to bring hiking up to the recreational standards enjoyed in the US, and France, Germany or elsewhere in western Europe.

Other guidebooks are available in Macedonian. However, even if you can read Macedonian, information on how to get to the trailhead, good route descriptions, a basic route map, water supply locations, etc are somewhat obscure, never mind grid references. Admittedly grid references were difficult to give when maps were once a state secret and only officers were taught how to read them!

This chapter offers information on 12 hikes of differing grades to whet your appetite. More routes are available at www.summitpost.org (type in the name of a mountain peak or hut) and at www.mkdmount.org, including GPS tracks, huts and further links. As with mountaineering anywhere in the world, respect the terrain and know your own limits especially if you intend to venture out without a guide. (See *Chapter 2*, page 83, for *Health and safety in the mountains*.) If you would like a guide and none of the clubs below can help, then Macedonia Travel (*www.macedoniatravel.com*) in Skopje or **Dea Tours** (*www.deatours.com.mk*) in Ohrid can arrange multi-day hikes starting from €195 depending on the number of hikers, length of tours and type of accommodation.

For more on where and how to buy maps, and the peculiarities of the new Macedonian maps, see page 76.

HIKING CLUBS

There are over 70 hiking clubs in Macedonia, some more active than others. You'll find somebody who speaks English at most of these clubs. A few are listed here, and are mentioned in relevant sections throughout this guidebook. For a complete list of all the clubs contact MMSF (see above).

Makedon Planinarski Klub m 076 456 056 (for English-speaking club president Iskra Gerazova); e kps@makedon.mk; www.makedon. mk. This new, young club meets every Wed at 20.00, at the faculty of mechanical engineering in Skopje (barrack No 5).

Korab Planinarski Klub m 071 564 086; e contact@korab.org.mk (for English-speaking club secretary Slobodan); www.korab.org. mk (inc their annual programme in English). Based in Skopje, the club's weekly meet takes place at the Sports Association Hall at Jordan Hadžikonstantinov-Džinot 12a (↘ 02 3117 687, 02 3227 672). Their national day (8 Sep) annual hike is to Mt Korab.

Ljuboten Planinarski Klub m 075 649 393 (for English-speaking club president Jovan Božinovski); e jovan@pkljuboten.org.mk; www.sharamountainguide.com.mk. Based in Tetovo, the club's national day hike is along the River Pena to Lešnica Waterfall. Their website highlights a number of hiking options in the Šar Mountains, & their costs include a guide.

MOUNTAIN HUT SYSTEM

Serving the needs of the clubs and individuals is an extensive system of over 30 mountain huts in Macedonia. Although most of these rarely require you to book ahead, it is best to phone before arrival as some are only staffed if they know there will be overnight visitors. The huts offer clean sheets in a dormitory bed space, and cost around 300MKD for the night. This does not include food and most huts offer only small snacks and drinks, so bring your own food. For a full list of huts see www.mkdmount.org/planinarski_domovi/refuges.html. Here is a list of most of the huts (called *planinarski dom* in Macedonian).

OUTSIDE SKOPJE

🏠 **Dare Džambaz** (25 beds) ↘ 02 3164 365; hut warden: Živko Temelkoski m 070 220 166; location: 1,066m, peak of Mt Vodno, south of Skopje.

🏠 **Karadžica** (50 beds) m 070 238 736; hut warden: Gospodin Časlav; location: 1,450m on Karadžica Mountain above the village of Aldinci, south of Dračevo.

🏠 **Kitka** (60 beds) ↘ 02 3117 100; m 070 246 419; hut warden: Sašo Popovski; location: 1,560m on Kitka Mountain near the village of Crvena Voda. The hut was recently destroyed by fire, but the chalets there are still in use.

VELES AREA

🏠 **Braka Janevi** (30 beds) m 078 492 014, 078 377 135; hut warden and president of Gemidžii Mountineering Club in Veles: Dragan Adamcevski ; location: near the village of Oreov Dol on Babuna Mountain.

🏠 **Čeples** (60 beds) m 070 887 678 for Jovan; m 070 216 059 for Vasko Gjorjievski; location: at 1,445m near the village of Nežilovo on Jakupica Mountain. Eat at the Nežilovo Trout Farm (↘ 043 811 812; m 070 594 682) on the way up or down to the hut. There is also a hotel by the farm where you can stay for 400MKD per night.

🏠 **Papradište** (30 beds) ↘ 043 211 411; m 075 757 297; hut warden Igor; location: the old school house, 1,000m, in Papradište village.

🏠 **Šeškovo** (50 beds) ↘ 043 413 639 for Ljupčo Binov, the president of Mountaineering Club Orle who run the hut; hut warden: Momčilo Gjorgjevik; location: near the village of Šeškovo, southwest of Lake Tikveš & Kavadarci.

🏠 **Strovje** (12 beds) m 072 212 264; hut warden: Stevče Čubrinovski; location: the village of Gostiraznik, near Bogomila.

STRUMICA AREA

Ezero (20 beds) 034 325 282 for hut warden Krume, 043 343 122 for Ilija or Lenče Končaliev of Mountaineering Club Ezero who run the hut; location: on Lake Vodoča near the village of Popčevo, southwest of Strumica.

Dedo Kožjo Murtinski (10 beds) m 070 535 688; hut warden: Vasko; location: 1,160m on Belasica Mountain near Strumica.

Gorna (30 beds) 034 178 150; hut warden: Slave Spasov; location: 1,420m on Pljačkovica Mountain near Radoviš.

Šarena Češma (16 beds) Contact details as for Dedo Kožjo Murtinski above; location: 1,300m near Šarena springs on Belasica Mountain near Strumica.

Vrteška (64 beds) m 070 210 063; hut warden: Sanev Aleksandar; location: on Plačkovica Mountain.

POPOVA ŠAPKA

SaraSki (14 beds) m 070 533 303; hut warden: Ilija; location: next to the church on Popova Sapka.

Smreka (100 beds) 02 3221 350; m 070 641 998; hut warden: Zoran Kostadinovski; location: ski resort of Popova Šapka.

NORTHEAST

Divlje (20 beds) 02 2781 686; hut warden: Mijalčo Nikolov; location: near the village of Divlje, east of Katlanovo.

Kozjak (15 beds) 031 430 990; hut warden: Momšilo Jakimovski; location: near the village of Malotino, northeast of Kumanovo, towards Prohor Pčjinski.

Pojak Kalman (22 beds) 031 373 216 for hut warden Ljubiša Ivanovski, or 031 430 990 or m 075 591 990 for Martin Veličkovski; location: near the village of Dejlovce, northeast of Kumanovo, south of Mt Peren.

Toranica (15 beds) as above; hut warden: Stojko Velkovski; location: near the village of Kostur, east of Kriva Palanka.

BABA MOUNTAIN

Golemo Ezero (50 beds) Lies 600m below Pelister peak at 2,225m. To arrange an overnight stay contact Petar Nolev m 075 458 782. Staffed at w/ends in summer only. No food available. Water & washing facilities are outside.

Kopanki (110 beds) 1,630m Mount Baba; m 075 458 782; hut warden: Petar Nolev. Serves food & drink (inc alcohol); washing facilities are indoors; TV & video available. A very popular outing for Bitolites & local people.

Neolica (48 beds) m 078 851 396; hut warden: Jovan Cvetkoski; location: 1,440m on the east side of Mt Baba. Or contact Slobodan Lazarevič, president of the Gjorgji Naumov Mountaineering Club to book ahead: 047 242 879. Staffed during the w/ends.

GOSTIVAR-KIČEVO

Sarski Vodi (8 beds) 042 214 505; m 070 298 757; hut warden: Gojko Gegovski; location: near the village of Gorno Jelovce, west of Gostivar.

Tajmište (40 beds) m 072 212 264; hut warden: Stevče Čubrinovski; location: near the village of Tajmište, northwest of Zajas, Kičevo.

1 VODNO CROSS TO MATKA DAM

Distance	10.5km (18km from the centre of Skopje)
Altitude	Skopje 245m, Sredno Vodno 600m, Vodno Cross 1,066m, Matka 310m
Rating	Moderate: ridge walk followed by steep downhill section
Timing	4 hours (+2 hours from Sredno Vodno to Vodno Cross)
In reverse	Possible, better light for taking photographs of the lake if starting from Matka, but more dramatic to end at Matka and then eat a late lunch afterwards
Trailhead	Taxi or hike to Sredno Vodno, then hike to Vodno Cross or during the week a taxi can take you to the Cross
Accommodation	Dare Džambaz mountaineering hut (see page 322) at Vodno Cross; Hotel Vodno (✆ 02 3178 866); Skopje town; Matka mountaineering hut (✆ 02 205 2655)
Map	1:25,000 SAGW Map Sheets Matka 731-2-1 and Skopje 731-2-2, January 2007. See page 154 for sketch map.

ROUTE DESCRIPTION The route is west-southwest along Vodno ridge and mostly gently downhill for about the first 7km. The last 3.5km is a steep descent, which ends with terrific views of the lake and a small boat crossing to reach Matka Hut and Sveta Andreja Monastery. The route is well marked until the last 4km when the trail veers off into the woods and is lost in overgrown fields and poor markings. For good orienteers with GPS, there is a detailed route card opposite. Grid bearings are not given here due to the lack of reliable mapping available at the time of writing. For the less orienteering-savvy, take a guide, such as one from **Korab Mountaineering Club** (m 071 564 086; e contact@korab.org.mk), where the club secretary, Slobodan, can set you up with a guide.

For a description of the route from Skopje to Sredno Vodno and to Vodno Cross see page 156.

Bring plenty of water for this hike as there is none along the way once you leave Vodno Cross until you reach the spring at Leg 10, some 7km into the hike and halfway down the other side. Hikers have been known to suffer from heat exhaustion hiking this route in the summer. If the Dare Džambaz Hut is (unusually) shut, there is signage for a tap pointing around the back of the cross. In fact it is for a spring that is very difficult to find unless somebody shows it to you.

Matka Hut serves refreshments year round, and the Restoran Peštera (see page 160) and other restaurants at Matka dam serve good traditional food. For details on getting there and back see page 148.

START POINT: DARE DŽAMBAZ HUT AT VODNO CROSS 1,066M

Leg	From Grid	Distance/ Time	To Grid	Height
1	332 468	approx 3km/40mins	3045 4658	907m

Starting at Dare Džĺambaz Hut at Vodno Cross – tank hideouts to left, right track goes to Krušopek. Continue straight on.

| 2 | 3045 4658 | approx 2.8km/40mins | 2812 4588 | 898m |

To this point is easy, frequently marked with fresh red-and-white paint along an easy trail. This point is the first key turn in the entire route, and turns SSW off main track into woods between recently burnt and cut-down trees. At the turning point there is a faded red-and-white mark on a pine tree. From here on the path is marked but infrequently, with faded paint and the path is often not visible for several metres ahead.

| 3 | 2812 4588 | 250m | 2780 4567 | 908m |

Top of small wooded hill

| 4 | 2780 4567 | 250m | 2756 4563874m | |

Bottom of hill, no trees, bear left along wide track for 50m then turn right up hill along small track

| 5 | 2756 4563 | 800m | 2710 4547 | 880m |

Alpine field

| 6 | 2710 4547 | 100m | 2695 4545 | 889m |

Follow ridge line SW

| 7 | 2695 4545 | 150m | 2678 4524 | 888m |

Turn W down gully

| 8 | 2678 4524 | 400m | 2653 4532 | 836m |

Turn NW down track (to right)

| 9 | 2653 4532 | 900m | 2618 4590 | 732m |

Turn W off the track

| 10 | 2618 4590 | 500m | 2605 4587 | 700m |

Spring running into a concrete container

| 11 | 2605 4587 | 400m | 2586 4542 | 488m |

Fork in the track; up to Sv Nikola Church (recommended), or down to the bottom of Matka dam

| 12 | 2586 4542 | 200m | 2564 4538 | 598m |

Sv Nikola Church. From here descend to the lake and sound the gong for a boatman to fetch you from the hut across the lake.

| 13 | 2564 4538 | 900m | 2525 4520 | 310m |

End Destination: Matka Hut (☏ 02 205 2655) and Sv Andrea Church

2 MARKO'S TOWER TO TRESKAVEC MONASTERY

Distance	6.5km
Altitude	Prilep town centre 640m, Markovi Kuli 945m, Treskavec Monastery 1,260m
Rating	Easy to moderate
Timing	2½ hours
Circular trail	Possible
Trailhead	Train or bus to Prilep, taxi or hike to Markovi Kuli entrance
Accommodation	Prilep town (page 223); Treskavec Monastery (page 228)
Map	1:25,000 SAGW Map Sheet Prilep 782-1-3, January 2007

ROUTE DESCRIPTION There are three routes to the monastery.

Route 1 By foot from Markovi Kuli (for directions to Markovi Kuli see page 226). This is the easiest route and is well trodden and relatively well marked by red-and-white hiking marks, paintings of saints, and a spring just over halfway along the route. Part of the hike is along some steep rocks, but the way is aided by a steel rope. The rocks along all three routes are what make Prilep's scenery famous.

Route 2 By foot along the old cobbled road from Dabnica. This route is only 4.5km if you take a taxi through the disgracefully neglected Roma slums of Prilep to within 1km of Dabnica. It is steeper over the shorter distance, however. Your hike begins when the road is no longer fenced off on the left and comes to the obvious opening onto the foothills of Zlatovrv. At the end of the fence there is another dirt track to the left leading to a nearby house. The cobbled path you require, which is not obvious at first, heads straight up the ridge of the spur leading up to Zlatovrv. It lies directly between where the dirt track divides, and if you have a compass, set it to 6,000 mils or 340° and follow this bearing until you come across the obvious path uphill. After an hour, the path, with large chunks of cobbling still intact, starts to wind back and forth and comes upon a water fountain. From the fountain the path is practically straight until you get to the back gate of the monastery. Follow the path around to the left and to the front of the monastery. If you drive yourself to the start point of the hike, then head west through the Roma settlement (ask for Dabnica).

Route 3 By 4x4 or foot along a dirt track to the southwest. To reach the dirt track head out of Prilep on Marksova and Orde Čopela, past the Tobacco Institute and Museum, and turn towards the town cemetery 5km from the centre of town. Follow the road left around to the back of the cemetery. At the junction where you lose the tarmac (500m from the main road) is a small sign, marked Monastir Sveta Bogorodica, Treskavec, pointing the way straight ahead. After another 2.5km turn right when you join another track through the valley, then left after another 250m. Follow this road uphill to the monastery in about 3km.

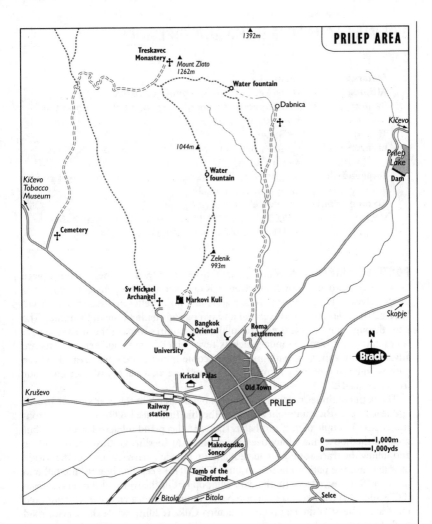

PRILEP AREA

1392m

Treskavec
Monastery ✝ ▲ Mount Zlato
                 1262m

Water fountain ○

Dabnica ○
✝

Kičevo

Prilep
Lake

Dam

1044m ▲

Water
fountain ○

Kičevo
Tobacco
Museum

Cemetery ✝

▲ Zelenik
 993m

Sv Michael
Archangel ✝

▥ Markovi Kuli

Skopje

Bangkok
Oriental ✗

Roma
settlement

N

University ●

Bradt

Kristal Palas 🏛

Kruševo

Old Town

PRILEP

Railway
station

0 ━━━━━ 1,000m
0 ━━━━━ 1,000yds

Makedonsko
Sonce ●

Tomb of the
undefeated ●

↙ Bitola   ← Bitola

Selce

3 DEMIR KAPIJA TO IBERLIJA AND KOREŠNICA

Distance	12km
Altitude	Demir Kapija 110m, Silananba Čuka 620m
Rating	Easy to moderate: short, steep wooded section at the summit
Timing	5–6 hours
In reverse	Possible, but more difficult to get a taxi back to Demir Kapija
Trailhead	Bus or train to Demir Kapija village, taxi to stopping place in the Iron Gate tunnel
Accommodation	Popova Kula Winery (see page 312)
Map	1:25,000 SAGW Map Sheets Demir Kapija West 783-1-2 and Demir Kapija East 783-2-1, January 2007

ROUTE DESCRIPTION A good summer hike directly from the stopping place between the two rock towers of Demir Kapija tunnel. The path goes along the canyon stream that created the rock feature and flows between them into the River Vardar. The sides are almost vertical and offer good shade in the hot summer. The path through the canyon is easy to follow but requires fording the stream several times in the first 1km, so sandals such as Tevas which have a good grip in water are advisable. Thereafter the path and stream come into a more open area where the path is wider and used by farm vehicles from **Čelevec** village (just over one hour from trailhead).

The path continues northeast alongside big boulders in the ever smaller stream and leads up to the mountain village of **Iberlija** (grid 0821 8997, two hours from trailhead). A couple of very old *babas* still tend sheep and tobacco leaves here, but most of the houses have long been abandoned. At Iberlija, go through the village and follow the track round to the west and up a steep narrow ravine. As the trickle of water and the path seem to run out (0759 9040) keep heading up the hill and in 30 to 40 minutes from Iberlija you will pop out of the brush at the service road (0674 9045 dirt track) for the water pipes feeding Korešnica village. A few hundred metres southeast is the trig point Silananba Čuka (620m), while the service road back to Korešnica heads off to the southwest. Some two to three hours gently downhill will lead you to the village shop where you can get refreshments and phone for a taxi to take you back to Demir Kapija.

For details on how to get to Demir Kapija and back, and for taxi contact details, see page 312. The best (and very popular) wine hotel in Macedonia, **Popova Kula**, offers rooms above Demir Kapija.

There is much more hiking to be had higher up the Čevlečka River, including to the ruined fortress of Prosek. To the southeast of Demir Kapija, towards the new ski resort Kožuf on the border with Greece, are some of Macedonia's many caves including the beautiful Golem Zmejovec (large dragon) and Mal Zmejovec (small dragon). Hiking the old road and railway on the right bank of the Vardar is also pleasant. The Demir Kapija canyon is home to some rare birds of prey including the griffon vulture *(Gyps fulvus)*, Egyptian vulture *(Neophron percnopterus)*, golden eagle *(Aquila chrysaetos)*, harrier eagle *(Circaetus gallicus)*, foxy buzzard *(Buteo rufinus)* and various falcons *(Falco peregrinus, Falco naumanni)*.

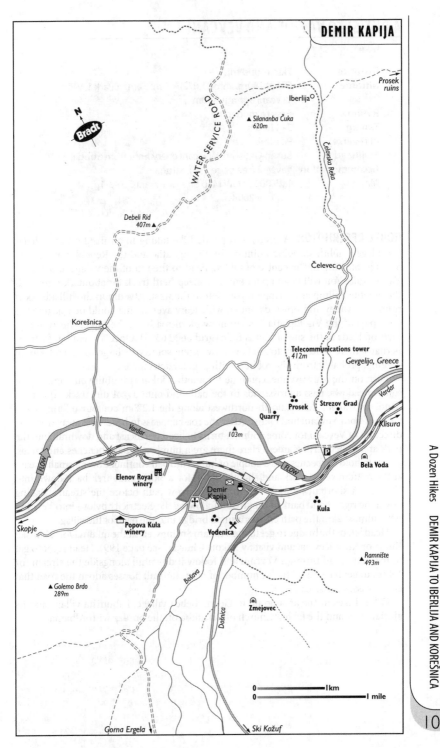

DEMIR KAPIJA

Prosek ruins

Iberlija

▲ Silananba Čuka
620m

WATER SERVICE ROAD

Čelovska Reka

Debeli Rid
407m ▲

Čelevec

Korešnica

Telecommunications tower
412m

Gevgelija, Greece

Vardar

Prosek

Strezov Grad

Quarry

Klisura

▲ 103m

FLOW

FLOW

Vardar

P

Bela Voda

Elenov Royal winery

Demir Kapija

Skopje

Kula

Popova Kula winery

Vodenica

Ramnište
493m

▲ Golemo Brdo
289m

Bošava

Došnica

Zmejovec

0 _____ 1km

0 _____ 1 mile

Gorna Ergela

Ski Kožuf

4 OKTISI TO VAJTOS AND VEVČANI

Distance	7km round trip
Altitude	Oktisi 780m, Varoš 1,072m, Crni Kamen Park 1,195m, Vevčani Springs 910m
Rating	Easy to moderate
Timing	3–4 hours
In reverse	Possible
Trailhead	Bus to Oktisi and Vevčani every hour from Struga
Accommodation	Vevčani (see page 199); Struga
Map	1:25,000 SAGW Map Sheet Vevčani 780-3-1, January 2007

ROUTE DESCRIPTION A pretty and gentle hike taking in a mixed ethnic village, the alleged eighth stopping point of the Via Egnatia, and the Republic of Vevčani Springs. Starting in the centre of Oktisi, head to the top of the village and ask for Vajtos Kale. You will head up an eroding sheep herd track for about 1km towards the obvious hilltop appearing on your left to the west. At a dip in the hillside, skirt round the valley and upwards onto a wide leafy avenue that could be imagined as once part of the Via Egnatia Roman network of roads. At the top of the avenue, a turn-off leads to the site of Vajtos Kale (grid 6600 6525). Once a Paeonian fortress, perhaps, there is little left to see here now except some very large rocks and a lot of digging, probably from site robbers with a metal detector.

Back on the leafy avenue, continue for another kilometre until you come out to some meadows, pass a crossroads in the path and onto a 4x4 dirt track. This road winds its way for 1.5km north-northwest along the 1,220m contour offering good views of both Vevčani and Oktisi. After the road appears to head west away from the direction of Vevčani for some 350m, it turns to head northeast and downhill into the park area called Crni Kamen. Here there are a number of park benches and tables, places to hold barbecues and a couple of huts. The road continues over a small stream at the bottom of the park and slightly uphill for a 3km gentle trek back down into Vevčani. A shortcut by foot is to follow a narrow path before the stream heading down the right-hand bank of the stream following the electricity pylons into Vevčani. After almost 2km the path crosses a small bridge into the back of the village.

Head left of the bridge to get to the Vevčani Springs, eat at the quaint Domakjinska Kukja or Kutmičevica, and visit Sv Nikola Church (see page 199). Head right to get to the main road through Vevčani and follow it downhill alongside the stream for 1.4km to get back to Oktisi. A number of old watermill houses adorn the road that criss-crosses the stream.

Other hikes in the area go up to Gorna Belica village, Labuništa village and its glacial lakes and the fabled Church of Perumba on the border with Albania.

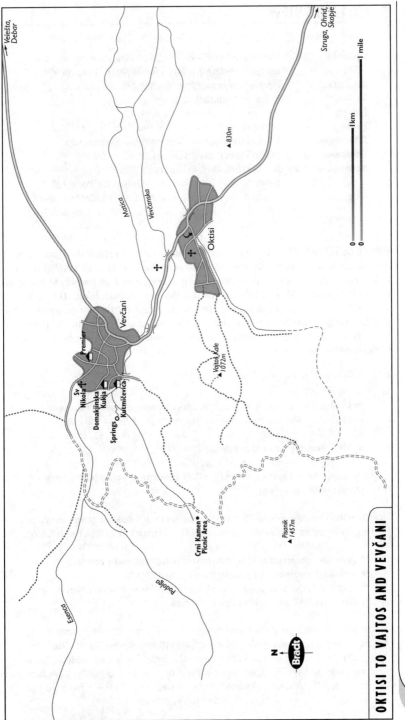

OKTISI TO VAJTOS AND VEVČANI

5 TWO LAKES VIEW

Distance	3km north to Galičica 1,985m; 3.5km south to Albanian border ridgeline 2,100m, a further 3km along the ridge
Altitude	Lipova Livada saddle 1,568m to highest point on Galičica range in Macedonia 2,275m
Rating	Easy to moderate: initially steep
Timing	To the viewpoint: north 1½ hours; south 2–3 hours
Alternative	2 hours to Bugarska Čuka from the plateau road
Trailhead	Bus to Trpejca, taxi to Lipova Livada
Accommodation	Bed and breakfast in Trpejca (✆ 070 261 751); Hotel Sveti Naum (page 180); camping in Ljubaništa (page 180)
Map	1:25,000 SAGW Map Sheets Ohrid 780-4-3, Gorno Dupeni 780-4-4, Ljubaništa 830-2-1, Oteševo 830-2-2, January 2007

ROUTE DESCRIPTION The route north is a steep climb to reach the Galičica peak (grid 8629 3648). It is the shortest route to gain the view of both Lake Ohrid and Lake Prespa. From Galičica peak, there is a good ridge walk all the way to Bugarska Čuka (5km, grid 8751 4018) that maintains the view of both lakes. The easier but slightly longer climb is to the south. This route is also to the highest point on the Galičica range inside Macedonia. The route is obvious at the bottom and peters out towards the top, but head towards the summit where you can see both lakes and then along the ridge.

NAISMITH'S RULE

When planning a hike, it is useful to apply Naismith's rule – rule of thumb developed by Scottish hiker, William Naismith, in 1892.

THE RULE The basic rule is as follows:

Allow one hour for every 5km (3 miles) forward, plus 1½ hours for every 300m (1,000ft) of ascent.

Over the years the rule has been expanded and the following can generally be applied – assuming you are carrying a well packed rucksack, allow one hour for:

- 5km easy going (on a road, flat/paved path, bridleway, etc)
- 3km easy scrambling (walking through fields, etc)
- 1.5km in extreme rough country (deep sand, snow, howling blizzard, etc)
- For every 5 hours walking due to fatigue

In addition, on a gentle decline (about 5–12°), subtract 10 minutes per 300m, of descent. On a steep decline (over 12°), add 10 minutes per 300m of descent.
    Very experienced walkers can lower the total time by one-third. If your party contains very inexperienced walkers or young children, the rules may be optimistic. Always calculate for the slowest walker. These rules do not include breaks, which must be added to the calculation.

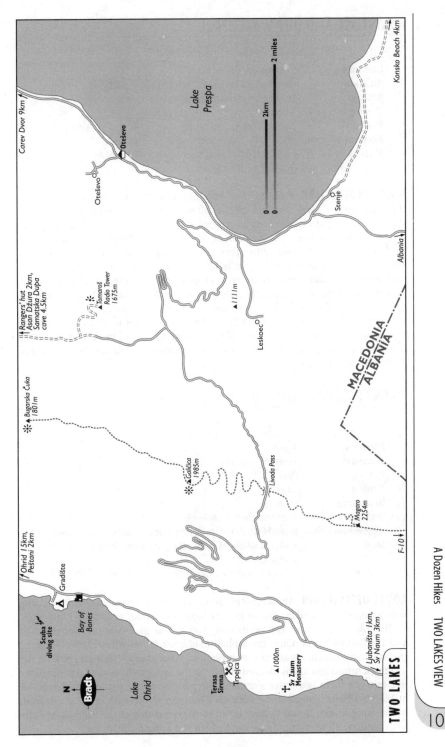

6 ROSTUŠE AND DUF WATERFALL

Distance	5km round trip
Altitude	River Radika bridge to Rostuše 700m, Duf Waterfall 840m
Rating	Easy, but narrow parts with steep drops
Timing	3 hours
Trailhead	Bus to River Radika bridge stop for Rostuše (Debar line)
Accommodation	Hotel Tutto (page 255); Hotel Besa (page 255)
Map	1:25,000 SAGW Map Sheet Debar 730-3-3, January 2010

ROUTE DESCRIPTION From the bus stop hike 1km to the village of Rostuše. At the entrance is a small fountain on the left next to the cemetery. At the back of the cemetery a path leads along an irrigation channel to the waterfall. The more conventional route is to take the route signposted above the church. If taking this route take care to descend rather than take the high road, which becomes very steep and turns into mountain goat tracks. The path along the irrigation ditch is well maintained and scenic. There are bridges at crossing points over the river and benches along the way. The path leads to Rostuše Waterfall 2, which is the most spectacular of all six waterfalls along the Duf ravine. It is not safe to try to access the higher waterfalls from number 2. It is better to attempt to do so by taking the higher path from before Vele Brdo village. The steep sides of the Duf ravine make it difficult to take good photos of the waterfall unless you arrive during midday. Return along the same route.

7 JANČE TO GALIČNIK (WEDDING FESTIVAL)

Distance	4.5km
Altitude	Janče bus stop 660m, Galičnik 1,415m
Rating	Easy
Timing	2 hours
In reverse	Possible
Trailhead	Bus to Janče (Debar line)
Accommodation	Hotel Tutto (page 255); Hotel Neda Galičnik (page 250)
Map	1:25,000 SAGW Map Sheet Lazarapole 730-3-4 January 2010

ROUTE DESCRIPTION An alternative route to see the annual summer wedding festival in mid-July and avoids the hordes taking the tarmac road from Mavrovo.

The hike takes almost two hours and gives spectacular views of Mount Korab and the Radika Valley. Once the asphalt road ends in the village, head left along the 4x4 track that curves around the mountain. After about 45 minutes by foot, the 4x4 track turns right and is blocked off, whilst the footpath heads left. After another five minutes there is a water fountain. The path is mostly shaded and levels out at Markovi Nogi, a small stone site with a foot-size depression in the stone, from where King Marko is said to have flown to the other side of the valley in the late 14th century. Views of the village can be seen just around the corner.

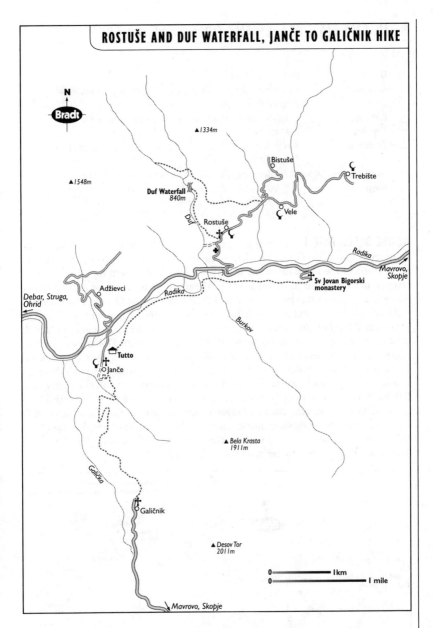

ROSTUŠE AND DUF WATERFALL, JANČE TO GALIČNIK HIKE

N

Bradt

▲1334m

Bistuše

Ç Trebište

▲1548m

Duf Waterfall
840m

Vele

Duf

Rostuše

Radika

Mavrovo,
Skopje

Adžievci

Radika

Sv Jovan Bigorski
monastery

Debar, Struga,
Ohrid

Burkov

Tutto

Jančе

▲ Bela Krasta
1911m

Galička

Galičnik

▲ Desov Tor
2011m

0 ——— 1km
0 ——— 1 mile

Mavrovo, Skopje

Note that Galičnik is accessible by public transport only in the summer. You can order a taxi at Hotel Neda to take you back down to Mavrovo or it is a beautiful 15km hike along the Mavrovo plateau and down to the lake. Alternatively, take the ski lifts down (even in the summer) if they are working (usually at the weekends).

8 BILJANA WATERFALLS AND DOLNA ALILICA CAVE

Distance	8km round trip
Altitude	Tresonče 1,005m, Alilica Cave 1,268m, Biljana Waterfall 2 1,296m
Rating	Easy: last 200m to the waterfall is impassable after rain
Timing	3–4 hours
Trailhead	Bus to Tresonče/Gari/Lazaropole stop (Debar line), taxi to Tresonče (12km)
Accommodation	Hotel Kalin (page 252); Hotel Besa (see page 255)
Map	1:25,000 SAGW Map Sheets Lazaropole 730-3-4 and Bistra 730-4-3, January 2010

ROUTE DESCRIPTION The ride to Tresonče along the pretty Mala Reka in the summer is beautiful. From the village church head along the valley and the 4x4 route through the meadows along the river. After about 1.5km the road becomes steeper, narrower and more damaged, making it difficult even for a 4x4 to pass. There is a spring at this point. Another 1.5km takes you to Obesen Izvor, a small waterfall-like spring on the right-hand north bank of the Tresončka River. There is also a small hut here for wood cutters and water service tools. A single-track path continues another 500m along sometimes slippery rocks to Dolna Alilica Cave, again on the north bank. Some large branches across the now narrow river will aid you across it. Hiking poles are useful at this stage. If you don't have a torch there are usually church candles on either side of the entrance, but you will need your own lighter. While the entryway is small and requires a bit of crouching, it is possible to stand up towards the rear. Back outside, it is only 200m or so to Biljana Waterfall 2, but this is difficult to negotiate unless it is the end of the summer and the water level is low. To reach the remaining ten waterfalls a higher path needs to be taken from Tresonče village. Access to the higher waterfalls is difficult.

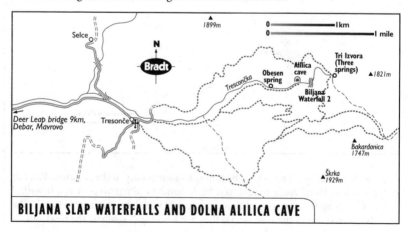

BILJANA SLAP WATERFALLS AND DOLNA ALILICA CAVE

Although Macedonia's natural beauties and countryside have long attracted people's interest and desire to go out in the mountains, organised mountaineering in Macedonia did not start until the 1920s. Before that time, visits were mainly organised around religious holidays, where people gathered at the monasteries often located in remote places. Soon after the first mountaineering club was founded in Prilep in 1924, the same initiative followed in other towns. Today's clubs offer weekend trips and courses for their members in a variety of outdoor disciplines: alpinism, speleology, mountaineering, climbing and orienteering. All mountain sports organisations in Macedonia are united under the umbrella of the Macedonian Mountaineering Sports (MMSF – see contact details on page 321). Located in Skopje, they are the contact point for all information and details about visiting the Macedonian mountains. The MMSF supports the protection of nature, mountains and hiking trails in close co-operation with local communities. Besides awareness campaigns and maintenance of mountain trails, MMSF has set up a training centre for professional mountain guides. Members of mountaineering clubs can follow the training for the Mountain Guide A Certificate through which they receive qualifications to guide organised mountain trips. Because of the remoteness of the Macedonian landscape it is highly recommended to make use of experienced mountain guides. If you wish to contact a mountain guide, contact the MMSF.

Another way to get in touch with active members of mountain clubs is to enlist on the forum at www.mkd-mount.org. The forum has over 100 members from inside and outside Macedonia. Although most of the messages are in Macedonian, the webmaster speaks excellent English and one part of the forum is reserved for international guests and questions. The website itself functions as an online magazine for mountaineering activities in Macedonia, of which most of the pages are translated into English.

If you prefer, however, to travel without a guide, there are a couple of ways to find more information. A few descriptions of hikes, and even the GPS co-ordinates of a couple of routes can be found on the website above under 'Mountains/GPS'. MMSF also publish two booklets with a concise description of the most well-known tracks: *The Mountains and the Mountaineering Huts in the Republic of Macedonia* and *Eastern Macedonian Mountaineering Transversal*. The first one covers hikes from all over Macedonia. Unfortunately the booklet lacks good maps and, since most tracks were last marked when Macedonia was still a part of Yugoslavia, only a few of the hikes are described extensively enough to be taken without a mountain guide. The maps in the second booklet are better, although the scale is still fairly large for orientation in an area visited for the first time. The booklet describes the newly marked international hiking trails, which connect with hikes in Bulgaria. In contrast to the more popular mountaineering destinations in western Macedonia, this booklet highlights less trodden trails in the east. A long overdue promotion!

A Dozen Hikes   BILJANA WATERFALLS AND DOLNA ALILICA CAVE

10

9 TITOV VRV

Distance	14km one-way
Altitude	Popova Šapka 1,782m, Titov Vrv 2,748m
Rating	Moderate: lengthy, steep ascent to the summit
Timing	5 hours one-way
Alternative	Return via Kriva Šija Waterfall (see below) possible
Trailhead	Bus or train to Tetovo, taxi to Popova Šapka
Accommodation	Smreka Hut (page 323); B&B at Popova Šapka (page 323)
Map	1:25,000 SAGW Map Sheets Bešala 680-4-3, Tetovo 680-4-4 and Titov Vrv 730-2-1, January 2010

ROUTE DESCRIPTION The fit can achieve the 37km round trip via Kriva Šija Waterfall (see below) in a long day, otherwise keep the hikes separate.

Titov Vrv is the highest mountain completely within Macedonia. Starting from Smreka mountain hut, head towards the top of the ski lifts until you cross the 4x4 track heading southeast. Follow this road just below the 2,000m contour for almost 5km until you reach a ravine. Follow the left/north bank of the ravine along a marked mountaineering path (red and white) in a northeasterly direction. The path crosses the ravine after 2km and heads southwest continuing to rise steeply for another 1.5km. The path then levels out and follows the 2,450m contour line for another 2km and rises onto the saddle southeast of Titov Vrv. From here there is a less trodden path directly to the summit or the well-trodden path heading west around the southern base of Titov Vrv to the shorter ascent to the summit. It's a 28km return hike on this route. A steep drop to the west of Titov Vrv will take you almost 4km to the beautiful Kriva Šija Waterfall (see below).

10 KRIVA ŠIJA WATERFALL

Distance	19km round trip
Altitude	Popova Šapka 1,782m, Kriva Šija Waterfall 1,865m
Rating	Moderate: lengthy, steep ascent to the summit
Timing	7+ hours
Alternative	Continuation over Titov Vrv (see above) possible
Trailhead	Bus or train to Tetovo, taxi to Popova Šapka
Accommodation	Smreka Hut (page 323); B&B at Popova Šapka (page 323)
Map	As above for Titov Vrv

ROUTE DESCRIPTION The hike from Popova Šapka can be shortened considerably if you can take a 4x4 to the end of the northern dirt track where the Lešnica River enters the Pena (the disused homes here were burned down in the 2001 conflict). From there it is a half-hour steep hike along the right/north bank of the Lešnica River to the **Lešnica Waterfall**, or a 1½- to two-hour hike to Kriva Šija Waterfall. The path along the Pena requires you to jump or ford the river several times. Once across the river of the Kriva Šija ravine, the path follows the left/west bank until it plateaus out after almost 3km. The waterfall can be seen across the other side of the alp.

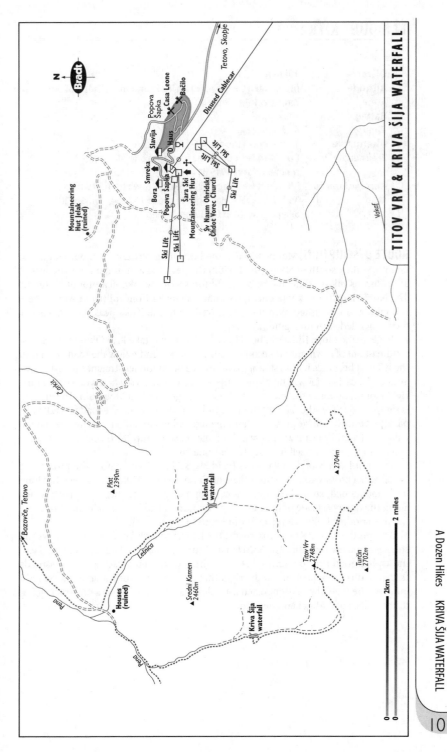

TITOV VRV & KRIVA ŠIJA WATERFALL

11 MOUNT KITKA

Distance	10km round trip
Altitude	Motel Kitka trailhead 903m, Kitka mountain hut 1,320m, Kitka peak 1,675m
Rating	Easy
Timing	4–5 hours
Alternative	14km round trip from Gorno Količani
Trailhead	Bus 74 to Gorno Količani or car/taxi to Motel Kitka trailhead (grid 3935 3140)
Accommodation	Kitka Hut (see page 322); Skopje town (page 134)
Map	1:25,000 SAGW Map Sheet Umovo 731-2-4, January 2010. See pages 144–5 for a sketch map.

ROUTE DESCRIPTION Mount Kitka is the beginning of the next mountain range behind Vodno, south of Skopje. At 1,675m the peak has a mountain hut and lots of adventurous hiking trails in the beautiful forests of the Jakupica mountain range. The No 74 bus from Skopje only goes as far as Gorno Količani (from where there is a faint and unmarked 5km mountain trail up to the Kitka peak, but this is not recommended without a guide).

To get to the Motel Kitka trailhead by car from Skopje, take 11th Oktomvri heading southeast out of town until it becomes Sava Kovačevič and follow the road around to the left as it becomes Ulica 1st Maj (Sava Kovačevič continues straight onto Markova Sušica). Ulica 1st Maj will take you to the village of Dračevo where you should turn right (south) opposite the village petrol station to get to Kitka Mountain. The turning is signposted in Cyrillic for Kitka and the Količani villages, and the road will take you past the Dračevo village graveyard and the red and white radio mast. Just before the village of Dolni Količani are many old marble Muslim gravestones. Keep right when you get to the village itself in order to continue on to Kitka.

The trail from Motel Kitka starts (grid 3935 3140) 200m before the prominent Motel Kitka crossroads after the village of Crvena Voda. Motel Kitka itself has long been abandoned, so no hopes of relaxing on a café terrace there. The path winds along the northeast side of the mountain for 3km to Kitka mountain hut. From the hut it is another 1.5km along a winding path to the summit.

Beyond the Motel Kitka crossroads, the left-hand fork heading east follows the steep Kadina ravine to the Torbeshi (Macedonian Muslim) village of Paligrad. Here the asphalt road runs out and a 4x4 is required to continue. Back at the crossroads there is a dirt track turn-off on the right that is signposted for Karadžica mountain hut, and the road ahead, signposted for Solunska Glava, becomes a dirt track going to the village of Aldinci and beyond.

Distance	12km Brajčino to Golemo Ezero Hut. Another 3km to Malo Ezero or 6km descent to Nižepole. From Malo Ezero 3km to Pelister peak, and another 5km to Hotel Molika.
Altitude	Brajčino 1,020m, Golemo Ezero 2,235m, Malo Ezero 2,250m, Nižepole 1,028m, Pelister peak 2,601m, Molika Hotel 1,400m
Rating	Moderate
Timing	5–7 hours to Golemo Ezero, plus 5–6 hours to Nižepole or Molika
In reverse	Possible
Trailhead	Bus to Brajčino (page 218), taxi to/from Molika or Nižepole
Accommodation	Brajčino (page 218); Golemo Ezero Hut (page 323); Molika Hotel (page 216)
Map	1:50,000 Geomap of Pelister (in Cyrillic); 1:25,000 SAGW Map Sheets Nakolec 831-1-1, Ljubojno 831-1-2 and Kažani 781-3-4, January 2007. See page 217 for a sketch map.

ROUTE DESCRIPTION This is a rewarding hike, which can be attempted in one day for the fit, or broken into two sections by overnighting at Golemo Ezero mountain hut. Taxis to Bitola from Molika can be ordered at the hotel.

The section from Brajčino to Golemo Ezero (Big Lake) has been well marked and several information boards about the surrounding area and wildlife are set at intervals on the way. Golemo Ezero mountain hut sits right on the edge of the waters of this glacial lake and is arguably the most picturesque of all Macdonia's mountain huts. It lies in the shelter of Veternica Peak (2,420m) and surrounding ridges. The original name of the hut is Dime Ilievski after the first and only Macedonian who died climbing Mount Everest, in 1989. Pictures of his life and the Everest expedition adorn the walls of the hut. The most common route to Golemo Ezero and back is from Nižepole although this route is also the steepest.

The ridge hike from Golemo Ezero to Malo Ezero (Little Lake) and along the Pelister Peak is above the treeline and affords beautiful vistas of the mountain range and surrounding countryside. Together the two lakes are called the Eyes of Pelister. Malo Ezero sits in the shelter of Partizanski Vrv (2,349m).

For those who can no longer face the remaining 400m ascent to Mount Pelister, or want a more gentle (and longer) descent to Molika, there is a 4x4 dirt track from Malo Ezero heading west around the next peak of Široko Stapalo (2,435m) and to the west of Pelister. The track heads down through the woods and ends up at the tarmac road just below the hotel.

Otherwise the ascent to Pelister heads north, passing Široko Stapalo and two more ridge peaks before summiting. The return route from Pelister heading northeast to Molika takes in two more panoramic viewpoints at Ilinden (2,542m) and Stiv (2,468m) and then descends into the woods. At the top of the ski lifts, 1km before Hotel Molika, is Kopanki mountain hut. Quite a wide range of food to eat and take away is for sale at Kopanki. The restaurant at Molika is also inviting after a long hike.

A Dozen Hikes   BRAJČINO TO PELISTER LAKES AND NIŽEPOLE

10

MOUNT GOLEM KORAB

At 2,753m, Mount Golem Korab (grid 627 275) is the highest peak touching Macedonia and shares the border with Albania. Mal Korab (2,683m), and beneath it the longest waterfall (138m) in the country, can be seen from the hike. Although permission is no longer required from the Ministry of the Interior Border Police to hike in the border area, it is a good idea to notify the border police hut at the start of the climb, in case of an accident. Once a year Korab Mountaineering Club arrange their annual climb on the weekend closest to Independence Day (8 September). It is a big event attracting over 1,000 hikers from all over the Balkans and further afield. It is usually a long and arduous walk of 25km in nine hours or more, and many enthusiasts go for the day out even if they don't make it to the top. Police escorts, guides and medical staff attend on the day. To find out more, contact Korab's English-speaking secretary, Slobodan (m *071 564 086;* e *contact@korab.org.mk*).

SAGW map sheet 730-1-3 (Korab Sever, 1:25,000, January 2009) covers the hike. Type in 'Korab' at www.summitpost.org for a good route description, photographs and a map.

Appendix 1

LANGUAGE

MACEDONIAN

Pronunciation and transliteration Like most languages (English being the prime exception) Macedonian is pronounced (almost!) exactly as it is written, so once you have mastered the sounds of each letter it is fairly straightforward to pronounce. Verbs are conjugated, but gratefully, unlike Serbian, nouns are not declined. There is no indefinite article, so the word for 'one' is used instead, and the definite article is added at the end of the noun (or adjective if one precedes the noun). There is a formal and informal conjugation of 'you' singular, as in French or Old English, and in this appendix the informal conjugation follows the formal where applicable. There are male, female and neuter genders for nouns, adjectives and verbal conjugations. For more information on the rules of the Macedonian language see Christina Kramer's excellent language book (full reference in *Appendix 4*, page 364).

Finally, a tip on sounding the correct stress on Macedonian words: with the exception of words of foreign origin, stress falls on the antepenultimate (third last) syllable. The stress in words of fewer than three syllables falls on the first or only syllable. The stress in words of foreign origin tends to fall as it would in the native language.

As it is usually too difficult for short-term visitors to learn a new alphabet like Cyrillic, it is not used in this book, but the standard transliteration is. Cyrillic, transliteration and pronunciation are given in the table below.

А	A	as in f<u>a</u>ther	М	M	as in <u>m</u>ade
Б	B	as in b<u>e</u>d	Н	N	as in <u>n</u>ot
В	V	as in <u>v</u>ery	Њ	Nj	as in ca<u>ny</u>on
Г	G	as in <u>g</u>ood	О	O	as in l<u>o</u>t
Д	D	as in <u>d</u>oor	П	P	as in <u>p</u>ut
Ѓ	Gj	as in Ma<u>gy</u>ar	Р	R	as in ma<u>r</u>k
Е	E	as in b<u>et</u>	С	S	as in <u>s</u>it
Ж	Ž	as in plea<u>s</u>ure	Т	T	as in <u>t</u>able
З	Z	as in <u>z</u>oo	Ќ	Kj	as in <u>c</u>ute
Ѕ	Dz	as in ad<u>ds</u>	У	U	as in t<u>oo</u>k
И	I	as in f<u>ee</u>t	Ф	F	as in <u>f</u>arm
Ј	J	as in <u>y</u>oung	Х	H	as in lo<u>ch</u>
К	K	as in <u>k</u>it	Ц	C	as in ca<u>ts</u>
Л	L	as in <u>l</u>og	Ч	Č	as in <u>ch</u>urch
Љ	Lj	as in Anato<u>l</u>ia; soft l pronounced at the back of the mouth	Џ	Dž	as in e<u>dge</u>
			Ш	Š	as in <u>sh</u>ovel

Words and phrases
Courtesies

Hello	*Zdravo*	I'm fine	*Dobro/super*
Goodbye	*Prijatno/čao*	Pleased to meet you	*Milo mi e što se zapoznavme*
Please	*Ve/te molam*		
Thank you	*Blagodaram/fala*	My pleasure	*Milo mi e*
Good morning	*Dobro utro*	Excuse me	*Izvenete*
Good afternoon	*Dobar den*	You're welcome/	*Povelete*
Good evening	*Dobra večer*	help yourself	
Good night	*Dobra nokj*	Welcome!	*Dobredojde!*
How are you?	*Kako ste/si?*		

Basics

yes/no	*da/ne*	excellent/terrible	*odlično/lošo*
OK	*može/važi*	hot/cold	*toplo/ladno*
maybe	*možebi*	toilet	*toalet/WC*
large/small	*golemo/malo*		(pronounced *ve-tse*)
more/less	*povekje/pomalku*	men/women	*maž/žena*
good/bad	*dobro/lošo*		

Basic questions

How?	*Kako?*	Who?	*Koj?*
How do you say in Macedonian?	*Kako se vika na makedonski?*	Why?	*Zošto?*
What?	*Što?*	Do you speak English?	*Zboruvate-li angliski?*
What is that?	*Što e toa?*	Do you understand French/German?	*Razbirate-li francuski/germanski?*
When?	*Koga?*	I do not understand Macedonian	*Ne razbiram makedonski*
When does the shop open/close?	*Koga otvora/zatvora prodavnicata?*	How much does it cost?	*Kolku čini?*
Where?	*Kade?*		
Where is there a telephone?	*Kade ima telefon?*	What time is it?	*Kolku e saat?*
The bill please?	*Smetkata molam?*	Which?	*Koj/koja/koe?*

Essentials

My name is …	*Jas se vikam/Jas sum …*
What is your name?	*Kako se vikaš?*
I am from … Britain/America/Australia	*Jas sum od … Anglija/Amerika/Avstralija*
Please would you speak more slowly	*Ve molam zboruvajte posporo*
What is your telephone number?	*Koj e vašiot telefonski broj?*
What is your address?	*Koja e vašata adressa?*
My address in Britain/America is …	*Mojata adresa vo Velika Britanija/ Amerika e …*
I want to change dollars to denar	*Sakam da smenam dolari vo denari*
How many denar for US$1?	*Kolku denari za eden dolar?*
I need a telephone	*Mi treba telefon*

Numbers

0	*nula*	21	*dvaeset i eden*
1	*eden*	30	*trieset*
2	*dva*	40	*četirieset*

3	tri	50	pedeset
4	četiri	60	šeeset
5	pet	70	sedumdeset
6	šest	80	osumdeset
7	sedum	90	devedeset
8	osum	100	sto
9	devet	200	dvesta
10	deset	300	trista
11	edinaeset	400	četiristo(tini)
12	dvanaest	500	petsto(tini)
13	trinaeset	one thousand	iljada
14	četirinaeset	two thousand	dve iljadi
15	petnaeset	one million	milion
16	šesnaeset	two million	dva milioni
17	sedumnaeset	quarter	četvrt
18	osumnaeset	half	pola/polovina
19	devetnaeset	three-quarters	tri četvrtini
20	dvaeset		

Time

hour	čas/saat	yesterday	včera
minute	minuta	morning	utro
week	nedela/sedmica	afternoon	popladne
day	den	evening	večer
year	godina	night	nokj
month	mesec	already	vekje
today	denes	soon	naskoro
tonight	večerva	now	sega
tomorrow	utre	this week	ovaa nedela
next week	slednata nedela	last week	minatata nedela
in the morning	sabaile	tonight	večerva
Monday	ponedelnik	Friday	petok
Tuesday	vtornik	Saturday	sabota
Wednesday	sreda	Sunday	nedela
Thursday	četvrtok		
January	Januari	July	Juli
February	Fevruari	August	Avgust
March	Mart	September	Septemvri
April	April	October	Oktomvri
May	Maj	November	Noemvri
June	Juni	December	Dekemvri
spring	prolet	autumn	esen
summer	leto	winter	zima

Getting around
Public transport

I'd like …	Sakam …	I want to go to …	Sakam da odam …
a one-way ticket	billet vo eden pravec	How much is it?	Kolku pari čini?
a return ticket	povraten billet	What time is it now?	Kolku e časot?

What time does it leave?	Vo kolku časot trgnuva?	bus	avtobus
The train has been	Vozot ...	train	voz
... delayed	... docni	plane	avion
... cancelled	... e otkažan	boat	brod
first class	prva klasa	ferry	feribrod
second class	vtora klasa	car	avtomobil/kola
sleeper	vagon za spienje	4x4	pogon na četiri trkala/džip
platform	peron	taxi	taksi
ticket office	biletara	minibus	minibus/kombe
timetable	vozen red	motobike/moped	motor/moped
from	od	bicycle	velosiped
to	do	arrival/departure	pristignuvanje/ trgnuvanje
airport	aerodrom	bon voyage!	srekjen pat!
port	pristanište		

Private transport

Is this the road to ...?	Dali e ova patot za ...?
Where is the service station?	Kade e benziskata stanica?
Please fill it up	Ve molam napolnete do gore
I'd like ... litres	Sakam ... litri
diesel	dizel
leaded petrol	benzin
unleaded petrol	bezoloven benzin
I have broken down	Mi se rasipa avtomobilot/kolata

Road signs

give way	prednost za premin	toll	patarina
danger	opasnost	no entry	zabranet vlez
entry	vlez	exit	izlez
detour	skršnuvanje	keep clear	zabraneto parkiranje
one way	ednonasočna		

Directions

Where is it?	Kade e ?
Which way is the ...?	Na kade e ...?
mosque/church	džamija/crkva
fortress/museum	zamok (kale)/museum
archaeological site/hotel	arxeologska naogjalište/xotel
cave/bridge	peštera/most
Go straight ahead	Odi pravo
turn left	svrti levo
turn right	svrti desno
... at the traffic lights	... na semaforite
... at the roundabout	... kaj obikolnicata
behind	pozadi
in front of	pred
near	blisku
opposite	sproti
here/there	tuka/tamu
on the left/right	na levo/na desno

straight on	pravo
forward/behind	napred/nazas
east/west	istok/zapad
north/south	sever/jug
Where is there a …?	Kade ima …?
taxi rank/travel agency	taksi stanica/putovanje agencija
bus station/train station	avtobus stanica/železnička stanica
doctor/hospital	doktor/bolnica
police station/bank	policiska stanica/banka
restaurant/shop	restoran/prodavnica
town/village	grad/selo
house/flat	kukja/stan
cinema/theatre	kino/teatar
When does the train arrive/leave?	Koga stignuva/poagja vozot?

Street signs

entrance	vlez	toilets –	toalet –
exit	izlez	men/women	maži/ženi
open	otvoreno	information	informacija
closed	zatvoreno		

Accommodation

Where is a cheap/good hotel?	Kade možam da najdam eftin/dobar hotel?
Could you please write the address?	Ve molam napišete ja adresata
Do you have any rooms available?	Dali imate slobodni sobi?
I'd like …	Bi sakal …
a single room	ednokrevetna soba
a double room	soba so francuski krevet
a room with two beds	soba so dva kreveta
a room with a bathroom	soba so kupatilo
to share a dorm	da delam soba
How much it is per night/person?	Kolku čini za edna nokj/eden čovek?
Where is the toilet?	Kade e toaletot?
Where is the bathroom?	Kade e kupatiloto?
Is there hot water?	Dali ima topla voda?
Is there electricity?	Dali ima struja?
Is breakfast included?	Dali e vклучен doručekot?
I am leaving today	Zaminuvam deneska

Food

Do you have a table for … people?	Dali imate masa za … lugje?
… a children's menu?	… detsko meni?
I am a vegetarian	Jas sum vegetarijanec
Do you have any vegetarian dishes?	Dali imate vegetarijanska hrana?
Please bring me …	Ve molam donesete mi …
a fork/knife/spoon	viljuška/nož/lažica
Please may I have the bill?	Ve molam donesete ja smetkata
What do you have to drink?	Što imate za pienje?
I would like to drink …	Sakam da pijam …
water/juice	voda/sok
sparkling/non-sparkling	gazirane/negazirane

tea/coffee	*čaj/kafe*
turkish coffee medium sweet/bitter	*tursko kafe sredno/gorko*
without sugar/milk	*bez šeker/mleko*
with lemon/honey	*so limun/med*
milkshake/milk	*frape/mljeko*
white coffee	*kafe so mleko*
red/white wine	*crno/belo vino*
beer/*rakija*	*pivo/rakija*
mulled wine	*vareno vino*
What do you have to eat?	*Što imate za jadenje?*
I want some bread, please	*Sakam malku leb, ve molam*
I want …	*Sakam …*
fish/meat	*riba/meso*
trout/eel	*pastrmka/jagula*
soup/salad	*supa/salata*
yellow cheese/white cheese	*kaškaval/sirenje*
tomatoes/eggs	*partližani/jajca*
vegetables/fruit	*zelenčuk/ovošje*
rice/potatoes	*oriz/kompir*
apples/oranges	*jabolko/portokal*
pears/grapes	*kruška/grozje*
figs/apricots	*smokva/kaijsija*
sugar/honey	*šeker/med*
hazelnuts/walnuts	*lešnici/orevi*
ice cream/pancakes	*sladoled/palačinke*
I don't eat meat/fish/flour	*Ne jadem meso/riba/brašno*

Shopping

I'd like to buy …	*Bi sakal/*	Do you accept …?	*Dali primate … ?*
	a da kupam …	credit cards	*kreditni kartički*
How much is it?	*Kolku čini?*	travellers' cheques	*čekovi*
I don't like it	*Ne mi se dopagja*	more	*povekje*
I'm just looking	*Samo razgleduvam*	less	*pomalku*
It's too expensive	*Premnogu e skapo*	smaller	*pomalo*
I'll take it	*Kje go kupam*	bigger	*pogolemo*
Please may I have …	*Ve molam dali*		
	može …		

Communications

I am looking for …	*Baram …*	embassy	*ambasada*
bank	*banka*	exchange office	*menuvačnica*
post office	*pošta*	telephone centre	*telefonska govornica*
church	*crkva*	tourist office	*turističko biro*

Health

diarrhoea	*dijarea*	antibiotics	*antibiotici*
nausea	*mi se loši*	antiseptic	*antiseptik*
doctor	*doktor*	tampons	*tamponi*
prescription	*recept*	condoms	*kondomi*
pharmacy	*apteka*	contraceptive	*kontracepcija*
paracetamol	*paracetamol*	sunblock	*zaštiten faktor*

Help!	Pomoš!	fire	požar
Call a doctor!	Povikajte doktor!	ambulance	ambulantna
There's been an	Se sluči nesreḱa		kola
accident		thief	kradec
I'm lost	Se izgubiv	hospital	bolnica
Go away!	Odi si!	I am ill	Bolen sum/
police	policija		bolna sum

I am …	Jas sum …	penicillin	penicillin
asthmatic	astmatičar	nuts – walnuts,	orevi,
epileptic	epileptičar	hazelnuts, almonds	lešnici, bademi
diabetic	dijabetičar	bees	pčeli
I'm allergic to …	aleričen sum na …	wheat	pšenica/brašno

Travel with children

Is there a …?	Dali ima …?
baby changing room	soba za presoblekuvanje bebinja?
a children's menu?	detsko meni?
Do you have …?	Dali imate …?
infant milk formula	deštačko mleko za bebinja?
nappies	peleni
potty	nokšir
babysitter	bebisiter
highchair	stolče za bebinja
Are children allowed?	Dali e dozvoleno za deca?

Other

my/mine/ours/yours	moj/moe/naše/vaše	good/bad	dobro/lošo
and/some/but	i/nekoi/no, osven, tuku	early/late	rano/kasno
this/that	ova/toa	hot/cold	toplo/ladno
expensive/cheap	skapo/eftino	difficult/easy	teško/lesno
beautiful/ugly	ubavo/neubavo	boring/interesting	dosadno/interesno
old/new	staro/novo		

Basic verbs

to be	da se bide		
I am	jas sum	we are	nie sme
you are	ti si	you are	vie ste
he/she/it is	toj/taa/toa e	they are	tie se

to have	ima		
I have	imam	we have	imame
you have	imas	you have	imate
he/she/it has	ima	they have	imaat

to want/like/love	saka		
I want	sakam	we want	sakame
you want	sakaš	you want	sakate
he/she/it wants	saka	they want	sakaat

Appendix 1 LANGUAGE

A1

ALBANIAN

Pronunciation Albanian nouns are declined and they are either feminine or masculine. There is no neuter, except in certain set phrases. The indefinite and definite articles are used, the latter being added to the end of the noun, as in Macedonian. Verbs are conjugated, and there is a formal and informal conjugation of 'you' singular, as in French or Old English. Here the informal conjugation follows the formal where applicable, and 'they' is translated as in standard representation with the masculine version first, followed by the feminine version. Unlike English, Albanian spelling is completely phonetic, so once you have mastered the sounds, you shouldn't have too much trouble with pronunciation. Good luck!

A	as in father	N	as in not
B	as in bed	Nj	as in canyon
C	as in cats	O	as in lot
Ç	as in church	P	as in put
D	as in door	Q	as in cute
Dh	as in the	R	as in mark
E	as in bet	Rr	as in burrito; pronounced with a
Ë	as in along; it is often not		resonant roll
	pronounced at all	S	as in sit
F	as in farm	Sh	as in shovel
G	as in good	T	as in table
Gj	as in Magyar	Th	as in thin
H	as in hit	U	as in took
I	as in feet	V	as in very
J	as in young	X	as in adds
K	as in kit	Xh	as in jam
L	as in log	Y	as in mural
Ll	as in fall; pronounced at the back	Z	as in zoo
	of the mouth	Zh	as in pleasure
M	as in made		

Words and phrases
Courtesies

Hello	*Tungjatjeta*	How are you?	*Si jeni/si je*
Goodbye	*Mirupafshim*	I'm fine	*Jam mirë*
Please	*Ju lutem/të lutem*	Pleased to meet you	*Më vjen mirë*
Thank you	*Faleminderit*	My pleasure	*Kënaqësia është e imja*
Good morning	*Mirëmëngjes*	Excuse me	*Më fal*
Good afternoon	*Mirëdita*	You're welcome	*S'ka përse*
Good evening	*Mirëmbrëma*	Help yourself	*Shëbehuni vetë*
Good night	*Natën e mirë*	Welcome!	*Mirëseardhët!*

Basics

yes/no	*po/jo*	good/bad	*mirë/keq*
OK	*mire/në regull*	hot/cold	*nxehtë/ftohtë*
maybe	*mundqë/mundet*	toilet	*nevojtore*
large/small	*madhe/vogël*	men/women	*mashkull/femër*
more/less	*më shumë/më pak*		

Basic questions

How?	*Si?*
How do you say in Albanian?	*Si thuhet në shqip?*
What?	*Çfarë?*
What is that?	*Çfarë është ajo?*
When?	*Kur?*
When does the shop open/close?	*Kur hapet/mbyullet shitorja?*
Where?	*Ku?*
Where is a public telephone?	*Kuka telefon publik?*
Who?	*Kush?*
Why?	*Pse?*
Which?	*Cili?*
Do you speak English?	*A flisni anglisht?*
Do you understand French/German?	*A kuptoni frëngjisht/gjermanisht?*
I do not understand Albanian	*Unë nuk kuptoj shqip*
How much does it cost?	*Sa kushton?*
What time is it?	*Sa është ora?*
The bill please?	*Llogarinë ju lutem?*

Essentials

My name is …	*Unë quhem …*
What is your name?	*Si quheni?*
I am from … Britain/America/Australia	*Unë jam nga … Anglia/Amerika/Australia*
Please would you speak more slowly	*Ju lutem, mund të flisni më ngadal*
What is your telephone number?	*Cili është numri i telefonit tënd/të juaj?*
What is your address?	*Cila është adressa tënde juaje?*
My address in Britain/America is …	*Adresa ime në Angli/Amerikë është …*
I want to change dollars to lek (the currency in Albania)	*Dua të këmbej dollarë për lekë*
How many leks will you give me for US$1?	*Sa lekë do më japish për një dollar?*
I need to make a telephone call	*Duhet të marr në telefon*

Numbers

0	zero	12	*dymbëdhjetë*
1	*një*	13	*trembëdhjetë*
2	*dy*	14	*katërmbëdhjetë*
3	*tre*	15	*pesëmbëdhjetë*
4	*katër*	16	*gjashtëmbëdhjetë*
5	*pesë*	17	*shtatëmbëdhjetë*
6	*gjashtë*	18	*tetëmbëdhjetë*
7	*shtatë*	19	*nëntëmbëdhjetë*
8	*tetë*	20	*njëzet*
9	*nëntë*	21	*njëzet e një*
10	*dhjetë*	30	*tridhjet*
11	*njëmbëdhjetë*	40	*dyzet*

GESTURES

Hand gestures in Macedonia are the same as in the rest of Europe, but do not offer your left hand to Muslims, or show them the soles of your feet or shoes.

50	pesëdhjet	500	pesëqind
60	gjashtëdhjet	one thousand	një mijë
70	shtatëdhjet	two thousand	dy mijë
80	tetëdhjet	one million	një miljon
90	nëntëdhjet	two million	dy miljonë
100	njëqind	quarter	çerek
200	dyqind	half	gjysmë
300	treqind	three-quarters	tre çerekë
400	katërqind		

Time

hour	orë	yesterday	dje
minute	minutë	morning	mëngjes
week	javë	afternoon	pas dite
day	ditë	evening	mbrëmje
year	vit	night	natë
month	muaj	already	veç më
today	sot	soon	së shpejti
tonight	sonte	now	tani
tomorrow	nesër	this week	këtë javë
next week	javën e ardhshme	last week	javën e kaluar

Monday	e hënë	Friday	e premte
Tuesday	e martë	Saturday	e shtunë
Wednesday	e mërkurë	Sunday	e dielë
Thursday	e ejte		

January	Janar	July	Korrik
February	Shkurt	August	Gusht
March	Mars	September	Shtator
April	Prill	October	Tetor
May	Maj	November	Nëntor
June	Qershor	December	Dhjetor

| spring | pranverë | autumn | vjeshtë |
| summer | verë | winter | dimër |

Getting around
Public transport

I'd like …	Dua …
a one-way ticket	një biletë njëdrejtimshe
a return ticket	një biletë kthyese
I want to go to …	Dua të shkoj në …
How much is it?	Sa kushton?
What time does it leave?	Kur niset?
What time is it now?	Sa është ora tani?
The train has been …	Treni do të …
delayed	vonohet
cancelled	anulohet
first class	klasa e parë	sleeper	vagon-shtrat
second class	Klasa e dytë	platform	platformë

ticket office	*sportel*	ferry	*ferribot*
timetable	*orar*	car	*veturë*
from	*prej*	4x4	*foristadë*
to	*gjer*	taxi	*taksi*
airport	*aeroport*	minibus	*minibus*
port	*liman*	motobike/moped	*motoçikletë*
bus	*autobus*	bicycle	*biçikletë*
train	*tren*	arrival/departure	*ardhje/nisje*
plane	*aeroplan*	bon voyage!	*rrugën e mbarë!*
boat	*anije*		

Private transport

Is this the road to …?	*A është kjo rruga për …?*
Where is the service station?	*Ku është pikë furnizimi?*
Please fill it up	*Ju lutem, mund ta mbushni plot?*
I'd like … litres	*Dua … litra*
diesel	*dizel/naftë*
leaded petrol	*benzin me plumb*
unleaded petrol	*benzin pa plumb*
I have broken down	*mu prish makina*

Road signs

give way	*jep përparësi*	toll	*tarifë*
danger	*rrezik*	no entry	*ndalohet hyrja*
entry	*hyrje*	exit	*dalje*
detour	*rrugë e tërthortë*	keep clear	*mos ndalo*
one way	*njëkahshe*		

Directions

Where is it?	*Ku është?*
Which way is the …?	*Nga është rruga për në …?*
mosque/church	*xhami/kishë*
castle/museum	*kala/muzeum*
archaeological site/hotel	*vend arkeologijike/hotel*
cave/bridge	*shpellë/urë*
Go straight ahead	*Shko drejt*
turn left	*kthe në të majtë*
turn right	*kthe në të djathtë*
… at the traffic lights	*… te semafori*
… at the roundabout	*… te qarkorja*
behind	*prapa*
in front of	*përpara*
near	*afër*
opposite	*përballë*
here/there	*këtu/atje*
on the left/right	*në të majtë/djathtë*
straight on	*drejt*
forward/behind	*përpara/mbrapa*
east/west	*lindje/perëndim*
north/south	*veri/jug*

Where is …?	Ku është …?
taxi rank/travel agency	*vendqëndrim i taksive/agjensioni turistik*
train station	*stacioni i trenit*
bus station	*stacion i autobusave*
ferry/train	*target/tren*
doctor/hospital	*doktor/spital*
police station/bank	*stacioni policior/bankë*
restaurant/shop	*restorant/shitore*
town/village	*qytet/fshat*
house/flat	*shtëpi/apartament*
cinema/theatre	*kinema/teatër*
When does the train arrive/leave?	*Kur arin/niset treni?*

Street signs

entrance	*hyrje*	closed	*mbyllur*
exit	*dalje*	toilets – men/women	*tualet – burra/gra*
open	*hapur*	information	*informacion*

Accommodation

Where is a cheap/good hotel?	*Ku ka një hotel të lirë/mire?*
Could you please write the address?	*A mund ta shkruani adresën ju lutem?*
Do you have any rooms available?	*A keni dhoma të lira?*
I'd like …	*Dua …*
a single room	*një dhomë njëkrevatshe*
a double room	*një dhomë me krevat dopio*
a room with two beds	*një dhomë me dy krevatë*
a room with a bathroom	*një dhomë me banjo*
to share a dorm	*të ndaj dhomën me dikë*
How much it is per night/person?	*Sa kushton për një natë/person?*
Where is the toilet?	*Ku është tualeti?*
Where is the bathroom?	*Ku është banjoja?*
Is there hot water?	*A ka ujë të nxehtë?*
Is there electricity?	*A ka rymë elektrike?*
Is breakfast included?	*A është mëngjesi i përfshirë?*
I am leaving today	*Unë shkoj sot*

Food

Do you have a table for … people?	*A keni një tavolinë për … persona?*
… a children's menu?	*… meny për fëmijë*
I am a vegetarian	*Unë jam vegjetarian*
Do you have any vegetarian dishes?	*A keni ndonjë ushqim vegjetarian?*
Please bring me …	*Ju lutem më sillni …*
a fork/knife/spoon	*një pirun/thikë/lugë*
Please may I have the bill?	*Ju lutem, mund ta sillni llogarinë?*
What do you have to drink?	*Çfarë ka për të pirë?*
I would like to drink …	*Do të doja të pi …*
water/juice	*ujë/lëng*
sparkling/non-sparkling	*i gazuar/i pa gazuar*
tea/coffee	*çaj/kafe*
hot chocolate/milk	*çokollatë e nxehtë/qumësht i nxehtë*
white coffee	*kafe me qumësht*

red/white wine	verë e kuqe/bardhë
beer/*rakija*	birrë/raki
mulled wine	verë e nxehtë
What do you have to eat?	Çfarë ka për të ngrënë?
I want some bread, please	Dua pak bukë, ju lutem
I want …	Dua …
fish/meat	peshk/mish
(Ohrid) trout/eel	troftë/ngjalë
soup/salad	supë/sallatë
cheese	djathë
tomatoes/eggs	domate/vezë
vegetables/fruit	zarzavate/fruta
rice/potatoes	oriz/patate
apples/oranges	mollë/portokaj
pears/grapes	dardha/rrush
figs/apricots	fiq/kajsi
sugar/honey	sheqer/mjaltë
hazelnuts/walnuts	lajthi/arra
ice cream/pancakes	akullore/petulla
I don't eat meat/fish/wheat products	Unë nuk ha mish/peshk/produkte të grurit

Shopping

I'd like to buy …	Dua të blej …	Do you accept …?	A pranoni …?
How much is it?	Sa kushton?	credit cards	kartela kreditore
I don't like it	Nuk më pëlqen	travellers' cheques	çeqje udhëtarësh
I'm just looking	Vetëm shoh	more	më shumë
It's too expensive	Është shumë shtrenjtë	less	më pak
I'll take it	Do ta marr	smaller	më e /i vogël
Please may I have …	Ju lutem, mund të ma jepni …	bigger	më e /i madh

Communications

I am looking for …	Kërkoj …		
bank	bankë	exchange office	këmbimore valutash
post office	postë	telephone centre	qendër telefonike
church	kishë	tourist office	zyrë turistike
embassy	ambasadë		

Health

diarrhoea	diarre	sunblock	mbrojtje nga dielli
nausea	të përzier	I am …	Unë jam …
doctor	mjek	asthmatic	asmatik
prescription	recetë	epileptic	epileptik
pharmacy	barnatore	diabetic	diabetik
paracetamol	paracetamoll	I'm allergic to …	Jam alergjik në …
antibiotics	antibiotik	penicillin	penicilin
antiseptic	antiseptik	nuts	lajthi, bajame, arra
tampons	tampona	bees	grera
condoms	prezervativ	wheat	miell/grurë
contraceptive	kontraceptiv		

Help!	*Ndihmë!*	fire	*zjarr*
Call a doctor!	*Thirni mjek!*	ambulance	*ndihmë e*
There's been an	*Ka një*		*shpejtë*
accident	*aksident*	thief	*vjedhës*
I'm lost	*Kam humbur*	hospital	*spital*
Go away!	*Largohu!*	I am ill	*Jam i sëmurë*
police	*polici*		

Travel with children

Is there a ...	*A ka ...*
baby changing room?	*dhomë pë të ndruar beben?*
a children's menu?	*meny për fëmijë?*
Do you have ...?	*A keni ...*
infant milk formula	*qumësht pluhur për bebe?*
nappies	*pelena*
potty	*oturak*
babysitter	*dado*
highchair	*karrige për fëmijë*
Are children allowed?	*A janë fëmijët të lejuar?*

Other

my/mine/ours/yours	*imi/imja/jona/jotja*	good/bad	*mirë/keq*
and/some/but	*edhe/disa/por*	early/late	*shpejt/vonë*
this/that	*kjo/ajo*	hot/cold	*nxehtë/ftohtë*
expensive/cheap	*shtrenjt/lirë*	difficult/easy	*rëndë/lehtë*
beautiful/ugly	*e bukur/e keqe*	boring/interesting	*banal/interesant*
old/new	*e vjetër/e re*		

Basic verbs

to be	*të jesh*		
I am	*unë jam*	we are	*ne jemi*
you are	*ti je*	you are	*ju jeni*
he/she/it is	*ai/ajo është*	they are	*ata/ato janë*

to have	*të kesh*		
I have	*unë kam*	we have	*ne kemi*
you have	*ti ke*	you have	*ju keni*
he/she/it has	*ai/ajo ka*	they have	*ato/ata kanë*

to want	*të duash*		
I want	*unë dua*	we want	*ne duam*
you want	*ti do*	you want	*ju doni*
he/she/it wants	*ai/ajo do*	they want	*ato/ata duan*

Appendix 2

GLOSSARY OF ARCHITECTURAL TERMS

acropolis	a fortified hill
amam	Turkish baths, usually using water from natural hot springs
amphitheatre	a Roman theatre, circular or semicircular in shape with tiered seats, used for animal or gladiatorial fights
an	an inn for travellers, usually four-sided around a well in an open courtyard, where travellers would sleep upstairs and animals and produce would be stored downstairs
apse	a semicircular recess in a wall
atrium	the inner courtyard of a Roman villa
basilica	a roofed Roman public hall, which by the 5th century BC had become a place of early Christian worship or formalised church
capital	distinctively decorated upper end of a column
cardac	a large niche in the wall on the second floor of a Turkish house
chancel	the altar end of a church; in the Orthodox Church this area is usually prohibited to women
čardak	first-floor balcony
cupola	domed roof
dolap	wardrobe or drawers for clothes
exonarthex	an open hall or lean-to built onto the side of a church
forum	a Roman marketplace or public square
iconostasis	the screen dividing the chancel from the nave of a church
konak	formerly describing a large Turkish house, now used for the inns of a monastery
madrese	a school teaching the Koran
methoses	land or estate owned by the Church
mihrab	the niche in the eastern wall of a mosque indicating the direction of Mecca
mimbar	the pulpit of a mosque, from where the sermon is preached
minaret	a thin circular or many-sided tower attached to an outside wall of a mosque
minder	cushion
minderlik	narrow fitted wooden benches with fitted cushions built into a room
mosaic	pictures usually depicting flora and fauna, people or buildings, made of small coloured tiles, usually laid as a flooring, but occasionally on a wall or ceiling
musandra	a built-in wardrobe for linen and bedding
narthex	the front lobby, porch or entrance hall of a church
nave	the main room of worship in a church
necropolis	a Roman graveyard

pithos	a large clay jar or jug used for storing foodstuffs
plinth	a square block of stone or marble at the bottom of a column
portico	a row of columns holding up the exonarthex roof of a church or mosque
sergen	a glass cupboard or shop window
teke	the Bektašii equivalent of a monastery
turbe	a tomb usually found outside a mosque but within its grounds

GLOSSARY OF ART TERMS

damp fold	painting or sculpting technique gathering folds of material to look as if wet and clinging to the body and used to emphasise depth and three-dimensionality
fresco	a wall painting
icon	portrait or likeness of a saint, often inlaid with silver and gold, and having holy and healing powers
iconoclasm	the destruction and prohibition of icons and artistic depiction of life forms, whether for religious or poltical reasons
scriptoria	place in a monastery for copying manuscripts; the body of written work of a monastery
zograph	title of a skilled fresco painter

GLOSSARY OF NAMES

As one might expect in a Balkan country as diverse as Macedonia, the names of famous people differ by language, and it can be quite confusing to figure out which names apply to which people. Here are some of the more commonly confusing names:

Aleksander III of Macedon	as usually found in Macedonian literature; more commonly known as Alexander the Great, especially by the Greeks, or as Aleksandar Veliki by some Macedonians; known as Iskander in Albanian, Turkish and lands further east; abbreviated to Aco
Basilius II	the Byzantium emperor known as Basil II in English, Vasilius II in some renditions (b and v are often interchangeable) and as Vasilie in Macedonia
Bogorodica	the Holy Mother of God (the Virgin Mary)
Gjorgi	George, also sometimes transliterated into English as Džordži
Jovan	John
Kliment	Clement in English
Pavle	Paul
Pantelejmon	meaning 'all merciful'; the patron saints of physicians
Skenderbej	also Skenderbeg, meaning literally 'Lord' (bej/beg) Iskander/Alexander
Spas	the Holy Saviour

Appendix 3

GUIDE TO WINES OF MACEDONIA

There are more than 50 small private wineries in Macedonia and the number is growing, as is quality. Few restaurants offer more than Tikveš or maybe Bovin, but supermarkets offer an increasing range, or go to www.winesofmacedonia.org to find out about some of the many wineries in the country. Tours to the wineries themselves are an easy way to sample many of these grape varieties.

Several are listed in the relevant chapters of this guidebook (Popova Kula and Tikveš are good places to start), or see a list of web addresses on page 366.

Macedonian wines are little known outside of its borders. There are two reasons for this: most of it is still exported in bulk for use in your local supermarket chain's own label wine; secondly, Macedonia's name dispute with Greece also affects wine exports. For more, see Mark Lowen's article at www.bbc.co.uk/news/world-europe-12884526.

Many of the usual varieties of grape found elsewhere are also grown in Macedonia, such as Chardonnay, Merlot, Pinot and Sauvignon. There are many indigenous varieties, however, and some of the grape varieties which you might be familiar with at home have a different name on a Macedonian wine bottle. Here is a guide:

Belan	Grenache. A grape which grows easily; herbaceous flavour.
Kratošija	A common indigenous red, similar to Vranec but not as full-bodied.
Muscat(el)	This name covers a wide variety of grapes, both red and white, which have a characteristic sweet musky perfume. A semi-sweet to sweet wine, often a desert wine.
Prokupec	A light yet nutty indigenous red, with dry fruit tones.
R'kacitel	From the Georgian *rkatsiteli*, meaning 'red stem'. Originating from Georgia, it is a very old white variety, similar to Riesling.
Smederevka	Peculiar to Macedonia and Serbia, the cultivation of this grape dates back to Roman times. Has a bitter acidic taste, best as a spritzer.
Stanušina	A refreshing semi-sweet red, usually made into a rosé or dark rosé.
Temjanika	Deriving its name from *temjanuška*, meaning violet or pansy, this floral scented semi-sweet white is a variety of Muscat.
Teran	An imported variety from Istria, which is sourish red, very high in iron derived from the red soil it requires to grow. Its medicinal properties are valued for combating anaemia, stimulating apetite and aiding digestion. Does not age well.
Traminec	A varient of Gewürztraminer, and akin to a semi-sweet Riesling. Unstable and difficult to age.
Vranec	This is the bulls' blood of the Balkans, deepest red, dry and intense.
Žilavka	A light, refreshing and fruity indigenous white, reflecting apple, pear and peach flavours.

You can order online for delivery to destinations in Macedonia from **www.wine.mk**. Sadly, only Tikveš and Bovin were on sale at Skopje Airport duty free at the time of writing, so if you want to take anything else home then stock up from www.wine.mk or at the supermarket.

Back in the UK you can order Bovin wine from **www.simplymacedonia.com**, or go to **Vardar** (*69 Askew Rd, London W12;* ☎ *020 8746 1844;* e *darko@vardar.co.uk; www.vardar. co.uk;* ⏰ *11.00–19.00 Mon–Fri, 11.00–18.00 Sat, 12.00–17.00 Sun*), a small shop near Shepherd's Bush market in west London, selling Tikveš and Bovin wines, as well as some from Serbia and Croatia, and other Macedonian food products. Elsewhere in the world try ordering through **www.snooth.com**.

Appendix 4

FURTHER INFORMATION

BOOKS If you are new to Macedonia and want to know where to start with further reading, I suggest the works of both John Phillips and Robert Kaplan. Books written on Macedonia by Macedonians abound, only some of which have been translated into English. These are listed separately, below the more internationally available books (which can be ordered through most bookshops or Amazon, or can be borrowed from a good university library). Old, rare and out-of-print titles can often be found on abebooks.co.uk (or .com). All the Macedonian books listed are available from Ikona, Kultura, Matica or Tabernakul bookshops in Skopje. Books specifically on ethnic Macedonians outside the Republic of Macedonia are not especially covered here, but many can be found at www.pollitecon.com.

History/politics

Brown, Keith *The Past in Question: Modern Macedonia and the Uncertainties of Nation* Princeton University Press, 2003. Looks at Macedonia's work on historiography of the Kruševo Republic of 1903 and how this has been an effort to create an identity for a nation uncertain of itself. Engaging reading in parts.

Carpenter, Teresa *The Miss Stone Affair: America's First Modern Hostage Crisis!* Simon & Schuster, 2003. A page-turner of a book on the kidnap of the American missionary, Ellen Stone, and her pregnant chaperone, Mrs Tsilka, by Jane Sandanski, a member of the Internal Macedonian Revolutionary Organisation (VMRO).

Cartledge, Paul *Alexander the Great: The Hunt for a New Past* Pan Books, 2005. This latest book on Alexander the Great by a professor of Greek history at Oxford University gives some clarity to all those who struggle with whether Alexander/Aleksandar was Greek or Macedonian. Interesting reading.

Chiclet, Christophe and Lory, Bernard (eds) *La République de Macédoine* Editions L'Harmattan, Paris, 1998. This is a useful update (in French) on a lot of Hugh Poulton's book (see below).

Clark, Victoria *Why Angels Fall: A Journey through Orthodox Europe from Byzantium to Kosovo* Picador, 2001. The 44 pages covering Macedonia also include Aegean Macedonia. They give an insight into the relationship between these two sides of geographical Macedonia and the role that the Church still plays.

Glenny, Misha *The Fall of Yugoslavia* (3rd edition) Penguin, London, 1996; and *The Balkans: Nationalism, War and the Great Powers, 1804–1999* Penguin, USA, 2001. Both books by this journalist are an excellent read, although depending on where you are in your knowledge of the Balkans, the books can either be too broad or too detailed! With the advantage of hindsight, the latter book has a weak ending.

Hammond, N G A *History of Macedonia*, Duckworth, 1979–88. The standard reference on the history of Macedonia up to the early 20th century. Three volumes.

Jezernik, Božidar *Wild Europe: The Balkans in the Gaze of Western Travellers* Saqi Books, 2004. An interesting critique of many of the books listed here. Good exposé of the Macedonian question in Chapter 9, 'A True Comedy of Errors'.

Kaplan, Robert D *Balkan Ghosts: A Journey through History* Vintage, New York, 1993. The one chapter on Macedonia is a fascinating read of historical and contemporary views of the country, especially considering it was written in 1990, before the country had even become independent.

Karakasidou, Anastasia *Fields of Wheat, Hills of Blood: Passages to a Nationhood in Greek Macedonia 1870–1990* University of Chicago Press, 1997. Originally banned in Greece and the source of death threats to the author, this book is a must-read for anyone wanting to understand Macedonia.

Moody, Simon and Wakefield, Alan *Under the Devil's Eye: Britain's Forgotten Army at Salonika 1915–1918* Sutton Publishing, 2004. Detailed reading taken from soldier accounts of their time on the Salonika Front, including the Battle of Dojran.

Mulley, Clare *The Woman Who Saved the Children: A Biography of Eglantyne Jebb* Oneworld Publications, 2009. Chapter 8 concentrates on Jebb's first and only trip to Macedonia and Kosovo to deliver aid to tens of thousands of refugees after the first Balkan War. The plight of children in particular spurs her to co-found Save the Children, and to author the Declaration of the Rights of the Child. A fascinating read. All book proceeds go to Save the Children.

Pekar, Harvey and Roberson, Heather *Macedonia: How Do You Stop a War?* Villard, 2007. Roberson's search to answer this question, through meetings with Macedonians as well as with foreigners working in Macedonia's many international organisations, is rendered into comic-book script and drawings by Pekar and illustrator Ed Piskor. The comic-book style leaves a lot out.

Pettifer, James (ed) *The New Macedonian Question* Palgrave, 2001. This is a collection of essays and articles covering a wide variety of topics concerning Macedonia. Extremely informative.

Phillips, John *Macedonia: Warlords and Rebels* I B Tauris, 2004. This book by a reporter for *The Times* is the first to give full coverage of the 2001 conflict in English. It is insightful and balanced until the last few pages, when his attempt to catch up on the last two years when he was not reporting on the country paints far too pessimistic a picture. Excellent review of Macedonian history.

Poulton, Hugh *Who Are the Macedonians?* Indiana University Press, 1995. A somewhat dry book that explores the origins of the peoples who now occupy the Republic of Macedonia and what they may mean in terms of their identity.

Silber, Laura et al *The Death of Yugoslavia* (revised edition) Penguin, 1996. An in-depth account of the ins and outs and minutiae that led up to the death of Yugoslavia. It is much easier to watch the BBC TV series.

Sokalski, Henryk J *An Ounce of Prevention: Macedonia and the UN Experience in Preventive Diplomacy* United States Institute of Peace, Washington DC, 2003. Analysis by the head of UNPROFOR/UNPREDEP of the UN's first military mission in preventive diplomacy. Could the conflict of 2001 have been avoided if UNPROFOR had not been pulled out?

Thucydides *History of the Peloponnesian War* Penguin, 1972. This is *the* account of the wars over the Greek city-states and islands, a foundation work in political science, and describes the beginning of the end of the Greek Empire. Paeonia and the royal house of Macedon are referred to in Book Two.

Macedonian authors

Koneska, Elizabeta *Yoruks* Museum of Macedonia, Skopje, 2004. Beautiful colour photographs by Robert Jankuloski and succinct text about the little-known Yoruk community of Macedonia.

Kumanovski, Risto *Ohrid and its Treasures* Mikena Publishing, Bitola, 2002. Gives an introduction to Ohrid's best sites, including 25 of its churches and monasteries.

Pavlovski, Jovan and Pavlovski, Mishel *Macedonia Yesterday and Today* (3rd edition) Mi-an Publishing, Skopje, 2001. A very readable, if very pro-Macedonian and anti-Bulgarian, account of Macedonia's history up until the first session of the Anti-fascist Assembly of the National Liberation of Macedonia (ASNOM) in October 1943.

Šeldarov, Nikola and Lilčikj, Viktor *Kralevite na antička Makedonija i nivnite moneti vo Republika Makedonija* (The Kings of Ancient Macedonia and their Coinage) National and University Library of Kliment Ohridski, Skopje, 1994. A good reference book on the ancient kingdom of the Macedons including maps of the kingdom, its tribes and towns, as well as drawings of many of their coins. Macedonian only.

Stojčev, Vanče *Military History of Macedonia*, Military Academy General Mihailo Apostolski, Skopje, 2004. Covering the period from 7BC through World War II. A beautiful compendium of maps accompanies the main 777-page volume.

Natural history

Gorman, Gerrard *Central and Eastern European Wildlife* Bradt Travel Guides, 2008. Although this guide does not cover Macedonia specifically, most of the animals to be found in Macedonia are covered in it, and it is a lot more affordable and easier to travel with than the Mitchell-Jones atlas below.

Hoffman, Helga and Marktanner, Thomas *Butterflies and Moths of Britain and Europe* HarperCollins, 1995. Small with a plastic cover, very handy for expeditions.

Karadelev, Mitko *Fungi Makedonci, Gabite na Makedonija* PGUP Sofija Bogdanci, Skopje, 2001. Available only in Macedonian, this is an excellent book with page-by-page descriptions and colour photos of all the mushrooms to be found in Macedonia.

Mitchell-Jones, A J et al *The Atlas of European Mammals* Academic Press, 1999. A weighty tome with lots packed in.

Polunin, Oleg *Flowers of Greece and the Balkans: A Field Guide* Oxford University Press, 1987. Invaluable.

Svensson, Lars *Collins Bird Guide* HarperCollins, 2010.

Historical travel writing

Čelebi, Evlija *Book of Travels: The Seyahatname* volumes V, VI & VIII, Brill Academic Publishers, Leiden, 1999. This is the best and often only source of what went on during the 17th century in the Ottoman Empire. Massively informative, if dense.

Lear, Edward *Journals of a Landscape Painter in Greece and Albania* Century, 1851, reprinted 1988. The more serious side of this most famous limerick writer offering sobering views.

Maclean, Fitzroy *Eastern Approaches* Penguin, 1991. An excellent account of Maclean's missions through the Balkans during World War I.

Moore, Frederick *The Balkan Trial* Smith, Elder and Co, 1906. An American journalist writes about his travels with other European travellers, including an English journalist, through Monastir (Bitola), Prilep and Üsküb (Skopje) and about the Kruševo Uprising from his time there in 1903, aged 29.

Pouqueville, F C H L (ed James Pettifer, Classic Balkan Travel Series, 1998) *Travels in Epirus, Albania, Macedonia, and Thessaly* Loizou Publications, Paris, 1820. Early 18th-century travels through Ottoman-held land; only a few pages on Vardar Macedonia.

West, Rebecca *Black Lamb and Grey Falcon* Canongate Books, Edinburgh, 1941, reprinted 1993. On the one hand it is one of the few accounts available of the Balkans in the early 20th century; on the other hand it is the account of a privileged upper-class lady with undisguised ethnocentric tendencies.

Willis, Martin P L *A Captive of the Bulgarian Brigand: An Englishman's Terrible Experiences in Macedonia* Ede Allum & Townsend, 1906. A revealing thriller, highlighting only one account of a more widespread problem debated by the Great Powers at the time.

Modern travel writing

Cho, Carol *A Hitchhiker's Guide to Macedonia ... and My Soul* Forum Publishing, 2002. Written by an Amerasian woman who spent three years living in the Macedonian community over the 2001 conflict period. Although the book mentions little of the conflict itself, it offers excellent insights into the trials and tribulations of a young woman coming to terms with her own self and with Macedonia.

Delisso, Christopher *Hidden Macedonia: The Mystic Lakes of Ohrid and Prespa* Haus Publishing, London, 2007. Delisso, a long-time Balkan-hand, brings his insights as editor of balkananalysis.com to bear on his 2006 journey through three countries around lakes Ohrid and Prespa. A short and readable introduction to the history, religions and races of the region.

Palin, Michael *New Europe* Weidenfeld & Nicolson, 2007. Palin's documentary takes him through all of new Europe and a few days in Ohrid and Prilep.

Macedonian literature

Pavlovski, Božin *The Red Hypocrite* AEA Publishers, Australia, 2001. One of the most famous modern authors to emerge from Macedonia, who now lives in Australia. Other books by Pavlovski available in English include: *Duva and the Flea*; *Eagle Coat of Arms*; *Egyptian Dreamer*; *Home is Where the Heart is*; *Journey with my Beloved*; *Miladin from China*; *Neighbours of the Owl*; *Return to Fairy Tales*.

Miscellaneous

Biegman, Nicolaas *God's Lovers: A Sufi Community in Macedonia* Kegan Paul, 2007. Biegman, a former Dutch diplomat in Macedonia and an expert on Islam, has produced a masterful photographic treatise of the little-understood Sufi community.

Biegman, Nicolaas *Living Sufism: Sufi Rituals in the Middle East and the Balkans* American University in Cairo Press, 2009. Complementing many of the gorgeous photographs from *God's Lovers*, this book compares the Sufi rituals across the Middle East and the Balkans and how they have developed over time and distance.

Biegman, Nicolaas *Oil Wrestlers*, Stylus Publishing, 2009. Close-up photography of pelivan wrestling in Macedonia. A male-only sport involving only a pair of sturdy breeches and total body coverage with sunflower oil.

Kornakov, Dimitar *A Guide to Macedonian Monasteries* Matica, Skopje, 2005. A guide in English on 29 of Macedonia's most revered monasteries. In-depth information on the building and reconstruction of the monastery buildings, on their frescoes and some of their history.

Kramer, Christina E *Macedonian: A Course for Beginning and Intermediate Students* University of Winsconsin Press, Madison, 1999. An extremely well-presented and comprehensive language-learning book with exercises. Explanations are in English and a separate CD-ROM can be purchased to accompany the book to listen to native Macedonian.

Kusevska, Maria and Mitovska, Liljana *Do You Speak Macedonian?* MEDIS-informatics, Skopje, 1995. This course book, accompanied by a workbook and cassette tape, is written entirely in Cyrillic Macedonian, so it is impossible to use as a beginner without the cassette tape. Vocabulary at the back is listed with English translations.

Murgoski, Zoze *Dictionary: English–Macedonian, Macedonian–English* National and University Library of Kliment Ohridski, Skopje, 1995. A handy little paperback dictionary for carrying in your back pocket or bag. The definitive *English–Macedonian Dictionary:*

The Unabridged Edition also by Murgoski, is all you will ever need for finding those awkward words like 'sovereignty' and 'fennel'. And the equivalent Macedonian–English version is also now out.

WEB RESOURCES There are a lot of outdated sites on Macedonia so check when the site was last updated before acting upon any of the information. Macedonian websites are generally quite good at having information available in English, but if not Google Chrome will translate entire webpages relatively accurately.

General

www.macedonia-timeless.com Site hosting the current internationally aired tourist advert for Macedonia directed by Macedonia's most famous film director, Milčo Mančevski. Offers hundreds of links to help you get to know, and get about, Macedonia.

news.bbc.co.uk/2/hi/europe/country_profiles/1067125.stm For a good overview of the recent history of Macedonia.

www.macedonia.co.uk The Macedonian Cultural and Information Centre for lots of useful information to help you get to know the country before you go.

www.mymacedonia.net Macedonian history from a nation-state perspective, including articles from leading Macedonian historians Risto Stefov and Alexander Donski.

www.manaki.com.mk Official site dedicated to the Manaki brothers, pioneers of film and photography in Macedonia.

www.kniga.com.mk Where you can find most Macedonian books, maps and software. Only available in Macedonian at the time of writing.

www.pollitecon.com A site offering books and views supporting the argument that there are ethnic Macedonians in Greece.

www.mhrmi.org The website of the Macedonian Human Rights Movement International, based in Toronto, Canada. Interesting dialogue in 2006 between MHRMI and *The Times* regarding the use of the word 'Slav'.

Travel and accommodation

www.exploringmacedonia.com The official tourist site for Macedonia. Very useful.

www.gomacedonia.com.mk An excellent site with up-to-date, accurate information on places worth visiting in Macedonia.

www.airports.com.mk Flight information for Skopje and Ohrid.

www.mz.com.mk Train information for national and international rail travel through Macedonia.

www.jsp.com.mk The Skopje city bus website with map and timetables (sometimes only working in Macedonian).

www.sas.com.mk The national and international bus service website (English timetable not working at the time of writing).

www.unet.com.mk/oldmacedonianmaps For all you map freaks.

www.cs.unca.edu/~boyd/touring/tour05/tour.htm An insightful personal account into bicycling around Macedonia on Professor Mark Boyd's 2005 European tour.

www.bicycletouringpro.com/blog/bicycling-in-macedonia Account of Darren Alff's 2009 account of cycling through Macedonia.

Sports clubs and associations

www.alpinizam.org Information about rock-climbing sites around Macedonia. Latest information available in Macedonian only.

www.amfora.com.mk Diving centre in Ohrid.

www.eskimo-freeride.com For the best skiing at the cheapest rates in Europe – too awesome for words.

www.korab.org.mk Korab mountaineering club, based in Skopje.

www.makedon.mk New, young mountaineering and climbing club, based in Skopje.

www.mkdmount.org A hub of information about mountaineering in Macedonia, has links to all the clubs, how to hire a guide, and latest information on the state of mountaineering in Macedonia. English pages not as up to date as Macedonian pages.

www.sharamountainguide.com.mk Homepage of Ljuboten mountaineering club, based in Tetovo, including hiring guides for Šar Planina hikes.

www.yoga.org.mk Macedonian yoga association.

Government, media, communications, etc

www.vlada.mk For the latest from the government.

www.president.gov.mk To see what the president is up to.

www.sobranie.mk Website of the Macedonian parliament.

www.zels.org.mk The Organisation of Local Self Government with links to all the municipalities. These sites in turn, many of which are available in English, offer the latest information on the local area including places of interest, transportation and accommodation.

www.culture.in.mk A very good site by the Ministry of Culture giving all the latest news on events and shows.

www.balkaninsight.com Reliable reporting of news coverage for the region.

www.mia.com.mk Macedonian Information Agency, the official independent national news agency – very informative and the most up to date.

www.setimes.com Southeast European Times – provides a very good overview of top news coverage by country in the Balkans.

imenik.telekom.mk Macedonia's on-line phone directory for private addresses.

www.t-home.mk Homepage of Makedonski Telekomunikacija now that it is owned by T-Mobile, with all the latest news in Macedonia and useful links to other sites.

www.yellowpages.com.mk Macedonia's online business phone directory, with an optional English interface. Useful links to other Yellow Pages around the world.

Business

www.bbgm.co.uk Homepage of the British Business Group Macedonia.

www.investinmacedonia.com A government-run portal.

www.see-business.biz A very useful website for an overview of doing business in the region.

www.doingbusiness.org/data/exploreeconomies/macedonia,-fyr/ Compares countries across the globe in various sectors of efficiency in doing business. Updated yearly.

www.bridgewest.eu/article/set-up-company-macedonia Runs you though how to actually set up a business in Macedonia.

Wines

www.bovin.com.mk Macedonia's most prestigious label. Bovin's award-winning Venus, Daron and Dissan red wines are distributed as far as California, while their Pinot Noir and Riesling are very recommendable, affordable wines. Bovin is open for wine tasting for groups of ten or more.

www.cekorovi.com.mk Based in Kavadarci, Čekorov specialises in Macedonia's indigenous Vranec grape and in Riesling. Quality comes with the specialisation.

www.chateaukamnik.com A bijou winery, hotel and restaurant based in the outskirts of Skopje. The hunting-themed restaurant has an extensive wine collection from around the world and of course is open for wine tasting.

www.dudinwinery.com.mk Near the old Roman town of Stobi, Dudin specialises in four wines: Chardonnay, Sauvignon Blanc, Cabernet Sauvignon and Merlot; and has a pleasant wine-tasting luncheon room. Old website but on Facebook.

www.ezimitvino.com.mk Near Veles, Ezimit is one of only four producers worldwide to receive the Honorable Panel of the Vine Knights of Austria. The award was received for their Vranac Reserve and Vranac Barrique, both of which are truly deserving of the award.

www.fonkowines.com Based in Negotino, Fonko offers seven wines, the most prestigious of which is their 2002 special limited edition Chardonnay.

www.popovwinery.com.mk Popov family wines went commercial in 2001, since when they have produced several excellent wines for public consumption. Their Temjanika (the Macedonian variety of Muscat-Frontignan), Vranec-Cabernet Sauvignon, Zilavka and Rose (Pinot Noir and Stanushina) are particularly noteworthy.

www.popovakula.com.mk A delightful winery with an impressive hotel/restaurant overlooking the ravine of Demir Kapija. Offers the widest variety of indigenous grape of the Tikveš region as well as more well-known varieties.

www.skovin.com.mk Based near Skopje, Skovin produces a variety of wines including a very good Muscat and a rosé.

www.tikves.com.mk Tikveš is the largest winery in Macedonia, producing the iconic T'ga za Jug red Vranec. Their impressive wine-cellar restaurant is also open for lunch (preferably by reservation a day in advance).

World War I Salonika Front

www.1914-1918.net/salonika.htm For family historians.

www.archive.org/stream/salonikafront00mannuoft/salonikafront00mannuoft_djvu. txt Online publication of *The Salonika Front* by Capt Arthur Mann, 1920.

www.gwpda.org/memoir/Salonica/salonTC.htm#TC Online publication of *The Story of the Salonika Army* by G Ward Price, 1918.

memorabilia.homestead.com/files/Salonika_and_Macedonia_1916_18.htm Listing of the battalions of each division who fought on the Salonika Front.

www.salonikabattlefieldtour.com A Strumica-based company providing informative tours of the Dojran battlefield and nearby graves.

www.srpska-mreza.com/library/facts/November-1918.html A Serbian site extolling the bravery of the Serbs in World War I using extracts from the book *November 1918* by Gordon Brook-Shepherd, 1981.

FILMS/DOCUMENTARIES

Cvetanovski, Vlado *The Secret Book*, 2005. A thriller based on a fictional search for the legendary secret Slavic book of the Bogomil Gnostic religion of the 11th century. The book is supposed to have ended up in France, where a father and son duo take up the search in the 21st century à la *Da Vinci Code*. In French and Macedonian, available with English and Macedonian subtitles.

Einarsson, Sigurjón *A Name is a Name*, 2010. A travelogue road movie considering the thorny issue of naming a nation. Controversial.

Horne, Robert *Edward Lear: An Exile in Paradise* Lear Productions, 2008. A fascinating reproduction of Lear's travels from Greece, through Monastir (Bitola), Prilep and Üsküb (Skopje) in 1848. Lear is better known for his nonsense poetry and sketches, but this documentary does a great job of showcasing his landscape paintings of the time and how they compare with the region today.

Leder, Mimi *The Peacemaker*, 1997. Nuclear warheads get in the wrong hands between Russia and the Balkans. A couple of the scenes are set in the church on the main square in Bitola. Starring George Clooney and Nicole Kidman. Usual Hollywood stuff.

Mančevski, Milčo *Before the Rain*, 1995. Set in London and Macedonia in the 1990s giving a chilling forecast of how inter-ethnic violence might start. English, Macedonian and Albanian with English subtitles. Gripping.

Mančevski, Milčo *Dust*, 2001. Set in New York and Macedonia at both ends of the 20th century. Wild West comes to Macedonia, starring Joseph Fiennes. Action packed.

Mančevski, Milčo *Mothers*, 2010. Set in contemporary Macedonia, two parts fiction, one part documentary, this movie looks at the nature of truth.

Mančevski, Milčo *Shadows*, 2008. A young doctor in Skopje has to lay to rest the wandering souls of several characters from bygone years. Not as 'insightful' of Macedonia per se, but a gripping drama all the same.

Mitrevski, Darko *Bal-kan-kan*, 2005. A fantastic parody of life in the Balkans at the turn of the 21st century. Available with English subtitles. Brilliant.

Mitrevski, Darko *The Third Half*, 2012. Based on true events set in World War II, when a Jewish German becomes the coach of a Macedonia football team and turns them around from failure to beating the Germans. But at what cost?

Mitrovic, Živorad *The Assasins of Salonika*, 1961. Classic feature of the fight for Macedonia at the end of the 19th century. Today's Macedonians grew up on this stuff. Macedonian and Serbo-Croat. Available with English subtitles.

Palin, Michael *New Europe* BBC documentary, 2007. Palin's documentary takes him all through New Europe stopping for a few days in Ohrid and Prilep.

Popov, Stole *Tetoviranje*, 1994. Set in Šutka detention centre and Idrižovo prison. A man is detained for having an empty suitcase and ends up being shot by a Macedonian crack sniper. English subtitles. Perks up in parts.

Stone, Oliver *Alexander*, 2004. This movie was never going to win any Oscars, not least because it is too long with too many up-close battles, but it's a revealing rendition of a legendary figure. Starring Colin Farrell and Angelina Jolie.

Trajkov, Ivo *The Great Water*, 2004. Based on the book of the same name by Živko Cingo, this story tells of an orphan after World War II, whose experience as a young pioneer in the orphanage allegedly creates one of the greatest democratic forces in Yugoslavia. English subtitles. Average.

Wood, Michael *In the Footsteps of Alexander* BBC documentary, 1997. An informative and interesting account of Alexander the Great's conquest of Persia.

WIN A FREE BRADT GUIDE
READER QUESTIONNAIRE

Send in your completed questionnaire and enter our monthly draw for the chance to win a Bradt guide of your choice.

To take up our special reader offer of 40% off, please visit our website at www.bradtguides.com/freeguide or answer the questions below and return to us with the order form overleaf.

(Forms may be posted or faxed to us.)

Have you used any other Bradt guides? If so, which titles? . . . .
. . . .

What other publishers' travel guides do you use regularly? . . . .
. . . .

Where did you buy this guidebook? . . . .

What was the main purpose of your trip to Macedonia (or for what other reason did you read our guide)? eg: holiday/business/charity . . . .
. . . .

How long did you travel for? (circle one)

weekend/long weekend   1–2 weeks   3–4 weeks   4 weeks plus

Which countries did you visit in connection with this trip? . . . .
. . . .

Did you travel with a tour operator?' If so, which one? . . . .
. . . .

What other destinations would you like to see covered by a Bradt guide?
. . . .

If you could make one improvement to this guide, what would it be?
. . . .

Age (circle relevant category) 16–25   26–45   46–60   60+

Male/Female (delete as appropriate)

Home country . . . .

Please send us any comments about this guide (or others on our list).
. . . .
. . . .
. . . .

Bradt Travel Guides
IDC House, The Vale, Chalfont St Peter, Bucks SL9 9RZ, UK
☎ +44 (0)1753 893444 **f** +44 (0)1753 892333
e info@bradtguides.com
www.bradtguides.com

TAKE 40% OFF YOUR NEXT BRADT GUIDE!
Order Form

To take advantage of this special offer visit www.bradtguides.com/freeguide and enter our monthly giveaway, or fill in the order form below, complete the questionnaire overleaf and send it to Bradt Travel Guides by post or fax.

Please send me one copy of the following guide at 40% off the UK retail price

No	Title	Retail price	40% price
1	. . . .	. . . .	. . . .

Please send the following additional guides at full UK retail price

No	Title	Retail price	Total
. . .	. . . .	. . . .	. . . .
. . .	. . . .	. . . .	. . . .
. . .	. . . .	. . . .	. . . .

Sub total . . . .
Post & packing . . . .
(Free shipping UK, £1 per book Europe, £3 per book rest of world)
Total . . . .

Name . . . .

Address . . . .

Tel . . . .   Email . . . .

☐ I enclose a cheque for £. . . . . . . made payable to Bradt Travel Guides Ltd

☐ I would like to pay by credit card. Number: . . . .

Expiry date: . . . / . . . . 3-digit security code (on reverse of card) . . . . .

Issue no (debit cards only) . . . . .

☐ Please sign me up to Bradt's monthly enewsletter, Bradtpackers' News.

☐ I would be happy for you to use my name and comments in Bradt marketing material.

Send your order on this form, with the completed questionnaire, to:

Bradt Travel Guides
IDC House, The Vale, Chalfont St Peter, Bucks SL9 9RZ, UK
☏ +44 (0)1753 893444   f +44 (0)1753 892333
e info@bradtguides.com   www.bradtguides.com

Bradt Travel Guides

www.bradtguides.com

Africa

Access Africa: Safaris for People with Limited Mobility	£16.99
Africa Overland	£16.99
Algeria	£15.99
Angola	£17.99
Botswana	£16.99
Burkina Faso	£17.99
Cameroon	£15.99
Cape Verde	£15.99
Congo	£16.99
Eritrea	£15.99
Ethiopia	£17.99
Ethiopia Highlights	£15.99
Ghana	£15.99
Kenya Highlights	£15.99
Madagascar	£16.99
Madagascar Highlights	£15.99
Malawi	£15.99
Mali	£14.99
Mauritius, Rodrigues & Réunion	£15.99
Mozambique	£15.99
Namibia	£15.99
Niger	£14.99
Nigeria	£17.99
North Africa: Roman Coast	£15.99
Rwanda	£15.99
São Tomé & Príncipe	£14.99
Seychelles	£16.99
Sierra Leone	£16.99
Somaliland	£15.99
South Africa Highlights	£15.99
Sudan	£15.99
Tanzania, Northern	£14.99
Tanzania	£17.99
Uganda	£16.99
Zambia	£18.99
Zanzibar	£14.99
Zimbabwe	£15.99

The Americas and the Caribbean

Alaska	£15.99
Amazon Highlights	£15.99
Argentina	£16.99
Bahia	£14.99
Cayman Islands	£14.99
Chile Highlights	£15.99
Colombia	£17.99
Dominica	£15.99
Grenada, Carriacou & Petite Martinique	£15.99
Guyana	£15.99
Nova Scotia	£14.99
Panama	£14.99
Paraguay	£15.99
Turks & Caicos Islands	£14.99
Uruguay	£15.99
USA by Rail	£15.99
Venezuela	£16.99
Yukon	£14.99

British Isles

Britain from the Rails	£14.99
Bus-Pass Britain	£15.99

Eccentric Britain	£15.99
Eccentric Cambridge	£9.99
Eccentric London	£14.99
Eccentric Oxford	£9.99
Sacred Britain	£16.99
Slow: Cornwall	£14.99
Slow: Cotswolds	£14.99
Slow: Devon & Exmoor	£14.99
Slow: Dorset	£14.99
Slow: Norfolk & Suffolk	£14.99
Slow: Northumberland	£14.99
Slow: North Yorkshire	£14.99
Slow: Sussex & South Downs National Park	£14.99

Europe

Abruzzo	£14.99
Albania	£16.99
Armenia	£16.99
Azores	£14.99
Baltic Cities	£14.99
Belarus	£15.99
Bosnia & Herzegovina	£14.99
Bratislava	£9.99
Budapest	£9.99
Croatia	£13.99
Cross-Channel France: Nord-Pas de Calais	£13.99
Cyprus see North Cyprus	
Dresden	£7.99
Estonia	£14.99
Faroe Islands	£15.99
Flanders	£15.99
Georgia	£15.99
Greece: The Peloponnese	£14.99
Helsinki	£7.99
Hungary	£15.99
Iceland	£15.99
Kosovo	£15.99
Lapland	£15.99
Lille	£9.99
Lithuania	£14.99
Luxembourg	£14.99
Macedonia	£16.99
Malta & Gozo	£12.99
Montenegro	£14.99
North Cyprus	£13.99
Serbia	£15.99
Slovakia	£14.99
Slovenia	£13.99
Spitsbergen	£16.99
Switzerland Without a Car	£14.99
Transylvania	£14.99
Ukraine	£15.99

Middle East, Asia and Australasia

Bangladesh	£17.99
Borneo	£17.99
Eastern Turkey	£16.99
Iran	£15.99
Iraq: Then & Now	£15.99
Israel	£15.99
Jordan	£16.99

Kazakhstan	£16.99
Kyrgyzstan	£16.99
Lake Baikal	£15.99
Lebanon	£15.99
Maldives	£15.99
Mongolia	£16.99
North Korea	£14.99
Oman	£15.99
Palestine	£15.99
Shangri-La: A Travel Guide to the Himalayan Dream	£14.99
Sri Lanka	£15.99
Syria	£15.99
Taiwan	£16.99
Tibet	£17.99
Yemen	£14.99

Wildlife

Antarctica: A Guide to the Wildlife	£15.99
Arctic: A Guide to Coastal Wildlife	£16.99
Australian Wildlife	£14.99
Central & Eastern European Wildlife	£15.99
Chinese Wildlife	£16.99
East African Wildlife	£19.99
Galápagos Wildlife	£16.99
Madagascar Wildlife	£16.99
New Zealand Wildlife	£14.99
North Atlantic Wildlife	£16.99
Pantanal Wildlife	£16.99
Peruvian Wildlife	£15.99
Southern African Wildlife	£19.99
Sri Lankan Wildlife	£15.99

Pictorials and other guides

100 Alien Invaders	£16.99
100 Animals to See Before They Die	£16.99
100 Bizarre Animals	£16.99
Eccentric Australia	£12.99
Northern Lights	£6.99
Swimming with Dolphins, Tracking Gorillas	£15.99
Through the Northwest Passage	£17.99
Tips on Tipping	£6.99
Total Solar Eclipse 2012 & 2013	£6.99
Wildlife and Conservation Volunteering: The Complete Guide	£13.99
Your Child Abroad	£10.95

Travel literature

Fakirs, Feluccas and Femmes Fatales	£9.99
The Marsh Lions	£9.99
Two Year Mountain	£9.99
Up the Creek	£9.99

Index

Page numbers in **bold** refer to major entries; those in *italics* indicate maps